Lecture Notes in Artificial Intelligence 10767

Subseries of Lecture Notes in Computer Science

More information about this series at http://www.springer.com/series/1244

Francesco Belardinelli · Estefanía Argente (Eds.)

Multi-Agent Systems and Agreement Technologies

15th European Conference, EUMAS 2017
and 5th International Conference, AT 2017
Evry, France, December 14–15, 2017
Revised Selected Papers

Springer

Editors
Francesco Belardinelli 🆔
University of Évry Val d'Essonne
Paris Saclay, France

Estefanía Argente 🆔
Polytechnic University of Valencia
Valencia, Spain

ISSN 0302-9743   ISSN 1611-3349 (electronic)
Lecture Notes in Artificial Intelligence
ISBN 978-3-030-01712-5   ISBN 978-3-030-01713-2 (eBook)
https://doi.org/10.1007/978-3-030-01713-2

Library of Congress Control Number: 2018957132

LNCS Sublibrary: SL7 – Artificial Intelligence

This Springer imprint is published by the registered company Springer Nature Switzerland AG
The registered company address is: Gewerbestrasse 11, 6330 Cham, Switzerland

Preface

This volume contains revised versions of the papers presented at the 15th European Conference on Multi-Agent Systems (EUMAS 2017) and the 5th International Conference on Agreement Technologies (AT 2017), which were both held at the Université d'Evry – Val d'Essonne, during December 14–15, 2017.

EUMAS 2017 followed the tradition of previous editions (Oxford 2003, Barcelona 2004, Brussels 2005, Lisbon 2006, Hammamet 2007, Bath 2008, Agia Napa 2009, Paris 2010, Maastricht 2011, Dublin 2012, Toulouse 2013, Prague 2014, Athens 2015, and Valencia 2016) in aiming to provide the prime European forum for presenting and discussing agents research as the annual designated event of the European Association of Multi-Agent Systems (EURAMAS).

AT 2017 was the fifth instalment in a series of events (after Dubrovnik 2012, Beijing 2013, Athens 2015, and Valencia 2016) that focus on bringing together researchers and practitioners working on computer systems in which autonomous software agents interact, typically on behalf of humans, in order to come to mutually acceptable agreements. A wide scope of technologies can help provide the support needed for reaching mutually acceptable agreements, such as argumentation and negotiation, trust and reputation, computational social choice, coalition and team formation, coordination and distributed decision-making, and semantic alignment, to name a few.

This year, for the third time, both events were co-located and run as a single, joint event. This joint organization aimed to encourage and continue cross-fertilization among the broader EUMAS and the more specialized AT communities, and to provide a richer and more attractive program to participants. While the technical program was put together by their independent committees into conference-specific thematic sessions, the conferences shared keynote talks and aligned their schedules to minimize overlap and enable participants to make the best possible use of the combined program of the two conferences.

Traditionally, both conference series have always followed a spirit of providing a forum for discussion and an annual opportunity for primarily European researchers to meet and exchange ideas. For this reason, they have always encouraged submission of papers that report on both early and mature research.

The peer-review processes carried out by both conferences put great emphasis on ensuring the high quality of accepted contributions. The EUMAS Program Committee accepted 30 submissions (48.39%) as full papers and another three submissions (4.84%) as short papers out of a total of 62 submissions. The AT review process resulted in the acceptance of eight full (57.14%) and two short papers (14.28%) out of 14 submissions overall.

This volume is structured as follows: In the first part, we present the invited paper of EUMAS; in the second, we present the EUMAS papers, and in the third we present the AT papers. The papers of each part are then grouped into thematic areas, where we first present full papers, followed by short papers. For the EUMAS papers, the thematic areas are:

- Agent-Based Modeling
- Logic and Formal Methods
- Argumentation and Rational Choice
- Simulation
- Games
- Negotiation, Planning, and Coalitions

For AT, the thematic areas are:

- Algorithms and Frameworks
- Applications
- Philosophical and Theoretical Studies

The editors would like to thank all authors for submitting to EUMAS and AT, all participants, the invited speakers, the members of the Program Committees, and the additional reviewers for putting together a strong joint program. We also thank the local organizers for their hard work organizing the events. Finally, we would like to express our gratitude to the sponsors of the conferences, the European Association for Artificial Intelligence (EurAi), the Agreement Computing Consortium (Spanish Government project TIN2015-68950-REDC), the IBISC laboratory, and the Université d'Evry Val d'Essonne – Paris Saclay, for their generous support, without which this event would not have been possible.

March 2018   Francesco Belardinelli
                                                                   Estefania Argente

Organization

EUMAS 2017 Organization

Conference Chair

Francesco Belardinelli   Université d'Evry val d'Essonne, Paris Saclay, France

Local Organization

Francesco Belardinelli   Université d'Evry val d'Essonne, Paris Saclay, France
Abbas Slimani   Université d'Evry val d'Essonne, Paris Saclay, France

Program Committee

Nadia Abchiche Mimouni	Université d'Evry val d'Essonne, Paris Saclay, France
Natasha Alechina	University of Nottingham, UK
Fred Amblard	IRIT - University of Toulouse 1 Capitole, France
Ana L. C. Bazzan	Universidade Federal do Rio Grande do Sul, Brazil
Francesco Belardinelli	Université d'Evry val d'Essonne, Paris Saclay, France
Olivier Boissier	Ecole des Mines Saint-Etienne, France
Vicent Botti	Universitat Politècnica de València, Spain
Ioana Boureanu	University of Surrey, UK
Cristiano Castelfranchi	Institute of Cognitive Sciences and Technologies, Italy
Georgios Chalkiadakis	Technical University of Crete, Greece
Vincent Chevrier	LORIA/CNRS Université de Lorraine, France
Amit Chopra	Lancaster University, UK
Massimo Cossentino	National Research Council of Italy, Italy
Natalia Criado	King's College London, UK
Mehdi Dastani	Utrecht University, The Netherlands
Tiago de Lima	University of Artois and CNRS, France
Marina De Vos	University of Bath, UK
Louise Dennis	University of Liverpool, UK
Catalin Dima	LACL, Université Paris Est - Créteil, France
Sylvie Doutre	IRIT - University of Toulouse 1 Capitole, France
Amal El Fallah Seghrouchni	LIP6 - Pierre and Marie Curie University, France
Piotr Faliszewski	AGH University of Science and Technology, Poland
Nicoletta Fornara	Università della Svizzera Italiana, Switzerland
Nicola Gatti	Politecnico di Milano, Italy
Benoit Gaudou	IRIT - University of Toulouse 1 Capitole, France
Umberto Grandi	IRIT - University of Toulouse 1 Capitole, France
Davide Grossi	University of Liverpool, UK
Andreas Herzig	IRIT - CNRS, France
Guillaume Hutzler	Université d'Evry val d'Essonne, Paris Saclay, France
Wojtek Jamroga	Polish Academy of Sciences, Poland

Franziska Klügl	Örebro University, Sweden
Joao Leite	Universidade NOVA de Lisboa, Portugal
Brian Logan	University of Nottingham, UK
Alessio Lomuscio	Imperial College London, UK
Dominique Longin	IRIT - CNRS, France
Maite Lopez-Sanchez	University of Barcelona, Spain
Emiliano Lorini	IRIT - CNRS, France
Samhar Mahmoud	King's College London, UK
Vadim Malvone	Università degli studi di Napoli Federico II, Italy
Frederic Moisan	Carnegie Mellon University, USA
Aniello Murano	Università degli studi di Napoli Federico II, Italy
Jörg P. Müller	TU Clausthal, Germany
Emma Norling	Manchester Metropolitan University, UK
Peter Novák	Science & Technology Corporation B.V., The Netherlands
Ingrid Nunes	Universidade Federal do Rio Grande do Sul, Brazil
Andrea Omicini	Università di Bologna, Italy
Nardine Osman	Artificial Intelligence Research Institute, Spain
Giuseppe Perelli	University of Oxford, UK
Laurent Perrussel	IRIT – University of Toulouse 1 Capitole, France
Sebastien Picault	Université de Lille, France
Alessandro Ricci	Università di Bologna, Italy
Antonino Rotolo	Università di Bologna, Italy
Nicolas Sabouret	LIMSI - CNRS, France
Olivier Simonin	INSA Lyon, Inria, France
Abbas Slimani	Université d'Evry val d'Essonne, Paris Saclay, France
Ingo J. Timm	University of Trier, Germany
Paolo Torroni	Università di Bologna, Italy
Paolo Turrini	Imperial College London, UK
Karl Tuyls	University of Liverpool and Google, UK
Leon van der Torre	University of Luxembourg, Luxembourg
M. Birna van Riemsdijk	Delft University of Technology, The Netherlands
Wamberto Vasconcelos	University of Aberdeen, UK
Laurent Vercouter	LITIS - INSA Rouen, France
Serena Villata	CNRS - Sophia-Antipolis, France
Neil Yorke-Smith	Delft University of Technology, The Netherlands

AT 2017 Organization

Conference Chair

Estefanía Argente	Universitat Politècnica de València, Spain

Local Organization

Francesco Belardinelli	Université d'Evry val d'Essonne, Paris Saclay, France
Abbas Slimani	Université d'Evry val d'Essonne, Paris Saclay, France

Program Committee

Giulia Andrighetto	Institute of Cognitive Sciences and Technologies (ISTC CNR), Rome, Italy
Floris Bex	Utrecht University, The Netherlands
Javier Bajo	Universidad Politécnica de Madrid, Spain
Holger Billhardt	Universidad Rey Juan Carlos, Madrid, Spain
Elena Cabrio	Université Côte d'Azur, Sophia Antipolis, France
Carlos Carrascosa	Universitat Politècnica de València, Spain
Carlos Chesñevar	Universidad Nacional del Sur, Bahia Blanca, Argentina
Paul Davidsson	Malmö University, Sweden
Sylvie Doutre	IRIT - University of Toulouse, France
Alberto Fernandez	Universidad Rey Juan Carlos, Madrid, Spain
Stella Heras	Universitat Politècnica de València, Spain
Floriana Grasso	University of Liverpool, UK
Mirjana Ivanovic	University of Novi Sad, Serbia
Gordan Jezic	University of Zagreb, Croatia
Vicente Julian	Universitat Politècnica de València, Spain
Jeroen Keppens	King's College London, UK
Matthias Klusch	DFKI Research Center for AI, Germany
Lea Kutvonen	University of Helsinki, Finland
Ryszard Kowalczyk	Swinburne University of Technology, Australia
Jerome Lang	LAMSADE, Université Paris-Dauphine, France
Joao Leite	Universidade Nova de Lisboa, Portugal
Emiliano Lorini	Université Paul Sabatier IRIT, France
Paulo Novais	University of Minho, Portugal
Viorel Negru	West University of Timisoara, Romania
Eugenio Oliveira	Universidade do Porto, Portugal
Nir Oren	University of Aberdeen, UK
Eva Onaindia	Universitat Politècnica de València, Spain
Sascha Ossowski	Universidad Rey Juan Carlos, Madrid, Spain
Marcin Paprzycki	Polish Academy of Sciences, Warsaw, Poland
Simon Parsons	King's College London, UK
Miguel Rebollo	Universitat Politècnica de València, Spain
Jörg Rothe	Universität Düsseldorf, Germany
Sara Rodriguez	University of Salamanca, Spain
Victor Sanchez-Anguix	Coventry University, UK
Jordi Sabater-Mir	Institut d'Investigació en Intelligència Artificial (IIIA-CSIC), Barcelona, Spain
Marco Schorlemmer	Artificial Intelligence Research Institute, Spain
Michael Ignaz Schumacher	University of Applied Sciences, Switzerland
Francesca Toni	Imperial College London, UK
Denis Trcek	University of Ljubljana, Slovenia

George Vouros   University of Piraeus, Greece
Antoine Zimmermann   ISCOD, ENS Mines Saint-Etienne, France
László Zsolt Varga   ELTE-IK, Hungary

Sponsoring Institutions

European Coordinating Committee for Artificial Intelligence

Université d'Evry Val d'Essonne, Paris Saclay

Agreement Computing Consortium (Spanish Goverment
project TIN2015-68950-REDC)

Contents

EUMAS 2017: Argumentation and Rational Choice

EUMAS 2017: Simulation

EUMAS 2017: Games

EUMAS 2017: Negotiation, Planning and Coalitions

AT 2017: Algorithms and Frameworks

AT 2017: Applications

AT 2017: Philosophical and Theoretical Studies

Invited Talks

Multiagent Learning Paradigms

K. Tuyls[1,2(✉)] and P. Stone[3]

[1] DeepMind, Paris, France
karltuyls@google.com
[2] University of Liverpool, Liverpool, UK
[3] University of Texas, Austin, USA
pstone@cs.utexas.edu

Abstract. *"Perhaps a thing is simple if you can describe it fully in several different ways, without immediately knowing that you are describing the same thing"* – Richard Feynman

This articles examines multiagent learning from several paradigmatic perspectives, aiming to bring them together within one framework. We aim to provide a general definition of multiagent learning and lay out the essential characteristics of the various paradigms in a systematic manner by dissecting multiagent learning into its main components. We show how these various paradigms are related and describe similar learning processes but from varying perspectives, e.g. an individual (cognitive) learner vs. a population of (simple) learning agents.

1 Introduction

Multiagent systems (MAS) are distributed systems of independent actors, called *agents*, that are each independently controlled, but that interact with one another in the same environment [47]. In their recent book entitled *Multiagent Systems*, Shoham and Leyton-Brown define multiagent systems as "those systems that include multiple autonomous entities with either diverging information or diverging interests, or both" [36]. Examples of multiagent systems applications include automated driving, disaster rescue aided by teams of robots, and autonomous bidding agents for electricity power markets. Because of the complexity of most MAS it is often impossible, or at least impractical, to engineer effective agent behaviors by hand. Rather, it is preferable for agents to be able to *learn* to behave effectively from experience in the environment, and from interactions with other agents. Tom Mitchell, in his book *Machine Learning* defines machine learning (ML) as "the study of computer algorithms that improve automatically through experience" [27]. Using these definitions of MAS and ML as bases, we consider "multiagent learning" to be:

> *The study of multiagent systems in which one or more of the autonomous entities improves automatically through experience.*

As stated, this definition is quite broad, leaving open the possibility for many types of autonomous entities, systems of these entities, and foci of learning. For

© Springer Nature Switzerland AG 2018
F. Belardinelli and E. Argente (Eds.): EUMAS 2017/AT 2017, LNAI 10767, pp. 3–21, 2018.
https://doi.org/10.1007/978-3-030-01713-2_1

example, there could be many simple agents (like an ant colony), or a small number of sophisticated agents (like a soccer team). The agents could interact over long periods of time with exactly the same other agents, or with a series of different randomly chosen other agents, each for a short interaction. And the agents could learn about the environment itself, about the behaviors of the other agents, or directly about what actions are most effective. The main commonality in all of these above scenarios, and indeed the prerequisite for learning in the first place (as pointed out by Shoham and Leyton-Brown), is that there is a temporal nature to the scenario that exhibits regularity across time. Thus past experience is somehow predictive of future expectations.

Multiagent learning (MAL) has received most attention from the reinforcement learning (RL) community [7,17,23,39]. For an overview see [18,44]. In [37] Shoham et al. explore what research questions multiagent learning is trying to answer by defining five research agenda's that MAL research is pursuing and classifying the state of the art therein. As not all work falls into one of these agenda's, this implies that either we need more agenda's, or some work needs to be revisited. The purpose of the paper was to inititiate a discussion within the community leading to several response articles, e.g. [34,38,41]. The current paper is different, in that it considers several multiagent learning paradigms, and not only RL, and furthermore aims to understand what the different MAL components are, bringing several of the paradigms together within one framework.

1.1 Multiagent Learning Components

In this paper, we consider the full spectrum of such scenarios, in which multiagent learning is possible. As illustrated in Fig. 1, we think of a multiagent learning scenario as consisting of four distinct components: the environment, the agents, the interaction mechanism, and the learning mechanism itself.

First, the environment, or domain, specifies the state space, action space, and transition function. The state space specifies the set of states that an *individual* agent can be in at any given time. The action space is the set of actions available to an individual agent at any given time, and the transition function, or the environment dynamics, specifies the (possibly stochastic) way in which the environment changes as a result of each agent (or a subset of agents) executing an action in a given state. For the purposes of exposition, we assume that the environment proceeds in discrete, evenly-spaced time steps and that all actions are available at all times. But these assumptions are easily relaxed, and indeed must be in many practical settings.

Second, the agents are defined by their communication channels with the environment for sensing the (possibly partial) state and for specifying actions; their communication channels between one another; their utility functions indicating their preferences over environmental states; and their policies for selecting actions.

Third, the interaction mechanism defines how long agents interact with one another, with which other agents, and what they observe about other agents. For

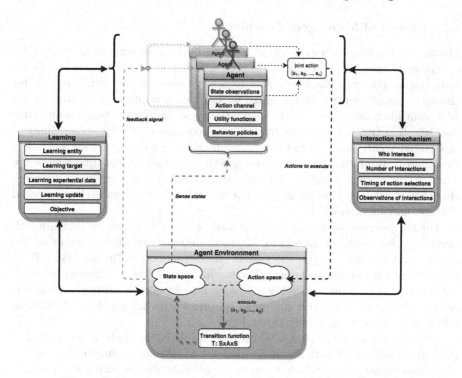

Fig. 1. A depiction of the general multiagent learning scenario.

example, at one extreme, agents may be fully aware of each other's behavior policies; or, at the other extreme, they may only observe the effects of their actions on the environment. As intermediate possibilities, they may observe each other's selected actions, their utilities (payoffs), or both. The interaction mechanism also dictates the frequency (or number) of interactions among any given agents, as well as whether their actions are selected simultaneously or sequentially (the timing of action selections).

Fourth, the learning mechanism is defined by the learning entity, learning target, the learning experiential data, the learning update, and the objective of learning. The learning entity specifies whether the learning happens at the individual agent level, e.g. by an intelligent cognitive agent, or at the group level, e.g. by a population of cognitively limited agents. The learning target describes what is being learnt. For example, it could be the interaction mechanism that is being learnt, or the policies of the individual agents. The learning experiential data describes what information is available to the learning entity as the basis for learning. The learning update defines how the learning entity is updated during the learning process; and the objective is a representation of the goal, or evaluation function, of the learning process.

1.2   Classes of Multiagent Learning

Multiagent learning scenarios are challenging both to design and to analyze for a number of reasons. To begin with, even defining an objective function is far from trivial. For example, is the goal to achieve some desired configuration for the entire set of agents with no regard for individual utility (e.g. disaster rescue with multiple robots); to achieve a game theoretic equilibrium (e.g. autonomous cars selecting travel routes); or to achieve maximum utility for some subset of designated agents (e.g. agents bidding in a marketplace on one person's behalf)? In addition, from the algorithmic perspective, as long as multiple agents are learning, multiagent learning scenarios are inherently non-stationary, meaning that they violate the Markov assumption that is typically leveraged by sequential decision making algorithms.

For the purpose of description and analysis, in this paper we divide multiagent learning scenarios into three distinct classes based on how many of the agents, and to what extent the system of interactions is "in our control" as designers of algorithms. Since each class has historically been addressed by different types of algorithms, we divide the paper into sections accordingly. However, we find that ultimately there are many commonalities among these algorithms, which we emphasize and unify throughout.

First, we consider the case in which just one of the agents is in our control as it interacts repeatedly with the same small set of relatively sophisticated agents. This class of scenarios, which we refer to as *individual learning* scenarios, is traditionally the realm of multiagent reinforcement learning (RL) algorithms. Second, we consider the case in which we have control over all of the agents and their interactions as they interact repeatedly with randomly chosen members of a large population of relatively simple agents. In such *population learning* scenarios, the next "state" may be defined by the distribution of other agents in the population (in particular their behaviors) that defines who the agents will interact with. This class of scenarios is traditionally the realm of co-evolutionary approaches and swarm algorithms. Third, we consider the case in which none of the agents are in our control, but we can define the system of interactions. We refer to this case as *protocol learning*. While much less common than the prior two cases, protocol learning covers multiagent systems research such as adaptive mechanism design for autonomous bidding agents.

While the distinctions among the three types of scenarios may appear sharp as stated, in practice they are quite fuzzy. For example, multiagent reinforcement learning algorithms can be analyzed from the perspective of all agents being in our control, and swarm algorithms can include relatively sophisticated agents.

In the next section we further refine the three classes of problems into five paradigmatic settings in which to consider the multiagent learning problem.

2   Paradigms

As stated above multiagent learning is a process by which agents learn to behave in order to achieve their goal(s), while interacting with other agents (possibly co-operative or adversarial) that are potentially learning as well. These learned behaviours can be generated by a variety of techniques coming from different paradigms. We distinguish five such paradigms from which such learning can be studied.

We distinguish between three higher level types of agents or learning scenarios, i.e., individual learning in which a relatively sophisticated agent learns at the individual level; population learning in which a population of cognitively-limited agents learn at the group level by using simple local interactions; and protocol learning in which the interaction mechanism among the agents is itself learned. The five paradigmatic settings, distributed over these three classes, we consider are:

1. *Online RL towards individual utility*
2. *Online RL towards social welfare*
3. *Co-evolutionary learning*
4. *Swarm Intelligence*
5. *Adaptive mechanism design*

Paradigms 1 and 2 concern *individual learners*, paradigms 3 and 4 concern *population learners*, and paradigm 5 concerns *protocol learning*. In addition to the 5 paradigms we also consider MAL tools for analyzing and predicting learning behaviour, and for building opponent models. Specifically, we consider:

– Analysis and prediction tools, for example to analyze the resulting equilibrium behavior of coevolutionary approaches; and
– Teammate and opponent modeling tools that can be useful for predicting agent behaviors in any of the five paradigms.

In the next section we describe the five paradigms systematically in prototypical multiagent learning scenarios that fully specify the environment, the agents, the interaction, and the objective, following the taxonomy laid out in Fig. 1.

3   Paradigm Descriptions

This section describes the five paradigms introduced above in more detail, and categorizes them according to the taxonomy introduced above.

3.1   Paradigm 1: Online RL Towards Individual Utility

One of the most-studied scenarios in multiagent learning is that in which multiple independent agents take actions in the same environment, and learn online to maximize their own individual utility functions.

This paradigm, in turn, is most often reduced to the abstract game-theoretic, artificial scenario of a repeated normal form game. In a normal form game, each agent (or "player") has a set of possible actions, players select an action simultaneously, and each player gets a payoff that is a function of the full set of actions. Perhaps the most famous normal form game is the Prisoner's Dilemma, a 2-player game with actions and utilities shown in Fig. 2. The motivation is that two prisoners committed a crime together and are being interrogated separately. If neither of them confesses to the crime (they both "cooperate"), then they will both get a small punishment (corresponding to a payoff of 3 in the figure). If one of them confesses (or "defects") but the other does not, then the one that confesses gets off for free (payoff of 5), but the other gets the worst punishment possible (payoff of 0). If they both defect, they both get a fairly bad punishment (payoff of 1). Normal form games can also have more than 2 players, and more than 2 actions per player.

$$
\begin{array}{cc}
 & D \quad C \\
\begin{array}{c} D \\ C \end{array} & \left(\begin{array}{cc} 1,1 & 5,0 \\ 0,5 & 3,3 \end{array} \right)
\end{array}
$$

Fig. 2. Payoff tables of the PD game. Strategies D and C correspond with Defect and Cooperate respectively.

Normal form games were initially introduced and studied as one-shot interactions. The players knew each other's full utility functions, and played the game only once. It was in this setting that the famous Nash equilibrium was introduced as a set of actions such that no player would be better off deviating given that the other players' actions are fixed. Games can have one, or multiple Nash Equilibria. In the prisoner's dilemma, the only Nash Equilibrium is for both agents to defect.

In these traditional one-shot settings, there is no opportunity for learning because there is no temporal nature to the scenario. However, it is also possible to consider *repeated* normal form games such that the same players interact with one another multiple times in the same game, with the objective of maximizing their (possibly discounted)[1] sum of utilities over time. In repeated normal form games, the repetition provides the temporal nature. The regularity across time comes from the assumption that players' past actions are somehow predictive of their future actions.

While normal form games are the common way to formulate this paradigm, it has also been studied extensively in the context of the pursuit domain [4], and applies also to a wide variety of more complex domains. The essential defining characteristics for multiagent learning settings that fall under this paradigm (i.e. the characteristic necessary to fall under this paradigm), are as laid out in Table 1. When many options are possible, they are enumerated, or the field is left blank.

---

[1] Discounted utilities are used to represent that near-term payoffs are more important to the agent than longer term payoffs.

Table 1. The essential characteristics of paradigm 1. When many options are possible, they are enumerated, or the field is left blank.

Online RL towards individual utility	
Component	Description
Agent Environment	
state space:	
action space:	
transition function:	
Agents	
state observations:	
action channel:	
utility functions:	(discounted) sum of rewards
behavior policies:	the other agents' policies are unknown; our agent's policy is the target of the learning (this is what is in our control)
Interaction mechanism	
who interacts:	same set of agents
frequency of interactions:	repeat multiple times or in one continual process
timing of action selections:	actions taken simultaneously or sequentially
observations of interactions:	agents may or may not observe the other agents' actions, payoffs, or policy
Learning	
learning entity:	individual learner
learning target:	agent's policy
learning experiential data:	agents' joint action, reward, next state observation
learning update:	behavior update from last experience
objective:	maximize our own agent's sum of utilities over time

3.2 Paradigm 2: Online RL Towards Social Welfare

A slight variation on the above scenario is that we may assume that all agents are using exactly the same learning-based behavior policy, and adopt the objective that, perhaps after some transient initial phase, they arrive at a steady state of always both selecting the cooperate action (which maximizes their sum of utilities).

In this case, the main things that change from Paradigm 1 are the behavior policies (in particular, what is in our control), and the objective.

The essential characteristics for this paradigm are laid out in Table 2.

Table 2. The essential characteristics of paradigm 2. When many options are possible, they are enumerated, or the field is left blank. The differences from Paradigm 1 are highlighted in bold.

Online RL towards social welfare	
Component	Description
Agent Environment	
state space:	
action space:	
transition function:	
Agents	
state observations:	
action channel:	
utility functions:	(discounted) sum of rewards
behavior policies:	**all agents' policy is the target of the learning (this is what is in our control)**
Interaction mechanism	
who interacts:	same set of agents
frequency of interactions:	repeat multiple times or in one continual process
timing of action selections:	actions taken simultaneously or sequentially
observations of interactions:	**each agent observes the other agents' actions and payoffs, but not policy**
Learning	
learning entity:	each agent learns individually
learning target:	each agent's policy
learning experiential data:	agents' joint action, reward next state observation
learning update:	behavior updates from last experience
objective:	**maximize the sum of all agents' utilities over time**

3.3   Paradigm 3: Co-evolutionary Approaches

Evolution can be used to learn agent behaviors as well. In this paradigm, abstract Darwinian models of evolution are applied to refine populations of agents (known as individuals) representing candidate solutions to a given problem [11, 26, 32]. This process consists of five steps: representation, selection, generation of new individuals (crossover and mutation), evaluation, and replacement. An evolutionary algorithm (EA) begins with an initial population of randomly-generated agents. Each member of this population is then evaluated and assigned a fitness value. The EA then uses a fitness-oriented procedure to select agents, breeds and mutates them to produce child agents, which are then added to the population, replacing older agents. One evaluation, selection, and breeding cycle is known as a generation. Successive generations continue to refine the population until time is exhausted or a sufficiently fit agent is discovered. Coevolution is an intuitive extension of evolutionary algorithms for domains with multiple learning agents. In co-evolution, the fitness of an individual is based on its interaction with other individuals in the population.

In essence EAs are training a "policy" to perform a state to action mapping. In this approach, rather than update the parameters of a single agent interacting with the environment as is done in reinforcement learning, one searches through a population of policies to find one that is appropriate for the task. This type of policy search approach is well suited to domains with continuous states and actions where traditional reinforcement learning approaches generally encounter difficulties. One can use a probability vector or distribution as representation of the policy, but an often-used policy in conjunction with evolutionary algorithms is a feed-forward neural network with non-linear activation functions (referred to as neuro-evolution [10, 20, 35, 45]). The aim of the neural network is to perform a mapping between its inputs (state) and its outputs (actions), that satisfies the agent's task. For example, a mobile robot using a neural network to navigate can map the sensory inputs it receives to direction and velocity. The key then is to find the correct parameters for the neural network that will provide the desired behavior.

The essential characteristics of this paradigm are laid out in Table 3.

3.4   Paradigm 4: Swarm Intelligence

Swarm Intelligence is a bio-inspired machine learning technique, largely based on the behavior of social insects (e.g. ants and honeybees), that is concerned with developing self-organized and decentralized adaptive algorithms [9, 24]. The type and form of learning in a swarm intelligence is characterized by a large population of cognition-limited agents that locally interact. Rather than developing complex behaviors for single individuals, as is done in reinforcement learning, swarm intelligence investigates the emerging (intelligent) behavior of a group of simple individuals that achieve complex behavior through their interactions with one another. Consequently, swarm intelligence can be considered as a cooperative multiagent learning approach in that the behavior of the full set of agents is determined by the actions of and interactions among the individuals.

In swarm intelligence, each individual in the group follows simple rules without central control structures. By interacting locally, a global behavior emerges, yet the individual has no knowledge of this 'big picture' behavior. Examples of such systems are ant foraging, bird flocking, fish schooling, and animal herding [3, 12, 14, 21]. Currently the most well-known swarm intelligence algorithms are pheromone-based (stigmergic), such as Ant Colony Optimization [8].

Ant Colony Optimization is a class name for ant-inspired algorithms solving combinatorial optimization problems. Algorithms belonging to it are stochastic search procedures in which the central component is the pheromone model. Pheromone-based algorithms are inspired by the behavior of ants and are the most well-known swarm intelligence algorithm. The algorithms are based on the fact that ants deposit a pheromone trail on the path they take during travel.

Table 3. The essential characteristics of paradigm 3. When many options are possible, they are enumerated, or the field is left blank.

Co-evolutionary approaches	
Component	Description
Agent Environment	
state space:	
action space:	
transition function:	
Agents	
state observations:	
action channel:	
utility functions:	payoff accumulated from utility matrix
behavior policies:	agents' policies are fixed parameterized functions
Interaction mechanism	
who interacts:	many sets of 2 agents, one from each population, randomly grouped
frequency of interactions:	repeat multiple times
timing of action selections:	actions taken simultaneously or sequentially
observations of interactions:	each agent may or may not observe the other agents' actions, payoffs, or policies
Learning	
learning entity:	population
learning target:	proportion of populations with each set of possible parameters
learning experiential data:	groupings of agents to generate utilities
learning update:	change of populations based on utilities of the individuals
objective:	maximize the sum of utilities over a group-wise interaction for the best agents in the populations

Using this trail, they are able to navigate toward their nest or food. Ants employ an indirect recruitment strategy by accumulating pheromone trails in the environment. The ants communicate indirectly via the environment, a phenomenon called *stigmergy*. When a trail is strong enough, other ants are attracted to it and, with high probability, will follow this trail toward a destination. In other words, the more ants follow a trail, the more that trail becomes attractive for being followed. However, pheromones evaporate over time, meaning that unless they are reinforced by other ants, they will disappear. Since long paths take more time to traverse, and pheromones evaporate, it will require more ants to sustain a long path. As a consequence, short paths will eventually prevail. The dissipation of pheromones ensures that "old" solutions can be forgotten, and that the ants will not get stuck in a local optimum.

Optimization problems best suited to be solved by ant colony optimization are those that can be cast as computational problems on a graph, implying that optimal solutions will correspond to specific paths in such a graph. Successful examples of such problems include the traveling salesman problem, various routing problems, job shop scheduling and even "coverage problems" with robots [2,6,9].

The essential characteristics of this paradigm are laid out in Table 4.

3.5   Paradigm 5: Adaptive Mechanism Design

Thus far, the thing under our control has been the algorithms of the agents, while their method of interaction has been taken as given. For example, in repeated games, it was given that the agents play the same game over and over again, taking actions simultaneously. The MAL algorithm defined the behavior(s) of the agent(s).

However, it is also possible to think of a multiagent learning setting as being one in which the agents are fixed (or at least beyond our control—so to the extent that they learn, they do so in a way that we cannot affect), but the interaction mechanism is to be learned [33].

Consider, for example, an auction house that interacts with a population of bidders. When auctioning several artworks, there are several parameters that can be adjusted, such as the reserve price, whether the auctions are simultaneous or sequential, and the mechanism by which the winner is determined and the price is set (e.g. English auction, Vickrey auction, Dutch auction, etc.). The auction house presumably wants to maximize the selling prices of the items, which will in turn maximize its commission.[2]

In this case, the auction house is not able to control the bidders (the interaction agents) themselves. As people tend to be, they may be irrational to varying degrees. Instead, it can only control the rules of interaction, in this case the bidding rules.

Note that the ideal auction mechanism may depend on the characteristics of the goods being auctioned. Compared to artwork, people bidding on electronic equipment may bid differently (or the auction may simply attract a different population). Furthermore, the population's bidding strategies as a whole may change over time (for example due to changes in the overall economy). Thus the auction house will need to continually adapt the parameters of its auctions if it is to maximize its profits [30,31].

The essential characteristics of this paradigm are laid out in Table 5.

---

[2] In some public auctions, the objective may instead be to maximize social welfare—striving to sell each item to the bidder who values it most.

Table 4. The essential characteristics of paradigm 4. When many options are possible, they are enumerated, or the field is left blank.

Swarm Intelligence	
Component	Description
Agent Environment	
state space:	pheromone levels and, or agent locations in the environment
action space:	
transition function:	changes in pheromone levels and, or agent locations after all take actions
Agents	
state observations:	pheromone levels and/or agent locations either globally or locally
action channel:	
utility functions:	
behavior policies:	agent's policy is a fixed function (simple control rules based on pheromone levels and/or agent locations
Interaction mechanism	
who interacts:	agents operate in the same environment
frequency of interactions:	repeated task executions by each agent
timing of action selections:	actions taken simultaneously
observations of interactions:	each agent alters the environment, affects other agents' decisions via stigmergy
Learning	
learning entity:	population
learning target:	proportion of pheromones in the environment dropped by the entire population
learning experiential data:	amounts of pheromones dropped in the environment that will determine optimal path (or utilities)
learning update:	change of pheromones levels in the environment based on ant utility
objective:	maximize the level of pheromones on the optimal path in the environment

4 Multiagent Learning Tools

In addition to the five MAL paradigms presented in Sect. 3, in this section we summarize two useful tools for the study and development of MAL algorithms. The first, using evolutionary game theory, is an analysis tool designed to enable researchers to predict the eventual stable state (fixed point) of an MAL system assuming self-interested agents continually adapt to each other's behaviors using known learning rules.

Table 5. The essential characteristics of paradigm 5. When many options are possible, they are enumerated, or the field is left blank.

Adaptive mechanism design	
Component	Description
Agent Environment	
state space:	
action space:	
transition function:	determined by the auction mechanism - how the prices change over time as a function of bids. This is one of the things we control
Agents	
state observations:	
action channel:	
utility functions:	
behavior policies:	various - not in our control
Interaction mechanism	
who interacts:	random subsets from populations of agents interact in a series of auctions
frequency of interactions:	repeat continually
timing of action selections:	Under our control, the subject of the adaptive algorithm
observations of interactions:	Under our control, the subject of the adaptive algorithm
Learning	
learning entity:	the mechanism; the entity that sets the rules of interaction
learning target:	the current mechanism: – do agents observe each other's bids? just prices? – is price set by highest bid or 2nd highest? – are auctions run sequentially or simultaneously? – are bids sequential or simultaenous?
learning experiential data:	alteration of the mechanism for next round
learning update:	objective value with new mechanism
objective:	maximize profit or social welfare

The second, opponent modeling, is a tool used by agents within a multiagent system themselves to predict the future actions of other agents in the environment. An opponent model could itself be learnt, in which case it falls under the "learning target" within our taxonomy shown in Fig. 1. However it may also be provided to the agent a priori. For this reason we treat it here as a tool to be used by an agent in a MAL system.

4.1   Analysis and Prediction Tool

The first MAL tool we discuss leverages Evolutionary Game Theory (EGT) as an analysis and prediction tool for the dynamics of MAL. It is well known that by using concepts from EGT, such as replicator equations and evolutionary stability, we can say something useful about the properties of learning trajectories and equilibria that are learnt by a variety of multi agent learning algorithms [13,22,40,43,48]. We now first briefly outline the differences between EGT and traditional Game Theory, and present some intuitions of the replicator equations and how they can be used as an analysis tool in MAL. For a good overview see [5].

Classical game theory assumes that full knowledge of the normal form game is available to all players, which together with the assumption of individual rationality, or perfectly logical players, does not necessarily reflect the dynamic nature of real world interactions. EGT relaxes the rationality assumption and replaces it by biological operators such as natural selection, crossover and mutation [15,16,25,46]. Central to evolutionary game theory are the replicator dynamics that describe how a population of individuals or agents evolves over time under evolutionary pressure. Each individual has a certain phenotype, using the same pure strategy during its lifetime, and individuals are randomly paired in interaction. The population mix evolves over time according to the reproduction rates of strategies under exponential growth or decay. Their reproductive success is determined by their fitness, which results from these interactions.

The replicator dynamics dictate that the population share of a certain phenotype will increase if the individuals of this type have a higher fitness than the population average when interacting with the current distribution of agents; otherwise their population share will decrease. The population can be described by the state vector $x = (x_1, x_2, ..., x_n)$, with $0 <= x_i <= 1$ for all i and $\sum_i x_i = 1$, representing the fractions of the population belonging to each of the phenotypes or strategies. Now suppose the fitness of type i is given by the fitness function $f_i(x)$, and the average fitness of the population is given by $f(x) = \sum_j [x_j f_j(x)]$. The population change over time can then be written as: $\frac{dx_i}{dt} = x_i[f_i(x) - f(x)]$ or,

$$\dot{x}_i = x_i \left[f_i(\mathbf{x}) - \bar{f}(\mathbf{x}) \right] \qquad (1)$$

which is known as the single population replicator equation.

Let us now consider an example of a population playing the prisoner's dilemma with payoff tables shown in Fig. 2. An individual playing the strategy $i = 1$, i.e. cooperate, on average encounters x_1 individuals also cooperating and x_2 individuals defecting. This means that the average fitness of an individual playing cooperate is $(Ax)_1 = 3x_1 + 0x_2$ Similarly, the average payoff of an individual playing defect is $(Ax)_2 = 5x_1 + 1x_2$. The payoff matrix A determines the payoff an individual receives when interacting with others. The state vector x describes the frequencies of all pure strategies within the population. Success of a strategy i is measured by the difference between its current payoff $(Ax)_i$ and the average payoff of the entire population xAx. Hence, strategies

that perform better than average grow in population share and those performing worse than average diminish. We can now also plot the phase plot of the
trajectories of the dynamical system, which will predict learning traces of various learning algorithms, for an extensive overview see [5]. An RL researcher or
experimentalist can now easily investigate the directional field plot of the learning behavior described by various replicator dynamics models, providing insight
into the equilibrium structure of games and their basins of attraction when various learning strategies are examined. Figure 3 shows the directional field plot
for the prisoner's dilemma using Eq. 1.

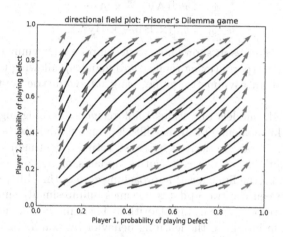

Fig. 3. Directional field plot of the replicator dynamics in the Prisoner's Dilemma
Game. The Nash equilibrium is situated at the top right corner.

On the one hand a population is a collection of individuals, each representing a certain phenotype, i.e., a pure strategy. An individual never changes its
phenotype during the course of its lifetime. Individuals are randomly matched
and play the game according to their predetermined phenotypes; subsequently,
phenotypes replicate according to the realized payoffs. Thus phenotypes compete with each other, fitter strategies prevail while inferior strategies eventually
die out. On the other hand, a **population** might also represent the behavior of
a **particular agent**. The population shares reflect the current preferences over
different strategies and thus defines the agent's policy. The asymmetric replicator dynamics provide a model for two learning agents pitted against each other
and thus, two populations co-evolving.

The single population replicator dynamics are only applicable to symmetric
games. An asymmetric two-player game comprises different payoff tables for the
two players and possibly different action sets (e.g. matching pennies). Likewise
we need two separate populations to describe the dynamics. At each time step
a random individual from one population interacts with a randomly matched
individual from the other population. Instead of one payoff matrix we will now

have two payoff matrixes A and B, which are of size $m \times n$. m is the number of actions the row player can choose from and n the number of actions the column player can choose from. The state vectors of the two populations will now be denoted as x and y, and the dynamics are now specified by a coupled dynamical system consisting of $m + n$ equations: m for the replicators of x and n for the replicators of y. The fitness of an individual of population x playing strategy i against population y is $f_i(x) = (Ay)_i$, and the expected fitness of a random individual of x against y is $f(x) = x^T Ay$. Similarly we can compute the fitness for individuals of population y. For the two populations the replicator equations now look as follows:

$$\dot{x}_i = x_i \left[(\mathbf{A}\mathbf{y})_i - \mathbf{x}^\top \mathbf{A}\mathbf{y} \right]$$
$$\dot{y}_i = y_i \left[(\mathbf{x}^\top \mathbf{B})_i - \mathbf{x}^\top \mathbf{B}\mathbf{y} \right].$$

(2)

Note that a recent result shows how to decompose an asymmetric game into its symmetric counterparts (using replicator dynamics), allowing to discover the Nash structure of an asymmetric game using its symmetric counterparts, for details see [42].

There exist RD models of various reinforcement learning algorithms such as: Q-learning [43], lenient Q-learning [28,29], regret minimization [19], FAQ-learning [18] etc. These are derived by constructing a continuous time limit of the difference equation of two consecutive updates of the respective learning update rule. Taking the limit for δt approaching zero of this difference equation, i.e. the time between the two updates becomes infinitesimally small, yields the RD model of the respective learning algorithm. These models can now be used by researchers to gain insight in the learning behavior by examining the respective phase-plots of the various dynamical systems in a specific game.

4.2   Opponent Modeling Tool

In contrast to replicator dynamics, which is a tool used by an MAL experimentalist or researcher, the second MAL tool we consider is one used by an agent within an MAL system. An opponent model predicts the future actions of other agents in the systems, and may be given a priori or itself learned. In the latter case, it is one example of a "learning" target within our taxonomy shown in Fig. 1.

A recently-published survey of methods for agents modeling other agents provides a comprehensive review of types of opponent modeling methods that can be used for constructing such a tool [1]. These methods include policy reconstruction, type-based reasoning, classification, plan recognition, recursive reasoning, graphical models, and group modeling.

An extended version of the current paper will describe opponent modelling in greater detail. For further details, we refer the reader to the survey [1], which compares and contrasts these methods and summarizes numerous examples from the literature.

5   Conclusion

The purpose of this paper has been to identify, compare, and contrast the main prevalent research paradigms within the multiagent learning literature. To this end, we begin with an overarching taxonomy of multiagent learning, as illustrated in Fig. 1. We then identify three high-level types of agent learning scenarios—individual learning in which a relatively sophisticated agent learns at the individual level; population learning in which a population of cognitively-limited agents learn at the group level by using simple local interactions; and protocol learning in which the interaction mechanism among the agents is itself learned—and then further subdivide them into the five paradigms specified in Sect. 3. We then conclude with coverage of two classes of MAL tools in Sect. 4: one for use by researchers or experimentalists to predict the dynamics of an MAL system, and one for use by the agents themselves.

While this paper provides a high-level classification of MAL paradigms, it does not survey the literature in any particular detail. We hope that the provided perspective and terminology will prove to be useful to the community for description of existing and future multiagent learning approaches.

References

1. Albrecht, S.V., Stone, P.: Autonomous agents modelling other agents: a comprehensive survey and open problems. Artif. Intell. **258**, 66–95 (2018)
2. Altshuler, Y., Bruckstein, A.M.: Static and expanding grid coverage with ant robots: complexity results. Theor. Comput. Sci. **412**(35), 4661–4674 (2011)
3. Banerjee, A.: A simple model of herd behavior. Q. J. Econ. **107**, 797–817 (1992)
4. Barrett, S., Stone, P., Kraus, S.: Empirical evaluation of ad hoc teamwork in the pursuit domain. In: 10th International Conference on Autonomous Agents and Multiagent Systems (AAMAS 2011), Taipei, Taiwan, 2–6 May, 2011, vol. 1–3, pp. 567–574 (2011)
5. Bloembergen, D., Tuyls, K., Hennes, D., Kaisers, M.: Evolutionary dynamics of multi-agent learning: a survey. J. Artif. Intell. Res. **53**, 659–697 (2015)
6. Broecker, B., Caliskanelli, I., Tuyls, K., Sklar, E.I., Hennes, D.: Hybrid insect-inspired multi-robot coverage in complex environments. In: Proceedings of the Towards Autonomous Robotic Systems - 16th Annual Conference, TAROS 2015, Liverpool, UK, 8–10 September 2015, pp. 56–68 (2015)
7. Claus, C., Boutilier, C.: The dynamics of reinforcement learning in cooperative multiagent systems. In: Proceedings of the Fifteenth National Conference on Artificial Intelligence and Tenth Innovative Applications of Artificial Intelligence Conference, AAAI 98, IAAI 98, Madison, Wisconsin, USA, 26–30 July, 1998, pp. 746–752 (1998)
8. Colorni, A., Dorigo, M., Maniezzo, V.: Distributed optimization by ant colonies. In: Varela, F.J., Bourgine, P. (eds.) Towards a Practice of Autonomous Systems: Proceedings of the First European Conference on Artificial Life, pp. 134–142. MIT Press, Cambridge (1992)
9. Dorigo, M., Stützle, T.: Ant Colony Optimization. MIT Press, Cambridge (2004)
10. Fogel, D.B.: Evolving behaviors in the iterated prisoner's dilemma. Evol. Comput. **1**(1), 77–97 (1993)

11. Fogel, D.B.: Evolutionary computation - toward a new philosophy of machine intelligence. IEEE (1995)
12. Galef, B.: Imitation in animals: history, definition, and interpretation of data from the psychological laboratory. In: Zentall, T., Galef, B. (eds.) Social Learning: Psychologicand Biological Perspectives. Lawrence Erlbaum Associates, Hillsdale (1988)
13. Gatti, N., Restelli, M.: Sequence-form and evolutionary dynamics: realization equivalence to agent form and logit dynamics. In: Proceedings of the Thirtieth AAAI Conference on Artificial Intelligence, Phoenix, Arizona, USA, 12–17 February 2016, pp. 509–515 (2016)
14. Genter, K.L., Stone, P.: Influencing a flock via ad hoc teamwork. In: Proceedings of the Swarm Intelligence - 9th International Conference, ANTS 2014, Brussels, Belgium, 10–12 September 2014, pp. 110–121 (2014)
15. Gintis, H.: Game Theory Evolving, 2nd edn. University Press, Princeton (2009)
16. Hofbauer, J., Sigmund, K.: Evolutionary Games and Population Dynamics. Cambridge University Press, Cambridge (1998)
17. Hu, J., Wellman, M.P.: Nash q-learning for general-sum stochastic games. J. Mach. Learn. Res. **4**, 1039–1069 (2003)
18. Kaisers, M., Tuyls, K.: Frequency adjusted multi-agent q-learning. In: 9th International Conference on Autonomous Agents and Multiagent Systems (AAMAS 2010), Toronto, Canada, 10–14 May, 2010, vol. 1–3, pp. 309–316 (2010)
19. Klos, T., van Ahee, G.J., Tuyls, K.: Evolutionary dynamics of regret minimization. In: Balcázar, J.L., Bonchi, F., Gionis, A., Sebag, M. (eds.) ECML PKDD 2010. LNCS (LNAI), vol. 6322, pp. 82–96. Springer, Heidelberg (2010). https://doi.org/10.1007/978-3-642-15883-4_6
20. Knudson, M., Tumer, K.: Policy transfer in mobile robots using neuro-evolutionary navigation. In: Genetic and Evolutionary Computation Conference, GECCO 2012, Philadelphia, PA, USA, 7–11 July, 2012, Companion Material Proceedings, pp. 1411–1412 (2012)
21. Laland, K., Richerson, P., Boyd, R.: Animal social learning: toward a new theoretical approach. In: Klopfer, P., Bateson, P., Thomson, N. (eds.) Perspectives in Ethology. Plenum Press, New York (1993)
22. Lanctot, M.: Further developments of extensive-form replicator dynamics using the sequence-form representation. In: International Conference on Autonomous Agents and Multi-Agent Systems, AAMAS 2014, Paris, France, 5–9 May, 2014, pp. 1257–1264 (2014)
23. Littman, M.: Markov games as a framework for multi-agent reinforcement learning. In: Proceedings of the Eleventh International Conference on Machine Learning, pp. 157–163 (1994)
24. Manderick, B., Spiessens, P.: Fine-grained parallel genetic algorithms. In: Proceedings of the 3rd International Conference on Genetic Algorithms, George Mason University, Fairfax, Virginia, USA, pp. 428–433, June 1989
25. Maynard Smith, J., Price, G.R.: The logic of animal conflict. Nature **246**(2), 15–18 (1973)
26. Mitchell, M.: An Introduction to Genetic Algorithms. MIT Press, Cambridge (1998)
27. Mitchell, T.M.: Machine Learning. McGraw Hill Series in Computer Science. McGraw-Hill, New York (1997)
28. Palmer, G., Tuyls, K., Bloembergen, D., Savani, R.: Lenient multi-agent deep reinforcement learning. Accepted for AAMAS 2018 (2018)

29. Panait, L., Tuyls, K., Luke, S.: Theoretical advantages of lenient learners: an evolutionary game theoretic perspective. J. Mach. Learn. Res. **9**, 423–457 (2008)
30. Pardoe, D., Stone, P., Saar-Tsechansky, M., Keskin, T., Tomak, K.: Adaptive auction mechanism design and the incorporation of prior knowledge. INFORMS J. Comput. **22**(3), 353–370 (2010)
31. Pardoe, D., Stone, P., Saar-Tsechansky, M., Tomak, K.: Adaptive mechanism design: a metalearning approach. In: Proceedings of the 8th International Conference on Electronic Commerce: The new e-commerce - Innovations for Conquering Current Barriers, Obstacles and Limitations to Conducting Successful Business on the Internet, 2006, Fredericton, New Brunswick, Canada, 13–16 August, 2006, pp. 92–102 (2006)
32. Paredis, J.: Coevolutionary computation. Artif. Life **2**(4), 355–375 (1995)
33. Parkes, D.C.: On Learnable Mechanism Design, p. 107–131. Springer-Verlag (2004)
34. Sandholm, T.: Perspectives on multiagent learning. Artif. Intell. **171**(7), 382–391 (2007)
35. Saravanan, N., Fogel, D.B.: Evolving neurocontrollers using evolutionary programming. In: Proceedings of the First IEEE Conference on Evolutionary Computation, IEEE World Congress on Computational Intelligence, Orlando, Florida, USA, 27–29 June, 1994, pp. 217–222 (1994)
36. Shoham, Y., Leyton-Brown, K.: Multiagent Systems - Algorithmic, Game-Theoretic, and Logical Foundations. Cambridge University Press, Cambridge (2009)
37. Shoham, Y., Powers, R., Grenager, T.: If multi-agent learning is the answer, what is the question? Artif. Intell. **171**(7), 365–377 (2007)
38. Stone, P.: Multiagent learning is not the answer. it is the question. Artif. Intell. **171**(7), 402–405 (2007)
39. Stone, P., Veloso, M.M.: Multiagent systems: a survey from a machine learning perspective. Auton. Robots **8**(3), 345–383 (2000)
40. Tuyls, K., Hoen, P.J., Vanschoenwinkel, B.: An evolutionary dynamical analysis of multi-agent learning in iterated games. Auton. Agents Multi-Agent Syst. **12**(1), 115–153 (2006)
41. Tuyls, K., Parsons, S.: What evolutionary game theory tells us about multiagent learning. Artif. Intell. **171**(7), 406–416 (2007)
42. Tuyls, K., Pérolat, J., Lanctot, M., Ostrovski, G., Savani, R., Leibo, J.Z., Ord, T., Graepel, T., Legg, S.: Symmetric decomposition of asymmetric games. Sci. Rep. **8**(1), 1015 (2018)
43. Tuyls, K., Verbeeck, K., Lenaerts, T.: A selection-mutation model for q-learning in multi-agent systems. In: Proceedings of the Second International Joint Conference on Autonomous Agents & Multiagent Systems, AAMAS 2003, Melbourne, Victoria, Australia, 14–18 July, 2003, pp. 693–700 (2003)
44. Tuyls, K., Weiss, G.: Multiagent learning: basics, challenges, and prospects. AI Mag. **33**(3), 41–52 (2012)
45. Urzelai, J., Floreano, D.: Evolutionary robotics: coping with environment change. In: Proceedings of the Genetic and Evolutionary Computation Conference (GECCO 2000), Las Vegas, Nevada, USA, 8–12 July, 2000, pp. 941–948 (2000)
46. Weibull, J.W.: Evolutionary Game Theory. MIT Press, Cambridge (1997)
47. Wooldridge, M.J.: Introduction to Multiagent Systems. Wiley, Hoboken (2002)
48. Wunder, M., Littman, M.L., Babes, M.: Classes of multiagent q-learning dynamics with epsilon-greedy exploration. In: Proceedings of the 27th International Conference on Machine Learning (ICML-10), Haifa, Israel, 21–24 June, 2010, pp. 1167–1174 (2010)

Multiagent Resource Allocation: The Power and Limitations of Bilateral Deals (Extended Abstract)

Nicolas Maudet[✉]

Sorbonne Université, CNRS, Laboratoire d'Informatique de Paris 6, LIP6,
75005 Paris, France
nicolas.maudet@lip6.fr

Abstract. This is a companion extended abstract to the invited talk given at EUMAS-2017. The talk was mostly based on [3,4].

1 Multiagent Resource Allocation: The Setting

In this talk I discussed multiagent resource allocation [2], more specifically a setting where *indivisible goods* have to be assigned to a number of agents. Agents have preferences over bundles they can receive—let us denote by $v_i(\pi(i))$ the value of the bundle $\pi(i)$ received by agent i. The objective is to allocate goods so as to optimize some social welfare measure. For instance we may wish the outcome to be Pareto-efficient, or to maximize the sum of agents' utilities (utilitarian social welfare) [8].

Several protocols can be used for that purpose. We study the decentralized approach first investigated in [9]. Its main features are as follows: (i) negotiation starts with an *initial allocation*; (ii) agents asynchronously *negotiate* resources; (iii) *deals* allow to move from one allocation to another, i.e. $\delta = (A, A')$; (iv) deals may or not involve *payments* (utility transfer), in which case a payment p summing up to 0 among agents takes place; (v) agents accept deals on the basis of a *rationality criterion*, and we assume myopic individual rationality, meaning that $v_i(A') - v_i(A) > p(i)$ for a deal $\delta = (A, A')$; and finally (vi) the dynamics converges when no more deal is possible (the outcome is *stable*).

Different *types of deals* can be considered. Sandholm [9] introduced several "natural" restrictions on the type of exchanges allowed between agents, in particular:

- *1-deals*: exchange of a single resource;
- *bilateral deal*: exchange involving two agents;
- *cyclic deals*: exchange among agents in a cycle.

Whereas positive results typically state that any sequence of individually rational deals eventually converge to some efficient outcome (e.g. to an outcome maximizing utilitarian social welfare in the setting with money), this comes at

F. Belardinelli and E. Argente (Eds.): EUMAS 2017/AT 2017, LNAI 10767, pp. 22–25, 2018.
https://doi.org/10.1007/978-3-030-01713-2_2

a price: deals must be potentially arbitrarily complex to guarantee this [7,9]. In many applications though, deals can only be "simple", and in particular involve only *two* agents (bilateral). Hence the following research question:

> *What can be said about dynamics of distributed multiagent resource allocation involving bilateral deals only? Are there domains restrictions on agents' preferences allowing to retrieve possible convergence results?*

In this talk I gave an overview of results characterizing the power and limits of such bilateral deals in this multiagent resource allocation setting. It is worth noticing that beyond the results described mentioned, the question of the length of sequences of such deals has also been studied [5,6]. For instance, Dunne [5] showed that they can still be exponential, even if restricted to individually rational 1-deals.

2   Bilateral Deals with Payments

It is rather easy to see that in *modular domains* (i.e. the utility of a bundle is the sum of utilities over single goods), any sequence of individually rational *1-deals* must converge to an outcome maximizing utilitarian social welfare. This is a sufficient condition, but does it exactly characterizes those domains guaranteeing the property? It cannot be, because there are certainly other domains offering the same guarantee—even if not very useful, like the *pseudo-constant* domain (agents equally like any allocation where they get at least *some* resource, whatever the resource(s)). But it is possible to show that there can be no domain of valuation functions that would be both sufficient and necessary. Suppose a necessary and sufficient domain (say, $\mathcal{D}$) exists. Let us take v_1 as being a modular function. Certainly if all agents are using v_1 convergence is guaranteed, so v_1 must belong to $\mathcal{D}$. Let us now take v_2 as being a pseudo-constant valuation. Here again, if all agents are using v_2 convergence is guaranteed, so v_2 must also belong to $\mathcal{D}$. As a consequence any scenario involving agents using either v_1 or v_2 must also necessarily converge. The counter-example of Table 1 shows that such a domain cannot exist.

Table 1. A scenario involving two agents

$u_1(\emptyset) =$	0	$u_2(\emptyset) =$	0	$u_1(\emptyset) =$	0	$u_2(\emptyset) =$	0
$u_1(\{\spadesuit\}) =$	4	$u_2(\{\spadesuit\}) =$	$\boxed{1}$	$u_1(\{\spadesuit\}) =$	$\boxed{4}$	$u_2(\{\spadesuit\}) =$	1
$u_1(\{\clubsuit\}) =$	$\boxed{4}$	$u_2(\{\clubsuit\}) =$	3	$u_1(\{\clubsuit\}) =$	4	$u_2(\{\clubsuit\}) =$	$\boxed{3}$
$u_1(\{\spadesuit,\clubsuit\}) =$	4	$u_2(\{\spadesuit,\clubsuit\}) =$	4	$u_1(\{\spadesuit,\clubsuit\}) =$	4	$u_2(\{\spadesuit,\clubsuit\}) =$	4

Note that the preferences of agent a_1 are pseudo-constant, while that of agent a_2 are modular. The table on the left is the initial allocation, yielding a utilitarian social welfare of 5. The table on the right shows the optimal allocation (the social welfare is 7). The reader can easily check that no sequence of individually rational 1-deal possibly leads to this allocation (a swap deal would be required here).

Maximal domains. Given the previous findings on the non-existence of domains exactly characterizing guaranteed convergence, we turned our attention to identify *maximal* domains exhibiting this property. A domain is said to be maximal when *any* larger domain (strictly including it) loses the property of guaranteeing convergence to maximal utilitarian social welfare. In [3] we were able to prove that the modular domain is maximal for guaranteed convergence by means of *bilateral deals*.

To prove this kind of results, we proceed by constructing a situation such that, (i) for an arbitrary agent's utility function *not* picked from the domain, we can construct a scenario where (ii) all the other agents' utility functions are, and such that (iii) from a given initial allocation no sequence of eligible deal can lead to the optimal outcome. This suffices to show failure of convergence, since this property should hold regardless of the initial state. The question is studied in detail in [3].

What this means is that a designer implementing a multiagent system where agents can only interact by means of bilateral deals can only hope to guarantee convergence as long as each agents' preferences are modular (of course, there may be *other* maximal domains, but the modular domain is arguably one of the most natural one). Still, for a specific scenario, convergence may be guaranteed, thus the designer could simply check whether the scenario at hand guarantees convergence. However this requires the designer to know exactly the full profile, *i.e.* the different preferences of all agents involved in the system (as opposed to just know that agents' preferences are drawn from a specific domain), and the computational complexity of the related decision problem is intractable for most representation languages, at least those sufficiently compact [3].

3   Bilateral Deals Without Payments

Regarding the setting without payments, I discussed the restricted variant of house allocation where agents must only receive a single good (and preferences are assumed to be given as linear orders). In that settings, bilateral deals correspond to *swap deals*: agents simply exchange one resource for another. This setting is well-studied and the *Top-Trading Cycle* algorithm [10] is the method of choice when a centralized approach is used. But in a distributed perspective, how do sequences of individual rational swap deals perform?

Certainly, bilateral (swap) deals are not sufficient to reach Pareto-optimal allocations, as agents may need to set up a deal involving all of them to reach it. On the following example, assuming that agents all hold their second best good, no individual rational swap is possible, while it would be possible to assign each agent her top one.

agent 1: ♣ ≻ ♠ ≻ ♡
agent 2: ♠ ≻ ♡ ≻ ♣
agent 3: ♡ ≻ ♣ ≻ ♠

However, interestingly, under the assumption that agents' preferences are *single-peaked* [1,8], we can also retrieve a positive result regarding convergence by means of individually rational swap deals to Pareto-efficient outcomes. In general, it is also possible to quantify the worst-case loss (in terms of average rank of the good obtained by agents) of the outcome obtained with this protocol, compared to the optimal one. This "price" is asymptotically 2, meaning that the average rank of agents may only be half of the one which would be obtained in the optimal allocation. In fact, it turns out to be the same as any protocol guaranteeing individual rationality.

References

1. Black, D., Newing, R.A., McLean, I., McMillan, A., Monroe, B.L.: The theory of committees and elections. Springer, Netherlands (1958)
2. Chevaleyre, Y., et al.: Issues in multiagent resource allocation. Informatica **30**, 3–31 (2006)
3. Chevaleyre, Y., Endriss, U., Maudet, N.: Simple negotiation schemes for agents with simple preferences: sufficiency, necessity and maximality. J. Auton. Agents Multiagent Syst. **20**(2), 234–259 (2010)
4. Damamme, A., Beynier, A., Chevaleyre, Y., Maudet, N.: The power of swap deals in distributed resource allocation. In: Proceedings of the 14th International Conference on Autonomous Agents and Multiagent Systems (AAMAS-15), Istanbul, Turkey, pp. 625–633. ACM, May 2015
5. Dunne, P.E.: Extremal behaviour in multiagent contract negotiation. J. Artif. Intell. Res. **23**, 41–78 (2005)
6. Endriss, U., Maudet, N.: On the communication complexity of multilateral trading: extended report. J. Auton. Agents Multiagent Syst. **11**(1), 91–107 (2005)
7. Endriss, U., Maudet, N., Sadri, F., Toni, F.: Negotiating socially optimal allocations of resources. J. Artif. Intell. Res. **25**, 315–348 (2006)
8. Moulin, H.: Axioms of Cooperative Decision Making. Cambridge University Press, New York (1988)
9. Sandholm, T.W.: Contract types for satisficing task allocation: I theoretical results. In: Proceedings of the 1998 AAAI Spring Symposium on Satisficing Models (1998)
10. Shapley, L., Scarf, H.: On cores and indivisibility. J. Math. Econ. **1**(1), 23–37 (1974)

EUMAS 2017: Agent-Based Modelling

Incentive Compatible Proactive Skill Posting in Referral Networks

Ashiqur R. KhudaBukhsh[✉], Jaime G. Carbonell, and Peter J. Jansen

Carnegie Mellon University, Pittsburgh, USA
{akhudabu,jgc,pjj}@cs.cmu.edu

Abstract. Learning to refer in a network of experts (agents) consists of distributed estimation of other experts' topic-conditioned skills so as to refer problem instances too difficult for the referring agent to solve. This paper focuses on the cold-start case, where experts post a subset of their top skills to connected agents, and as the results show, improve overall network performance and, in particular, early-learning-phase behavior. The method surpasses state-of-the-art, i.e., proactive-DIEL, by proposing a new mechanism to penalize experts who misreport their skills, and extends the technique to other distributed learning algorithms: proactive-ϵ-Greedy, and proactive-Q-Learning. Our proposed new technique exhibits stronger discouragement of strategic lying, both in the limit and finite-horizon empirical analysis. The method is shown robust to noisy self-skill estimates and in evolving networks.

Keywords: Active learning · Referral networks
Proactive skill posting

1 Introduction

Learning-to-refer in expert referral networks is a recently proposed active learning setting where an expert can refer problem instances to appropriate colleagues if she finds the task at hand difficult to solve [1]. Such a network draws inspiration from the real world examples of expert networks, such as among physicians or within consultancy firms. Initially designed for uninformative priors, an extension of the learning setting is proposed in [2] where experts are allowed a one-time local-network advertisement of a subset of their skills to their colleagues. The success in the extended learning setting depends on a *truthful mechanism* to elicit the true skills of the experts in the network. The experts, as selfish agents, try to maximize the number of tasks they receive to maximize fees. In this paper, we propose a novel penalty mechanism (applied to a diverse set of action selection algorithms) that shows stronger discouragement to strategic lying, including incentive compatibility for some referral algorithms, and also obtains a modest performance improvement.

While we study and contrast the behavior in the limit of our proposed mechanism against past work (see, Sect. 3.3), and show that theoretically, our mechanism discourages willful misreporting better than previous work, many of our

© Springer Nature Switzerland AG 2018
F. Belardinelli and E. Argente (Eds.): EUMAS 2017/AT 2017, LNAI 10767, pp. 29–43, 2018.
https://doi.org/10.1007/978-3-030-01713-2_3

experimental results deal with finite-horizon behavior (see, Sect. 5.2), acknowledging that in a practical setting, we cannot afford an unbounded number of samples to identify truthful, skilled workers. Although our primary focus is on referral networks, the challenge that we are addressing is relevant to the multi-armed bandit problem with partially-available noisy priors, a fairly general problem that may arise in several applications. We also see our work as a part of the growing trend of several lines of research on adversarial Machine Learning [3].

A key aspect on which we differ from past works on multi-armed bandits [4–7] is our choice of data sets: in addition to constructing traditional synthetic data that obeys well-known distributions, we evaluate algorithms on a referral network of high-performance SAT (propositional satisfiability problem) solvers where neither expertise nor noise in estimating skill obey known parameterized distributions.

2   Related Work

Our starting point for this work was the augmented setting of referral learning [1,9] first proposed in [2] and then extended in [8]. [2] proposed several modifications to Distributed Interval Estimation Learning (DIEL), up to then the best referral learning algorithm on uninformative priors. The modified algorithm, *proactive*-DIEL, demonstrated superior performance, especially during the initial learning phase, even in the presence of noise in skill self-estimates. It also showed empirical evidence of being near-Bayesian-Nash Incentive Compatible, i.e., misreporting skills to receive more referrals provided little or no benefit when all other experts report truthfully. More recently, [8] showed that the mechanism proposed in proactive-DIEL can be adapted with minor modifications to another algorithm (ϵ-Greedy), and that the new algorithm is robust to noisy self-skill estimates. Compared to the experiments reported in [8], we achieve stronger incentive compatibility covering a wider range of referral algorithms while showing comparable or better resilience to noise and dynamic network changes (Table 1).

Table 1. Summary of contributions: Blue columns represent new algorithms first proposed in this paper. Blue cells indicate new experimental results (e.g., cell (3,1), (3,5)), a check mark indicates that a property holds, and two check marks indicate we improve the known state of the art (including the case where there were no known previous baselines to compare against).

	proactive-DIEL [2]	proactive-DIEL$_t$	proactive-ϵGreedy [8]	proactive-ϵGreedy$_t$	proactive-Q-Learning$_t$
Incentive Compatibility	✓ [2]	✓✓	✓	✓✓	✓✓
Tolerance to noisy skill-estimates	✓ [2]	✓	✓	✓	✓✓
Early performance gain	✓ [2]	✓✓	✓	✓✓	✓✓
Steady-state performance gain	✓ [2]	✓✓	✓	✓✓	✓✓
Robustness to evolving networks	✓ [8]	✓✓	✓	✓✓	✓✓

In our work, the baseline algorithms are the non-proactive referral algorithms, of which DIEL is the known state of the art in the non-proactive setting. DIEL, a reinforcement learning technique balancing the exploration-exploitation trade-off, traces back to a chain of research on interval estimation learning, first proposed in [10,11] and has been successfully used in jointly learning the accuracy of labeling sources and obtaining the most informative labels in [12]. Adversarial Machine Learning focuses on a wide variety of issues, ranging from adversarial attempts to alter or influence the training data [13] to intrusion attacks by crafting negatives that would pass a classifier (false negatives) [14]. A comprehensive survey is available in [3]. In our work, deliberate skill misreporting from an expert would not only make it difficult for connected experts to learn appropriate referral choices, but it may potentially enable a weaker expert receive more business at the expense of a stronger expert and thus reducing the overall network performance.

While we note that there exists a large body of literature on truthful mechanism design [7,15–17], a few key differences set us apart from *budgeted multi-armed bandit mechanism* motivated by crowdsourcing platforms presented in [16]. Our setting is *distributed*; hence it consists of many parallel multi-armed bandit problems. Also, experts have *varying topical expertise*, which increases the scale of the problem as each expert needs to estimate the expertise of her colleagues for each of the topics. In contrast, [16] considered only homogenous tasks. Reflecting real-world scenarios where experts have differential expertise across topics, and communication/advertisement is focused on the top skills, proactive-DIEL deals with partially available priors, i.e., experts are restricted to bidding for business in their top skill areas only, (a factor [16] did not need to consider because of homogeneous tasks). Unlike budget-limited MAB [16,18,19], the budget restriction in our case is on the advertisement; although we focus on a finite-horizon performance analysis, there is no restriction on exploration or exploitation as such. Finally, we present proof sketches for incentive compatibility in the limit, as well as empirical performance evaluation on both synthetic data and real-world data without distributional assumptions.

3   Referral Network

3.1   Preliminaries

We summarize our basic notation, definitions, and assumptions, mostly from [1,2], where further details regarding expertise, network parameters, proactive skill posting mechanism and simulation details can be found.

Referral Network: Represented by a graph (V, E) of size k in which each vertex v_i corresponds to an expert e_i $(1 \leq k)$ and each bidirectional edge $\langle v_i, v_j \rangle$ indicates a *referral link* which implies e_i and e_j can co-refer problem instances.

Subnetwork of an expert e_i: The set of experts linked to an expert e_i by a referral link.

Scenario: Set of m instances $(q_1, \ldots, q_m)$ belonging to n topics $(t_1, \ldots, t_n)$ addressed by the k experts $(e_1, \ldots, e_k)$.

Expertise: Expertise of an expert/question pair $\langle e_i, q_l \rangle$ is the probability with which e_i can solve q_l.

Referral Mechanism: For a query budget Q (following [1,2], we kept fixed to $Q = 2$ across all our current experiments), this consists of the following steps.

1. A user issues an *initial query* q_l to a randomly chosen *initial expert* e_i.
2. The initial expert e_i examines the instance and solves it if possible. This depends on the *expertise* of e_i wrt. q_l.
3. If not, a *referral query* is issued by e_i to a *referred expert* e_j within her sub-network, with a query budget of $Q - 1$. *Learning-to-refer* involves improving the estimate of who is most likely to solve the problem.
4. If the referred expert succeeds, she sends the solution to the initial expert, who sends it to the user.

Advertising Unit: a tuple $\langle e_i, e_j, t_k, \mu_{t_k} \rangle$, where e_i is the *target expert*, e_j is the *advertising expert*, t_k is the topic and μ_{t_k} is e_j's (advertised) topical expertise.

Advertising Budget: the number of advertising units available to an expert, following [2], set to twice the size of that expert's subnetwork; each expert reports her top two skills to her subnetwork.

Advertising Protocol: a one-time advertisement that happens at the beginning of the simulation or when an expert joins the network. The advertising expert e_j reports to each target expert e_i in her subnetwork the two tuples $\langle e_i, e_j, t_{best}, \mu_{t_{best}} \rangle$ and $\langle e_i, e_j, t_{secondBest}, \mu_{t_{secondBest}} \rangle$, i.e., the top two topics in terms of the advertising expert's topic means.

Explicit Bid: A topic advertised in the above protocol.

Implicit Bid: A topic that is not advertised, for which an upper skill bound $<$ expert's two top advertised skills.

3.2 Referral Algorithms

From an individual expert's point of view, the referral decision is an action selection problem. We give a short description of action selection for the non-proactive referral algorithms, and then extend to proactive skill positing.

DIEL: DIEL uses Interval Estimation Learning to select action a for which the upper-confidence interval $UI(a)$ is largest, where

$$UI(a) = m(a) + \frac{s(a)}{\sqrt{n}}$$

$m(a)$ is the mean observed reward, $s(a)$ is the standard deviation of the observed rewards and n is the number of observations so far. The intuition behind DIEL is to combine exploitation (via high mean) and exploration (via high variance). As in [1,2], we initialized the mean reward, standard deviation and number of observations for all actions to 0.5, 0.7071 and 2 respectively as a non-informative prior.

ϵ-Greedy: Unlike DIEL, ϵ-Greedy only considers the mean observed reward to determine the most promising action [4]. It explores via an explicit probabilistic diversification step – randomly selecting a connected expert for referral. We set ϵ as in in [8]: Letting $\epsilon = \frac{\alpha * K}{N}$ (where K is the subnetwork size and N is the total observations) we configured α by a parameter sweep on a training set as in [1].

Q-Learning: Q-Learning [20] is a model-free reinforcement learning technique used to learn an optimal action selection policy provided that all actions are sampled repeatedly in all states. To ensure this, we combined Q-Learning with ϵ-Greedy as an action-selection component. For all of the above algorithms, a successful task receives a reward of 1 and a failed task receives a reward of 0.

3.3   Proactive Referral Algorithms

We extend the non-proactive referral algorithms to the augmented setting with proactive skill posting, both in previous work [2,8] and the current work.

proactive-DIEL: In [2], proactive-DIEL was derived from DIEL by enabling each expert to post a self-estimated skill prior initializing the mean expected reward. Given advertisement unit $\langle e_i, e_j, t_k, \mu_{t_k} \rangle$ the $reward_{mean}(e_i, t_k, e_k)$ (mean reward received by expert e_k on topic t_k as observed by expert e_i) is initialized to μ_{t_k} (explicit bid). When not, proactive-DIEL initializes $reward_{mean}(e_i, t_k, e_k)$ to $\mu_{t_{secondBest}}$, which is in effect an upper bound.

Since each expert has an incentive to maximize its income by drawing new business, a probabilistic penalty mechanism was added to discourage misreporting. The probability *penaltyProbability* with which a *penalty* (kept to 0.35 in [2]) is applied, is computed as described in Algorithm 1 below.

> **if** *referredExpert* succeeds **then**
>   *penaltyProbability* ← 0
> **else**
>   **if** *topic t* is *explicitBid* **then**
>   *penaltyProbability* ← $\mu_{advertised}$
>   **else**
>   *penaltyProbability* ← $\hat{\mu}_{observed}$
>   **end**
> **end**

Algorithm 1. Penalty mechanism proposed in [2]

proactive-ϵ-Greedy: proactive-ϵ-Greedy was adapted essentially the same way as proactive-DIEL, the only minor difference being that a failed task does not receive a penalty if it was a diversification step. Since one of our primary contributions is a better mechanism to prevent strategic misreporting, we describe this in the context of proactive-Q-Learning$_t$, an algorithm also first proposed here.

proactive-Q-Learning$_t$ uses the same initialization and a similar technique to bound unknown priors with reported second-best skills as proactive-DIEL and proactive-ϵ-Greedy. The Q-function for each action is initialized with its advertised mean or corresponding $\mu_{t_{secondBest}}$ in absence of such advertisement unit.

However, we take a marked deviation in defining the penalty function, which incorporates a factor we may call *distrust*, as it estimates a likelihood the expert is lying, given our current observations:

$$penalty = C_2 distrust, \text{where}$$
$$distrust = distrustFactor_1 + distrustFactor_2;$$
$$distrustFactor_1 = |\mu_{t_{best}} - \hat{\mu}_{t_{best}}|\zeta(n_{t_{best}}) \text{ and,}$$
$$distrustFactor_2 = |\mu_{t_{seconBest}} - \hat{\mu}_{t_{secondBest}}|\zeta(n_{t_{secondBest}})$$

where $\zeta(n_t) = \frac{n_t}{n_t + C_1}$, a factor ramping up to 1 in the steady state, where n_t is the number of observations for topic t.

Basically, $distrustFactor_1$ and $distrustFactor_2$ estimate how much the advertised skill is off from its estimated mean, for the best skill and second-best skill respectively. C_1 and C_2 are the two configurable parameters of this mechanism; the larger the value, greater is the discouragement for strategic lying. In all our experiments, C_1 was set to 50. C_2 was set to 1, 2 and 3 for proactive-DIEL$_t$, proactive-ϵ-Greedy$_t$, and proactive-Q-Learning$_t$, respectively.

The newly proposed penalty mechanism differs from the old method in that all tasks receive a penalty regardless of whether the referred expert solves it or not. Second, the two mechanisms penalize the extent of misreporting in different ways, as the previous method fails to penalize underbidding. We can show a simple two-expert subnetwork to illustrate how underbidding could be used to attract more business in the earlier scheme. Consider two experts, e_1 and e_2, have identical expertise ($1 - \epsilon$, $\epsilon \leq 0.5$) across all tasks. e_1 reports truthfully while e_1 underbids and advertises ($1 - 2\epsilon$). For a penalty of r ($r > 0$), the expected mean reward for e_1 will be ($1 - \epsilon$) $- \epsilon$ ($1 - \epsilon$) r. Due to underbidding, e_2 will have an unfair advantage over e_1 as her expected mean reward will be ($1 - \epsilon$) $- \epsilon$ ($1 - 2\epsilon$) r, larger than e_1.

proactive-DIEL$_t$ **and proactive-ϵ-Greedy**$_t$: proactive-DIEL$_t$ and proactive-ϵ-Greedy$_t$ denote the corresponding proactive versions with the new penalty mechanism.

We provide proof sketches demonstrating Bayesian-Nash incentive compatibility in the limit for our new mechanism.

Theorem 1. *Under the assumption that all actions are visited infinitely often, in the limit, strategic lying is not beneficial in proactive-Q-Learning$_t$.*

Proof. We give a proof sketch by showing that a lying expert will have a non-zero penalty in the limit.

$$\lim_{n \to \infty} \hat{\mu}_{t_{best}} = \mu_{t_{best}} \tag{1}$$

$$\lim_{n \to \infty} \hat{\mu}_{t_{secondBest}} = \mu_{t_{secondBest}} \tag{2}$$

$$\lim_{n \to \infty} \zeta(n) = 1 \tag{3}$$

Hence, for a truthful expert both *distrust* and *penalty* approach zero in the limit. However, for a lying expert at least one of the estimates ($distrustFactor_1$ or $distrustFactor_2$) is off by a positive constant c. Hence, in the limit, $distrust \geq c$ and $penalty \geq C_2 c$, therefore a truthful expert will always receive more reward than if she lies and since Q-Learning considers a discounted sum of rewards, eventually, a truthful expert will have a larger Q-value than if she lies. Ergo, strategic lying is not beneficial when all other experts are truthful.

Theorem 2. *Under the assumption that all actions are visited infinitely often, in the limit, strategic lying is not beneficial in proactive-ϵ-Greedy$_t$.*

Proof. The proof is essentially the same as the previous proof.

Theorem 3. *Under the assumption that all actions are visited infinitely often, in the limit, strategic lying is not beneficial in proactive-DIEL$_t$.*

Proof. In our previous proof, we already showed that in the limit, a lying expert will always receive a higher penalty than a truthful expert which will effectively lower the reward mean.

For any reward sequence $r_1, r_2, \ldots, r_n$, and a penalty sequence $p_1, p_2, \ldots, p_n$, $-max(p_1, p_2, \ldots, p_n) \leq r_i \leq 1 - min(p_1, p_2, \ldots, p_n)$, $1 \leq i \leq n$.

Now, $distrust \leq 2$. Hence, $0 \leq p_i \leq 2C_2, 1 \leq i \leq n$.

Hence, $-2C_2 \leq r_i \leq 1$, i.e., all rewards are finite and bounded. This means, in the limit, the variance of the reward sequence is finite and bounded. Hence,

$$\lim_{n \to \infty} UI(a) = \lim_{n \to \infty} (m(a) + \frac{s(a)}{\sqrt{n}}) = m(a) \tag{4}$$

This means, in the limit, the reward for DIEL will be dominated by its mean reward. Since a lying expert will always incur higher penalty than a truthful expert, an expert will have a higher reward mean when it behaves truthfully.

Unlike the Q-learning variants and ϵ-Greedy algorithms, there is no guarantee for DIEL that all actions are visited infinitely often, although a variant can guarantee that condition with random visits at ϵ probability, and perform similarly in the finite case for small enough ϵ.

4   Experimental Setup

Data set: as our synthetic data set, we used the same 1000 scenarios used in [1,2]. Each scenario consists of 100 experts connected through a referral network and 10 topics. For our experiments involving SAT solvers, we used 100 SATenstein (version 2.0) solvers obtained from the experiments presented in [21] as experts. As topics we use the six SAT distributions on which SATenstein is configured. The details of the SAT distributions can be found in [21].

Algorithm Configuration: The version of DIEL we used is parameter free. The remaining parameterized algorithms are configured by selecting 100 random instantiations of each algorithm and running them on a small background data set (generated with the same distributional parameters as our evaluation set). We selected the parameter configuration with the best performance on the background data.

Performance Measure: following [1,2], we used overall task accuracy as our performance measure. In order to empirically evaluate Bayesian-Nash incentive compatibility, we followed the same experimental protocol followed in [2] (described in Sect. 5.2).

Computational Environment: experiments on synthetic data were carried out on Matlab R2016 running Windows 10. Experiments on SAT solver referral networks were carried out on a cluster of dual-core 2.4 GHz machines with 3 MB cache and 32 GB RAM running Linux 2.6.

5   Results

5.1   Overall Performance Gain

Figure 1 compares the performance of the proactive algorithms with their non-proactive versions under the assumption of truthful reporting and accurate self-skill estimates. We also compare against the older proactive algorithms of which proactive-DIEL can be considered state of the art. The two main aspects of note are performance in the early learning phase, and steady state performance. We first observe that, as expected, all new proactive algorithms did better than their non-proactive counterparts, both in steady state and during the early phase of learning, while noting that the gap between DIEL and its proactive versions was less than the corresponding difference for the other two algorithms. We also obtained a modest performance gain over the state of the art and both proactive-DIEL$_t$ and proactive-ϵ-Greedy$_t$ did slightly better than the earlier proactive referral algorithms.

5.2   Incentive Compatibility

Next, we focus on the case of deliberate (strategic) misreporting, i.e. experts trying to get more business by overstating (or counter-intuitively, understating)

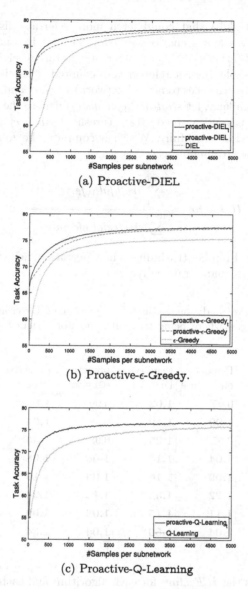

(a) Proactive-DIEL

(b) Proactive-ϵ-Greedy.

(c) Proactive-Q-Learning

Fig. 1. Performance comparison with previous proactive algorithms and corresponding non-proactive versions

their skills. While our theoretical results (see, Sect. 3.3) indicate *proactive*$_t$ algorithms are incentive compatible in the limit, empirical evaluation on a finite horizon addresses practical benefits.

Following [2], we treat the number of referrals received as a proxy for expert benefit, and we empirically analyze Bayesian-Nash incentive compatibility by examining all specific strategy combination (e.g., truthfully report best-skill but overbid second-best skill) that could fetch more referrals (listed in Table 2). For a given strategy s and scenario $scenario_i$, we first fix one expert, say e_l^i. Let $truthfulReferrals(e_l^i)$ denote the number of referrals received by e_l^i beyond a steady-state threshold (i.e., a referral gets counted if the initial expert has referred 1000 or more instances to her subnetwork) when e_l^i and all other experts report truthfully. Similarly, let $strategicReferrals(e_l^i)$ denote the number of referrals received by e_l^i beyond a steady-state threshold when e_l^i misreports while everyone else advertises truthfully. We then compute the following Incentive Compatibility factor ($ICFactor$) as:

$$ICFactor = \frac{\sum_{i=1}^{1000} truthfulReferrals(e_l^i)}{\sum_{i=1}^{1000} strategicReferrals(e_l^i)}.$$

A value greater than 1 implies truthfulness in expectation, i.e., truthful reporting fetched more referrals than strategic lying.

Table 2. Comparative study on empirical evaluation of Bayesian-Nash incentive-compatibility. Strategies where being truthful is no worse than being dishonest are highlighted in bold.

$\mu_{t_{best}}$	$\mu_{t_{secondBest}}$	Penalty on Failure	Penalty on Distrust	proactive ϵGreedy	proactive ϵGreedy$-t$	proactive Q-Learning$_t$
Truthful	Overbid	0.99	**1.02**	0.99	**1.03**	0.97
Overbid	Truthful	**1.00**	**1.19**	0.98	**1.24**	**1.35**
Overbid	Overbid	0.97	**1.25**	0.98	**1.36**	**1.39**
Truthful	Underbid	**1.04**	**1.15**	**1.00**	**1.08**	**1.21**
Underbid	Truthful	**1.09**	**1.16**	**1.06**	**1.10**	**1.17**
Underbid	Underbid	**1.22**	**1.32**	**1.12**	**1.24**	**1.56**
Underbid	Overbid	**1.11**	**1.15**	**1.09**	**1.09**	**1.14**
Overbid	Underbid	**1.04**	**1.50**	**1.04**	**1.34**	**1.63**

Table 2 presents the $ICFactors$ for each algorithm and each strategy combination. We see that, beyond the steady-state threshold, strategic misreporting is hardly beneficial and in fact counterproductive in most cases. Proactive-DIEL$_t$ was (slightly but consistently) better at discouraging each strategy combination than proactive-DIEL. The only case truthful advertising fetched slightly fewer referrals for proactive-Q-Learning$_t$ is when an expert truthfully reports her top skill but overbids her second-best skill (in fact a hard case for all the algorithms). This is likely the result of the way the posted second-best skill is used to bound implicit bids. However, on doubling the horizon (i.e., considering 10,000 samples per subnetwork), we found that proactive-Q-Learning$_t$'s $ICFactor$ improved to 1.04.

5.3   Robustness to Noisy Skill Estimates, Evolving Networks

So far, we have shown that our proposed proactive referral algorithms address the cold start problem better than their non-proactive counterparts and provide stronger discouragement to strategic lying. However, even when experts post their skills truthfully, their self-estimates may not be precise. Imprecise skill estimation in proactive skill posting was first explored in [2,8]. Note that, since a noisy bid can be interpreted as deliberate misreporting and vice-versa, robustness to noisy self-skill estimates and robustness to strategic lying are two major goals and there lies an inherent trade-off between them. Following [2], we assume Gaussian noise on the estimates in the form of $\hat{\mu} = \mu + \mathcal{N}(0, \sigma_{noise})$, where $\hat{\mu}$ is an expert's own estimate of her true topic-mean μ, and σ_{noise} is a small constant (0.05 or 0.1 in our experiments).

Figure 2 compares the performance of the proactive referral algorithms with noisy estimates with the noise-free case and their non-proactive versions. Resilience to the noise depends on the algorithm. In proactive-DIEL$_t$, a small amount of noise (0.05) degrades the steady-state performance, but retains a small advantage over the non-proactive version. While both versions of noisy proactive-DIEL$_t$ do substantially better in the early-learning phase, there is no steady-state performance gain in the presence of larger noise. Proactive-ϵ-Greedy$_t$ was the most resilient (not shown in the figure): even with a larger noise value, it kept a significant lead over the non-proactive version even in the steady state (task accuracy: 77.33% ($\sigma_{noise} = 0.1$), 76.76% ($\sigma_{noise} = 0.05$), and 75.26% for the non-proactive version). Proactive-Q-Learning$_t$ was the most sensitive: with smaller noise value, the early-learning-phase gain disappears again in the steady state; with higher noise value, proactive skill posting became counter-productive.

Referral networks may be dynamic, with new experts joining in and old experts leaving. We have already seen that a primary benefit of proactive methods is that they address the cold-start problem. Rapid improvement in the early learning phase is perhaps even more important for evolving networks. Figure 2(c) presents an extreme case of 20% network change at regular interval. We found that the proactive algorithms handled the network changes much better than the original DIEL, with proactive-DIEL$_t$ marginally outperforming proactive-DIEL.

5.4   SAT Solver Referral Network

As in [8], we also ran several experiments on a referral network of high-performance Stochastic Local Search (SLS) solvers, a more realistic situation in which expertise or noise in self-skill estimates do not obey known parameterized distributions. Our experts are 100 SATenstein solvers with varying expertise on six SAT distributions (map to topics). We ran experiments on 10 randomly chosen referral networks from our synthetic data set. In order to save computational cycles, in these experiments, we only focus on the referral behavior. This explains why our choice of horizon is smaller (also, the number of topics is less than the synthetic data set). On a given SAT instance, the referred SATenstein solver is run with a cutoff time of 1 CPU second. A solved instance

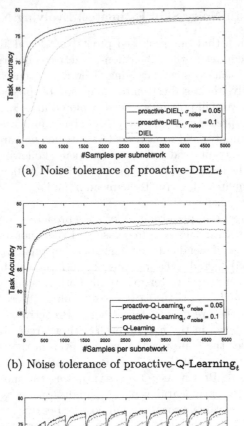

(a) Noise tolerance of proactive-DIEL$_t$

(b) Noise tolerance of proactive-Q-Learning$_t$

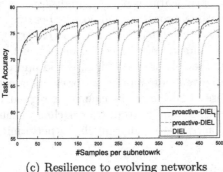

(c) Resilience to evolving networks

Fig. 2. Robustness to noisy skill estimates, evolving networks

(a satisfying model is found) fetches a reward of 1, a failed instance (timeout) fetches a reward of 0.

Figure 3 compares the performance of proactive and non-proactive algorithms on this data set. Figure 3(a) shows that proactive-DIEL$_t$ retains the early-learning phase advantage over DIEL, but the slight performance gain in steady state is missing. On the other hand, Fig. 3(b) shows qualitatively similar behavior as the synthetic data set: throughout the learning phase, proactive-ϵ-Greedy$_t$ maintained a modest lead over its non-proactive version.

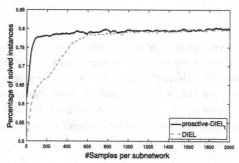

(a) Performance comparison between DIEL and proactive-DIEL$_t$

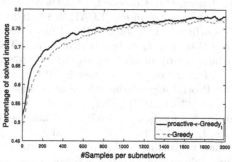

(b) Performance comparison between ϵ-Greedy and proactive-ϵ-Greedy$_t$

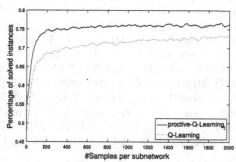

(c) Performance comparison between Q-Learning and proactive-Q-Learning$_t$

Fig. 3. Performance comparison on SAT solver referral network

6 Conclusions

We proposed an incentive compatible mechanism improving the state of the art for referral learning, both in overall performance and in discouraging strategic lying. We extended the algorithms (DIEL, ϵ-Greedy) as well as proposed a new one (Q-Learning) to use the new mechanism, and compared their behavior both with and without noise on the self-skill estimates, indicating ϵ-Greedy to be the most and Q-Learning the least robust. Similar experiments on automated agents (SAT solvers) confirmed the results on synthetic data.

References

1. KhudaBukhsh, A.R., Jansen, P.J., Carbonell, J.G.: Distributed learning in expert referral networks. Eur. Conf. Artif. Intell. (ECAI) **2016**, 1620–1621 (2016)
2. KhudaBukhsh, A.R., Carbonell, J.G., Jansen, P.J.: Proactive skill posting in referral networks. In: Kang, B.H., Bai, Q. (eds.) AI 2016. LNCS (LNAI), vol. 9992, pp. 585–596. Springer, Cham (2016). https://doi.org/10.1007/978-3-319-50127-7_52
3. Huang, L., Joseph, A.D., Nelson, B., Rubinstein, B.I., Tygar, J.: Adversarial machine learning. In: Proceedings of the 4th ACM Workshop on Security and Artificial Intelligence, pp. 43–58. ACM (2011)
4. Auer, P., Cesa-Bianchi, N., Fischer, P.: Finite-time analysis of the multiarmed bandit problem. Mach. Learn. **47**(2–3), 235–256 (2002)
5. Chakrabarti, D., Kumar, R., Radlinski, F., Upfal, E.: Mortal multi-armed bandits. In: Advances in Neural Information Processing Systems, pp. 273–280 (2009)
6. Xia, Y., Li, H., Qin, T., Yu, N., Liu, T.: Thompson sampling for Budgeted Multi-armed Bandits. CoRR abs/1505.00146 (2015)
7. Tran-Thanh, L., Chapman, A.C., Rogers, A., Jennings, N.R.: Knapsack based optimal policies for budget-limited multi-armed bandits. In: Proceedings of the Twenty-Sixth AAAI Conference on Artificial Intelligence (2012)
8. KhudaBukhsh, A.R., Carbonell, J.G., Jansen, P.J.: Proactive-DIEL in evolving referral networks. In: Criado Pacheco, N., Carrascosa, C., Osman, N., Julián Inglada, V. (eds.) EUMAS/AT -2016. LNCS (LNAI), vol. 10207, pp. 148–156. Springer, Cham (2017). https://doi.org/10.1007/978-3-319-59294-7_13
9. KhudaBukhsh, A.R., Carbonell, J.G., Jansen, P.J.: Robust learning in expert networks: a comparative analysis. In: Kryszkiewicz, M., Appice, A., Ślęzak, D., Rybinski, H., Skowron, A., Raś, Z.W. (eds.) ISMIS 2017. LNCS (LNAI), vol. 10352, pp. 292–301. Springer, Cham (2017). https://doi.org/10.1007/978-3-319-60438-1_29
10. Kaelbling, L.P.: Learning in Embedded Systems. MIT Press, Cambridge (1993)
11. Kaelbling, L.P., Littman, M.L., Moore, A.P.: Reinforcement learning: a survey. J. Artif. Intell. Res. **4**, 237–285 (1996)
12. Donmez, P., Carbonell, J.G., Schneider, J.: Efficiently learning the accuracy of labeling sources for selective sampling. In: Proceedings of KDD 2009, p. 259 (2009)
13. Newsome, J., Karp, B., Song, D.: Paragraph: thwarting signature learning by training maliciously. In: Zamboni, D., Kruegel, C. (eds.) RAID 2006. LNCS, vol. 4219, pp. 81–105. Springer, Heidelberg (2006). https://doi.org/10.1007/11856214_5
14. Papernot, N., McDaniel, P., Jha, S., Fredrikson, M., Celik, Z.B., Swami, A.: The limitations of deep learning in adversarial settings. In: IEEE European Symposium on Security and Privacy (EuroS&P), pp. 372–387. IEEE (2016)

15. Babaioff, M., Sharma, Y., Slivkins, A.: Characterizing truthful multi-armed bandit mechanisms. In: Proceedings of the 10th ACM conference on Electronic commerce, pp. 79–88. ACM (2009)
16. Biswas, A., Jain, S., Mandal, D., Narahari, Y.: A truthful budget feasible multi-armed bandit mechanism for crowdsourcing time critical tasks. In: Proceedings of the 2015 International Conference on Autonomous Agents and Multiagent Systems, pp. 1101–1109 (2015)
17. Tran-Thanh, L., Stein, S., Rogers, A., Jennings, N.R.: Efficient crowdsourcing of unknown experts using multi-armed bandits. In: European Conference on Artificial Intelligence, pp. 768–773 (2012)
18. Xia, Y., Qin, T., Ma, W., Yu, N., Liu, T.Y.: Budgeted multi-armed bandits with multiple plays. In: Proceedings of 25th International Joint Conference on Artificial Intelligence (2016)
19. Xia, Y., Ding, W., Zhang, X.D., Yu, N., Qin, T.: Budgeted bandit problems with continuous random costs. In: Proceedings of the 7th Asian Conference on Machine Learning, pp. 317–332 (2015)
20. Watkins, C.J., Dayan, P.: Q-Learning. Mach. Learn. **8**(3), 279–292 (1992)
21. KhudaBukhsh, A.R., Xu, L., Hoos, H.H., Leyton-Brown, K.: Satenstein: automatically building local search SAT solvers from components. Artif. Intell. **232**, 20–42 (2016)

Multi-agent Interactions on the Web Through Linked Data Notifications

Jean-Paul Calbimonte[1(✉)], Davide Calvaresi[1,2], and Michael Schumacher[1]

[1] University of Applied Sciences and Arts Western Switzerland,
HES-SO Valais-Wallis, Sierre, Switzerland
{jean-paul.calbimonte,davide.calvaresi,michael.schumacher}@hevs.ch
[2] Scuola Superiore Sant'Anna, Pisa, Italy

Abstract. The evolution of the Web towards a semantically-enriched information space has risen several challenges and opportunities concerning the interaction, knowledge representation, and design of multi-agent systems. Many of these have been explored in the past, such as the usage of ontologies for defining agent knowledge bases, the definition of semantic web services, or the usage of reasoning for intelligent agent behavior. Although these efforts have resulted in important research achievements, there is still a need to provide a simple –yet comprehensive– way of interconnecting decentralized intelligent agents through a generic Web-based infrastructure. In this paper we analyze how multi-agent systems can use extensions of the Linked Data Notifications W3C recommendation as the backbone for a Semantic Web-enabled infrastructure for agent communication.

1 Introduction

Multi-agent systems have shown an enormous potential for solving different types of tasks in several domains, such as health-care [7], financial technologies [19], traffic monitoring [10], and e-commerce [8]. Agents are capable, through different paradigms and strategies, to act according to their knowledge, goals, and dynamic environment, using intelligent algorithms, continuous learning, and knowledge management techniques [13]. The decentralized nature of multi-agent systems (MAS) requires them to rely on coordination and communication mechanisms that may require heterogeneous interactions over complex networks. This allows agents to exchange information and cooperate regardless of their physical location. The Web provides a natural environment for such interactions, thanks to the standards and protocols developed in the last decades.

However, the evolution towards a *Semantic Web* [5] has risen several challenges and opportunities concerning the interaction, knowledge representation, and design of MAS. Many of these have been explored in the past, such as the usage of ontologies for defining and exploring agent knowledge bases [18], the definition of Semantic Web services [20] for orchestration and negotiation, or the usage of reasoning for intelligent agent behavior [12]. Although these efforts

© Springer Nature Switzerland AG 2018
F. Belardinelli and E. Argente (Eds.): EUMAS 2017/AT 2017, LNAI 10767, pp. 44–53, 2018.
https://doi.org/10.1007/978-3-030-01713-2_4

have resulted in important research milestones, there is still a need to provide a simple and comprehensive way of enabling a generic Web-based communication among decentralized intelligent agents. Even if the initial vision of the Semantic Web explicitly evoked the emergence of these agents, in practice most implementations of the Semantic Web have focused on ontology models, reasoning, Linked Data, or RDF data management and querying.

In this paper we analyze how multi-agent systems can use extensions of existing W3C recommendations to interact on the Web, under a decentralized scheme. We describe a work-in-progress proposal how the W3C Linked Data Notifications (LDN) [9] recommendation can be used as the backbone for a Web-enabled infrastructure for agent data interchange.

As an example of an application for such environment, let us consider the following use case (Fig. 1). Roy, a middle-aged trekking enthusiast takes a trailing path near the Alps. He is equipped with an agent-based smart-watch with health monitoring capabilities, which can collect several physiological data on real time. At the same time, as he has recently had episodic breathing difficulties, his smart-watch can coordinate with a health recommendation application, which depending on the sensor readings, history, and current location/path difficulty/trekking time, etc. is able to propose alternative paths that are better suited for Roy. The health recommendations also take into account different characteristics of the nearby points-of-interest. For example, as

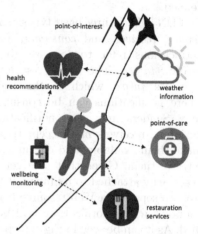

Fig. 1. Use-case: agent interactions on the Web for health recommendations.

Roy has vertigo issues, cliffs and voids in the trekking paths are avoided. Additionally, the local weather service is consulted in order to avoid local strong winds. Finally, depending on Roy's tiredness, sugar levels and stress, point of care and catering services can be proposed, coordinated and booked through his smart-watch agent.

To make these interactions possible, agents for the different described instances need a common language and a communication interface. The Web and its foundational standards, along with explicit semantics for data interchange, can pave the way for decentralized agent interactions, as argued in this work. The paper is organized as follows: we introduce LDN in Sect. 2, the main requirements for Web Agent interactions in Sect. 3. Section 4 described the use of LDN for agent messaging. Section 5 presents related work, before discussion in Sect. 6.

2   Linked Data Notifications

Linked Data Notifications (LDN) [9] is a recently endorsed W3C Recommendation[1] for decentralized data interchange of notifications on the Web. This protocol is designed as a generic and simple mechanism to send and consume data, based on the Linked Data [4] principles and usage of RDF (Resource Description Framework) for data representation. LDN has the potential to be used for virtually any type of notifications, including social media activity, sensor updates, or document updates, to name some examples. Although the adoption of LDN is still to be assessed, its characteristics make it an interesting option for different types of applications on the Web, for which extensions and/or profiles could be defined.

LDN defines three basic types of actors: *sender*, *receiver*, and *consumer*, and the notifications refer to (or are about) a certain *target*. The target is detached from its *inbox*, which is the endpoint where notifications can be consumed or sent. Senders may send notifications to an inbox, receivers may accept them and make them available, and consumers may retrieve them. Given that a target is not necessarily attached to its inbox, it is possible to separate a Web resource from the endpoint where notifications will be handled.

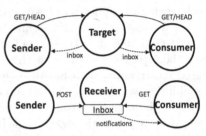

Fig. 2. LDN. Top: Discovery process of a target inbox. Bottom: send and retrieve notifications from an LDN inbox.

As it can be seen in Fig. 2 (top), a discovery process allows senders and consumers to retrieve the inbox location through a simple GET/HEAD HTTP request. Once the inbox location is known, senders can POST notifications to it, and consumers may GET the references to notifications contained in the inbox (Fig. 2, bottom).

3   Requirements for Interactions in the Web of Agents

Agent communication and protocols have been long studied, designed and implemented in the past, as presented in Sect. 5. Although there have been attempts to standardize these interactions, which could make it possible to integrate agents on the Web, these efforts (e.g. KQML [14], FIPA ACL [1]) have reached little adoption in practice. In the following, we identify a set of requirements for agent interactions on the Web.

R1: Standard and extensible messaging. Agents on the Web should be able to exchange any type of data, in different formats and representation means. **R2: Standard metadata.** Agents may use Web standards for representing metadata in their interactions. Metadata may include information such as participants, time constraints, performatives, conditions, etc. **R3. Asynchronous**

---

[1] https://www.w3.org/TR/ldn/.

and distributed communication. Agents on the Web should be able to send and receive messages, as well as coordinating among them without the need of a central entity that governs their interaction flow. **R4. Standard Web protocols.** Communication among agents should be implemented on top of widely supported Web Standards such as HTTP, but not excluding others. This implies no commitments to a particular agent implementation or framework. **R5. Web identifiers.** Agents and their resources, including message items, should all be named using identifier standards for the Web (i.e. URL/URI/IRIs), which provide unicity and de-referenceability. **R6. Semantic representation.** To allow agents to understand and act accordingly to a given message, semantic representations should be used. These should align with Web standards (e.g. OWL, RDF), and allow extensibility and high expressiveness.

4 LDN for Agents on the Web

This section provides a high-level overview of how decentralized agents can communicate on the Web using the LDN recommendation. In this proposal we take into account the requirements presented in the previous section, while considering the characteristics and principles behind LDN. In the following, we explain the main aspects of this proposal, including technical and design features.

HTTP-Based Communication. Given that LDN is entirely based on HTTP requests and responses, agents using LDN should also rely on this protocol for most of their interactions. The ubiquity of HTTP on the Web makes it the natural candidate for most types of exchanges, although –as the LDN specification states– other protocols could be used in certain circumstances, e.g. WebSockets for push-subscriptions.

Agent Identification. Given that LDN relies on the principles of Linked Data [4], URIs (or IRIs) are used to identify all entities involved. This includes the agents themselves, which should be de-referenceable in order to obtain more information about them. This feature would overcome the agent visibility, which in the traditional framework is limited to their single or federated container [3]. Moreover, introducing proper encoding mechanisms, the perception of agent's environment can be enriched and enhanced, thus fostering wider understanding and exploitation. As an example, an agent can be de-referenced through a GET operation over its IRI, e.g.:

```
GET http://example.org/agents/health-agent
```

The response to this request should include metadata about the agent, such as its name, scope, endpoint, ontologies, etc. [1] As prescribed by LDN, each of these agents can provide an endpoint to which messages can be sent, i.e. the inbox. This inbox does not need to be located within the same environment as the agent itself, providing further flexibility.

Endpoint Discovery. Each agent may advertise its inbox as indicated by LDN, with the LDP `inbox` predicate. As an example, consider the following JSON-LD message content response for the previous agent request:

```
{ "@context": "http://www.w3.org/ns/ldp",
  "@id": "http://example.org/agents/health-agent",
  "inbox": "http://example.org/agents/health-agent/inbox" }
```

The content indicates the inbox location, and potentially other useful metadata. This discovery phase would indeed be the first interaction between two agents that wish to establish a conversation or initiate a negotiation.

RDF Data Representation. Agent messages in practice could adopt any representation format and/or model. However, LDN agent implementations may preferably use RDF as a common and standard representation framework. RDF natively integrates the use of URIs for identifiers, allows using extensible vocabularies, and makes it possible to attach explicit semantics to all statements. Metadata annotations should be expressed in RDF, i.e. sender, receiver, performative, protocol, date-time, reply information, conversations, etc. (see FIPA ACL for common metadata information [1]). As an example, the metadata below, represented in RDF (JSON-LD serialization) contains information about an *agree* message, indicating the sender agent, receiver, conversation information, etc.

```
{ "@id": "ex:agree_request1",
  "ag:permormative": "ag:Agree",
  "ag:sender": "ex:agent1",     "ag:receiver": "ex:agent2",
  "ag:reply-to": "ex:agent3",   "ag:protocol": "ag:RequestWhen",
  "ag:conversationId": "ex:conversation3",    "ag:inReplyTo": "ex:conversation1",
  "ag:ontology": "http://example.org/ontology#",
  "ag:content": "..."    },
```

Sending Agent Notifications. An LDN agent may POST notifications to an agent inbox endpoint, as it is specified in LDN. Essentially, the POST body should contain the agent message (e.g. an RDF graph) that will be fed to the inbox of another agent. As an example consider the JSON-LD representation of a call for proposals agent message:

```
POST /agents/health-agent/inbox HTTP/1.1
Host: example.org
Content-Type: application/ld+json

{"prov:generatedAtTime": "2017-09-14T04:00:00.000Z",
  "@id": "ex:callForProposals1",
  "@graph": [
  { "@id": "ex:cfp1", "ag:permormative": "ag:CallForProposals",
    "ag:sender": "ex:agent1", "ag:protocol": "ag:ContractNet",
    "ag:ontology": "http://example.org/healthOntology#", "ag:content": "..."   }],
  "@context": {
    "prov": "http://www.w3.org/ns/prov#", "ex": "http://example.org#", "ag": "https://w3id.
        org/rdf-agents/msg#"}  }
```

Notice that the call is made against the agent inbox URI, and that the message indicates metadata information such as the sender, identified with its own URI (`eg:agent1`). It also includes the reference to the ontology used to represent the message content, the protocol (e.g. `ContractNet`), the type of message (i.e. *performative*), etc. The message content is not included for space reasons, but one could specify an type of arbitrary message, given the flexibility of RDF.

Interaction Protocols. Agent languages have been proposed in the past, even reaching a certain level of standardization. Agreement is not only necessary at format or message level, but also for the type of interactions themselves. For instance, the FIPA ACL standards identify several protocols for agent interactions. As an example, consider the Request Interaction Protocol[2] partially depicted in Fig. 3. The sequence diagram shows how an agent performs a request, which can be refused or agreed by a second agent, leading then to an *inform* or *failure* message. The generic nature of such protocols allows implementers to reuse them for different scenarios in practically any domain.

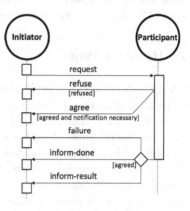

Fig. 3. FIPA ACL request interaction.

An LDN agent implementation should be able to support these interaction protocols, using the technical mechanisms provided by LDN. As an example, consider the diagram in Fig. 4. It depicts part of a Contract Net interaction protocol, according to FIPA ACL. Intuitively, it consists of a call for proposals which is made available to an agent inbox. These can later be accessed by the inbox owner (or owners), thus allowing them to respond to it by sending proposals. These proposals can afterwards be accepted by the initiator agent. Using LDN, all these messages should conform to the RDF structure presented above, and would be exchanged preferably through HTTP, with GET and POST operations as shown in Fig. 4.

Publishing Inbox Elements. As indicated by LDN, consumers may access an agent inbox in order to obtain the messages available there. Although LDN does not impose a fixed access control mechanism, it should be noted that different *security*, *privacy* and *ownership* schemes should be enforced at this level. Putting aside the security constraints, LDN specifies that per-

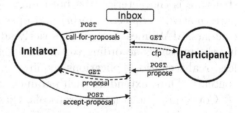

Fig. 4. LDN agent interactions for a CfP protocol.

forming a GET over an inbox should return the notification URIs listed as objects to the LDP `ldp:contains` predicate.

---

[2] http://www.fipa.org/specs/fipa00026/SC00026H.html.

Agent Reasoning. Regardless of any specific architecture (e.g., BDI), the LDN adoption do not affect traditional reasoning engines, since the implementation of a simple data-parser can guarantee the retro-compatibility with already existing mechanisms and foster the development of new ones with increased capabilities due to the semantic expressiveness and the simplified and extended interactions.

5 Related Work

Internet of Things, knowledge-based, and network-based/oriented systems are gaining momentum in the market. Therefore, it is a major challenge to integrate uncountable heterogeneous devices, virtual entities and human end-users. Such fast-paced growing networks wrap or connect several frameworks, mostly exploiting ad-hoc interaction methods, or over-complicating already structured communication standards. However, to achieve a common understanding, the definition of common formats and semantics (preferably standard) are necessary. Under the hypothesis of agents' rationality, the scientific community has defined a number of agent communication languages. For example, KQML [14] is a simple protocol mainly used in the academic world defining the basics of interaction among intelligent entities, in particular in MAS [17]. Later on, the Foundation for Intelligent Physical Agents (FIPA) [2] improved and extended the previous languages, defining the FIPA ACL (Agent Communication Language) in 1997.

Although such protocols provide a relevant support for agent communication, there is still no clear understanding/definition of the semantics of individual speech acts. Moreover, basic concepts required to define the semantics are still missing. Hence, a variety of semantic simplification strategies need to be employed when designing MAS. For example, JADE [3] and JASON [6], two of the most used multi-agent platforms, are compliant with the FIPA standards. Thereby, the agents running on such platforms could interact with any agent (language and platform independent) FIPA compliant. The FIPA ACL message structure is characterized by both mandatory (e.g., message type indicated as performative - *request, inform*) and optional (e.g., recipient, sender, ontology) contents. MAS' messages might strictly adhere to the ACL standard just encoding the messages according to the parameters listed in Table 1 in [1]. Nevertheless, real-scenario applications require handling more complex and articulated contents. Thus, extending such parameters is an obliged path.

Concerning negotiation protocols, these are mainly characterized by 1-to-1 or 1-to-n interactions between *initiators* (who proposes, the task to be performed and its boundary conditions) and *contractors* (who propose themselves as "solvers" replying to the required conditions with a bid) dynamically [16]. Although argumentation and negotiation in MAS can involve sophisticated, high-level reasoning, the relevance of the information representation and encoding for a common understanding is crucial. For example, in the context of agents operating in and crawling the web, the information can be expressed both in natural language or exploiting a multitude of different formats. Thus, although the agents know how to interact, they need a common knowledge base and/or an ontology to give an actual meaning to their interaction. Currently, markup languages such as XML are heavily used for agent data representation. Nevertheless, there is a growing trend on moving beyond the implicit semantic agreements inherent in languages such as XML and JSON. Standards and mechanisms such as RDF are developed to tie the information on machine-readable objects, finally allowing semantic interoperability [15].

6   Discussion

Multi-agent systems have proven to be useful in a wide range of application domains, especially when autonomous coordination and intelligent behavior is required. When such systems scale to the Web, additional needs arise, regarding heterogeneity, message semantics, mutual understandability, and decentralization. Although there have been important efforts targeting scenarios where Web agents interact for a given task (see Sect. 5), most of these approaches are either too complex, or have been abandoned in the last years.

While on the Semantic Web community, the idea of Web agents relies at the core of its original vision, in practice there is still not a commonly agreed mechanism for enabling these agents to communicate with each other, using well established standards. The challenges to achieve this vision are still numerous:

- Adoption of semantically rich messaging mechanisms (e.g. RDF-based) among Agents on the Web.
- Usage of ontologies and vocabularies that link existing Web protocols (e.g. LDN) and Agent-communication standards (e.g. FIPA ACL).
- Definition and agreement of system-agnostic Agent communication primitives, based on existing MAS languages.
- Provision of agent discovery, selection and orchestration services, based on existing standards.
- Implementation and adoption of best practices of agent-based mechanisms for Web interactions.

These high-level challenges describe only some of the urgent needs in this scope, but they already show the need for MAS and Semantic Web communities to work on research topics that address these issues. In this paper, we present a vision of how this could be implemented in practice, using existing Web standards, and specifically relaying on the Linked Data Notifications protocol. Although the generic nature of this specification may not be enough to describe interaction protocols among agents, an extension, or a profile for LDN, can fill this gap. This effort is complementary to recent developments towards MAS deployed as hypermedia applications [11] and Semantic Web services [20]. The examples and scenarios described in this paper provide an initial work-in-progress vision of how this can be done, although a more detailed specification of these extensions needs to be made and implemented, thus stepping towards its validation. In the future, we plan to continue developing this vision, and providing a feasibility evaluation using real use-cases. We believe that this approach may open new research perspectives for designing Web-scale solutions governed by intelligent agent-based systems.

References

1. FIPA ACL Message Structure Spec. http://www.fipa.org/specs/fipa00061/
2. Foundation for Intelligent Physical Agents Standard. http://www.fipa.org/
3. Bellifemine, F., Poggi, A., Rimassa, G.: JADE: a FIPA2000 compliant agent development environment. In: Proceedings of the 5th International Conference on Autonomous Agents, pp. 216–217 (2001)
4. Berners-Lee, T., Bizer, C., Heath, T.: Linked data-the story so far. IJSWIS 5(3), 1–22 (2009)
5. Berners-Lee, T., Hendler, J., Lassila, O.: The semantic web. Sci. Am. 284(5), 34–43 (2001)
6. Bordini, R.H., Hübner, J.F., Wooldridge, M.: Programming Multi-Agent Systems in AgentSpeak using Jason, vol. 8. Wiley, Hoboken (2007)
7. Calvaresi, D., Cesarini, D., Sernani, P., Marinoni, M., Dragoni, A., Sturm, A.: Exploring the ambient assisted living domain: a systematic review. J. Ambient Intell. Humaniz. Comput. 8(2), 1–19 (2016)
8. Calvaresi, D., Marinoni, M., Sturm, A., Schumacher, M., Buttazzo, G.: The challenge of real-time multi-agent systems for enabling IoT and CPS. In: WI, pp. 356–364 (2017)
9. Capadisli, S., Guy, A., Lange, C., Auer, S., Sambra, A., Berners-Lee, T.: Linked data notifications: a resource-centric communication protocol. In: Blomqvist, E., Maynard, D., Gangemi, A., Hoekstra, R., Hitzler, P., Hartig, O. (eds.) ESWC 2017. LNCS, vol. 10249, pp. 537–553. Springer, Cham (2017). https://doi.org/10.1007/978-3-319-58068-5_33
10. Chen, B., Cheng, H.H., Palen, J.: Integrating mobile agent technology with multi-agent systems for distributed traffic detection and management systems. Transp. Res. Part C Emerg. Technol. 17(1), 1–10 (2009)
11. Ciortea, A., Boissier, O., Zimmermann, A., Florea, A.M.: Give agents some REST: a resource-oriented abstraction layer for internet-scale agent environments. In: AAMAS, pp. 1502–1504 (2017)
12. d'Inverno, M., et al.: The dMARS architecture: a specification of the distributed multi-agent reasoning system. Auton. Agents Multi-Agent Syst. 9(1), 5–53 (2004)
13. Ferber, J.: Multi-Agent Systems: An Introduction to Distributed Artificial Intelligence. Addison-Wesley, Reading (1999)
14. Finin, T., Fritzson, R., McKay, D., McEntire, R.: KQML as an agent communication language. In: ICIKM, pp. 456–463 (1994)
15. Hendler, J.: Agents and the semantic web. IEEE Intell. Syst. 16(2), 30–37 (2001)
16. Kraus, S.: Negotiation and cooperation in multi-agent environments. Artif. Intell. 94(1–2), 79–97 (1997)
17. Labrou, Y., Finin, T.: Semantics for an agent communication language. In: Singh, M.P., Rao, A., Wooldridge, M.J. (eds.) ATAL 1997. LNCS, vol. 1365, pp. 209–214. Springer, Heidelberg (1998). https://doi.org/10.1007/BFb0026760

18. Luke, S., Spector, L., Rager, D., Hendler, J.: Ontology-based web agents. In: Proceedings of the First International Conference on Autonomous Agents, pp. 59–66. ACM (1997)
19. Luo, Y., Liu, K., Davis, D.N.: A multi-agent decision support system for stock trading. IEEE Netw. **16**(1), 20–27 (2002)
20. McIlraith, S.A., Son, T.C., Zeng, H.: Semantic web services. IEEE Intell. Syst. **16**(2), 46–53 (2001)

A Model Driven Methodology
for Developing Multi Agent Solutions
for Energy Systems

Lamia Ben Romdhane[1(✉)], Hassan A. Sleiman[1], Saadia Dhouib[2],
and Chokri Mraidha[2(✉)]

[1] CEA, LIST, Laboratory of Data Analysis and Systems' Intelligence,
PC 19, 91191 Gif-sur-Yvette, France
{lamia.benromdhane,hassan.sleiman}@cea.fr
[2] CEA, LIST, Laboratory of Model Driven Engineering for Embedded Systems,
PC 94, 91191 Gif-sur-Yvette, France
{saadia.dhouib,chokri.mraidha}@cea.fr

Abstract. The complexity and intelligence of energy systems has
increased in the recent years, whereas using Multi-agent Systems (MAS)
has been recommended by IEEE for developing software solutions for
modeling, controlling, and simulating their behaviors. Existing proposals on MAS solutions for energy systems proposed ad-hoc solutions
for resolving specific problems, without considering interoperability and
reusability. We propose a methodology, based on the Model-Driven Engineering (MDE) technique, for developing MAS solutions for energy systems. Our methodology uses the Common Information Model standard
(CIM), recommended by IEEE, and the existing Platform Independent
agent metamodel PIM4Agents. The proposed methodology allows modeling MAS solutions for power engineering applications, by means of
a platform-independent model that abstracts developers from existing
agent-oriented methodologies and platforms. Applying model transformations, the generated models can be transformed and executed within
several agent platforms such as JACK and JADE. Our proposal has been
validated by means of a well-known test case from the literature.

Keywords: Energy systems · Model Driven Engineering
Multi-agent system · IEC common information model

1 Introduction

Modern Energy Systems (ESs) are composed of different interacting entities
that allow an intelligent production, distribution, and consumption of energy,
which increases the complexity of their management [10]. In the recent years,
Multi-agent Systems (MAS) have emerged as one of the most promising technologies to optimize the production, distribution, and consumption of electricity,
and to regulate the flow of electricity between suppliers and consumers [18,19].

© Springer Nature Switzerland AG 2018
F. Belardinelli and E. Argente (Eds.): EUMAS 2017/AT 2017, LNAI 10767, pp. 54–69, 2018.
https://doi.org/10.1007/978-3-030-01713-2_5

MAS technology enables the implementation of large, scalable, complex, and distributed applications by enabling the development of autonomous control agents that are able to coordinate in a cooperative and fault-tolerant environment [27].

Existing MAS solutions for ESs generally proposed ad-hoc solutions; i.e., they were designed for resolving specific problems and that were not intended to be reused [16]. Furthermore, these solutions were designed to run on a specific agent platform, without considering the interoperability among different agent systems, neither with other technologies. On the other hand, Model Driven Engineering (MDE) techniques have proven to be a feasible solution that enhances reusability, portability, and interoperability of designs and implementations [25].

Model Driven Architecture (MDA) is an approach to define and implement software applications. MDA allows an efficient reuse of the system models and is supported by automated tools and services [13]. MDA has two levels of models, namely: a Platform-Independent Model (PIM) that describes a given system without referring to the platform-specific choices, and a Platform Specific Model (PSM), which is considered as the realization of PIM with all the details of the chosen platform. Our proposal goes beyond the existing MAS solutions for ESs by proposing a model driven methodology for developing MAS solutions dedicated to ESs. We follow an MDE perspective, which is based on the classical Model-Driven Architecture approach (MDA) [13]. The use of MDA techniques in the development of MASs shall allow the interoperability between agent systems and the reusability of the agents' models.

The proposed model driven methodology is intended to guide power engineers in the design and implementation of MAS solutions, and to simplify the design tasks by reusing models. We propose a five-phase methodology, in which we start by instantiating an abstract and generic platform independent metamodel called PIM4Agents [11]. The output of the previous step is an abstract and specific agent model (PIM), which is specific to ESs, where the standardized CIM is part of the generated agent model, representing the components of the ES. The provided PIM abstracts the developers from the existing specific agent-oriented methodologies and platforms. The resulted Platform Independent Model (PIM) is used to model a MAS solution dedicated to ES, and can be transformed into a different Platform Specific Models (PSMs). By instantiating the PSM, a concrete and specific application can be modeled to be run on a specific agent platform.

Our methodology uses the Common Information Model (CIM) standard [26], which is a standardized model for exchanging information between different companies, and among company applications in the electricity domain. CIM defines the components in the power system using the Unified Modeling Language (UML). CIM standard is used to model the entities of the ES, and provides an upper ontology for power engineers to be used in the agents' communications. This ontology allows agents in different MASs to share a common vocabulary in their interactions allowing interoperability between them. Our methodology has been validated by developing a MAS for demand side management, tested in a smart grid which is a 1.5 MW residential smart grid.

The rest of the paper is organized as follows: Sect. 2 reviews the existing work in the literature related to our proposal; Sect. 3 describes our methodology; a case of study related to the development of energy systems is used in Sect. 4 to illustrate and validate the methodology; and finally, Sect. 5 concludes our work.

2   Related Work

Several surveys have been performed on the application of MAS for modeling ESs [16,18]. In the following, we first review the proposed agent models for energy systems, and then we study the model-driven approaches proposed for MASs.

Koritarov et al. [14] proposed an agent model and a simulation approach by modeling the participants and their reactions to the changing economic, financial, and regulatory environments in ESs. Hernández et al. [12] presented a MAS model for Virtual Power Plants based on two aspects: demand forecasting and the coordination of producers and consumers in order to balance the energy production. In the distributed control of energy systems field, Pipattanasomporn et al. [23] proposed a MAS model to detect upstream outages, by proposing four types of agents with their own roles and responsibilities, namely: a control agent, a distributed energy resource (DER) agent, a user agent, and a database agent.

The use of the MDE approach for MAS development has been the focus of several proposals in the literature [2,22]. The Malaca agent model [2] proposed a mapping from the design models produced by existing agent oriented methodologies to the Malaca model, which is a common and neutral agent model (PIM) that implements all the concepts required by FIPA-compliant agent platforms [21], and from Malaca to the different agent platforms (PSMs). Pavón et al. [22] introduced the INGENIAS Development Kit (IDK), which is a set of tools for modeling, verifying, and transforming agent models, accompanied by Model Driven Development (MDD) tools for MAS development based on the INGENIAS metamodel.

Some authors have tried to provide a standardized metamodel for MAS [4,6]: Bernon et al. [4] proposed a metamodel based on three existing metamodels for MAS, namely: Gaia [28], PASSI [8], and ADELFE [5]; Beydoun et al. [6] proposed the FAML model, which is intended to resolve the interoperability issues among the agent-oriented methodologies, and based on five existing metamodels: ADELFE [5], PASSI [8], Gaia [28], INGENIAS [22] and Tropos [7].

Recently, Hahn et al. [11] proposed PIM4Agents, which is a Platform Independent MetaModel (PIMM), that is intended to contribute to the interoperability between domain-specific architectures and agent platforms. It aims to abstract the developers from existing agent-oriented methodologies and platforms. This metamodel provides the core language to be used in an agent-oriented software development process, which conforms to the principles of MDD. It describes the MAS aspects, namely: agent, organization, interaction, behaviors and environment. Furthermore, Hahn et al. [11] provided two model transformations that allow to transform the created models into textual code that can be executed with JACK [1] and JADE [3].

Our review of the literature reveals that existing MAS solutions for energy systems are generally based on ad-hoc models for resolving specific problems, which run on specific agent platforms, without considering the interoperability among different agent platforms [11] and that were not intended to be reused [16]. Furthermore, none of the existing MAS metamodels is intended for modeling MAS for ESs.

We propose a model driven methodology to help developers and power engineers in modeling MAS solutions for managing ESs, following the principle of MDE [24]. The methodology is intended to simplify the design process, to resolve the interoperability issue, and to allow reusing the models. Compared to the existing proposals, our methodology is not a specific agent-based solution for modeling a given energy system, but a methodology that can be used to develop MAS solutions. The result of the methodology is a MAS solution that can be either implemented and deployed in a real ES, or used to perform an agent-based simulation of a given ES.

3   Our Proposal

We propose a methodology for developing MAS solutions dedicated to energy systems. We follow an MDE [25] perspective based on the classical MDA [13]. MDA techniques are applied in our proposal by providing a PIM that abstracts developers from existing specific agent-oriented methodologies and platforms. The methodology is intended to contain the stages required to design and implement a MAS solution for any ES, allowing the reuse of models and considering the interoperability between MASs.

Our methodology is a five-phase model driven methodology that provides a starting point for power engineers interested in devising MAS solutions for intelligent ESs. Following the proposed methodology, the developer can make use of already existing models and mapping rules to accelerate the development process of these solutions; i.e., the designer shall only focus on the behaviors in the target ES and on the problem to be solved (optimization, control, simulation, etc.), without focusing on the modeling process.

The methodology is based on the CIM standard [26] and on the PIM4Agents metamodel [11]. It consists of five phases (c.f. Fig. 1), namely: (i) the CIM Restriction phase, in which we create a CIM profile to model our target ES; (ii) the Specific and Abstract Modeling phase, in which we instantiate the PIM4Agents metamodel to define the platform-independent MAS for ES model (MAS4ES), in which we connect the agents to their assigned equipment from the resulted CIM profile of the previous phase; (iii) the Model to Model Transformation phase (M2M), which allows mapping the concepts of MAS4ES model to the concepts of the specific agent platform model (from PIM to PSM); (iv) the Specific and Concrete Modeling phase, which aims to model the real world objects of the MAS solution by instantiating the concepts of the MAS4ES model from the previous phase; and (v) the Code Generation phase, which allows the code generation from of the specific and concrete application model. In the following subsections, we describe each of the previous phases in detail.

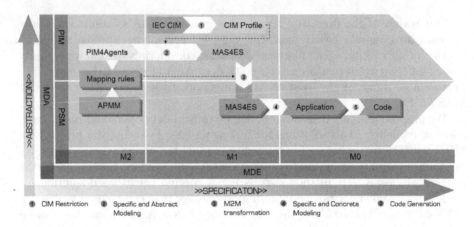

Fig. 1. The methodology's process for developing MAS solutions dedicated to energy system.

3.1 CIM Restriction Phase

The International Electrotechnical Commission IEC CIM standard is used in the electricity domain, covering transmission, distribution, markets, generation, and related business processes [26]. The key idea of the CIM is to define a common language in order to allow both: exchanging data between different companies, and exchanging data between company applications. The core packages of CIM are defined in the IEC standard 61970-301 [18], which defines the components in the power system using the Unified Modeling Language (UML). Generally, only a part of the CIM (so-called CIM profile) is used for modeling a given energy system solution. CIM profiles allow defining a subset of the CIM, including only the classes and associations required for modeling a specific solution.

The objective of our methodology is to develop a MAS solution to manage ESs. The MAS environment in these systems contains the agents, the objects they manage or interact with, and other resources. The controlled objects can be the electrical equipment that compose the ES.

During this phase, the developer uses the IEC CIM standard to model the agent's knowledge on the ES components and how they are physically connected. This shall simplify the design task by defining a consistent and unified administration system of the managed elements.

This phase produces a CIM profile for the ES to be modeled. This profile contains the CIM concepts, which model the electrical components that are managed by the agents within the MAS solution. It will then be used in the next steps, and can be reused whenever the components of the ES being modeled are already represented in the defined CIM profile.

3.2   Specific and Abstract Modeling Phase

In this phase, the designer will instantiate the PIM4Agents metamodel (c.f. upper part of Fig. 5) to model a MAS solution to ESs by connecting both models. The resulted MAS4ES model is intended to provide the essential concepts for modeling a given energy system, and the agents that manage their entities.

This phase is considered as a specification step since starting from a PIM metamodel, namely the PIM4Agents metamodel, which is abstract and platform independent, a PIM agent model (called MAS4ES), that is specific to energy systems, is created. MAS4ES is still a PIM since it is still abstract from the target agent platform where the application shall be executed.

To create the MAS4ES PIM, the designer starts by defining the types of the agents needed in the MAS solution with their behaviors in order to handle the approved MAS solution. Two major recommendations to make an agent model suitable for the energy field: first, the designer must model the relevant concepts of a given energy system, and the agent-object relation to reflect the interaction between each agent and the ES components; second, he or she has to model the ontology's concepts used by the agents to carry out a comprehensible conversation.

Agents in a MAS generally interact with objects or other agents to solve particular tasks. These objects are modeled as resources in the MAS environment according to the PIM4Agents metamodel. Thus, the user can instantiate the object concept to model the used equipment in the ES. The resulted CIM profile of the previous phase is imported into the MAS4ES model in order to model the ES itself by instantiating all its concepts from the object class in the PIM4Agents metamodel. Then, for each agent type, the designer assigns the equipment that will be managed by this agent, in order to model the agents-object relationship.

Developers of multi-agent systems tend to use application-specific ontologies, which do not allow further agents from different MASs to understand the message contents. To tackle with this interoperability issue, the designer can use the existing common ontology (CIM ontology) that is based on the CIM standard and recommended by IEEE [19]. This ontology shall allow the interoperability between the MAS agents in power engineering applications. The ontology aspect is already addressed in the PIM4Agents metamodel. Indeed, the metamodel contains the *resource* concept that is used to reference an ontology [11]. The resulting MAS4ES model can be reused to model different MAS applications for different scenarios.

3.3   Model to Model Transformation Phase

This phase allows the mapping of a PIM to one or more PSMs. The resulting MAS4ES from the previous phase is independent from the specific agent platform where the solution will be executed. This phase aims to map the concepts of the MAS4ES model to the concepts of the specific agent platform model such as JADE, JACK, etc. In this phase, the designer can apply the existing mapping rules [11] on the MAS4ES model.

The mapping rules define the transformations that shall be carried out to map the concepts of the MAS4ES to the concepts of the selected Agent Platform MetaModel (APMM). These rules are specified only one time and can be reused. The concepts derived from the CIM profile are instances of the object concept in PIM4Agents, they will be implemented directly in a programming language (such as Java and C++).

This phase is considered as a concretization since it transforms a given model into another one of a lower level of abstraction, i.e., starting from a MAS4ES (PIM) to generate a MAS4ES (PSM) that is specific to the agent platform where the application will be executed.

The generated MAS4ES model (which is a PSM) can be instantiated later to model a real energy system application runnable on a specific agent platform (e.g. JADE [3]). Below we present the most relevant mappings rules to transform the PIM4Agents metamodel's concepts to the JADE metamodel's concepts defined in [11]:

1. PIM4Agents: Agent → JadeMM: Agent
2. PIM4Agents: Organisation → JadeMM: Agent
3. PIM4Agents: Message → JadeMM: ACLMessage
4. PIM4Agents: Behaviour → JadeMM: Behaviour
5. PIM4Agents: resource → JadeMM: ConceptSchema
6. PIM4Agents: Object → JAVA.lang.object

3.4   Specific and Concrete Modeling Phase

The MAS4ES model (PSM), produced by the previous phase, should be refined and then instantiated to model the specific and concrete MAS application with the real controlled objects and agents to manage a real ES from the given system. The generated model (Application) is then deployed on the selected agent platform. The Application model shall be executed in a specific agent platform.

3.5   Code Generation phase

The last phase of our methodology is the generation of the code from the PSM model (Application model in our methodology) generated by the previous phase. For this step, we propose the use of the Java code generator within the papyrus UML tool [9], which generates only the structural part of classes i.e., it generates the classes with their attributes and the function headers, and implements the connection between the classes. The next version of the Java code generator will take into account the behavioral part of the classes. Now, it is up to the user to implement the behavior code of the agents, depending on the MAS being developed.

4   Test and Validation

In the following subsections, we first define the test case we have considered for validation, and then we provide more details on the work undergone at each step of our proposed methodology.

4.1 Validation Use Case

Our proposal has been validated on a well-known circuit for a residential area from the literature [17] (c.f. Fig. 2). The devices that will be controlled by the MAS in this residential area have small power consumption ratings, whereas their operations have short durations. The grid contains more than 2600 controllable devices, which are from 14 different types of devices. The consumption profiles of the loads under the control are given in Table 1. Table 1 shows also the initial schedule, flexibility, priority and number of devices for each controllable load.

Our aim is to develop a MAS solution for a demand side management system, where the agents schedule the controllable loads to reduce their consumption during peak hours. The objective is to optimize the consumption of the controllable loads by shifting their schedules; i.e., the consumption demands of shiftable loads are shifted to off peak times in order to reduce the overall operational cost of the network. The wholesale electricity prices are hourly-based and are reported beside the hourly energy demand of the residential area in Fig. 3.

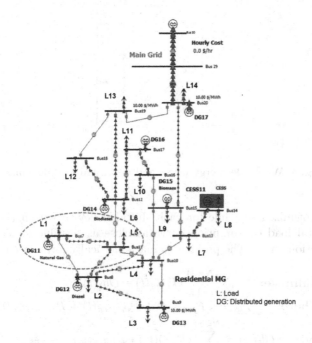

Fig. 2. Network diagram of the residential smart grid

Since our aim is to validate our methodology and not to propose a new optimization technique, we have used a simple centralized optimization algorithm, inspired by [17], which runs on a daily basis. As input, this algorithm takes the forecasted load demands and the energy prices for a given day. It then calculates the objective load curves and tries to find the best load scheduling. The

Table 1. Data of controllable devices in the residential area

Device type	Initial schedule	Profile			Flexibility	Priority	Number of devices
		1st Hr	2nd Hr	3rd Hr			
Dryer	17:00	1.2	-	-	6	3	189
Dish washer	13:00	0.7	-	-	5	3	288
Washing machine	15:00	0.5	0.4	-	6	3	268
Oven	12:00	1.3	-	-	3	2	279
Iron	18:00	1.0	-	-	5	3	340
Vacuum cleaner	10:00	0.4	-	-	1	2	158
Fan	12:00	0.20	0.20	0.20	1	2	288
Kettle	21:00	2.0	-	-	2	2	406
Toaster	8:00	0.9	-	-	1	1	48
Rice-cooker	12:00	0.85	-	-	1	1	59
Hair dryer	8:00	1.5	-	-	1	2	58
Blender	9:00	0.3	-	-	1	1	66
Frying pan	00:00	1.1	-	-	1	3	101
Coffee maker	8:00	0.8	-	-	1	1	56

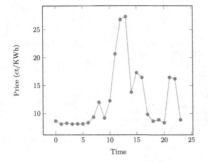 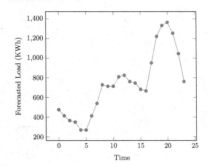

Fig. 3. Wholesale energy prices and forecasted load demands

result is an optimized schedule for each shiftable device within the grid that brings the total load consumption curve as close as possible to the objective load consumption curve. The problem is mathematically formulated as follows:

Minimize: $\quad \sum_{t=1}^{N=24} (P_{load}(t) - Obj(t))^2$

Where: $\quad P_{load} = P_{fixed}(t) + P_{shifted}(t) + P_{unshifted}(t)$

and $\quad Obj(t) = \sum_{t=1}^{N=24} (P_{load}(t)) * Pice_{Avg} * \dfrac{1}{Price(t)}$

In the following, we describe each step of our proposed methodology to model a MAS for managing the described ES of the residential area. The validation example was implemented using the Papyrus UML tool [9].

4.2   Step 1: Restriction Phase

In this phase we need to restrict the CIM metamodel by creating a CIM profile, in which we select the CIM classes, associations and attributes to be used in our example. In the following we describe the three substeps for creating this profile.

Identifying the Equipment's CIM Classes: The residential area shown in Fig. 2 represents an energy system with 14 buses, 8 generators, 20 lines and 14 loads. The line, load and bus map to the CIM *ACLineSegment*, *Energy-Consumer* and *BusBarSection* classes respectively. The *EnergyConsumer* class in CIM is used to model the load which is a point of consumption where many devices are connected. The generator is mapped to a single piece of conducting equipment (class *SynchronousMachine*). When operating as a generator, the *SynchronousMachine* object must have an association with an instance of the *GeneratingUnit* class. The *GeneratingUnit* class does not represent a piece of conducting equipment that physically connects to the network, but a single or set of synchronous machines for converting mechanical power into alternating current.

Defining Components' Interconnections: CIM uses *ConnectivityNodes* and *Terminals* to define the components' interconnections. The electrical components (e.g. breaker, loads, and lines) are not directly associated with each other, instead, any conducting equipment has one or more terminals. The relationship between *Terminal*, *ConnecitivtyNode* and *ConductingEquipment* classes is shown in Fig. 4.

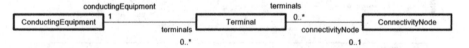

Fig. 4. Conducting equipment and connectivity class diagram.

Defining Containments: Besides the component interconnections defined using the *ConductingEquipment-Terminal-ConnectivityNode* association, the CIM has an *EquipmentContainer* class that provides a means of grouping pieces of Equipment together to represent both electrical and non-electrical containments [20], which are as follows:

Voltage levels: the conducting equipment do not have a voltage attribute, but they are associated with a *VoltageLevel*. The *VoltageLevel* class itself has an associated *BaseVoltage* object that contains a single attribute to define the nominal voltage. It contains only the interconnected pieces of equipment at the same voltage level.

Substation: the *Substation* class is a subclass of *EquipmentContainer* that can contain multiple *VoltageLevels* and is used to define a collection of equipments. In the running example, the four different voltage levels are contained within a single *Substation* instance. The *Substation* class can also contain other instances of *Equipment*, such as *PowerTransformer*, which is itself a container. The Substation class represents non-electrical containment since it contains pieces of equipment that are physically grouped, but not necessarily electrically connected.

Line: the *ACLineSegment* is not contained within a *VoltageLevel*, but within an instance of the *Line* class. A line may contain multiple Alternating Current (AC) or Direct Current (DC) line segments, but does not itself represent a piece of physical conducting equipment. The *AC-* and *DC- LineSegment* classes contain a direct association to the *BaseVoltage* class to define their nominal voltage level.

Many tools allow the creation of CIM profile such as CimConteXtor, CIM EA and CIMTool [26]. The red part of the Fig. 5 shows a part of the CIM Profile created using the CimConteXtor tool[1].

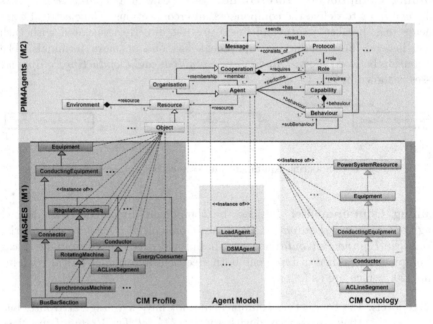

Fig. 5. Partial view of the resulted MAS4ES model (PIM). (Color figure online)

---

[1] http://www.cimcontextor.net/.

4.3   Step 2: Specific and Abstract Modeling

In this phase, we propose a PIM for the development of MAS applications dedicated to energy systems (MAS4ES); i.e., we instantiate the PIM4Agents metamodel to model the relevant concepts for the MAS application that manages a residential area. We propose to define two *Agent* instances, namely:

1. *LoadAgent*: this agent manipulates a controllable load in the ES, which is represented by the *EnergyConsumer* class.
2. *DSMAgent*: the Demand Side Management Agent (DSMAgent) is responsible for running the centralized optimization algorithm defined before and to provide the new schedule with load shifting to the *LoadAgents*.

The partial view of the MAS4ES is presented in the lower part of Fig. 5. It shows the *LoadAgent* that can manipulate an energy consumer, whereas the *DSMAgent* is part of the agents model but does not manipulate any energy consumer. The *DSMAgent* is able to shift energy demand within certain constraints from peak hours to off-peak hours to minimize the operational cost of the system. The *LoadAgent* can access to the data of the load (the *EnergyConsumer* class) it controls such as the consumption schedule, its flexibility, initial schedule, and the number of connected devices. The *DSMAgent* sends a request to all the *LoadAgents* to send the data needed for the optimization and for preparing the new optimized schedules. The *DSMAgent* collects the data from the *LoadAgents*, and based on the energy price and the total forecasted load data for twenty four hours, it optimizes the plans and sends the instructions to each *LoadAgent* as day ahead schedules.

4.4   Step 3: Model to Model Transformation

For this test case we chose to map our MAS4ES model to the JADE platform model, which is a FIPA compliant platform that is considered as the most popular agent platform in the literature [15]. For this purpose, we applied the mapping rules to transform the PIM4Agents metamodel's concepts to the JADE metamodel's concepts defined by [11], and previously described in Sect. 3.3.

In this phase, we apply these rules on the MAS4ES model to make it specific to the JADE platform. The resulting model (c.f. Fig. 6) can now be instantiated to model a real MAS application runnable on the JADE platform.

4.5   Step 4: Specific and Concrete Modeling

The circuit illustrated in Fig. 2 contains fourteen *EnergyConsumer* objects. A unique instance of the *DSMAgent* class is created for the side demand management and for each *EnergyConsumer* object, we assign an instance of *LoadAgent*. Due to space constraints, in this phase we show only the surrounded part in the circuit (Fig. 2).

Figure 7 shows the electrical components of the surrounded part in the residential area modeled as CIM objects, and for each of the components, it shows the *Agent* that manipulates it.

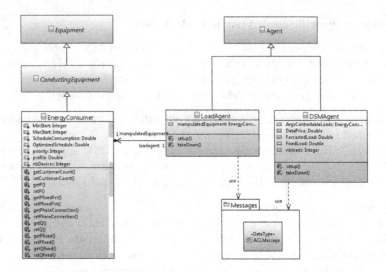

Fig. 6. Partial view of the resulted MAS4ES model specific for JADE (PSM).

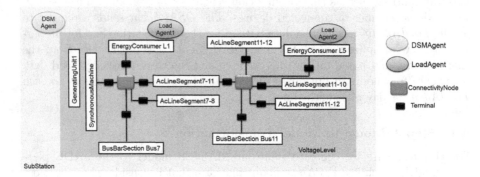

Fig. 7. The residential area as CIM objects and agents.

4.6   Step 5: Coding Phase

Now that we have created the models of the agents and the circuit objects, we can generate the MAS code that shall run on the JADE platform. Figure 8 shows a part of the generated code of the MAS solution (platform-specific for JADE), that allows managing the CIM components in our test case. Figure 8a shows part of the code of the *LoadAgent* class, where its manipulated load is given through its arguments array. This equipment is sent as an argument from the main class shown in Fig. 8b.

The results obtained from the proposed optimization algorithm for the residential smart grid is illustrated in Fig. 9. The figure shows how the load shifting algorithm tried to bring the final consumption curve closer to the objective load curve. For instance, the amount of the forecasted load consumption between 12

```java
public class LoadAgent extends Agent {

    /**[]
    private static final long serialVersionUID = 1L;
    private EnergyConsumer manipulatedEquipment= new EnergyConsumer();
    @Override
    protected void setup() {

        Object[]args=getArguments();
        if(args.length==1){
            manipulatedEquipment=(EnergyConsumer) args[0];
            System.out.println( "Hello I'am "+ getAID() +" I control: " + manipulatedEquipment);
```

(a) Generated *LoadAgent* class.

```java
EnergyConsumer Dryer= new EnergyConsumer("Dryer",17,23,new double[]{0,0,0,0,0,0,0,0,0,0,0,
EnergyConsumer DishWasher= new EnergyConsumer("DishWasher",13,18,new double[]{0,0,0,0,0,0,0,
EnergyConsumer WashingMachine= new EnergyConsumer("WashingMachine",15,21,new double[]{0,0,
EnergyConsumer oven= new EnergyConsumer("oven",12,15,new double[]{0,0,0,0,0,0,0,0,0,0,0,0,
AgentController load1 = mainContainer.createNewAgent( Dryer.name, "Agents.LoadAgent", new
                load1.start();
AgentController load2 = mainContainer.createNewAgent( DishWasher.name, "Agents.LoadAgent",
                load2.start();
AgentController load3 = mainContainer.createNewAgent( WashingMachine.name, "Agents.LoadAge
                load3.start();
```

(b) Main class.

Fig. 8. Part of the generated Java code of the MAS application.

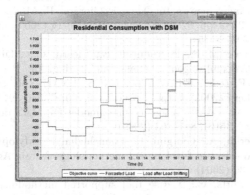

Fig. 9. Results for the residential smart grid

and 2 p.m. was reduced after applying the shifting technique, since the selling price of energy at that time is expensive. The simulation outcomes show that proposed technique achieves sustainable saving by reducing the system peaks during the peak periods and as result the total consumption cost has decreased from 2302.87\$ to 2129.27\$.

5   Conclusions

We propose a model driven methodology for the development of MAS solutions to manage ESs using the CIM standard and applying the IEEE recommendation. Our proposal follows the MDE process in order to guide the power engineers in the design and implementation of MAS applications, and to simplify the design task by reusing models. The MDA approach is applied to create a PIM, called MAS4ES, which can be transformed into different PSMs, allowing the interoperability between agent systems. The proposed methodology has five phases, namely: CIM Restriction, Specific and Abstract Modeling, Model to Model Transformation, Specific and Concrete Modeling and Code Generation phases. The methodology was presented and validated by developing a MAS optimization solution for a well-known test case.

References

1. JACK Intelligent Agents: The agent oriented software group (AOS) (2006)
2. Amor, M., Fuentes, L., Vallecillo, A.: Bridging the gap between agent-oriented design and implementation using MDA. In: Odell, J., Giorgini, P., Müller, J.P. (eds.) AOSE 2004. LNCS, vol. 3382, pp. 93–108. Springer, Heidelberg (2005). https://doi.org/10.1007/978-3-540-30578-1_7
3. Bellifemine, F., Poggi, A., Rimassa, G.: JADE-A FIPA-compliant agent framework. In: Proceedings of PAAM, London, vol. 99, p. 33 (1999)
4. Bernon, C., Cossentino, M., Gleizes, M.-P., Turci, P., Zambonelli, F.: A study of some multi-agent meta-models. In: Odell, J., Giorgini, P., Müller, J.P. (eds.) AOSE 2004. LNCS, vol. 3382, pp. 62–77. Springer, Heidelberg (2005). https://doi.org/10.1007/978-3-540-30578-1_5
5. Bernon, C., Gleizes, M.-P., Peyruqueou, S., Picard, G.: ADELFE: a methodology for adaptive multi-agent systems engineering. In: Petta, P., Tolksdorf, R., Zambonelli, F. (eds.) ESAW 2002. LNCS (LNAI), vol. 2577, pp. 156–169. Springer, Heidelberg (2003). https://doi.org/10.1007/3-540-39173-8_12
6. Beydoun, G., et al.: FAML: a generic metamodel for MAS development. IEEE Trans. Softw. Eng. **35**(6), 841–863 (2009)
7. Bresciani, P., Perini, A., Giorgini, P., Giunchiglia, F., Mylopoulos, J.: Tropos: an agent-oriented software development methodology. Auton. Agents Multi-Agent Syst. **8**(3), 203–236 (2004)
8. Cossentino, M., Potts, C.: A case tool supported methodology for the design of multi-agent systems. In: International Conference on Software Engineering Research and Practice (SERP 2002) (2002)
9. Gérard, S., Dumoulin, C., Tessier, P., Selic, B.: 19 Papyrus: a UML2 tool for domain-specific language modeling. In: Giese, H., Karsai, G., Lee, E., Rumpe, B., Schätz, B. (eds.) MBEERTS 2007. LNCS, vol. 6100, pp. 361–368. Springer, Heidelberg (2010). https://doi.org/10.1007/978-3-642-16277-0_19
10. Gungor, V.C., Sahin, D., Kocak, T., Ergut, S., Buccella, C., Cecati, C., Hancke, G.P.: Smart grid technologies: communication technologies and standards. IEEE Trans. Ind. Inform. **7**(4), 529–539 (2011)
11. Hahn, C., Madrigal-Mora, C., Fischer, K.: A platform-independent metamodel for multiagent systems. Auton. Agents Multi-Agent Syst. **18**(2), 239–266 (2009)
12. Hernandez, L., et al.: A multi-agent system architecture for smart grid management and forecasting of energy demand in virtual power plants. IEEE Commun. Mag. **51**(1), 106–113 (2013)
13. Kleppe, A.G., Warmer, J.B., Bast, W.: MDA Explained: the Model Driven Architecture: Practice and Promise. Addison-Wesley Professional, Reading (2003)
14. Koritarov, V.S.: Real-world market representation with agents. IEEE Power Energy Mag. **2**(4), 39–46 (2004)

15. Kravari, K., Bassiliades, N.: A survey of agent platforms. J. Artif. Soc. Soc. Simul. **18**(1), 11 (2015)
16. Kremers, E.A.: Modelling and Simulation of Electrical Energy Systems Through a Complex Systems Approach using Agent-Based Models. KIT Scientific Publishing, Karlsruhe (2013)
17. Logenthiran, T., Srinivasan, D., Shun, T.Z.: Demand side management in smart grid using heuristic optimization. IEEE Trans. Smart Grid **3**(3), 1244–1252 (2012)
18. McArthur, S.D., et al.: Multi-agent systems for power engineering applications–Part I: concepts, approaches, and technical challenges. IEEE Trans. Power Syst. **22**(4), 1743–1752 (2007)
19. McArthur, S.D.: Multi-agent systems for power engineering applications–Part II: technologies, standards, and tools for building multi-agent systems. IEEE Trans. Power Syst. **22**(4), 1753–1759 (2007)
20. McMorran, A.W.: An introduction to IEC 61970–301 & 61968–11: The common information model. vol. 93, p. 124. University of Strathclyde (2007)
21. O'Brien, P.D., Nicol, R.C.: FIPA–towards a standard for software agents. BT Technol. J. **16**(3), 51–59 (1998)
22. Pavón, J., Gómez-Sanz, J., Fuentes, R.: Model driven development of multi-agent systems. In: Rensink, A., Warmer, J. (eds.) ECMDA-FA 2006. LNCS, vol. 4066, pp. 284–298. Springer, Heidelberg (2006). https://doi.org/10.1007/11787044_22
23. Pipattanasomporn, M., Feroze, H., Rahman, S.: Multi-agent systems in a distributed smart grid: design and implementation. In: Power Systems Conference and Exposition, PSCE 2009, pp. 1–8. IEEE/PES (2009)
24. Romdhane, L.B., Sleiman, H.A., Mraidha, C., Dhouib, S.: Multi-agent solutions for energy systems: a model driven approach. In: 2017 22nd IEEE International Conference on Emerging Technologies and Factory Automation (ETFA), pp. 1–4, September 2017
25. Schmidt, D.C.: Model-driven engineering. Comput. IEEE Comput. Soc. **39**(2), 25 (2006)
26. Uslar, M., Specht, M., Rohjans, S., Trefke, J., González, J.M.: The Common Information Model CIM: IEC 61968/61970 and 62325-A practical introduction to the CIM. Springer, Heidelberg (2012). https://doi.org/10.1007/978-3-642-25215-0
27. Wooldridge, M., Jennings, N.R.: Intelligent agents: theory and practice. Knowl. Eng. Rev. **10**(2), 115–152 (1995)
28. Wooldridge, M., Jennings, N.R., Kinny, D.: The Gaia methodology for agent-oriented analysis and design. Auton. Agents Multi-Agent Syst. **3**(3), 285–312 (2000)

Active Situation Reporting: Definition and Analysis

Jennifer Renoux[✉]

Machine Perception and Interaction Lab, AASS, Örebro Universitet,
Fakultetsgatan 1, 702 81 Örebro, Sweden
jennifer.renoux@oru.se

Abstract. In a lot of situations a human is incapable to observe their environment properly. This can be due to disabilities, extreme conditions or simply a complex and changing environment. In those cases, help from an artificial system can be beneficial. This system, equipped with appropriate sensors, would be capable of perceiving things that a human cannot and inform them about the current state of the situation. In this short position paper, we introduce the notion of Active Situation Reporting, in which an agent can inform another agent about the evolution of a situation. We define this notion, study the challenges such a system raises and identify the open research questions by reviewing the state of the art.

1 Introduction

Alice is blind and love to sing in a choir. She uses her autonomous car every Mondays to go to her singing lesson. She is very involved and would not like to miss or be late to a lesson without warning the teacher. This Monday, the route Alice's car usually uses is blocked by a wide load. The traffic information system in the car detects that taking an alternative route would take 15 min more to travel while waiting for the wide load to leave takes an unknown amount of time (from 5 to 60 min). Alice notices that the car slows down and stops unusually and she is a bit stressed she might miss her lesson. She would like the car to be able to tell her what is happening and why it is acting unusually.

Barbara is a firefighter. Today she is entering a burning building with her teammates to try to find any victim. The team is accompanied by a robot that can perceive and navigate even in deep smoke. The robot can explore the environment and guide Barbara through the building, warning her if a roof collapses or if path is becoming too dangerous to take. Since the firefighters can hardly manipulate a tablet or other computer device in these extreme conditions, the robot is guiding them with voice.

Carl is living alone at home with an AI assistant to help him in his everyday life. The hospital just called him to tell him that his daughter had an accident and has been injured. Carl decides to go to the hospital right away but in his precipitation, he does not manage to find his car keys. His artificial assistant

F. Belardinelli and E. Argente (Eds.): EUMAS 2017/AT 2017, LNAI 10767, pp. 70–78, 2018.
https://doi.org/10.1007/978-3-030-01713-2_6

monitored that Carl took his keys in the bedroom the night before instead of putting them in the usual bowl in the entrance. It needs to inform Carl about it as soon as it detects that Carl is preparing to go out and is looking for something.

These three simple examples illustrate the advantages of having a system capable of helping a human understanding the environment they evolves in when this human cannot observe their environment properly. We refer this ability as *Active Situation Reporting*. In this paper, we study the problem of Active Situation Reporting and propose a definition in Sect. 2. Then, in Sect. 3, we highlight the different research challenges encountered while dealing with active situation reporting, study possible leads from the literature and identify open research questions. Finally, Sect. 4 identifies related research topics.

2   The Problem of Active Situation Reporting

Active Situation Reporting is not bound to an artificial system, and we define it as follows:

Definition 1. *Active Situation Reporting (ASR) is the process for an agent (called the reporter) to give relevant information about an evolving environment to another agent (called the user) without the user explicitly asking for this information. Automatic Active Situation Reporting is Active Situation Reporting performed by an artificial system.*

As we see, the reporter in an ASR system can as well be a human. Human journalists are in fact performing ASR for the newspaper or channel they work for by selecting information to deliver at a certain moment in time in order to give the reader or viewer an overview of a situation they cannot perceive directly. The nature of the information reported depends of what the journalist considers important and relevant. Automatic Active Situation Reporting works on the same principle: the reporter needs to select information that it considers relevant for its user at a certain moment in time and deliver it in the most appropriate way. We can already point out the main aspect (and challenge) of automatic ASR: how to automatically select the relevant information as it greatly depends on the user's preferences and knowledge as well as on the state of the situation at a certain time.

We can also note, as illustrated in the scenarios described in Sect. 1, that ASR can be the main goal of an artificial system (as for the firefighter case) or a mission to improve the user's comfort (as for the autonomous car). In the latter case, it is important that the situation reporting does not interfere with the main goal of the system.

Active Situation Reporting is at the crossroads of three different research areas which are Active Sensing, Semantic Perception and Human-Machine Interaction, as shown on Fig. 1.

3   Research Challenges and Open Questions

3.1   Active Sensing, Change Detection and Relevance

Active Sensing is defined as the "problem of controlling strategies applied to the data acquisition process which will depend on the current state of the data interpretation and the goal or the task of the process" [2]. A system performing active sensing will therefore act in order to maximize the amount of information it can gather. This can be the sole purpose of the system, as in exploration or surveillance applications, but can also be combined with other type of mission performed by the agent such as in [31]. The reader can refer to Chap. 1 of [25] for a review about active sensing. As stated in Definition 1, an ASR system notifies the user about changes in their environment. Those changes can happen gradually (a staircase burning and finally being destroyed) or be encountered suddenly (the wide load on the road), which raise the question of their detection.

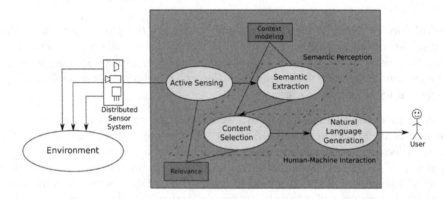

Fig. 1. Overview of an Active Situation Reporting system

In Computer Vision, change detection algorithms aim at detecting significant changes occurring in a video by analyzing the frames of this video. State of the art algorithms use statistical methods such as Kalman filter [5] or Bayesian models [34], non-parametric methods [32] and machine learning [17]. In the domain of pervasive computing, multiple sources of information need to be combined in order detect changes. Small changes on single individual sensors might be considered insignificant but the fusion of signals coming from different sources may reveal important changes in the environment. Several algorithms have been proposed to detect changes in multivariate time series [11,16] but they are computationally expensive and require a large amount of data for the model training. To overcome this issue, an information-theoretic change detection method for IoT systems has been recently proposed in [13]. One common aspect of all these methods is that they focus on anomaly detection, meaning detecting when the system changes from a *normal* state (often learned) to an *abnormal* state.

However in the case of ASR, the changes are not related to anomaly detection but concern changes compared to previous states. In Data Mining and Machine Learning, the term *Concept Drift* refers to the possible change through time in the underlying model of a data stream and are usually tackled through adaptive learning algorithms [15]. One of the main challenges of concept drift detection algorithms is not to mistake noise with true drift. Many of existing algorithms assume sudden drifts [20], which is a big limitation compared to what can be observed in reality.

An ASR system cannot report all changes it detects in the environment but should select those that are *relevant* for the user at this moment. The concept of relevance is mostly studied in Information Science [29] and, technically, in Information Retrieval (IR) systems [10] and is usually called *system-based relevance*. In this topic, the goal of the system is to retrieve all the documents relevant to a request [27]. Here the relevance is objective and defined related to a subject. However, in intelligent autonomous systems, the relevance can be subjective and depends on the user's current state of beliefs and is referred to as *agent-based relevance, user-based relevance* or *epistemic relevance*. Agent-based relevance has received a lot of interest in knowledge theory and its different properties has been defined [14]. These properties have been used to derive a formal model of relevance within modal logic [28]. However, this model still assumes that the system knows with certainty the information need of the agent receiving the information, which is an unrealistic hypothesis when this agent is a human. In [26], Renoux et al. suggested a model in which each agent uses approximations of other agent's beliefs in order to compute a degree of relevance. This system does not require an explicit request but depends on a lot of communication between the agents for the relevance computation to be efficient. In addition, the correspondence between the degree developed and what a human would consider relevant has not been directly demonstrated. Only indirect clues has been provided by experiments using this degree, as presented in [25].

With this study of the literature about active sensing, two important open research questions have already been identified:

1. How to detect gradual changes in an environment? As mentioned, all the methods we have encountered so far are hypothesizing (implicitly or not) sudden changes to detect. However, the environment will often change gradually and those changes are important for humans. Therefore a methods to detect such changes needs to be developed.
2. How to construct an efficient framework to quantify agent-based relevance? Such a framework would need to be able to compute the relevance of a piece of information for a human, based on a model of the human mind and knowledge. The degree proposed by Renoux et al. could be a interesting starting point but needs to be expanded with more advanced theories of mind such as the one suggested in [12].

3.2 Semantic Perception

Sensor data as captured by artificial systems are not of much use for a human without their meaning. A human expert is capable, by analyzing the data, to extract meaning from them. An automatic ASR system needs to be able of the same in order to communicate meaningful information to its user.

Semantic perception is the systematic automation of observing/sensing the environment via sensors and the ability of extracting semantics from the data [23]. The Semantic Sensor Web proposes to annotate sensor data with semantic metadata in order to provide contextual information [30]. In this direction, the Semantic Sensor Network (SSN) ontology [7] provides a terminology to represent contextual knowledge and has been successfully used in various applications [1,18]. In addition to being able to abstract sensors data to reason upon, artificial systems acting in the real wold need to make and maintain a connection between what concepts they reason upon and the actual real-world object these concepts represent or apply to, despite possible changes of the object in time (in position, shape, aspect...). This is the Physical Symbol Grounding Problem [8]. This problem has been tackled from different angles and learning methods have been used [33] as well as spatio-temporal reasoning [22] and, more recently, ontologies [4].

Despite those recent advances in semantic perception and symbol grounding, some questions remain open and are being investigated by the research community, such as the problem of *shared symbol grounding*, or humans and machines using the same terms to denote the same entity [4]; and perceptual anchoring, which is a subset of symbol grounding focused on maintaining a link between the object and the concept over time [9].

3.3 Human-Machine Interaction

The information perceived and abstracted needs to be reported in an adequate format to the user and therefore mapped to human-understandable language. Natural Language Generation (NLG) is concerned about "building software systems that can produce meaningful texts in English or other human languages from some underlying nonlinguistic representation of information" [24]. NLG has been used in various applications to describe physiological data [3], to interact with the semantic web [6] or for spoken dialog. Despite recent advances in content selection and text generation, recent NLG systems are still rudimentary with regard to context-adaptation. They are capable of selecting a target language and adapt to a user's preferences but the modeling of the context remains rather simple. However, the semantic web and its modeling capabilities could be an excellent framework to model rich contexts and include them in a Natural Language Generation system [6].

4 Related Work

In the previous sections, we studied ASR with regards to the fields of research needed to achieve it. In this section, we will give an overview of approaches that are similar or related to our problem and see where they differ from ASR.

First of all, one cannot fail to notice that Active Situation Reporting is some kind of monitoring. A lot of monitoring systems already exist and are doing very good job in verifying the state of an environment and its evolution. One could therefore rightfully wonder what Active Situation Reporting would do more or better. First of all, current monitoring systems are not *active*, in the sense that the user needs to request the information to be reported in order to get it. An ASR system is proactive by detecting that the user might need some piece of information and deciding to report it. In addition, classic monitoring systems do not select relevant information to report but report everything. They can highlight anomalies (usually based on thresholds) but offer a full access to all the information they are monitoring, which can be overwhelming for the user in large and complex environment such as the surrounding of a car. Finally, monitoring systems usually require the user to be trained at using them as the interface they offer is usually specialized for one type of operator. Active Situation Reporting aims at integrating flexibility, adaptability and user-friendliness in monitoring.

Two trendy topics currently in human-machine interaction are transparency [21] and explainable agency [19]. Autonomous agents are required to be able to explain their behavior, their beliefs, their intentions and their reasoning to a human user. Transparency and explainable agency are required to enable humans to trust artificial agents in critical situations where they are expected to collaborate. Similar challenges are encountered in those two topics and ASR, such as the human-machine communication, the extraction of semantics from data, etc. However, ASR aims at describing the environment around the agent more than the behavior of the agent itself, hence the importance of active sensing. Of course, agents describing their behavior and reasoning can be relevant for active situation reporting system, such as the autonomous car explaining that it decided to modify the planned route because of a closed road.

5 Conclusion

In this paper we described the problem of Active Situation Reporting, looked at the state of the art to determine what are the still open research questions in order to be able to build ASR systems and identified the following open questions:

1. how to detect gradual and incremental changes in the environment?
2. how to quantify the relevance of a piece of information for a human?
3. how to perform efficiently shared symbol grounding and perceptual anchoring?

In addition to those research questions, challenges arise in the combination of those fields that are Active Sensing, Semantic Perception and Human-Machine Interaction. Indeed, those three field use methods, assumptions and tools very different from one another and achieving interoperability between the components required by an ASR system is a great challenge. Finally, the complexity of the tasks considered by ASR involves a very complex modeling task. If ontologies seem to be a good tool to enable interoperability and rich context-modeling, connections between active sensing and semantic perception still need to be drawn in order to create an Active Situation Reporting system.

Acknowledgment. This work has been funded by the MoveCare project (ID 732158), which is funded by the European Commission under the H2020 framework program for research and innovation.

References

1. Alirezaie, et al.: An ontology-based context-aware system for smart homes: E-care@ home. Sensors **17**(7), 1586 (2017)
2. Bajcsy, R.: Active perception. Proc. IEEE **76**(8), 966–1005 (1988)
3. Banaee, H., Loutfi, A.: Data-driven rule mining and representation of temporal patterns in physiological sensor data. IEEE J. Biomed. Health Inform. **19**(5), 1557–1566 (2015)
4. Beeson, P., Kortenkamp, D., Bonasso, R.P., Persson, A., Loutfi, A., Bona, J.P.: An ontology-based symbol grounding system for human-robot interaction. In: Proceedings of the 2014 AAAI Fall Symposium Series, Arlington, pp. 13–15 (2014)
5. Benezeth, Y., Jodoin, P.M., Emile, B., Laurent, H., Rosenberger, C.: Comparative study of background subtraction algorithms. J. Electron. Imaging **19**(3), 033003–033003 (2010)
6. Bouayad-Agha, N., Casamayor, G., Wanner, L.: Natural language generation in the context of the semantic web. Semant. Web **5**(6), 493–513 (2014)
7. Compton, M., et al.: The SSN ontology of the W3C semantic sensor network incubator group. Web Semant. Sci. Serv. Agents World Wide Web **17**, 25–32 (2012)
8. Coradeschi, S., Loutfi, A., Wrede, B.: A short review of symbol grounding in robotic and intelligent systems. KI - Künstliche Intelligenz **27**(2), 129–136 (2013)
9. Coradeschi, S., Saffiotti, A.: An introduction to the anchoring problem. Robot. Auton. Syst. **43**(2–3), 85–96 (2003)
10. Croft, B., Lafferty, J.: Language Modeling for Information Retrieval, vol. 13. Springer, Dordrecht (2013). https://doi.org/10.1007/978-94-017-0171-6
11. Desobry, F., Davy, M., Doncarli, C.: An online kernel change detection algorithm. Trans. Signal Process. **53**(8), 2961–2974 (2005)
12. Devin, S., Alami, R.: An implemented theory of mind to improve human-robot shared plans execution. In: The Eleventh ACM/IEEE International Conference on Human Robot Interaction, HRI 2016, pp. 319–326. IEEE Press, Piscataway (2016)
13. Faivishevsky, L.: Information theoretic multivariate change detection for multisensory information processing in Internet of Things. In: IEEE International Conference on Acoustics, Speech and Signal Processing (ICASSP), pp. 6250–6254. IEEE, March 2016. http://ieeexplore.ieee.org/document/7472879/
14. Floridi, L.: Understanding epistemic relevance. Erkenntnis **69**(1), 69–92 (2008)

15. Gama, J., Žliobaitė, I., Bifet, A., Pechenizkiy, M., Bouchachia, A.: A survey on concept drift adaptation. ACM Comput. Surv. (CSUR) **46**(4), 44 (2014)
16. Glazer, A., Lindenbaoum, M., Markovitch, S.: Learning high-density regions for a generalized Kolmogorov-Smirnov test in high-dimensional data. In: Proceedings of the 25th International Conference on Neural Information Processing Systems, NIPS 2012, pp. 728–736. Curran Associates Inc., USA (2012). http://dl.acm.org/citation.cfm?id=2999134.2999216
17. Han, B., Davis, L.S.: Density-based multifeature background subtraction with support vector machine. IEEE Trans. Pattern Anal. Mach. Intell. **34**(5), 1017–1023 (2012)
18. Henson, C., Thirunarayan, K., Sheth, A.: An ontological approach to focusing attention and enhancing machine perception on the web. Appl. Ontol. **6**(4), 345–376 (2011)
19. Langley, P.: Explainable agency in human-robot interaction. In: AAAI Fall Symposium Series (2016)
20. Liu, A., Zhang, G., Lu, J., Lu, N., Lin, C.-T.: An online competence-based concept drift detection algorithm. In: Kang, B.H., Bai, Q. (eds.) AI 2016. LNCS (LNAI), vol. 9992, pp. 416–428. Springer, Cham (2016). https://doi.org/10.1007/978-3-319-50127-7_36
21. Lyons, J.B.: Being transparent about transparency: a model for human-robot interaction. In: AAAI Spring Symposium Series (2013)
22. Milliez, G., Warnier, M., Clodic, A., Alami, R.: A framework for endowing an interactive robot with reasoning capabilities about perspective-taking and belief management. In: 2014 RO-MAN: The 23rd IEEE International Symposium on Robot and Human Interactive Communication, pp. 1103–1109. IEEE (2014)
23. Nevatia, R.: Machine perception, p. 209. Prentice-Hall Inc., Englewood Cliffs (1982). 07632
24. Reiter, E., Dale, R.: Building Natural Language Generation Systems. Cambridge University Press, New York (2000)
25. Renoux, J.: Contribution to multiagent planning for active information gathering. Ph.D. thesis, Normandie Université (2015)
26. Renoux, J., Mouaddib, A.-I., LeGloannec, S.: Distributed decision-theoretic active perception for multi-robot active information gathering. In: Torra, V., Narukawa, Y., Endo, Y. (eds.) MDAI 2014. LNCS (LNAI), vol. 8825, pp. 60–71. Springer, Cham (2014). https://doi.org/10.1007/978-3-319-12054-6_6
27. Rijsbergen, C.J.V.: Information Retrieval, 2nd edn. Butterworth-Heinemann, Newton (1979)
28. Roussel, S., Cholvy, L.: Cooperative interpersonal communication and relevant information. In: ESSLLI Workshop on Logical Methods for Social Concepts, Bordeaux. Citeseer (2009)
29. Saracevic, T.: Why is relevance still the basic notion in information science. In: Re: inventing Information Science in the Networked Society. Proceedings of the 14th International Symposium on Information Science (ISI 2015), pp. 26–35 (2015)
30. Sheth, A., Henson, C., Sahoo, S.S.: Semantic sensor web. IEEE Internet Comput. **12**(4), 78–83 (2008)
31. Spaan, M.T.J., Veiga, T.S., Lima, P.U.: Decision-theoretic planning under uncertainty with information rewards for active cooperative perception. Auton. Agents Multi-Agent Syst. **29**(6), 1157–1185 (2015)

32. St-Charles, P.L., Bilodeau, G.A., Bergevin, R.: Flexible background subtraction with self-balanced local sensitivity. In: Proceedings of the 2014 IEEE Conference on Computer Vision and Pattern Recognition Workshops, CVPRW 2014, pp. 414–419. IEEE Computer Society, Washington, DC (2014)
33. Vavrečka, M., Farkaš, I., Lhotská, L.: Bio-inspired model of spatial cognition. In: Lu, B.-L., Zhang, L., Kwok, J. (eds.) ICONIP 2011. LNCS, vol. 7062, pp. 443–450. Springer, Heidelberg (2011). https://doi.org/10.1007/978-3-642-24955-6_53
34. Wang, R., Bunyak, F., Seetharaman, G., Palaniappan, K.: Static and moving object detection using flux tensor with split Gaussian models. In: Proceedings of the IEEE Conference on Computer Vision and Pattern Recognition Workshops, pp. 414–418 (2014)

Agent-Based Security Constrained Optimal Power Flow with Primary Frequency Control

Maxime Velay[1,2]([✉]), Meritxell Vinyals[1], Yvon Bésanger[2], and Nicolas Retière[2]

[1] CEA, LIST, Laboratoire d'Analyse des Données et d'Intelligence des Systèmes, Gif-sur-Yvette 91191, France
maxime.velay@cea.fr, maxime.velay@g2elab.grenoble-inp.fr
[2] Univ. Grenoble Alpes, CNRS, Grenoble INP, Institute of Engineering Univ. Grenoble Alpes, G2Elab, 38000 Grenoble, France

Abstract. We propose in this paper a distributed method to solve the security constrained optimal power flow problem (SCOPF) that considers not only contingencies on transmission lines but also on generators. With this aim, we extend the formulation of the SCOPF problem to consider the primary frequency response of generators as well as the short term constraints of generators and transmission lines. Then, we distribute the problem among different agents and we use a decentralized decision making algorithm, based on the Alternating Direction Method of Multipliers (ADMM), to optimize the grid power supply while being resilient to violations that would occur during contingencies. Finally, we validate the effectiveness of our approach on a simple test system.

Keywords: Distributed optimization · Multi-agent system
Security-constrained optimal power flow · Primary frequency control

1 Introduction

The planning and operation of power systems is one of the more challenging problems faced by system operators given the complex interplay of multiple objectives to be achieved, including economic, security and reliability aspects. On one side, electricity is a commodity that cannot be easily stored so system operators need to keep the balance between generation and consumption at all times while minimizing the total operation cost of the power system and enforcing the network's operational constraints (e.g. the capacity of the transmission lines). On the other side, transmission system operators also need to perform contingency analysis to guarantee not only that no operational constraint is violated during the normal operating case, but also on potential contingency scenarios when the outage of some components occurs. Most of the transmission system operators (TSOs) must operate at least in compliance with the N-1 criteria so that any single element contingency (either transmission line or generator)

© Springer Nature Switzerland AG 2018
F. Belardinelli and E. Argente (Eds.): EUMAS 2017/AT 2017, LNAI 10767, pp. 79–95, 2018.
https://doi.org/10.1007/978-3-030-01713-2_7

can be handled and lead to a stable operating point, i.e., with no propagation of the disturbance [10]. In other words, the loss of any transmission line should not overload the remaining ones, and the loss of any generator can be compensated by the other remaining generators.

Consequently, system operators employ optimization techniques to guarantee that all constraints above are respected as well as to minimize the cost of operation, to solve the so-called Security-Constrained Optimal Power Flow (SC-OPF) [3]. The SC-OPF problem is a fundamental optimization problem in power systems and has been extensively investigated by many researchers.

In current practices, transmission system operators adopt centralized optimization approaches for solving SCOPF problem, which gather all information and make decisions for their own systems. However, during the last decade, power systems have been extended by applying interconnections to the neighboring systems in order to achieve technical and economical advantages, leading to problems of unprecedented scale (e.g. 36 countries interconnected in Europe). As large interconnected power networks come into existence (i.e. covering parts of or even whole continents), such centralized approach raises more and more computation and communication concerns [12].

To avoid these drawbacks, new distributed optimization techniques have been proposed so that the computation can be parallelized (and so it does not increase exponentially with the size of the problem) and control is as much as possible autonomous. Under such approaches, the problem is usually modeled by means of a network of autonomous entities (aka agents) where each entity cooperate by solving a local problem (with local constraints and local data) providing an holistic view for power network operation. Of particular interest here is the Alternating Direction Method of Multipliers (ADMM), a distributed algorithm intended to blend the decomposability of dual ascent with the superior convergence properties of the method of multipliers for constrained optimization [2].

ADMM has been recently applied to a wide variety of a large-scale power system optimization problems. In particular, Kranning et al. in [7], have shown how a decentralized algorithm based on ADMM, can be efficiently applied to the optimal power flow problem (i.e. without considering any contingency scenario) and solved distributively by autonomous agents [11]. More recently, Chakrabarti et al. [4] extended the framework presented in [7] to be able to solve the SCOPF problem. Despite its potential, the model proposed in [4] has an important drawback: it does not take into account the automatic response of generators after a power disturbance and hence it is not able to model any contingency scenario that leads to power imbalance. As a result, such model can not support any contingency involving the loss of a generator and the solution found under such model will never meet the N-1 criteria.

In practice, generators implement primary frequency control (PFC) strategies to steer away the power system from frequency instability. Primary frequency control involves all actions performed locally at the generator to stabilize the system frequency (i.e. within specified stable limits but different from its nominal value) after a power disturbance. Since the power system frequency reflects the power balance and it is the same across the whole power system, the generating units use the frequency to regulate the power supplied (i.e. with a contribution that depends on the frequency deviation and on the generator's characteristics).

Against this background, this paper overcomes this drawback by extending the framework in [4] in order to take into account the automatic primary frequency response of generators. By doing so we are able to model contingency states in SCOPF due to an incident involving a modification of the active power balance and, in particular, those involving generation outages. The major modeling issue is the codependent relationship between the control variables (i.e. the output of generators) in the normal operating scenario and the automatic frequency response of generators following the incident. In summary, the SCOPF problem considering the PFC setting is complex, and in this paper we provide the first agent-based totally distributed solution to this challenge.

In more detail, this work can be seen as having the following contributions to the state-of-the-art:

- We illustrate the limitations of the SCOPF formulation without PFC by means of a simple numerical example.
- We extend the SCOPF formulation from [4] by: (1) introducing a new variable representing the frequency deviation which is computed by distributed consensus among agents and used to coordinate the power reallocation process after an incident; (2) enhancing the local problem of each generator to consider how it will adjust its production after a contingency following its primary frequency regulation curve.
- We distribute the resulting SCOPF problem among different agents and we use the ADMM algorithm as a coordination mechanism among these agents.
- We evaluate our approach on a IEEE test system to validate its efficiency.

The rest of this paper is structured as follows. A review of the related literature is provided in Sect. 2. Section 3 gives some background on the decentralized SCOPF formulation and on the ADMM algorithm. Section 4 uses a 3-bus circuit to illustrate the operation and importance of taking into account PFC in SCOPF. Section 5 extend the existing decentralized SCOPF formulation (in particular agent's objective functions and the corresponding ADMM updates) in order to be able to consider PFC. Finally Sect. 6 presents results on the IEEE 14-bus test system and Sect. 7 concludes.

2   Related Work

The main challenges and techniques for solving the SCOPF are reviewed in [3]. Most of the literature takes into account medium term post-contingency or tertiary frequency control scenarios that correspond to an optimal response of the ISO, like in [8]. Moreover, SCOPF models in the literature are classified into two types: (i) the *preventive* [2], in which there is no post-contingency re-scheduling of control variables (the solution found for the normal state is also feasible for all contingencies scenarios); and the *corrective/curative* [9], in which the control variables are allowed to be re-scheduled to rectify any violated operating constraint in post contingency network. The focus of this paper is on short term post-contingency scenarios with automatic reactions, i.e. preventive SCOPF model, of the system that include the primary frequency control as modeled in [6].

Related work on distributed optimization for power system operation can be found in [12] and the references cited therein. Based on the type of information being exchanged, [12] divides the distributed methodologies applied in power system operation into two categories: (i) generator-based decomposition with price/cost information exchange and (ii) geography-based decomposition with physical information exchange.

On the one hand, generator-based decomposition with price/cost information exchange approaches set each generator as a local control agent. Under this category, a lot of works have been proposed based on different techniques, varying from the incremental cost consensus based methods [13] to the flooding-based consensus approaches [5]. However, by decomposing the central power system operation at generator level, such approaches require significant information exchange at the bus level and hence, they are only efficient when neglecting system-level constraints (e.g. network constraints and capacity limits of transmission lines). Therefore, such approaches are not suitable for solving large-scale OPF problems and even less for solving the extended SCOPF problems (i.e. with system-level security constraints), which is the focus of this paper.

On the other hand, geography-based decomposition methods exchange, instead of cost information of generators, information related to the physical measures (i.e. voltage and power flows). A major advantage of geography-based decomposition approaches is that they divide the large system into several smaller-scale geographical regions coupled by lines and hence they can provide a natural decomposition structure which is consistent with the topology of power physical systems. In this context, ADMM has been identified as one of the most applicable and efficient decomposition methods given its good computational performance and linear convergence rate. ADMM [2] is a distributed solution that combines the fast convergence properties of augmented Lagrangian-based methods with the separability of alternating optimization.

In particular, Kraning et al. proposed in [7] a methodology for decomposing the OPF problem among a collaborative agent network and a fully-distributed ADMM-based OPF algorithm to solve it. The convergence criterion is provided and experiments on large systems are conducted. Chakrabarti et al. [4] extended that model in order to deal with the SCOPF problem, handling different reliability constraints across multiple scenarios. However, they only consider contingencies on transmission lines and hence the primary frequency control is not modeled as the power balance is kept after each contingency. Moreover, the paper lacks empirical evaluation: the framework is only evaluated in a single two bus system.

In summary, to the best of the authors knowledge, the preventive SCOPF including the primary frequency control has never been addressed using a

ADMM based distributed algorithm. Hence, this work is the first to propose a decentralized formulation of the preventive SCOPF problem, and a subsequent implementation solved by distributed autonomous agents, that is able to consider contingencies generating power imbalance, and specifically, on generators.

3 Background

In this section, we review the ADMM algorithm and its application to the SC-OPF problem. Following the network model proposed by Kraning et al. [7], we divide the set of power system network components into two groups: (i) the set of *nets* (N), that similarly to the electrical bus concept contains all the lossless components that connect devices and enforce Kirchoff's physical laws; and (ii) the set of *devices* (D), that is composed of all power components that are not buses namely transmission lines, generators and loads. These components are the agents of our system. Then, each agent $a \in N \cup D$ (i.e. either net or device) is associated to a local objective function $f_a(x_a)$ that returns the exploitation cost of agent a for the set of variables x_a and a set of constraints, denoted as C_a, that x_a should satisfy in order to be a feasible solution. In this model, the global objective function is factorized into smaller functions, one for each network agent:

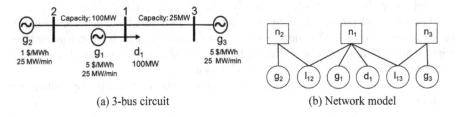

(a) 3-bus circuit   (b) Network model

Fig. 1. A simple bus test circuit (left); its graphical representation in the network model from [7] (right).

$$\min_x \sum_{d \in D} f_d(x_d) + \sum_{n \in N} f_n(x_n)$$

$$\text{subject to } \forall d \in D : x_d \in C_d, \ \forall n \in N : x_n \in C_n \tag{1}$$

Now, we create an edge for every pair of agents whose objective function have some variable in common (i.e. the cost and/or the feasibility of both agents depends on at least some shared variables). We will refer to this set of edges as *terminals* (T). For each agent $a \in N \cup D$, we use a to refer to both the agent itself as well as to the set of terminals associated with it, i.e., we say $t \in a$ if terminal t is associated with agent a. As shown in [7], for a power network this leads to a bipartite graph between nets and devices in which each terminal t connects a device and a net. For example, Fig. 1a shows a simple 3-bus circuit whereas Fig. 1b shows its network model where nets are represented by rectangles, terminals by lines and devices by circles. Moreover, the set of variables associated to terminal ($x_t = x_d \cap x_n$) results on the classic power flow variables, namely active power (p) and other quantities that depend on the transmission line and power flow model used. In this paper, we restrict ourselves to the DC-model and thus, only the voltage phase angle (θ) will be considered for transmission lines and nets, in addition to the active power. The global objective function is intended to find the active power and voltage phase angle schedules (i.e. the variable x) that satisfy the power flow equations and that minimize the operating cost.

This model is used in [4] to solve a SC-OPF problem in which the optimization is performed over a number of possible contingency scenarios, $\mathcal{L} \in \mathbb{N}^+$, each related to a contingency. Here we assume that the first scenario, (0), is the one that stands for the base case (with no contingency). Given a contingency (c) we define $D^{(c)}$ as the set of devices that are disconnected in that scenario.

Thus, in a SC-OPF problem, each terminal $t \in T$ has associated one (active) power schedule over the set of contingencies $\mathcal{L}$ $p_t = (p_t(0), \ldots, p_t(\mathcal{L})) \in \mathbb{R}^{\mathcal{L}}$. Then, for all $\tau \in [(0), \mathcal{L}]$, $p_t(\tau)$ is the (real) power consumed (if $p_t(\tau) > 0$, otherwise produced) by device d through terminal t, for the contingency scenario τ. Similarly, we use an analogous notation for other quantities that are associated to each terminal, i.e. each terminal $t \in T$ is associated with a voltage phase angle schedule over the set of contingencies $\theta_t = (\theta_t(0), \ldots, \theta_t(\mathcal{L})) \in \mathbb{R}^{\mathcal{L}}$.

The set of all power schedules associated with an agent $a \in D \cup N$ (being a either a device or a net) is denoted by $p_a = \{p_t | t \in a\}$, which we can associate with a $|a| \times \mathcal{L}$ matrix. For voltage phase angle schedules we use an identical notation to power schedules, i.e. $\theta_a = \{\theta_t | t \in a\}$.

Formally, an energy coordination network models the following optimization problem:

$$\min_{p, \theta \in \mathbb{R}^{|T| \times \mathcal{L}}} \sum_{d \in D} f_d(p_d, \theta_d) + \sum_{n \in N} f_n(p_n, \theta_n) \tag{2}$$

$$\text{subject to } \forall d \in D: p_d, \theta_d \in C_d, \ \forall n \in N: p_n, \theta_n \in C_n$$

where p, θ are respectively the set of all terminal power schedules ($p = \{p_t | t \in T\}$) and voltage phase angle schedules ($\theta = \{\theta_t | t \in T\}$).

Following [4,7], this optimization problem can be solved by a distributed coordination protocol based on the Alternating Direction Method of Multipliers (ADMM) [2]. ADMM is an algorithm that blends the decomposability of dual ascent with the superior convergence properties of the method of multipliers for constrained optimization (i.e. guarantees of achieving convergence without assumptions such as strict convexity for functions f_d and f_n). Under ADMM formulation, first, the nets agents objective functions are defined over a duplicated copy of the original variables (i.e. denoted as $\dot{p}, \dot{\theta}$) to form the augmented Lagrangian, then the equality constraint ($p = \dot{p}, \theta = \dot{\theta}$) is relaxed via a Lagrange multiplier.

In a nutshell, the ADMM algorithm consists in iteratively applying the following three steps at a given iteration $k + 1$:

The *device-minimization* step (i.e. parallelized among devices agents) minimizes the operating cost of the device, encoded by f_d and C_d, and a penalty designed for coordination with its neighboring nets:

$$(p_d^{k+1}, \theta_d^{k+1}) = \arg \min_{p_d, \theta_d \in C_d} (f_d(p_d, \theta_d) + \frac{\rho}{2}||p_d - \dot{p}_d^k + u_d^k||_2^2$$
$$+ \frac{\rho}{2}||\theta_d - \dot{\theta}_d^k + v_d^k||_2^2), \quad \forall d \in D \tag{3}$$

The *net-minimization* step (i.e. parallelized among nets agents) enforces the Kirchhoff's physical laws, encoded by means of f_n and C_n, with a penalty designed to coordinate the net and its neighboring devices:

$$(\dot{p}_n^{k+1}, \dot{\theta}_n^{k+1}) = \arg \min_{\dot{p}_n, \dot{\theta}_n \in C_n} (f_n(\dot{p}_n, \dot{\theta}_n) + \frac{\rho}{2}||p_n^{k+1} - \dot{p}_n + u_n^k||_2^2$$
$$+ \frac{\rho}{2}||\theta_n^{k+1} - \dot{\theta}_n + v_n^k||_2^2), \quad \forall n \in N \tag{4}$$

The (price) *scaled dual variables* update (i.e. parallelized among nets agents) aims at coordinating nets and devices through the scaled dual variables:

$$\forall n \in N, \quad u_n^{k+1} = u_n^k + (p_n^{k+1} - \dot{p}_n^{k+1}) \tag{5}$$

$$\forall n \in N, \quad v_n^{k+1} = v_n^k + (\theta_n^{k+1} - \dot{\theta}_n^{k+1}) \tag{6}$$

with iteration index k and some scaling parameter $\rho > 0$.

The problem, is by construction, already separated in local sub-problems which allows each agent (either net or device) to solve its sub-problem in parallel and coordinate via message-passing through terminals. At each iteration, every device agent computes a minimization step for its local objective function (Eq. 3) with an argument that depends on messages passed to it through its terminals by its neighboring nets agents in the previous iteration ($\dot{p}_n^{k+1}$, $\dot{\theta}_n^{k+1}$, u_n^{k+1} and v_n^{k+1}). Similarly, each net agent computes its minimization (Eq. 4) and scaled dual variables steps (Eq. 6) with an argument that depends on messages passed to it through its terminals by its neighboring devices agents in the previous iteration (p_n^{k+1}, θ_n^{k+1}). This is done iteratively until a sufficient consistency is reached at each net.

4 Considering Contingencies Involving Power Imbalance – Primary Frequency Control

This section first highlights the importance of taking into account the primary frequency control in the SCOPF problem by means of a simple example and second, it provides a formal definition of the primary frequency control scheme in power systems.

4.1 Motivation

The model proposed in [4] is the first attempt to use the ADMM to solve a preventive SC-OPF problem. However, this model has a major drawback, it neglects the fact that in reality generator controllers are designed to balance the power in emergency cases by means of the so-called primary frequency control (PFC). As a result, the solution found by the SCOPF model formulated in [4] can not guarantee to satisfy the N-1 criteria because it deals with outages of lines but not of generators. To illustrate the limits of the mentioned formulation and to present the preventive SC-OPF with PFC, we take as example the 3-bus circuit depicted in Fig. 1a. Notice that a solution compliant with the N-1 criteria in this circuit is one that guarantees that the system will be able to operate in a normal state (i.e. respecting the constraints of the system such as line capacities or ramp of generators) following the loss of any single device, either generator (g_1 or g_2 or g_3) or line (l_{12} or l_{13}).

Table 1. (a) Different models base case solutions and (b) contingency scenarios SCOPF with PFC solutions for the 3-bus circuit in Fig. 1a

	g_1	g_2	g_3	$
OPF	0MW	100MW	0MW	100$
SCOPF	100MW	0MW	0MW	500$
SCOPF with PFC	50MW	50MW	0MW	300$

(a) Base scenario (pre-contingency) dispatch.

Contingency	Post-contingency dispatch		
	g_1	g_2	g_3
g_2 or l_{12}	75MW	0MW	25MW
g_1	0MW	75MW	25MW
g_3 or l_{13}	50MW	50MW	0MW

(b) SCOPF with PFC post-contingency scenarios dispatch

Table 1a states the base case solutions for this 3-bus circuit and the different models considered. Observe that the OPF solution (e.g. without considering any security constraint) for this circuit is that the cheapest generator (i.e. g_2) produces all active power consumed by d_1 with a cost of 100$/h. Now, consider a solution that is not only feasible under normal operating limits, but also after a contingency happened. Notice that in this circuit, any contingency related to the loss of a line also results in the disconnection of a generator (i.e. the loss of line l_{12} disconnects g_2 and of line l_{13} disconnects g_3). Therefore, the only solution to the SC-OPF problem with no PFC is that generator g_1 produces all power consumed by d_1 with a cost of 500$/h. The difference between the OPF cost and the SCOPF cost is called cost of security and is equal to $500 - 100 = 400\$/h$. However, notice that this solution is not N-1 resilient since it does not support the loss of generation g_1 and as we will see next the cost of the security can be lowered.

Now consider the case of SC-OPF with PFC and the contingency on line l_{12}. In this case, generators g_1 and g_3, both taking part into the PFC, will automatically increase their output to compensate the loss of g_2 according to their characteristics and droop. Considering that both generators have the same char-acteristics (e.g. same size and same droop), the units produced by g_2 will be equally compensated by the remaining generators, namely g_1 and g_3. However, the primary response of generators is limited by their ramp rate, and hence generators g_1 and g_3 are able to compensate a maximum of 25 MW each. Con-sequently, in the dispatch, the output of g_2 should be limited to 50 MW whereas the remaining generation is distributed between g_1 and g_3. Since the output of generator g_3 is limited by the maximum capacity of line l_{12}, the only way to avoid the overload of the line is to set the production of g_3 in the base case to 0.

Moreover, as summarized in Table 1b, considering contingencies on line 2–3, and even on any generator, does not add anymore constraint to the problem and hence the solution of the SCOPF when taking into account PFC meets the N-1 criterion. The cost of security is $300 - 100 = 200\$/h$ when considering the PFC, and represents half the one found by the SC-OPF without PFC.

As a results, taking into account the PFC allows to consider the disconnec-tions of generators and lines that connect generators to the grid. The security of the system is then improved and the N-1 security criteria can be totally enforced.

4.2 Primary Frequency Control

The primary frequency control (PFC) aims at regulating the frequency of the power system by adapting the generation [1]. Since this paper focuses on pre-ventive SC-OPF, the change in generation production variables, following a con-tingency, is only due to the response of the power system automatic control:

$$p_g^{(c)} = p_g^{(0)} + \Delta p_g^{(c)} \tag{7}$$

where $p_g^{(c)}$ is the generation after PFC due to contingency (c) and $p_g^{(0)}$ is the generation in the base case (0), i.e. prior any contingency.

The primary frequency response follows the following five principles:

1. The active power imbalance due to contingency is completely compensated by the active production of generators, taking part to the primary frequency control.

$$\sum_{g \in G} p_g^{(0)} - \sum_{g \in G} p_g^{(c)} = 0 \tag{8}$$

   where $G \subseteq D$ is the set of generators of the system.
2. The units taking part to the primary frequency control recover the active power imbalance according to its coefficient: each generator g participating in the PFC responds proportionally to the frequency deviation $\Delta f^{(c)}$ due to contingency (c). $\Delta p_g^{(c)}$ is the contribution of the generator to the regulation of the frequency of the system for a deviation of $\Delta f^{(c)}$ on a base frequency of f_0.

$$\Delta p_g^{(c)} = -K_g \cdot \frac{\Delta f^{(c)}}{f_0} \tag{9}$$

   where:

K_g is the ratio of the nominal active power and the speed droop of the generator (both constants and depending on the generators characteristics)

f_0 is regulated frequency of the grid (50 Hz or 60 Hz depending of the country)

3. The active production of each generator has to remain within its production limits

$$P^{min} \leq p_g^{(c)} \leq P^{max} \tag{10}$$

4. The primary response of each generator does not exceed the ramp constraints, $\Delta p_g^{(c)}$ is limited because generators cannot change their production at any speed.

$$R^{min} \leq \Delta p_g^{(c)} \leq R^{max} \tag{11}$$

5. Once a generator reaches its (ramp or production) limits the other generators have to compensate the non-allocated power according to their own speed droop. Thus, when generators do not change as expected because they reached some constraints, this is reflected into the frequency deviation $\Delta f^{(c)}$ which increases to have the rest of generators compensate more.

For the rest of the paper, we introduce the variable $\alpha^{(c)}$ for the contingency (c) so that $\alpha^{(c)}$ is the relative frequency deviation related to contingency (c). Formally:

$$\alpha^{(c)} = -\frac{\Delta f^{(c)}}{f_0} \tag{12}$$

5   Formulation of Nets and Devices Agents Objective Functions, Constraints and Their Proximal Functions

In this section, we present the objective functions introduced in Eq. 1, we consider buses and three types of devices, i.e. generators, loads and lines.

5.1   Nets Agents

Nets are loss-less energy carriers (i.e. buses) with zero cost function but with constraints on the power and phase schedules of their terminals.

A net $n \in N$ requires *power balance* in each scenario, which is represented by the constraints:

$$\sum_{t \in n} \dot{p}_t^{(c)} = 0, \quad \forall (c) = (0), \dots, \mathcal{L} \tag{13}$$

In addition to power balance, each net imposes *phase consistency* via the constraints:

$$\dot{\theta}_t^{(c)} = \dot{\theta}_{t'}^{(c)}, \quad \forall t, t' \in n, c = (0), \dots, \mathcal{L}^{`} \tag{14}$$

Thirdly, to consider primary frequency control, each net constrains that in each scenario all the terminals have the same frequency deviation:

$$\dot{\alpha}_t^{(c)} = \dot{\alpha}_{t'}^{(c)}, \quad \forall t, t' \in n, c = (0), \dots, \mathcal{L} \tag{15}$$

Then, the computation of the net-minimization step to calculate the desired values $\dot{p}_n$, $\dot{\theta}_n$ and $\dot{\alpha}_n$ can be simplified as in [7][1] as follows: $\forall (c) \in \mathcal{L}, \forall t \in n$,

$$\dot{p}_t^{k+1(c)} = p_t^{k+1(c)} - \frac{1}{|n|} \sum_{t \in n} p_t^{k+1(c)} \tag{16}$$

$$\dot{\theta}_t^{k+1(c)} = \frac{1}{|n|} \sum_{t \in n} \theta_t^{k+1(c)} \tag{17}$$

$$\dot{\alpha}_t^{k+1(c)} = \frac{1}{|n|} \sum_{t \in n} \alpha_t^{k+1(c)} \tag{18}$$

5.2 Generators Agents

A generator is a single terminal device which produces power. The local problem of a generator depends on its power production in each case, p_g, and on a variable that represents the strength of the corresponding steady-state relative frequency deviation for each contingency, α_g.

Generators have a local cost for operating the generator at a given power level. This cost of operation only accounts for the base case. Indeed, contingencies are not expected to happen in a regular basis so the solution found by the SCOPF is expected to be resilient in front of a contingency but the cost of operation of the generation in such a case is not so important. A quadratic cost function for generating costs:

$$f_g(p_g^{(0)}) = \beta \cdot (p_g^{(0)})^2 + \gamma \cdot p_g^{(0)} \tag{19}$$

where β, $\gamma > 0$ are respectively linear and quadratic cost coefficients.

If the contingency case implies the outage of the generator, the power output of the generator in this case should be zero:

$$p^{(c)} = 0, \quad \forall \{(c) \in (1) \dots \mathcal{L} | g \in D^{(c)}\} \tag{20}$$

In the rest of contingencies cases, the primary frequency response of a generator is proportional to its coefficient and bounded by its ramp limits. Formally, $\forall (c) \in \{(1) \dots \mathcal{L} | g \notin D^{(c)}\}$:

$$\Delta p_g^{(c)} = \begin{cases} R_g^{min} & \text{if } K_g \alpha_g^{(c)} \leq R_g^{min} \\ K_g \alpha_g^{(c)} & \text{if } R_g^{min} \leq K_g \alpha_g^{(c)} \leq R_g^{max} \\ R_g^{max} & \text{if } K_g \alpha_g^{(c)} \geq R_g^{max} \end{cases} \tag{21}$$

---

[1] Equation 13 is a projection on an hyperplane.

In each case, the power output of the generator has to remain within its production limits. Formally, $\forall(c) \in \{(1)\ldots\mathcal{L}|g \notin D^{(c)}\}$:

$$p_g^{(c)} = \begin{cases} P_g^{min} & \text{if } p_g^{(0)} + \Delta p_g^{(c)} \leq P_g^{min} \\ p_g^{(0)} + \Delta p_g^{(c)} & \text{if } P_g^{min} \leq p_g^{(0)} + \Delta p_g^{(c)} \leq P_g^{max} \\ P_g^{max} & \text{if } p_g^{(0)} + \Delta p_g^{(c)} \geq P_g^{max} \end{cases} \qquad (22)$$

$$P_g^{min} \leq p_g^{(0)} \leq P_g^{max} \qquad (23)$$

Unfortunately, the step functions in Eqs. 21 and 22 leads to a non-convex device-minimization problem. To overcome this, we substitute them by simpler constraints that directly bound the domain of variable $\alpha^{(c)}$ so that $-R_g^{min} \leq K_g\alpha^{(c)} \leq R_g^{max}$ and variable $p_g^{(c)}$ so that $P_g^{min} \leq p_g^{(0)} + \Delta p_g^{(c)} \leq P_g^{max}$. Notice that those are more restrictive constraints. In particular, under this assumption when a generator reaches its ramp/production limit, $\alpha^{(c)}$ will not increases and the generators left provide the power that is then missing but instead the base case solution will be modified in order for each generator to contribute to the PFC as planned. This assumption allow us to keep the device-minimization problem for generators convex and hence we can rely on off-the-shelf optimization tools to solve it efficiently.

5.3 Transmission Lines Agents

A (transmission) line is a two-terminal device used to transfer power from one net (i.e. bus) to another. The AC power flow equations are non-convex, so they are often either approximated or relaxed. Here, we use a linear DCOPF model, often used in the literature to get rid of the non-convexity of the physics of AC circuits. Under this model the power flow equations ignore real power losses as well as reactive power and voltage magnitude is assumed to be equal to 1 pu. A line has zero cost function but the power flows and voltage phase angles are constrained. In particular, the power flow through the line depends on: (i) the power schedules (p_{l_1} and p_{l_2}) and voltage phase angles (θ_{l_1} and θ_{l_2}) at both sides of the line; and on the susceptance of the line (b_l). In particular, the power and voltage phase angle schedules should satisfy the relations:

$$p_{l_1}^{(c)} = -p_{l_2}^{(c)} = b_l \cdot (\theta_{l_2}^{(c)} - \theta_{l_1}^{(c)}), \quad \forall(c) \in \{(0)\ldots\mathcal{L}|g \notin D^{(c)}\} \qquad (24)$$

$$p_{l_1}^{(c)} = -p_{l_2}^{(c)} = 0, \quad \forall(c) \in \{(0)\ldots\mathcal{L}|g \in D^{(c)}\} \qquad (25)$$

Moreover, each line constrains that in each scenario the power going through the line to be lower than its maximum capacity (i.e. long-term capacity in the base case and short-term capacity in a contingency case):

$$-C_l^{max} \leq p_{l_1}^{(c)} \leq C_l^{max}, \quad \forall(c) \in \{(0)\ldots\mathcal{L}|g \notin D^{(c)}\} \qquad (26)$$

Finally, the line also constrains that the steady-state frequency deviation on both sides of the line are equal:

$$\alpha_{l_1}^{(c)} = \alpha_{l_1}^{(c)}, \forall (c) \in (0)..\mathcal{L}, \tag{27}$$

To be able to provide a solution we need to change variables to reformulate this problem.

Let's introduce:

$$X_{l_1}^{(c)} = \begin{bmatrix} p_{l_1}^{(c)} \\ \theta_{l_1}^{(c)} \end{bmatrix}, \quad ZU_{l_1}^{k(c)} = \begin{bmatrix} \dot{p}_{l_1}^{k(c)} - u_{l_1}^{k(c)} \\ \dot{\theta}_{l_1}^{k(c)} - v_{l_1}^{k(c)} \end{bmatrix}, \text{ and } B_l = \begin{bmatrix} -1 & 0 \\ \frac{1}{b_l} & 1 \end{bmatrix}.$$

B_l is a matrix that include the susceptance b_l of the line.

We can then write the proximal problems as the minimization of the sum of the augmented Lagrangian terms of each side of the line with the power flow equation and the maximum capacity of the line as constraints. Note that we consider the short-term capacity of lines equals to the long-term capacity for simplicity. The term depending on $\alpha^{(c)}$ is independent. Then for all $(c) \in \{(0)..\mathcal{L}\}$:

$$\begin{aligned} \underset{X_{l_1}^{(c)}, X_{l_2}^{(c)}}{\text{minimize}} \quad & \frac{\varrho}{2} \| ZU_{l_1}^{k(c)} - X_{l_1}^{(c)} \|_2^2 + \frac{\varrho}{2} \| ZU_{l_2}^{k(c)} - X_{l_1}^{(c)} \|_2^2 \\ \text{subject to} \quad & X_{l_2}^{(c)} = B_l X_{l_1}^{(c)} \\ & \begin{bmatrix} -P_l^M \\ -2\pi \end{bmatrix} \le X_i \le \begin{bmatrix} P_l^M \\ +2\pi \end{bmatrix} \end{aligned} \tag{28}$$

Lines Agents Proximal Problem Solution. When the capacity limit is not reached the solution is simply:

$$X_{l_1}^{(c)} = (I + B_l^T B_l)^{-1}(ZU_{l_1}^{k(c)} + B_l^T ZU_{l_2}^{k(c)})$$

$$\alpha_{l_1} = \alpha_{l_2} = \frac{\dot{\alpha}_{l_1}^{(c)} - w_{l_1}^{(c)} + \dot{\alpha}_{l_2}^{(c)} - w_{l_2}^{(c)}}{2} \tag{29}$$

When the capacity limits of the line are reached the problem is simplified as the optimal power flow through the line in this case is equal to the maximum capacity.

5.4   Fixed Loads Agents

Therefore, a fixed load is a single terminal device with zero cost function which consists of a desired consumption $l \in \Re$. In this paper we assume that only generation will adapt in front of a contingency (i.e. loads will remain fixed) and hence the solution for a fixed load can be simply summarized as $\forall (c) \in \mathcal{L}, p_l^{(c)} = l$.

6 Experiments

The framework described in the previous sections is implemented as a multi-agent system, where agents solve the sub-problems developed in Sect. 5. The CEA LIST multi-agent system platform based on JADE was used to create those agents and the communication framework.

Table 2. Power generation in MW for each generating unit, comparison between the OPF schedule and the schedule of each case in $\{1, 2, 3, 4, 5\}$.

	OPF	Base case	Case 1	Case 2	Case 3	Case 4	Case 5
$\alpha = -\frac{\Delta f}{f_0}$ (%)	–	–	1.58	0.28	0.35	0.08	0.21
Gen. 1	−168.0	−138.6	0.0	−156.8	−161.8	−144.0	−152.6
Gen. 2	−43.3	−34.5	−78.6	0.0	−44.2	−36.7	−40.4
Gen. 3	−43.0	−46.8	−78.3	−52.2	0.0	−48.4	−51.0
Gen. 4	0.0	−10.8	−42.3	−16.3	−17.8	0.0	−15.0
Gen. 5	−4.7	−28.3	−59.8	−33.7	−35.3	−29.9	0.0

The test system we employed is the IEEE 14-bus model available in Mat-Power. This test is composed of 11 loads, 5 generators with quadratic cost and 20 lines. We modified the model to include ramp constraints of generators and line capacity limits that were missing. In particular, each generator is modeled with a ramp limit of 50 MW and with a speed droop of 5%. Moreover all lines capacity limits have been set to 110 MW for both, short-term and long-term settings. Regarding ADMM parameters, the scaling parameter was set to $\rho = 1$ and the absolute tolerance to $\epsilon = 10^{-5}$ for all scenarios.

To validate the extension presented in this paper, we restrict our experiments to consider contingencies on generators. Different contingency lists are tested, from a single to all generators. Table 2 presents in detail the case where all single-generator contingencies are considered: case $\{1, 2, 3, 4, 5\}$. It provides the power generation of each generator for the base case and in each contingency scenario, compared to the OPF schedule, as in the example of Sect. 4.1. It also provides the value of α for each contingency, for example, if the generator 1 is disconnected the steady-state frequency deviation on a 50 Hz system would be equal to 0.79 Hz.

Figure 2 compares the generation cost of our SCOPF solution with respect to those of the OPF solution to illustrate the cost of security. The different contingency lists are then sorted from the cheapest to the more expensive. Notice that the considerations of generators 2 and 3 have the greatest impact on the cost of security even though these generators disconnection imply a relatively small frequency deviation. It thus justifies the need of considering the more contingencies possible, and so deal with large number of contingency scenarios, even when the contribution of the devices do not seem significant compare to others, like generator 1.

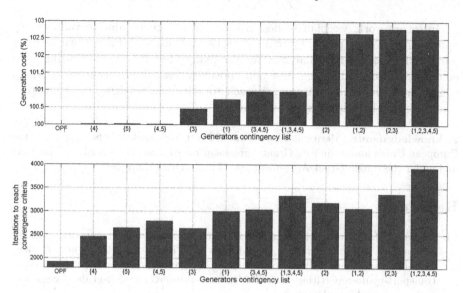

Fig. 2. Comparison of the SCOPF with different contingency lists with the OPF. Number of iterations needed to converge and SCOPF cost in percentage of OPF cost.

We also compare the number of iterations needed to reach the convergence criteria and this comparison highlights the strength of this type of distributed method. In particular, observe that there are 5 control variables for generators in the OPF and 14 for the bus angles and for contingency cases $\{1, 2, 3, 4, 5\}$ there are 5 more for the frequency deviations and 5 times 14 bus angles to determine with different constraints considered in each case and between cases. We notice here that the number of iterations needed to converge did not increase as much as the complexity of the problem solved. This result is promising because it proves a good scalability of the method to the number of contingency scenarios.

7   Conclusions and Future Work

We extend a previous decentralized security-constrained optimal power flow framework to take into account the automatic primary frequency control of generators and we solve it in a fully distributed way using a ADMM-based algorithm. The contribution of this paper allows this distributed SCOPF model to find solutions that remain stable after the disconnection of generators in the system. We have also presented a multi-agent implementation of the method in which individual local agents are restricted to access their own data and exchange relevant information with their neighbors following ADMM iterative equations. To evaluate the efficiency of our approach we provide results on the IEEE 14-bus test system. Empirical results show how our method is able to find optimal SCOPF solutions for this circuit, defining for each contingency case the corresponding power flows and steady-state frequency deviation.

In future work, we plan to design a benchmark to be able to validate our approach on larger power system networks and quantify its performance, in particular regarding its scalability. We also plan to test the approach using more complex device models, e.g. the non convexity brought by generators' ramp constraints. The ability of our approach to solve the resulting more complex problem should then be tested extensively.

Acknowledgments. Meritxell Vinyals would like to acknowledge the support of the European Union under the FP7 Grant Agreement no. 619682 (MAS2TERING project) and under the H2020 Grant Agreement no. 774431 (DRIVE project).

References

1. Bornard, P., Pavard, M.: Réseaux d'interconnexion et de transport: réglages et stabilité. Technival report, Téchniques de l'ingénieur (1993). http://www.techniques-ingenieur.fr/base-documentaire/energies-th4/reseaux-electriques-de-transport-et-de-repartition-42263210/reseaux-d-interconnexion-et-de-transport-reglages-et-stabilite-d4092/
2. Boyd, S., Parikh, N., Chu, E., Peleato, B., Eckstein, J.: Distributed optimization and statistical learning via the alternating direction method of multipliers. Found. Trends Mach. Learn. **3**(1), 1–122 (2011). https://doi.org/10.1561/2200000016
3. Capitanescu, F., et al.: State-of-the-art, challenges, and future trends in security constrained optimal power flow. Electr. Power Syst. Res. **81**(8), 1731–1741 (2011)
4. Chakrabarti, S., Kraning, M., Chu, E., Baldick, R., Boyd, S.: Security Constrained Optimal Power Flow via proximal message passing. In: 2014 Clemson University Power Systems Conference, pp. 1–8 (2014). https://doi.org/10.1109/PSC.2014.6808131. http://ieeexplore.ieee.org/lpdocs/epic03/wrapper.htm?arnumber=6808131
5. Elsayed, W.T., El-Saadany, E.F.: A fully decentralized approach for solving the economic dispatch problem. IEEE Trans. Power Syst. **30**(4), 2179–2189 (2015). https://doi.org/10.1109/TPWRS.2014.2360369
6. Karoui, K., Crisciu, H., Platbrood, L.: Modeling the primary reserve allocation in preventive and curative security constrained OPF. In: 2010 IEEE PES Transmission and Distribution Conference and Exposition, pp. 1–6. IEEE (2010)
7. Kraning, M., Chu, E., Lavaei, J., Boyd, S.P.: Dynamic network energy management via proximal message passing. Found. Trends Optim. **1**(2), 73–126 (2014)
8. Monticelli, A., Pereira, M.V.F., Granville, S.: Security-constrained optimal power flow with post-contigency corrective rescheduling. IEEE Trans. Power Syst. **2**(1), 175–180 (1987)
9. Phan, D.T., Sun, X.A.: Minimal impact corrective actions in security-constrained optimal power flow via sparsity regularization. IEEE Trans. Power Syst. **30**(4), 1947–1956 (2015)
10. Pinar, A., Meza, J., Donde, V., Lesieutre, B.: Optimization strategies for the vulnerability analysis of the electric power grid. SIAM J. Optim. **20**(4), 1786–1810 (2010)
11. Scott, P., Thiébaux, S.: Distributed multi-period optimal power flow for demand response in microgrids. In: Proceedings of the 2015 ACM Sixth International Conference on Future Energy Systems, e-Energy 2015, Bangalore, India, 14–17 July 2015, pp. 17–26 (2015)

12. Wang, Y., Wang, S., Wu, L.: Distributed optimization approaches for emerging power systems operation: a review. Electr. Power Syst. Res. **144**, 127–135 (2017). http://dx.doi.org/10.1016/j.epsr.2016.11.025
13. Zhang, Z., Chow, M.Y.: Convergence analysis of the incremental cost consensus algorithm under different communication network topologies in a smart grid. IEEE Trans. Power Syst. **27**, 1761–1768 (2012)

Local Scheduling in Multi-Agent Systems: Getting Ready for Safety-Critical Scenarios

Davide Calvaresi[1,2]([✉]), Mauro Marinoni[1], Luca Lustrissimini[3],
Kevin Appoggetti[3], Paolo Sernani[3], Aldo F. Dragoni[3], Michael Schumacher[2],
and Giorgio Buttazzo[1]

[1] Scuola Superiore Sant'Anna, Pisa, Italy
{d.calvaresi,m.marinoni,g.buttazzo}@sssup.it
[2] University of Applied Sciences Western Switzerland, Sierre, Switzerland
michael.schumacher@hevs.ch
[3] Università Politecnica delle Marche, Ancona, Italy
{p.sernani,a.f.dragoni}@univpm.it

Abstract. Multi-Agent Systems (MAS) have been supporting the development of distributed systems performing decentralized thinking and reasoning, automated actions, and regulating component interactions in unpredictable and uncertain scenarios. Despite the scientific literature is plenty of innovative contributions about resource and tasks allocation, the agents still schedule their behaviors and tasks by employing traditional general-purpose scheduling algorithms. By doing so, MAS are unable to enforce the compliance with strict timing constraints. Thus, it is not possible to provide any guarantee about the system behavior in the worst-case scenario. Thereby, as they are, they cannot operate in safety-critical environments. This paper analyzes the agents' local schedulers provided by the most relevant agent-based frameworks from a cyber-physical systems point of view. Moreover, it maps a set of agents' behaviors on task models from the real-time literature. Finally, a practical case-study is provided to highlight how such "MAS reliability" can be achieved.

Keywords: Multi-Agent Systems · Cyber-Physical Systems
Real-time systems · Scheduling algorithms · Real-time MAS

1 Introduction

Cyber models and the physical world are merging into increasingly complex systems since human beings began to use Cyber-Physical Systems (CPS) to control and interact with their surrounding environment. Data are collected through distributed sensors, locally or remotely processed, possibly composing feedback to be sent to other entities, or triggering actions directly affecting the physical world (e.g., via actuators). In domains such as e-health [1,2], telerehabilitation [3], manufacturing [4], retails [5], and automotive [6], regardless of

© Springer Nature Switzerland AG 2018
F. Belardinelli and E. Argente (Eds.): EUMAS 2017/AT 2017, LNAI 10767, pp. 96–111, 2018.
https://doi.org/10.1007/978-3-030-01713-2_8

dimensions and distribution, the safety of the system and its users is the major requirement. Assuming there is an absence of hardware failures and errors in the design phase [7], to operate in safety-critical scenarios, a system has to be able to guarantee its correct execution and the compliance with strict timing constraints even in the worst-case scenario [7]. The distributed nature of such CPS relies on a multitude of elements operating simultaneously. Hence, the interaction among entities of a decentralized system requires an *(i)* "intelligent/strategic" layer (i.e., a layer to allow single components and the CPS as a whole to achieve their goals), *(ii)* a communication middleware (i.e., to allow the exchange of information and requests among the components of the CPS), and *(iii)* local policies (e.g., schedulers and heuristics enabling each component execute its tasks). Thus, to have a reliable system, its components (both singularly and altogether) have to provide timing guarantees on delays and response/execution times. Dealing with hard-coded, automatic or semi-automatic actions imposes different requirements with respect to scenarios characterized by highly unpredictable and uncertain behaviors. Nevertheless, mechanisms such as negotiation, communication, and local scheduling have to operate in either one.

Considering Multi-Agent Systems (MAS) as one of the most prominent and promising "approaches" supporting Internet of Things (IoT) technologies and CPS [8], the capability of MAS to comply with strict timing constraints is a crucial arising challenge. Adopting an agent-based framework can facilitate the implementation of robust and reconfigurable systems. In particular, seeking for distributed thinking, the capabilities of having partial technology independence (smooth migrations between diverse technologies) [9–11] and "reusing" components, capabilities, functionalities, and knowledge, are extremely relevant. However, concerning strict dependability, stringent safety and security policies, resources efficiency, and real-time guarantees [12], at present no agent-based framework can yet support the development of an MAS able to guarantee full compliance [8].

Contribution
Investigating the most used and still active agent frameworks, this paper focuses on the single agent's internal scheduler (hereafter referred to as local scheduler) used to regulate the execution of its tasks and behaviors. Considering the review conducted in [13, 14] as common ground and adopting the safety-critical systems point of view, this paper:

(i) analyzes local schedulers for handling agent's tasks/behaviors, *(ii)* motivates adoption and adaption of schedulers from the real-time literature, *(iii)* proposes to map agent's behaviors on real-time task models, and finally *(iv)* proposes a practical example as a case-study of the proposed approach.

Summarizing, the outcome of this study aims at supporting the development of real-time multi-agent systems (RT-MAS) that can finally satisfy all the requirements of a safety-critical scenario. The paper is organized as follows: Sect. 2 presents and elaborates the state of the art, Sect. 3 organizes and describes the obtained results, Sect. 4 briefly discusses the obtained results in key CPS. Finally, Sect. 5 concludes the paper.

2   Local Scheduling in Agent-Based Frameworks

Kravari and Bassiliades [13] proposed a detailed and comprehensive study of multi-agent frameworks (referred as *Agent Platforms*). However, the notion of *scheduling* appears only to refer to mechanisms that distribute and organize tasks and resources among the agents within a specific platform. By doing so, they took for granted the behavior execution and the compliance with the agreements stipulated during the negotiation phase. Such an assumption is naive and too optimistic, thus resulting in being unacceptable for safety-critical applications [8]. For example, in the case of a telerehabilitation system, a delayed, wrong, or miss-aligned (in terms of content - time) feedback may cause severe injuries to the patient [3]. Nevertheless, almost all the agent-based platforms present and have implement at least one local scheduler. Table 1 collects them detailing *programming language, platform purpose* (where GP is general purpose, M is Modeling, and S is simulations), *status* (where A is Active, N is inactive, and U is unclear), *last update* (according to the last platform release or push in the official repository), and finally the *agent's scheduling algorithm*. Excluding two agent platforms, all other analyzed ones have implemented specific schedulers. Although it provides a default event-driven mechanism to process the agent behavior, the first exception is NetLogo, which declares that no particular scheduler is implemented. The second is Cormas, which, differently from the previous one, if no custom/Ad-Hoc scheduler is provided, the behaviors are not executed (nothing in the system would happen). Allowing the platforms' users to directly implement their version of a behavior scheduler ensures a high flexibility. Hence, not only pure algorithms are admitted, (e.g., heuristics such as RR, random selection, less workload first, early starting time first) but the custom mix development of the one mentioned above is also encouraged [15].

MaDKit, RePast, and Swarm implement the classic FCFS, GAMA and MASON [16] implement a type of priority scheduler (e.g., SJF-like), Jason implements an RR applied to structured behaviors, and finally JADE implements a non-preemptive RR. The Jason and Jade's implementations of RR result in being FCFS of *intentions* [17] in the first case and of *behaviors* in the second, eventually treated like single entities. Aiming at emphasizing the safety-critical systems point of view, an analysis of those algorithms is presented below and organized as *non-priority* and *priority* schedulers.

2.1   Analysis of *non-priority* Local Schedulers in MAS

The FIFO and RR scheduling algorithms are two of the most known algorithms and inspired a multitude of variants. On the one hand, FIFO (also referred as FCFS) executes *tasks* in the exact order of their arrival (according to their position in the ready queue). The absence of preemption or re-ordering in this mechanism allows to classify the FCFS "the simplest scheduling policy with minimal scheduling overhead". On the other hand, RR is mainly appreciated for its fairness (which plays an important role in general-purpose applications) and prevention from tasks-starvation. Its mechanism is based on the concept of

Table 1. Brief overview of the major agent platforms.

Agent platform	Programming language	Platform purpose	Status	Last update	Scheduling algorithm
JADE	Java, .NET (via add-ons)	GP	A	Jun 2017[a]	Non-Preemptive RR (FCFS)
Cormas	SmallTalk	M, S	A	Aug 2017[b]	No default scheduler (nothing happen)
Swarm	Java, Objective-C	M, S	U	Oct 2016[c]	Event-driven (Priority Scheduling, FCFS)
GAMA	Java	M, S	A/N	Jul 2017[d]	Priority Scheduling
MASON	Java	GP	A	-	Event-driven (Priority Scheduling)
Jason	AgentSpeak	GP	A	(?) Aug 2017[e]	RR
MaDKit	Java	GP	A	Jul 2017[f]	FCFS
NetLogo	Logo Dialect	M, S	A	Aug 2017[g]	No default scheduler (nothing happen)
RePast	Java, Python, .NET, C++, ReLogo, Groovy	M, S	A	Sep 2016[h]	FCFS
Jadex	Java	GP	A	Mar 2017[i]	FCFS

[a] https://goo.gl/TKGqT6 [b] https://goo.gl/9sxKtt [c] https://goo.gl/WYJAK2
[d] https://goo.gl/USVVbe [e] https://goo.gl/Wtbm5T [f] https://goo.gl/ysJZRH
[g] https://goo.gl/kngRWj [h] https://goo.gl/yDsqyH [i] https://goo.gl/ZK7fAf

slicing the tasks' computing time on the processor in equal time-quantum. Thus, the tasks in the ready queue are cycled to get the processor. If a running task is completed, the processor directly computes the next one; otherwise, it saves the task status and puts it back in the ready-queue before computing the next one (context switch).

Given this conceptually simple mechanism, minor adjustments are enough to make it suitable for handling a structured queue of "tasks". A practical example, showing how Jason revisited the RR scheduler, is presented in Fig. 1. Such a platform is characterized by the adoption of the *Beliefs, Desires,* and *Intentions*" software model (BDI) [17]. Thus, simple actions compose a plan which aims at

satisfying a desire according to the agent's beliefs and knowledge. Assuming to
have an agent with multiple and concurrent intentions, the way Jason applies
the RR is to execute one *action* from the *plan* at the top of the plans stack
composing one *intention*. At completion, the next action scheduled is the first on
top of the *actions*-stack of the next *intention*. Referring to Fig. 1 the scheduling
is: $P_1(A_1)$, $P_2(A_1)$, $P_3(A_1)$, $P_1(A_2)$, $P_2(A_2)$, and so forth. Note that, the second
action of Plan 1 is scheduled only after the execution of at least one *action*
per *plan*. Moreover, the concept of time-quantum has been overridden by the
actual duration of the selected *action*. So, the time-quantum actually coincide
with the computational time required by the currently running task. Finally,
this mechanism is repeated for all the intentions owned by the agent. In case a
new *intention* is generated, it is placed on the top of the queue.

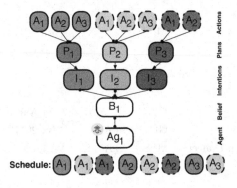

Fig. 1. Jason's implementation of RR scheduling: A graphical representation.

This simple mechanism cannot be implemented/applied in real-time operating systems because of the long waiting time and significant response time,
which has to be recalculated for any new task arrival [18]. The latter, given its
complexity due the dependency from the queue characteristics, is too complex to
be actually considered feasible at run-time. Therefore, in-light of these factors,
the risk of missing deadlines (not taken into account at all by the algorithm)
might dramatically increment, thus degrading system performance and compro-
mising its reliability and safety. Nevertheless, tuning the parameters as proposed
in [18] leads to minor improvements, which are still not enough the breach into
the world of the real-time systems.

In the Jade platform, the agents' *tasks* are referred as *"behaviors"*, which can
be primitive or composite [8], and might be compared to the roles played by the
actions in Jason. The most relevant for the purpose of our study are:

Primitive behaviors:

SimpleB.: an extendable basic class; **CyclicB.:** a behaviour performing actions
repeatedly, reactivating itself after its execution is completed. It stays active
as long as its agent is alive; **TickerB.:** a periodic behavior which unlike the

CyclicBehaviour is re-executed after a set time (customized activation period); **OneShotB.:** an instance can only be executed once along with its agent life-cycle; **WakerB.:** it allows defining the activation time (delay from the agent life-cycle start); **MsgReceiverB.:** it is triggered if a timeout expires or a specific type of message is received.

Composite behaviors are enabled by complex combination of *primitive* behaviors:

ParallelB.: it enables the parallel execution of children behaviors allowing the definition of the termination conditions: it terminates if *all, n,* or *any* child is completed. **SequentialB.:** it executes its children behaviors consecutively and terminates when the last child is terminated.

To handle such behaviors, Jade proposes another customization of the RR algorithm, called *non-preemptive RR* [19]. However, the reference to the term "Round Robin" is inappropriate since preemption is not admitted and, consequently, time-quantum varies from task-to-task (i.e. the computational time of the running behavior). Therefore, the non-preemptive RR turns to operate like a classic FIFO/FCFS which treats both simple and composite *behaviors* as "atomic task". The only variant is that when the action method of a behavior can return true (it is removed from the list of active behaviors") or false (it is appended back in the ready queue).

Jadex is a JADE-based platform relying on the BDI notion [20] and based on four JADE elements which operate concurrently on the internal data-structures of the agent. The message receiver listens for ACL messages from other agents creating corresponding message events. The timing behavior releases the events on the timetable, appending them to the list of events to be dispatched. The dispatcher adopts goals by placing them on the intention stack and selecting plans to be handled from the event list. The selected plans are subsequently executed step-by-step by the scheduler (which also implements the plan supervision).

Implementing the functionalities into separate behaviours allows a flexible behavior replacement with custom implementations (e.g., alternative schedulers and BDI implementations). However, the dispatcher is responsible for selecting plans to handle events and goals inside the agent, thus facilitating reactive and proactive behavior. It also manages the interrelation between plan instances and goals. The dispatcher cyclically removes the next entry from the event list, checks if a goal is associated with the event, and then creates the applicable plans list (APL) for the event. When a goal is finished (success or failure), the owner of the goal will be notified. For a failed goal, the dispatcher may choose another plan for execution depending on the BDI flags of the goal. The scheduler executes the ready-to-run plan instances one at a time, and step by step, applying an FCFS scheme. In each scheduling cycle, the first plan instance is removed from the ready list, and then a single step is executed. The scheduler waits until the plan step finishes or an error occurs. Afterwards, it checks if any of the associated goals are already achieved. At the last step of the plan, the plan instance is removed from the agent.

The schedulers implemented in JADE (non-preemptive RR) and Jadex (FCFS) are essentially extensions of FIFO and thus, are not suitable to provide strong real-time guarantees. For example, *(i)* it has no means to handle task priorities, *(ii)* the schedulability under FIFO can only be guaranteed for systems with a considerably low utilization factor[1] and with uniform period ranges, *(iii)* response time has to be recalculated for any new task arrival (unsustainable), and *(iv)* waiting and response time are affected by the tasks set features even then in the RR case.

Although FIFO guarantees simplicity and fairness (which can apply to general-purpose but not for the real-time systems), the real-world applications often operate under unfavorable conditions and high task-set utilization. Thus, in the best hypothesis, FIFO can only be considered a viable option for soft real-time" systems. However, Altmeyer et al. [21] revisited FIFO scheduling altering its operating conditions to increase its predictability and improve its real-time performance. They provided a schedulability test for FIFO with and without offsets. Moreover, studying a case with strictly periodic *tasks* and offsets, they proved the competitiveness of such a scheduling policy when predictability and simplicity matter. Finally, two significant advantages can be achieved by enforcing strictly periodic task releases and adding offsets: *(i)* performance limitations are mitigated and the number of schedulable task sets is increased (even in the case of high utilization rates and task-sets with harmonic or loosely-harmonic periods, and *(ii)* defined by the order of job arrivals, a unique execution order is enforced, thus simplifying validation and testing.

To overcome some of the real-time limitations introduced in MAS by RR, FCFS, and their customization above-mentioned, the *Priority schedulers* have been introduced.

2.2   Analysis of *priority* Local Schedulers in MAS

The class of priority schedulers is based on assigning a priority to all the tasks in the task-set which discriminates their position in the ready queue and so their turn to get the CPU. Usually, tasks with higher priorities are carried out first, whereas tasks with equal priorities are treated on the FCFS basis. A general example of a priority-scheduling algorithm is the shortest-job-first (SJF) algorithm. There two main types of priority algorithms:

- The *fixed priority*, which schedule general-purpose systems by assigning a "priority-based" value to the tasks offline. Then, the dispatcher sorts them by relevance and time-by-time it executes the first in the ready queue;
- The *dynamic priority*, which have similar mechanisms, but they assign the priority depending on the systems' behaviors at run-time. Thus such values can change over the time.

According to the developers, the MASON platform is not *yet* a distributed toolkit. It requires a single unified memory space, and has no facilities for distributing models over multiple processes or multiple computers [22]. Designed to

---

[1] The fraction of processor time spent in the execution of the task set [7].

be efficient on a single process, such a simulation tool could also be run simultaneously (e.g., multiple MASON instances on multiple threads). In MASON, the concept of agent has a particular specific interpretation: *"a computational entity which may be scheduled to perform some action, and which can manipulate the environment.* Thus, considering the single process nature of such a platform, the agent is a series of behaviors associated with its logic model. The time is conceived discrete, and the agents' behaviors are scheduled as discrete events composed of steps [22]. They are:

- **scheduleOnce(Steppable agent):** Schedules the given agent at the current time + 1.0, with an ordering of 0, and returns true;
- **scheduleOnceIn(double delta, Steppable agent):** Schedules the given agent at the current time + delta, with an ordering of 0, and returns true;
- **Stoppable scheduleRepeating(Steppable agent):** Schedules the given agent at the current time + 1.0, with an ordering of 0.

Moreover, such methods can be called adding more parameters (e.g., ordering, steppable agents, time, and intervals) [22].

Similar per time and scheduler discretization, GAMA refers to the agents as *species* and to the tasks/behaviors as *actions* (activable anytime – like the OneShot behaviors in Jade) and *reflex* (periodic behavior – like the cyclic in Jade, with the only difference that they are activable only in the contex in which they are defined). Recalling that, these kind of schedulers rely on the concept of *fixed* and *dynamic priority*. In both MASON and GAMA, such priority is implemented by using the release time of the behaviors. Despite a broad applicability of such algorithms, there are significant limitations. Considering the fixed priority, the task set might become not schedulable due to two main reasons: *(i)* in the case the other tasks have a higher priority, the task added at run-time might risk the starvation (it can be overcome by implementing aging mechanisms), and *(ii)* although respecting all the deadlines, the priority of the old task set cannot be updated. With respect to RR and FCFS, this class of scheduling algorithms can guarantee a higher utilization factor. However, the schedulability analysis has still to be re-computed at any new task activation.

To finally improve performance and guarantee reliability of the MAS, the next section addresses the adoption and adaption of the most fitting scheduling algorithm among the models typical of real-time systems.

3   Improving MAS' Local Scheduling

This section formalizes the objectives and performance that have been set to define the most fitting scheduler for MAS discussing pro and cons of the analyzed algorithms. Moreover, it proposes the mapping of the most relevant agent's behaviors with tasks-set model from the real-time theory.

A *high utilization factor* guarantees a better exploitation of systems with scarcity of resources. Aiming at employing MAS in IoT systems, this is a crucial feature. Hence, distributed technologies are mainly characterized by limited dimensions, which involve limited battery life-time and limited computational capabilities [3].

In a real-time system, the correct resource allocation to guarantee the timing constraints is based on an analysis that considers the worst-case scenario for the set of tasks under evaluation. With respect to the classical approaches, introducing the concept of a schedulability test to be kept into consideration in a reservation based negotiation protocol [8] is already a remarkable improvement. Moreover, *incrementing the tasks acceptance ratio*, with mechanisms tractable during the negotiation phases is strategic objective which introduces directly the most important, which are introducing the *possibility of handling aperiodic requests* and *being able to guarantee isolation among tasks*, thus avoiding interference due to deadline misses, overrun, and crashes.

Given the features described in Sect. 2.1, we consider the set of behaviors present in Jade as the most suitable to match the real-time task models. Thus, to determine the best combination of task models and schedulers enabling the compliance with strict timing constraints and the maximization of the agents' resource utilization, we propose the following as possible mapping:

(i) the *OneShotBehavior* and *(ii)* the *WakerBehavior* can be represented with the *aperiodic task model*. Moreover, a natural mapping occur for the *(iii)* *TickerBehavior* which fits perfectly the feature of the *periodic task model* [7]. Finally, assuming the knowledge about external activities and incoming packets (i.e., *minimum* inter-arrival) the *(iv)* *MsgReceiverBehaviour* can be modeled on the *sporadic task*. All the other *behaviors* and *activities* not mentioned in the direct mapping can be expressed as combinations of *(i)*, *(ii)*, and *(iii)* models. In particular, the *CompositeBehaviors* can be modeled according to the scheduling theory based on the directed cyclic graphs (DAG) representation [23].

According to such a mapping, the objectives, and the several constraints imposed by the real-time theory, several scheduling algorithms such as Rate Monotonic (RM) [24], Earliest Deadline First (EDF) [7], Constant Bandwidth Server (CBS), Sporadic Server (SS), and Total Bandwidth Server (TBS) can be considered eligible [25].

3.1   RM and EDF Analysis

Considering a scenario solely involving periodic (and sporadic) tasks, the scheduling can be performed using RM or EDF (depending on specific requirements).

Let us consider a generic task-set Γ composed of periodic and sporadic tasks τ_i. They have to at least be characterized by *release time* (r_i), *computation time* (C_i), and *relative deadline* (D_i). Moreover, the parameter (T_i) indicates the *period* for the periodic tasks and the *minimum-interarrival time* for the sporadic tasks.

The assumptions characterizing the traditional schedulability analysis are: *(A1)* The instances of a periodic task τ_i are regularly activated at a constant rate. The interval T_i between two consecutive activations is the period of the task. *(A2)* All instances of a periodic task τ_i have the same worst-case execution time C_i. *(A3)* All instances of a periodic task τ_i have the same relative deadline D_i, which is equal to the period T_i. *(A4)* All tasks in Γ are independent; that is, there are no precedence relations and no resource constraints.

For completion, it is worth to also mention the implicit assumption involved by *A1,A2,A3*, and *A4*: *(A5)* No task can suspend itself, for example on I/O operations. *(A6)* All tasks are released as soon as they arrive. *(A7)* All overheads in the kernel are assumed to be negligible.

Recalling that the *processor utilization factor* U is the fraction of processor time spent in the execution of the task set [7], it is calculated as show in Eq. 1. If U is $U > 1$ the schedule is not feasible for any algorithm. If $U \leq 1$ the schedule is feasible for EDF and might be schedulable for the others algorithms mentioned above.

$$U = \sum_{i=1}^{n} \frac{C_i}{T_i} \tag{1}$$

RM follows a simple rule, assigning priorities to tasks according to their request rates. In particular, tasks with higher request rates (shorter periods) get higher priorities. Being the periods constant, RM performs offline the assignment of fixed-priorities P_i which being static cannot change at run-time. The preemption mechanism is intrinsic in RM. Hence, the running task can be preempted by a newly arrived task if it has a shorter period.

Although RM optimality has been proved [7], the maximum U it can guarantee is low, and it is dramatically dependent on the task set' features. The *lower upper bound* is shown in Eq. 2, and for $n \to \infty$, $U_{lub} \to ln2$.

$$U_{lub}^{RM} = n(2^{1/2} - 1) \tag{2}$$

Finally, it is not always possible to assign and sort the priorities. Hence, in MAS scenarios, assigning offline priorities based on the tasks' period is not viable. It would mean handling coordinately all the priority in the system. Moreover, it would not cope with the necessity of updating the task-set at run-time.

Thus, it has been investigated which algorithms can satisfy real-time guarantees with dynamic priority. The first algorithm analyzed is EDF.

Such an algorithm handles the priority according to the task's absolute deadline (D). Hence, the ready queue is sorted accordingly, and the task getting the CPU is always the one with earliest deadline. In the case a task with a deadline earlier than the deadline of the running task is released, a preemption take place and so forth. According to Horn [26], given a set of n independent tasks with arbitrary arrival times, any algorithm that at any instant executes the task with the earliest absolute deadline among all the ready tasks is optimal with respect to minimizing the maximum lateness.

The EDF complexity is $O(n)$ per task if the ready queue is implemented as a list, or $O(nlogn)$ per task if the ready queue is implemented as a heap. In the case of asynchronous activations it goes to $O(n^2)$. According to Dertouzos [27] EDF is optimal. In particular, if a feasible schedule for a given task-set exists, EDF is able to find it.

Scheduling with EDF, Eq. 1 is still valid for the calculation of the *task-set utilization factor*. However, in this case, the maximum U guaranteed is $U = 1$.

The acceptability test performed by this algorithm is based on the calculation of U, which is quite easy to compute, sustainable to be done at run-time, and incremental. For example, if the U of a given running task-set is 0.7, according to Eq. 1, by adding a task τ_i with $C_i = 2$ and $T = 20$ we have $U = 0.8$. Checking if a new task can be added in run-time to the task-set has a considerably low computational impact on the CPU and does not require to recompute the whole algorithm.

EDF improves considerably the performance offered by RM, however, it is still not enough to fully satisfy MAS needs. Hence, recalling that agents make a massive use of negotiating services and resources with each other, it highlights the unsatisfiable requirements by EDF which are *(i)* the need of mechanisms to handle aperiodic requests (major outcome of sporadic and unpredictable negotiations) and *(ii)* the need of guaranteeing isolation among tasks (in real-case scenarios, the tasks' computational time cannot always be considered ideal and be trusted by default).

To overcome these two limitations characterizing the basic EDF algorithm, mainly due to tasks' dynamic activations and arrival times not known a priori, the CBS has been analyzed. It maintains the same advantages of EDF (implementing the same mechanism). In addition, it can deal with dynamic admission tests (whenever a new task might to be added to the system) and provides isolation mechanism, proposing and efficiently implementing a bandwidth reservation strategy.

The CBS mechanism relies on the basic idea of introducing the concept of server, which is a periodic task whose purpose is to serve aperiodic requests as soon as possible. Its computational time (budget) is indicated with Q_s, its period is indicated with P_s, and the ratio $U_s = Q_s/P_s$ denotes its bandwidth.

When a new task enters the system (maintaining the task-set still schedulable), it get assigned a suitable scheduling deadline (to bound its execution in the reserved bandwidth) and it is inserted (accordingly to its deadline) in the EDF ready queue. If the job tries to execute more than expected, its deadline is postponed. Such a task is still eligible for being executed, but its priority is decreased minimizing its interference on the other tasks.

For those schedulers which make various use of the concept of server, the *system utilization factor* is the sum of the *processor utilization factor* (see Eq. 1) and *server utilization factor* (see Eq. 3). Thus the final value is given by Eq. 4.

$$U_s = \sum_{s=1}^{m} \frac{Q_s}{P_s} \qquad (3)$$

$$U_{sys} = U_p + U_s \leq 1 \qquad (4)$$

Finally, if a subset of tasks is handled by a single server, all the tasks in that subset will share the same budget/bandwidth, so there is no isolation among them. Nevertheless, all the other tasks in the system are protected against overruns occurring in any server.

Summarizing, Table 2 collects the requirements set for a scheduler to be eligible as local scheduler in real-time compliant MAS. The following table summarizes the most characterizing features of the analyzed scheduling algorithm with respect to the requirements formalized in Table 3.

Table 2. Improvements required for Local Scheduler.

ID	Requirements
1	High utilization with bounded response times[a]
2	Respect of strict timing constraints (no deadline misses)
3	Tractable acceptance test (executed during bid)
4	Isolation among periodic and aperiodic tasks to avoid/minimize interference.

[a]Sum of reading data/sensors, elaboration, communications, and possible actuation

Table 3. Improvements required for Local Scheduler.

FCFS	RR	EDF	CBS	Features
☹	☹	☺	☺	No deadline missed for $U \leq 1$
☹	☹	☺	☺	Utilization based acceptance test
☹	☹	☹	☺	Providing schedulability test for aperiodic request
☹	☹	☹	☺ [a]	Isolation among tasks
☹	☹	☹	☺	Server support and admission test

[a]Only between the sub-set of the tasks handled by the server and the periodic task-set

4 Case-Study Evaluation

This section presents the analysis of an agent-based system for telerehabilitation as a practical case study modeled implementing the CBS mechanism as the local scheduler. The system is composed of three agents ($\mathcal{A}$, $\mathcal{B}$, and $\mathcal{C}$). Let us assume that $\mathcal{B}$ and $\mathcal{C}$ are similar agents deployed on wearable sensors capable of sharing inertial information. $\mathcal{A}$ runs on a tablet and is in charge of integrating and displaying the values received from $\mathcal{B}$ and $\mathcal{C}$. The behaviors/tasks running in the system are:

τ_1 : reading messages,
τ_2 : writing messages,
τ_3 : computing inertial information,
τ_4 : displaying graphically the elaborated inertial information, and
τ_5 : generating the need of inertial information.

For simplicity, in this example the communication delays among the agents are assumed to be constant (i.e., $\delta_{A,B} = \delta_{B,A} = \delta_{A,C} = \ldots = \delta_{comm}$). Such a value is included in the computation time of each communication task (i.e., τ_1 and τ_2).

The task-set of agent A is composed of $\tau_1, \tau_2, \tau_4, \tau_5$. The task-sets of agents B and C have the same composition which is τ_1, τ_2, τ_3. The tasks' computation time and period are specified in Table 4a. The system's dynamics are represented in Fig. 2a.

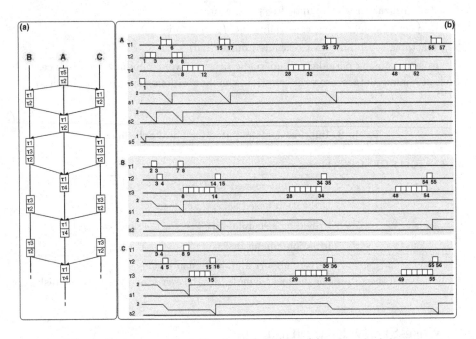

Fig. 2. System representation in: *(a)* AUML, *(b)* tasks scheduling.

As introduced in the previous section, the CBS can provide isolation among aperiodic and periodic tasks. In this case study, τ_1, τ_2, and τ_5 are aperiodic, having different characteristics and scopes. Therefore, the common practice is to assign them to independent servers [7] (e.g., $\tau_1 \rightarrow s_1$, $\tau_2 \rightarrow s_2$, and $\tau_5 \rightarrow s_5$) characterized as shown in Table 4b where $P_s = T_s$ and $C_s = Q_s$.

When the system starts, at $t = 0$, A has only scheduled τ_1, τ_2, τ_5. Thus, according to Eq. 4 its *utilization factor* is $U = 0,25$. At the same instant, according to the same formula, B and C have $U = 0,2$, since they only have τ_1 and τ_2 in the set task.

The execution of task τ_5 (at $t = 1$) generates in A the need for information produced by the execution of task τ_3 from both B and C. If adding such a task to the analysis Eq. 4 is still respected and if the negotiation for on agents B and C get accomplished, task τ_4 is added to the task-set. Considering that $U_{\tau_4} = 0,2$,

Table 4. Agents' task-sets

(a) tasks parameters

Agent	t	C	T
$\mathcal{A}, \mathcal{B}, \mathcal{C}$	τ_1	1	–
$\mathcal{A}, \mathcal{B}, \mathcal{C}$	τ_2	1	–
$\mathcal{B}, \mathcal{C}$	τ_3	6	20
$\mathcal{A}$	τ_4	4	20
$\mathcal{A}$	τ_5	1	–

(b) Servers' parameters

Server	Q	T
s_1	2	20
s_2	2	20
s_5	1	20

we have $U^{\mathcal{A}} = 0,6 \leq 1$, so the task-set of $\mathcal{A}$ is still schedulable. The contribution in terms of U_i given by τ_3 in $\mathcal{B}$ and $\mathcal{C}$ is $U_3 = (6/20) = 0,3$. Thus the admission control executed during the negotiation phase at $t = 2$ (in $\mathcal{B}$) and $t = 3$ (in $\mathcal{C}$) gives a positive response to its activation, being $U^{\mathcal{B},\mathcal{C}} = 0,5 \leq 1$. Therefore, τ_4 is activated for the first time at $t = 8$ (see Fig. 2b).

This practical example aims at *(i)* showing how the CBS scheduling algorithm would operate if employed in MAS, *(ii)* confirming its crucial support for a reservation-based negotiation protocol [8], *(iii)* confirming the capability of satisfying the requirement presented in Table 2, and finally *(iv)* ow it is fully compliant with the MAS standards for agent interactions [28].

5   Conclusions

A plethora of scientific contributions deal with resource/task allocation among distributed entities. In particular, the agent-based approach revealed to be prominent to foster the development of such systems. In most of the proposed solutions, the execution of the allocated task is given for granted. Nevertheless, in real safety-critical applications, this is a naive and unsustainable assumption. This paper showed that general-purpose scheduling algorithms neither consider the deadline notion nor can provide any timing guarantee. Therefore, to purse MAS reliability, the local scheduler is a crucial component that needs to be updated, in current and/or future platforms. Aiming at providing a better understanding of the limitations of current local scheduling algorithms of MAS, their mechanisms have been presented and analyzed. The proposed solution is to adopt and adapt real-time scheduling models for multi-agent applications and scenarios. Thus, based on the current approaches, it has been proposed a mapping of agent's tasks/behaviors/actions with real-time scheduling models. Finally, the case study of an agent-based telerehabilitation system it has been proposed to prove the suitability of the aforementioned discussion while respecting the MAS standards.

Guaranteeing bounded execution times is a fundamental building block to support a reservation-based negotiation protocol. Moreover, although formal verification methodologies checking on time and resource bounds have been proposed [29], integrating real-time scheduling algorithms into agent-oriented platforms requires ad-hoc adaptations based on the actual framework used in the systems if possible (e.g., due to the unpredictability of the JVM, java-based platform make impossible to provide anyhow strict guarantees). Thus, assembling an infrastructure for real-time compliant MAS is a priority.

References

1. Calvaresi, D., Cesarini, D., Sernani, P., Marinoni, M., Dragoni, A.F., Sturm, A.: Exploring the ambient assisted living domain: a systematic review. J. Ambient Intell. Humanized Comput. 8(2), 239–257 (2017)
2. Calvaresi, D., Claudi, A., Dragoni, A.F., Yu, E., Accattoli, D., Sernani, D.: A goal-oriented requirements engineering approach for the ambient assisted living domain. In Proceedings of the 7th International Conference on PErvasive Technologies Related to Assistive Environments, PETRA 2014, pp. 20:1–20:4 (2014)
3. Calvaresi, D., Schumacher, M., Marinoni, M., Hilfiker, R., Dragoni, A.F., Buttazzo, G.: Agent-based systems for telerehabilitation: strengths, limitations and future challenges. In: Proceedings of X Workshop on Agents Applied in Health Care (2017)
4. Hsieh, F.-S.: Modeling and control of holonic manufacturing systems based on extended contract net protocol. In: Proceedings of the 2002 American Control Conference, vol. 6, pp. 5037–5042. IEEE (2002)
5. Paolanti, M., Liciotti, D., Pietrini, R., Mancini, A., Frontoni, E.: Modelling and forecasting customer navigation in intelligent retail environments. J. Intell. Robot. Syst. Theory Appl. 91(2), 165–180 (2018). www.scopus.com
6. Biondi, A., Di Natale, M., Buttazzo, G.: Response-time analysis for real-time tasks in engine control applications. In: Proceedings of the ACM/IEEE Sixth International Conference on Cyber-Physical Systems, pp. 120–129. ACM (2015)
7. Buttazzo, G.: Hard Real-Time Computing Systems: Predictable Scheduling Algorithms and Applications, vol. 24. Springer Science & Business Media, Berlin (2011)
8. Calvaresi, D., Marinoni, M., Sturm, A., Schumacher, M., Buttazzo, G.: The challenge of real-time multi-agent systems for enabling iot and cps. In: Proceedings of IEEE/WIC/ACM International Conference on Web Intelligence (WI 2017), August 2017
9. Wooldridge, M., Jennings, N.R.: Intelligent agents: theory and practice. Knowl. Eng. Rev. 10(2), 115–152 (1995)
10. Bellifemine, F.L., Caire, G., Greenwood, D.: Developing Multi-Agent Systems with JADE, vol. 7. Wiley, Hoboken (2007)
11. Calvaresi, D., et al.: A framework based on real-time os and multi-agents for intelligent autonomous robot competitions. In: 2016 11th IEEE Symposium on Industrial Embedded Systems (SIES), pp. 1–10, May 2016
12. Rajkumar, R.R., Lee, I., Sha, L., Stankovic, J.: Cyber-physical systems: the next computing revolution. In: Proceedings of the 47th Design Automation Conference, pp. 731–736. ACM (2010)
13. Kravari, K., Bassiliades, N.: A survey of agent platforms. J. Artif. Soc. Soc. Simul. 18(1), 11 (2015)
14. Leon, M.G.F., Paprzycki, M.: A review of agent platforms. Technical report, ICT COST Action IC1404, Multi-Paradigm Modelling for Cyber-Physical Systems (MPM4CPS) (2015)

15. Chen, S., Tang, A., Stephens, P., Hsing-bung (HB) Chen: Simulation of multi-agent based scheduling algorithms for waiting-line queuing problems. Challenge, New Mexico Supercomputing (2012)
16. Luke, S., Cioffi-Revilla, C., Panait, L., Sullivan, K.: Mason: a new multi-agent simulation toolkit. In: Proceedings of the 2004 Swarmfest Workshop, pp. 316–327. Department of Computer Science and Center for Social Complexity, George Mason University Fairfax, VA (2004)
17. Bordini, R.H., Hübner, J.F.: BDI agent programming in agentspeak using *Jason*. In: Toni, F., Torroni, P. (eds.) CLIMA 2005. LNCS (LNAI), vol. 3900, pp. 143–164. Springer, Heidelberg (2006). https://doi.org/10.1007/11750734_9
18. Yaashuwanth, C., Ramesh, R.: Intelligent time slice for round robin in real time operating systems. IJRRAS **2**(2), 126–131 (2010)
19. JADE - Programmer Manual. http://jade.tilab.com/doc/programmersguide.pdf. Accessed 24 Sep 2017
20. Braubach, L., Lamersdorf, W., Pokahr, A.: Implementing a bdi-infrastructure for jade agents, Jadex (2003)
21. Altmeyer, S., Manikandan Sundharam, S., Navet, N.: The case for fifo real-time scheduling. Technical report, University of Luxembourg (2016)
22. MASON - Manual. https://cs.gmu.edu/~eclab/projects/mason/manual.pdf. Accessed 24 Sep 2017
23. Saifullah, A., Li, J., Agrawal, K., Lu, C., Gill, C.: Multi-core real-time scheduling for generalized parallel task models. Real-Time Syst. **49**(4), 404–435 (2013)
24. Liu, C.L., Layland, J.W.: Scheduling algorithms for multiprogramming in a hard-real-time environment. J. ACM (JACM) **20**(1), 46–61 (1973)
25. Biondi, A., Melani, A., Bertogna, M.: Hard constant bandwidth server: comprehensive formulation and critical scenarios. In: Proceedings of the 9th IEEE International Symposium on Industrial Embedded Systems, pp. 29–37, June 2014
26. Horn, W.A.: Some simple scheduling algorithms. Naval Res. Logist. (NRL) **21**(1), 177–185 (1974)
27. Dertouzos, M.L.: Control robotics: the procedural control of physical processes. In: Proceedings IFIP Congress (1974)
28. Foundation for Intelligent Physical Agents Standard. http://www.fipa.org/. Accessed 24 Sep 2017
29. Alechina, N., Logan, B., Nguyen, H.N., Rakib, A.: Verifying time, memory and communication bounds in systems of reasoning agents. Synthese **169**(2), 385–403 (2009)

EUMAS 2017: Logic and Formal Methods

Strategic Knowledge of the Past - Expressivity and Complexity

Christophe Chareton[⊠]

LORIA, CNRS, Université de Lorraine, Lorraine, France
christophe.chareton@loria.fr

Abstract. In this article we present theoretical results for an epistemic strategy logic with past operators, PKSL. In PKSL, agents are able to choose their strategies depending on past moves of other agents. This strictly extends the expressive power of some well-known epistemic strategy logics, which we illustrate by modelling forward induction: a rationality criterion, called admissibility, may be defined over agent's strategies. Admissibility specifies coherence conditions between past and future actions, inducing new conditions for the availability of optimal strategies. We also give a resolution algorithm for PKSL model-checking. It runs in exponential time, while the satisfiability problem is undecidable, as is the case for similar logics for strategies such as Strategy Logic.

1 Introduction

Strategy Logic (SL), provides formal tools to model the ability of agents or coalitions of agents to ensure temporal properties in strategic contexts. Two versions of SL actually exist in the literature: the first one [1] considered interactions between two players in a turn-based game. The second one [2] extends it to concurrent games between any finite number of agents. In the remainder of this paper, we only refer to the latter.

In SL, one considers sequences of transitions between possible *states* of a modelled system. In these states agents can concurrently perform *actions*, determining *transitions* to other states.

Strategy logic has powerful modelling possibilities. But more may be needed. In SL, an agent is able to reach a goal if she can perform (play) a conditioned sequence of actions (a strategy) ensuring the realisation of that goal. But how to build this strategy is not addressed. A classical illustration of this restriction is the problem of how to open a strong-box: for any password, any agent is able to compose it. So, the agent has a winning strategy to open the strong-box. But she cannot be called able to open the strong-box.

This problem can be solved by modelling our agent's knowledge: in order to open the strong-box, the agent needs to *know* the password. Knowledge is interpreted by identifying, for every agent, an equivalence relation over state descriptions. This means that the agent cannot distinguish between two states in this relation. To realise a goal, the agent must have an efficient *uniform strategy*,

© Springer Nature Switzerland AG 2018
F. Belardinelli and E. Argente (Eds.): EUMAS 2017/AT 2017, LNAI 10767, pp. 115–130, 2018.
https://doi.org/10.1007/978-3-030-01713-2_9

selecting the same action in two states she is unable to distinguish. This notion of ability therefore combines knowledge and performing actions. Formal approaches include epistemic multi-agent logics [3,4] and epistemic strategy logics (ESL) [5–7].

Combining agents' knowledge and their ability to achieve goals raises the question of how agents observe the actions performed by other agents. For example in a semantic game featuring two agents *Alice* and *Bob*, if *Alice* performs an action, is it (always/sometimes/conditionally) the case that, after she did, *Bob* knows it? How does *Bob's* ability to achieve his goals depend on his observance of *Alice* actions? This consideration reaches the concern of Dynamic Epistemic Logic (DEL) [8], in which agents perform actions that may or may not be observed by the other agents.

In this article, we exhibit a situation where *Bob's* ability to anticipate *Alice's* moves depends on his knowledge about her past actions. Assuming that *Alice* moves are coherent along time, *Bob* may partially deduce her future moves, based on his knowledge about her past moves. Therefore, he can decide on his strategy to play. So, the knowledge *Bob* has about what happened so far affects the payoff he can ensure in the game.

To formalise such *forward inductive reasoning*, we use an epistemic strategy logic with past temporal operators called Past Knowledge Strategy Logic (PKSL) [9]. Past temporal logics have already been widely explored [10,11] and studied in multi-agent settings [12–14] but, to the best of our knowledge, PKSL is the first formalism featuring past time and explicit strategy quantification. Therefore it is the first formalism enabling the characterisation of forward inductive reasoning.

We close the introduction with an overview of our contribution. In Sect. 2 we introduce forward induction reasoning. In Sect. 3 we present the syntax and the semantics of PKSL. As an example of the use of past temporal operators we formalise forward induction in Sect. 4, and we show that the use of past temporal operators is strictly necessary for this formalisation. In Sect. 5 we give the main complexity results for PKSL: we give an EXPTIME executing model-checking algorithm and we prove that PKSL satisfiability problem is undecidable. Section 6 contains the conclusions.

2 Forward Induction

Figure 1(a) features a classical example of a *coordination game*, commonly referred to as the *stag hunt* [15]. There are two players, *Alice* (A) and *Bob* (B). The game starts at state s_0, in which each agent $P \in \{A, B\}$ can play either a risky action R_P or a safe one S_P. This leads them to a state in $\{s_1, s_2, s_3, s_4\}$ for which payoffs are indicated in the figure. For example, if the game reaches state s_2, then *Alice* gets payoff 0 and *Bob* gets payoff 7.

By taking a risk, each player can expect the highest payoff (10) if her partner also takes the risk, but may also not gain anything otherwise. And by playing safely she ensures herself a payoff of at least 7 but she renounces to a payoff larger than 8. For each player, considering as fixed the other player's strategy ς,

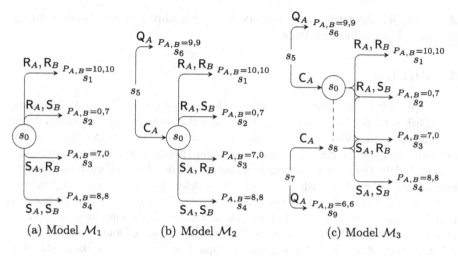

Fig. 1. An illustration of forward induction

the *optimal* strategy is to play ς as well. But there is no strategy that is *optimal* against any strategy of the other player (we say players do not have *dominant strategies*). In a nutshell, each player has interest in playing the same strategy as her partner, but has no means to identify it.

Things may differ depending on what led to this situation. Look at state s_0 in model $\mathcal{M}_2$ (Fig. 1(b)). The only difference with $\mathcal{M}_1$ lies in the circumstances which have led to state s_0. Indeed, the initial state of the model is still s_0. But now this state has an incoming transition from state s_5. For an execution, being in state s_0 therefore means having been in state s_5 before. From state s_5, *Alice* has two choices: either play Q_A and get an ensured payoff of 9 in state s_6 or play C_A and enter a game similar to the one in Fig. 1(a) from state s_0.

So, a game starting at state s_0 is a game for which *Alice* has already renounced to an ensured payoff of 9. Then, playing S_A for a maximal expected payoff of 8 would not make her overall strategy *rational* (also called *admissible* [16,17]) and *Bob* has some reasons to think *Alice* would better play R_A. Assuming that, *Bob* can either play S_B and get payoff 7 or play R_B and get payoff 10. Clearly, given that *Alice* is rational and will play R_A, *Bob's optimal* strategy is to play R_B. *Bob* does not have a *dominant strategy* (he has no strategy that is optimal against any strategy for *Alice*), but he has a strategy (playing R_A) that is *optimal* against any *admissible* strategy for *Alice*.

In such reasoning, called *forward induction* [18,19], *Bob* eliminates certain future moves for *Alice*, based on his observations of her past moves. We illustrate this point with model $\mathcal{M}_3$ in (Fig. 1(c)). The dashed edge between states s_0 and s_8 is a modelling of *Bob's* knowledge. More precisely, it means that *Bob* is not able to distinguish between s_0 and s_8. When the game is in state s_0, *Bob* does not know if *Alice* just made the choice not to take payoff $(9,9)$, or if she renounced to payoff $(6,6)$ instead. In this last case, S_A would still be an *admissible* choice for

Alice. So, playing action R_B is optimal for *Bob* against any *admissible* strategy for *Alice*, but he does not know it is.

3   PKSL

Let us present PKSL syntax. It distinguishes between state and path formulas. In addition to boolean operators, state formulas bring strategic material: for each agent a, an existential quantifier $\exists^a x$, over the set of strategies that are available for a, a binder $\downarrow_x$, stating that the (previously quantified) strategy x is played in the current semantic game (it is added to the current context) and an unbinder $\uparrow^x$, by which a strategy is deleted from the current context. Our logic enables strategy refinements for agents: in a given context, an agent may be committed to different strategies at a time. Then she plays the actions enabled by these different strategies. In case she cannot (if she is committed to contradictory strategies), the execution stops. For more details about strategy refinement see [20,21]. Path formulas describe the future, with classical LTL operators X and U, or the past, with symmetrical operators P (*previous*) and S (*since*). We also define Forward Knowledge Strategy Logic (FKSL), the fragment of PKSL without past temporal formulas.

Definition 1 (PKSL,FKSL). *Let Ag be a set of agents, let At be a set of propositions, and let X be a set of (strategy) variables. Then the set of PKSL pseudo-formulas is defined by the following grammar:*

- *State formulas:* $\quad \psi ::= p \mid \neg\psi \mid \psi \wedge \psi \mid \exists^a x\psi \mid \downarrow_x \varphi \mid \uparrow^x \varphi \mid K_a\psi$
- *Path formulas:* $\quad\quad\quad\quad\quad \varphi ::= \zeta \mid \xi$
  - *Future:* $\quad\quad\quad\quad\quad \zeta ::= \psi \mid \neg\zeta \mid \zeta \wedge \zeta \mid X\zeta \mid \zeta U \zeta$
  - *Past:* $\quad\quad\quad\quad\quad\quad \xi ::= \psi \mid \neg\xi \mid \xi \wedge \xi \mid P\xi \mid \xi S\xi$

where $a \in Ag, p \in At$ and $x \in X$. The set of FKSL pseudo-formulas is defined by deleting past path formulas from the above grammar.

As strategy variable *names* are taken into account in the semantics of formulas, some care must be taken when a quantifier is encountered. Thus, well-formed formulas are pseudo-formulas such that every quantifier introduces a fresh strategy variable with regard to the scope in which it appears. The universal quantifiers $\forall^a x$ and booleans $\vee$, $\rightarrow$ and $\leftrightarrow$ are introduced in the usual way. The *some time in the future* operator is given by F (for any future formula, $F\zeta := \top U \zeta$) and its dual *always in the future* by G. Their respective past counterparts are written F^{-1} (some time in the past) and G^{-1} (always in the past). Formulas are evaluated in *Concurrent Epistemic Transition Systems* (CETSs):

Definition 2. *Let us consider a given set of propositions At and a given set of agents Ag. Then, a CETS is a tuple $\mathcal{M} = \langle St, v, \{\mathcal{R}_a\}_{a \in Ag}, Act, s_0 \rangle$ where:*

- *St is an enumerable non-empty set of states.*
- *$v : St \rightarrow \mathcal{P}(At)$ is a valuation function which maps each state s to the set of propositions true at s.*

- For each $a \in Ag$, $\mathcal{R}_a$ is an equivalence accessibility relation, inducing a partition $[St]_a$ of St. For any state s, we write $[s]_a$ for $\{s' \in St \mid (s, s') \in \mathcal{R}_a\}$

- For each $a \in Ag$, Act_a is an enumerable set of actions, each action being a binary relation between elements of St. Then, $Act = \bigcup_{a \in Ag} Act_a$. In a semantic game, agents know the set of actions they may play and the set of actions they may have just played. So, an action $ac \in Act_a$ is such that there are C_1 and C_2 in $\mathcal{P}([St]_a)$ such that $\mathrm{dom}(ac) = \cup C_1$ and $\mathrm{img}(ac) = \cup C_2$ (where $\mathrm{dom}(ac)$ and $\mathrm{img}(ac)$ respectively denote the left and right projection of ac).

- $s_0 \in St$ is the initial state.

In SL, agents use *full-memory* strategies, deciding their actions, at each state of an execution, depending on the full history of previously visited states. This use implicitly assumes that agents have perfect knowledge about the history of previously visited states. In PKSL no *a priori* assumption is made about the knowledge agents have about the past. Therefore agents make use of *uniform memoryless* strategies, depending only on their knowledge of the current state. Since the notion of memory refers to the particular knowledge of agents, the restriction to memoryless strategies is relative to the different agents for which strategies are considered. This is why the existential quantifier of PKSL is parameterised by an agent (see Definition 1). This is also why we introduce definition for both a *strategy* and a *strategy for an agent*, the former being the couple of an agent and a strategy for this agent:

Definition 3 (Strategy)

- A strategy ς for an agent a is a map with domain of definition $\mathrm{dom}(\varsigma) = \bigcup_{ac \in Act_a} \mathrm{dom}(ac)$. Given an equivalence class $[s]_a \subseteq \mathrm{dom}(\varsigma)$, it yields an action ac_a for a such that $[s]_a \subseteq \mathrm{dom}(ac_a)$.
- A strategy is the couple $\varsigma_a = \langle \pi_1(\varsigma_a), \pi_2(\varsigma_a) \rangle$ of an agent $\pi_1(\varsigma_a) = a$ and a strategy $\pi_2(\varsigma_a) = \varsigma$ for a.

As for SL or USL [20,21], the evaluation of PKSL formulas is relative to a strategic *context*. However, contrary to SL, in a strategy context PKSL adopts the USL distinction between the part keeping track of the strategy variables instanciations (the *assignment*) and the part storing binding of agents to strategies (the *commitment*):

Definition 4 (Assignment, commitment, context)

- An assignment α is a map which, given a strategy variable x in its domain of definition, yields a strategy $\alpha(x)$.
- A commitment γ is a set of variables gathering bindings of strategies to their relative agents.
- A context κ is a "well-formed" pair $\langle \alpha, \gamma \rangle$ of an assignment α and a commitment γ, that is a pair such that each strategy variable in the commitment is instantiated: $\gamma \subseteq \mathrm{dom}(\alpha)$.

During the semantic evaluation of a formula, a context $\kappa = \langle \alpha, \gamma \rangle$ must be transformed as we encounter a strategy quantifier $\exists^a x$, a binding $\downarrow_x$ or an unbinding $\uparrow^x$ operator. We write $\alpha[x \mapsto \varsigma]$ the assignment of domain $\operatorname{dom}(\alpha) \cup \{x\}$ such that $\alpha[x \mapsto \varsigma](x) = \varsigma$ and for all $y \in \operatorname{dom}(\alpha) \setminus \{x\}, \alpha[x \mapsto \varsigma](y) = \alpha(y)$. This notation is extended to contexts: $\kappa[x \mapsto \varsigma] = \langle \alpha[x \mapsto \varsigma], \gamma \rangle$. We also write $\kappa \cup \{x\}$ (respectively $\kappa \setminus \{x\}$) for the context $\langle \alpha, \gamma \cup \{x\} \rangle$ (respectively $\langle \alpha, \gamma \setminus \{x\} \rangle$). Furthermore, if $\gamma = \operatorname{dom}(\alpha) = \{x_0, x_1, \ldots, x_i\}$, then we commonly write $\langle \alpha(x_0), \alpha(x_1), \ldots, \alpha(x_i) \rangle$ for the context $\langle \alpha, \gamma \rangle$.

A context κ induces possible *incomes* and *outcomes* from a state s. These are the set of executions that can be if, from (respectively up to) s, agents play (respectively have played) according to the strategies stored in κ. To define the income and outcome functions, we need to introduce *executions* and the set of possible immediate *successors* of a state, given a context.

Definition 5 (Execution, Successor). *Let $\mathcal{M}$ be a CETS, let $\kappa = \langle \alpha, \gamma \rangle$ be a context for $\mathcal{M}$ and let s be a state in $\mathcal{M}$.*

- *An execution λ is a non-empty finite or infinite $]\inf_\lambda, \sup_\lambda[$-indexed sequence of state λ_i (with $i \in]\inf_\lambda, \sup_\lambda[$). It is such that $\inf_\lambda \in \mathbb{Z}^- \cup \{-\infty\}$ and $\sup_\lambda \in \mathbb{Z}^+ \cup \{\infty\}$. Given $i \in]\inf_\lambda, \sup_\lambda[$, we write $\lambda_{\leqslant i}$ for the subsequence of λ ending at index i, and $\lambda_{\geqslant i}$ for its subsequence starting at index i.*
- *The successor function $succ_\kappa : St \to \mathcal{P}(St)$ induced by κ characterises, for any state s, the set of transitions that are possible if each agent respects the different strategies it is bound to. It is defined by the intersection of the different sets of potential successors allowed by these different strategies from this state:*

$$succ_\kappa(s) = \{s' \in St \mid \text{for all } x \in \gamma,$$
$$\text{if } \alpha(x) = \langle a, \varsigma_a \rangle \text{ and } [s]_a \in \operatorname{dom}(\varsigma), \text{ then } (s, s') \in \varsigma([s]_a)\}$$

Now, one can decide wether a sequence of states λ is possible under context κ, by checking wether for each subsequence $s_i \cdot s_{i+1}$ of λ, it is the case that s_{i+1} is a potential successor of s_i (that is whether $s_{i+1} \in succ_\kappa(s_i)$). This yields a set of potential executions under context κ. Given a state s, we call *in-outcomes* of κ and s the set of potential executions under κ which contain at least one occurence of s. Given state s, the *in-outcomes* of κ and s can alternatively be introduced as the set of scenarios that may be occuring if the execution is in state s.

Definition 6 (In-outcomes)

- *The in-outcomes of κ and s in $\mathcal{M}$ is the set $I/O(\kappa, s)$ of executions λ such that $\lambda_0 = s$ and, for any $i \in \mathbb{Z}$, if $\inf_\lambda < i$ and $i+1 < \sup_\lambda$, then $\lambda_{i+1} \in succ_\kappa(\lambda_i)$. We also call outcomes (respectively incomes) of κ and s and we write $O(\kappa, s)$ (respectively $I(\kappa, s)$) the set $\{\lambda_{\geqslant 0}\}_{\lambda \in I/O(\kappa, s)}$ (respectively $\{\lambda_{\leqslant 0}\}_{\lambda \in I/O(\kappa, s)}$).*

Note that the successor function induced by a context κ may indicate the empty set. So the outcomes, and incomes, of a context in a given state may contain finite executions. In such cases, we adopt the classical interpretation of temporal operators from Linear Temporal Logic in finite traces (LTL_f) [22]. Now we give the truth conditions for PKSL formulas. Truth conditions for FKSL formulas are obtained by ignoring clauses for P and S in the following definition.

Definition 7 (Satisfaction). *Let $\mathcal{M}$ be a CETS, with the notations of Definition 2. Let κ be a context, s be a state in St and λ be an execution. Then:*

- *State formulas*
  - $\mathcal{M}, \kappa, s \models p$ *iff* $p \in v(s)$, *with* $p \in At$
  - $\mathcal{M}, \kappa, s \models \neg\psi$ *iff* $\mathcal{M}, \kappa, s \not\models \psi$
  - $\mathcal{M}, \kappa, s \models \psi_1 \wedge \psi_2$ *iff* $\mathcal{M}, \kappa, s \models \psi_1$ *and* $\mathcal{M}, \kappa, s \models \psi_2$
  - $\mathcal{M}, \kappa, s \models \exists^a x\psi$ *iff there is a strategy ς for a such that* $\mathcal{M}, \kappa[x \mapsto \varsigma], s \models \psi$
  - $\mathcal{M}, \kappa, s \models \downarrow_x \varphi$ *iff for all* $\lambda \in I/O(\kappa \cup \{x\}, s), \mathcal{M}, \kappa \cup \{x\}, \lambda \models \varphi$
  - $\mathcal{M}, \kappa, s \models \uparrow^x \varphi$ *iff for all* $\lambda \in I/O(\kappa \setminus \{x\}, s), \mathcal{M}, \kappa \setminus \{x\}, \lambda \models \varphi$
  - $\mathcal{M}, \kappa, s \models K_a\psi$ *iff for all* $s' \in [s]_a, \mathcal{M}, \langle a, \emptyset \rangle, s' \models \psi$
- *Path formulas*
  - $\mathcal{M}, \kappa, \lambda \models \psi$ *iff* $\mathcal{M}, \kappa, \lambda_0 \models \psi$, *if ψ is a state formula*
  - $\mathcal{M}, \kappa, \lambda \models \neg\varphi$ *iff* $\mathcal{M}, \kappa, \lambda \not\models \varphi$
  - $\mathcal{M}, \kappa, \lambda \models \varphi_1 \wedge \varphi_2$ *iff* $\mathcal{M}, \kappa, \lambda \models \varphi_1$ *and* $\mathcal{M}, \kappa, \lambda \models \varphi_2$
  - $\mathcal{M}, \kappa, \lambda \models X\zeta$ *iff* $|\lambda_{\geq 0}| > 1$ *and* $\mathcal{M}, \kappa, \lambda_{\geq 1} \models \zeta$
  - $\mathcal{M}, \kappa, \lambda \models \zeta_1 U \zeta_2$ *iff there is a number $i \in \mathbb{N}$ such that* $|\lambda_{\geq 0}| > i$, *such that* $\mathcal{M}, \kappa, \lambda_{\geq i} \models \zeta_2$ *and such that for any $0 \leq j \leq i$, $\mathcal{M}, \kappa, \lambda_{\geq j} \models \zeta_1$.*
  - $\mathcal{M}, \kappa, \lambda \models P\xi$ *iff* $|\lambda_{\leq 0}| > 1$ *and* $\mathcal{M}, \kappa, \lambda_{\leq -1} \models \xi$
  - $\mathcal{M}, \kappa, \lambda \models \xi_1 S \xi_2$ *iff there is a number $i \in \mathbb{N}$ such that* $|\lambda_{\leq 0}| > i$, *such that* $\mathcal{M}, \kappa, \lambda_{\leq -i} \models \xi_2$ *and such that for any $0 \leq j \leq i$, $\mathcal{M}, \kappa, \lambda_{\leq -j} \models \xi_1$.*

Given the empty context $\kappa_\emptyset$ and a formula ψ, we write $\mathcal{M}, s \models \psi$ for $\mathcal{M}, \kappa_\emptyset, s \models \psi$, and $\mathcal{M} \models \psi$ for $\mathcal{M}, s_0 \models \psi$.

4 Expressive Power

In this section we discuss the expressive power of PKSL. First, we formalise forward induction in PKSL (Sect. 4.1). Then we prove that forward induction is not expressible in FKSL (Sect. 4.2).

4.1 PKSL and Forward Induction

First we formalise, in PKSL, the notions of admissible and forward inductive optimal strategies at stake with models $\mathcal{M}_1, \mathcal{M}_2$ and $\mathcal{M}_3$.

To formalise admissible strategies, let us first give a logical interpretation of payoffs labelling states in models. One can find similar such embedding of game utilities in a logical model in, eg., [23]. In models $\mathcal{M}_1, \mathcal{M}_2$ and $\mathcal{M}_3$, expression $P_{A,B} = n, f$ means that *Alice* gets payoff n and *Bob* get payoff k. This syntax does not fit PKSL. To adapt it, for each agent a and $k \in [0, \ldots 10]$ we introduce a proposition p_k^a stating that the payoff obtained by a is at least k. Then, for all $n, k \in [0, \ldots 10], P_{A,B} = n, k$ is interpreted as a shortcut for the set of propositions $\{p_i^A\}_{i \in [0,\ldots n]} \cup \{p_j^B\}_{j \in [0,\ldots k]}$. This comes with the definition for a subclass of CETSs for the interpretation of finite games that we call *CETSs for finite games*.

Definition 8. *Let $\mathcal{M} = \langle St, v, \{\mathcal{R}_a\}_{a \in Ag}, Act, s_0 \rangle$ be a CETS and let $n \in \mathbb{N}$. Then $\mathcal{M}$ is a CETS for finite game with payoffs up to n (written n-CETS) if the following conditions are met:*

- *The domain is partitioned into terminal states St^t and non-terminal states St^{nt}: $St = St^t \cup St^{nt}$.*
- *For each integer $k \leqslant n$ and each agent a, there is a proposition p_i^a.*
- *For each $s \in St^t$ and for each $a \in Ag$ there is an integer $k^a \leqslant n$ such that $v(s) = \bigcup_{a \in Ag} (\{p_k^a\}_{k \leqslant k^a})$.*
- *For each $s \in St^{nt}, k \leqslant n$ and $a \in Ag, p_k^a \notin v(s)$.*
- *For each $a \in Ag$, there is a specific action $null^a$. It is such that $null^a = \{(s,s)\}_{s \in St^t}$. Furthermore, for each $ac \in Act \setminus \{null^a\}_{a \in Ag}, \mathrm{dom}(ac) \subseteq St^{nt}$.*
- *There is no infinite sequence $ac_0 \cdot ac_1 \cdots$ of elements in $Act \setminus \{null^a\}_{a \in Ag}$ such that for all $k \in \mathbb{N}, \mathrm{img}(ac_k) \cap \mathrm{dom}(ac_{k+1}) \neq \emptyset$.*

Now we can define optimal, dominant and admissible strategies in a two player game. First, given a strategy y for agent b, strategy x is better for a against y than x' ($\mathsf{better}_y^{a;b}(x, x')$) if and only if, given that b plays y, then by playing x, a ensures herself a payoff at least equal to that ensured by playing x'. Given strategy y for b, strategy x is an optimal strategy for a ($\mathsf{opt}_y^{a;b}(x)$) if and only if it is better than any strategy for a. Now, strategy x for a (weakly) dominates strategy x' ($\mathsf{dom}^a(x, x')$) if it is better than x against any strategy y for b and there is a strategy y for b against which x' is not better than x. A strategy for an agent is admissible ($\mathsf{adm}^a(x)$) if it is not dominated by any strategy for this agent. Formally:

Definition 9. *Let a and b be two agents, let x and x' be strategies for a and y be a strategy for b. Then:*

- $\mathsf{better}_y^{a;b}(x, x') := \bigwedge_{k \in K} \left((\downarrow_y \downarrow_{x'} \mathsf{F} p_k^a) \rightarrow (\downarrow_y \downarrow_x \mathsf{F} p_k^a) \right)$
- $\mathsf{opt}_y^{a;b}(x) := \forall^a x' \mathsf{better}_y^{a;b}(x, x')$
- $\mathsf{dom}^a(x, x') := \left(\forall^b y \; \mathsf{better}_y^{a;b}(x, x') \right) \wedge \left(\exists^b y_b \; \neg\mathsf{better}_y^{a;b}(x', x) \right)$
- $\mathsf{adm}^a(x_a) := \forall^a x' \neg\mathsf{dom}^a(x', x)$

We also need to identify those strategies that, at some point of a game, may have been played so far. From any state s, a *potentially played* strategy is a strategy that may have been played to reach state s. More formally, it is a strategy enabling incoming transitions to s. As an illustration, consider model $\mathcal{M}_2$ from Fig. 1(b). State s_0 is reachable only by a transition from state s_5, for which *Alice* plays action C_A. Therefore at s_0, the strategy binding *Alice* to action C_A is a strategy potentially played by *Alice*. On the other hand, state

s_0 cannot be reached if *Alice* plays a strategy binding her to action Q_A from state s_5. Therefore, this strategy is not a *potentially played* strategy at s_0. This notion is characterised by a PKSL formula in the following definition. Intuitively, formula $Pot^a(x)$ is true at state s if and only if x stands for a strategy ς for a such that either

- there is no incoming transition to s
- or there is a state s' and a transition to s (from s') such that ς is played (*i.e.* such that $s \in \varsigma(s')$) and $Pot^a(x)$ is true at s'.

Definition 10 ($Pot^a(x)$). *Let x be a strategy variable and let a be an agent. Then,*

$$Pot^a(x) := \downarrow_x G^{-1}\Big(\uparrow^x \big(\bigvee_{a \in Ag} \exists^a y \downarrow_y (P\top)\big) \to \big(\downarrow_x (P\top)\big)\Big)$$

In models from Fig. 1, forward inductive reasoning for *Bob* consists in the identification of a strategy that is optimal against any admissible strategy potentially played so far by *Alice*. Predicate $Opt\text{-}FI^{b;a}$ generalises the existence of such a strategy in a two players game:

$$Opt\text{-}FI^{b;a} := \exists^b y\Big\{ K_b \forall^a x\big((Pot^a(x) \wedge \downarrow_x (G^{-1}(\uparrow^x adm^a(x)))) \to opt_x^{b;a}(y)\big)\Big\}$$

Formula $Opt\text{-}FI^{b;a}$ states that b has a strategy she knows to be optimal against any admissible strategy a may have been playing so far. We illustrate its satisfaction conditions with models $\mathcal{M}_1, \mathcal{M}_2$ and $\mathcal{M}_3$ from Fig. 1:

Proposition 1. $\mathcal{M}_1 \nvDash Opt\text{-}FI^{B;A}$ $\mathcal{M}_2 \vDash Opt\text{-}FI^{B;A}$ $\mathcal{M}_3 \nvDash Opt\text{-}FI^{B;A}$

Proof. In models $\mathcal{M}_1, \mathcal{M}_2$ and $\mathcal{M}_3$, a strategy for *Bob* consists in a choice of an action in $\{R_B, S_B\}$ from either state s_0 (in $\mathcal{M}_1$ and $\mathcal{M}_2$) or set of states $\{s_0, s_8\}$ (in $\mathcal{M}_3$). we write them τ_r and τ_s.

Similarly, in $\mathcal{M}_1$ strategies for *Alice* consist in choosing between actions R_A and S_A in s_0. We write them ς_r and ς_s. There is no possible transition to s_0 in the model, so $\mathcal{M}_1, s_0 \nvDash \bigvee_{a \in Ag}(\exists^a y \downarrow_y (P\top))$ and, for any $\varsigma \in \{\varsigma_r, \varsigma_s\}, \mathcal{M}_1, \langle\langle(x \mapsto \langle A, \varsigma\rangle)\rangle, \gamma_\emptyset\rangle, s_0 \vDash Pot^A(x)$. Now, since $\mathcal{M}_1, \langle\varsigma_r, \tau_r\rangle, s_0 \vDash Fp_{10}^A$ and $\mathcal{M}_1, \langle\varsigma_s, \tau_r\rangle, s_0 \nvDash Fp_{10}^A$, we have that $\mathcal{M}_1, \langle\langle(x \mapsto \langle A, \varsigma_s\rangle), (x' \mapsto \langle A, \varsigma_r\rangle), (y \mapsto \langle B, \tau_r\rangle)\rangle, \gamma_\emptyset\rangle, s_0 \nvDash better_y^{A;B}(x, x')$ and so, $\mathcal{M}_1, \langle\langle(x \mapsto \langle A, \varsigma_s\rangle), (x' \mapsto \langle A, \varsigma_r\rangle)\rangle, \gamma_\emptyset\rangle, s_0 \nvDash dom^A(x, x')$. Similarly, since $\mathcal{M}_1, \langle\varsigma_s, \tau_s\rangle, s_0 \vDash Fp_8^A$ and $\mathcal{M}_1, \langle\varsigma_r, \tau_s\rangle, s_0 \nvDash Fp_8^A$, we have that $\mathcal{M}_1, \langle\langle(x \mapsto \langle A, \varsigma_s\rangle), (x' \mapsto \langle A, \varsigma_r\rangle)\rangle, \gamma_\emptyset\rangle, s_0 \nvDash dom^A(x', x)$. Thus for any $\varsigma \in \{\varsigma_r, \varsigma_s\}, \mathcal{M}_1, \langle\langle(x \mapsto \langle A, \varsigma\rangle),\rangle, \gamma_\emptyset\rangle, s_0 \vDash adm^A(x)$. Since $\mathcal{M}_1, \langle\varsigma_r, \tau_r\rangle, s_0 \vDash Fp_{10}^B$ and $\mathcal{M}_1, \langle\varsigma_r, \tau_s\rangle, s_0 \nvDash Fp_{10}^B$, we have that $\mathcal{M}_1, \langle\langle(x \mapsto \langle A, \varsigma_r\rangle), (y \mapsto \langle B, \tau_s\rangle), (y' \mapsto \langle B, \tau_r\rangle)\rangle, \gamma_\emptyset\rangle, s_0 \nvDash better_x^{B;A}(y, y')$ and thus $\mathcal{M}_1, \langle\langle(x \mapsto \langle A, \varsigma_r\rangle), (y \mapsto \langle B, \tau_s\rangle)\rangle, \gamma_\emptyset\rangle, s_0 \nvDash opt_x^{B;A}(y)$. Similarly, $\mathcal{M}_1, \langle\langle(x \mapsto \langle A, \varsigma_s\rangle), (y' \mapsto \langle A, \tau_r\rangle)\rangle, \gamma_\emptyset\rangle, s_0 \nvDash opt_x^{B;A}(y')$. Hence for any $\tau \in \{\tau_r, \tau_s\}$, formula

$$K_B \forall^A x\big((Pot^A(x) \wedge \downarrow_x (G^{-1}(\uparrow^x adm^A(x)))) \to opt_x^{A;B}(y)\big)$$

is true in s_0 with context $\langle\langle(y \mapsto \langle B, \tau\rangle)\rangle, \gamma_0\rangle$.

In $\mathcal{M}_2$, strategies for *Alice* reduce to a pair of choices in $\{\varsigma_{qr} = (Q_A, R_A), \varsigma_{qs} = (Q_A, S_A), \varsigma_{cr} = (C_A, R_A), \varsigma_{cs} = (C_A, S_A)\}$ from states s_5 and s_0. Strategies ς_{qr} and ς_{qs} do not enable any incoming transition to state s_0, so they don't satisfy predicate Pot^A at state s_0. Strategies for *Bob* reduce to a choice between S_B and R_B. As for model $\mathcal{M}_1$, we denote them by τ_s and τ_r. Now, we claim that ς_{cs} is dominated by ς_{qs}. Indeed, for any $\tau \in \{\tau_s, \tau_r\}$, $\mathcal{M}_2, \langle\tau, \varsigma_{qs}\rangle, s_5 \models \mathsf{F}p_9^A$ and $\mathcal{M}_2, \langle\tau, \varsigma_{cs}\rangle, s_5 \not\models \mathsf{F}p_9^A$. So $\mathcal{M}_2\langle\langle(x \mapsto \langle A, \varsigma_{cs}\rangle)\rangle, \gamma_0\rangle, s_5 \not\models \mathsf{adm}^A(x)$. One also checks that ς_{cr} is not dominated by any strategy in s_5, so that $\mathcal{M}_2\langle\langle(x \mapsto \langle A, \varsigma_{cr}\rangle)\rangle, \gamma_0\rangle, s_0 \models \mathsf{adm}^A(x)$. Now, since $\mathcal{M}_2, \langle\varsigma_{cr}, \tau_r\rangle, s_0 \models \mathsf{F}p_{10}^A$ and $\mathcal{M}_2, \langle\varsigma_{cr}, \tau_s\rangle, s_0 \not\models \mathsf{F}p_{10}^A$ we have that by playing τ_r *Bob* would ensure himself the maximal payoff against the unique admissible strategy ς_{cr} (predicate $\mathsf{opt}_{\varsigma_{cr}}^{B;A}(\tau_r)$ is satisfied). Since $[s_0]_B = \{s_0\}$, it is the case that for any $s \in [s_0]_B$, formula

$$\forall^A x\left(\left(\mathsf{Pot}^A(x) \wedge \downarrow_x (\mathsf{G}^{-1}(\uparrow^x \mathsf{adm}^A(x)))\right) \to \mathsf{opt}_x^{B;A}(y)\right)$$

is true in s with context $\langle\langle(y \mapsto \langle B, \tau_r\rangle)\rangle, \gamma_0\rangle$.

The situation in model $\mathcal{M}_3$ is the same, except that *Bob* does not know whether *Alice* renounced to payoff $(9,9)$ or $(6,6)$. So he does not know whether ς_{cs} is an admissible strategy for *Alice*. It happens not to be, so that strategy τ_r is optimal against any admissible strategy for *Alice*, but *Bob* does not know it: with context $\langle\langle(y \mapsto \langle B, \tau_r\rangle)\rangle, \gamma_0\rangle$, formula

$$\forall^A x\left(\left(\mathsf{Pot}^A(x) \wedge \downarrow_x (\mathsf{G}^{-1}(\uparrow^x \mathsf{adm}^A(x)))\right) \to \mathsf{opt}_x^{B;A}(y)\right)$$

is true in state s_0, but false in state s_8. So we have $\mathcal{M}_3 \not\models \mathsf{Opt\text{-}FI}^{B;A}$.

4.2   PKSL Is Strictly More Expressive than Its Version Without Past

We do not give comparison theorems between PKSL and existing formalisms such as SL [2], USL [20,21], ESL [5] or ESL [6], but instead we prove that the framgent of PKSL without past operators (FKSL) is strictly less expressive than PKSL. The reasons for this treatment are twofold:

- The fragment FKSL is very similar to ESL [5] and ESL [6], which extend SL with epistemic operators. Still, there are some technical particularities for each of these languages. In particular, the definition of actions in CETSs relaxes some intersection constraints from models used in [2,5,6]. This USL [20,21] flavour of PKSL and FKSL enables the assignment of an agent to several strategies at a time and contexts resulting in finite executions. Treating this kind of differences would have led us far from our main focus, which is the expressivity of backward operators.
- Therefore, we give a theorem that isolates the expressivity of backward operators, stating that PKSL is strictly more expressive than FKSL. This result

holds for any language with backward operators: one can add backward operators to any logic $\mathcal{L}$ in { SL [2], ESL [5], ESL [6]}, call the logic obtained $P\mathcal{L}$ and prove that $P\mathcal{L}$ is strictly more expressive than $\mathcal{L}$ just has we give this result for $\mathcal{L} = $ FKSL.

Basically, without past time operators, one cannot distinguish between two models $\mathcal{M}$ and $\mathcal{M}'$ differing only in parts that are not accessible from their initial state. To formalise this idea, we introduce notions of *forward reachable states* and *forward submodels*. Let $\mathcal{M}$ be a CETS and let s be a state in $\mathcal{M}$, then for any state s', we say that s' is *forward reachable from* s if and only if there is a finite sequence of state $s_0, s_1, \ldots, s_k$ such that $s_0 = s, s_k = s'$ and for all $i \in [0, \ldots k-1]$, either $s_{i+1} \in succ_{\kappa_\theta}(s_i)$ or there is $a \in Ag$ such that $s_{i+1} \in [s_i]_a$. Now, let us define *forward submodels*:

Definition 11. *Let* $\mathcal{M} = \langle St, v, \{\mathcal{R}_a\}_{a \in Ag}, s_0 \rangle$ *be a CETS and let* s *be a state in* $\mathcal{M}$. *We call the* forward submodel *of* $\mathcal{M}$ *the CETS* $\mathcal{M}_{\restriction F} = \langle St_{\restriction F}, v_{\restriction F}, \{\mathcal{R}_{a \restriction F}\}_{a \in Ag}, \bigcup_{a \in Ag} \{ac_{\restriction F}\}_{ac \in Act_a}, s_0 \rangle$ *such that :*

- $St_{\restriction F} = \{s' \in St \mid s' \text{ is forward reachable from } s_0\}$
- $v_{\restriction F}$ *is the projection of* v *upon* $St_{\restriction F}$.
- *For each* $a \in Ag$, $\mathcal{R}_{a \restriction F} = \mathcal{R}_a \cap (St_{\restriction F} \times St_{\restriction F})$ *and for each* $ac \in Act_a$, $ac_{\restriction F} = ac \cap (St_{\restriction F} \times St_{\restriction F})$.

The restriction to reachable states extends to strategies and contexts: let $\mathcal{M}$ be a CETS and let a be an agent in $\mathcal{M}$. Let also ς be a strategy for a in $\mathcal{M}$. Then $\varsigma_{\restriction F}$ designates the strategy for a in $\mathcal{M}_{\restriction F}$ such that $dom(\varsigma_{\restriction F}) = dom(\varsigma) \cap St_{\restriction F}$ and for all $[s]_a \in dom(\varsigma_{\restriction F}), \varsigma_{\restriction F}([s]_a) = \varsigma([s]_a)_{\restriction F}$. Now, let $\kappa = \langle \alpha, \gamma \rangle$ be a context, then $\kappa_{\restriction F} = \langle \alpha_{\restriction F}, \gamma \rangle$, where $dom(\alpha_{\restriction F}) = dom(\alpha)$ and for all $s \in dom(\alpha), \alpha_{\restriction F}(x) = \langle \pi_1(\alpha(x)), \pi_2(\alpha(x))_{\restriction F} \rangle$.

Theorem 1. *Let* $\mathcal{M} = \langle St, v, Ag, \{\mathcal{R}_a\}, s_0 \rangle$ *be a CETS, let* κ *be a context and* s *be a state in* $\mathcal{M}$. *Then for any FKSL formula* ψ: $\mathcal{M}, \kappa, s_0 \models \psi$ *iff* $\mathcal{M}_{\restriction F}, \kappa_{\restriction F}, s_0 \models \psi$.

Proof. By structural induction upon φ.

Now, from Proposition 1 in Sect. 4.2, we have that formula Opt-FI$^{B;A}$ distinguishes between models $\mathcal{M}_1$ and $\mathcal{M}_2$ from Fig. 1. This brings the following corollary:

Corollary 1. *PKSL is strictly more expressive than FKSL. Specifically, let* a *and* b *be two agents, then formula* Opt-FI$^{b;a}$ *is not expressible in FKSL.*

5   Complexity

In this section we tackle the model-checking (MC(PKSL)) and satisfiability (SAT(PKSL)) problems for PKSL.

5.1   Model-Checking

Here, we give a lower bound for MC(PKSL), which is PSPACE-hard and we describe a decision algorithm for this problem. For lack of space, we cannot include the full algorithm here. It runs in exponential time.

First, let us identify any instance of MC(LTL) as an instance of MC(PKSL):

Proposition 2. *Let φ be an LTL formula, let $\mathcal{K} = \langle St, v, R, s_0 \rangle$ be a Kripke structure. Let us also consider the CETS $\mathcal{M}_\mathcal{K} \langle St, v, \{a\}, \{\mathcal{R}_a = St^2\}, \{ac_a = R\}, s_0 \rangle$. Then it is the case that $\mathcal{M}_\mathcal{K}, s_0 \models \forall^a x \downarrow_x \varphi$ iff for any path λ in $\mathcal{K}$ such that $\lambda_0 = s_0, \lambda \models_{LTL} \varphi$.*

Proof. In $\mathcal{M}_\mathcal{K}$, the only strategy ς that the only agent a may play is the one consisting in playing ac_a from any state. Then we have that $\mathcal{M}_\mathcal{K}, s_0 \models \forall^a x \downarrow_x \varphi$ iff for any $\lambda \in \mathsf{I/O}(\langle \varsigma \rangle, s_0), \mathcal{M}_\mathcal{K}, \langle \varsigma \rangle, \lambda \models \varphi$, iff for any path λ in $\mathcal{K}$ such that $\lambda_0 = s_0, \lambda \models_{LTL} \varphi$.

This proposition straightly brings our lower bound for MC(PKSL):

Corollary 2. MC($PKSL$) *is* PSPACE-*hard.*

Now, our decision procedure makes use of restrictions of CETSs and strategy contexts to Kripke models. Let φ be a PKSL path formula. We first introduce a notation enabling to treat φ as an LTL formula whose atoms are the state subformulas of φ: we write $\mathcal{Q}(\varphi)$ the set of maximal state subformulas of φ (*i.e.* its set of state subformulas ψ such that ψ is not a proper subformula of any other state proper subformula of φ). We then write $LTL(\varphi)$ the formula obtained from φ by:

- replacing each subformula ψ in $\mathcal{Q}(\varphi)$ by a new atom $\overline{\psi}$.
- if the resulting formula is a past formula, then replacing each occurrence of P by X and each occurrence of S by U.

Let $\mathcal{M} = \langle At, v, \{\mathcal{R}_a\}_{a \in Ag}, Act, s_0 \rangle$ be a CETS, κ be a context for $\mathcal{M}$, s be a state in $\mathcal{M}$, and φ be an LTL formula. We define two Kripke models, $\mathcal{K}^+_{\mathcal{M},\kappa} = \langle At, v, R^+ \rangle$ and $\mathcal{K}^-_{\mathcal{M},\kappa} = \langle At, v, R^- \rangle$. They are such that : $R^+ = \{(s, s') \in St^2 \mid s' \in succ_\kappa(s)\}$ and $R^- = \{(s', s) \in St^2 \mid s' \in succ_\kappa(s)\}$. To decide MC(PKSL($\mathcal{M}, \kappa, s, \varphi$)), our procedure is recursive: quantifiers are treated by enumeration of strategies, binders and unbinders update models $\mathcal{K}^+_{\mathcal{M},\kappa}$ and $\mathcal{K}^-_{\mathcal{M},\kappa}$. For temporal subformulas φ we call, as oracle, the model-checking for Linear Temporal Logic on finite traces MC(LTL_f) [22] of formula $LTL(\varphi)$, either in model $\mathcal{K}^+_{\mathcal{M},\kappa}$ (for future subformulas) or in model $\mathcal{K}^-_{\mathcal{M},\kappa}$ (for past subformulas).

Proposition 3. MC($PKSL$) *can be decided in exponential time.*

Proof. A strategy context can be stored in space $\bigcirc(|St| \times |Act|)$ and the problem used as oracle (MC(LTL_f)) is PSPACE-complete [22]. Now, cases for K_a and $\exists^x a$ quantify over executions of MC(PKSL) and case for $\neg$ introduces a quantifier alternation. So, MC(PKSL) can be solved by an alternating Turing machine using polynomial space. Therefore it is in class APSPACE, which is equivalent to EXPTIME [24].

5.2   Satisfiability

Just as for SL, there is no recursive procedure to decide the satisfiability of PKSL. More precisely, neither epistemic nor past time operators are needed to make this problem undecidable. In this section, we sketch a reduction of SAT(FKSL) to the highly undecidable *recurrent tiling problem* (RTC) [25]. For a full detailed similar reduction, one can refer to the proof for SL in [26].

An instance of the recurrent tiling problem $\mathcal{I} = \langle \mathcal{T}, H, V, t_0 \rangle$ is given by: a set $\mathcal{T}$ of tile types, two type relations H and V in $\mathcal{T} \times \mathcal{T}$ and a distinguished type $t_0 \in \mathcal{T}$. For any RTC instance $\mathcal{I}$, RTC($\mathcal{I}$) asks whether there is a mapping $f : \mathbb{N} \times \mathbb{N} \to \mathcal{T}$ such that : for all $i, j \in \mathbb{N}$, $H\big(f(i,j), f(i+1,j)\big)$ and $V\big(f(i,j), f(i,j+1)\big)$ and there is an infinite set $I_0 \subseteq \mathbb{N}$ such that for all $i \in I_0, f(0,i) = t_0$. For each such instance $\mathcal{I}$, one can build a FKSL sentence $\varphi_{\mathcal{I}}$ such that $\varphi_{\mathcal{I}}$ is satisfiable if and only if $\mathcal{I}$ has a solution.

Formula $\varphi_{\mathcal{I}}$ is the conjunction of two formulas φ^{grid} and $\varphi^{spec}(\mathcal{I})$. For sake of place, we just give a brief description of these formulas.

Formula φ^{grid} is common for all instances of RTC. It ensures the existence of a supporting grid matching $\mathbb{N} \times \mathbb{N}$. In a model of φ^{grid}, the set of states is made of an initial state p_s and for any $i, j \in \mathbb{N} \times \mathbb{N}$, a state $s_{i,j}$ figuring the corresponding node in the grid. From state p_s there is exactly one possible transition to any state $s_{i,j}$. This transition results from two agent's choices, A choosing the column by playing action $ac_{A,i}$ and B choosing the row by playing $ac_{B,j}$. From any state $s_{i,j}$ in the grid there are exactly two possible transitions, one going to $s_{i+1,j}$ and the other one going to $s_{i,j+1}$. These transitions result from choices of a third agent C, playing either action S_H or S_V.

Formula $\varphi^{spec}(\mathcal{I})$ induces the proper tiling specifications for $\mathcal{I}$. So, it ensures that each state $s_{i,j}$ in the grid is labelled by a type in $\mathcal{T}$ such that relations H and V are respected. It also formalises the satisfaction of the recurrent tile condition.

Our undecidability result lies on the following lemmas:

Lemma 1. *Let $\mathcal{I}$ be an instance of the recurrent tiling problem, then any model of $\varphi^{grid} \wedge \varphi^{spec}(\mathcal{I})$ is a solution to RTC($\mathcal{I}$).*

Lemma 2. *Let $\mathcal{I} = \langle \mathcal{T}, H, V, t_0 \rangle$ be an instance of the recurrent tiling problem and let $f : \mathbb{N} \times \mathbb{N} \to \mathcal{T}$ be a solution for $\mathcal{I}$. Then f induces a model for $\varphi^{grid} \wedge \varphi^{spec}(\mathcal{I})$.*

These two lemmas together state that for any instance $\mathcal{I}$ of RTC, $\mathcal{I}$ has a solution if and only if $\varphi^{grid} \wedge \varphi^{spec}(\mathcal{I})$ has a model, which brings our undecidability result:

Theorem 2. SAT(*FKSL*) *is higly undecidable.*

6   Conclusion and Future Works

In this article we presented some theoretical results for PKSL. This logic builds upon Epistemic Strategy Logics [5–7], by introducing past temporal operators.

In PKSL we can specify the knowledge that agents may have about the evolution of a system, be it about its future or about its past. We proved that PKSL is strictly more expressive than FKSL, its fragment without past temporal operators. To illustrate this additional expressive power we formalised, in PKSL, forward induction reasoning and a characterisation of the related solution concept. We also gave an exponential time running algorithm for PKSL model checking problem, and showed that its satisfiability problem is undecidable.

Since we can reason about knowledge agents have about the past, PKSL opens research directions on the concept of memory. Memory is usually a metalogical property constraining the set of available strategies for agents. Model-checking games with imperfect information and full memory is proved to be undecidable. On an other hand, model checking epistemic strategy logics with memoryless strategies is implementable [27]. Therefore, a contemporary research effort consists in searching fragments of SL and restrictions over the knowledge structure that bring decidable model-checking [28,29].

We adopt a different perspective. In PKSL indeed, memory is not assumed but becomes a set of verifiable logical properties. Even though the semantics exclusively uses memoryless strategies, agents are able to choose strategies depending on their knowledge of the past. The use of memoryless strategies instead of full-memory strategies is the reason why the model checking remains decidable, with a relatively low complexity. We conjecture that full memory strategies would make model-checking NONELEMENTARY for PKSL, as it is for SL. Therefore, we would like to further investigate to what extent memoryless strategies are sufficient for modelling game situations and multi-agent systems.

Acknowledgments. The author acknowledges financial support from ERC project EPS 313360 and thanks Hans van Ditmarsch for his useful comments on the presented research. He also gives thanks to the anonymous reviewers of conference SR 2017 for their comments on a previous version of this article.

References

1. Chatterjee, K., Henzinger, T.A., Piterman, N.: Strategy logic. Inf. Comp. **208**(6), 677–693 (2010)
2. Mogavero, F., Murano, A., Perelli, G., Vardi, M.Y.: Reasoning about strategies: On the model-checking problem. ACM Trans. Comput. Log. **15**(4), 1–47 (2014)
3. Ågotnes, T., Goranko, V., Jamroga, W., Wooldridge, M.: Knowledge and ability. Volume In: van Ditmarsch, H., Halpern, J.Y., van der Hoek, W., Kooi, B. (eds.) Handbook of Epistemic Logic, pp. 543–589. College Publications (2015)
4. Jamroga, W., Ågotnes, T.: Constructive knowledge: what agents can achieve under imperfect information. J. Appl. Non-Class. Log. **17**, 423–475 (2007)
5. Belardinelli, F.: Reasoning about knowledge and strategies: epistemic strategy logic. In: Proceedings of 2nd International Workshop on Strategic Reasoning, SR, pp. 27–33 (2014)
6. Knight, S., Maubert, B.: Dealing with imperfect information in strategy logic. In: Proceedings of 3rd International Workshop on Strategic Reasoning, SR (2015)

7. Huang, X., van der Meyden, R.: An epistemic strategy logic. In: Proceedings of 2nd International Workshop on Strategic Reasoning, SR, pp. 35–41 (2014)

8. Van Ditmarsch, H., van Der Hoek, W., Kooi, B.: Dynamic Epistemic Logic, vol. 337. Springer Science & Business Media, Netherlands (2007). https://doi.org/10.1007/978-1-4020-5839-4

9. Chareton, C., van Ditmarsch, H.: Strategic knowledge of the past in quantum cryptography. In: Baltag, A., Seligman, J., Yamada, T. (eds.) LORI 2017. LNCS, vol. 10455, pp. 347–361. Springer, Heidelberg (2017). https://doi.org/10.1007/978-3-662-55665-8_24

10. Lichtenstein, O., Pnueli, A., Zuck, L.: The glory of the past. In: Parikh, R. (ed.) Logic of Programs 1985. LNCS, vol. 193, pp. 196–218. Springer, Heidelberg (1985). https://doi.org/10.1007/3-540-15648-8_16

11. Vardi, M.Y.: Reasoning about the past with two-way automata. In: Larsen, K.G., Skyum, S., Winskel, G. (eds.) ICALP 1998. LNCS, vol. 1443, pp. 628–641. Springer, Heidelberg (1998). https://doi.org/10.1007/BFb0055090

12. French, T., van der Meyden, R., Reynolds, M.: Axioms for logics of knowledge and past time: synchrony and unique initial states. In: Proceedings of AiML, vol. 5, pp. 53–72 (2004)

13. Sack, J.: Logic for update products and steps into the past. Ann. Pure Appl. Logic **161**(12), 1431–1461 (2010)

14. Guelev, D.P., Dima, C.: Model-checking strategic ability and knowledge of the past of communicating coalitions. In: Baldoni, M., Son, T.C., van Riemsdijk, M.B., Winikoff, M. (eds.) DALT 2008. LNCS (LNAI), vol. 5397, pp. 75–90. Springer, Heidelberg (2009). https://doi.org/10.1007/978-3-540-93920-7_6

15. Skyrms, B.: The Stag Hunt and the Evolution of Social Structure. Cambridge University Press, Cambridge (2004)

16. Brenguier, R., Pérez, G.A., Raskin, J.F., Sankur, O.: Admissibility in quantitative graph games. arXiv preprint arXiv:1611.08677 (2016)

17. Berwanger, D.: Admissibility in infinite games. In: Thomas, W., Weil, P. (eds.) STACS 2007. LNCS, vol. 4393, pp. 188–199. Springer, Heidelberg (2007). https://doi.org/10.1007/978-3-540-70918-3_17

18. Van Damme, E.: Stable equilibria and forward induction. J. Econ. Theory **48**(2), 476–496 (1989)

19. Cooper, R., De Jong, D.V., Forsythe, R., Ross, T.W.: Forward induction in coordination games. Econ. Lett. **40**(2), 167–172 (1992)

20. Chareton, C., Brunel, J., Chemouil, D.: Towards an updatable strategy logic. In: Proceedings of 1st International Workshop on Strategic Reasoning, SR, pp. 91–98 (2013)

21. Chareton, C., Brunel, J., Chemouil, D.: A logic with revocable and refinable strategies. Inf. Comput. **242**, 157–182 (2015)

22. De Giacomo, G., Vardi, M.Y.: Linear temporal logic and linear dynamic logic on finite traces. In: Proceedings of 22th IJCAI, pp. 854–860 (2013)

23. Baltag, A.: A logic for suspicious players: Epistemic actions and belief-updates in games. Technical report, Amsterdam, The Netherlands (2000)

24. Chandra, A.K., Stockmeyer, L.J.: Alternation. In: 17th Annual Symposium on Foundations of Computer Science, pp. 98–108. IEEE (1976)

25. Harel, D.: Recurring dominoes: making the highly undecidable highly understandable. North-Holl. Math. Stud. **102**, 51–71 (1985)

26. Mogavero, F., Murano, A., Perelli, G., Vardi, M.Y.: Reasoning about strategies: on the satisfiability problem. Log. Methods Comput. Sci. **13**(1), 1–37 (2017)

27. Čermák, P., Lomuscio, A., Mogavero, F., Murano, A.: MCMAS-SLK: a model checker for the verification of strategy logic specifications. In: Biere, A., Bloem, R. (eds.) CAV 2014. LNCS, vol. 8559, pp. 525–532. Springer, Cham (2014). https://doi.org/10.1007/978-3-319-08867-9_34

28. Belardinelli, F., Lomuscio, A., Murano, A., Rubin, S.: Verification of broadcasting multi-agent systems against an epistemic strategy logic. In: Proceedings of the Twenty-Sixth International Joint Conference on Artificial Intelligence, IJCAI 2017, Melbourne, Australia, August 19–25, 2017, pp. 91–97 (2017)

29. Berthon, R., Maubert, B., Murano, A., Rubin, S., Vardi, M.Y.: Strategy logic with imperfect information. In: 32nd Annual ACM/IEEE Symposium on Logic in Computer Science, LICS 2017, Reykjavik, Iceland, June 20–23, 2017, pp. 1–12 (2017)

The Expected Duration
of Sequential Gossiping

Hans van Ditmarsch[1,2] and Ioannis Kokkinis[3](✉)

[1] CNRS, LORIA, University of Lorraine, Nancy, France
hans.van-ditmarsch@loria.fr
[2] ReLaX UMI 2000, IMSc, Chennai, India
[3] TU Dortmund University, Dortmund, Germany
ioannis.kokkinis@tu-dortmund.de

Abstract. A gossip protocol aims at arriving, by means of point-to-point communications (or telephone calls), at a situation in which every agent knows all the information initially present in the network. If it is forbidden to have more than one call at the same time, the protocol is called sequential. We generalise a method, that originates from the famous coupon collector's problem and that was proposed by John Haigh in 1981, for bounding the expected duration of sequential gossip protocols. We give two examples of protocols where this method succeeds and two examples of protocols where this method fails to give useful bounds. Our main contribution is that, although Haigh originally applied this method in a protocol where any call is available at any moment, we show that this method can be applied in protocols where the number of available calls is decreasing. Furthermore, for one of the protocols where Haigh's method fails we were able to obtain lower bounds for the expectation using results from random graph theory.

Keywords: Sequential gossip · Networks
Coupon collector's problem · Expectation

1 Introduction

1.1 Background

The *coupon collector's problem* [13] (CCP) is a classical problem in probability theory. It can be stated as follows: Assume that we have n different objects. Each time, we are allowed to pick a single object. All the objects have the same probability of being selected and all of them are available at every selection. How many picks are we expected to make until we complete a collection of all the n objects? A solution for this problem [13] goes as follows: It costs us one pick to get the first object. The event of a getting a new object in the second pick follows the geometric distribution with parameter $\frac{n-1}{n}$. So we are expected to make $\frac{n}{n-1}$ picks until we pick a new object. Similarly, given that we already have two different objects, we are expected to make $\frac{n}{n-2}$ picks until we get a third object

© Springer Nature Switzerland AG 2018
F. Belardinelli and E. Argente (Eds.): EUMAS 2017/AT 2017, LNAI 10767, pp. 131–146, 2018.
https://doi.org/10.1007/978-3-030-01713-2_10

and so on. In total we are expected to make $n \cdot H_n$ picks, where $H_n = \sum_{i=1}^{n} \frac{1}{i}$ is the n-th harmonic number. It is well known [13] that asymptotically, i.e. for large n:

$$H_n \approx \log n + \gamma + \frac{1}{n} + \mathcal{O}\left(\frac{1}{n^2}\right), \tag{1}$$

where $\gamma \approx 0.5772156649$ is the Euler-Mascheroni constant and log without subscripts represents the natural logarithm. So, asymptotically we are expected to make $n \log n + \Theta(n)$ picks until we complete the collection.

Now we state the problems of *gossiping*, *broadcasting* and *gathering*. Assume that we have a set of n agents which can communicate via telephone calls. Initially, each agent holds a single piece of information that is unknown to the others (a secret). When two agents call each other, they share all the secrets they knew exactly before the call. An agent who knows all secrets is an *expert*. The goal of gossiping is that all agents get to know all secrets. The goal of broadcasting is that all agents learn a single secret. The goal of gathering is that a specific agent becomes expert. A protocol achieving gossiping, broadcasting or gathering is usually called a *gossip protocol* [17]. Five gossip protocols of a more epistemic nature [3–5,9] are (for $a \neq b$):

ANY: Until all agents are experts, select two agents a and b, and let a call b.

TOK: Until all agents are experts, select two agents a and b such that agent a has not been in prior calls or the last call involving a was *to* a, and let a call b.

SPI: Until all agents are experts, select two agents a and b such that agent a has not been in prior calls or the last call involving a was *from* a, and let a call b.

CO: Until all agents are experts, select two agents a and b who did not call each other, and let a call b.

LNS: Until all agents are experts, select two agents a and b such that a does not know b's secret, and let a call b.

These acronyms are also mnemonic devices indicating how calls are selected: in ANY, any call can be made. In the protocols TOK and SPI every agent is initially endowed with a token. In TOK when a call is made the caller passes the token to the callee, whereas in SPI when a call is made the callee passes the token to the caller (provided that the callee had one). All the tokens received by an agent at a time merge into one token before the next call and a token is required to make a call. So, TOK's name originates from the TOKen and SPI stands for a SPIder in the web that gobbles up all tokens from the agents it calls. CO only allows to Call Once; and LNS means Learn New Secrets.

We assume that at each point in time a single call is selected, uniformly at random. So, our protocols are discrete time random processes. We characterize our protocols as *sequential* in order to distinguish them from *parallel* gossip protocols, where at each point in time all (or some of) the agents (randomly or with respect to some criterion) select a communication partner.

An important property for all the protocols studied here is that the condition for selecting a call can be checked *locally*, i.e. agent a can decide whether she is allowed to call b, based only on a's calling history. In the present paper we assume that only one call is selected at a time (e.g. by a central scheduler) so the locality of the protocol's conditions is not important. However, in future work we might want agents to act independently: e.g. if we consider parallel extensions of our protocols; in such an approach we may even assume that the agents are not following the same protocol. So, the nature of the protocol condition is the main reason for studying ANY, TOK, SPI, CO and LNS: a local protocol condition makes it easier to extend our protocols to distributed gossiping mechanisms.

We always assume a complete directed network topology without self loops (i.e. for any $a \neq b$, there is a link from a to b and a link from b to a). So, initially all the agents can call each other. However only in ANY all the communications remain possible at every point in time. In TOK and SPI, since a call cannot increase the number of tokens, the number of available calls is (non-strictly) decreasing. In CO and LNS it is impossible to select the same call twice, so in CO and LNS we can have only finite call sequences. It is easy to see that CO and LNS always succeed: in the worst case, after all the calls have been selected all the agents are experts. On the other hand in ANY, TOK and SPI we can have infinite call sequences: take $ba; ab; ba; ab; \ldots$ in TOK, $ab; ab; ab; \ldots$ in SPI and any infinite call sequence in ANY (ab represents the call from a to b). So, there are unsuccessful executions of ANY, TOK and SPI. However it is not difficult to show that, in a complete network, the success of gossiping, broadcasting and gathering under ANY, TOK or SPI has positive probability after every call sequence. So, the expected duration of the aforementioned processes can be defined for all the protocols in complete networks.

The number of agents knowing a secret can increase by at most 1 during a call. Therefore, broadcasting needs at least $n - 1$ calls. There are several proofs for the fact that gossiping needs at least $2n - 4$ calls [18, 20] and also that this bound is tight for all the protocols. In CO and LNS the maximum length of a call sequence achieving gossiping, broadcasting or gathering is $\binom{n}{2}$ [5, 11]. The previous numbers give the trivial bounds for the expectation of gossiping and broadcasting for our protocols.

1.2   Related Work

While in the CCP there is a single person that needs to complete a collection of objects, in the gossip problem there are several persons that have this task. So, it seems natural to employ the ideas from the solution of CCP in gossiping. According to [17], the first person to make use of this idea was J. W. Moon, who provided some bounds for the expected duration of ANY [19]. Moon observed that, given that i persons know a secret, the probability that $i + 1$ persons learn it (we will refer to this probability as the transition probability) is $\frac{2i(i-1)}{n(n-1)}$. With this observation the expectation of broadcasting can be computed as in the CCP and afterwards, by applying some variations of the same idea, some bounds for gossiping can be obtained. The results of Moon were later sharpened by Boyd and Steele [7], and later by Haigh [16] who showed that the expected duration of ANY is $\frac{3}{2} n \log n + \mathcal{O}(n)$.

Recently, there have been several publications in distributed sequential gossiping [1,2,10] addressing interesting computational issues: decidability of termination, complexity of deciding whether a specific distribution of secrets among the agents can be achieved, deciding whether a specific condition holds after a sequence of calls. However the expected duration has been investigated only for parallel gossip protocols. For example parallel, distributed versions of LNS-like protocols are presented in [15] with an expectation (called *connection communication complexity*) of order $n \log_2^2 n$, and a version of CO (for a different communicative setting, not for sharing— so-called push-pull—but for *sending*— push— secrets) in [12]. It is also common to employ ideas from the CCP in the analysis of parallel gossip algorithms [6,8]. We are unaware of similar results for sequential gossip protocols other than ANY, and this stimulated our research. Except from the present work we have addressed the expected duration of sequential gossiping in [11], where we presented an algorithm that computes the exact value of the expected duration of ANY and LNS for small numbers of agents and some simulation results for the asymptotic behaviour of LNS.

1.3 Our Contribution

We show that broadcasting and gathering have the same expectation in all the protocols. We also show that gossiping has the same expectation in SPI and TOK. We show that broadcasting and gathering in SPI and TOK are between $1.38 \cdot n + \log n + \Theta(1)$ and $2n \log n - \Theta(n)$ and also that gossiping in TOK and SPI is between $1.64 \cdot n + \log n + \Theta(1)$ and $3n \log n - \Theta(n)$. We also show that, for large n, broadcasting in and gossiping in CO are bounded below by $\frac{1}{2}n(\log n + c_n)$ and $\frac{1}{2}n(\log n + \log \log n + c_n)$ respectively, where $\lim_{n \to \infty} c_n \to -\infty$.

1.4 Outline of the Paper

In Sect. 2 we present some definitions and lemmata that are necessary for our analysis. In Sect. 3 we give a formal presentation of Haigh's method. In Sect. 4 we obtain upper and lower bounds for TOK and SPI using Haigh's method. In Sect. 5 we explain why the method fails for CO and LNS and we also present some lower bounds for CO. In Sect. 6 we summarize our results and present an interesting conjecture.

2 Preliminaries

In this section we present some definitions, notation and lemmata that are necessary for our presentation. We use the (possibly primed) lower-case letters $a, b, c, d, \ldots$ for agents and the corresponding upper case letters $A, B, C, D, \ldots$ for the relevant secrets. The number of agents, and the set of agents are represented by, respectively, n, and Ag. P represents an arbitrary protocol.

We informally define the notions of (P-permitted) calls and call sequences, since for the purposes of this paper no formal definition is necessary. Complete formal definitions of these notions can be found for example in [9,10]. A *call* is an ordered pair (a, b) for $a, b \in \mathsf{Ag}$ and $a \neq b$. We write ab instead of (a, b). A *call sequence* is a (possibly empty) finite or infinite sequence of calls. After the call ab takes place, a and b exchange all the secrets they knew before the call. For example after the call sequence $ab; bc$, a knows the secrets A and B, and b and c know the secrets A, B, and C. A call ab is P-permitted after a call sequence σ iff a can call b under the restrictions of P when all the calls in σ have taken place. A call sequence σ is P-permitted iff every call in σ is P-permitted given that the previous calls have taken place.

In the gossip community considering the reverse of a given call sequence has provided a lot of results [7,16,18–20]. Based on this idea, we give the following definitions and prove Lemma 1.

Definition 1 (Reverse Call Sequence). *Let τ be a finite call sequence. The reverse of τ is the call sequence τ^{-1}, which is inductively defined as follows:*

$$\epsilon^{-1} = \epsilon \qquad and \qquad (ab; \sigma)^{-1} = \sigma^{-1}; ba.$$

Definition 2 (Reverse Property). *P has the reverse property iff the reverse of every P-permitted call sequence is a P- permitted call sequence.*

Lemma 1. *Protocols* ANY, CO *and* SPI *have the reverse property.*

Proof. For ANY the claim is obvious. CO has the reverse property since, if no call is repeated in σ then no call can be repeated in σ^{-1}. For SPI, we show the claim by contradiction:

Assume that σ is a SPI-call sequence and that σ^{-1} is not a SPI-call sequence. Then σ^{-1} looks like:

$$\ldots ; \ ca \ ; \ \sigma' \ ; \ ab \ ; \ \ldots$$

where σ' does not contain any calls involving a. But then σ has the same shape as σ^{-1}. So, σ is not a SPI call sequence, which is absurd. □

We continue with the following interesting theorem, which will allow us to study SPI and TOK together.

Theorem 1. SPI *and* TOK *can be modelled by the same Markov Chain.*

Proof. In [11] we have shown that ANY can be modelled by a Markov Chain in the space of unordered tuples. As an example assume that we have only 4 agents. Using the notation of [11] we can represent the initial knowledge of the agents with the state (i.e. unordered tuple) $\{A, B, C, D\}$. The previous state means that a knows A, b knows B etc. After call ab, we go to the state $\{AB, AB, C, D\}$ (i.e. to the state where a knows A and B etc.) and so on. The fact that in ANY, each call can be selected at any time, gives us the right to use unordered tuples: the knowledge of any two agents can be freely interchanged, with no effect in the future selection of calls.

A similar idea can be used for modelling the execution of SPI and TOK. In order to select the next call in SPI and TOK, except from the agents' knowledge, we need to know which agents have a token. Therefore, we can use unordered tuples with underlined elements. An underlined element refers to an agent who has a token. So, the initial state for 4 agents is the following: $\{\underline{A}, \underline{B}, C, D\}$. After the TOK-call ab we go to the state $\{AB, \underline{AB}, C, D\}$ and so on. Clearly the knowledge of any two agents who have a token can be interchanged and the same holds for the knowledge of any two agents who do not have a token, since this does not affect the selection of new calls. That is why we can use unordered tuples as states in the Markov chain.

Assume that we have the state $\{S_1, \ldots, \underline{S_i}, S_j, \ldots S_n\}$. The TOK-call ij will lead us to the state $\{S_1, \ldots, \underline{S_i \cup S_j}, S_i \cup S_j, \ldots S_n\}$ and the SPI-call ij will lead us to the state $\{S_1, \ldots, \underline{S_i \cup S_j}, S_i \cup \overline{S_j}, \ldots S_n\}$. Observe however that ,since the tuples are unordered the two previous states are the same. We conclude that the Markov chains which model TOK and SPI have exactly the same transitions in the space of unordered tuples with underlined elements. The probability of this transitions depends only on the current state, therefore we conclude that SPI and TOK can be modelled by the same Markov chain.   □

Let $T_{v \to n}^{P}$, $T_{v \leftarrow n}^{P}$ and T_n^{P} denote the number of calls until the broadcasting of V, v becomes expert and all agents become experts, for the first time respectively. We will refer to the previous random variables as the T-variables. Observe that an arrow directed to v denotes the gathering of all the secrets to v and an arrow pointing out from v denotes broadcasting of V. We will use the T-variables without superscripts when this causes no confusion. For a random variable T, $\mathbb{E}(T)$ represents the expectation of T. As a direct consequence of Theorem 1 we have that gossiping has the same expectation in SPI and TOK (and the same holds for broadcasting and gathering). So, in the rest of the paper we will simply write $\mathbb{E}(T_n^{SPI,TOK})$, $\mathbb{E}(T_{v \to n}^{SPI,TOK})$ and $\mathbb{E}(T_{v \leftarrow n}^{SPI,TOK})$. The next corollary follows from Lemma 1 and Theorem 1.

Corollary 1. *For any agent v we have that:*

$$\mathbb{E}\left(T_{v \to n}^{ANY}\right) = \mathbb{E}\left(T_{v \leftarrow n}^{ANY}\right) \quad , \quad \mathbb{E}\left(T_{v \to n}^{CO}\right) = \mathbb{E}\left(T_{v \leftarrow n}^{CO}\right)$$

$$\mathbb{E}\left(T_{v \to n}^{LNS}\right) = \mathbb{E}\left(T_{v \leftarrow n}^{LNS}\right) \quad and \quad \mathbb{E}\left(T_{v \to n}^{SPI,TOK}\right) = \mathbb{E}\left(T_{v \leftarrow n}^{SPI,TOK}\right).$$

Finally we need a standard Lemma about random experiments. Let A be an experiment which has the outcome "success" or "failure". The Bernoulli trials of A are independent trials of A such that the probability of success remains constant in every trial. On the contrary, the Poisson trials of A are independent trials of A, such that the probability of success varies from trial to trail. The proof of the Lemma is straightforward.

Lemma 2. *Let A be an experiment and assume that we are performing Poisson trials of A where in the i-th trial the probability of success is p_i. Let T_A be the number of independent trials of A until we get the first success and let $0 < p \leq 1$. Then we have the following:*

1. *if for all i we have that $p_i \geq p$, then $\mathbb{E}(T_A) \leq \frac{1}{p}$.*
2. *if for all i we have that $p_i \leq p$, then $\mathbb{E}(T_A) \geq \frac{1}{p}$.*

The next Lemma contains all the arithmetical computations needed for this paper.

Lemma 3

(i.)

$$\frac{n-i+1}{(n-i)(i+1)} = \frac{1}{n+1}\left(\frac{1}{n-i} + \frac{n+2}{i+1}\right)$$

(ii.)

$$\sum_{i=1}^{\lfloor \frac{n}{2} \rfloor} \frac{1}{p_i(i,0)} \overset{(6)}{=} \sum_{i=1}^{\lfloor \frac{n}{2} \rfloor} \frac{n-1}{n-i} = (n-1)\left(H_{n-1} - H_{n-\lfloor \frac{n}{2} \rfloor -1}\right)$$

(iii.)

$$\sum_{i=\lfloor \frac{n}{2} \rfloor +1}^{n-1} \frac{1}{p_i(1,n-i)} \overset{(6)}{=} \sum_{\lfloor \frac{n}{2} \rfloor +1}^{n-1} \frac{(n-i+1)(n-1)}{(n-i)(i+1)}$$

$$\overset{(i.)}{=} \frac{(n-1)}{(n+1)} \sum_{\lfloor \frac{n}{2} \rfloor +1}^{n-1}\left(\frac{1}{(n-i)} + \frac{n+2}{(i+1)}\right)$$

$$= \frac{n-1}{n+1}\left(H_{n-\lfloor \frac{n}{2} \rfloor -1} + (n+2)\left(H_n - H_{\lfloor \frac{n}{2} \rfloor +1}\right)\right)$$

(iv.)

$$\sum_{i=1}^{\lfloor \frac{n}{2} \rfloor} \frac{1}{p_i(1,n-i)} \overset{\text{as in (iii.)}}{=} \frac{n-1}{n+1}\left(H_{n-1} - H_{n-\lfloor \frac{n}{2} \rfloor -1} + (n+2)\left(H_{\lfloor \frac{n}{2} \rfloor +1} - 1\right)\right)$$

(v.)

$$\sum_{i=\lfloor \frac{n}{2} \rfloor +1}^{n-1} \frac{1}{p_i(i,0)} \overset{(6)}{=} \sum_{i=\lfloor \frac{n}{2} \rfloor +1}^{n-1} \frac{n-1}{n-i} = (n-1)H_{n-\lfloor \frac{n}{2} \rfloor -1}$$

(vi.)

$$\sum_{i=2}^{\lfloor \frac{n}{2} \rfloor} \frac{i}{np_i(1,n-i)} \overset{(6)}{=} \sum_{i=2}^{\lfloor \frac{n}{2} \rfloor} \frac{i(n-i+1)(n-1)}{n(n-i)(i+1)} \overset{(i.)}{=} \frac{n-1}{n(n+1)}\left(\sum_{i=2}^{\lfloor \frac{n}{2} \rfloor} \frac{i}{n-i}\right.$$

$$\left. + (n+2)\sum_{i=2}^{\lfloor \frac{n}{2} \rfloor} \frac{i}{i+1}\right) = \frac{n-1}{n(n+1)}\left(n\left(H_{n-2} - H_{n-\lfloor \frac{n}{2} \rfloor -1}\right)\right.$$

$$\left. - \lfloor \frac{n}{2} \rfloor + 1 + (n+2)\left(\lfloor \frac{n}{2} \rfloor - H_{\lfloor \frac{n}{2} \rfloor +1} + \frac{1}{2}\right)\right)$$

(vii.)

$$\sum_{i=\lfloor\frac{n}{2}\rfloor+1}^{n-1} \frac{i}{np_i(i,0)} \overset{(6)}{=} \frac{n-1}{n} \sum_{i=\lfloor\frac{n}{2}\rfloor+1}^{n-1} \frac{i}{n-i} \overset{j:=n-i}{=} \frac{n-1}{n} \sum_{j=1}^{n-\lfloor\frac{n}{2}\rfloor-1} \frac{n-j}{j}$$

$$= (n-1)H_{n-\lfloor\frac{n}{2}\rfloor-1} - \left(\frac{n-1}{n}\right)\left(\left\lfloor n-\frac{n}{2}\right\rfloor-1\right).$$

3   Haigh's Method

In this section we formally present John Haigh's method [16] for obtaining bounds in broadcasting, gathering and gossiping. All the T-variables refer to an arbitrary protocol. In the rest of the paper we fix an arbitrary agent v.

Broadcasting and Gathering. We divide the time in $n-1$ phases. The i-th phase starts when i nodes know V and ends when $i+1$ nodes know V ($1 \leq i \leq n-1$). Let $T_{v\to i}$ be the number of calls spent in phase i. Then it holds that:

$$T_{v\to n} = \sum_{i=1}^{n-1} T_{v\to i} \quad \text{and} \quad \mathbb{E}\left(T_{v\to n}\right) = \sum_{i=1}^{n-1} \mathbb{E}\left(T_{v\to i}\right). \tag{2}$$

Assume that we are in phase i. The set $\mathcal{K}$ contains the i agents that *know* V. The *available calls* in phase i are all the P-permitted calls in phase i. The *useful calls* in phase i are the calls that lead in one more agent learning V. Let p_i^P be the probability of one more agent learning V, i.e. the transition probability from phase i to phase $i+1$ (see Fig. 1). Since all the available calls have the same probability of being chosen, we have:

$$p_i^P = \frac{\text{number of useful calls}}{\text{number of available calls}}.$$

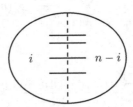

Fig. 1. The situation in phase i. There are i agents that know V and $n-i$ that do not know V. If we select one of the displayed edges then we go from phase i to phase $i+1$.

Let A be the event "going to phase $i+1$". Each time we select a call we have an independent trial of A. In the ANY protocol there are always $2i(n-i)$

useful and $n(n-1)$ available calls. So, in ANY the selection of calls represents Bernoulli trials, but in all the other protocols the selection of calls represents Poisson trials. If we have bounds for p_i we can apply Lemma 2 in order to obtain bounds for $T_{v\to i}$ and by (2) for $T_{v\to n}$ (broadcasting). For all the protocols except TOK these bounds will also refer to $T_{v\leftarrow n}$ (gathering), because of Corollary 1. Clearly $T_{v\to i}^{\text{ANY}}$ follows the geometric distribution with parameter $\frac{2i(n-i)}{n(n-1)}$. As it was shown in [19] we have:

$$\mathbb{E}\left(T_{v\to n}^{\text{ANY}}\right) = \sum_{i=1}^{n-1} \mathbb{E}\left(T_{v\to i}^{\text{ANY}}\right) = \sum_{i=1}^{n-1} \frac{n(n-1)}{2i(n-i)} = (n-1)\cdot H_{n-1} \overset{(1)}{\approx} n\log n + \Theta(n).$$

Gossiping. In any realization of the protocol the agents will become experts in some order, e.g.:

$$T_{a_5\leftarrow n} \leq T_{a_7\leftarrow n} \leq \ldots \leq T_{a_8\leftarrow n}.$$

The position of $T_{v\leftarrow n}$ in the above inequality is the order, compared to the rest of the agents, in which v becomes expert. Observe that in the above inequality we have that at most two $T_{a_i\leftarrow n}$'s can tie at a given value: it is impossible to make more than two agents experts with a single call. Let Z be the number of agents that are experts at time $T_{v\leftarrow n}$. It holds that $2 \leq Z \leq n$. Let $2 \leq k \leq n$ and consider the event $Z \leq k$. In every realisation of the protocol there will be at most k positions that satisfy $Z \leq k$: at position $k+1$ we will certainly have $k+1$ experts. We conclude that:

$$\Pr(Z \leq k) \leq \frac{k}{n}. \tag{3}$$

Upper Bound for Gossiping. Assume that we are at time $T_{v\leftarrow n}$. We now modify the original process as follows: each time a non-expert a communicates with an expert, a becomes expert. Let T_{UB} be the completion time for the new process. The new process cannot end before gossiping is achieved, thus:

$$T \leq T_{v\leftarrow n} + T_{\text{UB}}. \tag{4}$$

Assume that $Z = r$. Let U_i be the number of calls, in the new process, for one more person to become expert, when i persons are experts ($r \leq i \leq n-1$). Then we have that $T_{\text{UB}} = U_r + U_{r+1} + \ldots + U_{n-1}$. We have that:

$$E(T_{\text{UB}}) = \sum_{r=2}^{n} P(Z=r) \sum_{i=r}^{n-1} U_i = \sum_{i=2}^{n-1} U_i \sum_{r=2}^{i} P(Z=r) = \sum_{i=2}^{n-1} U_i P(Z \leq i).$$

And by (3) and (4) we get:

$$\mathbb{E}\left(T_n\right) \leq \mathbb{E}\left(T_{v\leftarrow n}\right) + \sum_{i=2}^{n-1} U_i \frac{i}{n}. \tag{5}$$

Now observe that for the U_i's we can apply the same analysis as for the $T_{v\to i}$'s. Thus, when we have i experts in the new process, the probability of one more person becoming expert is again p_i. So any bounds for the p_i's will lead us to bounds for the U_i's.

Using similar arguments, John Haigh [16] was able to find lower bounds for the expectation of ANY which lead to: $\mathbb{E}\left(T_n^{\mathsf{ANY}}\right) \approx \frac{3}{2}n\log n + \mathcal{O}\left(n\right)$. Since, these arguments do not yield any useful for SPI and TOK we do not present them here.

4   The Protocols TOK and SPI

4.1   Bounding $\mathbb{E}\left(T_{v\to n}^{\mathsf{TOK}}\right)$ and $\mathbb{E}\left(T_{v\to n}^{\mathsf{SPI}}\right)$

In this section the T-variables refer to TOK and SPI. Assume that we are in phase i and that the sets $\mathcal{K}$ and $\mathsf{Ag}\setminus\mathcal{K}$ contain x and y agents that have a token respectively (Fig. 2). The set $\mathcal{K}$ should contain at least the token initially held by v, but the set $\mathsf{Ag}\setminus\mathcal{K}$ may contain no tokens at all. Each of the x agents can make $(n-i)$ useful calls and each of the y agents can make i useful calls. Further only $x+y$ agents are allowed to make calls. So, the transition probability depends on x and y:

$$p_i^{\mathsf{P}} = p_i(x,y) = \frac{x(n-i)+yi}{(x+y)(n-1)},\ 1\le x\le i,\ 0\le y\le n-i, 1\le i\le n-1. \quad (6)$$

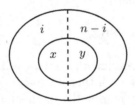

Fig. 2. The situation in phase i for protocols TOK and SPI. There are i agents that know V, but only x of them have a token. There are $n-i$ agents that do not know V, but only y of them have a token.

We have that:

$$\frac{\partial p_i(x,y)}{\partial x} = \frac{y(n-2i)}{(x+y)^2(n-1)} \quad \text{and} \quad \frac{\partial p_i(x,y)}{\partial y} = \frac{x(2i-n)}{(x+y)^2(n-1)}.$$

So, for $1\le i\le \frac{n}{2}$, p_i is increasing on x and decreasing on y. Also, for $\frac{n}{2}< i\le n-1$, p_i is decreasing on x and increasing on y. Taking into account that p_i is defined for $1\le x\le i$ and for $0\le y\le n-i$ we obtain:

$$p_i(1,n-i)\le p_i(x,y)\le p_i(i,0), \qquad\qquad \text{for } 1\le i\le \frac{n}{2}$$

$$p_i(i,0)\le p_i(x,y)\le p_i(1,n-i), \qquad\qquad \text{for } \frac{n}{2}< i\le n-1.$$

And from Lemma 2 we get:

$$\frac{1}{p_i(i,0)} \leq T_{v \to i} \leq \frac{1}{p_i(1,n-i)}, \qquad \text{for } 1 \leq i \leq \frac{n}{2} \qquad (7)$$

$$\frac{1}{p_i(1,n-i)} \leq T_{v \to i} \leq \frac{1}{p_i(i,0)}, \qquad \text{for } \frac{n}{2} < i \leq n-1. \qquad (8)$$

We have that:

$$\mathbb{E}\left(T_{v \to n}\right) = \sum_{i=1}^{n-1} \mathbb{E}\left(T_{v \to i}\right) = \sum_{i=1}^{\lfloor \frac{n}{2} \rfloor} \mathbb{E}\left(T_{v \to i}\right) + \sum_{i=\lfloor \frac{n}{2} \rfloor+1}^{n-1} \mathbb{E}\left(T_{v \to i}\right).$$

So, by (7) and (8):

$$\sum_{i=1}^{\lfloor \frac{n}{2} \rfloor} \frac{1}{p_i(i,0)} + \sum_{i>\lfloor \frac{n}{2} \rfloor}^{n-1} \frac{1}{p_i(1,n-i)} \leq \mathbb{E}\left(T_{v \to n}\right) \leq \sum_{i=1}^{\lfloor \frac{n}{2} \rfloor} \frac{1}{p_i(1,n-i)} + \sum_{i>\lfloor \frac{n}{2} \rfloor}^{n-1} \frac{1}{p_i(i,0)}.$$

And by Lemma 3 (ii.)–(v.) and (1) we have that for large n:

$$1.38n + \log n + \Theta(1) \leq \mathbb{E}\left(T_{v \to n}^{\mathsf{SPI,TOK}}\right) \leq 2n \log n - \Theta(n). \qquad (9)$$

4.2   Bounding $\mathbb{E}\left(T_n^{\mathsf{SPI,TOK}}\right)$

Because of Corollary 1, Eq. (9) holds for $\mathbb{E}\left(T_{v \leftarrow n}\right)$ too. Therefore we can continue the application of Haigh's method for protocols SPI and TOK.

The Upper Bound. By (5) and by recalling that (7) and (8) hold for the U_i's too we get:

$$\mathbb{E}\left(T_n\right) \leq \mathbb{E}\left(T_{v \leftarrow n}\right) + \sum_{i=2}^{\lfloor \frac{n}{2} \rfloor} U_i \frac{i}{n} + \sum_{i=2}^{\lfloor \frac{n}{2} \rfloor+1} U_i \frac{i}{n}$$

$$\leq \mathbb{E}\left(T_{v \leftarrow n}\right) + \sum_{i=2}^{\lfloor \frac{n}{2} \rfloor} \frac{i}{n p_i(1,n-i)} + \sum_{i=\lfloor \frac{n}{2} \rfloor+1}^{n-1} \frac{i}{n p_i(i,0)}.$$

By (1) and Lemma 3 (iv.)–(vii.) we get the upper bound:

$$\mathbb{E}\left(T_n^{\mathsf{SPI,TOK}}\right) \leq 3n \log n - \Theta(n).$$

5   The Protocols CO and LNS

The lack of infinite call sequences in CO and LNS, makes one believe that the expected duration of the processes we study is faster in these protocols. This might be true, but as we will show in this section obtaining bounds for CO and LNS seems much harder than for ANY, TOK and SPI.

Assume that during an execution of CO or LNS we are in phase i. It is possible that all the calls inside the sets $\mathcal{K}$ and $\mathsf{Ag} \setminus \mathcal{K}$ have been selected and therefore are not available any more. This means that the any selection of an available call leads to one more agent learning V which implies that $p_i = 1$; and this can happen for any value of i. So, in the case of CO and LNS we cannot obtain a useful upper bound for the transition probability.

Now we will provide some examples of CO and LNS-call sequences which lead to phase i and leave very little useful and too many available calls. This implies that the transition probability can take very small values in CO and LNS, which will lead to useless bounds.

In CO it is possible to reach phase i with the following sequence of calls:

- First, we make all the possible calls between the agents in $\mathcal{K}$ and the agents in $\mathsf{Ag} \setminus \mathcal{K}$ with the exception of the $n - i$ calls between v and the agents $\mathsf{Ag} \setminus \mathcal{K}$ (these are $(i-1)(n-1)$ calls).
- Then we use $i - 1$ calls to spread V to all the agents in $\mathcal{K}$

Now, the transition probability is:

$$p_i^{\mathsf{CO}} = \frac{2(n - i)}{n(n - 1) - 2(i - 1)(n - i) - 2(i - 1)}.$$

So the minimum value of the transition probability is at most p_i^{CO}. So, if we apply Haigh's method, we will find an upper bound for $\mathbb{E}\left(T_{v \to n}^{\mathsf{CO}}\right)$ that is at least:

$$\sum_{i=1}^{n-1} p_i^{\mathsf{CO}} = \frac{1}{2}n(n - 1)H_{n-1} - (n - 1)(n - 2) - (n - 1)H_{n-1} + n - 1$$

which is a trivial upper bound since for sufficiently large n it is greater than $\binom{n}{2}$, i.e. the maximum number of calls.

Assume that $v = a_1$ and that $\mathcal{K} = \{a_1, \ldots, a_i\}$. In LNS it is possible to reach phase i with the following sequence of calls:

$$
\begin{array}{ll}
a_2 a_{i+1}; \quad a_2 a_{i+2}; \quad \ldots; \quad a_2 a_n & (a_2 \text{ collects all the secrets from } \mathsf{Ag} \setminus \mathcal{K}) \\
a_{i+1} a_3; \quad a_{i+1} a_4; \quad \ldots; \quad a_{i+1} a_i & (a_{i+1} \text{ collects all the secrets from } \mathcal{K}) \\
a_{i+1} a_{i+2}; \, a_{i+1} a_{i+3}; \, \ldots; \, a_{i+1} a_n & (a_{i+1} \text{ spreads the secrets of } \mathcal{K} \text{ to } \mathsf{Ag} \setminus \mathcal{K}) \\
a_1 a_2; & \\
a_2 a_3; \quad a_2 a_4; \quad \ldots; \quad a_2 a_i & (\text{the agents in } \mathcal{K} \text{ learn } V \text{ and} \\
& \quad \text{the secrets in } \mathsf{Ag} \setminus \mathcal{K})
\end{array}
$$

The reader can verify that after the above call sequence, no agent in $\mathsf{Ag} \setminus \mathcal{K}$ knows V. So it is indeed a call sequence that leads to phase i. After the above call sequence, the agents can make the following calls:

a_1	a_2	a_3	a_4	...	a_{i-2}	a_{i-1}	a_i	a_{i+1}	a_{i+2}		a_{i+3}	...	a_{n-2}	a_{n-1}	a_n
$i-2$	0	$i-3$	$i-4$	...	2	1	0	1		$n-i-1$	$n-i-2$	...	3	2	1

Now the available calls are $\frac{(i-2)(i-1)}{2} + \frac{(n-i-1)(n-i)}{2} + 1$ and the useful only $n-i$ (the only communications allowed between $\mathsf{Ag} \setminus \mathcal{K}$ and $\mathcal{K}$ are all the call from $\mathsf{Ag} \setminus \mathcal{K}$ to a_1). So, the transition probability is:

$$p_i^{\mathsf{LNS}} = \frac{n-i}{\frac{(i-2)(i-1)}{2} + \frac{(n-i-1)(n-i)}{2} + 1}.$$

So, any upper bound for $\mathbb{E}\left(T_{v\rightarrow}^{\mathsf{LNS}}\right)$ will be at least:

$$\sum_{i=1}^{n-1} p_i^{\mathsf{LNS}} = \frac{(n-2)(n-1)}{2}(H_{n-1}-1) - \frac{(n-1)^2}{2} + \frac{n(n-1)}{4} + H_{n-1} > \binom{n}{2}$$

which is again a trivial upper bound.

We conclude that an immediate application of Haigh's method in CO and LNS seems impossible, therefore bounding the expectation of CO and LNS seems much harder than bounding the expectation of the other protocols.

As we already observed in [11] the execution of CO can be modelled by an undirected graph where the nodes are agents and there is an edge from a to b if there has been a call between a and b. This leads us to the following theorem, for which we give only a proof sketch.

Theorem 2 *Let c_n be such that $\lim_{n\rightarrow\infty} c_n = -\infty$. Then, for $n \rightarrow \infty$:*

1. $\mathbb{E}\left(T_{v\rightarrow n}^{\mathsf{CO}}\right) \geq \frac{1}{2}n(\log n + c_n)$
2. $\mathbb{E}\left(T_n^{\mathsf{CO}}\right) \geq \frac{1}{2}n(\log n + \log\log n + c_n)$

Proof Using some standard results from random graph theory [14] we can show that when at most $\frac{1}{2}n(\log n + c_n)$ edges have been added in the random graph that models the execution of CO (i.e. when at most $\frac{1}{2}n(\log n + c_n)$ calls have taken place), then the random graph contains isolated nodes with high probability. Since isolated nodes correspond to agents who have not communicated with anyone, this means that broadcasting and gathering cannot be successful. This proves 1.

Similarly, we can prove that when the aforementioned random graph contains at most $\frac{1}{2}n(\log n + \log\log n + c_n)$ edges, then it contains at least two nodes of degree at most one with high probability. This means that there are two agents, call them a and b, that have made at most 1 call each. In order for a to learn B, a's single call should have taken place before b's single call. Similarly, in order for b to learn A, b's call should have preceded a's. This contradiction proves 2. □

6   Conclusion and Further Work

In Table 1 we present all the known bounds for sequential information dissemination. Observe that the transition probability of ANY is a special case of the transition probability for SPI and TOK (one can see this by setting $x = i$ and $y = n - i$ in (6)). So, any bound for SPI and TOK is also a bound for ANY. This explains why our bounds for SPI and TOK are not tight.

Table 1. All the known bounds for sequential gathering, broadcasting and gossiping. The *trivial bounds are in italic font and it also holds that* $\lim_{n \to \infty} = -\infty$.

	Lower bound broadcasting gathering	Upper bound broadcasting gathering	Lower bound gossiping	Upper bound gossiping
ANY	$n \log n + \Theta(n)$		$\frac{3}{2}n \log n + \mathcal{O}(n)$	
SPI TOK	$1.38n + \log n + \Theta(1)$	$2n \log n - \Theta(n)$	$2n - 4$	$3n \log n - \Theta(n)$
CO	$\frac{1}{2}n(\log n + c_n)$	$\binom{n}{2}$	$\frac{1}{2}n(\log n + \log \log n + c_n)$	$\binom{n}{2}$
LNS	$n - 1$	$\binom{n}{2}$	$2n - 4$	$\binom{n}{2}$

By simulating the execution of the protocols, we obtained the results in Fig. 3 which lead us to the following conjecture:

$$\mathbb{E}\left(T_n^{\mathsf{LNS}}\right) < \mathbb{E}\left(T_n^{\mathsf{CO}}\right) < \mathbb{E}\left(T_n^{\mathsf{ANY}}\right) < \mathbb{E}\left(T_n^{\mathsf{SPI,TOK}}\right).$$

It is natural to think that our protocols try to improve the performance of ANY, which is clearly the simplest and most intuitive sequential protocol. Having

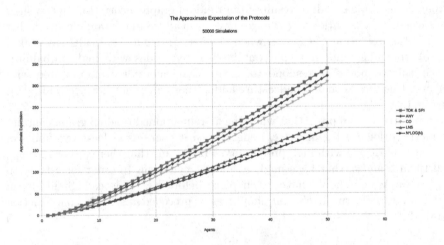

Fig. 3. The simulated expected duration of the protocols

this in mind we can draw the following information from Fig. 3: if the protocol condition simply restricts the number of available calls, without any guarantee that the amount of information will grow (as it is the case for TOK, SPI and CO) then the protocol does not necessarily become faster. However, if the protocol condition guarantees than at least one agent will learn something new (like in the case of LNS), the protocol can become very fast.

Acknowledgements. We acknowledge financial support from ERC project EPS 313360. We are also grateful to Aris Pagourtzis for useful discussions.

References

1. Apt, K.R., Wojtczak, D.: Decidability of fair termination of gossip protocols. In: Proceedings of the IWIL Workshop and LPAR Short Presentations, pp. 73–85. Kalpa Publications (2017)
2. Apt, K.R., Wojtczak, D.: On the computational complexity of gossip protocols. In: Proceedings of the Twenty-Sixth International Joint Conference on Artificial Intelligence, IJCAI 2017, Melbourne, Australia, 19–25 August 2017 , pp. 765–771 (2017)
3. Apt, K.R., Grossi, D., van der Hoek, W.: Epistemic protocols for distributed gossiping. In: Proceedings of 15th TARK (2015)
4. Attamah, M., van Ditmarsch, H., Grossi, D., van der Hoek, W.: The pleasure of gossip. In: Başkent, C., Moss, L.S., Ramanujam, R. (eds.) Rohit Parikh on Logic, Language and Society. OCL, vol. 11, pp. 145–163. Springer, Cham (2017). https://doi.org/10.1007/978-3-319-47843-2_9
5. Attamah, M., Van Ditmarsch, H., Grossi, D., van der Hoek, W.: Knowledge and gossip. In: Proceedings of the Twenty-first European Conference on Artificial Intelligence, pp. 21–26. IOS Press (2014)
6. Berenbrink, P., Elsässer, R., Friedetzky, T., Nagel, L., Sauerwald, T.: Faster coupon collecting via replication with applications in gossiping. In: Murlak, F., Sankowski, P. (eds.) MFCS 2011. LNCS, vol. 6907, pp. 72–83. Springer, Heidelberg (2011). https://doi.org/10.1007/978-3-642-22993-0_10
7. Boyd, D.W., Steele, J.M.: Random exchanges of information. J. Appl. Prob. **16**, 657–661 (1979)
8. Deb, S., Médard, M., Choute, C.: Algebraic gossip: a network coding approach to optimal multiple rumor mongering. IEEE Trans. Inf. Theory **52**(6), 2486–2507 (2006)
9. van Ditmarsch, H., van Eijck, J., Pardo, P., Ramezanian, R., Schwarzentruber, F.: Epistemic protocols for dynamic gossip. J. Appl. Log. **20**, 1–31 (2017)
10. van Ditmarsch, H., van Eijck, J., Pardo, P., Ramezanian, R., Schwarzentruber, F.: Dynamic gossip. CoRR abs/1511.00867 (2015)
11. van Ditmarsch, H., Kokkinis, I., Stockmarr, A.: Reachability and expectation in gossiping. In: An, B., Bazzan, A., Leite, J., Villata, S., van der Torre, L. (eds.) PRIMA 2017. LNCS (LNAI), vol. 10621, pp. 93–109. Springer, Cham (2017). https://doi.org/10.1007/978-3-319-69131-2_6
12. Doerr, B., Friedrich, T., Sauerwald, T.: Quasirandom rumor spreading. ACM Trans. Algorithms **11**(2), 1–35 (2014)
13. Ferrante, M., Saltalamacchia, M.: The coupon collector's problem. Materials Matemátics 2014(2), 35 (2014), www.mat.uab.cat/matmat

14. Frieze, A., Karoński, M.: Introduction to Random Graphs. Cambridge University Press, Cambridge (2015)
15. Haeupler, B.: Simple, fast and deterministic gossip and rumor spreading. J. ACM **62**(6), 47 (2015)
16. Haigh, J.: Random exchanges of information. J. Appl. Probab. **18**, 743–746 (1981)
17. Hedetniemi, S., Hedetniemi, S., Liestman, A.: A survey of gossiping and broadcasting in communication networks. Networks **18**, 319–349 (1988)
18. Hurkens, C.A.: Spreading gossip efficiently. Nieuw Archief voor Wiskunde **1**, 208–210 (2000)
19. Moon, J.: Random exchanges of information. Nieuw Archief voor Wiskunde **20**, 246–249 (1972)
20. Tijdeman, R.: On a telephone problem. Nieuw Archief voor Wiskunde **3**(19), 188–192 (1971)

Decidable Term-Modal Logics

Eugenio Orlandelli$^{(\boxtimes)}$ and Giovanna Corsi

Department of Philosophy and Communication Studies, University of Bologna,
Via Zamboni 38, 40126 Bologna, Italy
{eugenio.orlandelli,giovanna.corsi}unibo.it

Abstract. The paper considers *term-modal logics* and introduces some decidable fragments thereof. In particular, two fragments will be introduced: one that simulates monotone non-normal logics and another one that simulates normal multi-agent epistemic logics with quantification over groups of agents. These logics are defined semantically. Then, each of them is proof-theoretically characterized by a labelled calculus with good structural properties. Finally, we prove that each fragment considered is decidable, and we characterize the complexity of the validity problem for some of them.

Keywords: Term-modal logics · Monotone modalities
Multi-agent epistemic logics · Decidability · Sequent calculi

1 Introduction

Propositional multi-modal epistemic logics (MELs) have been a key tool for reasoning about knowledge and belief in multi-agent systems (MASs), cf. [9]. Given a set of agents $\{1, \ldots, n\}$, we have formulas $\Box_i \phi$, which may be read as *agent i knows that* ϕ, and given a group of agents G – i.e. a subset of the set of agents – we may have formulas such as $E_G \phi$, $D_G \phi$, and $C_G \phi$ which may be read, respectively, as *every G knows/it is distributed/common knowledge among the Gs that* ϕ. Most applications are based on the multi-agent logic of belief **KD45^n** or on the multi-agent logic of knowledge **S5^n** – e.g., interpreted systems [9] are captured by **S5^n**; but in some cases also other logics, such as **K^n** or **S4^n**, are used. One key aspect of these logics is that they are decidable and have a good computational complexity: if $n \geq 2$, the validity problem is PSPACE-complete if common knowledge is omitted, else it is EXPTIME-complete [16].

Even if MELs allow us to reason about agents' knowledge, they do not allow to reason about agents and groups thereof. The problem, roughly, is that agents are (denoted by) a finite set of indexes that, so to say, live outside of the logic. Therefore, as it is noted in [15], we can only reason about a finite and known set of agents where each name (i.e. index) denotes a different agent and where

Thanks are due to three anonymous referees and to the audience at EUMAS 2017, especially to Valentin Goranko, for helpful comments.

F. Belardinelli and E. Argente (Eds.): EUMAS 2017/AT 2017, LNAI 10767, pp. 147–162, 2018.
https://doi.org/10.1007/978-3-030-01713-2_11

the naming relation is common knowledge. One elegant way of overcoming these limitations is provided by term-modal logics (TMLs) [10]. These are first-order epistemic logics with increasing domains and rigid designators, cf. [2,3], where each epistemic operator is indexed by a term. The term-modal operator $[x]$ – to be read as *the agent (denoted by the possibly bound) x knows that* – is semantically modeled by a three place relation of x-dependent compatibility relation. TMLs enhance our ability to reason about agents and groups in that (i) we do not have to reason about a finite and known set of agents, and (ii) we can express:

- knowledge of a particular agent: $[x]A$ means that *x knows that A*;
- knowledge of a generic agent: $\exists x[x]A$ means that *someone knows that A*;
- knowledge of a first-order definable group: $\forall x(Gx \supset [x]A)$ means that *every member of the group G knows that A*;
- relations between groups of agents: $\forall x(Gx \supset Hx) \wedge \forall y(Hy \supset [y]A)$ means that *each G is an H and each H knows A*, and it entails that $\forall x(Gx \supset [x]A)$.

Despite their great expressive power, the TMLs considered in [10] are not suited for practical applications because: (i) [10] introduces only logics where the negative introspection axiom 5 is not valid, and (ii) being extensions of first-order modal logics, TMLs are undecidable.[1]

We first show that TMLs with any combination of the axioms $D, T, 4$, and 5, as well as their extensions with interaction axioms like the Barcan Formulas, can be proof-theoretically characterized by labelled sequent calculi. This would allow us to introduce the term-modal version of useful quantified MELs such as, e.g., the objectual quantified interpreted systems considered in [2]; see also [5,10,15,19] for scenarios where term-modal-like logics can be applied. Then, we introduce two decidable fragments of TMLs. The first fragment has very limited expressive power, but it is interesting in that it simulates monotone non-normal logics [4,17,25] in a way that is more natural than that in [13,18]. The second fragment – which extends both MELs and the epistemic logic with names $\mathbf{AX}_{\mathcal{N}}$ of [15] – allows us to reason about the propositional knowledge of individual agents and of groups of agents denoted by monadic predicates. Moreover, it allows us to express whether individual agents are members of these groups or not (but not to reason about the relations between groups). The logics defined over this latter fragment are interesting for reasoning about MASs in that they increase the expressive power of MELs without thereby increasing their complexity.

The paper proceeds as follows. Section 2 introduces TMLs and shows that they can be proof-theoretically characterized by labelled sequent calculi with the good structural properties that are typical of **G3**-style calculi. Then, in Sects. 3 and 4, we present two decidable fragments of TMLs. More specifically, in Sect. 3, we consider non-normal monotone logics based on a generalization of multi-relational semantics [4]; we introduce TMLs expressing them; and we characterize their complexity. In Sect. 4, we consider TMLs that simulate MELs with

---

[1] See [19] for a term-modal like extension of the logic of belief **KD45**; and see [5–7] for extensions of TMLs, called indexed epistemic logics, with non-rigid designators.

explicit quantification over groups of agents; we show that they are decidable; and we characterize the complexity of (most of) them. We conclude, in Sect. 5, by sketching some future direction of research.

2   Term-Modal Logics

2.1   Syntax and Semantics

Language. Let us consider a first-order language $\mathcal{L}$ whose signature contains only predicate symbols of any arity n (each result of the paper can be extended straightforwardly to a signature containing also individual constants). Let Var be an infinite set of variables. The primitive logical symbols are $\neg, \wedge, \forall$, and $[\cdot]$. $\mathcal{L}$-formulas are defined by the following grammar, where P^n is an arbitrary n-ary predicate symbol and $y, x_1, \ldots, x_n \in Var$,

$$A ::= P^n x_1, \ldots, x_n \mid \neg A \mid A \wedge A \mid \forall y A \mid [y]A. \tag{$\mathcal{L}$}$$

We use the following metavariables, all possibly with numerical subscripts: x, y, z for variables; p for atomic formulas; and A, B, C for formulas. The formulas $\bot, \top, A \vee B, A \supset B, \exists x A$ are defined as usual, and $\langle x \rangle A := \neg [x] \neg A$. The notions of *free and bound occurrences of a variable* are defined as expected; in particular, the displayed occurrence of x in $[x]A$ is free, and each occurrence of x in $\forall x A$ is bound. The *height* of a formula, $He(A)$, is the height of the longest branch of its generation tree; its *length*, $Le(A)$, is the number of nodes of its generation tree.

We use $\equiv$ to denote syntactic identity. Without loss of generality, we assume that the variables occurring free in a formula are different from the bound ones, and we identify formulas that differ only in the name of bound variables. By $A(y/x)$ we denote the formula that is obtained from A by substituting each (free) occurrence of x with an occurrence of y. In particular, we have that $([z]A)(y/x) \equiv [z(y/x)](A(y/x))$. Having identified formulas differing only in the name of bound variables, we can assume that y is free for x in A whenever we write $A(y/x)$ – that is to say, no free occurrence of any variable becomes bound after having applied a substitution.

Semantics. We mostly follow [10] in introducing the semantics. The main novelties are (i) that we consider a more general varying domain semantics instead of an increasing domains semantics where the Converse Barcan Formula holds in every frame, cf. [3]; and (ii) that we consider also Euclidean frames.

Definition 1 (Frame). *A frame is a tuple $\mathcal{F} := < \mathcal{W}, \mathcal{U}, \mathcal{D}, \{\overset{a}{\rightsquigarrow} : a \in \mathcal{U}\} >$, where:*

1. *$\mathcal{W}$ is a non-empty set of worlds, denoted by $u, v, w, \ldots$;*
2. *$\mathcal{U}$ is a non-empty set of objects/agents, denoted by $a, b, c, \ldots$. $\mathcal{U}$ is called the outer domain of $\mathcal{F}$;*

3. $\mathcal{D}$ is a set containing, for each $w \in \mathcal{W}$, a possibly empty subset of $\mathcal{U}$ denoted by D_w. D_w is called the inner domain of w and it represents the objects existing at w;

4. each $\overset{a}{\rightsquigarrow}$ is an agent-dependent compatibility relation between worlds – $\overset{a}{\rightsquigarrow} \subseteq \mathcal{W} \times a \times \mathcal{W}$ – for which we use infix notation. Intuitively, $w \overset{a}{\rightsquigarrow} v$ means that world v is compatible with what agent a knows in world w.

Definition 2 (Models and assignments). A model (based on $\mathcal{F}$) is a pair $\mathcal{M} := \langle \mathcal{F}, \mathcal{I} \rangle$ where $\mathcal{F}$ is a frame and $\mathcal{I}$ is an interpretation function mapping each n-ary $\mathcal{L}$-predicate to a set of $n + 1$-tuples made of a world and of n objects from the outer domain $\mathcal{U}$. Formally $\mathcal{I}(P^n) \subseteq \{\langle w, a_1, \ldots, a_n \rangle : w \in \mathcal{W} \,\&\, a_i \in \mathcal{U}\}$. An assignment is a mapping from Var to $\mathcal{U}$. We use σ, τ, ν to denote assignments. By $\sigma^{x \triangleright a}$ we denote the assignment that behaves like σ save for the variable x that is mapped to the object a.

Definition 3 (Satisfaction). Satisfaction of a formula A at a world w of a model $\mathcal{M}$ under the assignment σ, to be denoted by $\sigma \vDash_w^{\mathcal{M}} A$, is defined by:

$$\sigma \vDash_w^{\mathcal{M}} P^n x_1, \ldots, x_n \quad iff \quad \langle w, \sigma(x_1), \ldots, \sigma(x_n) \rangle \in \mathcal{I}(P^n)$$

$$\sigma \vDash_w^{\mathcal{M}} \neg B \quad iff \quad \sigma \nvDash_w^{\mathcal{M}} B$$

$$\sigma \vDash_w^{\mathcal{M}} B \wedge C \quad iff \quad \sigma \vDash_w^{\mathcal{M}} B \text{ and } \sigma \vDash_w^{\mathcal{M}} C$$

$$\sigma \vDash_w^{\mathcal{M}} \forall x B \quad iff \quad \text{for all } a \in D_w, \sigma^{x \triangleright a} \vDash_w^{\mathcal{M}} B$$

$$\sigma \vDash_w^{\mathcal{M}} [x]B \quad iff \quad \text{for all } v \in \mathcal{W}, w \overset{\sigma(x)}{\rightsquigarrow} v \text{ implies } \sigma \vDash_v^{\mathcal{M}} B$$

The notions of truth in a world, $\vDash_w^{\mathcal{M}} A$, truth in a model, $\vDash^{\mathcal{M}} A$, validity in a frame, $\mathcal{F} \vDash A$, and validity in a class $\mathcal{C}$ of frames, $\mathcal{C} \vDash A$, are as usual.

Logics. By an $\mathcal{L}$-*logic* we mean the set of all $\mathcal{L}$-formulas that are valid in some class of frames. In this paper we will consider all $\mathcal{L}$-logics that are defined by some combination of the properties in the following correspondence results, whose straightforward proofs can be omitted.

Proposition 4 (Correspondence results). *The following formulas are valid in all and only the frames satisfying the following properties, where $w, v, u \in \mathcal{W}$ and $a, b \in \mathcal{U}$ (the universal closure of T–BF would correspond to the same properties restricted to agents of the inner domains: $\forall a \in D_w$ instead of $\forall a \in \mathcal{U}$),*

- $T := [x]A \supset A$ iff $\mathcal{F}$ is reflexive: $\forall a \forall w (w \overset{a}{\rightsquigarrow} w)$
- $D := \neg[x]\bot$ iff $\mathcal{F}$ is serial: $\forall a \forall w \exists v (w \overset{a}{\rightsquigarrow} v)$
- $4 := [x]A \supset [x][x]A$ iff $\mathcal{F}$ is transitive: $\forall a \forall w, v, u (w \overset{a}{\rightsquigarrow} v \,\&\, v \overset{a}{\rightsquigarrow} u \supset w \overset{a}{\rightsquigarrow} u)$
- $5 := \langle x \rangle A \supset [x]\langle x \rangle A$ iff $\mathcal{F}$ is Euclidean: $\forall a \forall w, v, u (w \overset{a}{\rightsquigarrow} v \,\&\, w \overset{a}{\rightsquigarrow} u \supset v \overset{a}{\rightsquigarrow} u)$
- $NE := \forall x A \supset \exists x A$ iff $\mathcal{F}$ has non empty domains: $\forall w (D_w \neq \varnothing)$
- $UI := \forall x A \supset A(y/x)$ iff $\mathcal{F}$ has single domain: $\forall w (D_w = \mathcal{U})$
- $CBF := [x]\forall y A \supset \forall y [x]A$ iff $\mathcal{F}$ has increasing domains:
  $\forall a, b \forall w, v (w \overset{a}{\rightsquigarrow} v \,\&\, b \in D_w \supset b \in D_v)$
- $BF := \forall y [x]A \supset [x]\forall y A$ iff $\mathcal{F}$ has decreasing domains:
  $\forall a, b \forall w, v (w \overset{a}{\rightsquigarrow} v \,\&\, b \in D_v \supset b \in D_w)$

We use the standard names for the $\mathcal{L}$-extensions of propositional logics in the cube of normal modalities. For example, **K** denotes the set of $\mathcal{L}$-formulas valid in the class of all frames; **T** denotes the set of $\mathcal{L}$-formulas valid in all reflexive frames; and **S5** denotes the set of $\mathcal{L}$-formulas valid in all reflexive, transitive, and Euclidean frames. Moreover, if **X** is the name of one of the $\mathcal{L}$-logics thus defined, $\mathbf{X} \oplus \mathbf{NE}$ is the logic of all non empty domains **X**-frames, and analogously for their extensions with UI, CBF, BF, and the combinations thereof. We use **L** for an arbitrary $\mathcal{L}$-logic among the ones we are considering.

2.2 Proof Systems

Labelled Sequent Calculi for TMLs. We are now going to introduce labelled sequent calculi that characterize $\mathcal{L}$-logics. We assume the reader is acquainted with sequent calculi. The calculi for TMLs are like the ones for propositional and quantified modal logics [20, Sects. 11 and 12.1], save that two-place relational atoms, wRv, are replaced by three-places compatibility atoms, $w \overset{x}{\twoheadrightarrow} v$. More precisely, we introduce an infinite set of fresh variables, called *(world) labels*, for which we use the metavariables w, v, u. A *labelled sequent* is an expression $\Omega; \Gamma \Rightarrow \Delta$, where Ω is a multiset of *domain atoms* $x \in w$ – meaning that x is in the inner domain of world w – and of *compatibility atoms* $w \overset{x}{\twoheadrightarrow} v$ – meaning that v is compatible with what agent x knows in w; and where Γ and Δ are multisets of *labelled formulas* $w : A$ – meaning that the $\mathcal{L}$-formula A holds at w.

The rules for the calculus **G3tm.K**, which characterizes the $\mathcal{L}$-logic **K**, are given in Table 1; the label u in rule $R\square$, as well as the variable z in $R\forall$, is an *eigenvariable* – i.e., it cannot occur free in the conclusion of that rule instance.

Table 1. Sequent calculus **G3tm.K**

Initial sequents:

$\Omega; w : p, \Gamma \Rightarrow \Delta, w : p \quad (p \text{ atomic})$

Logical rules:

$$\dfrac{\Omega; \Gamma \Rightarrow \Delta, w : A}{\Omega; w : \neg A, \Gamma \Rightarrow \Delta} \; L\neg \qquad\qquad \dfrac{\Omega; w : A, \Gamma \Rightarrow \Delta}{\Omega; \Gamma \Rightarrow \Delta, w : \neg A} \; R\neg$$

$$\dfrac{\Omega; w : A, w : B, \Gamma \Rightarrow \Delta}{\Omega; w : A \wedge B, \Gamma \Rightarrow \Delta} \; L\wedge \qquad\qquad \dfrac{\Omega; \Gamma \Rightarrow \Delta, w : A \quad \Omega; \Gamma \Rightarrow \Delta, w : B}{\Omega; \Gamma \Rightarrow \Delta, w : A \wedge B} \; R\wedge$$

$$\dfrac{y \in w, \Omega; w : A(y/x), w : \forall x A, \Gamma \Rightarrow \Delta}{y \in w, \Omega; w : \forall x A, \Gamma \Rightarrow \Delta} \; L\forall \qquad\qquad \dfrac{z \in w, \Omega; \Gamma \Rightarrow \Delta, w : A(z/x)}{\Omega; \Gamma \Rightarrow \Delta, w : \forall x A} \; R\forall, z \text{ eig.}$$

$$\dfrac{w \overset{x}{\twoheadrightarrow} v, \Omega; v : A, w : [x]A, \Gamma \Rightarrow \Delta}{w \overset{x}{\twoheadrightarrow} v, \Omega; w : [x]A, \Gamma \Rightarrow \Delta} \; L\square \qquad\qquad \dfrac{w \overset{x}{\twoheadrightarrow} u, \Omega; \Gamma \Rightarrow \Delta, u : A}{\Omega; \Gamma \Rightarrow \Delta, w : [x]A} \; R\square, u \text{ eig.}$$

To obtain calculi for the other $\mathcal{L}$-logics, we use non-logical rules expressing the geometric semantic conditions given in Proposition 4, cf. [20, Sect. 8]. For any $\mathcal{L}$-logic $\mathbf{L}$, the calculus $\mathbf{G3tm.L}$ is obtained by extending $\mathbf{G3tm.K}$ with the non-logical rules from Table 2 that express the semantic conditions defining $\mathbf{L}$. The label u in rule L_D and the variable z in rule L_{NE} are *eigenvariables*. If a calculus contains rule L_5, it also contains its contracted instances L_{5c}. The other rules in Table 2 are such that we do not have do add contracted instances.

Table 2. Non-logical rules

$$\frac{w \overset{x}{\twoheadrightarrow} w, \Omega; \Gamma \Rightarrow \Delta}{\Omega; \Gamma \Rightarrow \Delta} \, L_T \qquad \frac{v \overset{x}{\twoheadrightarrow} u, w \overset{x}{\twoheadrightarrow} v, w \overset{x}{\twoheadrightarrow} u, \Omega; \Gamma \Rightarrow \Delta}{w \overset{x}{\twoheadrightarrow} v, w \overset{x}{\twoheadrightarrow} u, \Omega; \Gamma \Rightarrow \Delta} \, L_5 \qquad \frac{v \overset{x}{\twoheadrightarrow} v, w \overset{x}{\twoheadrightarrow} v, \Omega; \Gamma \Rightarrow \Delta}{w \overset{x}{\twoheadrightarrow} v, \Omega; \Gamma \Rightarrow \Delta} \, L_{5c}$$

$$\frac{w \overset{x}{\twoheadrightarrow} u, \Omega; \Gamma \Rightarrow \Delta}{\Omega; \Gamma \Rightarrow \Delta} \, L_{D}, u \text{ eig.} \qquad \frac{w \overset{x}{\twoheadrightarrow} u, w \overset{x}{\twoheadrightarrow} v, v \overset{x}{\twoheadrightarrow} u, \Omega; \Gamma \Rightarrow \Delta}{w \overset{x}{\twoheadrightarrow} v, v \overset{x}{\twoheadrightarrow} u, \Omega; \Gamma \Rightarrow \Delta} \, L_4$$

$$\frac{x \in w, \Omega; \Gamma \Rightarrow \Delta}{\Omega; \Gamma \Rightarrow \Delta} \, L_{UI} \qquad \frac{z \in v, z \in w, w \overset{x}{\twoheadrightarrow} v, \Omega; \Gamma \Rightarrow \Delta}{z \in w, w \overset{x}{\twoheadrightarrow} v, \Omega; \Gamma \Rightarrow \Delta} \, L_{CBF}$$

$$\frac{z \in w, \Omega; \Gamma \Rightarrow \Delta}{\Omega; \Gamma \Rightarrow \Delta} \, L_{NE}, z \text{ eig.} \qquad \frac{z \in w, z \in v, w \overset{x}{\twoheadrightarrow} v, \Omega; \Gamma \Rightarrow \Delta}{z \in v, w \overset{x}{\twoheadrightarrow} v, \Omega; \Gamma \Rightarrow \Delta} \, L_{BF}$$

The notion of substitution of world labels is defined as expected. Substitutions are extended to domain and compatibility atoms. Substitutions are extended to sequents by applying them componentwise. A derivation $\mathcal{D}$ of a sequent $\mathcal{S}$ in $\mathbf{G3tm.L}$ is a tree of sequents that is obtained by applying rules of $\mathbf{G3tm.L}$, whose root is $\mathcal{S}$, and whose leaves are initial sequents. The *height* of a derivation $\mathcal{D}$, $He(\mathcal{D})$, is the height of the longest branch of $\mathcal{D}$. We write $\mathbf{G3tm.L} \vdash^{(n)} \mathcal{S}$ if the sequent $\mathcal{S}$ is $\mathbf{G3tm.L}$-derivable (with a derivation of at most height n). We say that a rule is *(height-preserving) admissible* in $\mathbf{G3tm.L}$ if whenever its premisses are $\mathbf{G3tm.L}$-derivable (with height n), its conclusion is $\mathbf{G3tm.L}$-derivable (with at most height n). Finally, in the rules in Tables 1 and 2, the multisets Ω, Γ, and Δ are called *contexts*, the formulas displayed in the conclusion are called *principal* and those displayed only in the premiss(es) are called *active*.

Properties of G3tm.L. We are now going to present some properties of the calculi $\mathbf{G3tm.L}$. The main results are (i) that these calculi have the good structural properties of $\mathbf{G3}$-style calculi – i.e. all rules are invertible, weakening and contraction are height-preserving admissible (hp-admissible), and cut is admissible; and (ii) that each calculus is sound and complete with respect to the corresponding $\mathcal{L}$-logic. Most proofs will be omitted for lack of space. They can be easily obtained by modifying the ones given in [20, Sect. 12.1] for quantified modal logics or the ones given in [6, Sects. 3–4] for indexed epistemic logics.

Lemma 5 (Substitution). *Substitutions are hp-admissible in* $\mathbf{G3tm.L}$:

1. *If* $\mathbf{G3tm.L} \vdash^n \mathcal{S}$ *then* $\mathbf{G3tm.L} \vdash^n \mathcal{S}(y/x)$;
2. *If* $\mathbf{G3tm.L} \vdash^n \mathcal{S}$ *then* $\mathbf{G3tm.L} \vdash^n \mathcal{S}(w/v)$.

Lemma 6 (Initial sequents). *Sequents of shapes (i)* $\Omega; w : \bot, \Gamma \Rightarrow \Delta$, *(ii)* $\Omega; \Gamma \Rightarrow \Delta, w : \top$, *and (iii)* $\Omega; w : A, \Gamma \Rightarrow \Delta, w : A$, *with A arbitrary $\mathcal{L}$-formula and w arbitrary world label, are derivable in* **G3tm.L**.

Lemma 7 (Weakening). *The following rules are hp-admissible in* **G3tm.L***:*

$$\frac{\Omega; \Gamma \Rightarrow \Delta}{\Omega', \Omega; \Gamma \Rightarrow \Delta} \, LW_\Omega \qquad \frac{\Omega; \Gamma \Rightarrow \Delta}{\Omega; \Pi, \Gamma \Rightarrow \Delta} \, LW \qquad \frac{\Omega; \Gamma \Rightarrow \Delta}{\Omega; \Gamma \Rightarrow \Delta, \Sigma} \, RW$$

Lemma 8 (Invertibility). *Each rule of* **G3tm.L** *is hp-invertible.*

Lemma 9 (Contraction). *The following rules are hp-admissible in* **G3tm.L***:*

$$\frac{\Omega', \Omega', \Omega; \Gamma \Rightarrow \Delta}{\Omega', \Omega; \Gamma \Rightarrow \Delta} \, LC_\Omega \qquad \frac{\Omega; \Pi, \Pi, \Gamma \Rightarrow \Delta}{\Omega; \Pi, \Gamma \Rightarrow \Delta} \, LC \qquad \frac{\Omega; \Gamma \Rightarrow \Delta, \Sigma, \Sigma}{\Omega; \Gamma \Rightarrow \Delta, \Sigma} \, RC$$

Theorem 10 (Cut). *The following rule of cut is admissible in* **G3tm.L***:*

$$\frac{\Omega; \Gamma \Rightarrow \Delta, w : A \qquad \Omega'; w : A, \Pi \Rightarrow \Sigma}{\Omega, \Omega'; \Gamma, \Pi \Rightarrow \Delta, \Sigma} \, Cut$$

In order to show that **G3tm.L** is sound and complete with respect to **L**-frames, we extend the notion of validity to sequents. Notice that a semantic proof of the admissibility of the structural rules of inference is an immediate corollary of the completeness theorem.

Definition 11. *Let $\sigma_{\mathcal{F}}$ be a function mapping world labels to worlds of a frame $\mathcal{F}$ and variables to objects of the outer domain of $\mathcal{F}$.*
A sequent $\Omega; \Gamma \Rightarrow \Delta$ is valid on $\mathcal{F}$ iff for all $\sigma_{\mathcal{F}}$ and all $\mathcal{M}$ based on $\mathcal{F}$,
if (i) for all $x \in w$ occurring in Ω we have that $\sigma_{\mathcal{F}}(x) \in D_{\sigma_{\mathcal{F}}(w)}$,

(ii) for all $w \overset{x}{\twoheadrightarrow} v$ occurring in Ω we have that $\sigma_{\mathcal{F}}(w) \overset{\sigma_{\mathcal{F}}(x)}{\twoheadrightarrow} \sigma_{\mathcal{F}}(v)$, and
(iii) for all $w : A$ occurring in Γ we have that $\sigma_{\mathcal{F}} \vDash^{\mathcal{M}}_{\sigma_{\mathcal{F}}(w)} A$,
then there is some $v : B$ occurring in Δ such that $\sigma_{\mathcal{F}} \vDash^{\mathcal{M}}_{\sigma_{\mathcal{F}}(v)} B$.

Theorem 12 (Soundness). *If a sequent S is derivable in* **G3tm.L***, then it is valid in the class of all frames for* **L***.*

Proof (Sketch). The proof is by induction on the height of the derivation $\mathcal{D}$ of S. The base case holds trivially. For the inductive step, we have to check that each rule of **G3tm.L** preserves validity over frames for **L**. Each logical rule preserves validity over any frame. Each non-logical rule preserves validity over frames satisfying the corresponding semantic property; cf. [20, Theorem 12.13]. □

Theorem 13 (Completeness). *If a sequent is valid in the class of all frames for* **L***, then it is derivable in* **G3tm.L***.*

Proof. The proof is in three steps. First, in Definition 14, we define a notion of **L**-saturated branch of a proof-search for a sequent S. Then, with Definition 15 and Lemma 16, we show that an **L**-saturated branch allows us to define a countermodel for S that is based on a frame for **L**. Finally, we give a root first **G3tm.L**-proof-search procedure, Proposition 17, that either gives us a **G3tm.L**-derivation of S – and, by Theorem 12, S is **L**-valid – or it has an **L**-saturated branch – and, therefore, S has a countermodel based on an appropriate frame.   □

Definition 14 (Saturation). *A branch B of a **G3tm.L**-proof-search tree for a sequent S is **L**-saturated if it satisfies the following conditions, where Γ (Δ) is the union of the antecedents (succedents) occurring in that branch,*

1. *no $w : p$ occurs in $\Gamma \cap \Delta$;*
2. *if $w : \neg A$ is in Γ, then $w : A$ is in Δ;*
3. *if $w : \neg A$ is in Δ, then $w : A$ is in Γ;*
4. *if $w : A \wedge B$ is in Γ, then both $w : A$ and $w : B$ are in Γ;*
5. *if $w : A \wedge B$ is in Δ, then at least one of $w : A$ and $w : B$ is in Δ;*
6. *if both $w : \forall x A$ and $y \in w$ are in Γ, then $w : A(y/x)$ is in Γ;*
7. *if $w : \forall x A$ is in Δ, then, for some z, $w : A(z/x)$ is in Δ and $z \in w$ is in Γ;*
8. *if both $w : [x]A$ and $w \overset{x}{\rightsquigarrow} v$ are in Γ, then $v : A$ is in Γ;*
9. *if $w : [x]A$ is in Δ, then, for some u, $u : A$ is in Δ and $w \overset{x}{\rightsquigarrow} u$ is in Γ;*
10. *if R is a non-logical rule of **G3tm.L**, then for any set of principal formulas of R that are in Γ also the corresponding active formulas are in Γ (for some eigenvariable of R, if any).*

Definition 15. *Let B be **L**-saturated. The model $\mathcal{M}^B$ is thus defined: (i) $\mathcal{W}^B$ is the set of world labels occurring in $\Gamma \cup \Delta$; (ii) $\mathcal{U}^B$ is the set of all variables occurring free in $\Gamma \cup \Delta$; (iii) for each $w \in W$, $x \in D_w$ iff $x : w$ is in Γ; (iv) for each $x \in \mathcal{U}$, $w \overset{x}{\rightsquigarrow} v$ iff the formula $w \overset{x}{\rightsquigarrow} v$ is in Γ; (v) $\mathcal{I}^B(P^n)$ is the set of all $n + 1$-tuples $< w, x_1, \ldots, x_n >$ such that the formula $w : P^n x_1, \ldots, x_n$ is in Γ. Given $\mathcal{M}^B$, σ_B denotes the assignment given by the identity mapping.*

Lemma 16. *Let B be an **L**-saturated branch. Then (1) for any $\mathcal{L}$-formula A we have that $\sigma_B \vDash_w^{\mathcal{M}^B} A$ iff $w : A$ is in Γ; and (2) $\mathcal{M}^B$ is based on a frame for **L**.*

Proof (Sketch). The proof of claim (1) is by induction on $He(A)$. The base case holds by construction of $\mathcal{M}^B$ and of σ_B, and the inductive cases depend on Definition 14.2–9. Claim (2) follows by Definition 14.10 and by construction of $\mathcal{M}^B$ and of σ_B.   □

Proposition 17. *A **G3tm.L**-proof-search tree for a sequent S is the tree of sequent that has S as root and whose branches grow according to the following procedure: if the leaf is an initial sequent the branch stops growing, else either no instance of rules of **G3tm.L** is applicable root first to it, or k instances are (where rules $L\forall, L\square, L_T, L_D, L_{UI}, L_{NE}$ are applied w.r.t. all free variables/labels occurring in the leaf). In the first case, the branch stops growing; in this case it is immediate to see that we have a finite **L**-saturated branch. In the second case,* *we apply the k rule instances that are applicable in some order (each one will be applied to all end-sequents that are generated at the previous step). If the tree never stops growing then, by König's Lemma, it has an infinite branch which, as the reader can easily check, is **L**-saturated.*

3   Monotone Non-Normal Modalities

The first decidable fragment of TMLs is obtained by restricting the language to 0-ary predicates – i.e., propositional variables – and by using quantifiers and term-modal operators only to introduce logical operators of shape $\exists x[x]$ and $\forall x\langle x\rangle$. This fragment simulates non-normal monotone epistemic logics [4,17,25] – i.e., logics not closed under deduction nor under necessitation, but only under the weaker rule RM – via normal TMLs. Roughly, the monotone formula $\Box\phi$ is expressed by $\exists x[x]\phi$. This simulation is simpler than that via polymodal normal modalities [13,18]. Moreover, as it is done in [14] building on the approach in [13,18], we easily obtain labelled calculi for monotone epistemic logics. Monotone epistemic logics are interesting in at least two respects. First, they model humans' knowledge more appropriately (than normal ones) in that agents need not know every tautology and their knowledge need not be closed under deduction, cf. [25] and [16, p. 377]. Second, and more related to applications, many important logics for reasoning in MASs, such as Parikh's Game Logic [22] and Pauly's Coalition Logic [23], are based on monotone modalities, cf [17].

Monotone Epistemic Logics. We give here a very short introduction to monotone epistemic logics. Given that this will simplify the simulation, we will make use of (a generalization of) multi-relational semantics for monotone epistemic logics [4], and not the usual neighbourhood semantics [17,25]. We generalize the (weak) semantics given in [4] by considering a 'varying domain' version of it where the *necessitation axiom* $\Box\top$ is not valid in all frames. The language $\mathcal{L}^\Box$ is generated by the following grammar, where Q^0 is an arbitrary 0-ary predicate,

$$\phi ::= Q^0 \mid \neg\phi \mid \phi \wedge \phi \mid \Box\phi \mid \Diamond\phi. \qquad (\mathcal{L}^\Box)$$

A *multi-relational frame* is a tuple $\mathscr{F} = < \mathcal{W}, \{R_1, \ldots, R_n\}, \mathcal{R} >$, where (i) $\mathcal{W}$ is a non-empty set of worlds; (ii) $n \geq 1$ and $R_i \subseteq \mathcal{W} \times \mathcal{W}$; and (iii) $\mathcal{R}$ is a mapping from worlds to possibly empty subsets of $\{R_1, \ldots, R_n\}$. A *multi-relational model* is a tuple $\mathscr{M} = < \mathscr{F}, \mathcal{V} >$, where $\mathcal{V}$ is a *valuation* mapping 0-ary predicates to subsets of $\mathcal{W}$. *Truth* of an $\mathcal{L}^\Box$-formula at a world w of a model $\mathscr{M}$ is defined as in Kripke semantics, save for $\Box\phi$ and $\Diamond\phi$ where we have, respectively

$$\vDash_w^{\mathscr{M}} \Box\phi \text{ iff some } R_i \in \mathcal{R}(w) \text{ is s.t. for all } v \in \mathcal{W}, \text{ if } wR_iv \text{ then } \vDash_v^{\mathscr{M}} \phi; \qquad (1)$$

$$\vDash_w^{\mathscr{M}} \Diamond\phi \text{ iff for each } R_i \in \mathcal{R}(w) \text{ there is } v \in \mathcal{W} \text{ s.t. } wR_iv \text{ and } \vDash_v^{\mathscr{M}} \phi. \qquad (2)$$

By a *monotone modal logic* we mean the set of all $\mathcal{L}^\Box$-formulas valid in some class of multi-relational frames. In particular, we will consider the classes of multi-relational frames that are defined by some combination of the properties given in Table 3, where $R_j(w) = \{v : wR_jv\}$, and w, v, u are generic worlds. The set $\mathbf{M}$ of the $\mathcal{L}^{\square}$-formulas valid in all multi-relational frames is the smallest set containing all $\mathcal{L}^{\square}$-instances of propositional tautologies, that is closed under modus ponens, and is closed under RM: if $(\phi \supset \psi) \in \mathbf{M}$ then $(\square\phi \supset \square\psi) \in \mathbf{M}$. The set $\mathbf{MN}$ of $\mathcal{L}^{\square}$-formulas valid in all $\mathscr{F}$ satisfying N^m is the smallest extension of $\mathbf{M}$ containing $N := \square\top$. The set $\mathbf{MC}$ of $\mathcal{L}^{\square}$-formulas valid in all $\mathscr{F}$ satisfying C^m is the smallest extension of $\mathbf{M}$ containing $C := \square\phi \wedge \square\psi \supset \square(\phi \wedge \psi)$; and so on for the logics containing all $\mathcal{L}^{\square}$-instances of the modal axioms $T, D, 4, 5$ (where if $5 \in \mathbf{X}$ then $N \in \mathbf{X}$, and where $D := \neg \square \bot$ is equivalent to $\square\phi \supset \Diamond\phi$ only if $C \in \mathbf{X}$), and for the combinations thereof. The proofs are like the ones in [4], save that in [4] it is imposed that $\mathcal{R}(w) \neq \varnothing$ and, therefore, N always holds and the 'existential constituents' of 4^m and 5^m hold trivially.

Table 3. Properties of $\mathscr{F}$

$N^m := \mathcal{R}(w) \neq \varnothing$ $\qquad\qquad\qquad C^m := \forall R_i, R_j \in \mathcal{R}(w) \exists R_k \in \mathcal{R}(w)(R_k(w) \subseteq R_i(w) \cap R_j(w))$
$T^m := \forall R_i(R_i \in \mathcal{R}(w) \supset wR_iw) \quad D^m := \forall R_i(R_i \in \mathcal{R}(w) \supset R_i(w) \neq \varnothing)$
$4^m := \forall R_i(R_i \in \mathcal{D}(w)\&wR_iv \supset \mathcal{R}(v) \neq \varnothing) \,\&\, \forall R_i, R_k \in \mathcal{D}(w)\forall R_j \in \mathcal{D}(v)(wR_iv\&vR_ju \supset wR_ku)$
$5^m := \mathcal{R}(w) \neq \varnothing \,\&\, \forall R_i, R_j \in \mathcal{D}(w)\forall R_k \in \mathcal{D}(v)(wR_iv\&wR_ju \supset vR_ku)$

Term-Modal Logics and Monotone Epistemic Logics. From the perspective of multi-relational semantics, the monotone modalities $\square$ and $\Diamond$ are similar to normal ones in Kripke semantics. The only novelty is that we have $\exists\forall$ and $\forall\exists$ modalities whose epistemic readings are, respectively, (i) *there is an agent such that in all worlds compatible with his knowledge...*; and (ii) *for each agent some world compatible with his knowledge is such that....* It should immediately be clear that we can capture these quantifier alternation in the term-modal language.[2] In order to do so, we introduce the following notational conventions: $\boxplus A := \exists x[x]A$ and $\diamondplus A := \forall x\langle x \rangle A$; and we consider TMLs based on the language $\mathcal{L}^{\boxplus}$ defined by the following grammar, where Q^0 is an arbitrary 0-ary predicate,

$$A ::= Q^0 \mid \neg A \mid A \wedge A \mid \boxplus A \mid \diamondplus A. \qquad (\mathcal{L}^{\boxplus})$$

Next, we consider correspondence results between $\mathcal{L}^{\boxplus}$-formulas and properties of term-modal frames.

Proposition 18. *The following $\mathcal{L}^{\boxplus}$-formulas are valid in all and only the term-modal frames satisfying the following conditions (for $w, v, u \in \mathcal{W}$ and $a, b, c \in \mathcal{U}$)*

---

[2] See [24] for another way of expressing the minimal monotone logic $\mathbf{M}$ via TMLs.

- $N^{\boxplus} := \boxplus \top$ *iff* $\forall w \exists a (a \in D_w)$
- $C^{\boxplus} := \boxplus A \wedge \boxplus B \supset \boxplus (A \wedge B)$ *iff* $\forall w, v, u \, \forall a, b$

  $(a \in D_w \,\&\, b \in D_w \supset \exists c (c \in D_w \,\&\, \forall w_1 (w \overset{c}{\rightsquigarrow} w_1 \supset (w \overset{a}{\rightsquigarrow} w_1 \,\&\, w \overset{b}{\rightsquigarrow} w_1))))$
- $T^{\boxplus} := \boxplus A \supset A$ *iff* $\forall w \, \forall a (a \in D_w \supset w \overset{a}{\rightsquigarrow} w))$
- $D^{\boxplus} := \neg \boxplus \bot$ *iff* $\forall w \, \forall a (a \in D_w \supset \exists v (w \overset{a}{\rightsquigarrow} v))$
- $4^{\boxplus} := \boxplus A \supset \boxplus \boxplus A$ *iff* $\forall w, v \, \forall a \in D_w (w \overset{a}{\rightsquigarrow} v \supset \exists b (b \in D_v)) \,\&\, \forall w, v, u$

  $\forall a, c \in D_w \forall b \in D_v (w \overset{a}{\rightsquigarrow} v \,\&\, v \overset{b}{\rightsquigarrow} u \supset w \overset{c}{\rightsquigarrow} u)$
- $5^{\boxplus} := \Diamond\!\!\!\!\boxplus\, A \supset \boxplus \Diamond\!\!\!\!\boxplus\, A$ *iff* $\forall w \exists a (a \in D_w) \,\&\, \forall w, v, u \forall a, b \in D_w \forall c \in D_v$

  $(w \overset{a}{\rightsquigarrow} v \,\&\, w \overset{b}{\rightsquigarrow} u \supset v \overset{c}{\rightsquigarrow} u)$

Now, we introduce a 1-1 mapping, TR, between $\mathcal{L}^{\square}$-formulas and $\mathcal{L}^{\boxplus}$-formulas and another 1-1 mapping, M, between multi-relational models and term-modal models defined over $\mathcal{L}^{\boxplus}$ (TR^{-1}and M^{-1} denote the inverse mappings).

Definition 19. *Let ϕ be an $\mathcal{L}^{\square}$-formula, A an $\mathcal{L}^{\boxplus}$-formula, $\mathcal{M}$ a multi-relational model, and $\mathcal{M}$ a term-modal model over $\mathcal{L}^{\boxplus}$. The mappings TR and M are:*

- $\mathrm{TR}(Q^0) = Q^0;$ $\mathrm{TR}(\neg \phi) = \neg \mathrm{TR}(\phi);$ $\mathrm{TR}(\phi \wedge \psi) = \mathrm{TR}(\phi) \wedge \mathrm{TR}(\psi);$
  $\mathrm{TR}(\square \phi) = \boxplus \mathrm{TR}(\phi);$ $\mathrm{TR}(\Diamond \phi) = \Diamond\!\!\!\!\boxplus\, \mathrm{TR}(\phi).$
- *For $\mathcal{M} = \, < W, \{R_1, \ldots, R_n\}, \mathcal{R}, \mathcal{V} >$, $\mathrm{M}(\mathcal{M})$ is $< W^{\mathcal{M}}, \mathcal{U}^{\mathcal{M}}, \mathcal{D}^{\mathcal{M}}, \rightsquigarrow^{\mathcal{M}}, \mathcal{I}^{\mathcal{M}} >$, where: (i) $W^{\mathcal{M}} = W$; (ii) $\mathcal{U}^{\mathcal{M}} = \{R_1, \ldots, R_n\}$; (iii) $\mathcal{D}^{\mathcal{M}} = \{D_w : R_i \in D_w$ iff $R_i \in \mathcal{R}(w)\}$; (iv) $\rightsquigarrow^{\mathcal{M}} = \bigcup \{\overset{R_i}{\rightsquigarrow} : w \overset{R_i}{\rightsquigarrow} v$ iff $w R_i v\}$; and (v) $\mathcal{I}^{\mathcal{M}}(Q^0) = \mathcal{V}(Q^0)$.*

We can now prove that $\mathcal{L}^{\boxplus}$-logics simulate monotone epistemic logics.

Lemma 20. *If $\phi, A, \mathcal{M}, \mathcal{M}$ are as in Definition 19, then (i) $\vDash_w^{\mathcal{M}} \phi$ iff $\vDash_w^{\mathrm{M}(\mathcal{M})}$ $\mathrm{TR}(\phi)$, and, vice versa, (ii) $\vDash_w^{\mathcal{M}} A$ iff $\vDash_w^{\mathrm{M}^{-1}(\mathcal{M})} \mathrm{TR}^{-1}(A)$.*

Proof (Sketch). We can prove that $\vDash_w^{\mathcal{M}} \phi$ iff $\vDash_w^{\mathrm{M}(\mathcal{M})} \mathrm{TR}(\phi)$ by an easy induction on the height of ϕ. If ϕ is atomic or of shape $\neg \psi$ or $\psi_1 \wedge \psi_2$, the proof is straight-forward. If $\phi \equiv \square \psi$, then: $\vDash_w^{\mathcal{M}} \square \psi \overset{(1)}{\Longleftrightarrow} \exists R_i \in \mathcal{R}(w) \forall v \in w (w R_i v \supset \vDash_w^{\mathcal{M}} \psi) \overset{IH}{\Longleftrightarrow}$ $\exists R_i \in \mathcal{R}(w) \forall v \in w (w R_i v \supset \vDash_w^{\mathrm{M}(\mathcal{M})} \mathrm{TR}(\psi)) \overset{\mathrm{Def.\ M}(\mathcal{M})}{\Longleftrightarrow} \exists R_i \in D_w \forall v \in W$ $(w \overset{R_i}{\rightsquigarrow} v \supset \vDash_w^{m(\mathcal{M})} \mathrm{TR}(\psi)) \overset{\mathrm{Def.\ 3}}{\Longleftrightarrow} \vDash_w^{\mathrm{M}(\mathcal{M})} \exists x [x] \mathrm{TR}(\psi) \overset{\mathrm{Def.\ } \boxplus + \mathrm{TR}}{\Longleftrightarrow} \vDash_w^{\mathrm{M}(\mathcal{M})} \mathrm{TR}(\square \psi)$. The proofs of case $\phi \equiv \Diamond \psi$ and of claim (ii) are similar and can be omitted.   □

Theorem 21. *Validity of $\mathcal{L}^{\boxplus}$-formulas over term-modal frames defined by properties in Proposition 18 and validity of $\mathcal{L}^{\square}$-formulas over multi-relational frames defined by the corresponding properties (see Table 3) are equivalent problems.*

Proof. An easy corollary of Lemma 20 and of Proposition 18.   □

Theorem 22. *The validity problem of $\mathcal{L}^{\boxplus}$-formulas over frames defined by properties in Proposition 18 is decidable. Moreover, for $\mathcal{L}^{\boxplus}$-logics without $C^{\boxplus}$ the validity problem is co-NP-complete, and for $\mathcal{L}^{\boxplus}$-logics with $C^{\boxplus}$ it is PSPACE-complete.*

Proof. The theorem follows by Theorem 21 and by [25, Theorem 2.3] (assuming that the conjecture [25, p. 251] that $\mathcal{L}^\square$-logics with C are PSPACE-hard is correct). □

Finally, Table 4, together with rule L_{NE} (see Table 2) which expresses condition N^m, gives the non-logical rules that allow us to introduce the labelled calculus **G3tm.X** which characterizes (via TR) the monotone logic **X**. If **G3tm.X** contains rule $L_{5⊞}$, then it contains also rule L_{NE}; and if it contains L_C ($L_{5⊞}$), then it contains also its contracted instances L_{Cc} ($L_{5c⊞}$) and, for $L_{5⊞}$ and $L_{4^⊞_2}$, those where $x \in w \equiv y \in w$. The semantic condition that corresponds to $C^⊞$ in Proposition 18 is not geometric, but the rule expressing it is made geometric by introducing the three places atomic predicate $\cap$ and rule $L_\cap$, cf. [8]. It can be easily shown that results analogous to Lemma 5–Theorem 13 hold for each calculus **G3tm.X**. It should be possible to define a terminating **G3tm.X**-proof-search procedure, cf. [12,20]. This would solve the open problem that multi-relational models have the finite model property, cf. [4, p. 318].

Table 4. Non-logical rules for monotone epistemic logics

$$\frac{z \in w, \cap(z,x,y), x \in w, y \in w, \Omega; \Gamma \Rightarrow \Delta}{x \in w, y \in w, \Omega; \Gamma \Rightarrow \Delta} \; L_C, z \text{ eig.}$$

$$\frac{w \overset{x}{\twoheadrightarrow} v, w \overset{y}{\twoheadrightarrow} v, w \overset{z}{\twoheadrightarrow} v, \cap(z,x,y), \Omega; \Gamma \Rightarrow \Delta}{w \overset{z}{\twoheadrightarrow} v, \cap(z,x,y), \Omega; \Gamma \Rightarrow \Delta} \; L_\cap$$

$$\frac{w \overset{x}{\twoheadrightarrow} u, x \in w, \Omega; \Gamma \Rightarrow \Delta}{x \in w, \Omega; \Gamma \Rightarrow \Delta} \; L_{D⊞}, u \text{ eig.}$$

$$\frac{v \overset{z}{\twoheadrightarrow} u, x \in w, y \in w, z \in v, w \overset{x}{\twoheadrightarrow} v, w \overset{y}{\twoheadrightarrow} u, \Omega; \Gamma \Rightarrow \Delta}{x \in w, y \in w, z \in v, w \overset{x}{\twoheadrightarrow} v, w \overset{y}{\twoheadrightarrow} u, \Omega; \Gamma \Rightarrow \Delta} \; L_{5⊞}$$

$$\frac{z \in v, x \in w, w \overset{x}{\twoheadrightarrow} v, \Omega; \Gamma \Rightarrow \Delta}{x \in w, w \overset{x}{\twoheadrightarrow} v, \Omega; \Gamma \Rightarrow \Delta} \; L_{4^⊞_1}, z \text{ eig.}$$

$$\frac{w \overset{y}{\twoheadrightarrow} u, x \in w, y \in w, z \in v, w \overset{x}{\twoheadrightarrow} v, v \overset{z}{\twoheadrightarrow} u, \Omega; \Gamma \Rightarrow \Delta}{x \in w, y \in w, z \in v, w \overset{x}{\twoheadrightarrow} v, v \overset{z}{\twoheadrightarrow} u, \Omega; \Gamma \Rightarrow \Delta} \; L_{4^⊞_2}$$

$$\frac{w \overset{x}{\twoheadrightarrow} w, x \in w, \Omega; \Gamma \Rightarrow \Delta}{x \in w, \Omega; \Gamma \Rightarrow \Delta} \; L_{T⊞} \quad \frac{z \in w, \cap(z,x,x), x \in w, \Omega; \Gamma \Rightarrow \Delta}{x \in w, \Omega; \Gamma \Rightarrow \Delta} \; L_{Cc}, z \text{ eig.}$$

$$\frac{v \overset{y}{\twoheadrightarrow} v, x \in w, y \in v, w \overset{x}{\twoheadrightarrow} v, \Omega; \Gamma \Rightarrow \Delta}{x \in w, y \in v, w \overset{x}{\twoheadrightarrow} v, \Omega; \Gamma \Rightarrow \Delta} \; L_{5c⊞}$$

4   Multi-Agent Epistemic Logics with Groups

The second decidable fragment of TMLs that we consider expresses MELs with quantification over groups of agents. This fragment simulates MELs by expressing the multi-agent modalities $\square_1, \ldots, \square_n$ via the term-modal ones $[x_1], \ldots, [x_n]$, and, if P is a monadic predicate, it allows to say that the individual agent x_i is a member of the group P and that each/some member of the group P knows something. Moreover, it simulates the epistemic logic with names AX_N introduced in [15]. Note that groups' knowledge can be expressed also in MELs, but the present formulation is preferable in that it is more succint in the sense of [11].

Formally, we introduce the following conventions: $[\forall P]A := \forall y(Py \supset [y]A)$ and $[\exists P]A := \exists y(Py \wedge [y]A)$. Then, for any $n \in \mathbb{N}$, we consider the language $\mathcal{L}^*_n$ defined by the following grammar, where we restrict the set of variables to $\{y, x_1, \ldots, x_n\}$; Q is a 0-ary predicate and P an 1-ary one; and, finally, B is an $\mathcal{L}^*_n$-formula with no subformula of shape Px_i

$$A ::= Q \mid Px_i \mid \neg A \mid A \wedge A \mid [x_i]B \mid [\forall P]B \mid [\exists P]B. \qquad (\mathcal{L}^*_n)$$

In $\mathcal{L}_n^*$-formulas, the variable y is always bound by a quantifier and the x_is are always free; therefore, the x_is can be thought as individual constants and $\mathcal{L}_n^*$ as a monodic fragment of TMLs [21]. The operators $\top, \bot, \vee, \supset$, and $\langle x_i \rangle$ are defined as before. We can also consider the 'group-diamond' operators $\langle \exists P \rangle$ and $\langle \forall P \rangle$ that are the dual of the primitive ones, e.g. the dual of $[\forall P]$ is $\langle \exists P \rangle$ that is defined as $\langle \exists P \rangle A := \neg[\forall P]\neg A$. $[\forall P]$ and $[\exists P]$ are not interdefinable.

$\mathcal{L}$-formulas involving interaction of modalities and quantifiers, like the Barcan Formulas, are not $\mathcal{L}_n^*$-formulas. Thus, the distinction between varying and single domain frames loses much of its interest over the language $\mathcal{L}_n^*$. For the sake of simplicity, we consider here only single domain frames (sd-frames, for short.) – i.e. frames where, for all $w \in \mathcal{W}$, $D_w = \mathcal{U}$. By an $\mathcal{L}_n^*$-logic we mean the set of all $\mathcal{L}_n^*$-formulas that are valid in some class of sd-frames obtained by some combination of the semantic properties corresponding to the schemes $T, D, 4$, and 5 (see Proposition 4). We name $\mathcal{L}_n^*$-logics according to the standard propositional conventions. To illustrate, $\mathbf{KD45_n^*}$ is the set of $\mathcal{L}_n^*$-formulas valid over all serial, transitive and Euclidean sd-frames; $\mathbf{S5_n^*}$ is the set of $\mathcal{L}_n^*$-formulas valid over all sd-frames where each $\overset{a}{\rightsquigarrow}$ is an equivalence relation. Theorems 12 and 13 imply that $\mathbf{G3tm.X} \oplus \mathbf{UI_n^*}$ is sound and complete w.r.t. theoremhood in $\mathbf{X_n^*}$.

Example 23. The $\mathcal{L}_n^*$-formula $Px_i \wedge [x_i]A \wedge [\forall P](A \supset B) \supset [\exists P]B$ – which expresses the sentence *if x_i is a P that knows that A and if every P knows that A implies B, then some P knows that B* – is valid in every sd-frame, but the $\mathcal{L}_n^*$-formula $[\exists P]A \wedge [\exists P](A \supset B) \supset [\exists P]B$ is not valid in every sd-frame, as it is shown by the following (compressed) $\mathbf{G3tm.K} \oplus \mathbf{UI_n^*}$-proof-searches (where rules $L\exists$, $R\exists$, and $L\supset$ are admissible).

$$
\cfrac{
\cfrac{
\cfrac{
\cfrac{
\cfrac{\cfrac{v:A \Rightarrow v:A \ ^{Lem.6} \quad v:B \Rightarrow v:B \ ^{Lem.6}}{w \overset{x_i}{\rightsquigarrow} v,\ldots,v:A \supset B, v:A \Rightarrow v:B} \ ^{L\supset}}{w:Px_i \Rightarrow w:Px_i \quad \ldots, w:[x_i](A \supset B), w:[x_i]A \Rightarrow w:[x_i]B} \ ^{R\Box + L\Box}}{w:Px_i \Rightarrow w:Px_i \quad \ldots, w:Px_i \supset [x_i](A \supset B) \Rightarrow w:[x_i]B} \ ^{L\supset}}{x_i \in w; w:Px_i, w:[x_i]A, w:Px_i \supset [x_i](A \supset B) \Rightarrow w:Px_i \wedge [x_i]B} \ ^{R\wedge}}{w:Px_i, w:[x_i]A, w:[\forall P](A \supset B) \Rightarrow w:[\exists P]B} \ ^{Defs.\ [\forall P]\&[\exists P]+L_{UI}+L\forall+R\exists}
$$

$$
\cfrac{
\cfrac{
\cfrac{
\cfrac{\cfrac{???}{\vdots} \quad \cfrac{\ldots v:A \Rightarrow v:B, u:B, u:A \quad \ldots u:B \Rightarrow v:B, u:B}{w \overset{y}{\rightsquigarrow} v, w \overset{z}{\rightsquigarrow} u, y, z \in w; v:A, u:A \supset B, \ldots \Rightarrow v:B, u:B} \ ^{Lem.6} \ ^{L\supset}}{\star \quad y, z \in w; w:Py, w:[y]A, w:Pz, w:[z](A \supset B) \Rightarrow w:[y]B, w:[z]B} \ ^{R\Box + L\Box}}{\star \quad y, z \in w; w:Py, w:[y]A, w:Pz, w:[z](A \supset B) \Rightarrow w:[y]B, w:Pz \wedge [z]B} \ ^{R\wedge}}{y, z \in w; w:Py, w:[y]A, w:Pz, w:[z](A \supset B) \Rightarrow w:Py \wedge [y]B, w:Pz \wedge [z]B} \ ^{R\wedge}}{w:[\exists P]A, w:[\exists P](A \supset B) \Rightarrow w:[\exists P]B} \ ^{Def.\ [\exists P]+L\exists+L\wedge+R\exists} \quad \Box
$$

We have now all the elements to prove the main result of this section, whose proof is based on that for the epistemic logic with names $AX_\mathcal{N}$ [15, Theorem 3.2].

Theorem 24. *Each $\mathcal{L}_n^*$-logic is decidable. Moreover, the validity problem for the $\mathcal{L}_n^*$-logics $\mathbf{K_n^*}$, $\mathbf{S4_n^*}$, $\mathbf{KD45_n^*}$, and $\mathbf{S5_n^*}$ is* PSPACE-*complete.*

Proof (Sketch). We fix an $\mathcal{L}_n^*$-logic $\mathbf{X_n^*}$ and an $\mathcal{L}_n^*$-formula A of length m. First, in (1), we show that the $\mathbf{X_n^*}$-satisfiability problem is decidable by outlining a terminating $\mathbf{G3tm.X} \oplus \mathbf{UI}_n^*$-proof-search procedure for $\mathcal{L}_n^*$-formulas. Then, in **(2)**, we prove that the problem is in PSPACE, and, in **(3)**, we prove that it is PSPACE-hard. Both **(2)** and **(3)** are proved by reduction to a satisfiability problem in propositional MELs which are known to be PSPACE-complete.

(1) First, it is possible to modify the proof-search procedure given in Proposition 17 into a terminating procedure for the sequent $\Rightarrow w : \neg A$. Let us call *agent-creating* any subformula of A that is either of shape $[\exists P]B$ and in the scope of an even number of negations, or of shape $[\forall P]B$ and in the scope of an odd number of negations. It can be shown that, if A is $\mathbf{X}_n^*$-satisfiable, each agent-creating subformula of A can be satisfied by exactly one individual. Thus, in the proof-search procedure, each time we consider an instance of rules $L\exists$ and $R\forall$ whose principal formula has been already analysed (root first) in that branch, we can instantiate it to the same variable (we apply an hp-admissible substitution to rename the *eigenvariable* we introduce). It follows that at most m different term-modal modalities $[z]$ occurs in the proof-search tree, and we can easily adapt the termination procedures for propositional labelled calculi given in [12,20].

(2) Next, we prove PSPACE-completeness. Let, from now on, $\mathbf{X}_n^*$ be one of $\mathbf{K}_n^*$, $\mathbf{S4}_n^*$, $\mathbf{KD45}_n^*$ and $\mathbf{S5}_n^*$. We start by showing that the problem is in PSPACE. Let A be $\mathbf{X}_n^*$-satisfiable, and let $\mathcal{M}^A$ be the model (based on a frame for $\mathbf{X}_n^*$) that is constructed as in Definition 15 from the terminating proof-search procedure for $\Rightarrow w : \neg A$. For each monadic predicate P occurring in A (A-group, for short.), let $|P|$ be the maximum number of agents (i.e. members of $\mathcal{U}^A$) satisfying P in some $w \in \mathcal{W}^A$; where, for each x_i occurring in A, we suppose there is a corresponding singleton A-group X_i. It is clear that for each A-group P, there is a $k \le m$, with $m = Le(A)$, such that $|P| = k$. We consider a propositional multi-modal logic $\mathbf{X}^A$ where, for each A-group P, we have the modalities $\{\Box_{P_i} : i \le |P|\}$ and where, if Px_i holds in some world, then $\Box_{X_i} \equiv \Box_{P_j}$ for some $j \le |P|$.

We map A to the $\mathbf{X}^A$-formula ϕ^A that is obtained by replacing each subformula of shape $[\exists P]B$ with $\bigvee_{i=1}^{|P|} \Box_{P_i} B$; each subformula of shape $[\forall P]B$ with $\bigwedge_{i=1}^{|P|} \Box_{P_i} B$ (if $|P| = 0$, we replace $[\exists P]B$ with $\bot$ and $[\forall P]B$ with $\top$); and each subformula of shape Px_i with a new atomic propositional formula p_{Px_i} having the same semantic value. It is clear that, for all $v \in \mathcal{W}$, $\vDash_v^{\mathcal{M}^A} A$ iff $\vDash_v^{\mathcal{M}^A} \phi^A$.

In [16] it is given a PSPACE algorithm for checking satisfiability of an $\mathbf{X}^A$-formula, which, if adequately implemented, depends on the number of its subformulas, and the number of subformulas of ϕ^A is at most m^2. Thus, the $\mathbf{X}_n^*$-satisfiability problem is in PSPACE.

(3) Finally, we show that the satisfiability problem is PSPACE-hard. Let's assume that the language of $\mathbf{X}_n^*$ is such that at least two agents/groups are expressible in it. To show that the $\mathbf{X}_n^*$-satisfiability problem is PSPACE-hard, it is enough to notice that the logic $\mathbf{X}^n$ is contained in $\mathbf{X}_n^*$, and that, save for $\mathbf{KD45}^1$ and $\mathbf{S5}^1$, the $\mathbf{X}^n$-satisfiability problem is PSPACE-hard.   □

5   Future Work

We have introduced two simple decidable fragments of TMLs, and we have characterized the complexity of the validity problem for logics in these fragments. In the future we plan to introduce terminating **G3tm.L**-proof-search procedures for these logics, and to consider more expressive fragments. One simple extension is the addition of distributed knowledge to $\mathcal{L}_n^*$-logics. Distributed knowledge represents 'what a wise man, who knows what every member of the group knows, would know' [16, p. 321], and, accordingly, it is possible to express the propositional epistemic formula $D_G\phi$ via the $\mathcal{L}$-sentence $\exists x \forall y (Gy \wedge [y]\phi \supset [x]\phi)$. The addition of distributed knowledge to $\mathbf{X^n}$ does not change its complexity [16], and the same should hold for $\mathbf{X_n^*}$.

Notice that the operators $[\exists P]$ and $\langle \forall P \rangle$ can be seen as a monotone epistemic operators over the group P. Since Coalition Logic ($\mathcal{CL}$) can be seen as a logic with monotone modalities, cf. [17], it should be possible to simulate $\mathcal{CL}$ via TMLs (the only interesting step is that of modeling *superadditivity*, see [23, p. 152], in the term-modal framework). Then, it would be natural to consider its PSPACE-complete epistemic extensions $\mathcal{ECL}$ and $\mathcal{CLD}$ [1].

The fragments of TMLs considered thus far are more expressive than MELs, but they cannot express relations between groups – e.g., $\forall x (Px \supset Qx)$ is not expressible – nor agents' knowledge about whether they are member of a group – e.g., $\exists x (Px \wedge [x]Px)$ is not expressible. An important direction for future research is to find 'maximal' decidable fragments of TMLs. It is known, cf. [21], that the monadic fragment of TMLs is not decidable, and that the propositional monodic fragment – which is, roughly, $\mathcal{L}_n^*$ without unary predicates – is decidable. It might well be that the *full* monodic fragment [3, p. 582–86] of TMLs and of indexed epistemic logics [5–7], or some interesting sublanguage thereof, is decidable.

References

1. Ågotnes, T., Alechina, N.: Epistemic coalition logic: completeness and complexity. In: Proceedings of AAMAS 2012, 1099–1106 (2012)
2. Belardinelli, F., Lomuscio, A.: Quantified epistemic logic for reasoning about knowledge in multi-agent systems. Artif. Intell. **173**, 982–1013 (2009)
3. Braüner, T., Ghilardi, S.: First-order modal logic. In: Blackburn, P., et al. (eds.) Handbook of Modal Logic, pp. 549–620. Elsevier, Amsterdam (2007)
4. Calardo, E., Rotolo, A.: Variants of multi-relational semantics for propositional non-normal modal logics. J. Appl. Non-Class. Log. **24**, 293–320 (2014)
5. Corsi, G., Orlandelli, E.: Free quantified epistemic logics. Stud. Log. **101**, 1159–1183 (2013)
6. Corsi, G., Orlandelli, E.: Sequent calculi for free quantified epistemic logics. In: Proceedings of ARQNL 2016, pp. 21–35. CEUR-WS (2016)
7. Corsi, G., Tassi, G.: A new approach to epistemic logic. In: Weber, E. (ed.) Logic, Reasoning, and Rationality, pp. 27–44. Springer, Dordrecht (2014). https://doi.org/10.1007/978-94-017-9011-6_2
8. Dyckhoff, R., Negri, S.: Geometrization of first-order logic. Bull. Symb. Log. **21**, 126–163 (2015)

9. Fagin, R., et al.: Reasoning about Knowledge. MIT Press, Cambridge (1995)
10. Fitting, M., et al.: Term-modal logics. Stud. Log. **69**, 133–169 (2001)
11. French, T., et al.: Succinctness of epistemic languages. In: Proceedings of IJCAI 2011, pp. 881–886. AAAI Press (2011)
12. Garg, D., et al.: Countermodels from sequent calculi in multi-modal logics. In: Proceedings of LICS 2012, pp. 315–324. IEEE Press (2012)
13. Gasquet, O., Herzig, A.: From classical to normal modal logics. In: Wansing, H. (ed.) Proof Theory of Modal Logic, pp. 293–311. Kluwer, Dordrecht (1996). https://doi.org/10.1007/978-94-017-2798-3_15
14. Gilbert, D., Maffezioli, P.: Modular sequent calculi for classical modal logics. Stud. Log. **103**, 175–217 (2015)
15. Grove, A., Halpern, J.: Naming and identity in epistemic logics part 1: the propositional case. J. Log. Comp. **3**, 345–378 (1993)
16. Halpern, J., Moses, Y.: A guide to completeness and complexity for modal logics of knowledge and belief. Artif. Intell. **54**, 319–379 (1992)
17. Hansen, H.: Monotone Modal Logic (M.Th.). ILLC Preprints, Amsterdam (2003)
18. Kracht, M., Wolter, F.: Normal monomodal logics can simulate all others. J. Symb. Log. **64**, 99–138 (1999)
19. Lomuscio, A., Colombetti, M.: QLB: a quantified logic for belief. In: Müller, J.P., Wooldridge, M.J., Jennings, N.R. (eds.) ATAL 1996. LNCS, vol. 1193, pp. 71–85. Springer, Heidelberg (1997). https://doi.org/10.1007/BFb0013578
20. Negri, S., von Plato, J.: Proof Analysis. CUP, Cambridge (2011)
21. Padmanabha, A., Ramanujam, R.: The monodic fragment of propositional term modal logic. Stud. Log. 1–25 (2018). Online First
22. Parikh, R.: The logic of games and its applications. In: Karpinski, M., van Leeuwen, J. (eds.) Topics in the Theory of Computation, pp. 119–139. Elsevier, Amsterdam (1985)
23. Pauly, M.: A modal logic for coalitional power in games. J. Log. Comput. **12**, 149–166 (2002)
24. Sedlar, I.: Term-modal logic of evidence (2016). Unpublished paper
25. Vardi, M.: On the complexity of epistemic reasoning. In: Proceedings of LICS 1989, pp. 243–252. IEEE Press (1989)

Reasoning About Additional Winning Strategies in Two-Player Games

Vadim Malvone[1](✉) and Aniello Murano[2]

[1] Université d'Évry, Évry, France
vadim.malvone@univ-evry.fr
[2] Università degli Studi di Napoli Federico II, Naples, Italy

Abstract. In game theory, deciding whether a designed player wins a game corresponds to check whether he has a winning strategy. There are situations in which it is important to know whether some extra winning strategy also exists. In this paper we investigate this question over two-player turn-based games under safety and fairness objectives. We provide an automata-based technique that allows to decide in polynomial-time whether the game admits more than one winning strategy.

1 Introduction

Game theory is a powerful framework, usefully applied in computer science to reason about *reactive* systems [15]. In recent years, it has been used efficiently to deal with the strategy reasoning in multi-agent systems [1,17,22,27,34].

In the basic setting, we consider two-player turn-based games. The configurations (states) of the game are partitioned between the two players, $Player_0$ and $Player_1$, and a player moves in a state whenever he owns it. Solving a two-player game amounts to checking whether $Player_0$ has a *winning strategy*, that is a complete plan of choices, one for each decision point of the player (*i.e.* a *strategy*), that allows him to satisfy the game objective, no matter how his opponent acts.

In several game settings it is mandatory to have a more precise (quantitative) information about *how many* winning strategies a player has at his disposal. For example, in Nash Equilibrium, such an information amounts to solving the question of checking whether the equilibrium is unique [2,3,13,23,24,30]. This problem impacts on the predictive power of Nash Equilibrium since, in case there are multiple equilibria, the outcome of the game cannot be uniquely pinned down [10,31,35].

A recent line of research aiming at addressing uniqueness in Nash Equilibria (as well as other solution concepts), with goals expressed in LTL, concerns extending Strategy Logic (a powerful logic able to express Nash Equilibria [27]) with graded modalities [2,3]. This approach however turns out to be less effective in practice as it requires double exponential-time. Conversely, the problem of checking the existence of a Nash equilibrium in games with LTL goals is in PSPACE [14]. This has spurred us to look for other and more efficient directions.

© Springer Nature Switzerland AG 2018
F. Belardinelli and E. Argente (Eds.): EUMAS 2017/AT 2017, LNAI 10767, pp. 163–171, 2018.
https://doi.org/10.1007/978-3-030-01713-2_12

In [25,26], we have investigated the existence of additional winning strategies in two-player finite games under the reachability condition in which the players have perfect or imperfect information about the moves performed by the opponent. In this paper we go further and consider as objectives *safety* and *fairness*. Precisely, we consider games in which the states are partitioned between *good* and *bad* states. Under the safety condition, $Player_0$ wins the game if he can induce a play that never visits a *bad* state. Under the fairness objective, instead, $Player_0$ wins the game whenever he can induce a play along which a *good* state is visited infinitely often.

We solve the problem of checking the existence of additional winning strategy under safety and fairness objectives by using an automata-theoretic approach. Precisely, we build an automaton that accepts only trees that are witnesses of more than one winning strategy for the designed player over the game arena. Hence, we reduce the addressed quantitative question to the emptiness of this automaton. This leads to a polynomial-time solution, thus not harder than the one required for the existence of a winning strategy in safety and fair games [9,16]. As a important consequence of this result we get that checking the uniqueness of a Nash Equilbrium under safety or fairness objectives can be done in polynomial-time. This motivates our work.

Related Works. Counting strategies has been deeply exploited in the formal verification of *reactive* systems by means of specification logics extended with *graded modalities*, interpreted over games of infinite duration [2,3,5,7,11,19,23,24,26]. It is worth recalling that the solution algorithms present in the literature for graded modalities have been conceived to address complicated scenarios and, consequently, they usually perform much worse than our algorithm on the restricted setting we consider.

Finally, we remark that the automata-theoretic solution we provide takes inspiration from those ones introduced in [4,6,11,12,20,25,26,32].

2   Preliminaries

In this section we introduce some preliminary concepts needed to properly define the game setting under exam as well as to describe the adopted solution approach. In particular, we introduce trees useful to represent strategies and automata to collect winning strategies.

Trees. Let Υ be a set. An Υ-*tree* is a prefix closed subset $T \subseteq \Upsilon^*$. The elements of T are called *nodes* and the empty word ε is the *root* of T. For $v \in T$, the set of *children* of v (in T) is $child(T,v) = \{v \cdot x \in T \mid x \in \Upsilon\}$. Given a node $v = y \cdot x$, with $y \in \Upsilon^*$ and $x \in \Upsilon$, we define $prf(v)$ to be y and $last(v)$ to be x. We also say that v *corresponds* to x. The complete Υ-tree is the tree Υ^*. For $v \in T$, a (full) path π of T from v is a *minimal* set $\pi \subseteq T$ such that $v \in \pi$ and for each $v' \in \pi$ such that $child(T,v') \neq \emptyset$, there is exactly one node in $child(T,v')$ belonging to π. Note that every word $w \in \Upsilon^*$ can be thought as a path in the tree Υ^*, namely the path containing all the prefixes of w. For an alphabet Σ, a Σ-labeled Υ-tree is a pair $< T, V >$ where T is an Υ−tree and $V : T \to \Sigma$ maps each node of T to a symbol in Σ.

Automata Theory. An *alternating tree automaton* (*ATA*, for short) is a tuple $A = < \Sigma, D, Q, q_0, \delta, F >$, where Σ is the alphabet, D is a finite set of directions, Q is the set of states, $q_0 \in Q$ is the initial state, $\delta : Q \times \Sigma \to \mathcal{B}^+(D \times Q)$ is the transition function, where $\mathcal{B}^+(D \times Q)$ is the set of all positive Boolean combinations of pairs (d, q) with d direction and q state, and $F \subseteq Q$ is the set of the accepting states. An *ATA* A recognizes (finite) trees by means of runs. For a Σ-labeled tree $< T, V >$, with $T = D^*$, a run is a $(D^* \times Q)$-labeled N-tree $< T_r, r >$ such that the root is labeled with (ε, q_0) and the labels of each node and its successors satisfy the transition relation. A run is *accepting* if all its leaves are labeled with accepting states. An input tree is accepted if there exists a corresponding accepting run. By $L(A)$ we denote the set of trees accepted by A. We say that A is not empty if $L(A) \neq \emptyset$.

As a special case of alternating tree automata, we consider *nondeterministic tree automata* (*NTA*, for short), where the concurrency feature is not allowed. That is, whenever the automaton visits a node x of the input tree, it sends to each successor (direction) of x at most one copy of itself. More formally, an *NTA* is an *ATA* in which δ is in disjunctive normal form, and in each conjunctive clause every direction appears at most once.

Finally, *Alternating Büchi tree automata* (*BATA*, for short) are *ATA* accepting infinite trees. Precisely, a run is *accepting* if all its branches visit *infinitely often* at least one state belonging to F. As before, we also consider *nondeterministic Büchi tree automata* (*BNTA*, for short). We refer to [21] for a formal definition of *BATA*.

3   The Game Model

In this section, we introduce two-player turn-based games. Precisely, we consider games consisting of an arena coupled with an objective. The arena describes the configurations of the game through a set of states, being partitioned between the two players. In each state, only the player that owns it can take a move. The formal definition of the considered game model follows.

Definition 1. *A two-player turn-based game (2TG, for short), played between Player$_0$ and Player$_1$, is a tuple $G \triangleq$ <St, s_I, Ac, tr, W, O>, where St $\triangleq$ St$_0 \cup$ St$_1$ is a finite non-empty set of states, with St$_i$ being the set of states of Player$_i$, $s_I \in$ St is a designated initial state, Ac $\triangleq$ Ac$_0 \cup$ Ac$_1$ is the set of actions, W is a set of target states, O is the objective of Player$_0$, and tr : St$_i \times$ Ac$_i \to$ St$_{1-i}$, for $i \in \{0, 1\}$ is a transition function mapping a state of a player and its action to a state belonging to the other player.*

In a *2TG* we only define the objective for *Player$_0$* since, the objective for *Player$_1$* is the opposite. In the following we only consider as objectives for *Player$_0$* *safety* and *fairness*. Regarding the former, *Player$_0$* wins the game if he has a strategy that prevents him from reaching all the states in St \ W. For the latter, $Player_0$ wins the game if he can induce plays along which he visits at least a target state infinitely often. These concepts will be formalized in the sequel.

To properly give the semantics of 2TGs, we now introduce some basic concepts such as path, track, strategy, and play.

A *path* is a finite or infinite sequence of states $s_1, s_2, \ldots$ such that $s_1 = s_I$ and for all i, if $s_i \in St_0$ then there exists an action $a_0 \in Ac_0$ such that $s_{i+1} = tr(s_i, a_0)$, else there exists an action $a_1 \in Ac_1$ such that $s_{i+1} = tr(s_i, a_1)$.

A *track* $\rho \in St^*$ is a finite path. For a track ρ, by $(\rho)_i$ we denote the i-st element of ρ, by $\rho_{\leq i}$ we denote the prefix track $(\rho)_0 \ldots (\rho)_i$, and by $last(\rho)$ we denote the last element of ρ. By $Trk \subseteq St^*$, we denote the set of tracks over St. By Trk_i we denote the set of tracks ρ in which $last(\rho) \in St_i$.

A *strategy* represents a scheme for a player containing a precise choice of actions along an interaction with the other player. It is given as a function over tracks. Formally, a *strategy* for $Player_i$ is a function $\sigma_i : Trk_i \to Ac_i$ that maps a track to an action.

The composition of strategies, one for each player in the game, induces a computation called *play*. Precisely, assume $Player_0$ and $Player_1$ take strategies σ_0 and σ_1, respectively. Their composition *induces* a play ρ such that $(\rho)_0 = s_I$ and for each $i \geq 0$ if $(\rho)_i \in St_0$ then $(\rho)_{i+1} = tr((\rho)_i, \sigma_0(\rho_{\leq i}))$, else $(\rho)_{i+1} = tr((\rho)_i, \sigma_1(\rho_{\leq i}))$. A play ρ satisfies a safety objective, if and only if it contains only states in W. Conversely, let $inf(\rho)$ the set of states occurring infinitely often in ρ, the play satisfies the fairness objective if and only if $inf(\rho) \cap W \neq \emptyset$.

A strategy is winning for a player if all the plays induced by composing such strategy with all the strategies of the adversarial player satisfies his objective. If such a winning strategy exists we say that the player wins the game. The formal definition of *winning condition* follows.

Definition 2. *Let G be a 2TG. $Player_0$ wins the game G if he has a strategy such that for all strategies of $Player_1$ the resulting induced play satisfies* O.

4   Searching for Additional Winning Strategies

In this section, we show how to check whether $Player_0$ wins the game under safety and fairness objectives. To proper introduce our solutions procedure we first need to provide some auxiliary notation. Precisely, we introduce the concepts of *decision tree*, *strategy tree*, and *additional strategy tree*.

A decision tree simply collects all the tracks that come out from the interplays between the players. In other words, a decision tree can be seen as an unwinding of the game structure along with all possible combinations of player actions. The formal definition follows.

Definition 3. *Given a 2TG G, a decision tree is an St-labeled Ac-tree collecting all tracks over G.*

We now introduce strategy trees that allow to collect, for each fixed strategy for $Player_0$, all possible responding strategies for $Player_1$. Therefore, the strategy tree is a tree where each node labeled with $s \in St_0$ has an unique successor determined by the strategy for $Player_0$ and each node labeled with $s \in St_1$ has all possible successors determined by the actions of $Player_1$. Thus, a strategy tree is an opportune projection of the decision tree. The formal definition follows.

Definition 4. *Given a 2TG and a strategy σ for $Player_0$, a strategy tree for $Player_0$ is an St-labeled Ac-tree $< T, V >$, with $T \subset Ac^*$ and V as follows: (i) $V(\varepsilon) = s_I$; (ii) for all $v \in T$, let $\rho = (\rho)_0 \ldots (\rho)_{|v|-1}$ be a track from s_I with $(\rho)_k = V(v_{\leq k})$ for each $0 \leq k \leq |v| - 1$, if $V(prf(v)) \in St_0$ then $V(v) = tr(V(prf(v)), \sigma(\rho))$, otherwise $V(v) = tr(V(prf(v)), last(v))$.*

Following the above definition and Definition 2, given a 2TG G, $Player_0$ wins the game and $Player_1$ loses it by simply checking the existence of a strategy tree for $Player_0$, that is a tree such that each path satisfies the objective O. Such a tree is called a *winning-strategy* tree for $Player_0$.

In case we want to ensure that at least two winning strategies exist then, at a certain point along the tree, $Player_0$ must take two successors. Let $succ :$ $St \to 2^{St}$ to be the function that for each state $s \in St$ in G gives the set of its successors, the formal definition of *additional strategy tree* follows.

Definition 5. *Given a 2TG G, an additional strategy tree for $Player_0$ is an St-labeled Ac-tree $< T, V >$ that satisfies the following properties:*

1. *the root node is labeled with the initial state s_I of G;*
2. *for each $x \in T$ that is not a leaf and it is labeled with state s of $Player_0$, it holds that x has as children a non-empty subset of $succ(s)$;*
3. *for each $x \in T$ that is not a leaf and it is labeled with state s of $Player_1$, it holds that x has as children the set of $succ(s)$;*
4. *there exists at least one $x \in T$ that corresponds to a state of $Player_0$ in G and it has at least two children.*

Note that, the above definition, but item 4, is the classical characterization of strategy tree. As before, given a 2TG G, $Player_0$ has an additional strategy to win the game if there is an additional strategy tree for him, that is a tree such that each path satisfies the objective O. Such a tree is called an *additional winning-strategy* tree for $Player_0$.

Now, we have all ingredients to solve 2TG in which the objective is safety or fairness. For the former we have the following result.

Theorem 1. *Given 2TG G with safety objective it is possible to decide in linear time whether $Player_0$ has more than one strategy to win the game.*

Proof. Consider a 2TG G with safety objective. We know that $Player_0$ wins G iff there exists a strategy for $Player_0$ that for all strategies for $Player_1$ the induced play does not reach any state in $St \setminus W$.

We build an *NTA* A that accepts all additional winning-strategy for $Player_0$ over G. The automaton A uses $Q = \text{St} \times \{ok, split, bad\}$ as set of states, where ok and $split$ are flags and the latter is used to remember that along the tree $Player_0$ has to ensure the existence of two winning strategies by opportunely choosing a point where to "split", and bad is used when a state $s \in \text{St} \setminus W$ is occurred. We set as alphabet $\Sigma = \text{St}$ and initial state $q_0 = (s_I, split)$. For the transitions, starting from a state $q = (s, flag)$ and reading the symbol a, we have that:

$$\delta(q, a) = \begin{cases} (s', bad) & \text{if } s \in \text{St} \setminus W; \\ (s', ok) & \text{if } s = a \wedge s \in \text{St}_0 \wedge flag = ok; \\ ((s', ok) \wedge (s'', ok)) \vee (s', split) & \text{if } s = a \wedge s \in \text{St}_0 \wedge flag = split; \\ succ(s) \times \{ok\} & \text{if } s = a \wedge s \in \text{St}_1 \wedge flag = ok; \\ (s_1, f_1) \wedge \cdots \wedge (s_n, f_n) & \text{if } s = a \wedge s \in \text{St}_1 \wedge flag = split; \\ \emptyset & \text{otherwise.} \end{cases}$$

where $s', s'' \in succ(s)$ with $s' \neq s''$, $\{s_1, \ldots, s_n\} = succ(s)$, and $f_1, \ldots, f_n$ are flags in which there exists $1 \leq i \leq n$ such that $f_i = split$ and for all $j \neq i$, we have $f_j = ok$. The set of accepting states is $W \times \{ok\}$.

The automaton checks if each path of an input tree does not reach a bad state. It is not hard to see that the automaton only needs to check the tree up to a depth of $|\text{St}| + 1$. Indeed, if a bad state does not occur within this bound, $Player_0$ can pump good states forever through some cycles in the game. To limit the automaton to check up to such a bound it is sufficient to use a binary counter along its states. For the sake of readability we omit this part. Finally, it is not hard to see that if A is not empty then $Player_0$ has at least two strategies to win G.

Since, the size of the automaton A is just linear in the size of the game and checking its emptiness can be performed in linear time (from [32]), the desired complexity result follows.   □

Theorem 2. *Given 2TG G with fairness objective it is possible to decide in quadratic time whether $Player_0$ has more than one strategy to win the game.*

Proof. Consider a 2TG G with fairness objective. We know that $Player_0$ wins G iff there exists a strategy for $Player_0$ that for all strategies for $Player_1$ the induced play reaches infinitely often a state in W. In particular, now to handle the winning condition we need a non-deterministic Büchi tree automaton.

We build a *BNTA* B that accepts all trees that are witnesses of more than a winning strategy for $Player_0$ over G. The automaton A uses $Q = \text{St} \times \{ok, split\}$ as set of states, $\Sigma = \text{St}$ as alphabet, and $q_0 = (s_I, split)$ as initial state. For the transitions, starting from $q = (s, flag)$ and reading the symbol a, we have that:

$$\delta(q,a) = \begin{cases} (s',ok) & \text{if } s = a \wedge s \in \text{St}_0 \wedge flag = ok; \\ ((s',ok) \wedge (s'',ok)) \vee (s',split) & \text{if } s = a \wedge s \in \text{St}_0 \wedge flag = split; \\ succ(s) \times \{ok\} & \text{if } s = a \wedge s \in \text{St}_1 \wedge flag = ok; \\ (s_1,f_1) \wedge \cdots \wedge (s_n,f_n) & \text{if } s = a \wedge s \in \text{St}_1 \wedge flag = split; \\ \emptyset & \text{otherwise.} \end{cases}$$

where $s', s'' \in succ(s)$ with $s' \neq s''$, $\{s_1, \ldots, s_n\} = succ(s)$, and $f_1, \ldots, f_n$ are flags in which there exists $1 \leq i \leq n$ such that $f_i = split$ and for all $j \neq i$, we have $f_j = ok$. The set of accepting states is $W \times \{ok\}$. Hence, if B is not empty then $Player_0$ has at least two strategies to win G.

Since, the size of the automaton B is just linear in the size of the game and checking its emptiness can be performed in quadratic time (from [33]), the desired complexity result follows.   □

5   Conclusion and Future Work

In this paper we have introduced a simple but effective automata-based methodology to check whether a player has more than one winning strategy in a two-player game under safety and fairness objectives. We believe that the solution algorithm we have conceived in this paper can be used as core engine to count strategies efficiently in more involved game scenarios and in many solution concepts reasoning as we plan to investigate as a continuation of this paper.

This work opens to several interesting questions and extensions, which we plan to investigate. An interesting direction is to consider the counting of strategies in multi-agent concurrent games. This kind of games have several interesting applications in artificial intelligence [34]. As another direction of work, one can consider some kind of hybrid game, where one can opportunely combine teams of players working concurrently with some others playing in a turn-based manner as in [17,18,29]. These games arise for example in case the interaction among the players behaves in a recursive way [8,28].

References

1. Alur, R., Henzinger, T., Kupferman, O.: Alternating-time temporal logic. J. ACM **49**(5), 672–713 (2002)
2. Aminof, B., Malvone, V., Murano, A., Rubin, S.: Extended graded modalities in strategy logic. In: SR 2016, pp. 1–14 (2016)
3. Aminof, B., Malvone, V., Murano, A., Rubin, S.: Graded strategy logic: reasoning about uniqueness of nash equilibria. In: AAMAS 2016, pp. 698–706 (2016)
4. Aminof, B., Murano, A., Rubin, S.: On ctl* with graded path modalities. In: LPAR-20, pp. 281–296 (2015)
5. Baader, F., Borgwardt, S., Lippmann, M.: Temporal conjunctive queries in expressive description logics with transitive roles. In: Pfahringer, B., Renz, J. (eds.) AI 2015. LNCS (LNAI), vol. 9457, pp. 21–33. Springer, Cham (2015). https://doi.org/10.1007/978-3-319-26350-2_3

6. Bianco, A., Mogavero, F., Murano, A.: Graded computation tree logic. Trans. Comput. Log. **13**(3), 25:1–25:53 (2012)
7. Bonatti, P., Lutz, C., Murano, A., Vardi, M.: The complexity of enriched mucalculi. Log. Methods Comput. Sci. **4**(3), 1–27 (2008)
8. Bozzelli, L., Murano, A., Peron, A.: Pushdown module checking. Form. Methods Syst. Des. **36**(1), 65–95 (2010)
9. Chatterjee, K., Henzinger, M.: An $O(n^2)$ time algorithm for alternating büchi games. In: SODA 2012, pp. 1386–1399 (2012)
10. Simchi-Levi, D., Chen, X., Bramel, J.: The Logic of Logistics: Theory, Algorithms, and Applications for Logistics Management. SSORFE. Springer, New York (2014). https://doi.org/10.1007/978-1-4614-9149-1
11. Ferrante, A., Murano, A., Parente, M.: Enriched mu-calculi module checking. Log. Methods Comput. Sci. **4**(3), 1–21 (2008)
12. Ferrante, A., Napoli, M., Parente, M.: Model checking for graded CTL. Fundam. Inf. **96**(3), 323–339 (2009)
13. Fraser, C.D.: The uniqueness of nash equilibrium in the private provision of public goods: an alternative proof. J. Publ. Econ. **49**(3), 389–390 (1992)
14. Gutierrez, J., Perelli, G., Wooldridge, M.: Iterated games with LDL goals over finite traces. In: AAMAS 2017, pp. 696–704 (2017)
15. Harel, D., Pnueli, A.: On the development of reactive systems. In: Apt, K.R. (ed.) Logics and Models of Concurrent Systems. NATO ASI Series (Series F: Computer and Systems Sciences), vol. 13. Springer, Heidelberg (1985). https://doi.org/10.1007/978-3-642-82453-1_17
16. Immerman, N.: Number of quantifiers is better than number of tape cells. J. Comput. Syst. Sci. **22**(3), 384–406 (1981)
17. Jamroga, W., Murano, A.: On module checking and strategies. In: AAMAS 2014, pp. 701–708 (2014)
18. Jamroga, W., Murano, A.: Module checking of strategic ability. In: AAMAS 2015, pp. 227–235 (2015)
19. Kupferman, O., Sattler, U., Vardi, M.Y.: The complexity of the graded mu-calculus. In: Voronkov, A. (ed.) CADE 2002. LNCS (LNAI), vol. 2392, pp. 423–437. Springer, Heidelberg (2002). https://doi.org/10.1007/3-540-45620-1_34
20. Kupferman, O., Vardi, M.Y.: Module checking revisited. In: Grumberg, O. (ed.) CAV 1997. LNCS, vol. 1254, pp. 36–47. Springer, Heidelberg (1997). https://doi.org/10.1007/3-540-63166-6_7
21. Kupferman, O., Vardi, M., Wolper, P.: An automata theoretic approach to branching-time model checking. J. ACM **47**(2), 312–360 (2000)
22. Kupferman, O., Vardi, M., Wolper, P.: Module checking. Inf. Comput. **164**(2), 322–344 (2001)
23. Malvone, V., Mogavero, F., Murano, A., Sorrentino, L.: Reasoning about graded strategy quantifiers. Inf. Comput. (to appear)
24. Malvone, V., Mogavero, F., Murano, A., Sorrentino, L.: On the counting of strategies. In: TIME 2015, pp. 170–179 (2015)
25. Malvone, V., Murano, A.: Additional winning strategies in two-player games. In: ICTCS 2016, pp. 251–256 (2016)
26. Malvone, V., Murano, A., Sorrentino, L.: Games with additional winning strategies. In: CILC 2015, pp. 175–180 (2015)
27. Mogavero, F., Murano, A., Perelli, G., Vardi, M.: Reasoning about strategies: on the model-checking problem. TOCL **15**(4), 34:1–34:42 (2014)
28. Murano, A., Perelli, G.: Pushdown multi-agent system verification. In: IJCAI 2015, pp. 1090–1097 (2015)

29. Murano, A., Sorrentino, L.: A game-based model for human-robots interaction. In: WOA 2015, pp. 146–150 (2015)
30. Papavassilopoulos, G., Cruz, J.B.: On the uniqueness of nash strategies for a class of analytic differential games. JOTA **27**(2), 309–314 (1979)
31. Pavel, L.: Game Theory for Control of Optical Networks. Springer, Heidelberg (2012). https://doi.org/10.1007/978-0-8176-8322-1
32. Thomas, W.: Infinite trees and automaton definable relations over omega-words. In: STACS 1990, pp. 263–277 (1990)
33. Vardi, M.Y.: Alternating automata and program verification. In: van Leeuwen, J. (ed.) Computer Science Today. Lecture Notes in Computer Science, vol. 1000. Springer, Heidelberg (1995). https://doi.org/10.1007/BFb0015261
34. Wooldridge, M.: An Introduction to Multi Agent Systems. Wiley, Hoboken (2002)
35. Zhang, Y., Guizani, M.: Game Theory for Wireless Communications and Networking. CRC Press, Boca Raton (2011)

Operational Semantics of an Extension
of ODRL Able
to Express Obligations

Nicoletta Fornara[1]([✉])[iD] and Marco Colombetti[2][iD]

[1] Università della Svizzera italiana, via G. Buffi 13, 6900 Lugano, Switzerland
nicoletta.fornara@usi.ch
[2] Politecnico di Milano, piazza Leonardo Da Vinci 32, Milan, Italy
marco.colombetti@polimi.it

Abstract. Nowadays economy is every day more and more a digital economy where many human activities are performed by means of digital devices. Those digital activities produce and operate on a big amount of digital assets, as the data stored in datasets, documents, images, videos or audio files. Rationally, it is useless that digital assets are made public without the specification of constrains on their usage and access. Many formal languages for expressing licenses, policies, norms, agreements, and contracts have been proposed in literature. Among them, the Open Digital Rights Language (ODRL) is a quite general one. In this paper, we present an extension of the syntax of ODRL for expressing conditional obligations. We present also an operational semantics of this extension with the goal of being able to perform automatic reasoning on the dynamic evolution in time of obligations. The definition of such operational semantics will be based on the specification of the lifecycle of obligations and on the definition of the mechanisms for computing their state using automatic reasoning. In particular, for doing that we use as far as possible, W3C standards: RDF and RDF Schema for the specification of obligations, and the Apache Jena general purpose rule engine for efficiently deducing the state of obligations on the bases of the state of the interaction among agents.

1 Introduction

Nowadays economy is every day more and more a digital economy where many human activities are performed by means of digital devices. Those digital activities produce and operate on a big amount of digital resources, as structured data stored in various datasets, documents, images, videos or audio files. Those digital resources may become digital assets when they are exchanged between peer agents or made available to data consumers, for example on the Internet, by data publishers.

Rationally, it is useless that digital assets are made public without the specification of constrains on their usage and access, this because the absence of a

F. Belardinelli and E. Argente (Eds.): EUMAS 2017/AT 2017, LNAI 10767, pp. 172–186, 2018.
https://doi.org/10.1007/978-3-030-01713-2_13

license or of a document attached to the data is not equivalent to the right to do whatever one wants with those data [11]. Nowadays, digital assets may be made available as Open Data (by adopting one of the Open Data Commons (ODC) licenses), or they can be associated to one of the Creative Commons licenses, or to other existing licenses like for example the Open Government License (OGL). Many other licenses with big or slight differences are created every day; therefore a standardization of the existing licenses with the goal of limiting their number to a finite set is far from the present situation [9]. Moreover, it is important to consider that instead of using pre-defined data licenses, data producers or data publishers may exchange digital assets with data consumers on the basis of an ad hoc agreement that may be reached by the parties in different ways, for example through a negotiation, by accepting an offer, by buying a ticket, and so on.

Licenses and agreements may be specified using human-readable formats, but the increasing usage and exchange of digital assets requires more formal and machine-readable mechanisms for the specification of licenses and agreements. This in order to enable machine-to-machine interactions combined with a number of useful services. Services like for example: (i) an advance search of resources based on their license; (ii) the possibility to aggregate different resources released under different licenses by computing license compatibility or conflicts; (iii) the automatic checking of the satisfaction or violations of the normative or legal relations that such an exchange of digital assets creates in the chain of interactions among data producers, data publishers, and data consumers.

In order to perform many of these services it is crucial not only to propose the syntax of a formal language for expressing licenses, policies, norms, and agreements, but also to express a formal semantics of such a language. This with the goal of being able to perform automatic reasoning on the normative or legal constrains, and to monitor the fulfilment or violation of a set of policies on the basis of the (usually partial) knowledge of the actions of the parties and of the state of their interaction. A formal semantics may be used also to simulate what will happen if one of the parties, related by a set of policies, perform certain actions.

Formal languages for expressing licenses (that can be used to waive some rights on a given resource), norms, agreements, and contracts have been developed in the Multiagent Systems (MAS) research community, and in its Normative MAS sub-community. Studies on Access Control Policies have been developed by the Access Control community; and studies on deontic logic developed by the Artificial Intelligence and Law community. Numerous of these proposals, which are related to this paper, are discussed in the Related Work section.

Among such formal languages, the most interesting and general one is the Open Digital Rights Language (ODRL), which uses Semantic Web languages for the formalization of policies. In its most recent version ODRL, as a language for expressing policies, presents some limits in its expressivity. In order to overcome one of these limits, in this paper we present an extension of the syntax of ODRL for expressing conditional obligations. We present also an operational semantics of this extension with the goal of being able to perform automatic reasoning on the temporal evolution of obligations. The definition of such operational semantics will be based on the specification of the lifecycle of obligations and on the definition of the mechanisms for computing the state of obligations using automatic reasoning. In particular, for doing that we use, as far as possible, W3C or de facto standards for the Semantic Web: RDF and RDF Schema for the specification of obligations, and the Apache Jena general purpose rule engine for efficiently deducing the state of obligations on the bases of the state of the interaction among agents.

The paper is organized as follows. In Sect. 2 formal languages for expressing licenses and agreements or contracts are presented, with a particular focus to the approaches that use semantic web technologies. In Sect. 3 we present the extension of the syntax of ODRL for expressing conditional obligations, and in Sect. 4 an operational semantics of such an extension is introduced. In Sect. 5 the implementation of a system able to simulate the evolution in time of a set of conditional obligations is evaluated and some conclusions and proposals for future work are discussed.

2   Related Work

Formal languages for expressing licenses (that can be used to waive some rights on a given resource) and agreements or contracts have been developed. Examples of such languages are: the MPEG21-Right Expression Language, which is mostly used for expressing rights on audio and video files; ccREL [1], an RDF-based language for expressing Creative Common licenses; and the Web Access Control (WAC) vocabulary[1], which provides a basic way to describe various forms of access to resources for users or groups who are identified by HTTP URIs.

Among such languages, the Open Digital Rights Language (ODRL) is the most general one, in that it is not focused on a file type nor only on access control. It can be used in different scenarios, as proved by the specification using ODRL 2.0 of the 126 licenses stored in the RDFLicense dataset [17]. Originally (in 2001), ODRL was an XML language for expressing digital rights, that is, digital content usage terms and conditions. In 2012, with version 2.0, and in 2015, with version 2.1 [10], ODRL evolved into a more general policy language: it is no longer focused only on the formalization of rights expressions, but also on the specification of privacy statements, like for example duties, permissions, and prohibitions. In version 2.0 and 2.1 ORDL is a Policy Language formalized in RDF with an abstract model specified by an ontology, and is developed and promoted by the ODRL W3C Community Group. In March 2016 the W3C "Permissions and Obligations Expression" (POE) Working Group was created with the goal of bringing the Community Group specifications through the W3C Process to "Recommendation" status. ODRL 2.1 has an informal semantics described in English in the Core Model, but there is not a formal specification of its semantics [19]. In [13] an OWL representation of ODRL 1.1 is presented, but it is

---

[1] http://www.w3.org/wiki/WebAccessControl.

limited to the representation of classes and properties, and no representation is given of the dynamic semantics of policies, that is, of how they evolve in time.

L4LOD (Licenses for Linked Open Data) is a lightweight vocabulary for expressing the licenses for Linked Open Data. It is presented in [9]. This language is able to express the semantics of the deontic component of licenses by using an extension of Defeasible Logic [8]. This extension is a non-monotonic logic able to take into account the idea of expressing obligations as defeasible rules, prohibitions as obligations to not do an action, and a simple notion of permission defined as defeaters of obligations (i.e. defeaters of prohibitions). The goal of the proposed work is to automatically compute the deontic components of a composite license l_c that can be obtained from a set of licenses $l_1,\ldots,l_n$. This is done by using deontic rules (having different type) and two heuristics for OR-composition and AND-composition of the deontic effects of licenses. The content of the formalized licenses is expressed using propositions like ShareAlike or Attribution, or Commercial. This is an interesting approach based on a non-monotonic logic that can be used only when it is not necessary to explicitly express the actor, the context, and other relevant attributes of the regulated actions.

In the field of studies on Access Control to data, an important XML standard language is the eXtensible Access Control Markup Language XACML [15] which is focused on the specification of access control policies. It is an important application independent policy language which is an OASIS industry standard. It is primarily an Attribute-Based Access Control system and an XML-based language for expressing and interchanging access control policies over the Web. It describes both a policy language and an access control decision request/response language. Policies in XACML are characterized by subjects, resources, environments, and actions. A subject element is the entity requesting access and it has one or more attributes. The resource element is a data, service, or system component and it has one or more attributes. The action element defines, by means of one or more attributes, the type of access requested on the resource. An environment element can optionally provide additional information. The formalization of access control obligations is barely supported by the XACML standard; indeed XACML only describes a general syntax for obligation specification, but focusses its core functionalities on permissions and prohibitions.

Among all these rights, policies, and access control languages, ODRL 2.1 is the most general one; in fact, it allows the specification of licenses, but also of more customizable offers of digital assets by data-provider, requests of digital data by data-consumer, or agreements that binds two parties.

The studies on Normative Multiagent Systems (NorMAS), concern mainly the formalization of norms used for expressing obligations, permissions, and prohibitions, and the definition and the realization of fundamental functionalities for norms promulgation, monitoring, enforcement, and for norms adoption and reasoning. In NorMAS literature there are various proposals for the specification of norms and policies using different languages [4,5,18] and of frameworks [3] for their management. In this paper, we propose to formalize policies using Semantic Web Technologies and therefore here we will mainly discuss other approaches where Semantic Web languages were adopted.

In [5,6] a proposal to specify and reason on commitments and obligations using OWL 2, SWRL rules, and OWL-API is presented (as widely discussed in next sections). In particular, in those papers an OWL ontology of obligations whose content is a class of possible actions that have to be performed within a given deadline is presented. The monitoring of those obligations (checking if they are fulfilled of violated on the basis of the actions of the agents) can be realized thanks to a specific framework required for managing the elapsing of time and to perform closed-world reasoning on certain classes. Unfortunately, the scalability of this approach is not good enough to make it usable in real applications.

Another interesting approach that uses Semantic Web Technologies for norms formalization and management is the OWL-POLAR framework for semantic policy representation and reasoning [18]. This framework investigates the possibility of using OWL ontologies for representing the state of the interaction among agents and SPARQL queries for reasoning on policies activation, for anticipating possible conflicts among policies, and for conflicts avoidance and resolution. In the OWL-POLAR model the activation condition and the content of the policies (that is what is prohibited, permitted or obliged by the policy) are represented using conjunctive semantic formulas, that is a conjunction of atomic assertions expressed using the concepts and the relations defined on an OWL ontology. Reasoning on a set of policies for deducing their state is quite expensive in OWL-POLAR, because it requires translating the activation condition and the content of a policy into the SPARQL query language and then evaluating the resulting queries on the OWL ontology used for representing the state of the world. In OWL-POLAR, there is no treatment of time. An interesting contribution of this framework is the study of conflicts among norms and a proposal for conflict resolution. The reasoning mechanisms proposed in this work are decidable, but if OWL DL is used, they are not tractable, in the worst case. If expressiveness is reduced to OWL Lite, decidability is guaranteed.

Another relevant proposal, where Semantic Web technologies are used for policy specification and management, is the KAoS policy management framework [3,20]. It is composed by three layers: (i) the human interface layer where policies, expressing authorizations and obligations, are specified in the form of constrained English sentences; (ii) the policy management layer used for encoding in OWL the policy-related information; (iii) the policy monitoring and enforcing layer used to compile OWL policies to an efficient format usable for monitoring and enforcement. Another approach where Semantic Web technologies are partially used is the Rei policy language [12] for modelling the deontic concepts of rights, prohibitions, obligations and dispensations. Rei is implemented in the logic language Prolog, but also includes some ontologies that enable the policy engine to interpret a subset of RDFS policies.

It is therefore clear that, even if the concept of norms and policies has been studied quite extensively in Multiagent research, a lot of work has to be done for improving the existing models and languages for norm and policy formalization. It is necessary to evaluate their expressivity on real-world use cases, to improve the performances and the scalability of the framework developed for policies management, i.e., for their creation, enforcement, and monitoring, and for making those approaches usable by practitioners and industry. This paper goes in this direction.

3   A Model of Obligation

Among the formal languages for expressing licenses, or more general normative or legal relations among autonomous parties/agents, presented in the previous section, ODRL is one of the most interesting, because of the following crucial characteristics: it is under study for becoming a W3C Recommendation, it has the possibility to be extended with profiles, there is an RDF specification of the Core Model of ODRL 2.1, and it has useful policy types like agreement, offer, request and ticket, that allow to manage personalized form of contracts for the distribution of digital assets. The last aspect is essential in all frequent situations where standard licenses do not meet the constraints that a data producer or a data provider may want to express.

In the ODRL 2.1 Core Model[2] a policy must contain at least one *permission* and may contain *prohibitions*. A permission may be conditioned by a *duty*. Permissions, prohibitions, and duties relate two *parties*, an *asset*, and an *action*. ODRL 2.1 has an informal semantics described in English in the Core Model. As a language for expressing licenses and more complex agreements or contracts, ODRL presents some limits in its expressivity, as it is clarified below and has been initially discussed in [2], where some syntactic changes to ODRL 2.0 were proposed.

In this section, we present a proposal to extend the syntax of ODRL in order to be able to express pure *obligations* to perform a certain class of actions. This is an important extension of ODRL 2.1 where it is only possible to express the duty to perform a specific action, as a requirement that must be fulfilled for obtaining a valid permission to perform another action.

Obligations are crucial for expressing the normative relationships in which an agent will become obliged to do a certain type of action a_1 as a consequence of the performance of another action a_2, where a_2 may be viewed as the *activation condition* of the obligation. Two concrete examples of this type of obligations are the following. A nurse may have the *possibility* to use an "emergency account" for getting access to sensitive health data of a patient, in case the emergency account is used the nurse becomes obligated to write within one week a report explaining the reasons why the account has been used. Another interesting example is given by the policy that regulates the access to the "limited traffic area" of certain big cities: people have the *possibility* to enter the "limited traffic area", but if they do so they become obligated to pay a certain sum within a given temporal limit, otherwise they will be sanctioned. Obligations without activation conditions are rare and it is quite hard to find interesting examples.

---

[2] https://www.w3.org/community/odrl/model/2.1/.

The temporal relationship between the activation condition and the consequent obligation makes it impossible to formalize such obligations using only the notion of permission or prohibition. For example, a conditional permission stating that if the nurse writes the report she gets the permission to use the emergency account, would change the temporal relation among the actions, and therefore is not equivalent to the conditional obligation described above. Similarly, if a prohibition coupled with a sanction is used (stating that using the emergency account is prohibited, and in case the prohibition is violated, the sanction of writing a report applies) the result is a counterintuitive specification. Moreover, the formalization by means of a prohibition will create a violation that may affect the reputation of the violator, even if this is not a desired consequence.

In the ODRL 2.1 core model, it is assumed that "any use not explicitly permitted is prohibited". In our view, it is not always reasonable to assume that all actions regulated by a set of policies are prohibited, except those that are explicitly permitted. In real use cases, it may happen that certain actions are simply *possible*, i.e. they are not explicitly permitted but they are not prohibited: this because in certain situations the request of explicitly permitting certain actions may complicate the overall specification of the set of policies. This assumption requires also that permissions are stronger than prohibitions or that the prohibition to perform an action is deleted when a permission to perform such an action is added.

In March 2016 the W3C "Permissions and Obligations Expression" (POE) Working Group was created with the goal of bringing the Community Group specifications of ODRL 2.1 through the W3C Process to "Recommendation" status. In the following sections we will refer to the most recent version of the Model[3].

In our proposal, a conditional obligation is characterized by the following properties: an *assigner*, an *assignee*, a *deadline*, an *activation condition*, and a *content*. Conditional obligations could be expressed in ODRL by introducing the following syntactic extensions to the RDF Core Model.

– We introduce the class Obligation as a subclass of the ODRL class Rule and we use the property obligation: Policy → Rule for connecting a policy with an obligation.
– Like in ODRL, an obligation may have none or one assigner and/or assignee, which are specified by using the property assigner: Role → Party and the property assignee: Role → Party.
– Differently from ODRL, in our model an obligation does not need to be connected by the target property with the asset whose use is regulated by the obligation. This because the regulated asset is specified by the activation condition of the obligation. In fact, in our model actions are not simply labels like "odrl:read", but they are specified using a richer content language, actions have a class/type and a certain number of properties. In our examples

---

[3] A preview of the new, even if unstable, ODRL Information Model is available at https://www.w3.org/TR/odrl-model/.

we will use the RDF Schema definition of the notion of action proposed by
Schema.org vocabulary[4].

- Moreover we introduce the following new properties:
  - hasActCond: Obligation → Action, which is used for connecting an obliga-
    tion with its activation condition. The activation condition may describe
    a specific action or a class of actions, this last option is possible by spec-
    ifying only the type of the action and some of its properties;
  - hasContent: Rule → Action, which is used for connecting an obligation to
    its content, that is, the description of the action that should be performed
    for fulfilling the obligation. This action, like for the activation condition,
    may be described in full details or by specifying only the type of the
    action and some of its properties;
  - hasDeadline: Obligation → TemporalEntity, which is used for connecting
    an obligation to the deadline within which the action, described in the
    content of the obligation, has to be performed.

Another example of conditional obligation, which is common in electronic
commerce of digital assets like music or video file, is the obligation to pay to a
music provider (for example Sony) a certain amount (for example 5 euros) before
a given deadline (for example the end of September 2017) when an agent (for
example Billy:888) plays a song recorded by the a certain artist, for example
the Beatles. Obviously, this conditional obligation may be initially formalized
at a high level of abstraction using roles and variables, like the role of music
provider, or the role of listener or the variable used for expressing the amount
to be paid. This high-level obligation may be transformed through various steps
into a low-level, concrete obligation without roles and variables. The specification
of a possible concrete obligation formalized in RDF using the Turtle serialization
format[5] is reported below. Thanks to the choice of using a semantic web language
like RDF for the specification of our example, we are able to exploit the crucial
advantage of importing other ontologies in our example. In particular our RDF
specification of obl:01 uses: the ODRL 2.1 RDF Ontology, the Time Ontology in
OWL[6], the RDF ontology of the notion of Action defined by schema.org, our
OWL Event Ontology[7] which defines the notion of Event and connects it with
the notion of Time[5], and the OWL Normative Language Ontology that results
from the previously discussed extension of ODRL[8].

```
@prefix rdfs: <http://www.w3.org/2000/01/rdf-schema#>.
@prefix rdf: <http://www.w3.org/1999/02/22-rdf-syntax-ns#>.
@prefix xsd: <http://www.w3.org/2001/XMLSchema#>.
@prefix odrl: <http://www.w3.org/ns/odrl/2/>.
@prefix schema: <http://schema.org/>.
@prefix time: <http://www.w3.org/2006/time#>.
```

---

[4] http://schema.org/Action.

[5] https://www.w3.org/TR/turtle/.

[6] https://www.w3.org/TR/2006/WD-owl-time-20060927/.

[7] Available at http://www.people.usi.ch/fornaran/ontology/Event.

[8] Available at http://www.people.usi.ch/fornaran/ontology/NormativeLanguage.

```
@prefix event: <http://www.people.usi.ch/fornaran/ontology/event#>.
@prefix nl: <http://www.people.usi.ch/fornaran/ontology/NormativeLanguage#>.

<http://example.com/policy:01>
    a odrl:Agreement;
    nl:obligation <http://example.com/obl:01>.
<http://example.com/obl:01>
    a nl:Obligation;
    nl:hasDeonState nl:conditional;
    odrl:assigner <http://example.com/sony:10>;
    odrl:assignee <http://example.com/billie:888>;
    nl:hasDeadline [
        time:inDateTime "2017-08-21T09:00:00"^^xsd:dateTime];
    nl:hasActCond [
        a schema:ListenAction;
        nl:hasState nl:unSatisfied;
        schema:agent <http://example.com/billie:888>;
        schema:object [
            a schema:MusicRecording;
            schema:byArtist <http://example.com/Beatles>]
    ];
    nl:hasContent [
        a schema:PayAction;
        nl:hasState nl:unSatisfied;
        schema:agent <http://example.com/billie:888>;
        schema:recipient <http://example.com/sony:10>;
        schema:price 5.00;
        schema:priceCurrency "euro"].
<http://example.com/sony:10> a odrl:Party.
<http://example.com/billie:888> a odrl:Party.
<http://example.com/Beatles> a schema:MusicGroup.
```

4   Operational Semantics of Obligations

One relevant limit of ODRL 2.1 is that it has only an informal semantics described in English in the Core Model document and it there is not a formal specification of its semantics [19]. Without a formal semantics, it is not possible to perform automatic reasoning on those policies and therefore it is almost impossible to automatically provide relevant services. One important service is *monitoring* of obligations, in order to automatically compute their activation, and fulfilment or violation on the basis of the (usually partial) knowledge of the actions of the parties involved and of the state of their interaction. Monitoring techniques together with a generator of events and/or the list of actions that one or more users would like to perform on a set of digital assets, can be used to *simulate* the evolution of the state of obligations and then perform a *"what if"* analysis on their fulfilment or violation. This is also a possible approach for evaluating norms *conflicts* or norms compatibility that is thought to work for obligations with a dynamic evolution from active to fulfilled or violated.

A concrete use case where the simulation service proposed may be used is to assist a user who wants to use different digital assets (some photos, one video, and certain data) for creating a conference presentation and then publish it on the Internet on a Social Network. The user wants to know if a given sequence of actions performed on the digital assets will bring to a violation of one of the policies connected to the digital assets used and, if the answer is in the positive, what are the reasons of the violation.

In this section, we present an operational semantics of the syntactic extension of ODRL for expressing conditional obligations, described in the previous section. In particular, the proposed semantics will be focused on the goal of performing automatic reasoning on the temporal evolution of obligations on the basis of the actions of the involved parties and of the elapsing of time. The first step, for the definition of such an operational semantics, consists in the unambiguous specification of the lifecycle of conditional obligations, which depends on the satisfaction of their condition and content. Figure 1 shows the lifecycle of conditional obligations. In this figure, boxes indicate states of the obligation, arrows indicates transitions between states, labels on arrow indicate the preconditions that must be satisfied for the transition to take place or the action that determines the transition.

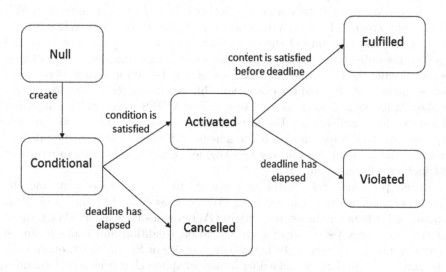

Fig. 1. Conditional obligations lifecycle

When an obligation is created, it becomes *conditional* if it has an unsatisfied condition. A *conditional* obligation becomes *activated* when its condition is satisfied (e.g., the song is played). The condition or the content of obligations becomes satisfied if, in the ontology used for representing the state of the interaction, there is an action whose attribute values match the values specified in the condition or content of the obligation. The condition or the content of an obligation is connected to the matched action or event by means of the reason property. An *active* obligation becomes *fulfilled* if its content becomes satisfied before the deadline. On the contrary, if the deadline of an active obligation has elapsed the obligation becomes *violated*.

The second step for the definition of the operational semantics of conditional obligations consists in specifying how the dynamic evolution of the various obligations can be automatically computed, in order to provide *monitoring* and *simulation* services.

Our approach in this phase is to adopt, as far as possible, W3C standards and in particular Semantic Web Technologies. This first of all because their diffusion among software practitioners and research communities is fundamental for the acceptance and adoption of the proposed formal semantics, and secondly because W3C Semantic Web Technologies are supported by tools (RDFS and OWL reasoners, editors, and API) that are suitable to implement a software framework for testing and evaluating our proposal. Moreover, in this paper we propose an extension of ODRL Version 2.1 Core Model, which is available in RDF 1.0. This choice makes it also feasible to re-use existing ontologies as discussed in the previous section, and to express policies that depend on the semantic content of the data when these are represented using Semantic Web Technologies, like for example Linked Open Data.

An open question at this point is whether it is a good solution to use OWL 2 (possibly integrated with SWRL whenever the expressivity of OWL is insufficient) to express the state of the interaction (i.e. the actions performed by the agents), the obligations and the axioms/rules for computing the state of obligations following their lifecycle. Alternatively, it may be better to express our data (state and obligations) and the obligations' lifecycle using RDFS ontologies, and exploit an RDFS reasoner, like the Apache Jena RDFS reasoner, for computing the state of the obligations. The latter option would allow us to integrate the Apache Jena RDFS reasoner with domain-specific rules, written in the rule language of the Jena general purpose rule engine[9], which can be used to represent the lifecycle of obligations.

In our previous works [5,16] we proposed to express the content and the activation condition of norms by using OWL classes defined by means of OWL axioms and, whenever the expressivity of OWL was insufficient, by SWRL rules. At runtime, the satisfaction of such activation condition and content can be evaluated using a standard OWL reasoning service or SPARQL-DL queries [7]. The main problem that we tackled with such an approach concerns performance, mainly due to the time required for reasoning on OWL ontologies when the number of assertions in the data ontology and the number of norms increase.

Therefore, in the work described in this paper we investigated the expressivity and performance of a solution where the state of the interaction and the obligations' components are formalized using RDFS and the state of obligations is computed by using the Apache Jena general-purpose rule engine. This rule engine integrates a general purpose rule-based reasoner, able to implement

---

[9] Documentation available at https://jena.apache.org/documentation/inference/.

RDFS and OWL reasoning, but is also available for general use[10]. In particular, we propose to exploit the Jena forward chaining RETE engine for reasoning on the state of the obligations formalized in RDFS using the RDFS Schema proposed in the previous section.

The Jena rules that can be used for computing if an obligation is cancelled, activated, fulfilled or violated are the following.

```
[cancelObligation:
(?obl    rdf:type    nl:Obligation),
(?obl    nl:hasDeonState    nl:conditional),
(?obl    nl:hasDeadline    ?deadLine),
(?deadLine time:inDateTime ?dateTime),
now(?now),
greaterThan(?now,?dateTime)        ->
(?obl    nl:hasDeonState    nl:cancelled),
drop(1)
]


[activateObligation:
(?obl    rdf:type    nl:Obligation),
(?obl    nl:hasDeonState    nl:conditional),
(?obl    nl:hasActCond ?activation),
(?activation nl:hasState nl:satisfied) ->
drop(1),
(?obl    nl:hasDeonState    nl:activated)
]


[fulfillObligation:
(?obl    rdf:type    nl:Obligation),
(?obl    nl:hasDeonState    nl:activated),
(?obl    nl:hasDeadline    ?deadLine),
(?deadLine time:inDateTime ?dateTimeDeadline),
(?obl    nl:hasContent    ?content),
(?content nl:hasState nl:satisfied),
(?content nl:reason ?instance),
(?instance event:atTime ?instant),
(?instant time:inDateTime ?dateTimeInstance),
lessThan(?dateTimeInstance,?dateTimeDeadline)    ->
(?obl    nl:hasDeonState    nl:fulfilled),
drop(1)
]
```

---

[10] More precisely "there are two internal rule engines one forward chaining RETE engine and one tabled datalog engine - they can be run separately or the forward engine can be used to prime the backward engine which in turn will be used to answer queries.".

```
[violateObligation:
(?obl    rdf:type     nl:Obligation),
(?obl    nl:hasDeonState    nl:activated),
(?obl    nl:hasDeadline     ?deadLine),
(?deadLine time:inDateTime ?dateTime),
now(?now),
greaterThan(?now,?dateTime)    ->
(?obl    nl:hasDeonState    nl:violated),
drop(1)
]
```

In order to compute the satisfaction of the condition and of the content of obligations we need to introduce had-hoc rules for every obligation. These rules change on the basis of the attributes specified in the description of the actions or events in the content and condition of obligations. For example the rule for computing the satisfaction of the condition of obligation obl:01 specified in the previous section is:

```
[satisfyCondObl01:
(<http://example.com/obl:01> nl:hasDeonState    nl:conditional),
(<http://example.com/obl:01> nl:hasActCond ?activation),
(?activation rdf:type ?actClass),
(?activation nl:hasState nl:unSatisfied),
(?activation schema:agent ?agent),
(?activation schema:object ?object),
(?object rdf:type ?objectClass),
(?object schema:byArtist ?artist),
(?inst   rdf:type ?actClass),
(?inst   schema:agent ?agent),
(?inst   schema:object ?object1),
(?inst   event:atTime ?instant),
(?instant time:inDateTime ?dateTime),
now(?now),
greaterThan(?now,?dateTime),
(?object1   rdf:type ?objectClass),
(?object1 schema:byArtist ?artist)   ->
(?activation nl:hasState nl:satisfied),
(?activation nl:reason ?inst),
drop(3)
]
```

5   Evaluations and Conclusions

We have implemented a Java prototype of the proposed approach. We formalized policies containing conditional obligations using RDF 1.0, and computed their state based on a RDF 1.0 representation of the actions performed by the parties involved in the obligations. The state of conditional obligations and the satisfaction of their condition and content have been computed using forward rules formalized for the Jena general-purpose rule engine. Tests were made with a PC with an Intel Core i5-6600 CPU 3.3 GHz processor, 8 GB RAM. The computation of the satisfaction of the content and condition of one obligation and of its state requires 555 ms. The computation time becomes 557 ms with 10 policies (having all the same content and condition), 569 ms with 20 policies, and 576 ms with 30 policies. From this experiment, we can conclude that the number of policies (and in our case the number of obligations) does not significantly influence the computation time.

We intend to continue this work by proposing an extension and a syntax of the ODRL notion of permission and prohibition. We plan to study how it is possible to integrate efficiently the automatic reasoning on the state of the obligations with the reasoning on the semantics of their content and conditions. This could be done by exploiting the possibility to combine the Jena RDFS reasoner with custom rules (like the one proposed in this paper) or by using one of the available external reasoners, like for example Pellet [14]. We plan also to investigate the possibility to express the activation condition of obligations based on the semantics of the protected digital assets and to study the process for automatically transforming high-level policies expressed in terms of roles and variables into concrete policies.

References

1. Abelson, H., Creative Commons (Organization): CcREL: The Creative Commons Rights Expression Language (2008)
2. Becker, S., Hück, B., Naujokat, K., Schmeiser, A.F., Kasten, A.: ODRL 2.0 revisited. In: Horbach, M. (ed.) GI-Jahrestagung. LNI, vol. 220, pp. 3081–3095. GI (2013)
3. Bradshaw, J.M., et al.: The KAoS Policy Services Framework. In: Eighth Cyber Security and Information Intelligence Research Workshop (CSIIRW 2013), Oak Ridge, p. 2013. Oak Ridge National Labs, TN (2013)
4. da Silva Figueiredo, K., Torres da Silva, V., de Oliveira Braga, C.: Modeling norms in multi-agent systems with NormML. In: De Vos, M., Fornara, N., Pitt, J.V., Vouros, G. (eds.) COIN -2010. LNCS (LNAI), vol. 6541, pp. 39–57. Springer, Heidelberg (2011). https://doi.org/10.1007/978-3-642-21268-0_3
5. Fornara, N.: Specifying and monitoring obligations in open multiagent systems using semantic web technology. In: Elçi, A., Koné, M.T., Orgun, M.A. (eds.) Semantic Agent Systems: Foundations and Applications. Studies in Computational Intelligence, vol. 344, pp. 25–46. Springer, Heidelberg (2011). https://doi.org/10.1007/978-3-642-18308-9_2
6. Fornara, N., Colombetti, M.: Representation and monitoring of commitments and norms using OWL. AI Commun. 23(4), 341–356 (2010)
7. Fornara, N., Marfia, F.: Modeling and enforcing access control obligations for SPARQL-DL queries. In: Fensel, A., Zaveri, A., Hellmann, S., Pellegrini, T. (eds.) Proceedings of the 12th International Conference on Semantic Systems, SEMANTICS 2016, Leipzig, Germany, 12–15 September 2016, pp. 145–152. ACM (2016)
8. Governatori, G., Rotolo, A.: BIO logical agents: norms, beliefs, intentions in defeasible logic. Auton. Agents Multi-Agent Syst. 17(1), 36–69 (2008)

9. Governatori, G., Rotolo, A., Villata, S., Gandon, F.: One license to compose them all. In: Alani, H., et al. (eds.) ISWC 2013, Part I. LNCS, vol. 8218, pp. 151–166. Springer, Heidelberg (2013). https://doi.org/10.1007/978-3-642-41335-3_10

10. Iannella, R., Guth, S., Paehler, D., Kasten, A.: ODRL Version 2.1 Core Model (2015). https://www.w3.org/community/odrl/model/2.1/. Accessed 15 Sept 2017

11. Jain, P., Hitzler, P., Janowicz, K., Venkatramani, C.: There's no money in linked data (2013)

12. Kagal, L., Finin, T.W., Joshi, A.: A policy language for a pervasive computing environment. In: 4th IEEE International Workshop on Policies for Distributed Systems and Networks (POLICY 2003), 4–6 June 2003, Lake Como, Italy, p. 63. IEEE Computer Society (2003)

13. Kasten, A., Grimm, R.: Making the semantics of ODRL and URM explicit using web ontologies. In: Virtual Goods, pp. 77–91 (2010)

14. Meditskos, G., Bassiliades, N.: Dlejena: a practical forward-chaining OWL 2 RL reasoner combining jena and pellet. J. Web Sem. 8(1), 89–94 (2010)

15. Moses, T.: Extensible access control markup language (xacml) version 2.0. OASIS Standard, 200502 (2005)

16. Nguyen, T.T., Fornara, N., Marfia, F.: Automatic policy enforcement on semantic social data. Multiagent Grid Syst. 11(3), 121–146 (2015)

17. Rodríguez-Doncel, V., Villata, S., Gómez-Pérez, A.: A dataset of RDF licenses. In: Hoekstra, R. (ed.) Legal Knowledge and Information Systems - JURIX 2014: The Twenty-Seventh Annual Conference. Jagiellonian University, Krakow, Poland, 10–12 December 2014. Frontiers in Artificial Intelligence and Applications, vol. 271, pp. 187–188. IOS Press (2014)

18. Sensoy, M., Norman, T.J., Vasconcelos, W.W., Sycara, K.P.: OWL-POLAR: a framework for semantic policy representation and reasoning. J. Web Sem. 12, 148–160 (2012)

19. Steyskal, S., Polleres, A.: Towards formal semantics for ODRL policies. In: Bassiliades, N., Gottlob, G., Sadri, F., Paschke, A., Roman, D. (eds.) RuleML 2015. LNCS, vol. 9202, pp. 360–375. Springer, Cham (2015). https://doi.org/10.1007/978-3-319-21542-6_23

20. Uszok, A., et al.: New developments in ontology-based policy management: Increasing the practicality and comprehensiveness of kaos. In: 9th IEEE International Workshop on Policies for Distributed Systems and Networks (POLICY 2008), 2–4 June 2008, Palisades, New York, USA, pp. 145–152. IEEE Computer Society (2008)

A Plausibility Model for Regret Games

Federico Bobbio[1] and Jianying Cui[2(✉)]

[1] Department of Mathematics, University of Pisa, Pisa, Italy
`federico.bobbio01@gmail.com`
[2] Institute of Logic and Cognition, Philosophy Department, Sun Yat-sen University,
Guangdong, China
`cuijiany@mail.sysu.edu.cn`

Abstract. In this paper we develop a plausibility model by defining a
new notion of rationality based on the assumption that a player believes
that she doesn't play a regret dominated strategy. Especially, we show
that the interactive epistemic outcomes of this type of rationality are
in line with the solutions of the Iterated Regret Minimization (IRM)
algorithm. So, we state that one can achieve a characterization of the
IRM algorithm by keeping upgrading the assumption of rationality, and
we obtain common belief of rationality in the limit model. A benefit of
our characterization is that it provides the epistemic foundation to the
IRM algorithm and solve a dynamic information problem best expressed
through the Traveler's Dilemma. Meanwhile, we also link solutions of the
IRM algorithm to modal μ-calculus to deepen our understanding of the
epistemic characterization.

Keywords: Regret games · Iterated regret minimization algorithm
Plausibility model · μ-calculus · Modal logic · Traveler's Dilemma
Information dynamics

1 Introduction

In this paper we study the Iterated Regret Minimization (IRM) algorithm introduced by Halpern and Pass ([7]). The IRM algorithm is able to give game
solutions in accordance to experimental results for some examples where the
Nash Equilibrium fails (e.g. the Traveler's Dilemma). In [6] Cui, Luo and Sim
characterized the IRM using the public announcement of rationality, we took
inspiration from this paper to look for another Modal Logic characterization of
the IRM. In their works [1] and [3], Baltag and Smets propose a new model for
describing belief-changing actions of the agents: they propose to create levels of
plausibility among the possible events in such a way that "uncertainty is never
reduced but the plausibility relations change". All this is done using Kripke
models. The purpose of our study is to give an epistemic characterization of the
IRM that uses the plausibility model introduced by Baltag and Smets. We will
see that this plausibility model characterization enables us to keep all strategies
by creating levels of plausibility among strategy profiles. In the literature it is

© Springer Nature Switzerland AG 2018
F. Belardinelli and E. Argente (Eds.): EUMAS 2017/AT 2017, LNAI 10767, pp. 187–200, 2018.
https://doi.org/10.1007/978-3-030-01713-2_14

often used the lexicographic order to describe the degree of belief of a player (for example [5]). We introduce one lexicographic ordering for each player, to describe which strategy profiles are more plausible to be used by the players; so, we define the Belief of a player as the set of strategy profiles at the top of the lexicographic order of that player.

We work under the assumption that both players believe that themselves and the other players are playing rationally, common belief of rationality is not presupposed but obtained in the limit of the IRM plausibility characterization; thanks to the plausibility model we are also able to overcome an information problem related to this assumption, which is best expressed through the Traveler's Dilemma. Firstly, our definition of rationality is as follows: a rational player plays a strategy which she believes to be not regret dominated. We will express this concept through the modal language [4], as a consequence the rational strategy profiles will be those that are rational for all the players in the game. Secondly, we state that the interactive epistemic outcomes from the common belief of this type of rationality are in line with the solutions of the IRM algorithm, thus we answer the problem above mentioned in a positive way and provide an epistemic foundation for the algorithm. Meanwhile, to deepen our understanding of the IRM, we also provide a modal μ-calculus characterization of the IRM.

The rest of this paper is organized as follows: in Sect. 2 we give the preliminaries to the IRM, the plausibility models and the modal μ-calculus. In Sect. 3 we provide the definition of our plausibility model and the theorem that confirms the correctness of our characterization. Finally we provide the μ-calculus characterization for the algorithm, which is showed in Sect. 4. Conclusions and future work are stated in Sect. 5.

2   Preliminaries

In this section we want to give the necessary preliminaries needed to build our new plausibility and modal μ-calculus characterizations of the IRM algorithm.

2.1   The IRM Algorithm

Let's start with some definitions from Game Theory.

Definition 1. *A strategic game is a tuple* $G = \langle N, \{S_i\}_{i \in N}, \{u_i\}_{i \in N} \rangle$*, where:*

- *N is the set of players in the game G.*
- *S_i is the set of strategies for player i.*
- *u_i is the utility function for player i that assigns a real value to every strategy profile $s = (s_1, \ldots, s_n)$. We denote by $S = S_1 \times \ldots \times S_n$ the set of all strategy profiles.*

Let $S' \subseteq S$*, we denote by* $S'_{-i} = \{s_{-i} = (s_1, \ldots, s_{i-1}, s_{i+1}, \ldots, s_n)|$ *where* $s_j \in S'_j$ *for* $j = 1, \ldots, n$ *and* $j \neq i\} = S'_1 \times .. \times S'_{i-1} \times S'_{i+1} \times .. \times S'_n$ *the set of strategy profiles other than the i-th in* S'*. When we want to focus on the strategy of player i, we denote the strategy profile* $s \in S$ *as* $s = (s_i, s_{-i})$ *where* $s_i \in S_i$ *and* $s_{-i} \in S_{-i}$*.*

Let's now define the regret of a given strategy:

Definition 2. *Given a strategic game $G = \langle N, \{S_i\}_{i \in N}, \{u_i\}_{i \in N} \rangle$, we define $re_i^{S'_i}(s_i, s_{-i})$ as the regret ex post of player i associated to any strategy profile (s_i, s_{-i}) with $s_i \in S'_i$. We calculate it as follows:*

$$re_i^{S'_i}(s_i, s_{-i}) = \max\{u_i(s'_i, s_{-i}) | \forall s'_i \in S'_i \subseteq S_i\} - u_i(s_i, s_{-i}).$$

It represents the regret of player i derived by choosing s_i among all strategies of S'_i when her opponents choose s_{-i}.

Let now s_i and s'_i be two strategies for player i in S'_i. We say that s_i is regret dominated by s'_i w.r.t. $S' \subseteq S$ if $Re_i^{S'}(s'_i) < Re_i^{S'}(s_i)$, where

$$Re_i^{S'}(s_i) :=: Re_i^{S'_i, S'_{-i}}(s_i) := \max\{re_i^{S'_i}(s_i, s_{-i}) | \forall s_{-i} \in S'_{-i}\}.$$

We say that a regret dominated strategy s_i is regrettable for player i.
Let's finally define

$$minRe_i^{S'} :=: minRe_i^{S'_i, S'_{-i}} := min_{s_i \in S'_i} Re_i^{S'}(s_i)$$

be the minimum regret for player i w.r.t. S'.

Now we can introduce[1] the recursive elimination process of IRM presented in [7] by Halpern and Pass:

Definition 3. *Given a strategic game $G = \langle N, \{S_i\}_{i \in N}, \{u_i\}_{i \in N} \rangle$, let IUD be the set of iterated regret un-dominated strategies of G recursively defined by the following Iterated Regret Minimization (IRM) algorithm:*
For the base case we ask that $IUD_i^0 = S_i$ for $i = 0, \ldots, n$. Then we have:

$$IUD_i^{m+1} = \{s'_i \in IUD_i^m | Re_i^{IUD^m}(s'_i) = min_{s_i \in IUD_i^m} Re_i^{IUD^m}(s_i)\}.$$

At the m-th iteration we find $IUD^m = \prod_{i \in N} IUD_i^m$. For the limit we have $IUD_i = \bigcap_{m \geq 0} IUD_i^m$ and $IUD = \prod_{i \in N} IUD_i$.

Let's see how the IRM works through an example.

---

[1] In [6], the definition of the algorithm didn't compute again the regrets of the strategies after the process of elimination of the regret dominated strategies, that's why it couldn't give the desired solution to the Traveler's Dilemma. In this paper we correct this fact.

pl.1-pl.2	a	b	c
A	(0,0)	(1,2)	(0,0)
B	(1,3)	(0,0)	(4,3)
C	(3,4)	(2,0)	(2,3)

Compute its regret game →

pl.1-pl.2	a	b	c
A	(3,2)	(1,0)	(4,2)
B	(2,0)	(2,3)	(0,0)
C	(0,0)	(0,4)	(2,1)

↓ Delete A and b

pl.1-pl.2	a	c
B	(2,0)	(0,0)
C	(0,0)	(2,1)

← Compute its regret game

pl.1-pl.2	a	c
B	(1,3)	(4,3)
C	(3,4)	(2,3)

↓ Delete c

pl.1-pl.2	a
B	(1,3)
C	(3,4)

Compute its regret game, delete B →

pl.1-pl.2	a
C	(0,0)

The following theorem assures us that for any given strategic game G, the IRM algorithm converges to a nonempty fixed point. The proof can be found in [7].

Theorem 1. *Let $G = \langle N, \{S_i\}_{i \in N}, \{u_i\}_{i \in N} \rangle$ be a strategic game. If S is a closed, non-empty set of strategies, then IUD is non-empty.*

2.2 Plausibility Model

Let's move toward the Epistemic Logic and give the definition of plausibility model presented by Baltag and Smets in [1]:

Definition 4. *A multi-agent plausibility model is a tuple $M = \langle W, \leq_i, \sim_i, \|\cdot\|, z^* \rangle_{i \in N}$, where:*

- *W is a set of possible worlds.*
- *N is a finite set of agents.*
- *$\leq_i$ is a preorder (i.e. reflexive and transitive) on W: it is agent i's plausibility relation.*
- *$\sim_i$ is an equivalence relation on W: it is agent i's epistemic possibility.*
- *$\|\cdot\| : \Phi \to \wp(W)$ is a valuation map for a set Φ of propositional constants (the truth value is assigned to each formula inductively).*
- *a designated world (the actual world) $z^* \in W$.*

We ask the following conditions to be satisfied:

1. *Plausibility implies possibility: $s \leq_i t$ implies $s \sim_i t$.*
2. *Indistinguishable worlds are comparable: $s \sim_i t$ implies $s \leq_i t$ or $s \geq_i t$.*
3. *The preorders $\leq_i$ are converse well-founded: there are not infinite ascending chains $s_0 \leq_i s_1 \leq_i \ldots$.*

Remark 1. Baltag in [2] provides some explanations for these conditions.

Condition (1): "Since different agents may have different ("hard") information about the worlds, we can't exclude worlds that an agent knows (in the "hard" sense) to be impossible". We will consider impossible worlds as implausible, i.e. worlds that are less plausible are those which are impossible.

Condition (2): "We do not ask the plausibility relation to be total (though there could be cases where it is); that's because condition (1) forces worlds that are distinguishable ($\neg(t \sim_i s)$) for an agent i, to be implausible with respect to each other (i.e. incomparable $t \not\leq_i s$ and $t \not\geq_i s$) for the agent".

So, given these conditions, two worlds are indistinguishable for an agent iff they are comparable w.r.t. the corresponding plausibility relation: $t \sim_i s$ iff either $t \geq_i s$ or $t \leq_i s$. Thus it is enough to specify the relations $\geq_i$. The possibility relation can simply be defined in terms of the plausibility relation.

There is a map that let us transform a plausibility model into a new plausibility model:

Definition 5. *The radical upgrade is an operator $\Uparrow$ that transforms plausibility models; it is a function that, given the plausibility model $\boldsymbol{M} = \langle W, \leq_i, \sim_i, \| \cdot \|, z^* \rangle_{i \in N}$, gives a new plausibility model $\Uparrow (\boldsymbol{M}) = \langle W, \leq_i', \sim_i, \| \cdot \|, z^* \rangle_{i \in N}$. The new plausibility model $\Uparrow (\boldsymbol{M})$ has a new plausibility relation $\leq_i'$, while the rest remains unchanged.*

Let ϕ be a formula, the radical upgrade $\Uparrow \phi$ does a lexicographic revision with ϕ: all the worlds that satisfy ϕ become more plausible than all the worlds that satisfy $\neg\phi$.

The plausibility relation among the ϕ ($\neg\phi$) worlds remains as it was before the application of the radical upgrade $\Uparrow \phi$.

We also define the repeated truthful[2] radical upgrade $\Uparrow \overrightarrow{\phi} = (\Uparrow \phi)_{n \in \mathbb{N}}$ to be an infinite sequence of radical upgrades. The repeated radical upgrade $\Uparrow \overrightarrow{\phi}$ induces a function mapping every plausibility model $\boldsymbol{M}$ into an infinite sequence $\Uparrow \overrightarrow{\phi}(\boldsymbol{M}) = (\boldsymbol{M})_{n \in \mathbb{N}}$ of plausibility models inductively defined as: $(\boldsymbol{M})_0 = \boldsymbol{M}$, $(\boldsymbol{M})_{n+1} = \Uparrow \phi(\boldsymbol{M}_n)$ (i.e. the radical upgrade applied to the n-th model). In [3] the authors prove that every repeated truthful radical upgrade definable in doxastic-epistemic logic stabilizes every model; then, under the condition that ϕ is true in $\boldsymbol{M}$, by writing $\Uparrow \overrightarrow{\phi}(\boldsymbol{M})$ we will directly refer to the fixed point model obtained.

The radical upgrade is an operator which represents a change in "soft"[3] information, we will use it to understand which strategy profiles are believed to be rational from the players of a strategic game.

Let's see an example to understand how the radical upgrade works. Given the plausibility model on the left, if we apply the radical upgrade $\Uparrow p$ we obtain the plausibility model on the right.

---

[2] An upgrade $\Uparrow \phi$ is truthful in a plausibility model $\mathbf{M}$ if ϕ is true at z^*.

[3] By "hard" information we mean an information, typically referred to Knowledge, whose truth is beyond any doubt. By "soft" information we mean an information, typically referred to Belief, which can be subject to a change.

2.3 Modal μ-calculus

Through modal μ-calculus we are able to express recursion. For our purposes we will refer to [9] and to [8], from the latter we take the following short introduction to modal μ-calculus.

The modal μ-calculus is an extension of Modal Logic with the operators for "smallest fixed points" $\mu p \cdot \phi(p)^4$, where p is a proposition variable and the modal formula $\phi(p)$ must satisfy a special requirement. The propositional variable p may occur only positively in $\phi(p)$, i.e. in the scope of an even number of negations.

This ensures that the approximation function F_ϕ^M defined on sets of worlds as

$$F_\phi^M(X) = \{s \in M \mid M, [p := X], s \vDash \phi\},$$

is monotonic in the inclusion order:

$$\text{whenever } X \subseteq Y, \text{then } F_\phi^M(X) \subseteq F_\phi^M(Y)$$

where M is a model of Modal Logic and X, Y are subsets of its domain. On complete lattices (posets where all subsets have both the supremum and the infimum), the Tarski-Knaster Theorem says that monotonic maps F always have a "smallest fixed point", i.e. a smallest set of worlds X where $F(X) = X$. One can reach this smallest fixed point F_* through a sequence of approximations indexed by ordinals until there is no more increase:

$$\emptyset, \ F(\emptyset), \ F(F(\emptyset)), \ldots F_*.$$

The formula $\mu p \cdot \phi(p)$ holds in a model M at just those worlds that belong to the smallest fixed point for the map $F_\phi^M(X)$. Dually, there are also "greatest fixed point" for monotonic maps, and these are denoted by formulas

$$\nu p \cdot \phi(p)$$

with p occurring only positively in $\phi(p)$. The greatest fixed points are definable from the smallest ones (and vice versa), as shown in the valid formula $\nu p \cdot \phi(p) \leftrightarrow \neg \mu p \cdot \neg \phi(\neg p)$.

---

[4] This formula has the following syntactic interpretation: $\|\mu p \cdot \phi(p)\|_i = \bigcap \{T \subseteq S \mid T \subseteq \|\phi(p)\|_{i[\|p\|=T]}\}$ where i is the interpretation map and S is the domain of the Kripke model.

3   A Plausibility Model for the IRM

In this section we will provide a plausibility characterization for the IRM algorithm. This characterization let players "change" their chosen strategies across time when a change occurs in their beliefs (for example through a radical upgrade caused by sources like friends, mentors, books, papers, et cetera).

Let's first build our modal language, we will ask it to contain special symbols.

Definition 6. *Given a strategic game* $G = \langle N, \{S_i\}_{i \in N}, \{u_i\}_{i \in N} \rangle$, *we define the set of atomic propositions* Γ *to be constituted by a general set of atomic propositions* P, *by the set of all the strategy profiles* S *and, for every player* i, *by the set of the strategies* S_i *of player* i. *The plausibility game language* $\mathcal{L}_{G_p}$ *is defined by the following grammar:*

$$\mathcal{L}_{G_p} ::= p \mid \neg\psi \mid \psi \wedge \theta \mid s_i \succcurlyeq_i s'_i \mid Ra_i^{re} \mid B_i\phi \mid Cb\phi \mid \Uparrow \phi \mid \overrightarrow{\Uparrow \phi}$$

where $p \in \Gamma$ *and* $s_i, s'_i \in S_i$; $s_i \succcurlyeq_i s'_i$ *means that player* i *prefers strategy* s_i *over strategy* s'_i, Ra_i^{re} *means that player* i *is rational*, $B_i\phi$ *means that player* i *believes* ϕ, $Cb\phi$ *means that* ϕ *is common belief among the players*, $\Uparrow \phi$ *and* $\overrightarrow{\Uparrow \phi}$ *are the radical upgrade of* ϕ *and the repeated radical upgrade of* ϕ.

Let's see the definition of the plausibility game model.

Definition 7. *Given a strategic game* G, *its plausibility game model in the* $\mathcal{L}_{G_p}$ *language is* $\boldsymbol{M}_{G_p} = \langle W, \{\leq_i\}_{i \in N}, z^*, \{f_i\}_{i \in N}, \|\cdot\| \rangle$, *where*

- W ($\neq \emptyset$) *consists of all the strategy profiles.*
- *For every* $i \in N$, $\leq_i$ *is a total, converse well-founded preorder on* W: *player* i'*s plausibility relation. For every player* i, *from* $\leq_i$ *we obtain the possibility relation* $\sim_i$.
- *a designated world (the actual world)* $z^* \in W$.
- *For every* $i \in N$, $f_i : W \rightarrow S_i$ *is a strategic function such that* $f_i(w) = s_i$ *where* s_i *is* w *i-th strategy.*
- $\|\cdot\| : \Gamma \rightarrow \wp(W)$ *is the valuation map.*

The interpretation of formulas in the plausibility game model is defined as follows:

Definition 8. *Let* G *be a strategic game and* $\boldsymbol{M}_{G_p}$ *be its plausibility game model. We ask the following rules for the semantics, where* $S' \subseteq S$, $s_i, s'_i \in S_i$ *and* $w, v, s, x, y \in W$:

1. $\boldsymbol{M}_{G_p}, w \vDash s \Longleftrightarrow w = s$.
2. $\boldsymbol{M}_{G_p}, w \vDash s_i \Longleftrightarrow w \in \|s_i\|$, *where* $\|s_i\| := \{w \in W \mid f(w) = w_i = s_i\}$.
3. [5] $\boldsymbol{M}_{G_p}, w \vDash s_i \succcurlyeq_i s'_i \Longleftrightarrow \forall x : x_i = s_i$ *and* $x \in Max_i(W)$, $\exists y : y_i = s'_i$ *and* $y \in Max_i(W)$

$$re_i^{Max_{\leq}(W)}(x) \leq re_i^{Max_{\leq}(W)}(y),$$

---

[5] We say that "player i prefers strategy s_i over strategy s'_i".

where $Max_{\leq_i}(W) = \{s \in W \mid s \geq_i v \; \forall v \in W\}$ and $Max_{\leq}(W) = \bigcap_{j \in N} Max_{\leq_j}(W)$.

4. $\boldsymbol{M}_{G_p}, w \vDash Ra_i^{re} \Longleftrightarrow w \in Max_{\leq}(W)$ and

$$\boldsymbol{M}_{G_p}, w \vDash \bigvee_{s \in W} \left(s \wedge \bigwedge_{\{s_i' \in S_i \mid \exists v \in Max_{\leq}(W) \text{ and } v_i = s_i'\}} s_i \not\succ_i s_i' \right)$$

5. [6] $\boldsymbol{M}_{G_p}, w \vDash B_i \phi \Longleftrightarrow$ for all $v \in Max_{\leq_i}(W)$ then $\boldsymbol{M}_{G_p}, v \vDash \phi$.

6. $\boldsymbol{M}_{G_p}, w \vDash Cb\phi \Longleftrightarrow \boldsymbol{M}_{G_p}, v \vDash \phi$ for all v and every finite chain (of length $n \geq 1$) of the form $w \sim_{i_1} w' \sim_{i_2} w'' \ldots \sim_{i_m} v$ where $w' \in Max_{\leq_{i_1}}(W)$, $w' \in Max_{\leq_{i_2}}(W), \ldots$ and $v \in Max_{\leq_{i_m}}(W)$.

Remark 2. According to item 4 in Definition 8, a strategy profile (represented by the world w) is rational for player i iff w is in $Max_{\leq}(W)$ and for all strategy profiles with the same i-th strategy (and which are in $Max_{\leq}(W)$) we have that their i-th regret ex post is less or equal than all the i-th regret ex post of all the strategy profiles in $Max_{\leq}(W)$ with a different i-th strategy.

For every player $i \in N$, we asked $\leq_i$ to be total so that we can represent the initial situation of a game where each player doesn't know which strategy she should choose. Then, by doing radical upgrades we change the plausibility game model according to the provided informations.

Definition 9. *Let G be a strategic game and $\mathcal{L}_{G_p}$ its language.*

The set of plausibility modal formulas which are satisfied by the plausibility game model $(\boldsymbol{M}_{G_p}, z^*)$, i.e. the plausibility modal logic theory of z^* in $\boldsymbol{M}_{G_p}$, is denoted $\mathcal{G}_p$.

Let's see now some theoretical results.

Theorem 2. *Let G be a finite strategic game and $\boldsymbol{M}_{G_p}$ its plausibility game model. $\boldsymbol{M}_{G_p}$ has worlds in which Ra^{re} is true, where $Ra^{re} = \bigwedge_{i \in N} Ra_i^{re}$.*

Proof. We do the proof in the special case where $N = \{1,2\}$. The general case is similar.

Let's take into consideration the strategy profiles that are in $Max_{\leq}(W)$, if all these worlds are preferred (look at footnote 7 and rule 3) for both players then all the worlds in $Max_{\leq}(W)$ are rationals for all players.

Suppose now that player 1 prefers all the worlds in $Max_{\leq}(W)$ with strategy s over those in $Max_{\leq}(W)$ with strategy t.

On the other hand, if player 2 has no preferred worlds in $Max_{\leq}(W)$, then also Ra_2^{re} holds at all those worlds. In particular Ra_2^{re} holds at those worlds in $Max_{\leq}(W)$ whose 1−st strategy is s. So, there are worlds at which Ra^{re} holds.

However if player 2 also prefers all the worlds in $Max_{\leq}(W)$ with strategy X over all the worlds in $Max_{\leq}(W)$ whose second strategy is Y, then Ra_2^{re} holds at all the worlds in $Max_{\leq}(W)$ with strategy X. Therefore Ra^{re} holds at (s, X).

---

[6] In case $\boldsymbol{M}_{G_p}, w \vDash B_i s_i$, where $s_i \in S_i$ is a (mixed or pure) strategy, we say that "player i believes she should play strategy s_i".

We now show that every iteration of the IRM over a game G is equivalent to a radical upgrade of Ra^{re} over its plausibility game model $\mathbf{M}_{G_p}$. Also, the interactive epistemic outcomes from the repeated radical upgrade of Ra^{re} are in line with the solutions of the IRM algorithm and Ra^{re} is common believed in the fixed point model of the repeated radical upgrade of Ra^{re}.

Theorem 3. *Let $\mathbf{M}_{G_p}$ be a plausibility game model of a finite strategic game G and let $\Uparrow \overrightarrow{Ra^{re}}(\mathbf{M}_{G_p}) = ((\mathbf{M}_{G_p})_n)_{n \in \mathbb{N}}$ be the infinite sequence of pointed models obtained by the repeated radical upgrade of rationality over $\mathbf{M}_{G_p}$.*

First of all, for all $n \in \mathbb{N}$ and for all $w \in W$

$$w \in Max_{\leq}((\mathbf{M}_{G_p})_n) \quad \text{iff} \quad f(w) \in IUD^n.$$

Hence, the repeated radical upgrade of rationality stabilizes the plausibility game model and for all $w \in W$

$$w \in Max_{\leq}((\mathbf{M}_{G_p})_k) \quad \text{iff} \quad f(w) \in IUD$$

where k is the iteration at which we find the fixed point. Also, $CbRa^{re}$ is valid in $(\mathbf{M}_{G_p})_k$.

Proof. Let's start by proving the first statement.

($\rightarrow$) If $w \in Max_{\leq}((\mathbf{M}_{G_p})_n)$, then $(\mathbf{M}_{G_p})_n, w \vDash Ra^{re}$, i.e. $(\mathbf{M}_{G_p})_n, w \vDash \bigwedge_{i \in N} Ra_i^{re}$. First we show: $\forall i \in N, f_i(w) \notin S_i \backslash IUD_i^1$. Suppose not. Then $\exists i \in N$ such that $f_i(w) \in S_i \setminus IUD_i^1$, that is, $f_i(w)$ of player i is regret-dominated in G by some other strategy $s_i' \in S_i = IUD_i^0$. It means $Re_i(f_i(w)) > Re_i(s_i')$, thus by definition of $Re_i(\cdot)$, we have

$$\max\{re_i(f_i(w), s_{-i}) | \forall s_{-i} \in S_{-i}\} > \max\{re_i(s_i', s_{-i}) | \forall s_{-i} \in S_{-i}\}.$$

Now set some $s_{-i}'' \in S_{-i}$ satisfying $re_i(f_i(w), s_{-i}'') = Re_i(f_i(w))$, and set $s_{-i}''' \in S_{-i}$ satisfying $re_i(s_i', s_{-i}''') = Re_i(s_i')$. Thus, by the previous inequality we have

$$re_i(f_i(w), s_{-i}'') > re_i(s_i', s_{-i}''').$$

Furthermore, set $v' \in R_i(w) \cap \|s_{-i}''\|$. Then by the previous inequality

$$re_i(f_i(w), f_i(v')) > re_i(s_i', s_{-i}''').$$

Thus, considering $\forall v \in \|s_i'\|, re_i(s_i', s_{-i}''') \geq re_i(s_i', f_{-i}(v))$, then we can then find from the previous inequality

$$\forall v \in \|s_i'\|, re_i(f_i(w), f_{-i}(v')) > re_i(s_i', f_{-i}(v)).$$

According to $f_i(w) = f_i(v')$, which follows from $v' \in R_i(w)$ and the definition of the plausibility frame, we find

$$\forall v \in \|s_i'\|, re_i(f_i(v'), f_{-i}(v')) > re_i(s_i', f_{-i}(v)).$$

Then we have that $\mathbf{M}_{G_p}, v' \nvDash f_i(v') \succ^S s'_i$. From $f_i(w) = f_i(v')$ we have that $\mathbf{M}_{G_p}, v' \nvDash f_i(w) \succ^S s'_i$, since $v' \in R_i(w) \cap Max_\leq(W)$, where $R_i(w) = \{v \in W \mid f_i(w) = f_i(v)\}$ is the set of worlds which have the same i-th strategy as w. Then, by definition, we obtain that $\mathbf{M}_{G_p}, w \nvDash Ra_i^{re}$. This is against our hypothesis. Since $\forall w \in W \ f_i(w) \in IUD_i^0$, it follows that $f_i(w) \in IUD_i^1$.

Let's see now the inductive step. For a given integer $m \geq 1$, suppose that $\forall j \in N, f_j(w) \in IUD_j^m$, then we need to show that $f_j(w) \notin IUD_j^m \setminus IUD_j^{m+1}$ for all j. Suppose not. Then there is player i such that $f_i(w) \in IUD_i^m \setminus IUD_i^{m+1}$. That is, $f_i(w)$ is a regret dominated strategy in IUD_i^m by some other strategy $s'_i \in IUD_i^m$. Then we have

$$\max\{re_i(f_i(w), s_{-i}) | \forall s_{-i} \in IUD_{-i}^m\} > \max\{re_i(s'_i, s_{-i}) | \forall s_{-i} \in IUD_{-i}^m\}.$$

By the induction hypothesis, $\forall j \in N, f_j(w) \in IUD_j^m$. Thus we have that

$$\max\{re_i(f_i(w), f_{-i}(v)) | \forall v \in R_i(w) \text{ s.t. } f_i(v) \in IUD_i^m\} >$$
$$\max\{re_i(f_i(w'), f_{-i}(v)) | \forall v \in R_i(w) \text{ s.t. } f_i(v) \in IUD_i^m\}.$$

Where $w' \in \|s'_i\|$. Similar to the above proof, we can conclude that $\mathbf{M}_{G_p}, w \nvDash Ra_i^{re}$. This is in contradiction with the hypothesis that $\mathbf{M}_{G_p}, w \vDash Ra_i^{re}$. So $f_i(w) \in IUD_i^{m+1}$. Then for induction we have that $\forall i \in N, f_i(w) \in IUD_i$.

($\leftarrow$) Let $f(w) \in IUD^n$. Then, given $m < n$ a natural number $\forall i \in N \ f_i(w)$ is never regret dominated in IUD^m. It means that after m radical upgrades of Ra^{re}, $(\mathbf{M}_{G_p})_m, w \vDash Ra^{re}$, where $(\mathbf{M}_{G_p})_m$ is the plausibility model after the application of m radical upgrades of rationality. So $w \in Max_\leq((\mathbf{M}_{G_p})_n)$.

Let's prove the second statement. We now know that every application of the radical upgrade of rationality to the plausibility model finds the same strategy profiles as an application of the IRM to the game. Thanks to Theorem 1 we know that the IRM deletion process reaches a non-empty fixed-point from a certain k-th iteration. Thanks to the above stated equivalence we find that all the worlds (strategy profiles) in $Max_\leq((\mathbf{M}_{G_p})_k)$ remain in there after any application of $\Uparrow Ra^{re}$. Note that all the worlds that are in $Max_\leq((\mathbf{M}_{G_p})_k)$, have always been in $Max_\leq((\mathbf{M}_{G_p})_m)$ for all $m < k$. Now we choose the actual world to be one of the worlds in this set. Baltag and Smets in [3][7] prove that the repeated truthful radical upgrade in epistemic-doxastic logic stabilizes every model (w.r.t. which it is truthful), thus we have our proof. The last statement follows from the definition of Cb.

Theorem 4. *Let $\mathcal{M}_G$ be a plausibility game model and denote the fixed-point model obtained by applying a repeated radical upgrade of rationality as $(\mathbf{M}_{G_p})^* = \Uparrow \overrightarrow{Ra^{re}}(\mathbf{M}_{G_p})$. For the fixed-point model $(\mathbf{M}_{G_p})^*$ rationality is doxastically introspective, i.e. the following formula is valid*

$$Ra_i^{re} \rightarrow B_i Ra_i^{re}.$$

---

[7] Corollary 6 says: Every repeated truthful radical upgrade definable in doxastic-epistemic logic (i.e. the language of simple belief and knowledge operators, without any conditional beliefs) stabilizes every model.

Proof. Consider the fixed-point model $(\mathbf{M}_{G_p})^*$ and an arbitrary world w in it such that $(\mathbf{M}_{G_p})^*, w \vDash Ra_i^{re}$ but $(\mathbf{M}_{G_p})^*, w \nvDash B_i Ra_i^{re}$. Then there is a $v \in Max_{\leq_i}(W)$ such that $(\mathbf{M}_{G_p})^*, v \nvDash Ra_i^{re}$. By definition, $f_i(v)$ is a regret dominated strategy for player i by some of her strategies. Since $v \in Max_{\leq_i}(W)$ and the model is a fixed-point of radical upgrade Ra^{re}, then v is not a dominated strategy for i.

3.1   Application to the Traveler's Dilemma

Let's introduce the Traveler's Dilemma: an air company looses the suitcases of two travelers which value is the same. The air company asks each traveler which was the value of her suitcase from a minimum value of 2 \$ to a maximum value of 100 \$. They will refund both travelers with the minimum value between the two. The air company also decides to apply a penalty p (where $p \geq 2$): $p\$$ will be taken from the refund of the traveler who gave a higher value and will be assigned to the other one.

In the following table we represent the Traveler's Dilemma with p = 2.

player 1 - player 2	100	99	98	...	3	2
100	(100,100)	(97,101)	(96,100)	...	(1,5)	(0,4)
99	(101,97)	(99,99)	(96,100)	...	(1,5)	(0,4)
98	(100,96)	(100,96)	(98,98)	...	(1,5)	(0,4)
⋮	⋮	⋮	⋮	⋱	⋮	⋮
3	(5,1)	(5,1)	(5,1)	...	(3,3)	(0,4)
2	(4,0)	(4,0)	(4,0)	...	(4,0)	(2,2)

As it was shown in [7], the IRM is able to find a solution to the Traveler's Dilemma, (97,97) if the penalty is 2, which is in accordance to experimental results. Thanks to Theorem 3 we know that we can reach the same solution through our plausibility characterization.

Halpern and Pass in their paper pointed out the following observation: "(..) the iterated deletion of weakly dominated strategies requires sufficiently high mutual assumption of rationality, where "assumption" is a variant of "knowledge", and "rationality" means "doesn't play a weakly dominated strategy". If we make this assumption (and identify rationality with minimizing regret) we seem to run into a serious problem with Iterated Regret Minimization. As we observed earlier, the strategy profile (97,97) is the only one that survives iterated regret minimization when p = 2. However, if agent 1 knows that player 2 is playing 97, then he should play 96, not 97!".

We can solve this problem thanks to the fact that our definition of rationality requires not only that a strategy profile is not regret dominated for player 1, but also that player 1 believes that such given strategy profile is among the more plausible strategy profiles. Let's introduce the plausibility game model of the Traveler's Dilemma, where each Kripke world represents a strategy profile and it is labeled by its ex posts; the labeled arrows represent the possibility ($\leftrightarrow$) and the plausibility ($\rightarrow$) relations for player 1 and player 2.

$$
(100,100) \underset{\longleftrightarrow}{1,2} (97,101) \underset{\longleftrightarrow}{1,2} (96,100) \underset{\longleftrightarrow}{1,2} (95,99) \underset{\longleftrightarrow}{1,2} (94,98) \underset{\longleftrightarrow}{1,2} (93,97) \cdots
$$

$$
2\updownarrow 1 \qquad 2\updownarrow 1 \qquad 2\updownarrow 1 \qquad 2\updownarrow 1 \qquad 2\updownarrow 1 \qquad 2\updownarrow 1
$$

$$
\vdots \quad \vdots \quad \vdots \quad \vdots \quad \vdots \quad \vdots \quad \vdots \quad \vdots \quad \vdots \quad \vdots \quad \ddots
$$

As we can see in the above picture, thanks to the fact that $\forall i \in N \leq_i$ is total, we can represent the initial situation where all the Kripke worlds are indistinguishable for both players.

If we apply the IRM plausibility characterization (i.e. we apply $\Uparrow^* Ra^{re}$ to the model) we find the following plausibility game model (we highlighted in red the plausibility relations changed by the repeated radical upgrade):

$$
\vdots \quad \vdots \quad \vdots \quad \vdots \quad \vdots \quad \vdots \quad \vdots \quad \vdots \quad \vdots \quad \vdots
$$

$$
(100,96) \underset{\longleftrightarrow}{1,2} (100,96) \underset{\longleftrightarrow}{1,2} (98,98) \underset{\longleftrightarrow}{1,2} (95,99) \underset{\longleftrightarrow}{1,2} (94,98) \underset{\longleftarrow}{1,2} \cdots
$$

$$
2\updownarrow 1 \qquad 2\updownarrow 1 \qquad 2\updownarrow 1 \qquad 2\downarrow 1 \qquad 2\updownarrow 1
$$

$$
(99,95) \underset{\longleftrightarrow}{1,2} (99,95) \underset{\longleftrightarrow}{1,2} (99,95) \underset{\longrightarrow}{1,2} (97,97) \underset{\longleftarrow}{1,2} (94,98) \underset{\longleftarrow}{1,2} \cdots
$$

$$
2\updownarrow 1 \qquad 2\updownarrow 1 \qquad 2\updownarrow 1 \qquad 2\uparrow 1 \qquad 2\updownarrow 1
$$

$$
(98,94) \underset{\longleftrightarrow}{1,2} (98,94) \underset{\longleftrightarrow}{1,2} (98,94) \underset{\longleftrightarrow}{1,2} (98,94) \underset{\longleftrightarrow}{1,2} (96,96) \underset{\longleftarrow}{1,2} \cdots
$$

$$
2\uparrow 1 \qquad 2\uparrow 1 \qquad 2\uparrow 1 \qquad 2\uparrow 1 \qquad 2\uparrow 1
$$

$$
\vdots \quad \vdots \quad \vdots \quad \vdots \quad \vdots \quad \vdots \quad \vdots \quad \vdots \quad \vdots \quad \ddots
$$

Now we encode the information that player 1 believes that player 2 believes that she plays strategy 97_2 by doing the radical upgrade $\Uparrow 97_2$. We thus obtain the following plausibility game model (again, we highlighted in red the plausibility relations changed by the radical upgrade):

$$
(100,100) \underset{\longleftrightarrow}{1,2} (97,101) \underset{\longleftrightarrow}{1,2} (96,100) \underset{\longrightarrow}{1,2} (95,99) \underset{\longleftarrow}{1,2} (94,98) \underset{\longleftarrow}{1,2} \cdots
$$

$$
\vdots \quad \vdots \quad \vdots \quad \vdots \quad \vdots \quad \vdots \quad \vdots \quad \vdots \quad \vdots \quad \vdots
$$

$$
(99,95) \underset{\longleftrightarrow}{1,2} (99,95) \underset{\longleftrightarrow}{1,2} (99,95) \underset{\longrightarrow}{1,2} (97,97) \underset{\longleftarrow}{1,2} (94,98) \underset{\longleftarrow}{1,2} \cdots
$$

$$
2\updownarrow 1 \qquad 2\updownarrow 1 \qquad 2\updownarrow 1 \qquad 2\uparrow 1 \qquad 2\updownarrow 1
$$

$$
(98,94) \underset{\longleftrightarrow}{1,2} (98,94) \underset{\longleftrightarrow}{1,2} (98,94) \underset{\longrightarrow}{1,2} (98,94) \underset{\longleftarrow}{1,2} (96,96) \underset{\longleftarrow}{1,2} \cdots
$$

$$
\vdots \quad \vdots \quad \vdots \quad \vdots \quad \vdots \quad \vdots \quad \vdots \quad \vdots \quad \vdots \quad \ddots
$$

Now, if we want to know which are the strategy profiles that the two players believe they are going to play, we do a radical upgrade of rationality and we find that the model remains unchanged; thus the game solution remains the strategy profile (97,97).

A strength of the plausibility model introduced by Baltag and Smets is that it is susceptible to change in soft information; for instance, if it is common belief that player 2 is playing strategy 100_2-before the IRM is applied-, we can encode such information through a radical upgrade $\Uparrow 100_2$. After that, if we do the IRM we find that the game solution is the strategy profile (99,100).

4   IRM Through the μ-calculus

As we have seen, through the IRM algorithm we find a fixed point model as our game solution. Since modal μ-calculus is one of the most used languages to describe automata and it can easily describe fixed point, it is interesting to see how we can characterize the IRM through a modal μ-calculus formula. The modal μ-calculus formula we provide tells us that the strategy profiles that survive the IRM are exactly those that are in the greatest fixed point of rationality.

Given a finite game G, let's provide the language with which we are going to work:

$$\mathcal{L}_{G_\mu} ::= p \mid \neg\psi \mid \psi \wedge \theta \mid s_i \succcurlyeq_i s_i' \mid Ra_i^{re} \mid B_i\phi \mid Cb\phi \mid \nu x.\psi(x)$$

where $p \in \Gamma$ and $s_i, s_i' \in S_i$ and x is positive in $\psi(x)$.

We define the μ-game model $\mathcal{M}_{G_\mu}$ over the language $\mathcal{L}_{G_\mu}$ in the same way we did for the plausibility game model in Definition 7 and by considering the semantics for the modal μ-calculus.

Now we provide a modal μ-formula which characterizes the strategy profiles that survive the IRM:

Theorem 5. *Let G be a finite strategic form game. The game solution given by the IRM is the same obtained by repeated radical upgrade of Ra^{re} ($= \bigwedge_{a \in N} Ra_a^{re}$) in the plausibility game model $\mathcal{M}_G$; the same game solution can be characterized inside the μ-game model $\mathcal{M}_{G_\mu}$ by the following modal μ-formula:*

$$\nu x. \bigwedge_{a \in N} Ra_a^{re} \wedge x$$

Proof. The first statement of the theorem follows from Theorem 3. Let's see the second statement.

By the definition of greatest fixed point, any world in the set P defined by $\nu x. \bigwedge_{a \in N} Ra_a^{re} \wedge x$ satisfies $\bigwedge_{a \in N} Ra_a^{re} \wedge x$. Thus the formula $\bigwedge_{a \in N} Ra_a^{re}$, being a logical consequence of this, also holds throughout P, and a further radical upgrade of rationality $\Uparrow Ra^{re}$ has no effect.

On the other hand, the repeated radical upgrade limit for $\bigwedge_{a \in N} Ra_a^{re}$ is by definition a subset P of the current model that is contained in the set $\bigwedge_{a \in N} Ra_a^{re} \wedge x$. Thus, it is contained in the greatest fixed point for the monotonic operator matching this formula.

5   Conclusions and Future Work

We have presented a plausibility model for the IRM and we have also linked the IRM to modal μ-calculus. Relatively to the work done in [6] we have given a developed definition of the IRM algorithm because it recomputes the regret after every iteration and we have characterized it in a model where changes in soft information is relevant for equilibrium outcomes. Similarly as in the paper [7] by Halpern and Pass, we have provided a lexicographic order to set levels of belief for each player, but thanks to the plausibility characterization we can take into account when a player changes her strategy and we still get a reasonable solution to the game by applying the IRM. The strength of our characterization is that it doesn't erase dominated strategies, but it gives them a lower plausibility level so that we can use them again in case there is a change in soft information.

The plausibility model represents a strong breakthrough for describing change of information, thus it would be interesting to see if it is possible to give a plausibility characterization for other algorithms.

Concerning further work it would also be interesting to see if it is possible to prove the completeness theorem for the logic presented in this work.

Acknowledgements. For this work the first author benefited financial support from the University of Pisa, the paper is also supported by Kep Programm of National Social Science Foundation of China (No. 16AZX017) and by Kep Programm of National Social Science Foundation of China (No. 15AZX020). The authors would like to thank Alexandru Baltag, Alessandro Berarducci, Davide Grossi and Johan van Benthem for their precious suggestions and comments.

References

1. Baltag, A., Smets, S.: Dynamic belief revision over multi-agent plausibility models. In: Proceedings of LOFT, vol. 6, pp. 11–24 (2006)
2. Baltag, A.: Lectures on Dynamic Epistemic Logic. University of Amsterdam (2016)
3. Baltag, A., Smets, S.: Group belief dynamics under iterated revision: fixed points and cycles of joint upgrades. In: Proceedings of the 12th Conference on Theoretical Aspects of Rationality and Knowledge, pp. 41–50 (2009)
4. Blackburn, P., De Rijke, M., Venema, Y.: Modal Logic. Cambridge University Press (2002)
5. Blume, L., Brandenburger, A., Dekel, E.: Lexicographic probabilities and equilibrium refinements. Econometrica. J Econ. Soc. **59**, 81–98 (1991)
6. Cui, J., Luo, X., Sim, K.M.: A new epistemic logic model of regret games. In: Wang, M. (ed.) KSEM 2013. LNCS (LNAI), vol. 8041, pp. 372–386. Springer, Heidelberg (2013). https://doi.org/10.1007/978-3-642-39787-5_31
7. Halpern, J.Y., Pass, R.: Halpern and rafael pass: iterated regret minimization: a new solution concept. Games Econ. Behav. **1**(74), 184–207 (2012)
8. Van Benthem, J.: Logic in games. MIT press, Cambridge (2014)
9. Venema, Y.: Lectures on the modal μ−calculus. University of Amsterdam (2012)

EUMAS 2017: Argumentation and Rational Choice

Two Forms of Minimality in ASPIC$^+$

Zimi Li[1], Andrea Cohen[2($\boxtimes$)], and Simon Parsons[3]

[1] Department of Computer Science, Graduate Center,
City University of New York, New York City, USA
zli2@gradcenter.cuny.edu
[2] Institute for Computer Science and Engineering,
CONICET-UNS, Department of Computer Science and Engineering,
Universidad Nacional del Sur, Bahía Blanca, Argentina
ac@cs.uns.edu.ar
[3] Department of Informatics, King's College London, London, UK
simon.parsons@kcl.ac.uk

Abstract. Many systems of structured argumentation explicitly require
that the facts and rules that make up the argument for a conclusion be
the minimal set required to derive the conclusion. ASPIC$^+$ does not place
such a requirement on arguments, instead requiring that every rule and
fact that are part of an argument be used in its construction. Thus
ASPIC$^+$ arguments are minimal in the sense that removing any element
of the argument would lead to a structure that is not an argument. In
this paper we discuss these two types of minimality and show how the
first kind of minimality can, if desired, be recovered in ASPIC$^+$.

1 Introduction

A large part of the work on computational argumentation is concerned with
structured, or *logic-based* argumentation. In this work, much of the focus is on
the way that arguments are constructed from some set of components, expressed
in some logic. At this point, perhaps the most widely studied system of structured
argumentation is ASPIC$^+$, which builds on what is now quite a lengthy tradition,
a tradition which goes back at least as far as [10]. In addition to Pollock's work
on OSCAR [9,11], we can count the work of Loui [7], Krause *et al.* [6], Prakken
and Sartor [13], Besnard and Hunter [2], Amgoud and Cayrol [1], García and
Simari [5] and Dung *et al.* [4] as being in the same lineage. ASPIC$^+$ [8,12] is more
recent, but very influential, providing a very general notion of argumentation
that captures many of the structured systems which precede it. In all these
systems, there is, often explicitly, a notion of an argument as a pair $\langle \Delta, c \rangle$ which
relates the conclusion of the argument, c, and the set of statements Δ from which
that conclusion is derived. The form of derivation, and what these "statements"
consist of, are two of the aspects of these systems which vary widely.

One difference between ASPIC$^+$ and other systems of structured argumentation is that many of the latter require that arguments be minimal in the sense
that the set Δ in any argument $\langle \Delta, c \rangle$ has to be minimal. That is, Δ has to

F. Belardinelli and E. Argente (Eds.): EUMAS 2017/AT 2017, LNAI 10767, pp. 203–218, 2018.
https://doi.org/10.1007/978-3-030-01713-2_15

be the smallest set from which c can be derived. We can find this explicitly expressed, for example, in [1,2,5]. In contrast, like the assumption-based system from [4], ASPIC$^+$ does not explicitly require arguments to be minimal in this sense. Instead ASPIC$^+$ arguments satisfy a different form of minimality in which arguments cannot include premises or rules that are not used in the derivation of their conclusion. In recent work using ASPIC$^+$[3], we discovered some cases in which the difference between these two forms of minimality was important, and so needed to investigate those differences in the context of ASPIC$^+$. In this paper we report our findings.

Note that while the first form of minimality is stronger than the native minimality of ASPIC$^+$, because there are ASPIC$^+$ arguments that are not minimal in this sense, this form of minimality is completely compatible with ASPIC$^+$, and indeed with assumption-based argumentation (which shares the same mechanism for defining an argument). As we show, when the stronger form of minimality is required, we can simply invoke a definition for arguments in ASPIC$^+$ which does require this form of minimality.

The rest of the paper is organized as follows. In Sect. 2 we introduce background notions from ASPIC$^+$. Then, in Sect. 3 we discuss the native form of minimality of arguments in ASPIC$^+$, and propose two equivalent ways of providing a stronger notion of minimality, which prevents redundancy and circularity in arguments. Section 3 also includes formal results regarding the characterization of arguments in ASPIC$^+$, as well as relating the forms of minimality we proposed. Later, in Sect. 4, we analyze related work, and finally, in Sect. 5, we draw some conclusions and comment on future lines of work.

2   Background

ASPIC$^+$ is deliberately defined in a rather abstract way, as a system with a minimal set of features that can capture the notion of argumentation. This is done with the intention that it can be instantiated by a number of concrete systems that then inherit all of the properties of the more abstract system. ASPIC$^+$ starts from a logical language $\mathcal{L}$ with a notion of negation. A given instantiation will then be equipped with inference rules, and ASPIC$^+$ distinguishes two kinds of inference rules: strict rules and defeasible rules. Strict rules, denoted using $\rightarrow$, are rules whose conclusions hold without exception. Defeasible rules, denoted $\Rightarrow$, are rules whose conclusions hold unless there is an exception.

The language and the set of rules define an *argumentation system*:

Definition 1 (Argumentation System [8]). *An argumentation system is a tuple $AS = \langle \mathcal{L}, ^-, \mathcal{R}, n \rangle$ where:*

- *$\mathcal{L}$ is a logical language.*
- *$^-$ is a function from $\mathcal{L}$ to $2^{\mathcal{L}}$, such that:*
  - *φ is a contrary of ψ if $\varphi \in \overline{\psi}$, $\psi \notin \overline{\varphi}$;*
  - *φ is a contradictory of ψ if $\varphi \in \overline{\psi}$, $\psi \in \overline{\varphi}$;*
  - *each $\varphi \in \mathcal{L}$ has at least one contradictory.*

- $\mathcal{R} = \mathcal{R}_s \cup \mathcal{R}_d$ *is a set of strict ($\mathcal{R}_s$) and defeasible ($\mathcal{R}_d$) inference rules of the form* $\phi_1, \ldots, \phi_n \rightarrow \phi$ *and* $\phi_1, \ldots, \phi_n \Rightarrow \phi$ *respectively (where* ϕ_i, ϕ *are meta-variables ranging over wff in* $\mathcal{L}$*), and* $\mathcal{R}_s \cap \mathcal{R}_d = \varnothing$.
- $n : \mathcal{R}_d \mapsto \mathcal{L}$ *is a naming convention for defeasible rules.*

The function $\overline{}$ generalizes the usual symmetric notion of negation to allow non-symmetric conflict between elements of $\mathcal{L}$. The contradictory of some $\varphi \in \mathcal{L}$ is close to the usual notion of negation, and we denote that φ is a *contradictory* of ψ by "$\varphi = \neg\psi$". Note that, given the characterization of $\overline{}$, elements in $\mathcal{L}$ may have multiple contraries and contradictories. The naming convention for defeasible rules is necessary because there are cases in which we want to write rules that deny the applicability of certain defeasible rules. Naming the rules, and having those names be in $\mathcal{L}$ makes it possible to do this, and the denying applicability makes use of the contraries of the rule names.

An argumentation system, as defined above, is just a language and some rules which can be applied to formulae in that language. To provide a framework in which reasoning can happen, we need to add information that is known, or believed, to be true. In ASPIC⁺, this information makes up a *knowledge base*:

Definition 2 (Knowledge Base [8]). *A knowledge base in an argumentation system* $\langle \mathcal{L}, \overline{}, \mathcal{R}, n \rangle$ *is a set* $\mathcal{K} \subseteq \mathcal{L}$ *consisting of two disjoint subsets* $\mathcal{K}_n$ *and* $\mathcal{K}_p$.

We call $\mathcal{K}_n$ the axioms and $\mathcal{K}_p$ the ordinary premises. We make this distinction between the elements of the knowledge base for the same reason that we make the distinction between strict and defeasible rules. We are distinguishing between those elements—axioms and strict rules—which are definitely true and allow truth-preserving inferences to be made, and those elements—ordinary premises and defeasible rules—which can be disputed.

Combining the notions of argumentation system and knowledge base gives us the notion of an *argumentation theory*:

Definition 3 (Argumentation Theory [8]). *An argumentation theory* AT *is a pair* $\langle AS, \mathcal{K} \rangle$ *of an argumentation system* AS *and a knowledge base* $\mathcal{K}$.

We are now nearly ready to define an argument. But first we need to introduce some notions which can be defined just understanding that an argument is made up of some subset of the knowledge base $\mathcal{K}$, along with a sequence of rules, that lead to a conclusion. Given this, $\mathtt{Prem}(\cdot)$ returns all the premises, $\mathtt{Conc}(\cdot)$ returns the conclusion and $\mathtt{TopRule}(\cdot)$ returns the last rule in the argument. $\mathtt{Sub}(\cdot)$ returns all the sub-arguments of a given argument, that is all the arguments that are contained in the given argument.

Definition 4 (Argument [8]). *An argument* A *from an argumentation theory* $AT = \langle \langle \mathcal{L}, \overline{}, \mathcal{R}, n \rangle, \mathcal{K} \rangle$ *is:*

1. ϕ *if* $\phi \in \mathcal{K}$ *with:* $\mathtt{Prem}(A) = \{\phi\}$; $\mathtt{Conc}(A) = \phi$; $\mathtt{Sub}(A) = \{A\}$; *and* $\mathtt{TopRule}(A) = undefined$.

2. $A_1, \ldots, A_n \to \phi$ if A_i, $1 \leq i \leq n$, are arguments and there exists a strict rule of the form $\text{Conc}(A_1), \ldots, \text{Conc}(A_n) \to \phi$ in $\mathcal{R}_s$. $\text{Prem}(A) = \text{Prem}(A_1) \cup \ldots \cup \text{Prem}(A_n)$; $\text{Conc}(A) = \phi$; $\text{Sub}(A) = \text{Sub}(A_1) \cup \ldots \cup \text{Sub}(A_n) \cup \{A\}$; and $\text{TopRule}(A) = \text{Conc}(A_1), \ldots, \text{Conc}(A_n) \to \phi$.

3. $A_1, \ldots, A_n \Rightarrow \phi$ if A_i, $1 \leq i \leq n$, are arguments and there exists a defeasible rule of the form $\text{Conc}(A_1), \ldots, \text{Conc}(A_n) \Rightarrow \phi$ in $\mathcal{R}_d$. $\text{Prem}(A) = \text{Prem}(A_1) \cup \ldots \cup \text{Prem}(A_n)$; $\text{Conc}(A) = \phi$; $\text{Sub}(A) = \text{Sub}(A_1) \cup \ldots \cup \text{Sub}(A_n) \cup \{A\}$; and $\text{TopRule}(A) = \text{Conc}(A_1), \ldots, \text{Conc}(A_n) \Rightarrow \phi$.

We write $\mathcal{A}(AT)$ to denote the set of arguments from the theory AT.

In other words, an argument is either an element of $\mathcal{K}$, or it is a rule and its conclusion such that each premise of the rule is the conclusion of an argument. From here on, we will use the symbol $\rightsquigarrow$ when we do not care about distinguishing whether an argument uses a strict rule $\to$ or a defeasible rule $\Rightarrow$. Thus, if we are making a statement about an argument $A = [B \rightsquigarrow a]$, then we are making a statement about both arguments $A' = [B \to a]$ and $A'' = [B \Rightarrow a]$. Similarly, when referring to a rule $a \rightsquigarrow b$, we are referring to both a strict rule $a \to b$ and a defeasible rule $a \Rightarrow b$.

The above is a standard presentation of an argument in ASPIC$^+$. In this paper we wish to refer to an additional element of an argument, and to describe an argument in a somewhat different way. In particular, we wish to refer to $\text{Rules}(A)$, which identifies the set of all the strict and defeasible rules used in the argument A.

Definition 5 (Argument Rules). Let $AT = \langle AS, \mathcal{K} \rangle$ be an argumentation theory and $A \in \mathcal{A}(AT)$. We define the set of rules of A as follows:

$$\text{Rules}(A) = \begin{cases} \varnothing & A \in \mathcal{K} \\ \{\text{TopRule}(A)\} \cup \bigcup_{i=1}^{n} \text{Rules}(A_i) & A = [A_1, \ldots, A_n \rightsquigarrow \text{Conc}(A)] \end{cases}$$

We can then describe an argument A as a triple (G, R, c), where $G = \text{Prem}(A)$ are the grounds on which A is based, $R = \text{Rules}(A)$ is the set of rules that are used to construct A from G, and $c = \text{Conc}(A)$ is the conclusion of A.

Example 1. Consider that we have an argumentation system $AS_1 = \langle \mathcal{L}_1, \bar{\ }, \mathcal{R}_1, n \rangle$, where $\mathcal{L}_1 = \{p, q, r, s, t, u, v, \neg p, \neg q, \neg r, \neg s, \neg t, \neg u, \neg v\}$, $\mathcal{R}_1 = \{p, q \rightsquigarrow r; t, u \rightsquigarrow r; r \rightsquigarrow s; u \rightsquigarrow v\}$. By adding the knowledge base $\mathcal{K}_1 = \{p, q, t, u\}$ we obtain the argumentation theory $AT_1 = \langle AS_1, \mathcal{K}_1 \rangle$, from which we can construct the following arguments:

$$A_1 = [p]; A_2 = [q]; A_3 = [A_1, A_2 \rightsquigarrow r]; A = [A_3 \rightsquigarrow s];$$
$$B_1 = [t]; B_2 = [u]; B_3 = [B_1, B_2 \rightsquigarrow r]; B = [B_3 \rightsquigarrow s]$$

such that $A_1 = (\{p\}, \varnothing, p)$, $A_2 = (\{q\}, \varnothing, q)$, $A_3 = (\{p, q\}, \{p, q \rightsquigarrow r\}, r)$, $A = (\{p, q\}, \{p, q \rightsquigarrow r; r \rightsquigarrow s\}, s)$, $B_1 = (\{t\}, \varnothing, t)$, $B_2 = (\{u\}, \varnothing, u)$, $B_3 = (\{t, u\}, \{t, u \rightsquigarrow r\}, r)$ and $B = (\{t, u\}, \{t, u \rightsquigarrow r; r \rightsquigarrow s\}, s)$.

3   Minimality

Now, as mentioned above, unlike some definitions of arguments in the literature—for example [1,5]—Definition 4 does not impose any minimality requirement on the grounds or the set of rules. However, this does not mean that ASPIC$^+$ arguments are not, in some sense, minimal, as we will now show.

The following example illustrates the fact that any element (proposition or rule) in the grounds and rules of an argument needs to be used in the derivation of the conclusion of that argument:

Example 2. Given the argumentation theory from Example 1, the structure

$$C = (\{p, q, t, u\}, \{p, q \rightsquigarrow r; t, u \rightsquigarrow r; r \rightsquigarrow s\}, s)$$

is not an argument. In particular, C is not an argument because the third clause of Definition 4 only justifies adding the rules and grounds of one argument for each premise of the rule that is the subject of the clause. Thus, it allows $p, q \rightsquigarrow r$ to be added to an argument with conclusion r, or it allows $t, u \rightsquigarrow r$ to be added, but it does not permit both to be added. Similarly,

$$D = (\{p, q\}, \{p, q \rightsquigarrow r; r \rightsquigarrow s; u \rightsquigarrow v\}, s)$$
$$E = (\{t, u\}, \{t, u \rightsquigarrow r; r \rightsquigarrow s; u \rightsquigarrow v\}, s)$$

are not arguments because Definition 4 does not allow rules that are not used in the derivation of the conclusion of an argument to be part of the set of rules of that argument. Finally, neither of

$$F = (\{p, q, t, u\}, \{p, q \rightsquigarrow r; r \rightsquigarrow s\}, s)$$
$$G = (\{p, q, t, u\}, \{t, u \rightsquigarrow r; r \rightsquigarrow s\}, s)$$

are arguments, because Definition 4 does not allow the addition of propositions to the grounds of an argument if they do not correspond to premises of a rule in the argument.

Thus, as the preceding example shows, an argument A, described by the triple $A = (G, R, c)$, cannot contain any elements in G or R that are not used in the derivation of c. Therefore, Definition 4 implies that arguments are minimal in the sense that they do not contain any extraneous propositions or rules. This intuition is also pointed out by the authors in [8], and we formalize it in the following proposition:

Proposition 1. Let $AT = \langle AS, \mathcal{K} \rangle$ be an argumentation theory and $A \in \mathcal{A}(AT)$. It holds that either:

(a) $A = (\{c\}, \varnothing, c)$; or
(b) $A = (G, R, c)$ and
  i. for every $g \in G$: there exists $A' \in \mathsf{Sub}(A)$ such that $A' = (\{g\}, \varnothing, g)$ and there exists $r \in R$ such that $r = p_1, \ldots, g, \ldots, p_n \rightsquigarrow p'$; and

ii. for every $r' \in R$ such that $r' = p_1, \ldots, p_m \rightsquigarrow p''$: there exists $A'' \in$ Sub(A) such that $A'' = (G'', R'' \cup \{r'\}, p'')$, with $G'' \subseteq G$ and $R'' \subseteq R$.

Proof. Definition 4 includes three clauses that define when $A = (G, R, c)$ is an argument. In the first clause, the base case of the recursive definition, $c \in \mathcal{K}$, R is the empty set and $G = \{c\}$, satisfying case (a).

The rest of this proof concerns case (b). Now, the second and third clauses of Definition 4, which define the recursive step of the definition, tells us that (G, R, c) is an argument if there exists a rule in R of the form $c_1, \ldots,$ $c_n \rightsquigarrow c$ and for each c_i $(1 \leq i \leq n)$ there exists an argument $A_i \in \mathcal{A}(AT)$ such that Conc$(A_i) = c_i$. In other words, for every premise c_i of the rule there is a sub-argument A_i of A whose conclusion is that premise. Unwinding each of those sub-arguments in turn, they are either of the form $(\{c_i\}, \varnothing, c_i)$, or can be deconstructed into a rule with sub-arguments for each premise, where that rule is in R. In the first of these cases, the first clause of Definition 4 tells us that $c_i \in G$, and so case (b.i) holds. From the second of these cases we can infer that for every rule $p_1, \ldots, p_m \rightsquigarrow p'' \in R$, there is a sub-argument $(G'', R'' \cup \{p_1, \ldots, p_m \rightsquigarrow p''\}, p'')$ of A, and case (b.ii) is proved. $\square$

Given an argument $A = (G, R, c)$, Proposition 1 states that every element in G is the conclusion of a sub-argument A' of A and is the premise of a rule in R, and that every rule in R is the TopRule$(\cdot)$ of a sub-argument A'' of A. In other words, it states that every element of the grounds G and the rules R is part of the derivation of c. However, as the following example shows, Definition 4 does not imply that for any argument (G, R, c) there is no argument (G', R', c) such that $G' \subset G$ and $R' \subset R$:

Example 3. Consider the argumentation system $AS_3 = \langle \mathcal{L}_3, \dot{-}, \mathcal{R}_3, n \rangle$, where $\mathcal{L}_3 = \{p, q, r, s, t, \neg p, \neg q, \neg r, \neg s, \neg t\}$ and $\mathcal{R}_3 = \{p, q \rightsquigarrow s; s \rightsquigarrow q; q, r \rightsquigarrow t\}$. By adding the knowledge base $\mathcal{K}_3 = \{p, q, r\}$ we obtain the argumentation theory $AT_3 = \langle AS_3, \mathcal{K}_3 \rangle$, from which we can construct the following arguments:

$$A_1 = [p]; A_2 = [q]; A_3 = [A_1, A_2 \rightsquigarrow s]; A_4 = [A_3 \rightsquigarrow q]; A_5 = [r];$$
$$A = [A_4, A_5 \rightsquigarrow t]; B = [A_2, A_5 \rightsquigarrow t]$$

such that $A = (\{p, q, r\}, \{p, q \rightsquigarrow s; s \rightsquigarrow q; q, r \rightsquigarrow t\}, t)$ and $B = (\{q, r\}, \{q, r \rightsquigarrow t\}, t)$. Here, it is clear that the grounds and rules of argument B are proper subsets of those of argument A.

Consider now the set of rules $\mathcal{R}_{3'} = \{p, q \rightsquigarrow r; r \rightsquigarrow s; s \rightsquigarrow t; t \rightsquigarrow r\}$. We can obtain a new argumentation system $AS_{3'} = \langle \mathcal{L}_3, \dot{-}, \mathcal{R}_{3'}, n \rangle$ and combine it with the knowledge base $\mathcal{K}_3$ to obtain the argumentation theory $AT_{3'} = \langle AS_{3'}, \mathcal{K}_3 \rangle$, from which we can construct the arguments:

$$C_1 = [p]; C_2 = [q]; C_3 = [C_1, C_2 \rightsquigarrow r]; C_4 = [C_3 \rightsquigarrow s]; C_5 = [C_4 \rightsquigarrow t];$$
$$C = [C_5 \rightsquigarrow r]; D = C_3 = [C_1, C_2 \rightsquigarrow r]$$

Here, $C = (\{p, q\}, \{p, q \rightsquigarrow r; r \rightsquigarrow s; s \rightsquigarrow t; t \rightsquigarrow r\}, r)$ and $D = (\{p, q\}, \{p, q \rightsquigarrow r\}, r)$; hence, Rules$(D) \subset$ Rules(C).

Finally, if we consider a set of rules $\mathcal{R}_{3''} = \{p \leadsto r; r \leadsto s; q \leadsto r; r, s \leadsto t\}$ and a knowledge base $\mathcal{K}_{3'} = \{p, q\}$ we can define an argumentation system $AS_{3''} = \langle \mathcal{L}_3, \bar{\cdot}, \mathcal{R}_{3''}, n \rangle$ and an argumentation theory $AT_{3''} = \langle AS_{3''}, \mathcal{K}_{3'} \rangle$, from which we obtain:

$$E_1 = [p]; E_2 = [E_1 \leadsto r]; E_3 = [E_2 \leadsto s]; E_4 = [q]; E_5 = [E_4 \leadsto r];$$
$$E = [E_5, E_3 \leadsto t]; F = [E_2, E_3 \leadsto t]$$

In this case, $E = (\{p, q\}, \{p \leadsto r; r \leadsto s; q \leadsto r; r, s \leadsto t\}, t)$ and $F = (\{p\}, \{p \leadsto r; r \leadsto s; r, s \leadsto t\}, t)$. As a result, the grounds and rules of F are proper subsets of those of E.

At first sight, this seems a bit contradictory. Example 2 and Proposition 1 show that arguments only contain elements that are used in the derivation of their conclusion, yet Example 3 shows that elements can be removed from the grounds or the rules of an argument, and what remains is still an argument. There is, however, no contradiction. Rather, there are two ways in which this phenomenon might arise. The first is illustrated by the first two cases in Example 3. There we have arguments that are *circular*[1]—if you follow the chain of reasoning from premises to conclusion in A in Example 3, we start with q, then derive q, then use q to derive the final conclusion; similarly, when considering C, we start with p and q to derive r, then derive s and t to derive (again) r. In B and D, these loops are removed to give us more compact arguments with the same conclusions. The second way in which this phenomenon might arise is illustrated by the third case in Example 3, where we have arguments that are *redundant*. There, the cause is that the set of rules provides two ways to derive r, one that relies on p and another that relies on q, and r appears twice in the derivation of t: once to produce s, and once when the rule $r, s \leadsto t$ is applied. Then E, the redundant argument, uses both of the rules for deriving r while F uses just one of them, again providing a more compact derivation.

Furthermore, as shown by the following example, circularity in arguments may lead to having two distinct arguments A and B such that their descriptions as a triple (G, R, c) coincide. Hence, while we can extract a unique description (G, R, c) from a given ASPIC$^+$ argument A, the reverse is not true.[2]

---

[1] We use the term *circular* to reflect the idea of circular reasoning [15] and "begging the question" [14].

[2] This is a version of the issue pointed out by [4, p.119], that any inference-based description of an argument allows multiple arguments to be described in the same way. In fact what we have here is a stronger version of the problem, because [4] pointed out the problem for arguments which, in our terms, were described just by their grounds and conclusion. What we have here is the problem arising even when we state the inference rules as well. This issue the is converse of the problem that describing arguments by their entire structure, as ASPIC$^+$ and the assumption-based argumentation of [4] do, allows for redundant elements in the arguments, as we have just shown.

Example 4. Consider that we have an argumentation system $AS_4 = \langle \mathcal{L}_4, \dot{\ }, \mathcal{R}_4, n \rangle$, where $\mathcal{L}_4 = \{a, b, c, \neg a, \neg b, \neg c\}$ and $\mathcal{R}_4 = \{a \rightsquigarrow c; c \rightsquigarrow b; b \rightsquigarrow a\}$. We then add the knowledge base $\mathcal{K}_4 = \{a\}$ to get the argumentation theory $AT_4 = \langle AS_4, \mathcal{K}_4 \rangle$. From this we can construct the following arguments:

$$A_1 = [a]; A_2 = [A_1 \rightsquigarrow c]; A_3 = [A_2 \rightsquigarrow b]; A = [A_3 \rightsquigarrow a];$$
$$B_1 = [A \rightsquigarrow c]; B_2 = [B_1 \rightsquigarrow b]; B = [B_2 \rightsquigarrow a]$$

Here, both arguments A and B are described by the triple (G, R, a), where $G = \mathtt{Prem}(A) = \mathtt{Prem}(B) = \{a\}$, $R = \mathtt{Rules}(A) = \mathtt{Rules}(B) = \mathcal{R}_4$ and $a = \mathtt{Conc}(A) = \mathtt{Conc}(B)$.

Given the preceding analysis we can note that, even though the characterization of ASPIC$^+$ arguments accounts for some form of minimality (see [8]), it allows for circular and redundant arguments. These notions of circularity and redundancy are formalized next.

Definition 6 (Circular Argument). *Let AT be an argumentation theory and $A \in \mathcal{A}(AT)$. We say that A is a circular argument if $\exists A_1, A_2 \in \mathtt{Sub}(A)$ such that $A_1 \neq A_2$, $\mathtt{Conc}(A_1) = \mathtt{Conc}(A_2)$ and $A_1 \in \mathtt{Sub}(A_2)$.*

Note that the usual definition of a circular argument in the literature [14,15] involves starting with some premise and then inferring that premise—a typical pattern is "Assume a, then a is true". What we define here as circular is more general.

Example 5. Considering Example 3 in the light of Definition 6 and looking at A, the two sub-arguments that define its circularity are $A_1 = (\{q\}, \varnothing, q)$ and $A_4 = (\{p, q\}, \{p, q \rightsquigarrow s, s \rightsquigarrow q\}, q)$. Then, if we consider argument C, the two sub-arguments that define its circularity are $C_3 = (\{p, q\}, \{p, q \rightsquigarrow r\}, r)$ and $C = (\{p, q\}, \{p, q \rightsquigarrow r, r \rightsquigarrow s, s \rightsquigarrow t, t \rightsquigarrow r\}, r)$. Here, A follows the classic form of a circular argument. In contrast, C illustrates the more general form of circularity, not related to the premises of the argument.

Next, we formalize the notion of redundancy:

Definition 7 (Redundant Argument). *Let AT be an argumentation theory and $A \in \mathcal{A}(AT)$. We say that A is a redundant argument if $\exists A_1, A_2 \in \mathtt{Sub}(A)$ such that $A_1 \neq A_2$, $\mathtt{Conc}(A_1) = \mathtt{Conc}(A_2)$, $A_1 \notin \mathtt{Sub}(A_2)$ and $A_2 \notin \mathtt{Sub}(A_1)$.*

Example 6. Considering Example 3 in the light of Definition 7, the two sub-arguments that define the redundancy of E are $E_2 = (\{p\}, \{p \rightsquigarrow r\}, r)$ and $E_5 = (\{q\}, \{q \rightsquigarrow r\}, r)$.

We say that arguments that are non-circular and non-redundant are *regular* arguments since they are the kinds of argument that one encounters most often in the literature. Clearly this is the same as saying:

Definition 8 (Regular Argument). *Let AT be an argumentation theory and $A \in \mathcal{A}(AT)$. We say that A is regular if $\nexists A_1, A_2 \in \mathtt{Sub}(A)$ such that $A_1 \neq A_2$ and $\mathtt{Conc}(A_1) = \mathtt{Conc}(A_2)$.*

Now, to tie this back to the notion of minimality frequently used in the literature (e.g., [1,2,5]), that of a minimal set of information from which a conclusion is derived, we need a notion of inference that works for ASPIC$^+$. We start with a notion of *closure*. Given an argumentation theory, we can define the closure of a set of propositions in the knowledge base under a set of rules of the theory.

Definition 9 (Closure). *Let $AT = \langle AS, \mathcal{K} \rangle$ be an argumentation theory, where AS is the argumentation system $AS = \langle \mathcal{L}, \dot{-}, \mathcal{R}, n \rangle$. We define the closure of a set of propositions $P \subseteq \mathcal{K}$ under a set of rules $R \subseteq \mathcal{R}$ as $Cl(P)_R$, where:*

1. *$P \subseteq Cl(P)_R$;*
2. *if $p_1, \ldots, p_n \in Cl(P)_R$ and $p_1, \ldots, p_n \rightsquigarrow p \in R$, then $p \in Cl(P)_R$; and*
3. *$\nexists S \subset Cl(P)_R$ such that S satisfies the previous conditions.*

Based on the notion of closure, we can define a notion of inference from a set of propositions and rules of an argumentation theory.

Definition 10 (Inference). *Let $AT = \langle AS, \mathcal{K} \rangle$ be an argumentation theory, where AS is the argumentation system $AS = \langle \mathcal{L}, \dot{-}, \mathcal{R}, n \rangle$. Given a set of propositions $P \subseteq \mathcal{K}$, a set of rules $R \subseteq \mathcal{R}$ and a proposition $p \in \mathcal{K}$, we say that p is inferred from P and R, noted as $P \vdash_R p$, if $p \in Cl(P)_R$.*

Now, with this notion of inference, we can characterize *minimal arguments*. These arguments are such that they have minimal (with respect to $\subseteq$) sets of grounds and rules that allow to infer their conclusion.

Definition 11 (Minimal Argument). *Let $AT = \langle AS, \mathcal{K} \rangle$ be an argumentation theory and $A \in \mathcal{A}(AT)$. We say that $A = (G, R, c)$ is a minimal argument if $\nexists G' \subset G$ such that $G' \vdash_R c$ and $\nexists R' \subset R$ such that $G \vdash_{R'} c$.*

The following example illustrates the first condition in Definition 11.

Example 7. Let $AT_7 = \langle AS_7, \mathcal{K}_7 \rangle$ be an argumentation theory, where $AS_7 = \langle \mathcal{L}_7, \dot{-}, \mathcal{R}_7, n \rangle$, $\mathcal{R}_7 = \{d \rightsquigarrow b; b \rightsquigarrow c; b, c \rightsquigarrow a\}$ and $\mathcal{K}_7 = \{b, d\}$. From AT we can construct the following arguments:

$$A_1 = [d]; A_2 = [A_1 \rightsquigarrow b]; A_3 = [A_2 \rightsquigarrow c]; A_4 = [b]; A = [A_4, A_3 \rightsquigarrow a];$$
$$B = [A_2, A_3 \rightsquigarrow a]; A_5 = [A_4 \rightsquigarrow c]; C = [A_4, A_5 \rightsquigarrow a]$$

Here, $A = (G, R, a)$, with $G = \{b, d\}$ and $R = \mathcal{R}_7$. In this case, A is not minimal since $\exists G' \subset G$, with $G' = \{d\}$, such that $G' \vdash_R a$; moreover, $B = (G', R, a)$. On the other hand, argument C is represented by the triple (G'', R', a), with $G'' = \{b\}$ and $R' = \{b \rightsquigarrow c; c \rightsquigarrow a\}$. In particular, argument C is minimal. Furthermore, B is also minimal since, even though $R' \subset R$, it is not the case that $G' \vdash_{R'} a$.

It should be noted that, since the notion of minimality characterized in Definition 11 explicitly accounts for the set of grounds of the arguments, this notion of minimality is different from those used in other structured argumentation systems such as DeLP [5]. Arguments in DeLP do not include the grounds:

they are specified by a pair $\langle \Delta, c \rangle$, where Δ is the set of defeasible rules used to derive the conclusion c. Thus, the notion minimality in DeLP considers only the defeasible rules used in an argument. As a result, if we consider the arguments given in Example 7, argument B would not be minimal in DeLP.

To illustrate the second condition of Definition 11, let us consider the situation depicted in Example 4. There, we have arguments A and B, which are both described by the triple (G, R, a), with $G = \{a\}$ and $R = \{a \rightsquigarrow c; c \rightsquigarrow b; b \rightsquigarrow a\}$. Also, there is argument $A_1 = (G', \varnothing, a)$, with $G' = \{a\}$. As a result, $\exists G' \subset G$ such that $G' \vdash_R a$ and therefore, arguments A and B are not minimal, in contrast with A_1.

Given the characterization of regular and minimal arguments, the following proposition shows that these notions are equivalent.

Proposition 2. *Let* $AT = \langle AS, \mathcal{K} \rangle$ *be an argumentation theory and* $A \in \mathcal{A}(AT)$, *with* $A = (G, R, c)$. A *is a regular argument iff* A *is a minimal argument.*

Proof. The proof follows the same form as that of Proposition 1, being based around the three clauses of Definition 4.

*Let us start with the if part. In the first clause of Definition 4, c is a proposition in $\mathcal{K}$, R is empty, and G contains just c. Clearly, in this case there is no $R' \subset R$, nor $G' \subset G$ such that $G' \vdash_R c$ or $G \vdash_{R'} c$, so A is minimal. It is also regular. The second and third clauses in Definition 4 define the recursive case. Here, $A = (G, R, c)$ is an argument if c is the conclusion of a rule, let us call it r, and there is an argument in $\mathcal{A}(AT)$ for each of the premises of r. G is then the union of the grounds of all the arguments with conclusions that are premises of r; we will call this set of arguments **Args**, and R is the union of all the rules for **Args**, call them **Rs**, plus r. If all the arguments in **Args** are minimal, then A will be minimal, so long as (i) adding r does not introduce any non-minimality, and (ii) the union of the grounds and the rules of the arguments in **Args** do not introduce any non-minimality. Let us consider case (i). For the addition of r to introduce non-minimality, it must be the case that $(G, \textbf{Rs}, c)$ is an argument. In that case, $(G, \textbf{Rs}, c)$ will be a sub-argument of A and thus, by Definition 6, A is circular, contradicting the hypothesis that it is a regular argument. Let us now consider case (ii). Here, in order for A not to be minimal, there have to be minimal arguments $(G_1, R_1, p_1), \ldots, (G_n, R_n, p_n)$ in **Args** such that $p_1, \ldots, p_n$ are the premises in rule r and $A = (\bigcup_{i=1}^{n} G_i, \bigcup_{i=1}^{n} R_i \cup \{r\}, c)$ is not minimal. Because we are taking the unions, no duplication can be introduced. Since $G_1, \ldots, G_n$ are just sets of propositions, their union cannot be the cause of any non-minimality, and we know from case (i) that any non-minimality is not due to r. So if any non-minimality is introduced, it is in $\bigcup_{i=1}^{n} R_i$. Since by Proposition 1 every rule in R_i must be used in deriving p_i, the only way that $\bigcup_{i=1}^{n} R_i$ can make A non-minimal is if there is some rule in R_j which allows the derivation of the same conclusion as a rule in R_k (with $1 \leqslant j, k \leqslant n$, and $j \neq k$). In such a case, A would have two distinct sub-arguments with the same conclusion, where one is not a sub-argument of the other; hence, by Definition 7, A would be redundant, contradicting the hypothesis that A is regular.*

Let us now address the only if part. In the first clause of Definition 4, c is a proposition in $\mathcal{K}$, R is empty, and G contains just c. Clearly, in this case A is regular since A is the only sub-argument of A; thus, there exist no distinct sub-arguments of A with the same conclusion. A is also minimal. The second and third clauses in Definition 4 define the recursive case. Here, $A = (G, R, c)$ is an argument if c is the conclusion of a rule, let us call it r, and there is an argument in $\mathcal{A}(AT)$ for each of the premises in rule r. G is then the union of the grounds of all the arguments with conclusions that are premises in r, and R is the union of all the rules for those arguments, plus r. Since by hypothesis $A = (G, R, c)$ is minimal, it must be the case that $\nexists G' \subset G$ such that $G' \vdash_R c$ and $\nexists R' \subset R$ such that $G \vdash_{R'} c$. Suppose by contradiction that A is not regular. Hence, there should exist two distinct sub-arguments $A_1 = (G_1, R_1, p')$ and $A_2 = (G_2, R_2, p')$ of A such that $G_1 \neq G_2$, $R_1 \neq R_2$, or both. However, this would imply that $\exists G' \subset G$ (with $G' = (G \backslash G_1) \cup G_2$, or $G' = (G \backslash G_2) \cup G_1$) or $\exists R' \subset R$ (with $R' = (R \backslash R_1) \cup R_2$, or $R' = (R \backslash R_2) \cup R_1$) such that $G' \vdash_R c$ and $\nexists R' \subset R$ such that $G \vdash_{R'} c$, contradicting the hypothesis that A is minimal.   □

Next, we illustrate the relationship between regular and minimal arguments.

Example 8. Let us consider the arguments from Example 7, where it was shown that B and C are minimal arguments, whereas A is not. Then, we have that B is also regular, since it has no pair of sub-arguments with the same conclusion. Specifically, $\text{Sub}(B) = \{B, A_2, A_3, A_1\}$, and $\text{Conc}(B) = a$, $\text{Conc}(A_2) = b$, $\text{Conc}(A_3) = c$, $\text{Conc}(A_1) = d$. Similarly, C is also regular since $\text{Sub}(C) = \{C, A_4, A_5\}$, where $\text{Conc}(C) = a$, $\text{Conc}(A_4) = b$ and $\text{Conc}(A_5) = c$. In contrast, if we consider argument A, which was shown to be non-minimal in Example 7, we have $\text{Sub}(A) = \{A, A_4, A_3, A_2, A_1\}$ where, in particular, $\text{Conc}(A_4) = b$ and $\text{Conc}(A_2) = b$; therefore, A is not a regular argument.

On the other hand, if we consider the arguments from Example 3, it was shown in Examples 5 and 6 that A, C and E are not regular arguments (the first two by being circular and the last one by being redundant). Then, if we look at the minimality of these arguments, we have that $A = (G_a, R_a, t)$, with $G_a = \{p, q, r\}$, $R_a = \{p, q \rightsquigarrow s; s \rightsquigarrow q; q, r \rightsquigarrow t\}$, and $\exists G'_a = \{r\}$, $\exists R'_a = \{r \rightsquigarrow t\}$ such that $G'_a \vdash_{R_a} t$ and $G_a \vdash_{R'_a} t$; hence, A is not a minimal argument. In the case of $C = (G_c, R_c, r)$, with $G_c = \{p, q\}$ and $R_c = \{p, q \rightsquigarrow r; r \rightsquigarrow s; s \rightsquigarrow t; t \rightsquigarrow r\}$, we have that $\exists R'_c = \{p, q \rightsquigarrow r\}$ such that $G_c \vdash_{R'_c} r$ and therefore, C is not minimal. Finally, given $E = (G_e, R_e, t)$, with $G_e = \{p, q\}$ and $R_e = \{p \rightsquigarrow r; r \rightsquigarrow s; q \rightsquigarrow r; r, s \rightsquigarrow t\}$, it is the case that $\exists G'_e = \{p\}$, $\exists G''_e = \{q\}$, $\exists R'_e = \{p \rightsquigarrow r; r \rightsquigarrow s; r, s \rightsquigarrow t\}$, $\exists R''_e = \{r \rightsquigarrow s; q \rightsquigarrow r; r, s \rightsquigarrow t\}$ such that $G'_e \vdash_{R_e} t$, $G''_e \vdash_{R_e} t$, $G_e \vdash_{R'_e} t$ and $G_e \vdash_{R''_e} t$; thus, E is not a minimal argument.

Let us consider another example regarding minimal and non-minimal arguments.

Example 9. Consider that we have an argumentation system $AS_9 = \langle \mathcal{L}_9, \bar{\ }, \mathcal{R}_9, n \rangle$, where $\mathcal{L}_9 = \{p, q, r, \neg p, \neg q, \neg r\}$ and $\mathcal{R}_9 = \{p \rightsquigarrow q; q \rightsquigarrow r\}$. By adding the knowledge base $\mathcal{K}_9 = \{p, q\}$ we obtain the argumentation theory $AT_9 = \langle AS_9, \mathcal{K}_9 \rangle$, from which we can build the following arguments:

$$H_1 = [p]; \; H_2 = [H_1 \rightsquigarrow q]; \; H = [H_2 \rightsquigarrow r];$$
$$I_1 = [q]; \; I = [I_1 \rightsquigarrow r]$$

such that $H = (\{p\}, \{p \rightsquigarrow q; q \rightsquigarrow r\}, r)$ and $I = (\{q\}, \{q \rightsquigarrow r\}, r)$.

Even though arguments H and I in Example 9 have the same conclusion and use the rule $q \rightsquigarrow r$ to draw that conclusion, they are both minimal. This is because, according to Definition 11, an argument is minimal if there is no argument for the same conclusion built from a smaller set of grounds (respectively, rules) combined with the set of rules (respectively, grounds) of the former. Thus it is possible to have two minimal arguments for the same conclusion, where the latter uses a subset of the rules of the former, so long as the grounds of the latter are not included in the grounds of the former. Similarly, we could have two minimal arguments for the same conclusion, where the latter uses a subset of the grounds of the former, so long as the rules of the latter are not included in the set of rules of the former.

On the other hand, the situation depicted in Example 9 relates to the one involving arguments $C_3 = (\{p, q\}, \{p, q \rightsquigarrow r\}, r)$ and $C = (\{p, q\}, \{p, q \rightsquigarrow r; r \rightsquigarrow s; s \rightsquigarrow t; t \rightsquigarrow r\}, r)$ in Example 3. However, even though C_3 and C have the same conclusion, differently from H and I, they are such that one is a sub-argument of the other (specifically, C_3 is a sub-argument of C, with the sets of grounds and rules of C_3 being contained in those of C). As a result, C is not regular nor minimal.

Finally, it should be noted that, since ASPIC$^+$ arguments are not required to be minimal in the sense of Definition 11, it can be the case that two different arguments A and B have the same description as a triple (G, R, c), as occurred in Example 4. However, as shown by the following proposition, that cannot be the case when considering minimal arguments.

Proposition 3. *Let $AT = \langle AS, \mathcal{K} \rangle$ be an argumentation theory and $A \in \mathcal{A}(AT)$, with $A = (G, R, c)$. If A is a minimal argument, then $\nexists B \in \mathcal{A}(T)$ such that $B \neq A$ and $B = (G, R, c)$.*

Proof. Suppose that $A = (G, R, c)$ is a minimal argument and $\exists B \in \mathcal{A}(T)$ such that $B \neq A$ and $B = (G, R, c)$. By Proposition 1, every element in the grounds G and every rule in R is used in the derivation of A's and B's conclusion c. Furthermore, since by hypothesis A is minimal, by Definition 11 it is the case that $\nexists G' \subset G$, $\nexists R' \subset R$ such that $G' \vdash_R c$ or $G \vdash_{R'} c$. If $B \neq A$, then it must be the case that the difference between them is on the number of times they use the rules in R. Since by hypothesis A is minimal, there must be a rule $r = p_1, \ldots, p_n \rightsquigarrow p \in R$ that is used more times in B than in A. Now consider the derivation of A and B. From what we have said so far, these must be largely the same, so we can think of them starting from the same set of grounds and applying rules, one by one. Thinking of the two arguments like this, side by side, so to speak, since B uses some rule r more times than A does, then at some stage B uses the rule r to derive p, whereas r is not used in A at that point. Hence, since p is needed at that point as part of the derivation for A's conclusion c, there *must be an alternative derivation for p in A, which does not require the use of the rule r. However, this would imply that there exists a rule $r' \in R$ such that $r' = p'_1, \ldots, p'_m \rightsquigarrow p$ or $p \in G$, contradicting the hypothesis that A is minimal. As a result, if A is a minimal argument, then $\nexists B \in \mathcal{A}(T)$ such that $B \neq A$ and $B = (G, R, c)$.* □

We finish by noting that even though arguments H and I in Example 9, are both minimal in the sense of Definition 11, argument I could be considered to be, in some sense, "more minimal" than H since the sets of grounds of both arguments are the same size, while I has a smaller set of rules. This suggests that further forms of minimality may be worth investigating.

4 Related Work

In this section we will discuss how the notion of minimality is handled by other approaches to structured argumentation.

As we have mentioned before, the formalism of *Assumption-Based Argumentation (ABA)* proposed in [4] shares some characteristics with ASPIC+. Arguments in ABA are deductions of claims using rules based on a set of assumptions. Deductions are defined as trees, where leaves correspond to assumptions and non-leave nodes correspond to sentences that are the heads of rules, whose children correspond to the sentences in the body of those rules. That is, arguments in ABA are built following the same strategy as ASPIC+, where some form of minimality is implicit. Specifically, like in ASPIC+, irrelevant pieces of information cannot be introduced in a deduction in ABA. Thus, ABA arguments have ASPIC+ native form of minimality, in which minimality relates to relevance.

In [2] the authors propose a framework for structured argumentation based on classical logic. In their approach, an argument A is a pair $\langle \Phi, \alpha \rangle$, where Φ is a minimal (w.r.t. $\subseteq$) set of formulae that is consistent and allows to prove α. Relating their proposal to ASPIC+, if we consider an argument $A = (G, R, \alpha)$, the set Φ would be the combination of the sets of grounds and rules of A (i.e., $\Phi = G \cup R$). Then, since Definition 11 establishes that A is minimal if there exists no $G' \subset G$ and no $R' \subset R$ such that $G' \vdash_R \alpha$ or $G \vdash_{R'} \alpha$, this is the same as saying that there is no $\Phi' \subset \Phi$ such that $\Phi \vdash \alpha$ in [2]. As a result, the characterization of minimality for ASPIC+ arguments that we proposed in this paper could be considered to be equivalent to the one given in [2]. Thus we might claim to have extended the notion of minimality from [2] to fit ASPIC+.

Another work in which the notion of minimality becomes present when defining the structure of arguments is [1], where a framework for dealing with preferences between arguments is proposed. There, arguments are assumed to be built from a propositional knowledge base, by means of classical inference. Then, an argument is defined as a pair (H, h), where H is a consistent and minimal (w.r.t. $\subseteq$) set of formulae from the knowledge base that allows to infer h. That is, the notion of minimality considered in [1] coincides with that of [2]. Therefore, as discussed above, it could be considered to be equivalent to the notion of minimality we proposed in this paper for ASPIC+.

Let us now consider *Defeasible Logic Programming (DeLP)*, the structured argumentation system proposed in [5]. An argument in DeLP is defined as a pair $\langle \Delta, c \rangle$, where Δ is a set of rules used to derive the conclusion c. The first difference between the characterization of arguments in DeLP and in ASPIC$^+$(as well as in the formaslisms of [1, 2, 4]) relies on the fact that DeLP does not include in Δ the set of grounds used for building the argument. Furthermore, the set Δ does not include *every* rule used in the derivation process, but only includes the *defeasible* rules. In other words, the set Δ only includes the defeasible knowledge of the argument. This is because arguments in [5] are required to be consistent with the strict knowledge of a DeLP program, which is determined by the facts and strict rules of the program. Then, the minimality requirement on DeLP arguments accounts only for the defeasible part of the arguments (i.e., Δ has to be a minimal set—w.r.t. $\subseteq$—that is consistent with the strict knowledge of the program and allows to derive the conclusion c).

The characterization of arguments in DeLP, leaving the strict knowledge aside, results in that minimal arguments cannot be uniquely mapped into a single derivation. This is because there might be alternative derivations for a given argument, which make use of different sets of facts and strict rules that allow to derive the same conclusions. Furthermore, the derivation for the conclusion of a given argument may not be minimal, in the sense that it may include irrelevant facts or strict rules. In addition, since minimality only accounts for the set of defeasible rules, it could be the case that ASPIC$^+$ arguments satisfying the notion of minimality from Definition 11 are not minimal under DeLP's notion of minimality, as discussed after Example 7. Finally, it should be noted that, since there exist scenarios (like the one in Example 7) where arguments are not 'valid' (thus, they are not arguments at all) in DeLP but they are 'valid' (furthermore, minimal) arguments in ASPIC$^+$, the outcome of the two argumentation systems in such scenarios may differ, because different sets of arguments are considered. This difference opens up a space that we are interested in exploring in the future.

5 Conclusion

In this paper we have studied the notion of minimality of arguments in the context of ASPIC$^+$. We have considered two forms of minimality. The first of these corresponds to the native minimality of ASPIC$^+$, which implies that arguments do not include irrelevant grounds or rules. We have noted that, under the native form of minimality, redundant and circular arguments may be obtained. Although there is nothing inherently wrong with circular and redundant arguments, in some cases it may be helpful to work with arguments that satisfy a stronger form of minimality. The second, stronger form of minimality that we considered, is satisfied by what we have identified as *regular* arguments, since these are the arguments that one encounters most often in the literature of argumentation. Specifically, regular arguments do not have two (or more) distinct sub-arguments with the same conclusion. It should be noted that an argument A satisfying the stronger form of minimality uses the same grounds and rules for deriving a proposition p at every step in which p is required in the derivation of A's conclusion. Furthermore, we have shown that regular arguments, satisfying the stronger form of minimality, can be unequivocally described by a triple (G, R, c), distinguishing their grounds, rules and conclusion. In contrast, that is not the case for arguments complying only with ASPIC$^+$ native form of minimality. Finally, as discussed in Sect. 4, the stronger form of minimality we proposed in this paper is related to the notion of minimality considered in other approaches for structured argumentation like [1,2], but not to others, such as [5]. As a result, we can say that the way in which arguments are characterized, and the way in which the minimality restrictions are imposed on arguments, heavily influence the outcome of an argumentation system.

In the future we are interested in further studying the notion of minimality in the context of ASPIC$^+$, and investigate whether alternative forms of minimality could provide results that align with the behavior of structured systems like [5]. In addition, we are interested in studying the impact the notion of minimality could have in determining the existence of interactions between arguments, including attack and support relations.

Acknowledgements. This work was partially funded by EPSRC EP/P010105/1 Collaborative Mobile Decision Support for Managing Multiple Morbidities.

References

1. Amgoud, L., Cayrol, C.: A reasoning model based on the production of acceptable arguments. Ann. Math. Artif. Intell. **34**(3), 197–215 (2002)
2. Besnard, P., Hunter, A.: A logic-based theory of deductive arguments. Artif. Intell. **128**, 203–235 (2001)
3. Cohen, A., Parsons, S., Sklar, E., McBurney, P.: A characterization of types of support between structured arguments and their relationship with support in abstract argumentation. Int. J. Approx. Reason. **94**, 76–104 (2018)
4. Dung, P.M., Kowalski, R.A., Toni, F.: Dialectic proof procedures for assumption-based, admissable argumentation. Artif. Intell. **170**(2), 114–159 (2006)
5. García, A.J., Simari, G.: Defeasible logic programming: an argumentative approach. Theory Pract. Logic Program. **4**(1), 95–138 (2004)
6. Krause, P., Ambler, S., Elvang-Gørannson, M., Fox, J.: A logic of argumentation for reasoning under uncertainty. Comput. Intell. **11**(1), 113–131 (1995)
7. Loui, R.P.: Defeat among arguments: a system of defeasible inference. Comput. Intell. **3**(3), 100–106 (1987)
8. Modgil, S., Prakken, H.: A general account of argumentation with preferences. Artif. Intell. **195**, 361–397 (2013)
9. Pollock, J.: Cognitive Carpentry. MIT Press, Cambridge (1995)
10. Pollock, J.L.: Defeasible reasoning. Cogn. Sci. **11**, 481–518 (1987)
11. Pollock, J.L.: OSCAR–a general-purpose defeasible reasoner. J. Appl. Non-Classical Logics **6**, 89–113 (1996)
12. Prakken, H.: An abstract framework for argumentation with structured arguments. Argum. Comput. **1**, 93–124 (2010)

13. Prakken, H., Sartor, G.: Argument-based logic programming with defeasible priorities. J. Appl. Non-classical Logics **7**, 25–75 (1997)
14. Sinnott-Armstrong, W.: Begging the question. Australas. J. Philos. **77**(2), 174–191 (1999)
15. Walton, D.N.: Plausible Argument in Everyday Conversation. State University of New York Press, Albany (1992)

Comparison Criteria for Argumentation Semantics

Sylvie Doutre[1] and Jean-Guy Mailly[2(✉)]

[1] IRIT, Université Toulouse 1 Capitole, Toulouse, France
doutre@irit.fr
[2] LIPADE, Université Paris Descartes, Paris, France
jean-guy.mailly@parisdescartes.fr

Abstract. Argumentation reasoning is a way for agents to evaluate a situation. Given a framework made of conflicting arguments, a semantics allows to evaluate the acceptability of the arguments. It may happen that the semantics associated to the framework has to be changed. In order to perform the most suitable change, the current and a potential new semantics have to be compared. Notions of difference measures between semantics have already been proposed, and application cases where they have to be minimized when a change of semantics has to be performed, have been highlighted. This paper develops these notions, it proposes an additional kind of difference measure, and shows application cases where measures may have to be maximized, and combined.

1 Introduction

Argumentation is a reasoning model which has proved useful for agents in many contexts (*e.g.* decision making [3], negotiation [2], persuasion [27]). Abstract argumentation frameworks (AFs) are classically associated with a semantics which allows to evaluate arguments' statuses, determining sets of jointly acceptable arguments called extensions [4,18].

In [7,8], a method to modify an AF in order to satisfy a constraint (a given set of arguments should be an extension, or at least included in an extension) is defined; this process is called extension enforcement. The authors distinguish between conservative enforcement when the semantics does not change (only the AF changes) and liberal enforcement when the semantics changes. A first study of semantic change in a situation of enforcement has recently been conducted in [17]: it shows how to minimize the changes to perform on an AF in order to enforce an extension, by changing the semantics, for a new one which is not too "different" from the current one.

A change of the semantics may be necessary for other reasons, for instance, for computational purposes: if a given semantics was appropriate at some point in a certain context for some AF, one may imagine that changes over time on the structure of the AF (number of arguments, of attacks, structure of cycles) may make this semantics too "costly" to compute. It may then be interesting to

© Springer Nature Switzerland AG 2018
F. Belardinelli and E. Argente (Eds.): EUMAS 2017/AT 2017, LNAI 10767, pp. 219–234, 2018.
https://doi.org/10.1007/978-3-030-01713-2_16

pick up another semantics to apply to the AF, possibly not too dissimilar to the former on its acceptability results, but quite dissimilar regarding computational complexity.

The other way round, in contexts like decision or deliberation, a given semantics may be interesting from a computational point of view, but the results that it returns may be found for instance too restrictive, in the sense that, if the agents agree on the extensions that it returns, they would like to have more options, as many as possible, including the ones which have been returned. It may then be interesting to change the semantics, for a new one which is not too dissimilar in complexity to the former, but which extends the set of extensions. *Difference measures* between semantics, to quantify how much a semantics is dissimilar to another one, allow to define different minimality and maximality *criteria*. Such criteria can be used and combined to select the new semantics among several options when a semantic change is required.

This paper recalls and presents several sensible ways to quantify the difference between two semantics, depending on:

- the computational complexity of semantics;
- the properties which characterize the semantics;
- the relations between semantics;
- the acceptance statuses of arguments the semantics lead to in a specific AF.

The first measure is new; the last three measures have been proposed in [16], and illustrated on a number of semantics; they are developed here, proofs of the properties that they satisfy (whether they are distances, semi-distances or pseudo-distances) are given, and additional semantics are considered.

2   Background Notions

An Argumentation Framework (AF) [18] is a directed graph $\langle A, R \rangle$ where the nodes in A represent abstract entities called *arguments* and the edges in R represent *attacks* between arguments. $(a_i, a_j) \in R$ means that a_i attacks a_j; a_i is called an *attacker* of a_j. Figure 1 gives an example of an argumentation framework.

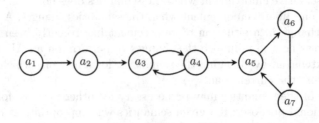

Fig. 1. The AF F_1

We say that an argument a_i (resp. a set of arguments S) defends the argument a_j against its attacker a_k if a_i (resp. any argument in S) attacks a_k. The *range* of a set of arguments S w.r.t. R, denoted S_R^+, is the subset of A which contains S and the arguments attacked by S; formally $S_R^+ = S \cup \{a_j \mid \exists a_i \in S$ s.t. $(a_i, a_j) \in R\}$. Different semantics allow to determine which sets of arguments can be collectively accepted [6,12,13,18–20,29].

Definition 1. *Let $F = \langle A, R \rangle$ be an AF. A set of arguments $S \subseteq A$ is*

- conflict-free *w.r.t.* F *if* $\nexists a_i, a_j \in S$ *s.t.* $(a_i, a_j) \in R$;
- admissible *w.r.t.* F *if S is conflict-free and S defends each of its arguments against all of their attackers;*
- a naive *extension of F if S is a maximal conflict-free set (w.r.t. $\subseteq$);*
- a complete *extension of F if S is admissible and S contains all the arguments that it defends;*
- a preferred *extension of F if S is a maximal complete extension (w.r.t. $\subseteq$);*
- a stable *extension of F if S is conflict-free and $S_R^+ = A$;*
- a grounded *extension of F if S is a minimal complete extension (w.r.t. $\subseteq$);*
- a stage *extension of F if S is conflict-free and there is no conflict-free T such that $S_R^+ \subset T_R^+$;*
- a semi-stable *extension of F if S is admissible and there is no admissible T such that $S_R^+ \subset T_R^+$;*
- an ideal set *of F if S is admissible and S is included in each preferred extension;*
- an ideal *extension of F if S is a maximal (w.r.t. $\subseteq$) ideal set of F;*
- an eager *extension of F if S is a maximal (w.r.t. $\subseteq$) admissible set that is a subset of each semi-stable extension.*

These semantics are denoted, respectively, $cf, adm, na, co, pr, st, gr, stg, sem, is, id$, eg. For each σ of them, $Ext_\sigma(F)$ denotes the set of σ-extensions of F.

Let us recall the definition of usual decision problems for argumentation.

Definition 2. *Let $F = \langle A, R \rangle$ be an AF and σ a semantics.*

$Cred_\sigma$ *An argument $a_i \in A$ is said to be credulously accepted by F w.r.t. σ if $\exists E \in Ext_\sigma(F)$ s.t. $a_i \in E$.*

$Skept_\sigma$ *An argument $a_i \in A$ is said to be skeptically accepted by F w.r.t. σ if $\forall E \in Ext_\sigma(F), a_i \in E$.*

$Exist_\sigma$ *F satisfies the non-trivial existence w.r.t. σ if F admits at least one non-empty σ extension.*

The set of credulously (resp. skeptically) accepted arguments in F w.r.t. σ is denoted $cr_\sigma(F)$ (resp. $sk_\sigma(F)$).

Example 1. *Let us consider the argumentation framework F_1 given at Fig. 1, and let us illustrate some of the semantics, and related decision problems.*

- $Ext_{adm}(F_1) = \{\emptyset, \{a_1\}, \{a_4\}, \{a_4, a_6\}, \{a_1, a_4, a_6\}, \{a_1, a_3\}, \{a_1, a_4\}\}$,
- $Ext_{st}(F_1) = \{\{a_1, a_4, a_6\}\}$,
- $Ext_{pr}(F_1) = \{\{a_1, a_4, a_6\}, \{a_1, a_3\}\}$,
- $Ext_{co}(F_1) = \{\{a_1, a_4, a_6\}, \{a_1, a_3\}, \{a_1\}\}$,
- $Ext_{gr}(F_1) = \{\{a_1\}\}$.

a_1 is skeptically accepted in F_1 w.r.t. the stable, preferred, complete and grounded semantics. a_4 is credulously accepted in F_1 w.r.t. the preferred and complete semantics, but it is not w.r.t. the grounded semantics.

Table 1 gives the complexity class of these decision problems[1]. Results come from [14,15,18,20–23,25]. We suppose that the reader is familiar with the basic notions of complexity. Otherwise, see [28] for instance. Computation of one extension and enumeration of all the extensions are not decision problems, so their complexity cannot be evaluated through the polynomial hierarchy as we do for credulous and skeptical acceptance. But the computational hardness of these functional problems can all the same be estimated. Indeed, the complexity of skeptical acceptance can be seen as a lower bound for the complexity of the enumeration of extensions, and the complexity of the non-trivial existence can be seen as a lower bound of the computation of an extension.

Table 1. Complexity of Inference Problems for the Usual Semantics. $C-c$ (resp. $C-h$) means that the considered decision problem is complete (resp. hard) for the complexity class C.

σ	$Cred_\sigma$	$Skept_\sigma$	$Exist_\sigma$
cf	Trivial	P	Trivial
adm	NP $-$ c	Trivial	NP $-$ c
na	P	P	L
co	NP $-$ c	P	NP $-$ c
pr	NP $-$ c	$\Pi_2^P - c$	NP $-$ c
st	NP $-$ c	coNP$-$c	NP $-$ c
gr	P	P	P
stg	$\Sigma_2^P - c$	$\Pi_2^P - c$	L
sem	$\Sigma_2^P - c$	$\Pi_2^P - c$	NP$-$c
id	coNP$-$h	coNP$-$h	P
eg	$\Pi_2^P - c$	$\Pi_2^P - c$	P

In order to compare, in the following section, the semantics, and propose measures of their differences, let us introduce a useful notation: given two sets X, Y, $X \Delta Y$ is the symmetric difference between X and Y. Let us recall also the definition of a distance and of an aggregation function.

---

[1] Up to our knowledge, the complexity class of $Cred_{is}$, $Skept_{is}$ and $Exist_{is}$ has not yet been determined.

Definition 3. *Given a set E, a mapping d from $E \times E$ to $\mathbb{R}^+$ is*

- *a pseudo-distance if it satisfies weak coincidence, symmetry and triangular inequality;*
- *a semi-distance if it satisfies coincidence and symmetry;*
- *a distance if it satisfies coincidence, symmetry and triangular inequality.*

weak coincidence $\forall x \in E, d(x, x) = 0$;
coincidence $\forall x, y \in E, d(x, y) = 0$ *iff* $x = y$;
symmetry $\forall x, y \in E, d(x, y) = d(y, x)$;
triangular inequality $\forall x, y, z \in E, d(x, y) + d(y, z) \geq d(x, z)$.

Definition 4. *An* aggregation function *is a function $\otimes$ which associates a non-negative real number to every finite tuple of non-negative numbers, and which satisfies:*

non-decreasingness *if* $y \leq z$ *then* $\otimes(x_1, \ldots, y, \ldots, x_n) \leq \otimes(x_1, \ldots, z, \ldots, x_n)$;
minimality $\otimes(x_1, \ldots, x_n) = 0$ *iff* $x_1 = \cdots = x_n = 0$;
identity $\forall x \in \mathbb{R}^+, \otimes(x) = x$.

For instance, we will use the sum $\sum$ as an aggregation function.

3   Complexity-Based Difference Measures

As mentioned in the introduction, the acceptability semantics may have to be changed because of the computational complexity of the reasoning tasks an agent is involved into. Indeed, depending on which kind of reasoning is actually used by the agent (computation of one extension, enumeration of all the extensions, credulous or skeptical acceptance), the use of a given semantics σ_1 may lead to a higher complexity than another semantics σ_2, as depicted in Table 1.

If the agent needs to change her semantics for practical purpose, it seems that she will choose the semantics which allows her to have the *lowest* possible *complexity* for her main reasoning task. For instance, if she uses skeptical acceptance frequently, and if she is currently using the preferred semantics, it is interesting to select a new semantics such that the complexity of skeptical acceptance is minimal. When we consider the set of semantics which select only complete extensions, the possible new semantics are $\{co, gr\}$. To choose among these two, the agent can use another criterion such as minimal change based on another of the measures defined here.

In some cases, the agent can be obliged to change her semantics to another one which has a *higher complexity*; it is not desirable in general, but it can be mandatory to satisfy a given constraint. In this case, if several options are possible, a notion of minimality can be used. It consists now in a minimal increase of the complexity. We formalize it by defining a difference measure between reasoning tasks, where such a task is parametrized by the semantics and the specific decision problem.

Definition 5. *Let $S = \{\sigma_1, \ldots, \sigma_n\}$ be a set of semantics, and $T = \{\tau_1, \ldots, \tau_m\}$ be a set of reasoning tasks. We define $\mathcal{C} = \{C(\tau_\sigma) \mid \tau \in T, \sigma \in S\}$, where $C(\tau_\sigma)$ denotes the complexity class which characterizes the decision problem τ_σ.*

The complexity graph on S and T is $Comp(S, T) = \langle \mathcal{C}, I \rangle$ with $I \subseteq \mathcal{C} \times \mathcal{C}$ defined by $\forall c_1, c_2 \in \mathcal{C}, (c_1, c_2) \in I$ iff $c_1 \subset c_2$ and $\nexists c_3 \in \mathcal{C}$ such that $c_3 \neq c_1, c_3 \neq c_2$ and $c_1 \subset c_3 \subset c_2$.[2]

The difference measure δ_T^S between decision problems τ_{σ_1} and τ'_{σ_2} is the non-negative integer $\delta_T^S(\tau_{\sigma_1}, \tau'_{\sigma_2})$ which is the length of the shortest non-oriented path between $C(\tau_{\sigma_1})$ and $C(\tau'_{\sigma_2})$ in $Comp(S, T)$.

In general, the complexity-based difference measure are not distances, they do not satisfy coincidence. They satisfy weak coincidence and symmetry.

Example 2. *Let us consider the classical Dung's semantics $S = \{co, pr, st, gr\}$ and the reasoning tasks $T = \{Cred_\sigma, Skept_\sigma, Exist_\sigma\}$. As we see in Table 1, $\mathcal{C} = \{\mathsf{P}, \mathsf{NP}, \mathsf{coNP}, \Pi_2^P\}$. The corresponding graph $Comp(S, T)$ is given in Fig. 2.*

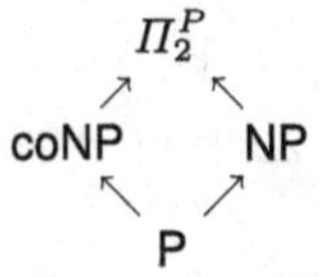

Fig. 2. Complexity Graph $Comp(S, T)$

Then, for instance, $\delta_T^S(Cred_{gr}, Cred_{co}) = 1$ and $\delta_T^S(Skept_{gr}, Skept_{pr}) = 2$. As soon as two decision problems have the same complexity, the measure of their difference is 0 (for instance, $\delta_T^S(Cred_{st}, Cred_{co}) = 0$); this explains why δ_T^S is not a distance.

Minimality of this complexity difference measure can be used when all the alternatives have a higher complexity than the previous one. For instance, if the agent is forced to change her semantics from gr to another one because she needs to be able to consider several solutions to her problem (which means that she needs to obtain several extensions), then she can choose the complete semantics when skeptical acceptance is important for her, because $\delta_T^S(skept_{gr}, skept_{co}) = 0$.

4   Property-Based Difference Measures

Semantics can be compared respectively to the set of properties that characterize them. Such a characterization can be defined as follows.

Definition 6 [16]. *A set of properties $\mathcal{P}$ characterizes a semantics σ if for each AF F,*

---

[2] Under the usual assumptions about inclusions between complexity classes.

1. *each σ-extension of F satisfies each property from $\mathcal{P}$,*
2. *each set of arguments which satisfies each property from $\mathcal{P}$ is a σ-extension of F,*
3. *$\mathcal{P}$ is a minimal set (w.r.t $\subseteq$) among those which satisfy 1. and 2.*

$Prop(\sigma)$ denotes the set of properties that characterizes a semantics σ.

[16] points out a set of properties, and shows how each semantics can be characterized given this set. Absolute properties, which concern only a set of arguments by itself (Definition 7) are distinguished from relative properties, which concern a set of arguments with respect to other sets of arguments (Definition 8).

Definition 7 [16]. *Given an AF $F = \langle A, R \rangle$, a set of arguments S satisfies*

- *conflict-freeness if S is conflict-free;*
- *acceptability if S defends itself against each attacker;*
- *reinstatement if S contains all the arguments that it defends;*
- *complement attack if each argument in $A \backslash S$ is attacked by S.*

Definition 8 [16]. *Given an AF $F = \langle A, R \rangle$ and a set of properties $\mathcal{P}$, a set of arguments S satisfies*

- *$\mathcal{P}$-maximality if S is maximal (w.r.t. $\subseteq$) among the sets of arguments satisfying $\mathcal{P}$;*
- *$\mathcal{P}$-minimality if S is minimal (w.r.t. $\subseteq$) among the sets of arguments satisfying $\mathcal{P}$;*
- *$\mathcal{P}$-inclusion if S is included in each set of arguments satisfying $\mathcal{P}$;*
- *$\mathcal{P}$-R-maximality if S has a maximal range (w.r.t. $\subseteq$) among the sets of arguments satisfying $\mathcal{P}$.*

It can be noticed that, by definition, if a set S satisfies $\mathcal{P}$-maximality (resp. $\mathcal{P}$-minimality, $\mathcal{P}$-R-maximality), then S satisfies $\mathcal{P}$.

A characterization of different semantics, that follows from the previous definitions, has been established in [16]; Proposition 1 recalls this characterization, and extends it to ideal sets, ideal and eager semantics.

Proposition 1. *The extension-based semantics considered in this paper can be characterized as follows:*

- *$Prop(cf) = \{conflict\text{-}freeness\}$.*
- *$Prop(adm) = Prop(cf) \cup \{acceptability\}$.*
- *$Prop(na) = Prop(cf)\text{-}maximality$.*
- *$Prop(co) = Prop(adm) \cup \{reinstatement\}$.*
- *$Prop(gr) = Prop(co)\text{-}minimality$.*
- *$Prop(pr) = Prop(adm)\text{-}maximality$.*
- *$Prop(sem) = Prop(adm)\text{-}R\text{-}maximality$.*
- *$Prop(stg) = Prop(cf)\text{-}R\text{-}maximality$.*
- *$Prop(st) = Prop(cf) \cup \{complement\ attack\}$.*
- *$Prop(is) = Prop(adm) \cup \{Prop(pr)\text{-}inclusion\}$.*

- $Prop(id) = Prop(is)$-maximality.
- $Prop(eg) = Prop(pr) \cup \{Prop(sem)$-inclusion$\}$.

Let us notice that we can consider other properties, and give alternative characterizations of the semantics (see [9,10] for contributions in this sense). Even if the value of the difference between two semantics (obviously) depends of the chosen characterizations, the general definition of property-based difference measures is the same whatever the characterizations.

The intuition which lead to define the characterization as the minimal set of properties is related to computational issues. Indeed, computing some reasoning tasks related to the semantics thanks to the semantics characterization can be done more efficiently with this definition. For instance, to determine whether a set of arguments is a stable extension of a given AF, checking the satisfaction of conflict-freeness and complement attack proves enough. For instance, $Prop(adm)$-maximality may be added in the characterization of the stable semantics, but computing the result of our problem would then be harder.

A weight can be associated to each property, depending on the importance of the property in a certain context.

Definition 9 [16]. *Let $\mathcal{P}$ be a set of properties. Let w be a function which maps each property $p \in \mathcal{P}$ to a strictly positive real number $w(p)$. Given σ_1, σ_2 two semantics such that $Prop(\sigma_1) \subseteq \mathcal{P}$ and $Prop(\sigma_2) \subseteq \mathcal{P}$, the property-based difference measure δ^w_{prop} between σ_1 and σ_2 is defined as:*

$$\delta^w_{prop}(\sigma_1, \sigma_2) = \sum_{p_i \in Prop(\sigma_1) \Delta Prop(\sigma_2)} w(p_i)$$

The specific property-based difference measure defined when all the properties have the same importance is as follows.

Definition 10 [16]. *Given two semantics σ_1, σ_2, the property-based difference measure δ_{prop} is defined by $\delta_{prop}(\sigma_1, \sigma_2) = |Prop(\sigma_1) \Delta Prop(\sigma_2)|$.*

Example 3. *Let us suppose that the initial semantics is the admissible one.*

- *When δ_{prop} is considered, naive and preferred semantics are "equivalent", since $\delta_{prop}(adm, na) = \delta_{prop}(adm, pr) = 3$.*
- *With a weighted measure δ^w_{prop} such that $w(Prop(cf)$-maximality$) = 1$ and $w(Prop(adm)$-maximality$) = 2$, the two semantics are no more equivalent, since $\delta_{prop}(adm, na) < \delta_{prop}(adm, pr)$.*

Proposition 2 [16]. *Given a set of semantics $\mathcal{S}$, the property-based measures defined on $\mathcal{S}$ are distances.*

5   Relation-Based Difference Measures

Most of the usual semantics are related according to some notions. For instance, it is well-known that each preferred extension of an AF is also a complete extension of it, and the grounded extension is also complete, but in general it is not a preferred extension. The preferred semantics may thus be seen closer to the complete semantics, than to the grounded semantics. This idea has been formalized with the notion of semantics relation graph.

Definition 11 [16]. *Let $S = \{\sigma_1, \ldots, \sigma_n\}$ a set of semantics. A semantics relation graph on S is defined by $Rel(S) = \langle S, D \rangle$ with $D \subseteq S \times S$.*

This abstract notion of relation graph, where the nodes are semantics, can be instantiated with the inclusion relation between the extensions of an AF.

Definition 12 [16]. *Let $S = \{\sigma_1, \ldots, \sigma_n\}$ a set of semantics. The extension inclusion graph of S is defined by $Inc(S) = \langle S, D \rangle$ with $D \subseteq S \times S$ such that $(\sigma_i, \sigma_j) \in D$ if and only if:*

- *for each AF F, $Ext_{\sigma_i}(F) \subseteq Ext_{\sigma_j}(F)$;*
- *there is no $\sigma_k \in S$ ($k \neq i, k \neq j$) such that for each AF F, $Ext_{\sigma_i}(F) \subseteq Ext_{\sigma_k}(F)$ and $Ext_{\sigma_k}(F) \subseteq Ext_{\sigma_j}(F)$.*

This idea has been discussed in [4], but the notion of relation between semantics had not been formalized before [16].

Example 4. *For instance, when $S = \{co, pr, st, gr, stg, sem, is, id, eg, adm, cf, na\}$, $Inc(S)$ is the graph given at Fig. 3.*

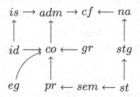

Fig. 3. Extension Inclusion Graph $Inc(S)$

A family of difference measures between semantics which is based on the semantics relation graphs has been defined, to measure what it costs for an agent to change her semantics.

Definition 13 [16]. *Given S a set of semantics, a S- relation difference measure is the mapping from two semantics $\sigma_1, \sigma_2 \in S$ to the non-negative integer $\delta_{Rel,S}(\sigma_1, \sigma_2)$ which is the length of the shortest non-oriented path between σ_1 and σ_2 in $Rel(S)$. In particular, the S-inclusion measure is the length of the shortest non-oriented path between σ_1 and σ_2 in $Inc(S)$, denoted by $\delta_{Inc,S}(\sigma_1, \sigma_2)$.*

Example 5. *Given two semantics σ_1 and σ_2 which are neighbours in the graph given at Fig. 3, the difference measure $\delta_{Inc,S}(\sigma_1, \sigma_2)$ is obviously 1. Otherwise, if several paths allow to reach σ_2 from σ_1, then the difference is the length of* the minimal one. For instance, $\delta_{Inc,S}(st, cf) = 3$ since the minimal path is $st \rightarrow stg \rightarrow na \rightarrow cf$, but other paths exist (for instance, $st \rightarrow sem \rightarrow pr \rightarrow co \rightarrow adm \rightarrow cf$). Since here the question is to define the difference between semantics, the possibility to obtain several minimal paths (for instance, there are two minimal paths between the ideal and admissible semantics: $id \rightarrow is \rightarrow adm$ and $id \rightarrow co \rightarrow adm$) is not problematic.

Proposition 3 [16]. *The S-inclusion difference measure is a distance.*

The relation graph can be instantiated with other relations between semantics. The skepticism relation studied in [5] would be an appropriate candidate. The graph resulting from the intertranslatability relationship of semantics [24] may also be considered. Such instantiations would require a deeper investigation.

It can be noticed that, for any instantiation of the relation graph as defined above, which is absolute, that is, independent of any specific AF, a relative version can also be defined. In this case, the edges in the graph would depend on the relations for a given AF; the initial proposal considers the relations which are true for any AF. Such AF-based relation graph may also lead to interesting difference measures, which would require investigation as well.

6   Acceptance-Based Difference Measures

In line with the remarks at the end of the last section, regarding absoluteness (that is, independence of the measure from any specific situation or AF) and relativity (dependence on a given AF) of difference measures, a family of relative measures is presented in this section. Now, the difference between semantics depends on the acceptance status of arguments in a given AF, w.r.t. the different semantics in consideration.

The first acceptance-based measure quantifies the difference between the σ_1-extensions and the σ_2-extension of the AF to quantify the difference between σ_1 and σ_2.

Definition 14 [16]. *Let F be an AF, d be a distance between sets of arguments, and $\otimes$ be an aggregation function. The F-d-$\otimes$-extension-based difference measure $\delta_F^{d,\otimes}$ is defined by $\delta_F^{d,\otimes}(\sigma_1, \sigma_2) = \otimes_{\epsilon \in Ext_{\sigma_1}(F)} \min_{\epsilon' \in Ext_{\sigma_2}(F)} d(\epsilon, \epsilon')$.*

Proposition 4. *In general, the extension-based difference measures are not distances, they do not satisfy coincidence, symmetry.*

Example 6. *For instance, we consider the Hamming distance between sets of arguments, defined as $d_H(s_1, s_2) = |s_1 \triangle s_2|$. Now, we define the F_1-d_H-$\sum$-extension-based difference measure $\delta_F^{d_H, \sum}$ from d_H and the AF F_1 given at Fig. 1. Its set of stable extensions is $Ext_{st}(F_1) = \{\{a_1, a_4, a_6\}\}$.*

When measuring the difference between the stable semantics and the other classical Dung's semantics, we obtain:

- $\delta_{F_1}^{d_H,\Sigma}(st, gr) = 2$ *since* $Ext_{gr}(F_1) = \{\{a_1\}\}$;
- $\delta_{F_1}^{d_H,\Sigma}(st, pr) = 0$ *since* $Ext_{pr}(F_1) = \{\{a_1, a_3\}, \{a_1, a_4, a_6\}\}$; *on the opposite,* $\delta_{F_1}^{d_H}(pr, st) = 3$;
- $\delta_{F_1}^{d_H,\Sigma}(st, co) = 0$ *since* $Ext_{co}(F_1) = \{\{a_1\}, \{a_1, a_3\}, \{a_1, a_4, a_6\}\}$.

The following result shows that the restriction of the extension-based measure to some particular sets of semantics leads to satisfy the coincidence property.

Proposition 5. *For a given F and a given set of semantics $S = \{\sigma_1, \ldots, \sigma_n\}$, if for all $\sigma_i, \sigma_j \in S$ such that $\sigma_i \neq \sigma_j$, $Ext_{\sigma_i}(F) \not\subseteq Ext_{\sigma_j}(F)$, then the extension-based measure $\delta_F^{d_H,\Sigma}$ satisfies coincidence.*

Even in this case, the measure does no satisfy all the properties of distances. However, we can use the intuition behind this measure to define another one.

Definition 15 [16]. *Let F be an AF, d be a distance between sets of arguments, and $\otimes$ be an aggregation function. The symmetric F-d-$\otimes$-extension-based difference measure $\delta_{F,sym}^{d,\otimes}$ is defined by $\delta_{F,sym}^{d,\otimes}(\sigma_1, \sigma_2) = \max(\delta_F^{d,\otimes}(\sigma_1, \sigma_2), \delta_F^{d,\otimes}(\sigma_2, \sigma_1))$.*

This measure satisfies the distance properties under some conditions.

Proposition 6 [16]. *For a given F and a given set of semantics $S = \{\sigma_1, \ldots, \sigma_n\}$, if for all $\sigma_i, \sigma_j \in S$ such that $\sigma_i \neq \sigma_j$, $Ext_{\sigma_i}(F) \neq Ext_{\sigma_j}(F)$, then the symmetric extension-based measure $\delta_{F,sym}^{d_H,\Sigma}$ is a semi-distance.*

As suggested in [16], we can also use the set of skeptically (resp. credulously) accepted arguments instead of the whole set of extensions to define a difference measure between semantics. We propose here a definition of such measures.

Definition 16. *Given F an AF, d a distance between sets of arguments, and S a set of semantics, the F-d-skeptical acceptance difference measure $\delta_{F,sk}^d$ is defined, for any $\sigma_1, \sigma_2 \in S$, by*

$$\delta_{F,sk}^d(\sigma_1, \sigma_2) = d(sk_{\sigma_1}(F), sk_{\sigma_2}(F))$$

The F-d-credulous acceptance difference measure $\delta_{F,sk}^d$ is defined, for any $\sigma_1, \sigma_2 \in S$, by

$$\delta_{F,cr}^d(\sigma_1, \sigma_2) = d(cr_{\sigma_1}(F), cr_{\sigma_2}(F))$$

If two semantics lead to the same set of credulously (resp. skeptically) accepted arguments, then these measures cannot distinguish between these semantics. Other properties are satisfied.

Proposition 7. *Given F and AF and d a distance, the F-d-skeptical acceptance difference measure and the F-d-credulous acceptance difference measure are pseudo-distances.*

7   Obtaining Comparison Criteria

In the context of a semantic change, the difference measures can be used to define different minimality or maximality criteria. With σ the initial semantics, and $\mathcal{S}$ the set of options for the new semantics, the new semantics should be $\sigma' \in \mathcal{S}$ such that, given δ the chosen measure:

- $\forall \sigma'' \in \mathcal{S}$, $\delta(\sigma, \sigma') \leq \delta(\sigma, \sigma'')$ to define a minimality criteria denoted $\min_{\delta, \sigma}$,
- $\forall \sigma'' \in \mathcal{S}$, $\delta(\sigma, \sigma') \geq \delta(\sigma, \sigma'')$ to define a maximality criteria denoted $\max_{\delta, \sigma}$.

Given σ a semantics and $\mathcal{S}$ a set of semantics, $\min_{\delta, \sigma}(\mathcal{S}) = \{\sigma_i \in \mathcal{S} \mid \forall \sigma_j \in \mathcal{S}, \delta(\sigma, \sigma_i) \leq \delta(\sigma, \sigma_j)\}$ is the subset of $\mathcal{S}$ of semantics which minimize the criterion $\min_{\delta, \sigma}$; the counterpart for maximality criteria is $\max_{\delta, \sigma}(\mathcal{S}) = \{\sigma_i \in \mathcal{S} \mid \forall \sigma_j \in \mathcal{S}, \delta(\sigma, \sigma_i) \geq \delta(\sigma, \sigma_j)\}$.

A single criteria may not be enough to compare, or distinguish between, some semantics, as shown in the examples in the Introduction. Combining criteria may allow an agent to do so. It can be noticed that the order of application of the different criteria may then lead to different results.

Definition 17. *Let* $X = \langle \chi_1, \ldots, \chi_n \rangle$ *a vector of (minimality or maximality) criteria. Let* σ *be a semantics, and* $\mathcal{S}$ *a set of semantics. The* X-*based semantic change selection function is defined by* $\chi_X(\sigma, \mathcal{S}) = \chi_X^n(\sigma, \mathcal{S})$

with χ_X^n *as follows:*

$$\gamma_X^1(\sigma, \mathcal{S}) = \chi_1(\mathcal{S})$$
$$\gamma_X^k(\sigma, \mathcal{S}) = \chi_k(\gamma_X^{k-1}(\sigma, \mathcal{S}))$$

Let us notice that this definition is general enough to encompass any difference measure yet to be defined.

Example 7. *Let* $\sigma = st$ *be the current semantics. A change of semantics has to be done. The reasoning task to complete by the agent is credulous reasoning ($Cred_\sigma$). The candidate new semantics are* $\mathcal{S} = \{pr, co, eg\}$. *The new semantics must be as close as possible in terms of computational complexity to the current one, but it should contain not only the current results, but as many results as possible (the agent wants as many options as possible). Hence, the vector of criteria to be considered is* $X = \langle \min_{\delta_{Cred}^S, \sigma}, \max_{\delta_{Inc}, S, \sigma} \rangle$. *Then, by first minimizing the complexity-based difference measure, the only semantics to be considered are* pr, co. *By maximizing then the inclusion measure, the X-based semantic change selection function returns* co.

8   Conclusion

This paper presents several ways to quantify the difference between extension-based semantics, building on [16]. Some of them are absolute (they only depend on the semantics), while the other ones are relative (they depend on the considered AF). Let us mention the fact that there is no general relation between these difference measures; for instance we have seen on several examples that it may occur that $\delta_1(\sigma_1, \sigma_2) > \delta_1(\sigma_1, \sigma_3)$ while $\delta_2(\sigma_1, \sigma_2) < \delta_2(\sigma_1, \sigma_3)$. When a semantic change occurs, this permits the agent to use some very different criteria to select the new semantics, depending on which difference measures make sense in the context of her application. The minimization, or the maximization of these measures, and their combinations, permit to express many comparison criteria.

Let us notice that only the relation-based and property-based measures are distances, other methods failing in general to satisfy the distance properties, which seem to be desirable to quantify the difference between objects. However, the skeptical and credulous acceptance difference measures are pseudo-distances. Further study could lead to identify the necessary conditions that a set of semantics must satisfy to ensure that these are distances.

Table 2. Summary of properties satisfied by the measures

	δ_T^S	δ_{prop}^w	$\delta_{Inc,S}$	$\delta_F^{d,\Sigma}$	$\delta_{F,sym}^{d,\Sigma}$	$\delta_{F,sk}^d$	$\delta_{F,cr}^d$
WC	✓	✓	✓	○	✓	✓	✓
Co	×	✓	✓	×	○	×	×
Sym	✓	✓	✓	×	✓	✓	✓
TI		✓	✓			✓	✓

Table 2 depicts the properties satisfied by our measures. WC, Co, Sym and TI stand respectively for weak coincidence, coincidence, symmetry and triangular inequality. A ✓ symbol means that the property is always satisfied, and × means that it is not satisfied in general. ○ means that the property is satisfied under some additional assumption.

Several tracks can be considered for future works. We have noticed that we can order semantics, with respect to an initial semantics σ and a measure δ: $\sigma_1 \leq_{\sigma,\delta} \sigma_2$ if and only if $\delta(\sigma, \sigma_1) \leq \delta(\sigma, \sigma_2)$. In this case, we can investigate the relation of the orderings defined by different measures. For instance, if some pairs (σ, δ_1) and (σ, δ_2) lead to the same ordering, then we can choose to use the measure which is the least expensive one to compute among δ_1 and δ_2.

We also plan to define a similar notion of difference measures for labelling-based semantics [4], and for ranking-based semantics [1,11,26]. In this last context, we need to determine whether some relevant properties characterize the ranking which is used to evaluate arguments, or to determine meaningful notions of difference between the rankings.

Finally, we will investigate more in depth the question which is mentioned in the introduction: using (minimal) semantic change in argumentation dynamics scenarios. In particular, [17] has shown that semantic change can be used to guarantee minimal change on the attack relation when performing an extension enforcement. We will investigate this question in other scenarios.

Acknowledgements. This work benefited from the support of the project AMANDE ANR-13-BS02-0004 of the French National Research Agency (ANR).

A   Proofs

Proof (Proof of Proposition 2). From our definition of characterizations, the mapping that associates a semantics σ to a set of properties $Prop(\sigma)$ guarantees that a semantics cannot be associated with two different sets of properties, and a same set of properties cannot correspond to different semantics.

The weighted sum on sets of properties obviously defines a distance (in particular, when all weights are identical, we obtain the well-known Hamming distance; other weights just define generalization of Hamming distance). Since we can identify the semantics to the sets of properties, δ_{prop}^{w} is a distance.

Proof (Proof of Proposition 3). From the definition of the Σ-relation graph,

- the difference between σ_1 and σ_2 is 0 iff they are the same node of the graph (i.e. $\sigma_1 = \sigma_2$), so coincidence is satisfied;
- the shortest path between two semantics σ_1, σ_2 has the same length whatever the direction of the path (from σ_1 to σ_2, or vice-versa), since we do not consider the direction of arrows, so symmetry is satisfied;
- the shortest path between σ_1 and σ_3 is at worst the concatenation of the paths $(\sigma_1, \ldots, \sigma_2)$ and $(\sigma_2, \ldots, \sigma_3)$, or (if possible) a shorter one, so triangular inequality is satisfied.

Proof (Proof of Proposition 4). Example 6 gives the counter-examples for coincidence and symmetry.

Proof (Proof of Proposition 5). We consider a given AF F and a set of semantics $\Sigma = \{\sigma_1, \ldots, \sigma_n\}$, such that for all $\sigma_i, \sigma_j \in \Sigma$ with $\sigma_i \neq \sigma_j$, $Ext_{\sigma_i}(F) \nsubseteq Ext_{\sigma_n}(F)$.

Obviously, for any semantics σ_i, $\delta_F^{d_H, \Sigma}(\sigma_i, \sigma_i) = 0$. Now, let us assume the existence of two semantics $\sigma_i, \sigma_j \in \Sigma$ such that $\delta_F^{d_H, \Sigma}(\sigma_i, \sigma_j) = 0$. We just rewrite this, following the definition of the measure: $\sum_{\epsilon \in Ext_{\sigma_i}(F)} \min_{\epsilon' \in Ext_{\sigma_j}(F)} d_H(\epsilon, \epsilon') = 0$. Since all distances are non-negative number, if the sum is equal to zero it means that $\forall \epsilon \in Ext_{\sigma_i}(F)$, $\min_{\epsilon' \in Ext_{\sigma_j}(F)} d_H(\epsilon, \epsilon') = 0$. Because of the properties of the Hamming distance, it means that $\epsilon \in Ext_{\sigma_j}$, and so $Ext_{\sigma_i} \subseteq Ext_{\sigma_j}$. From our starting assumption, we deduce that $\sigma_i = \sigma_j$.

Proof (Proof of Proposition 6). From the definition of the measure, $\delta_{F, sym}^{d_H, \Sigma}(\sigma_1, \sigma_2) = 0$ iff $Ext_{\sigma_1}(F) = Ext_{\sigma_2}(F)$. Under our assumptions, this is possible only if $\sigma_1 = \sigma_2$. The other direction is trivial, so coincidence is satisfied. Symmetry is obviously satisfied, since σ_1, σ_2 can be inverted in $\max(\delta_F^{d, \otimes}(\sigma_1, \sigma_2), \delta_F^{d, \otimes}(\sigma_2, \sigma_1))$.

Proof (Proof of Proposition 7). Weak coincidence and symmetry are trivial from the definition of the measures.

$$\delta^d_{F,sk}(\sigma_1, \sigma_2) + \delta^d_{F,sk}(\sigma_2, \sigma_3) = d(sk_{\sigma_1}(F), sk_{\sigma_2}(F)) + d(sk_{\sigma_2}(F), sk_{\sigma_3}(F))$$
$$\geq d(sk_{\sigma_1}(F), sk_{\sigma_3}(F)) = \delta^d_{F,sk}(\sigma_1, \sigma_3)$$

The same reasoning apply for the credulous acceptance measure. So both satisfy the triangular inequality. Coincidence is not satisfied by the skeptical acceptance measure. For instance, for each AF F, $\emptyset \in Ext_{cf}(F)$ and $\emptyset \in Ext_{adm}(F)$, so $sk_{cf}(F) = sk_{adm}(F) = \emptyset$, and so $\delta^d_{F,skep}(cf, adm) = 0$. The same conclusion holds as soon as two semantics yield the same skeptically or credulously accepted arguments.

References

1. Amgoud, L., Ben-Naim, J.: Ranking-based semantics for argumentation frameworks. In: Liu, W., Subrahmanian, V.S., Wijsen, J. (eds.) SUM 2013. LNCS (LNAI), vol. 8078, pp. 134–147. Springer, Heidelberg (2013). https://doi.org/10.1007/978-3-642-40381-1_11
2. Amgoud, L., Dimopoulos, Y., Moraitis, P.: A unified and general framework for argumentation-based negotiation. In: Proceedings of AAMAS 2007, p. 158 (2007)
3. Amgoud, L., Dimopoulos, Y., Moraitis, P.: Making decisions through preference-based argumentation. In: Proceedings of KR 2008, pp. 113–123 (2008)
4. Baroni, P., Caminada, M., Giacomin, M.: An introduction to argumentation semantics. Knowl. Eng. Rev. **26**, 365–410 (2011)
5. Baroni, P., Giacomin, M.: Skepticism relations for comparing argumentation semantics. Int. J. Approx. Reason. **50**(6), 854–866 (2009)
6. Baroni, P., Giacomin, M., Guida, G.: SCC-recursiveness: a general schema for argumentation semantics. Artif. Intell. **168**, 162–210 (2005)
7. Baumann, R.: What does it take to enforce an argument? Minimal change in abstract argumentation. In: Proceedings of ECAI 2012, pp. 127–132 (2012)
8. Baumann, R., Brewka, G.: Expanding argumentation frameworks: Enforcing and monotonicity results. In: Proceedings of COMMA 2010, pp. 75–86 (2010)
9. Besnard, P., Doutre, S., Herzig, A.: Encoding argument graphs in logic. In: Laurent, A., Strauss, O., Bouchon-Meunier, B., Yager, R.R. (eds.) IPMU 2014. CCIS, vol. 443, pp. 345–354. Springer, Cham (2014). https://doi.org/10.1007/978-3-319-08855-6_35
10. Besnard, P., Doutre, S., Ho, V.H., Longin, D.: SESAME - a system for specifying semantics in abstract argumentation. In: Thimm, M., Cerutti, F., Strass, H., Vallati, M. (eds.) Proceedings of SAFA 2016, vol. 1672, pp. 40–51. CEUR Workshop Proceedings (2016)
11. Bonzon, E., Delobelle, J., Konieczny, S., Maudet, N.: A comparative study of ranking-based semantics for abstract argumentation. In: Proceedings of AAAI 2016 (2016)
12. Caminada, M.: Semi-stable semantics. In: Proceedings of COMMA 2006 (2006)
13. Caminada, M.: Comparing two unique extension semantics for formal argumentation: ideal and eager (2007)

14. Coste-Marquis, S., Devred, C., Marquis, P.: Symmetric argumentation frameworks. In: Godo, L. (ed.) ECSQARU 2005. LNCS (LNAI), vol. 3571, pp. 317–328. Springer, Heidelberg (2005). https://doi.org/10.1007/11518655_28

15. Dimopoulos, Y., Torres, A.: Graph theoretical structures in logic programs and default theories. Theor. Comput. Sci. **170**(1–2), 209–244 (1996)

16. Doutre, S., Mailly, J.G.: Quantifying the Difference between Argumentation Semantics. In: Computational models of argument (COMMA), vol. 287, pp. 255–262. IOS Press (2016)

17. Doutre, S., Mailly, J.-G.: Semantic change and extension enforcement in abstract argumentation. In: Moral, S., Pivert, O., Sánchez, D., Marín, N. (eds.) SUM 2017. LNCS (LNAI), vol. 10564, pp. 194–207. Springer, Cham (2017). https://doi.org/10.1007/978-3-319-67582-4_14

18. Dung, P.M.: On the acceptability of arguments and its fundamental role in nonmonotonic reasoning, logic programming, and n-person games. Artif. Intell. **77**(2), 321–357 (1995)

19. Dung, P., Mancarella, P., Toni, F.: Adialectic procedure for sceptical, assumption-based argumentation. In: COMMA 2006 (2006)

20. Dunne, P.E.: The computational complexity of ideal semantics. Artif. Intell. **173**, 1559–1591 (2009)

21. Dunne, P.E., Bench-Capon, T.J.M.: Coherence in finite argument systems. Artif. Intell. **141**(1/2), 187–203 (2002)

22. Dunne, P.E., Caminada, M.: Computational complexity of semi-stable semantics in abstract argumentation frameworks. In: Hölldobler, S., Lutz, C., Wansing, H. (eds.) JELIA 2008. LNCS (LNAI), vol. 5293, pp. 153–165. Springer, Heidelberg (2008). https://doi.org/10.1007/978-3-540-87803-2_14

23. Dunne, P.E., Dvorák, W., Woltran, S.: Parametric properties of ideal semantics. Artif. Intell. **202**, 1–28 (2013)

24. Dvorák, W., Spanring, C.: Comparing the expressiveness of argumentation semantics. In: Proceedings of COMMA 2012, vol. 245, pp. 261–272. IOS Press (2012)

25. Dvorák, W., Woltran, S.: Complexity of semi-stable and stage semantics in argumentation frameworks. Inf. Process. Lett. **110**(11), 425–430 (2010)

26. Grossi, D., Modgil, S.: On the graded acceptability of arguments. In: Proceedings of IJCAI 2015, pp. 868–874 (2015)

27. Hunter, A.: Opportunities for argument-centric persuasion in behaviour change. In: Fermé, E., Leite, J. (eds.) JELIA 2014. LNCS (LNAI), vol. 8761, pp. 48–61. Springer, Cham (2014). https://doi.org/10.1007/978-3-319-11558-0_4

28. Papadimitriou, C.H.: Computational complexity. Addison-Wesley, Reading (1994)

29. Verheij, B.: Two approaches to dialectical argumentation: admissible sets and argumentation stages. In: Proceedings of BNAIC 1996 (1996)

Permutation-Based Randomised Tournament Solutions

Justin Kruger$^{(\boxtimes)}$ and Stéphane Airiau

Université Paris-Dauphine, PSL Research University,
CNRS, LAMSADE, 75016 Paris, France
{justin.kruger,stephane.airiau}@dauphine.fr

Abstract. Voting rules that are based on the majority graph typically output large sets of winners. In this full original paper our goal is to investigate a general method which leads to randomized version of such rules. We use the idea of parallel universes, where each universe is connected with a permutation over alternatives. The permutation allows us to construct resolute voting rules (i.e. rules that always choose unique winners). Such resolute rules can be constructed in a variety of ways: we consider using binary voting trees to select a single alternative. In turn this permits the construction of neutral rules that output the set the possible winners of every parallel universe. The question of which rules can be constructed in this way has already been partially studied under the heading of agenda implementability. We further propose a randomised version in which the probability of being the winner is the ratio of universes in which the alternative wins. We also briefly consider (typically novel) rules that elect the alternatives that have maximal winning probability. These rules typically output small sets of winners, thus provide refinements of known tournament solutions.

Keywords: Tournament · Probabilistic rules · Refinements
Condorcet consistency

1 Introduction

In general, social choice theory studies the problem of making group decisions: the problem of selecting a single alternative from a set of alternatives, about which different members of the group have different opinions. Stated as such this is a rather vague problem. One attempt to make it more tractable is to restrict attention to two alternatives at a time. Such a focus leads to structures called *tournaments*. In a tournament, if a majority of people in the society prefer a to b, then there is a directed edge from a to b. The hope is that using a tournament to determine the selected alternative will allow us to fairly select the best option in a consistent and transparent manner.

There are many methods designed to select alternatives from a tournament. Called rules, these include, but are not restricted to: Copeland, the Top Cycle,

© Springer Nature Switzerland AG 2018
F. Belardinelli and E. Argente (Eds.): EUMAS 2017/AT 2017, LNAI 10767, pp. 235–250, 2018.
https://doi.org/10.1007/978-3-030-01713-2_17

Banks, Slater and the Markov solution concepts [7]. All of these satisfy what is known as the *Condorcet criterion*. This requires that if a single alternative wins every pairwise competition when it is compared to any other alternative, then any reasonable rule will select this alternative.

What about in less clear cut cases, where there is no obvious winner? Another, less fortunate, property that rules based on tournaments typically exhibit is *irresoluteness*. They often cannot decide between alternatives; instead of selecting a unique alternative they output a set of multiple alternatives. *Resoluteness* (always selecting a single alternative) is often a required property, either for actual implementations or to facilitate particular analyses of social choice rules. Effectively, an irresolute rule hasn't completed the decision procedure. Thus irresolute rules are often equipped with an exogenous tie-breaking method that is applied after the rule. In terms of fairness using an exogenous tie-breaker violates the property of neutrality; it is no longer the case that all the alternatives are considered equal.

Arguably the simplest general tie-breaker is a priority ordering on the alternatives. There are $m!$ of these, where m is the number of alternatives. We think of each of these possible tie-breakers as a *possible universe*. Now, for a given irresolute set, each winning alternative wins in the same proportion of universes when we apply the tie-breaker at the end. What we do, roughly speaking, is apply the tie-breaker at an earlier stage in the decision procedure. This means that, within a given irresolute set, some alternative may win more often than another. Of course, in order to retain neutrality it will sometimes be necessary to select sets of alternatives, notably for completely symmetric tournaments; still, we will see that using this technique we can create more discriminating rules.

So far we have only discussed social choice theoretic issues concerning methods for selecting from tournaments, or tournament solutions. However tournament solutions are also interesting from an algorithmic standpoint. In particular, computing the full set of selected alternatives can be difficult while at the same time it is easy to find some winner. This is perhaps best exemplified by the gap between Woeginger's [21] result showing it is hard to tell if a particular alternative is in the Banks set and Hudry's [14] greedy algorithm for calculating some Banks winner. Tournament solutions are not alone in having this gap between "finding some" and "finding all". In general, social choice functions based on some parallel computations often seem to have this characteristic. This idea of parallel computations seems to originate from Tideman's work on Ranked Pairs [20], although it is first explicitly mentioned by Conitzer et al. [9], with respect to instant-runoff voting. Freeman et al. [11] continued this study in a similar direction, while Brill and Fischer [8] applied a similar approach to Tideman's [20] Ranked Pairs. For these parallel computation methods a trade-off was encountered between neutrality on the one hand, and resoluteness and tractability on the other. We know that full resoluteness is not achievable at the same time as neutrality; instead we ask whether it can be possible that the rule can be *more* resolute while remaining neutral. We can pose this question in two ways: (i) are there more cases where a single winner is selected? and (ii) in those cases where multiple winners are still selected, is the set smaller than before?

In general, this paper is concerned with applying parallel computation to tournament solutions. This can be used to define neutral refinements. It can also be used to define randomised voting rules, also known as social decision schemes. Social decision schemes have received growing interest in the literature recently. Randomised rules have received some particular attention in the recent years, for at least three reasons: first, as said, they reconcile neutrality and anonymity while being more informative than irresolute rules; second, they are less subject to results concerning manipulation [12]; third, they are very useful for repeated collective decision making, where probabilities can be viewed as fraction of time in a time sharing context.

Surprisingly, tournament solutions don't appear much in the landscape of randomised rules. We may wonder whether there are natural majoritarian randomised rules that are also Condorcet-consistent, or in other words, *randomised tournament solutions*. An obvious choice would be to start with an existing tournament solution and output all winning alternatives with uniform probability — we would then obtain a rule that we call *uniform F*, where F is an irresolute tournament solution. However, there is often no good reason for choosing a uniform probability, and the uniform distribution is, in many senses, the least discriminating of all probability distributions with a fixed support.

1.1   Previous Work

There is a large literature on tournaments, refer to [17] and [7] for general and extensive treatments. As already mentioned, particularly relevant results about tournaments concern the Banks set's easy/hard nature [14,21]. Also already mentioned, there is a recent literature that has started to explore the explicit use of parallel universes within social choice theory, for a variety of purposes [8,9,11].

Several randomised rules, or classes of randomised rules, have been considered: random dictatorship and its variants, proportional Borda (resp. Copeland), where the probability of an alternative is proportional to its Borda or Copeland score [5]; the *maximal lottery* rule [15]; the *leximin* rule (for dichotomous preferences) [6] and its extension to weak orders, the *egalitarian simultaneous reservation* rule [3]; the *maximal recursive* rule [2]. We observe that apart from the proportional Copeland rule, none is *majoritarian* (that is, computable from the majority graph associated with the preference profile, also called a *tournament solution*). Moreover, the only one on the list that is Condorcet-consistent (that is, which outputs the Condorcet winner with probability 1 when there exists one) is the maximal lottery rule.

1.2   Outline

We start in Sect. 2 by defining the underlying concepts that we will need concerning tournaments and binary trees. In Sect. 3 we consider irresolute tournament solution concepts based upon these rules. We consider what properties these rules satisfy and the effectiveness of argmax rules as refinements. In Sect. 4 we move on to consider randomised versions of the rules. Section 5 provides some final remarks.

2 Tournaments and Binary Trees

In this section we give preliminary definitions. All of these are given with reference to a set X of m alternatives. We will label specific alternatives of X as $1, 2, 3, \ldots$ and refer to arbitrary elements as $a, b, c, \ldots$

The typical comparison method between two alternatives is majority voting: alternative a defeats alternative b if a wins in a pairwise majority election. We will refer to this as the domination relation, i.e. "a dominates b" expresses the relation aTb. If we assume that such a relation holds between every pair of alternatives, we end up with a tournament. Formally, a *tournament* is a trichotomous [1] binary relation T over some set X. Perhaps the smallest interesting example involves four alternatives, see Fig. 1 for a visual representation. In this figure, we obtain T' from T by switching the arrow between 1 and 3. In general we will write $T_{\langle a,b \rangle}$ for the tournament obtained by reversing the relation between a and b in T.

Fig. 1. Visual representation of two example tournaments over four candidates: T and T'. The relation aTb or $aT'b$ holds if there is an arrow from a to b in the respective graphs.

A *tournament function* F is a function from the set of all tournaments over some set X to subsets of X. A *tournament solution* S a collection of tournament functions for each set X. Although we must be aware of the above distinction, it would tedious to take too much time to redefine every concept that applies to tournament functions to apply it also tournament solutions.

One common way to define tournament functions is using binary trees. Figure 2 contains an example. The binary tree in Fig. 2 is usually called the simple tree [17], but has also been called the voting caterpillar [10].[2] We also give a compact representation of the tree as a left-associative word, where parentheses (i) are assumed to exist between the two leftmost elements in a triple and (ii) indicate that two nodes are siblings.

---

[1] A binary relation $R \subseteq X \times X$ *trichotomous* if for all $a, b \in X$, either aTb, bTa or $a = b$.

[2] More precisely, this is one instance of the simple tree. We give a full recursive definition later in this section.

Fig. 2. An example binary tree. Its compact representation is 1(2(34)).

The basic idea behind using a binary tree to select an alternative is simple: alternatives are placed at the leaves of the tree, and compete against their siblings, the winners moving up to the parent node until we have a final winner at the root. Formally, for a tree τ, the tournament solution $[\![\tau]\!]$ has the following recursive definition:

$$[\![xy]\!](T) = \begin{cases} x & \text{if } xTy \\ y & \text{otherwise} \end{cases}$$

$$[\![\tau\tau']\!](T) = [\![\, (\, [\![\tau]\!](T) \,) \, (\, [\![\tau']\!](T) \,) \,]\!](T)$$

It can be verified that for the tournaments in Fig. 1 the simple tree has the same output.

$$[\![1(2(34))]\!](T) = [\![1(2(34))]\!](T')$$
$$= \{1\}$$

Clearly, any tournament function defined by a binary tree will always select a single alternative: we say the tournament solution is *resolute*. Resoluteness is incompatible with *neutrality*, which requires that permuting the alternatives in the tournament results in an identical permutation of the alternatives in the output set. The *Condorcet criterion*, which requires that if there is an alternative that pairwise defeats all other alternatives, this alternative is selected. The *two-leaf tree* below violates this when $m > 2$. In fact, only *complete* binary trees, those that have every alternative instantiated by some leaf, satisfy the Condorcet criterion.

Proposition 1. *A binary tree satisfies the Condorcet criterion iff it is complete.*

Proof. For the only if, consider the contrapositive: if a Condorcet winner is not in the tree, some other alternative will be selected. For the if, suppose the tree is complete. A Condorcet winner will defeat any other alternative it meets up until the root.

Monotonicity requires that whenever a winner is reinforced it does not become a loser. Formally, if T is a tournament such that bTa, and a is selected under this tournament then a should also be selected under $T_{\langle a,b \rangle}$. Notice that alternative 1 has been reinforced between T and T' in Fig. 1, and that the simple tree outputs 1 for both of these tournaments; in fact, the simple tree is monotonic. Further, all *non-repetitive* binary trees with no repeated alternatives in their leaves are monotonic.

Proposition 2. *Every non-repetitive binary tree is monotonic.*

Proof. Suppose an alternative is winning; as the alternative only appears once in a non-repetitive tree this implies that it defeats every other alternative it meets. If the only change to the tournament involves a change between this winning alternative and an alternative that used to defeat the winning alternative, then within the tree there will be no changes to which alternatives proceed to the parent nodes.

Other trees may not be monotonic [17]. Figure 3 provides a minimal counter example.

Fig. 3. A binary tree τ that is not monotonic. Taking T and T' from Fig. 1, we have $[\![\tau]\!](T) = \{1\}$, but $[\![\tau]\!](T') = \{3\}$. The compact representation of τ is 4(13)21, note that by left associativity many of the brackets here are left out.

The properties in the preceding paragraph were all either *intra-* or *inter-profile*, i.e. they either applied to all profiles or concerned relationships between pairs of profiles. The properties in the following paragraph have an *inter-agenda* character, in that they concern changes to the set of alternatives. In order to describe these properties we must first give some more definitions. For a tournament T over X, its *restriction* to $Y \subseteq X$ is the tournament $T_Y = \{(x, y) \in T \mid x, y \in Y\}$. This subtournament T_Y is further a *component* if all its alternatives have the same relation to any element outside the component. Formally, T_Y is a component iff for all $a, b \in Y$ and $c \in X \backslash Y$, aTc iff bTc. If a tournament has components, if can be sensibly decomposed into smaller parts. Thus a *decomposition* of a tournament is a division of the tournament into components T_{X_i}, fully written as $(T^*, T_{X_1}, \ldots, T_{X_k})$ such that the X_is are (i) pairwise disjoint, (ii) cover the set X, and (iii) form components when the tournament T is restricted to them. The tournament T^* is then the *summary* of the decomposition: a tournament over $\{1, \ldots, k\}$ such that iT^*j iff xTy for $x \in X_i$ and $y \in X_j$. See Fig. 4 for an example.

Weak composition consistency requires that local changes to a component (i) do not change the winners on other components and (ii) do not change the fact that either no element or some element wins on the component itself. Formally, a tournament *function* F satisfies weak composition consistency if, for all $\{x, y\} \subseteq Y \subseteq X$, (i) $F(T) \cap (X \backslash Y) = F(T_{\langle x,y \rangle}) \cap (X \backslash Y)$ and (ii) $F(T) \cap Y \neq \emptyset \leftrightarrow F(T_{\langle x,y \rangle}) \cap Y \neq \emptyset$. *Composition consistency* requires that the winners of the overall tournament should be winners of the winners in a decomposition: one can first determine the winners of the summary and

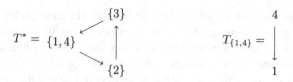

$$T^* = \{1,4\} \quad \begin{matrix} \{3\} \\ \uparrow \\ \{2\} \end{matrix} \qquad\qquad T_{\{1,4\}} = \begin{matrix} 4 \\ \downarrow \\ 1 \end{matrix}$$

Fig. 4. A decomposition of T from Fig. 1. into $(T^*, T_{\{1,4\}}, T_{\{3\}}, T_{\{2\}})$.

then determine the winners of these winning tournaments. Formally, a tournament *solution* S satisfies composition consistency if: for any decomposition $T = (T^*, T_{X_1}, \ldots, T_{X_k})$, $a \in S(T)$ iff $S(T^*) = i$ where $a \in X_i$ and $a \in S(T_{X_i})$. Composition consistency implies weak composition consistency.

2.1   Families of Trees

In order to use trees to obtain tournament solutions, we need a *family of binary trees* for all possible sets of alternatives. These can be defined by a recursive function g that takes permutations of different lengths as an argument. To terminate the recursion, for a permutation of two elements x and y we set $g(xy) = xy$. The simple tree can thus be described:

Simple tree $\mathsf{st}(12\ldots m) = 1\,(\mathsf{st}(2\ldots m))$

Another well known tree is named after one of its early investigators [4].

Banks tree $\mathsf{bn}(12\ldots m) = \mathsf{bn}(13\ldots m)\,(\mathsf{bn}(23\ldots m))$

The Banks tree for four alternatives is shown in Fig. 5. Clearly the Banks tree is repetitive. Although this means it doesn't fall under the claim of Proposition 2, it is nonetheless monotonic.

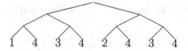

Fig. 5. The Banks tree for four alternatives. Its compact representation is $14(34)(24(34))$.

Proposition 3. *For any number of alternatives,* bn *is monotonic.*

Proof. This result is well known, see [4], so we only provide a high level description of the proof. Consider the following intuitive definition of the Banks tree. First, we suppose that the rightmost alternative in the Banks tree is the preliminary winner. We then successively examine the other alternatives (as arguments in the recursive definition from right to left), potentially setting them as new preliminary winners. For an alternative to become the new preliminary winner, it must defeat every member of the set of previous preliminary winners. After all the alternatives have been tested, we select the current preliminary winner. Clearly, if an alternative was selected then it defeated all previous preliminary winners: changing only this alternative so that it defeats more alternatives will not change the fact that it is selected.

A simple example of a non-complete tree (for $m > 2$) is the following.

Two-leaf tree $tt(12 \ldots m) = 12$.

The fact that this is non-complete implies that this violates the Condorcet criterion. We can also extract another non-repetitive family from the literature, "fair" or "balanced" voting trees [16]; trees which, for a given number of nodes, have minimal height.

Balanced tree

$$\mathrm{ft}\left(1 \ldots \left\lceil \frac{m}{2} \right\rceil \left[\left\lceil \frac{m}{2} \right\rceil + 1\right] \ldots m\right) = \mathrm{ft}\left(1 \ldots \left\lceil \frac{m}{2} \right\rceil\right) \left(\mathrm{ft}\left(\left[\left\lceil \frac{m}{2} \right\rceil + 1\right] \ldots m\right)\right)$$

We note that if $\log_2 |X|$ is not an integer there are multiple non-repetitive tree structures that have minimum height. However, our particular implementation is perhaps the most natural, as it also minimises the difference in the amount of nodes in the left and right subtrees of any particular node. There is one final family of trees, that we will return to early in the next section, that we consider.

Iterative Condorcet tree $ic(12 \ldots m) = 12 \ldots m \; ic(2 \ldots m)$

3   Irresolute Rules Based on Binary Trees

In this section we move from resolute rules to neutral rules. The idea behind one well-known method is simple: return all winners for all possible permutations of the leaves of the tree.[3] Following Conitzer et al. [9], we use the terminology "universe" to refer to each possible permutation. Thus this method forms the parallel universe solution concept. We indicate this with a superscript PU; formally, for a family of trees τ,

$$\tau^{\mathsf{PU}}(T) = \{ [\![\tau(\sigma)]\!](T) : \sigma \in S_X \}$$

The outcomes of many of these parallel universe versions are well studied,[4] and for others it is easy to see what the result is. However, although much work has been done on these rules, we are not aware of anyone explicitly remarking that different trees can return the same parallel universe rule.

---

[3] By permutation here do not mean all possible assignments of alternatives to the leaves: indeed, this would imply that all alternatives are trivially returned, as the tree where all leaves are the same alternative must return that alternative. We are not aware of any work that considers possible winners under some generalised "multiple assignment procedure" of the leaves of a binary tree.

[4] The question of what tournament rules are implementable by parallel universes in this manner has been studied by Horan [13], who gives necessary and sufficient conditions.

Proposition 4. *We have the following equivalences between parallel universe rules and known rules:*

1. st^{PU} returns the top cycle.[5]
2. bn^{PU} returns the Banks set, see [4].
3. tt^{PU} returns the set of undominated alternatives.[6]
4. The tournament solution ic^{PU} is identical to the top cycle.

Proof. Only 4. deserves comment, the other results are well known or obvious. The binary tree ic implements the iterative Condorcet rule described by Altman and Kleinberg [1] into a binary tree rule. Intuitively, this rule successively removes alternatives from the tournament until the contracted tournament has a Condorcet winner; this Condorcet winner is then selected. This produces every element in the top cycle: for an arbitrary element in the top cycle, consider successively removing the elements following the cycle starting with the alternative dominated by the arbitrary element. It is similarly easy to see that no element *not* in the top cycle can be produced by this procedure.

To see that the iterative Condorcet tree $\mathsf{ic}(1 \dots m)$ implements this, note that after the first $m-1$ comparisons if m is still a possible winner it will have defeated every other candidate, if not it has been eliminated as it does not reappear higher in the tree; in the latter case the process then continues by comparing $m - 1$ against all alternatives $< m - 1$, etc.

The parallel universe mindset suggests an obvious way to refine the above solution concepts: instead of taking the union over all universes, only take those alternatives that win in *most* universes. We refer to this as the *argmax* solution concept, and use AM as the corresponding superscript. For a family of trees τ,

$$\tau^{AM}(T) = \arg \max_{x \in X} | \{ \sigma \in S_X : [\![\tau(\sigma)]\!](T) = \{x\} \} |$$

We have noted that $\mathsf{st}^{PU} = \mathsf{ic}^{PU}$, however the same is not true for the argmax versions.

Proposition 5. *The tournament solutions st^{AM} and ic^{AM} are distinct.*

Proof. The counterexample was found by computer: the actual counting of universes is slightly tedious; we provide the example in Appendix A.

This suggests that we have to choose our refinement with care: in fact, there doesn't seem to be any principled reason to choose one of these versions over the other in order to obtain a refinement of the top cycle.

---

[5] The top cycle of a tournament is the maximal set of alternatives such that the restriction of the tournament to these alternatives contains a cycle.

[6] An alternative is undominated if it there is some alternative that does not dominate it.

3.1   Properties of Irresolute Rules

In general, a parallel universe version of a binary tree need not be monotonic: see [17]. However, our parallel universe rules are well known to be monotonic, and indeed inherit this property from the fact that the resolute binary trees are monotonic. It is also known that parallel universe versions are weakly composition consistent: for proof, see [17,19].

The big question here is whether or not the argmax versions of our rules also satisfy monotonicity. Unfortunately, it seems difficult to prove the monotonicity property here, which is a basic desirable property. The only rule for which we are sure that this holds is the argmax version of tt, which corresponds to Copeland. It would be somewhat surprising if monotonicity did not also apply to the other argmax versions of the rules.

We can show that no argmax rule is composition consistent, for $m \geq 5$.

Proposition 6. *There is no family of trees τ such that τ^{AM} satisfies weak composition consistency.*

Proof. Consider the tournament $T = (T^*, T_1, 2, 3)$ and $T' = (T^*, T_2, 2, 3)$ such that T^* and T_1 are cyclic tournaments with 3 alternatives, T_2 is a transitive tournament, and 2 and 3 are tournaments with single alternatives. Suppose for a contradiction that there is a tree τ such that τ_{AM} is composition consistent. This must make all five alternatives winners in T, by composition consistency and neutrality. However, in the second, only one alternative in T_2 can win (by Condorcet consistency), and 2 and 3 must also win. Now, consider the number of permutations for which 2 and 3 win for the tree τ under tournaments T and T': these must be the same. Similarly, the number of permutations for which some alternative in T_1 wins must be the same as the number of permutations for which some alternative in T_2 wins. As in T all alternatives are winning, 2 and 3 must win 20 times. But in T' the Condorcet winner of T_2 must win 60 times, contradiction.

3.2   Success of Argmax Rules as Refinements

Assuming, as we conjecture, that our argmax rules satisfy the basic property of monotonicity, the other issue at hand is how effective they actually are at refining the set of winners. Let us start by considering tt: for $\mathsf{tt}^{\mathsf{PU}}$, the undominated set is an extremely undiscriminating solution concept. However, $\mathsf{tt}^{\mathsf{AM}}$ corresponds to the *Copeland set*, which is much more discriminating even than many other solution concepts we consider. Here moving to the argmax universe version certainly provides a large gain in discriminating power.

The same seems to be the case for the other solution concepts. We have tested this on some example tournaments. The outcome of all of our rules only concern alternatives in the top cycle: any Condorcet losers will not affect the outcome of the vote. Thus we restrict attention to *non-reducible tournaments*, where there is a cycle throughout the whole tournament. Equivalently, the top cycle returns all

Table 1. Alternatives selected for various rules for all non-reducible tournaments of size 6. The alternatives are labelled from 0 to 5. The Markov solution concept [7] is provided to allow for comparison with a particularly decisive tournament solution concept.

st^{AM}	bn^{AM}	ft^{AM}	tt^{AM}	ic^{AM}	markov
0	0	0	0,1	0	0
0	0	0	0,1	0	0
0	0	0	0,1	0	0
0	0	0	0,1	0	0
0	1	0	0	0	0
1	1	1	1	1	1
0	0	0	0	0	0
0	0	0	0,1	0	0
0	0	0	0,1	0	0
0	0	0	0,1	0	0
0	0	0	0	0	0
0	0	0	0	0	0
0	0	0	0	0	0
0	0	0	0	0	0
0	0	0	0	0	0
2	2	2	0	0	0
0	0,1	0	0	0	0
0	0	0	0	0	0
0	4	0	0	0	0
0	0	0	0	0	0
0	0	0	0	0	0
0	0	0	0,1,2,3	0	0
4	4	0	0,1,2,4	0	4,0
0	0	0	0,1,2,3	0	0
1	1	1,2	1,2,3,4	1	1
0	0	0	0	0	0
0	0	0	0	0	0
0	0	0	0	0	0
2	2	2	2,3,4	2	2
1	1	1,3,4	1,3,4	1,3	1
4	4	4	1,4,5	4	4
3,4,5	3,4,5	3,4,5	3,4,5	3,4,5	3,4,5
3,4,5	3,4,5	3,4,5	3,4,5	3,4,5	3,4,5

Table 2. Candidates selected by each permutations σ of an tree g, applied to the tournament T of Fig. 1. The values in the top half of the table are $[\![g(\sigma)]\!](T)$.

σ	$g = $ sa	$g = $ ba	$g = $ fa	$g = $ ta	$g = $ ic
1234	1	3	3	1	3
2134	2	3	3	1	3
3214	3	3	4	2	4
2314	2	3	4	2	3
3124	3	3	3	3	4
1324	3	3	3	3	4
4321	3	3	3	3	1
3421	3	3	3	3	4
3241	3	3	4	2	4
4231	4	3	3	4	3
2431	2	3	3	4	3
2341	2	3	4	2	3
4123	4	2	4	4	2
1423	4	2	4	4	2
1243	1	2	3	1	3
4213	4	2	3	4	3
2413	2	2	3	4	3
2143	2	2	3	1	3
4132	4	4	4	4	2
1432	4	4	4	4	2
1342	3	4	3	3	4
4312	3	4	3	3	1
3412	3	4	3	3	4
3142	3	4	3	3	4
Number of times a is selected:					
$a = 1$	2	0	0	4	2
$a = 2$	6	6	0	4	4
$a = 3$	10	12	16	8	10
$a = 4$	6	6	8	8	8

alternatives. Moon [18] provides a list of all (small) non-isomorphic tournaments, from which we see that there are only 34 non-reducible tournaments of size 6. We applied our rules to all of these, and compared them with the (discriminating) Markov solution concept. The specific results are found in Table 1.

From Table 1 it can be verified that all these solution concepts are distinct. We can also see that the Banks set contains three alternatives 14 times, four alternatives 8 times, five alternatives 9 times and six alternatives 3 times. In contrast bn^{AM} outputs a single winner 32 times, two winners 1 time and three winners 2 times. Both st^{AM} and ic^{AM} get similar (though distinct) results. Copeland, equivalent to tt^{AM}, outputs a single winner 18 times, two winners 7 times, three winners 5 times and four winners 4 times. Thus it appears that the argmax rules are significantly more decisive than the full parallel universe versions.

4   Probabilistic Versions of Binary Trees

Counting universes also provides a method for returning probabilistic rules based upon a binary tree. For a family of binary trees τ, define a function τ^{FR}, which has all possible tournaments as its domain and probability distributions of the alternatives in each tournament as its range, as

$$\tau^{FR}(T)(x) = \frac{|\{\sigma \in S_X : [\![\tau(\sigma)]\!](T) = \{x\}\}|}{m!} .$$

We now define Condorcet consistency, monotonicity and composition consistency in the context of randomised tournament solution. To each of these we prepend "prob" to indicate that it is the probabilistic version. We start with the notion of Condorcet consistency: if a tournament has a Condorcet winner, no other alternative should have a positive probability to be elected.

Definition 1 (Prob-Condorcet consistency). *For a family of binary trees τ, τ^{FQ} satisfies Prob-Condorcet consistency if, whenever a tournament T has as a Condorcet winner a, then $\tau^{FQ}(T)(a) = 1$.*

A weaker version only requires that the Condorcet winner, when it exists, has the largest probability of winning of all alternatives.

Definition 2 (Weak prob-Condorcet consistency). *For a family of binary trees τ, τ^{FQ} satisfies Prob-Condorcet consistency if, whenever a tournament T has as a Condorcet winner a, then $R(T)(a) > R(T)(b)$ for all $b \neq a$.*

In a probabilistic setting, the simplest definition of monotonicity simply requires that if we reinforce a winner, her probability of winning cannot decrease.

Definition 3 (Prob-monotonicity). *We say that τ^{FQ} is prob-monotonic if for any tournament T where bTa we have $\tau^{FQ}(T_{\langle a,b \rangle})(a) \geq \tau^{FQ}(T)(a)$.*

Note that this is not the only possible definition: an alternative definition would also take the probability of other alternatives winning into account. It is precisely a property along these lines that we have failed to prove for the argmax version of the rules.

As with the deterministic versions, probabilistic composition consistency conditions concern changes to components of the tournament.

Definition 4 (Weak prob-composition consistency). *Given a decomposable tournament* $T = (T^*, T_{X_1}, \ldots, T_{X_k})$ *and two alternatives* $a, b \in X_i$ *in some component, we require, for any* $c \notin X_i$,

$$\tau^{\mathsf{FQ}}(T)(c) = \tau^{\mathsf{FQ}}(T_{\langle a,b \rangle})(c) \ ,$$

and

$$\sum_{d \in X_i} \tau^{\mathsf{FQ}}(T)(d) = \sum_{d \in X_i} \tau^{\mathsf{FQ}}(T_{\langle a,b \rangle})(d) \ .$$

Definition 5 (Prob-composition consistency). *If a tournament* T *can be decomposed into* $(T^*, T_{X_1}, \ldots, T_{X_k})$ *then for all* $j \in \{1, \ldots, k\}$ *and for all* $x \in X_j$

$$\tau^{\mathsf{FQ}}(T)(x) = \tau^{\mathsf{FQ}}(T_{X_j}) \cdot \tau^{\mathsf{FQ}}(T^*)(j) \ .$$

To show which of these properties are satisfied, we will refer to Table 2, which shows the outcome for all permutations of our trees for the four alternative tournament T of Fig. 1. Even for this small example we see that the counts for each alternative are different for the simple tree and the iterative Condorcet tree.

Proposition 7. *For any family of trees* τ, τ^{FR} *is weakly prob-Condorcet consistent. If* τ *is also complete,* τ^{FR} *is prob-Condorcet consistent.*

Proof. Supposing there are k different alternatives in the tree, a Condorcet winner will win in $k \cdot (m - 1)!$ universes (k choices for the Condorcet winner within the tree, $m - 1$ choices for the other alternatives). Any other alternative can only win in at most $k \cdot (m - k) \cdot (m - 2)!$ universes (k choices for the alternative within the tree, $m - k$ choices for the Condorcet winner outside the tree, $m - 2$ choices for the other alternatives). As the tree is non-singleton, $k > 1$.

Prob-monotonicity is inherited from the monotonicity of a resolute tree.

Proposition 8. *If* τ *is monotonic, so too is* τ^{FQ}.

Proof. The count of universes for which an alternative wins can only increase if this alternative has its position improved.

Weak prob-composition consistency holds for all probabilistic versions.

Proposition 9. *For any tree* τ, τ^{FR} *is weakly prob-composition consistent.*

Proof. Suppose a tournament only changes on some component $Y \subseteq X$. Fix any order over which we move the pairs of alternatives up the tree. At each such step, if an element not in the component won, it will still win. If an element in the component won, either it will still win or another element from the component will win. Thus this will not affect the number of permutations for which alternatives not in the component win.

However, we only have negative inheritance (from the parallel universe rule) of full composition consistency.

Proposition 10. *For any τ, if τ^{PU} is not composition consistent then τ^{FR} is not prob-composition consistent.*

Proof. By contraposition: suppose τ^{FR} is prob-composition consistent, consider the support of the rule for the components and the summary of the decomposition.

By observing Table 2, we see that Banks tree provides a counterexample to the inheritance of this property from parallel rules to probabilistic rules. That is, we know that bn^{PU} is composition consistent [7], but from the table we see that bn^{FR} is not.

5   Final Remarks

In this paper, we propose a general principle for constructing randomised voting rules (or social decision schemes) and neutral refinements of voting rules. We use the idea that, given a voting rule, some object that we call a universe can ensure that the voting rule is resolute. One example is to consider that a universe is defined by a tie-breaking rule. In this paper, we have considered that a universe is defined by a particular assignment of alternatives to a voting tree. There are three types of rules that are naturally definable with respect to a universe: parallel rules that output all winners for all possible universes, probabilistic (frequency) rules that randomly pick a universe and output the winner from that universe, and argmax rules that output the winners of the most universes. We summarise the status of these rules in Table 3.

Table 3. Summary of tree based rules.

	Parallel universe	Argmax	Randomised
Simple tree	Top cycle [17]	New	[10]
Banks tree	Banks [17]	New	New
Fair tree	Cup rule	New	New
Two-leaf tree	Condorcet non-losers	Copeland	New
Iterative Condorcet tree	Top cycle [1]	New	[1]

We have studied whether properties are inherited between these different rules. We summarise the known properties for our specific trees in Table 4. The particular attraction of the argmax rules is that they are more decisive than their parallel version counterparts. However, the real test of their attractiveness hinges upon whether or not they are monotonic, a property we have not been able to prove or disprove.

Table 4. Known properties (deterministic/randomised) for trees.

	Condorcet Consistency			Monotonicity			Composition Consistency		
	PU	AM	FR	PU	AM	FR	PU	AM	FR
Simple tree	✔	✔	✔	✔	?	✔	✘	✘	Weak
Iter. Cond. tree	✔	✔	✔	✔	?	✔	✘	✘	Weak
Banks tree	✔	✔	✔	✔	?	✔	✔	✘	Weak
Balanced tree	✔	✔	✔	✔	?	✔	✘	✘	Weak
Two-leaf tree	Weak	✔	weak	✔	✔	✔	✘	✘	Weak

Acknowledgement. Justin Kruger and Stéphane Airiau are supported by the ANR project CoCoRICo-CoDec.

A Tournament for which st^{AM} is distinct from ic^{AM}

We note that this tournament was found by computer; the actual counting of the different universes for which a particular alternative wins is slightly tedious. The tournament itself is shown in Fig. 6.

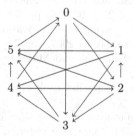

Fig. 6. A six alternative tournament T for which st$^{AM} = \{4\}$ and ic$^{AM} = \{0\}$.

References

1. Altman, A., Kleinberg, R.: Nonmanipulable randomized tournament selections. In: AAAI (2010)
2. Aziz, H.: Maximal recursive rule: a new social decision scheme. In Proceedings of IJCAI 2013, pp. 34–40. AAAI Press (2013)
3. Aziz, H., Stursberg, P.: A generalization of probabilistic serial to randomized social choice. In: Proceedings of the Twenty-Eighth AAAI Conference on Artificial Intelligence, 27–31 July 2014, Québec City, Québec, Canada, pp. 559–565 (2014)
4. Banks, S.J.: Sophisticated voting outcomes and agenda control. Soc. Choice Welfare **1**(4), 295–306 (1985)
5. Barberà, S.: Majority and positional voting in a probabilistic framework. Rev. Econ. Stud. **46**(2), 379–389 (1979)
6. Bogomolnaia, A., Moulin, H., Stong, R.: Collective choice under dichotomous preferences. J. Econ. Theory **122**(2), 165–184 (2005)
7. Brandt, F., Brill, M., Harrenstein, P.: Tournament solutions. In: Handbook of Computational Social Choice, chap. 3. Cambridge University Press, Cambridge (2016)
8. Brill, M., Fischer, F.: The price of neutrality for the ranked pairs method. In: Proceedings of AAAI-2012, pp. 1299–1305 (2012)
9. Conitzer, V., Rognlie, M., Xia, L.: Preference functions that score rankings and maximum likelihood estimation. In: Proceedings of IJCAI-2009, pp. 109–115 (2009)
10. Fischer, F., Procaccia, A.D., Samorodnitsky, A.: A new perspective on implementation by voting trees. In: Proceedings of the 10th ACM Conference on Electronic Commerce, pp. 31–40. ACM (2009)
11. Freeman, R., Brill, M., Conitzer, V.: General tiebreaking schemes for computational social choice. In: Proceedings of AAMAS-2015 (2015)
12. Gibbard, A.: Manipulation of schemes that mix voting with chance. Econometrica **45**, 665–681 (1977)
13. Horan, S.: Implementation of majority voting rules. Preprint (2013)
14. Hudry, O.: A note on "Banks winners in tournaments are difficult to recognize" by G. J. Woeginger. Soc. Choice Welfare **23**(1), 113–114 (2004)
15. Kreweras, G.: Aggregation of preference orderings. In: Mathematics and Social Sciences I: Proceedings of the Seminars of Menthon-Saint-Bernard, France, 1–27 July 1960, Gösing, Austria, 3–27 July 1962, pp. 73–79 (1965)
16. Lang, J., Pini, M.S., Rossi, F., Venable, K.B., Walsh, T.: Winner determination in sequential majority voting. In: IJCAI 2007, vol. 7, pp. 1372–1377 (2007)
17. Laslier, J.-F.: Tournament Solutions and Majority Voting. Springer, Heidelberg (1997)
18. Moon, J.W.: Topics on Tournaments in Graph Theory. Holt, Rinehart and Winston (1968)
19. Moulin, H.: Choosing from a tournament. Soc. Choice Welfare **3**(4), 271–291 (1986)
20. Nicolaus, T.: Independence of clones as a criterion for voting rules. Soc. Choice Welfare **4**(3), 185–206 (1987)
21. Woeginger, G.J.: Banks winners in tournaments are difficult to recognize. Soc. Choice Welfare **20**(3), 523–528 (2003)

EUMAS 2017: Simulation

Designing Co-simulation
with Multi-agent Tools: A Case Study
with NetLogo

Thomas Paris, Laurent Ciarletta, and Vincent Chevrier[✉]

Université de Lorraine, LORIA, INRIA-Lorraine BP 506,
54506 Vandoeuvre-lès-Nancy, France
{thomas.paris,laurent.ciarletta,vincent.chevrier}@loria.fr

Abstract. Multi-agent approach has demonstrated its benefits for complex system modeling and simulation. This article focuses on how to represent and simulate a system as a set of several interacting simulators, with a focus on the case of multi-agent simulators. This raises a major challenge: multi-agent simulators are not conceived (in general) to be used with other simulators.

This article presents a preliminary study about the rigorous integration of multi-agent simulators into a co-simulation platform. The work is grounded on the NetLogo simulator and the co-simulation platform MECSYCO.

Keywords: Complex system · Multi-agent system · Co-simulation
MECSYCO · NetLogo

1 Introduction

The modeling and simulation (M&S) of complex systems is one of the key challenges in research. One of the difficulties is to combine several perspectives of the same system (Seck and Honig 2012) into a coherent one (multi-modeling). It needs to manage the system with several levels (micro, macro), different scales (time, space, ...), etc. Handling such heterogeneities calls for the development of new approaches and tools.

One of the most promising approaches to face these challenges is co-simulation (Gomes et al. 2017). It consists in making different simulators interact into a simulation by ensuring the synchronization and the data exchanges between them. It enables the reuse of existing simulators used in specific domains. However, this implies to be able to manage the heterogeneities of the simulators both at software level (how to control simulators execution to make them interact?) and at formal one (how to make compatible the different dynamics?).

In parallel, multi-agent approach is convenient to represent and simulate systems composed of numerous interacting entities (which is a definition of complex

© Springer Nature Switzerland AG 2018
F. Belardinelli and E. Argente (Eds.): EUMAS 2017/AT 2017, LNAI 10767, pp. 253–267, 2018.
https://doi.org/10.1007/978-3-030-01713-2_18

systems (Ramat 2007)). It makes possible to represent both the individual and collective levels (Michel et al. 2009). Then multi-agent approach is a relevant choice to model and simulate complex systems.

The general question we address in this paper is *How can we represent and simulate a complex system with different multi-agent systems*, each representing a complementary perspective of the whole. We adopt a co-simulation approach to answer it. The issue we are now facing becomes how to make the multi-agent simulators interact to exchange information and synchronize their execution. We limit our scope in this article to spatial coupling of multi-agent systems: one agent is present in one simulator at a time, agents in different simulators can not interact. Interactions are restricted to events that pass from one simulator to another. Our goal is to rigorously integrate multi-agent simulators in an hybrid co-simulation which uses both continuous and discrete simulators. We do not consider ad-hoc solutions (potentially source of errors), nor the rewriting of models into one single simulator (source of errors, waste of time,...).

The problem we focus on can be solved by answering two questions: (i) how to manage the time and the synchronization of the multi-agent simulator with the rest of the simulation?; and (ii) how to manage information exchanges between the simulator and the other simulators of the co-simulation?

We demonstrated that these questions can be answered in the MECSYCO middleware (Camus 2015) by using the DEVS formalism as a formal basis for integration. This article details how we answer these questions and build a DEVS wrapper in the case of the NetLogo multi-agent simulator.

The remaining of the article is structured as follows: The Sect. 2 presents related works; next Sect. 3 introduces concepts used to build our proposal. The Sect. 4 presents the principles of our proposal which is detailed in 5. The Sect. 6 presents different use-cases that illustrate the possibilities of the proposal. Section 7 discusses the approach and Sect. 8 concludes the article.

2   Related Works

Several works dealt with the simulation of a multi-agent system as the integration of different subsystems.

A first question is to position that integration with respect to the modeling and simulation process. We use the structuring of (Galán et al. 2009) which distinguishes four steps as represented in Fig. 1. From this point of view, the integration of subsystems is possible at the interface of these 4 levels.

In the first case, a conceptual formulation describes the integration by proposing means of exchanges of information between components and of components synchronization, as for example, patterns (Gangat et al. 2012), or models (Morvan et al. 2013, Maudet et al. 2013). These works limit the integration of the different components of the multi-agent system into the same conceptual framework and the same tool.

The second case considers a formalism as a pivot for a rigorous integration. It is the case of the VLE (Virtual Laboratory Environment) (Quesnel et al. 2009), from which we retain its ideas under the wrapping perspective.

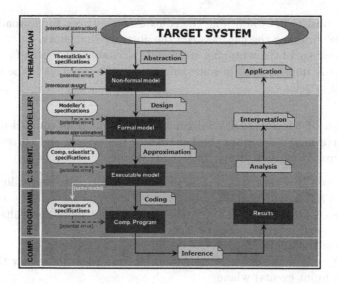

Fig. 1. The different steps of the modeling process. Source (Galán et al. 2009)

The third case envisages the integration as a software interoperability problem, the conceptual and formal issues are solved from an ad-hoc manner.

Alternatively, different multi-agent simulators are able to simulate a system as a set of different (logical or physical) environments (such as Madkit[1], or Repast (North et al. 2013)), but are not open to include environments coming from other tools. An effort for a more standard integration has been done in (Behrens et al. 2011) by considering an interface for agent/environment interaction. As far as we know, the issue of integrating a multi-agent simulator into a co-simulation is not tackled, nor the rigorous management of synchronization. Existing works we know (except (Quesnel et al. 2009)) propose different multi-agent concepts to define the integration of components into a simulation but are not open to a wider scope.

3 Prerequisites

3.1 DEVS

DEVS (Discrete EVent System specification) is an event-based formalism proposed by Bernard P. Zeigler in 1970 (Zeigler et al. 2000). One interesting properties of DEVS is its ability to integrate different formalisms. Thanks to its universality property, DEVS has a pivot place for the integration of formalisms (Vangheluwe 2000).

As summarized by (Quesnel et al. 2005), the integration of a formalism in DEVS can be performed either by a mapping or a wrapping strategy. While

---

[1] http://www.madkit.net/madkit/.

the former consists in establishing the equivalence between the formalisms, the latter implies bridging the gap between the abstract simulators.

The advantage of the wrapping strategy is to enable the reuse of preexisting models already implemented in some simulation software. This is the choice we make in this article.

Description of Models. DEVS distinguishes atomic from coupled models. A DEVS atomic model describes the behavior of the system and corresponds to this structure: $M = (X, Y, S, \delta_{ext}, \delta_{int}, \lambda, ta)$ where:

$X = \{(p, v)|p \in InPorts, v \in X_p\}$ is the set of input ports and values. These ports can receive external input events,

$Y = \{(p, v)|p \in OutPorts, v \in Y_p\}$ is the set of output ports and values. These ports can send external output events,

S is the set of the model states,

$\delta_{ext} : Q \times X \to S$ is the external transition function (describing how the model reacts to input events) where

$Q = \{(s, e)|s \in S, 0 \le e \le ta(s)\}$ is the total state of the model,

e is the elapsed time since the last transition,

$\delta_{int} : S \to S$ is the internal transition function describing the internal dynamic of the model -i.e. the function processes an internal event which changes the model state,

$\lambda : S \to Y$ is the output function describing the output events of the model according to its current state,

$ta : S \to \mathbb{R}^+_{0,\infty}$ is the time advance function describing the time during which the model will stay in the same current state (in the absence of input event). The function is used to get the date of the next internal event.

A coupled model describes the structure of the system, that is how atomic models are connected together to describe a system. As we do not refer directly to this concept for our proposal we shall not detail it here.

Wrapping and Simulation. DEVS formalism proposes different abstract simulation algorithms. It imposes five functions (detailed below) in order to perform a simulation with an atomic model. Defining a wrapper for a multi-agent system corresponds to define an interface with the simulator that implements these five functions. Once implemented, the simulator can be used as an atomic model and be rigorously integrated in a DEVS co-simulation.

3.2   NetLogo

NetLogo (Wilensky 1999) is an environment for modeling and simulating multi-agent systems. NetLogo can be controlled through an API that eases its integration in a wider project. A NetLogo model is composed of a graphical interface which makes possible for a user to interact with the simulation and view its evolution; a script (written in the NetLogo language) that describes the behavior of the agents (called *turtles*), the dynamics of the environment and, more generally, which actions to perform during simulation. NetLogo language permits the definition of methods; the *command* ones that act on the world and the *report* ones that collect data; and a model documentation that explains the model, its functioning and how to experience it.

Conventionally, the simulation parameters are initialized by the *setup* method and the simulation is ran with successive calls to the *go* command that makes the simulation progress step by step. The graphical interface proposes buttons associated with these commands, and sliders to select parameters values.

3.3   MECSYCO

MECSYCO (Camus et al. 2015) is a DEVS wrapping platform[2] that takes advantage of the DEVS universality for enabling multi-paradigm co-simulation of complex systems. It is currently used for the M&S of smart electrical grids in the context of a partnership between LORIA/Inria[3] and EDF R&D (leading French electric utility company) (Vaubourg et al. 2015).

MECSYCO is based on the AA4MM (Agents & Artifacts for Multi-Modeling) paradigm (Siebert et al. 2010) (from an original idea of Bonneaud (Bonneaud 2008)) that sees an heterogeneous co-simulation as a multi-agent system. Within this scope, each couple model/simulator corresponds to an agent, and the data exchanges between the simulators correspond to the interactions between the agents[4]. Originality with regard to other multi-agent multi-model approaches is to consider the interactions in an indirect way thanks to the concept of passive computational entities called artifacts (Ricci et al. 2007). By following this multi-agent paradigm from the concepts to their implementation, MECSYCO ensures a modular, extensible (i.e. features such as an observation system can be easily added), decentralized and distributable parallel co-simulation. MECSYCO implements the AA4MM concepts according to DEVS simulation protocol for coordinating the executions of the simulators and managing interactions between models.

So far, we successfully define DEVS wrappers for discrete and continuous modeling tools like the telecommunication network simulators NS-3 and OMNeT++ (Vaubourg et al. 2016), the FMI standard (Blochwitz et al. 2012), or application-specific wrapper for the NetLogo simulator (Camus et al. 2015).

4   Proposal

Til now, the integration of NetLogo in MECSYCO obliges to specify a new wrapper each time a new NetLogo model is used. This drawback comes from the absence

---

[2] MECSYCO is available on www.mecsyco.com under AGPL license.

[3] French IT research institute.

[4] Please note that multi-agent systems appear at two levels in this article: as a middleware architecture for co-simulation, and as simulation models to be integrated in a co-simulation.

of declarative representation of DEVS concepts; i.e., the declaration of inputs, outputs and parameters (model specific elements) were made directly in the code of the wrapper, making it model specific.

Specifying a DEVS wrapper for MECSYCO implies to create an interface between the simulator and the five functions of the DEVS simulation protocol:

- `init` sets the parameters and the initial state of the model,
- `processExternalEvent` makes the simulator process its external input event(s) coming from other simulators, it is dependent of the input ports of the model and the kinds of information associated with,
- `processInternalEvent` makes the simulator process its internal event(s) at a given time (makes the simulator progress according time),
- `getOutputEvent` returns external output event(s) to be sent to other simulators, it is dependent of the output ports of the model
- `getNextInternalEventTime` returns the time of the earliest scheduled internal event. The simulator scheduling policy must have temporal meaning in order to determine that value.

These five methods handle the time management, the synchronization and the date exchanges between a simulator and the remaining of the co-simulation. To design a generic wrapper, these functions must be independent of the simulated models. In particular, this implies for each model m to specify the sets of input and output ports (X and Y respectively). These information are rarely present in multi-agent system (mostly because there are not conceived to be connected to other models and not thought as a port-based architecture). We propose to define explicitly these sets and the corresponding events in a documentation associated with the model (in the same sense as the XML description of the FMI standard). Similarly, we have to express what has to be done when input events are received, how to get the data corresponding to output events and how to set initial parameters.

As the multi-agent simulators adopt various strategies of implementation and metamodel, we don't target a unified way to design wrapper, but rather try to propose a generic wrapper for NetLogo for which we take advantage of the possibility to send commands to the simulator thanks to an interpreter provided by the API.

It must be underlined that the *processInternalEvent* function makes evolve the simulation state and cannot be broken into different subfunctions. As a consequence, we have no mean to make agents from different simulator interact together in the same simulation step (or we stop respecting DEVS simulation protocol).

5   The DEVS Wrapper for NetLogo

This part details the wrapping of the NetLogo tool through the definition of the wrapper documentation. Figure 2 summarizes the principles behind it.

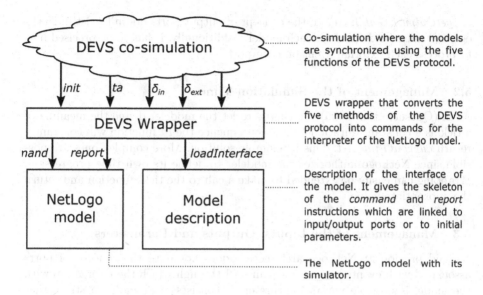

Fig. 2. Principle of the NetLogo wrapper.

5.1 Documentation Information

Until now, the NetLogo wrappers of MECSYCO embedded in their Java code the information related to the input and output ports, as well as the statements to process when executing each of the five DEVS methods. We propose to provide them separately in the wrapper documentation. That means providing the name of input and output ports, and what to process for each method of the DEVS protocol.

init(): We suppose the *setup* method of NetLogo can be used as the *init* method[5]. We add the concept of parameters in the documentation in order to provide values to set instead of the default ones used by setup (generally defined by sliders in the interface).

getNextInternalEventTime(): We suppose a constant time step simulation strategy in which each tick has no special temporal meaning. It is the responsibility of the modeler to propose a meaning of a tick in term of co-simulation time (e.g. one tick represent 0.1 unit of time simulation).

processInternalEvent(): We suppose[6] the *go* method corresponds to the statements to process at each tick and can correspond to the processInternalEvent one.

processExternalEvent(): The concept of input ports doesn't exist in NetLogo and must be defined for each model. Additionally, it has to be precised how to process each incoming event on each port.

---

[5] In other cases, either the documentation provides the command to call, either it provides the code to execute.

[6] In other cases, it has to be specified the same as for setup.

getOutputEvent(): Again, the concept of output ports doesn't exist in NetLogo and must be defined for each model. Additionally, it has to be precised how to process each external event on each port.

5.2   Management of the Simulation Time

As in (Quesnel et al. 2005), we choose to let the modeler define the meaning of a tick as a constant duration t (as a consequence the ta function will constantly return $currentTime + t$. This is a simple solution. More complex ones are possible since NetLogo authorizes the modeler to define its own time progression. Wrapping can easily be extended to make a call to the ticks function and return the appropriate value.

5.3   Management of the Inputs, Outputs and Parameters

As said previously, NetLogo architecture does not have the concept of ports associated with events but proposes an API through which the interaction with the model is possible via an interpreter. It consists in providing a string that corresponds to a NetLogo *command* to execute in order to modify the model or to a NetLogo *report* to fetch data from the model.

We propose to define in the wrapper documentation the port names of the inputs and outputs in association with the NetLogo methods to execute.

In the case of input events, we distinguish three cases:

(1) the port accepts events which do not depend of data from other simulators: the model has to run some commands (with no parameters) defined by the modeler;
(2) the port accepts events which contains only single data from other simulators: this data should be integrated in the simulation through a NetLogo command that modifies environment variables or turtles attributes;
(3) the port accepts events which contains a list of data from other simulators: the command has to be adapted to process these data.

In case of output events, two cases can be envisaged:

(1) the event corresponds to one or several data (the value of one attribute, . . .). In this case, one or several reports will be used to access these values. This kind of event has no impact on the NetLogo model
(2) In the second case, the event has an impact on the model (for example, turtles are exiting the model). One or more commands should be used to define this impact (e.g., suppress the turtles from the model).

The δ_{ext} of the DEVS interface processes input events with NetLogo *command*, whilst the λ one makes use of *report* to collect data and to convert them into events (some commands can be used to maintain a coherent state of the model, e.g., suppress turtles).

The parameters specified in the documentation will be set by a single *command* to modify a value before the call to *setup*.

5.4 The Wrapper

The basic principle of definition of the wrapper is to associate each function of the DEVS protocol to the corresponding NetLogo code. This is done by a java code using the NetLogo API facilities.

As the code to be executed is specified in the wrapper documentation, the wrapper becomes generic and can be used for any NetLogo models.

To summarize, as NetLogo proposes two functions associated to initialization (*init*) and to the simulation of one step (*go*), we reuse them. When one step of simulation is executed, the time progress of a constant value. As the simulation of one step is atomic (it can not be broken and we don't have something equivalent to the elapsed time function), processing of incoming events is undertaken at the next time step of the simulator by modifying the model state, the next invocation of "go" will perform the reaction of the model.

6 Proofs of Concepts

6.1 Experiment Goal

The goal of the following experiments is to illustrate what can be done with such an approach, notability by showing how a NetLogo component can be used in a co-simulation with MECSYCO.

```
model WolfSheepPredationExample version "1.0"
path "My Models/NetLogo/Wolf Sheep Predation.nlogo"
interface
    parameters // model parameters
        grass : true command "set grass? %s" // always true
        grass_regrowth_time : 10 command "set grass-regrowth-time %s" //small value in order to see effect of e
        // the following just put the same values as the GUI. Only for illlustration purposes.
        initial_number_sheep : 100 command "set initial-number-sheep %s"
        initial_number_wolves : 50 command "set initial-number-wolves %s"

    inputs
        //Inputs with the commands to process accordingly
        grass_regrowth : Integer initOption parameter command "set grass-regrowth-time %s"
        wolf_hunt : Integer initOption no command "ask n-of %s wolves [die]"
        sheep_coming : Integer initOption no command "create-sheep %s [set color white set size 1.5  set label-
    outputs
        //outputs (NB we use double instead of int because of some trouble with netlogo representation ... :-(
        nb_sheep : Double initOption no report Double "count turtles with [breed = sheep]"
        nb_wolves : Double initOption no report Double "count turtles with [breed = wolves]"
        nb_grass : Double initOption no report Double "grass"

information
    keywords
        "Predation"
        "NetLogo"
    description
        "This model represents wolf-sheep predation system example of NetLogo, it is an example of the integrat
simulator
    simulation variables
        //simulation variable
        stopTime: 1000. variability parameter // Time of the end of simulation
        discretization: 1. variability parameter //correspondence between Netlogo tick and the simulation time
```

Fig. 3. DSL definition for example 1.

Two experiments are detailed. The first shows how we can modify the state of the simulation by modifying variables that impact the agents behavior (as the GUI could have done). The second illustrates the spatial coupling between several NetLogo models by a transfer of agents between them.

Before describing these proofs of concepts we make two remarks. First, we do not recall what a MECSYCO co-simulation is but just provide an intuitive definition through the example. We orient the reader who wishes more details to the MECSYCO website where several tutorials explain the main concepts used and illustrate co-simulation. Second, we use a DSL (see Fig. 3) to describe the wrapper documentation. It is out of the article scope to detail the possibility of the DSL. We just provide the key elements necessary to the understanding.

6.2 Variation on Prey-Predator Model

The NetLogo Wolf-Sheep-Predation model[7] describes how the populations of wolves and sheep interact and evolve according to time as in a prey-predator ecosystem. Several parameters can be changed to observe their impact and the populations dynamics. We do not modify the original model but extend it in order to illustrate the possibility to modify model parameters, to define input events that modify at runtime some features of the model. Namely we want to:

- set initial values of some parameters,
- provide some input events that modify environment features,
- collect periodically information about the population to draw graphics (externally to NetLogo).

These elements are detailed below. They are summarized in Table 1 and followed by their definition in the NetLogo DSL we defined in MECSYCO. Note that parameters of NetLogo commands are denoted by %s.

We use the following parameters: `grass`, the grass dynamics is active (contrarily to the default value of the GUI); `grass_regrowth_time`, the time needed for grass to regrow in *tick*); `initial_number_sheep`, the initial number of sheep; and, `initial_number_wolves`, the initial number of wolves.

We create the following input ports (each event contains the value to be applied for the modification): `grass_regrowth` implies a modification of the time of grass to regrow (We have defined a port name that is different of the name of the environment variable); `sheep_coming`, results in an increase of the sheep number; and `wolf_hunt` that results in a decrease of the wolves number. Each port corresponds to one event coming from separate simple models (each sends a single event at a specified time).

We define the following output ports that are connected to a graphic drawer in order to display graphics: `nb_sheep`, the current number of sheep; `nb_wolves`, the current number of wolves; and `nb_grass`, the grass quantity.

Figure 4 shows the results obtained with that configuration. We can observe the impact of the different events (arrivals of 100 sheep at t=100; death of 25 wolves at t=175, increase of the time needed for grass to regrow at t =400).

---

[7] Provided in the models library.

Table 1. Summary of wrapper documentation.

PARAMETERS		
Name	**Value**	**Command**
grass	true	"set grass? %s"
grass_regrowth_time	10	"set grass-regrowth-time %s"
initial_number_sheep	100	"set initial-number-sheep %s"
initial_number_wolves	50	"set initial-number-wolves %s"
INPUT PORTS		
Name	**Command**	
grass_regrowth	"set grass-regrowth-time %s"	
sheep_coming	"create-sheep %s [set color white set size 1.5 set label-color blue - 2 set energy random (2 * sheep-gain-from-food) setxy min-pxcor max-pycor]"	
wolf_hunt	"ask n-of %s wolves [die]"	
OUTPUT PORTS		
Name	**Report statement**	
nb_sheep	"count turtles with [breed = sheep]"	
nb_wolves	"count turtles with [breed = wolves]"	
nb_grass	"grass"	

This proof of concept shows that we are able to provide initial values (e.g. the grass is active), to modify some characteristics of the model (remove wolves, add sheep or modify environment features) by input events (coming from other models) and to collect information from the simulation (here the numbers of wolves and sheep, and the grass quantity) through output events that will be used in other model (here a graphical drawer).

6.3 Spatial Coupling

In this experiment, we show the possibility to transfer turtles from one NetLogo model to another. We connect three models together as follows: a prey-predator model "sends" sheep to a pedestrian model (a model in which turtles travel from left to right as pedestrians in a corridor do) which, when turtles arrive at the right extremity, sends them to another prey-predator model.

The first model is the same as the previous experiment, we add a new output port **sheep_escaping** that is associated to the sheep present at the right side of the model. Data are collected as a list of sheep features (ordinate and energy).

The second model is initially empty and sheep, coming from the **sheep_escaping** port, arrive through the input port (called **left_in**). Sheep move from left to right. An output port (**right_out**) is associated to the sheep present at the right side.

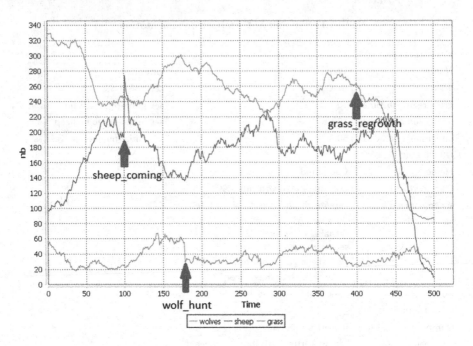

Fig. 4. Impact of different events on the prey-predator model.

The third model is again a prey-predator model on which we add an input port `sheep_loop_arrival` that accepts a list of sheep to be created on the left side of the environment with attributes whose values are specified in the event coming from he `sheep_escaping` port). This model is initialized with empty populations of wolves and sheep. Figure 5 illustrates the connections and shows a snapshot of the three NetLogo windows.

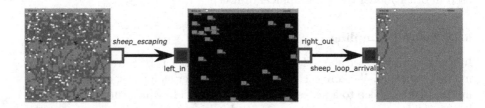

Fig. 5. Connections between model for spatial coupling.

These connections are possible because the types of events are compatible between the ports we use here and the pedestrian model for coherence purpose does define an "energy" attribute.

One interesting thing to notice is that the pedestrian model definition we used here enables the connection of several instances, one following the other, by the reuse of the same wrapper documentation. A model becomes a modular component for the co-simulation platform.

7   Discussion

The possibility of integrating a NetLogo model into a co-simulation as a component that can be added/removed or switched enables to define models of systems as the coupling of different sub-models.

One question not addressed in our approach is in what extend does an existing NetLogo model be adapted to be integrated in DEVS co-simulation. Currently, we do not propose any generic answer because of the variety of models available in NetLogo. However some directions can be proposed. Concerning the modification of the models, NetLogo GUI authorizes the user to modify parameters, to execute some actions at runtime. This is compatible with our approach: an input event can do the same. As we restricted our proposal to spatial coupling, we authorize agents to enter or exit the model. The exit of agents can be handled by providing some properties these agents have to respect and i) getting their features to be "exported" as a list and ii) removing them from the model. Agents entering the models can be represented by an event having a list of properties from which we create turtles.

We simplified the NetLogo integration by considering the use of *setup* and *go* commands instead of user defined ones. These choices can be revoked without putting into question the principles used.

As a system can be composed of many subsystems, the performance and the scalability of simulations can be put into question. Even if we did not focus on efficiency in the design of MECSYCO, a first answer is its architecture that can distribute the simulators execution among several machines. This enables to scale-up in terms of simulators number whilst keeping execution time.

This article focuses on the DEVS wrapping of NetLogo. We claim a declarative approach to bridge the gap between the DEVS simulation protocol and the model/simulator primitives. Readers may wonder on the generalization of this to other multi-agent system. From our experience, having a systematic approach is difficult because of the diversity of multi-agent platform architectures and multi-agent models structures, there is still no multi-agent standard to rely on.

8   Conclusion and Perspectives

This article presented a preliminary work on the integration of a multi-agent simulator in a co-simulation. Our proposal (implemented on the NetLogo platform) is grounded on a wrapper documentation which precises i) the initial parameters, the input and output ports; and ii) the NetLogo codes that correspond to the implementation of the DEVS protocol functions in the model. This documentation can be written within a dedicated DSL and is used inside the generic NetLogo wrapper (a Java code in our case) of the MECSYCO platform.

We provide two proofs of concepts that showed the possibility to integrate NetLogo models in MECSYCO, and to make them interact together or with other already integrated simulators without any additional coding (except the one provided in the documentation).

This integration opens the possibility to reuse the wide variety of existing NetLogo models in a co-simulation (with or without other multi-agent simulators).

However, our proposal imposes that the model has been adapted in order to be used inside a co-simulation. A second limitation coming from the wrapping strategy imposes that the information exchanges make the time to progress; this forbids interactions between agents situated in different simulators.

As perspectives, we want to confront our proposal with more NetLogo models in order to gain a better understanding of how a NetLogo model has to be modified to be integrated and to validate conceptually the approach before confronting the principles of our proposal to other multi-agent simulators (with which we will be faced to the same conceptual issues and to new software integration problems).

References

Behrens, T.M., Hindriks, K.V., Dix, J.: Towards an environment interface standard for agent platforms. Ann. Math. Artif. Intell. **61**(4), 261–295 (2011)

Blochwitz, T., Otter, M., Åkesson, J., et al. (2012). Functional mockup interface 2.0: the standard for tool independent exchange of simulation models. In Proceedings of the 9th International Modelica Conference, pp. 173–184 (2012)

Bonneaud, S.: Des agents-modèles pour la modélisation et la simulation de systèmes complexes - Application à l'écosystémique des pêches. PhD thesis (2008)

Camus, B.: Environnement Multi-agent pour la Multi-modélisation et Simulation des Systèmes Complexes. PhD thesis, Université de Lorraine (2015)

Camus, B., Bourjot, C., Chevrier, V.: Combining DEVS with multi-agent concepts to design and simulate multi-models of complex systems (WIP). In: Proceedings of TMS/DEVS 15, pp. 85–90. SCS (2015)

Galán, J.M., Izquierdo, L.R., Izquierdo, S.S., Santos, J.I., del Olmo, R., López-Paredes, A., Edmonds, B.: Errors and artefacts in agent-based modelling. J. Artif. Soc. Soc. Simul. **12**(1), 1 (2009)

Gangat, Y., Payet, D., Courdier, R.: Methodology for a new agent architecture based on the MVC pattern. In: Ramsay, A., Agre, G. (eds.) AIMSA 2012. LNCS (LNAI), vol. 7557, pp. 230–239. Springer, Heidelberg (2012). https://doi.org/10.1007/978-3-642-33185-5_26

Gomes, C., Thule, C., Broman, D., Gorm Larsen, P., Vangheluwe, H.: Cosimulation: State of the art. In: International Mediterranean Modeling Multiconference (2017)

Maudet, A., Touya, G., Duchêne, C., Picault, S.: Improving multi-level interactions modelling in a multi-agent generalisation model: first thoughts. In: Proceedings of 16th ICA Workshop on Generalisation and Multiple Representation, Dresden, Germany (2013)

Michel, F., Ferber, J., Drogoul, A.: Multi-agent systems and simulation: a survey from the agents community's perspective. In: Uhrmacher, A., Weyns, D. (eds.) Multi-Agent Systems: Simulation and Applications, Computational Analysis, Synthesis, and Design of Dynamic Systems, pp. 3–52. CRC Press - Taylor and Francis, Boca Raton (2009)

Morvan, G., Veremme, A., Dupont, D.: IRM4MLS: The Influence Reaction Model for Multi-level Simulation. ArXiv e-prints (2013)

North, M.J., et al.: Complex adaptive systems modeling with repast simphony. Complex Adapt. Syst. Model. 1(1), 3 (2013)

Quesnel, G., Duboz, R., Ramat, E.: Wrapping into DEVS simulator: a study case. In: International Mediterranean Modeling Multiconference, pp. 374–382 (2005)

Quesnel, G., Duboz, R., Ramat, E.: The virtual laboratory environment - an operational framework for multi-modelling, simulation and analysis of complex systems. Simul. Model. Pract. Theory 17, 641–653 (2009)

Ramat, E.: Introduction to discrete event modelling and simulation. In: Phan, D., Amblard, F. (eds.) Agent-based Modelling and Simulation in the Social and Human Sciences, Lavoisier. The Bardwell Press, Oxford (2007)

Ricci, A., Viroli, M., Omicini, A.: Give agents their artifacts: the A&A approach for engineering working environments in MAS. In: AAMAS 2007. ACM (2007)

Seck, M.D., Honig, H.J.: Multi-perspective modelling of complex phenomena. Comput. Math. Organ. Theory 18(1), 128–144 (2012)

Siebert, J., Ciarletta, L., Chevrier, V.: Agents and artefacts for multiple models co-evolution: building complex system simulation as a set of interacting models. In Proceedings of AAMAS 2010. AAMAS/ACM (2010)

Vangheluwe, H.L.: DEVS as a common denominator for multi-formalism hybrid systems modelling. In: IEEE International Symposium on Computer-Aided Control System Design, CACSD 2000, pp. 129–134. IEEE (2000)

Vaubourg, J., Chevrier, V., Ciarletta, L., Camus, B.: Co-simulation of IP network models in the cyber-physical systems context, using a DEVS-based platform. In: SCS/ACM, editor, Communications and Networking Simulation Symposium (CNS 2016) (2016)

Vaubourg, J., et al.: Multi-agent multi-model simulation of smart grids in the MS4SG Project. In: Demazeau, Y., Decker, K.S., Bajo Pérez, J., de la Prieta, F. (eds.) PAAMS 2015. LNCS (LNAI), vol. 9086, pp. 240–251. Springer, Cham (2015). https://doi.org/10.1007/978-3-319-18944-4_20

Wilensky, U.: Netlogo (and netlogo user manual). Center for connected learning and computer-based modeling, Northwestern University (1999). http://ccl.northwestern.edu/netlogo

Zeigler, B.P., Praehofer, H., Kim, T.G.: Theory of modeling and simulation. integration Discrete Event and Continuous Complex Dynamic Systems. Academic Press, Cambridge (2000)

Multi-agent Simulation of a Real Evacuation Scenario: Kiss Nightclub and the Panic Factor

Vinicius Silva[✉], Marcos Scholl, Bruna Correa, Diana Adamatti, and Miguel Zinelli Jr.

Program of Post Gradution in Computational Modelling,
Universidade Federal do Rio Grande (FURG), Rio Grande, RS, Brazil
{vinicius.montenegro,marcos.vinicius.scholl}@furg.br,
bruna_a_correa@gmail.com, dianaada@gmail.com, mzinelli95@gmail.com
http://www.furg.br

Abstract. This paper is based on the evacuation scenario of Kiss Nightclub Tragedy in 2012. Marked by imprudence of the responsible people to the national security standards, the event has resulted in many victims. The simulations were modeled with NetLogo using Multi-Agents approach based on real data of the Nightclub and an 'ideal' scenario using security standard NBR 9.077 of ABNT (Brazilian National Regulamentation). The environment was modeled using Kiss blueprint. Panic was modeled using psychology basement of the literature. Results show the importance of follow the security standards imposed by ABNT to give secure evacuations of Brazilian buildings. The conclusion shows how important can be the application of this standard in the control of panic disseminate on emergency scenarios in order to provide effective evacuations.

Keywords: Evacuation model · Kiss nightclub · Security standards
NBR · Tragedy

1 Introduction

The managers of nightclubs are respecting the technical security standards? Is this effectiveness to provide secure evacuations? Some supervisors negligence for the security project of a social gathering building can cause several consequences in evacuation scenarios? These questions are asked in many events where are scenarios of big tragedies, like in 2013 on the Brazilian Kiss Nightclub in Santa Maria, Rio Grande do Sul.

The Kiss fire occurred in January 27th of 2013 and some of the factors that caused the large rate of victims (242) and injured (680) were the poor signaling to emergency exits combined with an overcrowded scenario with just one exit door in the night of this tragedy [2,13,18].

© Springer Nature Switzerland AG 2018
F. Belardinelli and E. Argente (Eds.): EUMAS 2017/AT 2017, LNAI 10767, pp. 268–280, 2018.
https://doi.org/10.1007/978-3-030-01713-2_19

This study is considered necessary to demonstrate through an agent-based simulation, the result of the application of Brazilian Association of Technical Standards (Associação Brasileira de Normas Técnicas - ABNT), specially the NBR 9.077 at nightclubs, defined in the resolution as 'places of social meetings', and also demonstrate its support minimizing the emotional factor 'panic'. The NBR 9.077 recommends the size and number of the emergency exit doors based on building dimensions and population [5].

The main objective of this research is to provide results that can be encouraging to demonstrate how the Brazilian security standards are good and effective give secure for emergency scenarios of evacuation of buildings. The results will serve to contribute as a possible reference to prevent future tragedies like the Kiss nightclub. Also, characteristics like exit signaling, number of exit doors and how people act on this kind of situation with and without these standards in the scenario, should provide parameters and conclusions that could help the responsible people to prevent tragedy events in another nightclubs.

To do, two environments were implemented, each with two different scenarios of a Multi-Agent simulation. Both being different in the characteristics: initial population, signallings and emergency exit doors (local and size).

The implementation the NBR 9.077 indicates the characteristics and dimensions of the emergency exits in buildings [5]. The panic emotion logic was developed based in the definition of Mawson and Anthony [14] and this study uses a Multi-agent modelling approach, that is a computational system where two or more agents interact/work each other to accomplish some tasks or objectives [23]. The choosen software was NetLogo 5.3.1., because of its capacity to simulate social behavior on the Multi-Agent context and its good representation of real world environments and objects.

This paper is structured as following: The Sect. 2 presents the background of this study. The Sect. 3 shows up the process of definition and description of the simulation scenarios. On the Sect. 4, there is an analysis of obtained results. Finally, the Sect. 5 presents the final considerations and contributions of this study and the future possibilities on this domain.

2   Background

To work with people safe and security evacuations, its important to know the local standards of emergency. Brazil have an important association (NBR) responsible to study and provide the rules of several things, between these are the standard of the ways to calculate the emergency exits and where should be placed the signaling boards referring to this exits, NBR 9.077.

2.1   NBR 9.077

The Brazilian security standard NBR 9.077 refers to the regulation of emergency exits in buildings, such as classification of buildings, components of emergency (stairs, ramps and loading and unloading terminal), calculation of maximum population, dimensioning of emergency exits, areas of refuge, signaling, and other specific conditions [5,20].

According to NBR 9.077, the number of emergency exits and their dimensions are calculated according to the maximum capacity of people in a building. The population of the building is given according to the Table 1 in Silva [20] and Table 5 from page 29 of [5]. As follow in the NBR 9.077 and those Tables, nightclubs are in the F-6 division and to define the maximum population, bathroom areas in occupations E or F division are excluded. The width of the outputs is given by the Equation $N = P/C(1)$, where N represents the number of units of passage, rounded to the first upper integer; P is the population; and C is the capacity of the gate unit [5].

The unit of passage (UP) is fixed at 0.55 m, considering the minimum width for the passage of a row of people. While the capacity of the gate unit of passage (C) is the number of people that pass by minute in that unit. The minimum width of doors in general occupation must correspond to at least 1.10 meters, corresponding to two units of passage, except for occupations of group H, division H-3 [5,20].

Provide security with the standards must be combined with the human psychological factors like emotions in critical situations. For this study were combined the application of the NBR with the panic factor. This emotion is directly related to the planning of emergency systems, once compliance with the ABNT security standard can help people to maintain their natural social behavior in the face of a critical situation, collaborating with the safeness of the evacuation.

2.2   Panic

The definition of "panic" by several authors is considered "a reaction involving fear and/or evasive actions that causes irrational and competitive behavior and in many situations involving aggressive physical interactions, breaking the natural order of the environment" [9–11,14,21].

It is noted that in the human behavior literature, "panic" is generally defined as irrational behavior, but research results consistently show that people do not always exhibit this behavior in fires [21]. However, altruistic behavior is seen as rule in severe fire situations. In fact, human behavior under stress is relatively controlled, rational and adaptive [17].

Quarantelli [16] explains that for the configuration of panic, three factors are necessary: people must have an imprisonment feeling, deep isolation and a sense of incapability. These emotions and feelings can be seen from witness of more than 80 survivors of the 'Kiss' case [7].

Panic in the Emergency Systems Project

If an emergency evacuation was designed only considering the trigger of an alarm, the escape speed of the individuals would depend of their physical abilities, their location in relation to the closest exit and the fire progression [22]. An event such as the fire at Kiss nightclub in 2013 was showed that this concept was incomplete.

In the old days engineers and people responsible for fire prevention and protection have defended the hypothesis that people would abandon the building immediately when the fire alarm triggers. This thought considered only technical aspects of security standards, without thinking about the human behavior [12].

Therefore, this work has implemented this theoretical foundation in its development, that simulate an emergency situation in the recreated scenario from the Kiss Nightclub tragedy, also in an ideal scenario following the rule NBR 9.077. Demonstrating the possible effectiveness and the importance of following the security standards in an emergency situation that envolves panic.

3 Methodology

This work has evolved based on the implementation defined by Silva [20], where a simplified version of the Kiss nightclub is simulated (see Fig. 1). In that work the main objective was to verify how the standard NBR 9.077 could be improved people evacuation time in an emergency situation.

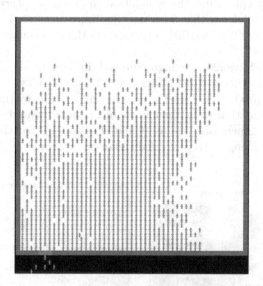

Fig. 1. Environment of Kiss nightclub evacuation in [20].

However, this present study proposes an evacuation scenario considering an additional emotional behavior in the people, that is considered an emotional factor in evacuation processes [14]. The Kiss parameters are the same as defined in Silva [20], that describes this one a smaller scale simulation due the proportion of computation simulation.

Also, this new simulation scenario considers a drawing of the nightclub's blueprint, once that the simulation begins to contemplate all the characteristics of the environment at the moment of the fire. These new parameters could be providing a more realistic simulation and more precise results.

According to [20], in the NBR 9.077, the maximum capacity of a building are provided by the division of all occupational area by the factor 0,5 m (measure that a person occupies in locals of social meetings of the division F-6), but in this new simulation, the non-occupiable areas (stages and bathrooms) weren't excluded.

Remembering, about the capacity, the nightclub had the maximum capacity of 691 people and the exit door width had an appropriate width to this capacity, but this specific door were the same entry door. However, at the moment of the incident the nightclub was overcrowded, according to reports there were about 1200 people there [2,13,18].

3.1 Environment

The environment of the simulations is based on agents, where they can perceive their environment and act on it. The implementation was created with the three main objects that constitute the simulation in NetLogo: *Turtles* agents that move in the world; *Patches* that form the two-dimensional environment, divided by a grid of patches; *Observer* that contemplates the environment formed by the turtles and patches [15].

As described in Silva [20], the nightclub had dimensions of 615 square meters, with a single access with a width of just over 2.5 m [2,13,18].

In order to reproduce a realistic scenario in relation to the tragedy, on a computational simulation scale, the environment was recreated (see Fig. 2). The implemented grid dimensions was recalculated assuming that the nightclub had an equal width and length, the obtained value was 24.8 m per wall. However, the

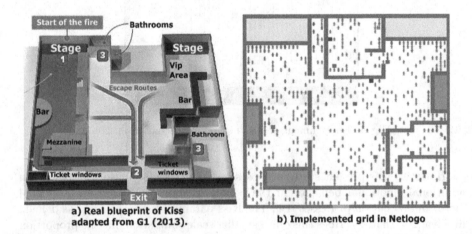

a) Real blueprint of Kiss adapted from G1 (2013).

b) Implemented grid in Netlogo

Fig. 2. Environment: In (a) the real blueprint of Kiss [8]. In (b) the implemented grid in NetLogo. (Color figure online)

software *NetLogo* has different measure values, so it was assumed that walls of the environment would occupy 24.85 patches, totalizing 615.05 patches squared. For the door, we have assumed 3 patches.

The reproduction of the nightclub's blueprint presents the fundamental characteristics of its real structure: two stages were represented by **light pink**; two bars were represented by **red**; two bathrooms represented by the places where they are "bad signalling": a **blue** colored patch (on top) and the other, **orange** colored patch (in the right bottom). At the time of the incident, the main access to the nightclub exit was blocked by security guards [7,13], considered in the simulation as a block continuous wall in the environment. The outer and inner walls consist in patches that are represented by gray and they are obstrutives, the people (turtles) inserted in the environment cannot cross them. This obstruction force people to move toward a free space "dancing" or seeking the exit in an evacuation scenario.

At the night of the incident, there were objects (obstacles as tables, chairs and environment divisors) present in the nightclub, causing small obstructions and difficulting the movement in the place. However, this object locations were not known and to represent this behavior closely of reality in the simulations, a number of obstacles was defined by the researchers (15), that were allocated in different random locations at the nightclub at each simulation starts.

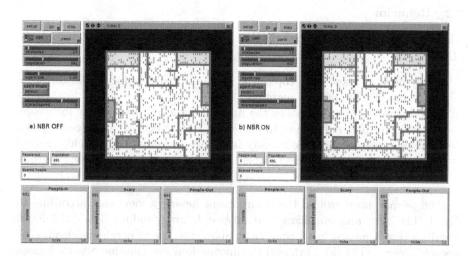

Fig. 3. Graphical Interface of Simulation Environment in NetLogo: (a) NBR OFF (b) NBR ON.

The simulation environment (Fig. 3) is configurable for six variables, the main three: *NBR*, that refers to the application of the safety rule; *obstacles*, referring to the number of obstructive random patches; *population*, that refers to the number of people present in the environment. And another three: *agent-size*; *agent-shape*, form of agents and; *scared-speed*, referring to the scared people velocity after the fire starts. These parameters were chosen because were considered relevant to customize the variations of the three simulations scenarios.

When the NBR is deactivated (**Fig. 3a**), the club presents an incorrect exit signaling and only one door for entry and exit. When the NBR is activated (**Fig. 3b**), the nightclub assume that it is in accordance with the current standards, so the environment is changed in order to accomplish the safety rules such as the following:

1. Two emergency exit doors placed in opposite localizations and with the recommended width in relation to the people capacity in the nightclub (as described on the NBR 9.077);
2. Lighting signaling placed correctly and indicative boards only to emergency exits (as described on the NBR 10.898).

The monitors People-out, Population, and Scared People present the updates of these variables in real time. People-In, Scary, and People-Out graphics plots present their values in function of time Fig. 3.

The nightclub's blueprint is not altered for all scenarios of simulation, allowing the analysis of the effects that the application of the rule would reflect in the scenario of the moment of the tragedy.

3.2   Behavior

The simulation describes a scenario that people present in the nightclub can be of two types:

- Happy-people: These are people who move normally (velocity and direction without panic) around the nightclub;
- Scared-people: People who saw the fire and enter in a panic state increasing your velocity and redirecting to the exits. Happy people also become panic when they see another one already in panic. According to Stroehle [21], in panic situations, people give up their own characteristics, inheriting a group behavior.

The people move around the environment having a view area according to Fig. 4. The view area considers that all people are standing. The NBR 9.050 describes that a person has a cone view, above the line of her/his horizon, s/he saw a 25-degree view (Fig. 4a), and the unconscious eye movement is 15 degrees (Fig. 4b).

The person's vision is presented in the context of the simulation as in the turtle vision. When the panic button is activated, the fire appears in red on the left top stage of the environment. A person that is currently looking to the stage, uses the 25 degree cone view to visualize the fire. At this point, this person changes from happy to panic and seeks luminous indications and/or exit doors, increasing her/his speed which is her/his movement in the environment. Based on the informations of the real tragedy, people did try to running out when the evacuation scenario began.

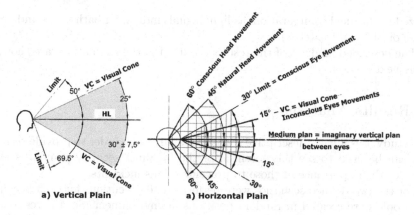

Fig. 4. (a) Vertical and (a) Horizontal Vision of people standing [4].

The people who had not seen the fire but see a person in panic, also change their state to panic. At this moment, this behavior shows that few people really seen the fire in fact, but many people see another one in panic. When in panic, turtles will movement to the nearest exit board signaling, calculated by the Euclidean distance of nearest exit board signal that would refers the exits of the environment and then to the exits.

3.3   Scenarios

The different parameters, such as population and the use of the NBR standard, make the analysis of the realistic scenario that caused the incident of the tragedy at Kiss nightclub possible. The scenario seen as "ideal" contemplates the safe rules, allowing the comparison of the results and validate the expected effectiveness of the standard application.

In the realistic scenario without the use of NBR 9.077, the population is 1200 people, configuring overcrowding, with only one exit door that is also the entry of the nightclub. Also it has luminous signals board that indicate people where are the bathrooms, a caracteristic which was consider one of the causes of greater number of victims, according to Luiz [13]. The variation of this scenario, uses the NBR partially, because it is still configured overcrowding.

In the "ideal" scenario with the NBR 9.077, the population is 691 people, as indicated by the calculation for the dimensions of the nightclub. In addition, the signal boards of the environment does not have signs to bathrooms, but indicative signs to the emergency exits strategic distributed in the environment, what facilitates the access to the exit doors, applied according to the suggestion in the standard NBR 10.898 [3], that describes that "persons in emergency situations tend to receive physical stimulus, or by means of communication". As suggested by the NBR 9.077, a second emergency exit door with a recommended width of 3 m (3 patches) is also defined. The variation of this scenario uses only the correct population of the nightclub, 691 people. Without the NBR indications utilized in the ideal configuration, as light signals indicating bathrooms and only one door of 3 m (3 patches).

The described analysis of the results obtained in the simulations are showed in the next section.

4   Results Analysis

This study uses a basic descriptive statistical analysis, in order to provide results that can be used to see the potential of the brazilian security standards and reinforce the importance of those to prevent serious incidents.

For the two defined scenarios were performed 10 executions for each because the people were created in random positions in environment. So, the results of those executions were tabulated and the arithmetic averages were calculated for each relevant variable for the analysis. Each execution of the "ideal scenario" presented difference between the number of people-in (trapped) and it was the reason that the researchers performed 10 executions.

The evacuation time average of the **realistic scenario**, population of 1200 people with NBR = ON and NBR = OFF, were respectively, **1215.3** and **1335.1** ticks. With the NBR = OFF, an average of **407,3** people died in the **bathrooms** (toilet room) after the evacuation ended, about **34%** of all population inside the nightclub. But when the NBR was activated, **no one** would have died, probably. These numbers are showed that with NBR, independing of the overcrowded situation, people should be evacuated with safety.

In the **ideal scenario** with the NBR configuration activated, it was obtained an evacuation in an average time of **784.3** ticks and just **16** people died, **2%** of the **691** current people. This result can be seen with surprise, but the explanation to deaths is: the place wasn't overcrowded, so a few people didn't saw the fire or someone in panic until the max time before the smoke spread throughout the environment. However, in the variation of this scenario, where the NBR was deactivated, the average evacuation time was **821.7** ticks, and **247.5** people died in the bathrooms, about **36%** of all people.

In the **ideal scenario** it is possible to note an important characteristc from behavioral vision, people die locked in. Even with the NBR activated and without overcrowding, the can be loss of lives because some people are far away from the fire and people that have seen the fire and panicked, can take time to perceive the situation, until the fire and the smoke are spreading throughout the environment, at the moment they panic, the reaction to evacuation can be belated.

Observing the linear tendency of the **people-outside** presented in the chart of Fig. 5, it can be noted that besides the difference of approximately of **100** ticks in time of evacuation between the two main scenarios in the chart, respectively: **realistic overcrowded and without the NBR** and ideal (crowded with NBR = ON), the difference in the percentage of victims (*people-inside*) is, considerably, relevant. While in the **realistic scenario** of the tragedy, about **34%** of the people were locked inside the nightclub, in the **scenario** told as **ideal**, only **2%** of the present people were victimized.

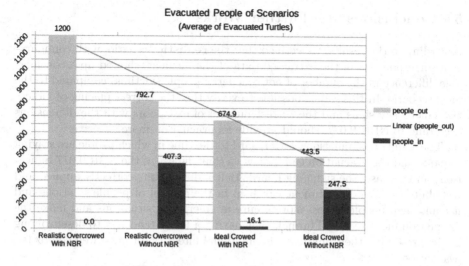

Fig. 5. Evacuated People of Scenarios

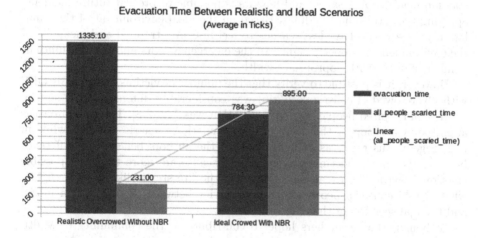

Fig. 6. Evacuation Time Between Realistic and Ideal Scenarios

An important aspect of the simulations is the time gap in which people panic, that is, change behavior. For that, the averages from the chart (Fig. 6) of the main scenarios: **realistic** (overcrowded and without the NBR) and **ideal** (crowded and with NBR), were also calculated.

When we observe the linear tendency of the chart of 'Time of Evacuation between the Realistic and the Ideal Scenarios' (Fig. 6), regarding **the time all people panic**, it is noted that in the **ideal** scenario, people take **74%** more time to begin panicking, compared with the **realistic** scenario.

5   Conclusions and Further Works

According to the results, we verified that the **realistic** scenario, with configuration correspondent of the extracted data of the incident, showed up a considerable difference in the number of not evacuated people (victims) compared to the ideal scenario. In this way is possible to verify that the correct placing of indicative emergency signs and the correct number of exit doors with the dimensions according to NBR 9.077, should provide an evacuation more effective.

The results of simulations with regard to the time in which people are staying in panic and the evacuation time, show us that the use of the NBR 9.077 indications, in this case, the signaling boards that indicate exits correctly applied and distributed in the environment can help in the control of people's actions and it could help people to feel more secure in emergency situations and make the evacuation more secure. Through that having a lesser tendency to desenvolving panic, preserving their physical and emotional integrity during a well-conducted evacuation.

Obviously this study is an simulation of the reality and their parameters, but this research is considered encouraging to show how important are the security standards on people's safety and how its is possible to prevent future incidents applying these rules on buildings. Based on the ideal environment of the simulation people would have less reasons to feel insecure, trapped and incapable if the environment is properly signed to the emergency exits and have a sufficient number of doors with appropriate width.

However, it is possible to verify that the number of victims in the NBR OFF with Overcrowed (Realistic scenario) was considerably different of the sum of victims and injured people of the tragedy that was 722 [7,8]. The rate of deaths after the evacuation of the overcrowded simulation scenario was 407 while in real tragedy this rate was 242. About this, the authors believe this difference between the rate of victims was provided because are more than one possible emotional factors acting at the moment of the fire starts (like flight or fight), what should causes a people different behavior between the simulation model and the real scenario of the tragedy.

Although, the researchers hope to contribute to the community of Multi-agent systems, regarding evacuation models. This through a study case using a real environment, applying the safety standards as NBR 9.077 of ABNT into the Brazilian nightclub.

In futher works, the authors aim to do the modelling of conflict behaviors, as momentary paralysis, 'fight or flight' and affiliation [12].

Dreaming higher, its possible to say that the researchers aim to develop an generic to the security standard NBR 9.077. An environment that would be receive a blueprint of an building and generate: their ideal population, an distribution of signal boards and the place of the exit doors and their widths.

References

1. Almeida, J.E., Kokkinogenis, Z., Rossetti, R.J.F.: NetLogo implementation of an evacuation scenario. In: 7th Iberian Conference on Information Systems and Technologies (CISTI), pp. 1–4. IEEE (2012)
2. Atiyeh, B.: Brazilian kiss nightclub disaster. Ann. Burns Fire Disasters **26**(1), 3 (2013)
3. Brazilian Association of Technical Standards: NBR 10.898. Rio de Janeiro, September 1999
4. Brazilian Association of Technical Standards: NBR 9050. Rio de Janeiro, September 2015
5. Brazilian Association of Technical Standards: NBR 9077. Rio de Janeiro, December 2001
6. Goldenson, R.M. (ed.): Longman Dictionary of Psychology and Psychiatry. Longman, New York (1984)
7. G1, RS. Como foi a tragédia em Santa Maria. Rio Grande do Sul (2017). http://g1.globo.com/rs/rio-grande-do-sul/tragedia-incendio-boate-santa-maria-entenda/platb/
8. G1, RS. Legista acredita que 90% dos mortos em incêndio tenham se asfixiado (2013). http://g1.globo.com/rs/rio-grande-do-sul/noticia/2013/01/legista-acredita-que-90-dos-mortos-em-incendio-tenham-se-asfixiado.html
9. Helbing, D.: Simulation of pedestrian crowds. In normal and evacuation situations. In: Schreckenberg, M., Sharma, S.D. (eds.) Pedestrian and Evacuation Dynamics, pp. 21–58. Springer, Berlin (2002)
10. Johnson, R.N.: Panic at the who concert stampede: an empirical assessment. Soc. Probl. **34**(4), 362–373 (1987)
11. Johnson, R.N.: Panic and the breakdown of social order: popular myth, social theory, empirical evidence. Sociol. Focus **20**(3), 171–183 (1987)
12. Ludovico, M.T.: Comportamento Humano e Planejamento de Emergências. 4th Edn of CCPS Latin American Process Safety Conference (2012)
13. Luiz, M.: Dois anos depois, veja 24 erros que contribuíram para trag édia na Kiss (2015). http://g1.globo.com/rs/rio-grande-do-sul/noticia/2015/01/dois-anos-depois-veja-24-erros-que-contribuiram-para-tragedia-na-kiss.html
14. Mawson, A.R.: Understanding mass panic and other collective responses to threat and disaster. Psychiatry Interpers. Biol. Process. **68**(2), 95–113 (2005)
15. NetLogo (1999). http://ccl.northwestern.edu/netlogo
16. Quarantelli, E.L.: The nature and conditions of panic. Am. J. Sociol. **60**(3), 267–275 (1954)
17. Quarantelli, E.L.: Panic Behavior: Some Empirical Observations. In: Conway, D.J. (ed.) Human Response to Tall Buildings, pp. 336–350. Dowden Hutchinson & Ross, 27 Stoudsburg (1977)
18. Souza D.V., Machado R.F., Montes R.G.E. e Souza I.C.: Incêndio da Boate Kiss: análise da conduta ética dos engenheiros civis. Revista Juris FIB. ISSN 2236–4498. vol. IV, Ano IV, Bauru - SP, Dezembro 2013
19. Seito, A.I., et al.: A Segurança Contra Incêndio No Brasil. São Paulo: Projeto Editora (2008)
20. Silva, V.M., Scholl, M.V., Correa, B.A., Adamatti, D.F.: Evacuação da Boate Kiss: Uma Simulação Multiagente do Cenário real em relacao ao ideal. In: 4a Conferêlncia Ibero Americana de Computação Aplicada, 2016, Lisboa. In: Proceedings of the IADIS Conferencias Ibero Americanas on WWW/Internet and Computação Aplicada 2016, pp. 334–338, Dezembro, 2016

21. Stroehle, J.: How do pedestrian crowds react when they are in an emergency situation: models and software (2008). http://guava.physics.uiuc.edu/nigel/courses/569/Essays_Fall2008/files/Stroehle.pdf
22. Winerman, L.: Criminal profiling: the reality behind the myth. American Psychological Association: Monitor on Psychology, vol. 35, no. 7, July/August 2004. http://www.apa.org/monitor/julaug04/criminal.aspx
23. Wooldridge, M., Jennings, N.R.: Intelligent agents: theory and practice. Knowledge Engineering Review (1994)

Lazy Fully Probabilistic Design: Application Potential

Tatiana V. Guy, Siavash Fakhimi Derakhshan$^{(\boxtimes)}$, and Jakub Štěch

Department of Adaptive Systems, Institute of Information Theory and Automation, The Czech Academy of Sciences, P.O. Box 18, 182 08 Prague 8, Czech Republic {guy,fakhimi,stech}@utia.cas.cz

Abstract. The article addresses a lazy learning approach to fully probabilistic decision making when a decision maker (human or artificial) uses incomplete knowledge of environment and faces high computational limitations. The resulting lazy Fully Probabilistic Design (FPD) selects a decision strategy that moves a probabilistic description of the closed decision loop to a pre-specified ideal description. The lazy FPD uses currently observed data to find past closed-loop similar to the actual ideal model. The optimal decision rule of the closest model is then used in the current step. The effectiveness and capability of the proposed approach are manifested through example.

Keywords: Lazy learning · Fully Probabilistic Design
Decision making · Linear quadratic gaussian control

1 Introduction

A closed decision-making (DM) loop consisting of *agent-environment* pair is described by the agent's actions and environment states (possibly partially observable). DM problem is to influence the environment behavior in a desired way by choosing and applying a tailored DM policy generating optional actions with respect to the environment. The DM formulation covers stochastic and adaptive control, estimation, filtering, prediction, classification, and others [1]. It has been shown that DM problem can be better treatable in a probabilistic way [2] such as Bayesian DM theory, [3], that provides well-justified solution of DM tasks. The applicability of Bayesian DM theory is limited by the curse of dimensionality, [4], therefore approximate non-linear estimation, [5], and approximate dynamic programming, [6], are mostly inevitable. Practically successful techniques rely on local approximations around the current realisation of the closed-loop behaviour.

This paper is a part of the project trying to lay a ground for *lazy* Fully Probabilistic Design. Lazy Learning (LL) is an approach that searches and uses relevant information from the past data. Inspired by human reasoning it decreases deliberation effort by employing early-developed solutions. A simple fact, that similar DM tasks tend to have similar solution, has caused the approach has

F. Belardinelli and E. Argente (Eds.): EUMAS 2017/AT 2017, LNAI 10767, pp. 281–291, 2018.
https://doi.org/10.1007/978-3-030-01713-2_20

evolved in many areas under different names. Lazy-learning philosophy [7] has been presented as case-based reasoning, memory-based learning, analogical modelling, memory-based prediction, just-in-time modelling, transfer learning, see for instance [8–10]. All of these experience-based methods are problem solving processes in which an actual problem, defined on the same domain as the past problems, is solved by searching for a similar situation and using its solution. These methods are used for transfer learning aiming at improving performance and learning on a new domain by learning from the past [11].

FPD, an extension of the Bayesian DM, solves a DM problem by considering probabilistic description of both environment behaviour and DM preferences [2]. The main aim is then to find an optimal policy minimising the divergence the probabilistic description of *actual* closed-loop behaviour from that of *ideal* closed-loop behaviour, which expresses DM preferences.

In this paper, a combination of LL and FPD is employed to utilize the competence of both techniques in opting tailored action at each time step when the knowledge of environment is incomplete. As a result the proposed solution not only provides the desired decrease of computation demands, but also its overall performance is comparable to the performance of the standard FPD. The proposed approach focuses on single-agent DM aiming at creating efficient and scalable solution that can easily be extended to multi-agent settings.

The layout of the paper is as follows. Section 2 introduces formal notations and necessary preliminaries together with a formal description of FPD. Section 3 formulates the lazy FPD problem and outlines its solution. Experimental section demonstrates the effectiveness of our approach on attitude control of the hovering helicopter. Finally, Sect. 5 summarises the main results and outlines the open problems remained.

2   Underlying Theory

This section introduces necessary conventions and notions.

2.1   Preliminaries

The sequence $(x_t, x_{t+1}, \ldots, x_{t+h})$ is shortened as $x(t, t + h)$. Discrete time instances are labelled by $\tau = 1, 2, \ldots, t$, $t \in \mathbb{N}$. Bold capital $\mathbf{X}$ represents a set of x values. An abbreviation *pdf* denotes probability density function. The Kullback-Leibler divergence (KLD), [12], measuring the proximity of two pdfs f and g, acting on a set $\mathbf{X}$, reads

$$\mathcal{D}(f\|g) = \int_{\mathbf{X}} f(x)\ln\frac{f(x)}{g(x)}\mathrm{d}x, \tag{1}$$

with $\mathcal{D}(f\|g) \geq 0$, $\mathcal{D}(f\|g) = 0$ iff $f = g$ almost everywhere on $\mathbf{X}$.

Let us consider an interacting agent-environment pair, see Fig. 1. The agent observes a new environment state $s_t \in \mathbf{S}$ at time t and chooses action $a_t \in \mathbf{A}$ to learn or influence the environment in accordance with the agent's DM preferences. Having action selected, the environment moves to the next state and the agent receives one-step reward. The aim of the agent is to find optimal policy maximizing the future reward.

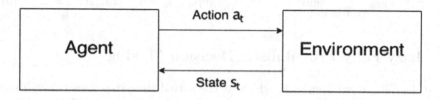

Fig. 1. The closed decision loop.

The closed-loop model of the *environment-agent* pair, is fully described by joint pdf $p(s_{t+h}, a_{t+h-1}, s_{t+h-1}, \ldots, s_{t+1}, a_t), s_\tau \in \mathbf{S}, a_\tau \in \mathbf{A}, t \leq \tau \leq t+h, t, \tau, h \in \mathbb{N}$, that can be factorised using the chain rule for pdfs, [13], as follows:

$$p_{(t,h)} = \prod_{\tau=t+1}^{t+h} p(s_\tau | s(t, \tau-1), a(t, \tau-1)) p(a_{\tau-1} | s(t, \tau-1), a(t, \tau-2)) p(s_t). \quad (2)$$

The first factor, $p(s_\tau | s(t, \tau-1), a(t, \tau-1))$, is environment model, the second factor, $p(a_\tau | s(t, \tau), a(t, \tau-1))$, is a randomised DM rule and $p(s_t)$ is a prior pdf of state. A sequence of DM rules, $\{p(a_\tau | s(t, \tau), a(t, \tau-1))\}_\tau$, up to time $t+h$, forms *DM policy* $\pi_\tau : (\mathbf{S}^\tau \times \mathbf{A}^{\tau-1}) \mapsto \mathbf{A}^\tau$.

2.2   Fully Probabilistic Design

Any systematic DM design selects a DM policy that makes the resulting closed-loop model (2) close to the desired one. FPD [2] considers the desired probabilistic closed-loop model as *ideal model* that expresses the agent's preferences. An advantage of FPD is an ability to explicitly describe multiple aims and constraints. The resulting optimal DM policy is randomised, unlike in the standard Bayesian DM. Let us consider the following simplified Markov version of (2):

$$p_{(t,h)} = \prod_{\tau=t+1}^{t+h} p(s_\tau | a_{\tau-1}, s_{\tau-1}) p(a_{\tau-1} | s_{\tau-1}) p(s_t). \quad (3)$$

In (3), t is a starting step and $h \in \mathbb{N}$ is a finite horizon. The corresponding ideal model reflecting agent's DM preferences reads:

$$^I p_{(t,h)} = \prod_{\tau=t+1}^{t+h} {}^I p(s_\tau | a_{\tau-1}, s_{\tau-1}) {}^I p(a_{\tau-1} | s_{\tau-1}) p(s_t). \quad (4)$$

FPD, provides a DM policy yielding minimum of the KLD, (1), from the *current* closed-loop description, (3), to the *ideal* one, (4). Thus optimal DM policy π^{opt} coming from the minimisation is

$$\pi^{opt} = \arg \min_{\{p(a_\tau|s(\tau))\}_{t \le \tau \le t+h-1}} \mathcal{D}(p_{(t,h)}||^I p_{(t,h)}), \quad \sum_{a_\tau \in \mathbf{A}} p(a_\tau|s(\tau)) = 1. \quad (5)$$

3   Lazy Fully Probabilistic Decision Making

Lazy learning is an approach, which at the actual time step goes through the stored data and searches the relevant data to deal with a current DM problem, see Fig. 2. In this figure, the red points indicate the similar situations in the past and different closed-loop sequences $(s_{\tau+1}, a_\tau, s_\tau)$. We are intending to find an optimal DM policy that respects our current ideal, based on the past optimal actions.

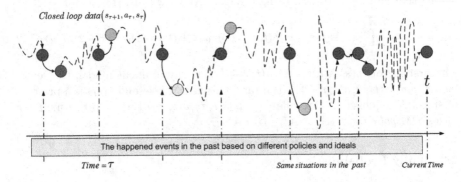

Fig. 2. Lazy-learning fully probabilistic decision making strategy.

This section describes the general idea of the proposed solution. Let us consider a DM task $Q_{(t,h)} = (p_{(t,h)}, {}^I p_{(t,h)})$ where $p_{(t,h)}$ and ${}^I p_{(t,h)}$ is given by (3) and (4), respectively. The collected historic data contain environment states $s_\tau \in \mathbf{S}$ and actions $a_\tau \in \mathbf{A}$, $\tau < t$, observed up to actual time t. The data describe past (solved) DM tasks $Q_{(\tau,h)}$, $\tau = 1, \ldots, t - h$. The following assumption is considered.

Assumption 1. *Actions $a_\tau, \tau < t$ applied in the past DM tasks sufficiently well approximate the optimal solution with respect to the past ideal models ${}^I p_{(\tau,h)}$.*

This assumption justifies considering the past actions and employing them to find current optimal action even without explicit knowledge of past ideal closed-loop models ${}^I p_{(\tau,h)}$, $\tau \le t - h$. Next, we need to find a_t^{opt} which makes closed-loop $p_{(t,h)}$ close to its ideal counterpart ${}^I p_{(t,h)}$. The proposed solution requires the following assumptions reflecting real-life DM tasks.

Assumption 2. *There exists at least one past ideal $^I p_{(\tau,h)}$ that is sufficiently close to the current ideal closed-loop model $^I p_{(t,h)}$.*

Assumptions 2 ensures that past experience is sufficiently rich to cover the current DM task. It also allows to search for the similar task in the whole past history.

Assumption 3. *The environment behaviour does not significantly change over time period considered.*

Technically Assumption 3 means that probabilities in (3) do not change with time. Note that Assumption 3 is not so restrictive. Once its violation is suspected, different forgetting-like techniques [14] can be applied.
The proposed solution of the lazy FPD is given by the following proposition.

Proposition 1. *Consider a set of past DM tasks $Q_{(\tau,h)} = (p_{(\tau,h)}, {}^I p_{(\tau,h)}), \tau = 1, \ldots, t - h$ respecting Assumptions 1–3. Then optimal action a_t^{opt} for the current DM task can be found as follows:*

$$\tau^{opt} = \arg \max_{\tau \in (0, t-h)} {}^I p(\tau, h)$$

$$a_t^{opt} = a_{\tau^{opt}}. \tag{6}$$

The maximisation in (6) runs over past sequence of states and actions

$$(s_{\tau+h}, a_{\tau+h-1}, s_{\tau+h-1}, \ldots, s_{\tau+1}, a_\tau), \quad \tau \in \mathbb{N}$$

such that states observed at times τ and t are virtually equal. An optimal action is then taken from a sequence maximising the current ideal closed-loop model.

4   Experiment

This section aims to verify the effectiveness of the proposed single-agent strategy. A linear model of the helicopter in hovering is considered as an example. The DM strategy designed by the presented approach is compared with a Linear Quadratic Gaussian (LQG) control strategy.

4.1   Lazy-Learning Fully Probabilistic LQG

The helicopter has six degrees of freedom in its motion, [15]. There are four control inputs concerning its flight in addition to throttle control. By coordinating these inputs the helicopter can make forward and backward flight, sideward flight, hovering, hovering turn, vertical climb and descent, etc.
    Assuming the main rotor is composed of two blades without dragging motion, the vehicle mass center is located under the rotor shaft, rotor angular velocity is constant in hovering, and the tail rotor is composed of two blades and its hub center is located on the fuselage longitudinal axis, the model of helicopter can

be separated into two parts. The first part represents main rotor dynamic and the second one models dynamics behaviour of the tail rotor.

In the hovering mode, only main rotor dynamics describes the roll and pitch movement of the craft. The aim is to move roll and pitch angle to zero values.

We consider the following linear model of helicopter, details see [16]:

$$
\begin{bmatrix} \phi_{t+1} \\ \dot{\phi}_{t+1} \\ \theta_{t+1} \\ \dot{\theta}_{t+1} \end{bmatrix} = \begin{bmatrix} 1 & 0.021 & 0 & 0.0002 \\ 0 & 0.99 & 0 & 0.025 \\ 0 & -0.0013 & 1 & 0.02 \\ 0 & -0.1820 & 0 & 0.848 \end{bmatrix} \begin{bmatrix} \phi_t \\ \dot{\phi}_t \\ \theta_t \\ \dot{\theta}_t \end{bmatrix} + \begin{bmatrix} 0.06 & 0.0032 \\ 4.75 & 0.45 \\ -0.0098 & 0.313 \\ -1.18 & 27.356 \end{bmatrix} \begin{bmatrix} \theta_t^s \\ \theta_t^c \end{bmatrix} \quad (7)
$$

In (7) t denotes discrete time step, $\dot{\theta}$ and θ are pitch angular velocity and pitch angle, $\dot{\phi}$ and ϕ are roll angular velocity and roll angle, and θ^s and θ^c are roll control (laterally cyclic) and pitch control (longitudinally cyclic), respectively. Under different strategies implied by various unknown ideals, roll and pitch movements are shown in Fig. 3. In order to gather the closed-loop data, the decentralised Proportional-Derivative (PD) controllers, [17], with different parameters are employed. Since system outputs are continuous, finding similar past data requires an infinite database. To solve this problem, control actions and system outputs are discretised in values, see Fig. 4. As it can be seen in Fig. 4, roll and pitch movements respond correctly and the helicopter moves to the hovering position from the different initial states. Figure 5 depicts a histogram of control actions when the current value of $\phi \in (0.798, 0.8)$ while the previous value of $\phi \in (0.998, 1.0)$. The diversity of actions guarantees that finding tailored set of control actions based on a given ideal FPD and past data is highly plausible.

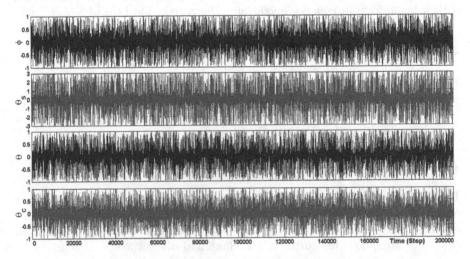

Fig. 3. The closed loop behaviour under different strategies.

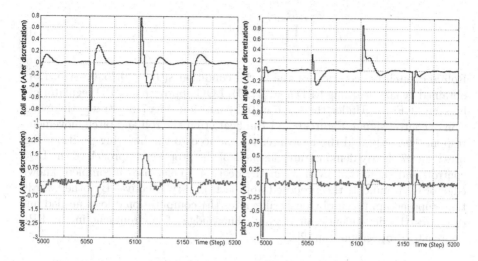

Fig. 4. The discrete-valued system outputs and control actions.

In order to formulate lazy-learning fully probabilistic LQG in hovering mode, the ideal state distribution and ideal controller strategy are assumed to be Gaussian with zero mean value and covariance matrices $\Sigma > 0$ and $R > 0$:

$$^I p(s_{\tau+1}|a_\tau, s_\tau) = \mathcal{N}_{s_{\tau+1}}(0, \Sigma) \tag{8}$$

$$^I p(a_\tau|s_\tau) = \mathcal{N}_{a_\tau}(0, R), \tag{9}$$

For the linear Gaussian state-space model, the controller found by FPD approach can be interpreted as a standard LQG with a state penalization matrix Σ^{-1} and input penalization matrix R^{-1}, details see [2].

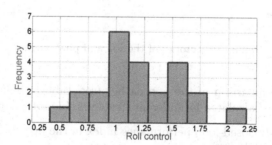

Fig. 5. The histogram of control actions.

By considering $\Sigma^{-1} = diag(1, 1, 0, 0)$ and $R^{-1} = \mathcal{I}_2$, where $\mathcal{I}$ is the identity matrix, and substituting (8) and (9) into (4), the ideal close-loop behaviour is defined as follows:

$$^I p_{(t,h)} \propto \prod_{\tau=t}^{t+h-1} e^{-(\hat{\theta}_{\tau+1}^2 + \hat{\phi}_{\tau+1}^2 + (\theta_{\tau}^s)^2 + (\theta_{\tau}^c)^2)}. \tag{10}$$

Roll and pitch trajectories for the initial condition $s(0) = \begin{bmatrix} 0.75, 0, -0.5, 1.0 \end{bmatrix}^T$ obtained by lazy-learning FPD $h = \{1, 10\}$, LQG approach and PD regulator can be seen at Fig. 6. Under the same initial condition, Fig. 7 illustrates the evolution of control signal. Figures 6 and 7 indicate that the roll and pitch movements respond correctly and the helicopter is conduced to the hovering position. Figures 6 and 7 clearly demonstrate closeness of the proposed approach to the LQG control, and show that even when the decision maker uses incomplete knowledge of environment, the proposed approach is very effective. By other words, the proposed approach obviously alleviates the computational load needed and decreases the dependency on accurate knowledge of environment in the FPD approach (Proposition 2 in [2]).

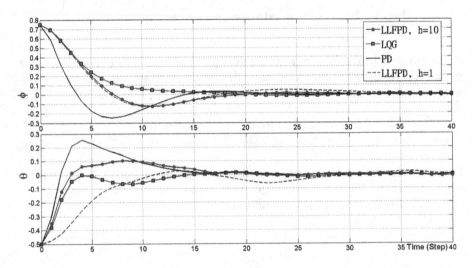

Fig. 6. Trajectories of the roll and pitch angle.

A detailed comparison of the approaches (see Table 1) is based on performance indices are calculated for different strategies. In particular we considered:

- *Transient cost*: closed-loop performance index in the first 20 steps under the influence of initial state.
- *Persistent cost*: value of closed-loop cost function in the last 100 steps under the influence of the process noise and the measurement noise.
- *Total cost*: value of the performance indices under the influence of initial state and Gaussian noise.

From Table 1, it can be seen that proposed approach (LLFPD LQG) with horizon $h = 10$ chooses the optimal control action. Compare to the standard LQG,

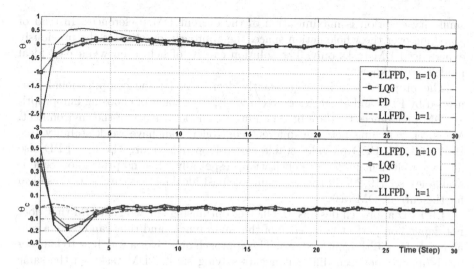

Fig. 7. Evolution of the control signals.

LLFPD with $h = 10$ had competitive responses in the transient and persistent state. Moreover under incomplete knowledge, LLFPD is a good alternative to FPD approach. The proposed approach provides results that highly outperform PD controller. Moreover it can reach visibly high control quality (see Table 1) with comparable computational effort.

Table 1. Performance quality

Method	Cost Function $J(t_{min}, t_{max}) = \Sigma_{t=t_{min}}^{t_{max}} (\theta_{t+1}^2 + \phi_{t+1}^2 + (\theta_t^s)^2 + (\theta_t^c)^2)$		
	Total cost	Transient cost	Persistent cost
	$J(0, 200)$	$J(0, 20)$	$J(100, 200)$
LQG	3.19623	3.10324	0.04751
PD	6.53832	6.37771	0.08482
LLFPD, $h = 1$	3.50326	3.19382	0.11641
LLFPD, $h = 2$	3.46451	3.22531	0.09185
LLFPD, $h = 5$	3.38828	3.20451	0.07306
LLFPD, $h = 10$	3.34851	3.21622	0.06081

5   Concluding Remarks

The paper describes lazy fully probabilistic design of DM strategies. The idea is based on searching similar previously experienced closed-loop models. The similarity criterion is maximisation of the current DM preferences. Instead of searching over the whole action space, the approach investigates the previously experienced DM tasks only. The solution can be of help even when past ideal models are unknown.

The proposed solution significantly decreases: (i) the computational load needed by FPD and other design techniques; (ii) danger of choosing inappropriate DM preferences that are based on little or no knowledge of the environment. Moreover switching between different controllers can have weak stability (see [18]) while LL FPD provides stable closed-loop behaviour. The lazy FPD also allows for efficient preference elicitation, (especially when no prior knowledge is available), see [19,20]. In this case suitable past ideal models can be used as ideal for the current DM task.

LL FPD approach designs an efficient optimising single-agent DM that does not depend on perfect knowledge of the environment and thus can create a reliable base for multi-agent systems. The approach also gives a way how to transfer ideals/models between different agents solving similar DM tasks on the same environment. This ability is highly demanded in many real-world applications where knowledge transfer cannot be easily ensured.

Acknowledgement. The authors would like to thank Miroslav Kárný for valuable discussions and comments. The research has been partially supported by the Czech Science Foundation, project GA16-09848S.

References

1. Kárný, M., et al. (eds.): Optimized Bayesian Dynamic Advising: Theory and algorithms. Springer, London (2006). https://doi.org/10.1007/1-84628-254-3
2. Kárný, M.: Towards fully probabilistic control design. Automatica **32**(12), 1719–1722 (1996)
3. Savage, L.J.: The Foundations of Statistics, pp. 188–190. Wiley, NY (1954)
4. Bellman, R.: Adaptive Control Processes. Princeton Press, NJ (1961)
5. Roll, J., Nazin, A., Ljung, L.: Nonlinear system identification via direct weight optimization. Automatica **41**(3), 475–490 (2005)
6. Powell, W.B.: Approximate Dynamic Programming: Solving the Curses of Dimensionality. vol. 703. Wiley (2007)
7. Aha, D.W.: Artif. Intell. Rev. Special Issue Lazy Learn. **11**, 1–5 (1997)
8. Aamodt, A., Plaza, E.: Case-based reasoning: foundational issues, methodological variations, and system approaches. AI Commun. **7**(1), 39–59 (1994)
9. Bitanti, S., Picci, G.: Identification, adaptation, learning. NATO ASI Series F on Computer and Systems Sciences (1996)
10. Weiss, K., Khoshgoftaar, T.M., Wang, D.: A survey of transfer learning. Journal of Big Data **3**(1), 9 (2016)
11. Klenk, M., Aha, D.W., Molineaux, M.: The case for case-based transfer learning. AI Mag. **32**(1), 54 (2011)
12. Kullback, S., Leibler, R.A.: On information and sufficiency. The Ann. Math. Stat. **22**(1), 79–86 (1951)

13. Peterka, V.: Bayesian approach to system identification. Trends Progress Syst. Ident. **1**, 239–304 (1981)
14. Kulhavy, R., Kárný, M.: Tracking of slowly varying parameters by directional forgetting. In: Proceedings of the 9th IFAC World Congress, vol. 10, pp. 78–83 (1984)
15. Adachi, S., Hashimoto, S., Miyamori, G., Tan, A.: Autonomous flight control for a large-scale unmanned helicopter. IEEJ Trans. Ind. Appl. **121**(12), 1278–1283 (2001)
16. Gil, I.A., Barrientos, A., Del Cerro, J.: Attitude control of a minihelicopter in hover using different types of control. Revista Técnica de la Facultad de Ingeniería. Universidad del Zulia **29**(3) (2006)
17. Ambrosino, G., Celentano, G., Garofalo, F.: Decentralized PD controllers for tracking control of uncertain multivariable systems. IFAC Proc. Vol. **18**(5), 1907–1911 (1985)
18. Hou, Z.S., Wang, Z.: From model-based control to data-driven control: Survey, classification and perspective. Inf. Sci. **235**(Suppl. C), 3–35 (2013)
19. Kárný, M., Guy, T.V.: Preference elicitation in fully probabilistic design of decision strategies. In: Proceedings of the 49th IEEE Conference on Decision and Control (2010)
20. Braziunas, D., Boutilier, C.: Preference elicitation and generalized additive utility (nectar paper). In: Proceedings of the 21st National Conference on AI (AAAI-2006), Boston, MA (2006)

Combination of Simulation and Model-Checking for the Analysis of Autonomous Vehicles' Behaviors: A Case Study

Johan Arcile[✉], Jérémy Sobieraj[✉], Hanna Klaudel, and Guillaume Hutzler

IBISC, Univ Evry, University of Paris-Saclay, 91025 Evry, France
{johan.arcile,jeremy.sobieraj,hanna.klaudel,
guillaume.hutzler}@univ-evry.fr
https://www.ibisc.fr

Abstract. Autonomous vehicles' behavioural analysis represents a major challenge in the automotive world. In order to ensure safety and fluidity of driving, various methods are available, in particular, simulation and formal verification. The analysis, however, has to cope with very complex environments depending on many parameters evolving in real time. In this context, none of the aforementioned approaches is fully satisfactory, which lead us to propose a combined methodology in order to point out suspicious behaviours more efficiently. We illustrate this approach by studying a non deterministic scenario involving a vehicle, which has to react to some perilous situation.

Keywords: Autonomous vehicles · Simulation · Verification

1 Introduction

Behavioural analysis of autonomous vehicles is a challenge for modellers for years [1–4]. It is often addressed by one of the following approaches:

- A road test consists in testing autonomous vehicles on existing roads or circuits in order to study their behaviour in the various situations they may have to deal with. Despite obvious advantages related to its realism, this method presents however serious limitations. Some countries simply do not allow the use of autonomous vehicles on existing roads, and even when it is legal, expensive prototypes are needed. Moreover, the time spent in testing is long, as it corresponds to the real time spent on the road. Finally, some scenarios cannot be studied with this approach, typically the dangerous ones, which potentially lead to crash. As a result, computer based approaches are generally prefered.
- More specifically, computer simulation enables to model vehicles' behaviours in a chosen environment so that various kinds of scenarios may be studied

© Springer Nature Switzerland AG 2018
F. Belardinelli and E. Argente (Eds.): EUMAS 2017/AT 2017, LNAI 10767, pp. 292–304, 2018.
https://doi.org/10.1007/978-3-030-01713-2_21

in a comparatively shorter time. As compared to the former method however, this implies that the vehicles and their environment are considered at some level of abstraction. Moreover, when vehicles present non-deterministic behaviours, simulation tools are generally not exhaustive since each simulation corresponds to a single path in the graph of all the possible behaviours;

– To improve the confidence in some model, the technique of model-checking, which is an exhaustive method, may be used. Model-checker analysers allow to automatically obtain binary answers (by yes or no) to questions about the dynamic behaviour of vehicles. To do so, specific models of vehicles in a given environment have to be provided. However, the use of the corresponding tools is generally limited, being quite prone to the well known state space explosion phenomenon.

We aim at proposing a method based on a combination of the latter two approaches in order to benefit from their respective comparative advantages when dealing with non-deterministic cases. The level of abstraction should therefore be carefully chosen so as to guarantee a convincing representation of the actual vehicles's behaviour in computer simulation. Because of the explosion of the state space, the same level of abstraction cannot be used in model checking. Since further abstractions are necessary to perform model checking analyses, it may lead to some gap as compared to computer simulation, so that we need to check that the obtained results are comparatively similar.

In order to define the desired levels of abstraction, it is necessary to determine the main properties of interest that are to be studied with these tools. Here, we focus on two main properties: the safety, which ensures that a vehicle always respects safety distances and minimises the risk of accidents; the fluidity of traffic, which consists in optimising the speed of each vehicle and in reducing the stop-and-go phenomenon (traffic jams) to lower atmospheric emissions and fuel consumption. The former can be addressed, for example, with *Time-To-Collision* (TTC) [5,6], which computes the time before two vehicles on the same lane collide if they keep their current speeds. The latter can be addressed, for example, with *Travel Time* [7,8], which computes the time required to travel a desired distance.

Our method is sketched in Fig. 1. The first step (step 0 in the figure) consists in producing data with the help of computer simulation. On the basis of such data, a human expert makes hypotheses about the behaviour of autonomous vehicles for a given initial situation. It could be for example: all vehicles are safe at all times. This kind of query needs an exhaustive check in the case of a non-deterministic evolution of the system. Step 1 consists in expressing the query in temporal logics[1] and model checking it. If the model checker finds some execution leading to a counter example, the corresponding execution is then confirmed by simulation, to ensure that it is not a false positive due to abstractions (step 2). In the case it is confirmed that some counter example invalidates the hypothesis, the process can go on with a new one, thanks to the enrichment of data through

---

[1] The translation of properties into temporal logics can be partly automatized using a predefined set of queries.

the verification process (step 3). More precisely, the method allows us to add particular executions to the data that will give critical informations in order to understand the behaviour of the vehicle and its causes.

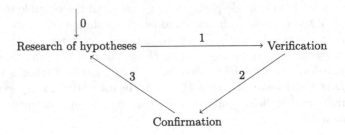

Fig. 1. Steps of the method.

To illustrate our method, we propose a case study, namely a car-following model in a given situation, which is rather straightforward for computer simulation but where the model checking has to face potential error accumulation due to the necessary discretisation of real number equations. A car following model is a mathematical model defining the vehicle's acceleration with respect to the dynamics of the vehicle that precedes it, such as Gipps [9] or IDM [10].

In particular, we are interested in the following questions:

- What conditions are needed for a vehicle in order to be in an unsafe situation?
- Are there executions where a vehicle is always safe?
- Is it possible to stop the car without overpassing a deceleration threshold?

The structure of the paper is as follows: Sect. 2 first presents the main elements of the computer simulation and model-checking approaches used in our case study on autonomous vehicles, as well as the corresponding tools. Section 3 is then devoted to the case study: first, a comparison between the simulation and model-checking tools is developed for more confidence in our results. Finally, our methodology is used on a non-deterministic scenario, where we aim at checking hypotheses on a vehicle's behaviour defined by a car-following model.

2   Presentation of the tools

2.1   Simulation

Simulation is a general method in which one first build a model to represent several aspects of a system (environment, behaviour, interactions, physical phenomena...). The simulation consists in the computational evaluation of the dynamics of the model over time. In the context of vehicles, it allows to reproduce their physics and interactions with the environment.

A level of abstraction should be defined in a way approaching the reality according to the desired observation. Various approaches have been developed for the simulation of autonomous vehicles, among which we could distinguish three main families.

A first approach consists in reproducing realistically the behaviour of vehicles by reproducing perfectly the laws of physics together with their specific parameters (such as inertia, impulse or friction). The simulation can then assess various aspects such as the study of a precise trajectory [11] or, in the context of communicating vehicles, a study of the reliability and integrity of the information transmitted between the vehicles [12].

A second approach focuses on traffic, in general, and its evolution over time through three points of view [13]: macroscopic, microscopic and mesoscopic. In particular, in the case of microscopic studies, where vehicles are handled individually in a small area, this approach allows to represent the longitudinal component of vehicles' motion thanks to car-following models, the majority of which are guaranteed without collision (such as IDM), and the lateral component thanks to lane change models (such as MOBIL [14]).

Finally, the third approach is agent-oriented in the sense that a vehicle is assimilated to an agent, which reacts according to the perception of its environment [15]. Each agent has also the possibility to communicate with other agents or with its environment to exchange information or negotiate a future decision to make.

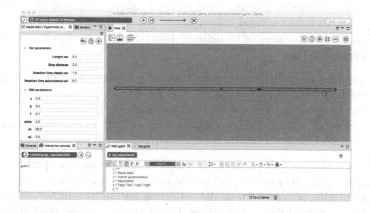

Fig. 2. Study of vehicles' behaviour with GAMA tool

The simulators allow to model and study various properties at different levels of realism and scale. We decided to illustrate our case study using the GAMA tool [16] (Fig. 2), which is a multi-agent systems simulator using an agent-oriented programming language (GAML). Each vehicle is characterised by a position, speed and acceleration and is in a two-dimensional environment: the longitudinal dimension (road direction) and the lateral dimension (neighboring lanes). At each time step, each vehicle updates its position while respecting the rectilinear motion with a uniform acceleration. It can perform the following actions: accelerate, slow down, keep the same speed or change lane in a road consisting in one or several lanes. The proposed abstraction is an effective way to observe complex phenomena between vehicles and is a first step before switching to a high level of realism.

2.2 Model-Checking

Model checking is a formal method for solving complex decision problems. More specifically, it allows for behavioural properties of a given system to be verified and provides examples of behaviours, which either respect or violate the checked property. A model checking tool can be seen as an operator which uses a model (for example a set of possible behaviours of vehicles on a portion of road) and a property (for example the possibility of a collision between the vehicles) and gives a binary result (true or false). This generally requires to model the system as a finite-state machine along with the formalisation of a behavioural property in temporal logics. The result of the checking is then obtained through the automated inspection of all states of the model, meaning that all the possible futures from a given initial situation are considered in order to assess the property. The main asset of such method is that it handles non-determinism while guaranteeing exhaustivity. But as a drawback, getting an answer may be difficult due to the number of states of the model. Indeed, as a formalisation of the system's characteristics is needed, the resulting model is often composed of a very large number of states (often several billions).

For instance, in the case of modelling of vehicles on a road portion, one must take into consideration:

- The variables needed to express the state of a vehicle (position, speed, acceleration, direction,...);
- The cost of non-deterministic decision making;
- The number of vehicles, whose growth exponentially increases the number of states.

Using abstractions allows to deal with the state explosion problem, while impacting the reliability of the system due to the necessary discretisation. Actually, accumulation of errors due to discretisation and finite number computation may lead to a totally different behaviour than the expected one. Having said that, model checking may be interesting in solving complex problems, but the model must present a satisfactory compromise between realism and computability.

In our combined analysis, we use a slightly modified version (without communication or lateral movement) of an existing model initially devoted to assess robustness of autonomous vehicles [17]. It runs on the model-checker UPPAAL [18,19], which allows the verification of properties expressed in a subset of CTL (computational tree logic) [20]. The expressivity of this query language is generally sufficient for the kind of information we want to obtain. The model considers a road section composed of several unidirectional lanes with several agents (vehicles) on it. This environment is represented by a data structure containing the state of each vehicle along with a set of constraints on their possible actions. A vehicle's state is kept as a set of values including position, speed, direction, knowledge on the environment, etc. The current position is expressed using discrete values, but with enough precision to model the vehicle's progression without leading to an abnormal behaviour due to the loss of information. More precisely, the position of a vehicle is considered as a point on a two-dimensional orthogonal grid. At a given frequency, each vehicle uses the information at its disposal to make a decision on the immediate action to be performed (it acts on acceleration and direction). It performs an action at its own frequency, i.e., vehicles are seen as independent agents. Vehicles' speeds and positions are updated in a simultaneous way, which means that the observation of the system is independent from the vehicles' decision making process frequency.

In the case study, we assume that each vehicle knows the exact position and speed of the vehicle that precedes it anytime a decision is made, meaning that the information from sensors is considered perfect. However, the challenge regarding this case study is to express the continuous function of a car-following equation using a discrete setting of model checking tools, while reaching a satisfactory precision and a state space small enough to be analysed in a reasonable time. In order to do so we scaled variables before division, implemented rounding, power and square root functions (which are not supported by UPPAAL because usually not needed in model-checking), and wisely chose the granularity of the variables used in the model. We obtained a model satisfying precision requirements that may be analysed by a model checker in (at most) a couple of minutes for a few vehicles on a portion of road of a few hundred meters.

3   Study of a Car-following Model: Intelligent Driver Model (IDM)

In this section we first present the Intelligent Driver Model (IDM, a decision making algorithm for autonomous vehicles) [10] and the interesting indicators for behavioural analysis. First, for more confidence in our results, a comparison between the simulation and model-checking tools is developed in order to find indicators not impacted by the used abstractions. Then, we use our methodology to check properties of IDM on some non-deterministic scenario.

3.1   Presentation

For our case study, we chose the Intelligent Driver Model (IDM) in order to observe suspicious situations by combining simulation and model-checking tools. This choice has several advantages:

- IDM allows to determine the acceleration of the follower vehicle for a given situation by observing the characteristics of the follower and leader vehicles;
- It can describe an autonomous vehicle using an Adaptive Cruise Control (ACC) system but it can also simulate the behavior of a human-driven vehicle;

- This variety of representations can be done through the ability to determine values for a set of initial parameters.

Let us consider two vehicles as depicted in Fig. 3: the follower vehicle i (whose behaviour is determined by IDM) and the leader vehicle $i-1$ (whose behaviour is not necessarily IDM). At each time step, vehicle i updates its acceleration, which varies according to two main criteria: on the one hand, vehicle i tends to reach a maximum speed allowed on the road portion, v_0 (cruise speed), and on the other hand, it must also respect a minimum safety distance s^* with the leading vehicle (which varies with the relative speed between the two vehicles).

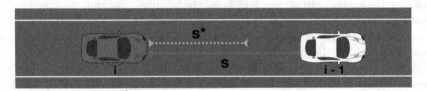

Fig. 3. IDM operation: at any time, vehicle i adapts its speed with respect to vehicle $i-1$

The IDM equation computing the acceleration of the follower vehicle is as follows:

$$acc_i = \frac{dv_i}{dt} = a \left[1 - \left(\frac{v_i}{v_0} \right)^\delta - \left(\frac{s^*(v_i, \Delta v_i)}{s} \right)^2 \right] \quad (1)$$

where the desired bumper-to-bumper distance $s^*(v_i, \Delta v_i)$ is:

$$s^*(v_i, \Delta v_i) = s_0 + \max \left[0, \left(v_i \times T + \frac{v_i \times \Delta v_i}{2\sqrt{ab}} \right) \right] \quad (2)$$

with a being the maximum acceleration, v_i the speed of vehicle i, v_0 the maximum allowed speed for vehicle i, δ the acceleration exponent ("aggressiveness" coefficient), $\Delta v_i = v_i - v_{i-1}$ the relative speed, s_0 the minimum bumper-to-bumper distance to the leading vehicle, T the estimated reaction time and b the desired deceleration.

The parameters, namely a, v_0, δ, s_0, T and b, should be fixed at the initialisation. For all the vehicles controlled with IDM, we decided to use the following values corresponding to a recent autonomous vehicle on a highway offering a comfortable deceleration and with a slightly shorter reaction time than that of a human driver [10]:

- $a : 5.0 \,\text{m.s}^{-2}$
- $v_0 : 30.0 \,\text{m.s}^{-1}$ (less than $110 \,\text{km.h}^{-1}$);
- $\delta : 4$;
- $s_0 : 2 \,\text{m}$;
- $T : 0.7 \,\text{s}$;
- $b : 3 \,\text{m.s}^{-2}$.

Note that in the IDM equation there is no limit on the maximum deceleration (only the desired deceleration b is fixed). This means that there are potentially situations where the value of deceleration exceeds b.

In what follows, we will use Time-to-Collision indicator TTC to study safety and therefore potential cases of abnormally high deceleration value involving unsafety or discomfort. TTC_i value depends on the speed and position of the two vehicles:

$$TTC_i = \frac{x_{i-1}(t) - x_i(t) - l(i)}{v_i(t) - v_{i-1}(t)} \quad \forall v_i(t) > v_{i-1}(t), \tag{3}$$

where $i - 1$ represents the leader, i the follower, v_i the speed of i, x_i the position of i and l_i the length of the vehicle i.

For all the scenarios presented in what follows, the observed portion of the road is 200 m long, each vehicle's length is exactly 5 m and their decision making process occurs every 100 ms.

3.2   Comparison

We first want to check the difference in behaviour between computer simulation and model checking approaches by comparing the travel time at the end of the road portion and the position at a given time (three seconds after the beginning of the scenario). Scenario 1 features three vehicles controlled by IDM. Initially, vehicle A is at position 0 m and its speed is 30 m.s^{-1}, vehicle B is at position 50 m and its speed is 25 m.s^{-1}, and vehicle C is at position 100 m and its speed is 20 m.s^{-1}. Figure 4 illustrates this scenario.

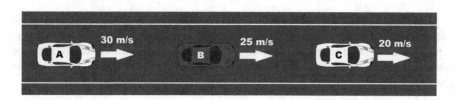

Fig. 4. Initial situation of Scenario 1 with the respective speeds of each vehicle.

Here, the vehicles A and B have to adapt their speed to avoid collision, which seems to be a good example to detect a possible error accumulation. The results are presented in Table 1 and show that the position and travel time of the vehicles are very close, with the higher percentage of error being on the travel time of B (0.52%). Such results show that the average behaviour obtained for both tools is similar enough to use position and travel time as reliable indicators.

Next, we check the behaviour regarding more sensitive indicators such as TTC or acceleration value. Scenario 2 features two vehicles: vehicle A controlled by IDM, initially at position 0 m with speed of 20 m.s^{-1}, and vehicle B initially

Table 1. Comparison of travel time and position at a given time for the three vehicles of Scenario 1.

Criterion	Travel time			Position at 3 s		
	Car A	Car B	Car C	Car A	Car B	Car C
Simulation	7.38 s	5.68 s	3.92 s	80.51 m	125.69 m	174.03 m
Model checking	7.39 s	5.71 s	3.92 s	80.74 m	125.26 m	173.99 m

at position 50 m with speed of 30 m.s^{-1}, controlled with the following rule: B starts by decelerating at -7 m.s^{-2} for one second, then accelerates at 5 m.s^{-2} for one second, and finally decelerates again at -7 m.s^{-2} until it stops, as depicted in Fig. 5.

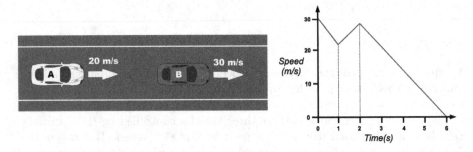

Fig. 5. Initial situation of Scenario 2 along with the evolution of vehicle B's speed.

One may notice that the initial situation is safe for the vehicle A (i.e., it respects the safety distance). On this scenario, we check the values and time of appearance of both the worst possible TTC value and the minimum acceleration value (i.e., the maximum deceleration) for vehicle A. From the same vehicle we also check the moment its acceleration value becomes negative.

Table 2. Comparison with respect to criteria based on acceleration and TTC of vehicle A's behaviour in Scenario 2.

Criterion	min TTC (value)	min TTC (time)	min acceleration (value)	min acceleration (time)	first deceleration (time)
Simulation	1.78 s	6.0 s	-7.36 m.s^{-2}	6.0 s	2.70 s
Model checking	1.76 s	6.0 s	-9.40 m.s^{-2}	6.0 s	2.70 s

The results are presented in Table 2 and show that for both tools, all the events occur in the same time units. Also, TTC values are very close with only 0.02 s of difference (1.13% of error), meaning that we can use TTC as an indicator with a reasonable confidence. On the other hand, the value of minimum acceleration is quite different with more than $2\,\mathrm{m.s^{-2}}$ of difference giving 27.71% of error. This is due to the propagation of errors of discrete value computation when making decision with the IDM controller. Due to a different level of abstraction, the acceleration computed at some step in the model checker is slightly different than the one obtained in simulation. If the acceleration computed by IDM equation with discrete domain of the model checker is greater than the real one, it implies that the speed at next step will be greater than needed and the time to collision lower than it should be. As a consequence, the next acceleration computed with IDM will be lower than the real one as it compensates this difference. One may therefore observe locally important differences on acceleration, even if the average values are close.

3.3   Application of the Method

In this section, we create a non-deterministic example on which we apply our method. We define scenario 3 as a non deterministic variant of scenario 2, where vehicle B starts with a $-7\,\mathrm{m.s^{-2}}$ acceleration, at some time changes this value to $5\,\mathrm{m.s^{-2}}$, and then at some time changes it back to $-7\,\mathrm{m.s^{-2}}$. We call the time of the first event e_1 and those of the second e_2, and define $\alpha = e_2 - e_1$ as the duration of vehicle B's positive acceleration. This values are illustrated in Fig. 6. Note that if e_2 never happend before the vehicle is out of the observed portion of road, we consider that α is infinite.

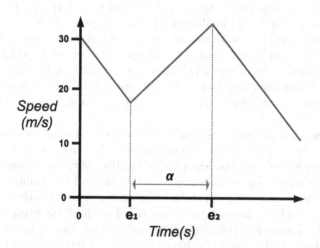

Fig. 6. Values of e_1, e_2 and α on a possible behaviour of vehicle B.

First, we run several random simulation executions and get both minimal TTC and acceleration values. On the basis of this data, we make three hypotheses:

1. There is a duration γ such that if $e_1 \leq \gamma$, TTC will never be under 1.7 s,
2. In order to have a TTC under 1.7 s, α must be comprised between $e_1 * 0.5$ and e_1,
3. There is no possible execution where vehicle B stops and its acceleration value is never less than to two times the desired deceleration parameter b (i.e. never less than $-6 \, \text{m.s}^{-2}$).

This leads to the following temporal logics queries:

1. Not Exists Finally $TTC < 1.7$ and $e_1 \leq \gamma$
2. Always Globally $(TTC < 1.7 \Rightarrow \alpha < e_1$ and $\alpha > e_1/2)$
3. Not Exists Globally $acceleration(A) \geq -6$ and $on\_the\_road(A)$, where $acceleration$ is the value of A's acceleration and $on\_the\_road(A)$ is a Boolean variable, which is $true$ if the vehicle A has not yet reached the end of the portion of the road.

The first hypothesis is easily confirmed, but it is more interesting to find a maximum for γ. Using model checker, we find by dichotomy a value of 2.3 s, however one must keep in mind that there may be a slight error in the computed TTC. Then, we explore the neighbourhood of this value by simulation in order to refine it. Simulation points out an execution with $e_1 = 2.2$ s, where a TTC under 1.7 s is found, but none at $e_1 = 2.1$ s. We can therefore assume that the actual maximum for γ is 2.1.

The second hypothesis appears to be wrong. Actually, the model checker finds an execution violating such property for both the upper bound (with $e_1 = 2.4$ and $e_1 = 4.9$) and the lower bound (with $e_1 = 3.3$ and $e_1 = 4.4$). We then refine the upper and lower bounds and finally get a result, where $\alpha \in [e_1 * 0.3, e_1 * 1.1]$. The exploration of these bounds by simulation does not show any counter example.

Finally, the third query gives a positive result, but we have to remember that, as we showed, the acceleration value may potentially be very different in the model checking and simulation. The verification of the same query with a value of $-7 \, \text{m.s}^{-2}$ instead of $-6 \, \text{m.s}^{-2}$ still gives a positive result adding some confidence to the result.

The verification process took less than 10 s for each query despite the complexity of the system due to the size of the variable ranges and a large number of positions in which each the agents may be. However, the system is still not so complex in terms of non determinism, as we limited the number of possible actions the leader vehicle may perform at any given time. This choice was made for the purpose of the case study, as it was easier to check the consistency of our result on such a case. For this reason one might argue that it might have been possible to check all the possible behaviours with simulation alone in a relatively reasonable time, which in this particular case, might indeed work. However, in case of more complex behaviours, this does not seem to be a reasonable method. Also, despite the fact that the verification time also increases with the size and complexity of the system, it is still possible, up to some extent, to exhaustively check hypotheses on complex non deterministic systems in a reasonable time (i.e., less than a few hours). Note that performance mainly depends on the level of non determinism. For instance, adding other deterministic vehicles on a scenario will have a very low cost, whereas adding more possible behaviours may seriously affect the performance.

4 Conclusion

We addressed the challenge of modelling autonomous vehicles' behaviour with both computer simulation and model checking through well chosen abstractions and discretisation. Both modelling approaches were studied and gave a satisfactory representation of reality. First, we succeeded to model with a good accuracy the behaviour of vehicles whose description needed a large number of variables. Second, we experimented and compared both in regards to suitable indicators which showed that obtained values coincided. Motivated by the complementarity of these techniques we proposed a method combining both of them in order to increase confidence in the results. Finally, thanks to this modelling and such a methodology, we provided a case study showing it was possible to obtain efficiently useful information on autonomous vehicles' behaviour. In particular, the analysis of the car-following model IDM pointed out some non trivial behaviours.

The tools used in this paper support more complex environments than those used in our case study. These features may be used to deal with more realistic situations (several lanes, communication between vehicles, various decision algorithms,...). Also, to cope with the error due to discrete values' computation, it should be possible to use finer granularity for the variables but at a cost of increased verification time. In the future we plan to use the infrastructure presented here to study communications protocols between agents in order to improve the quality of decision making of autonomous vehicles.

References

1. Ekren, B.Y., Heragu, S.S.: Simulation based performance analysis of an autonomous vehicle storage and retrieval system. Simul. Model. Pract. Theor. **19**(7), 1640–1650 (2011)
2. Dia, H.: An agent-based approach to modelling driver route choice behaviour under the influence of real-time information. Transp. Res. Part C: Emerg. Technol. **10**(5), 331–349 (2002)
3. Shamir, T.: How should an autonomous vehicle overtake a slower moving vehicle: design and analysis of an optimal trajectory. IEEE Trans. Automat. Control **49**, 607–610 (2004)
4. Hybrid-state driver/vehicle modelling, estimation and prediction. In: 13th International IEEE Conference on Intelligent Transportation Systems, pp. 806–811 (2010)
5. Vogel, K.: A comparison of headway and time to collision as safety indicators. Accid. Anal. Prev. **35**(3), 427–433 (2003)
6. Minderhoud, M.M., Bovy, P.H.: Extended time-to-collision measures for road traffic safety assessment. Accid. Anal. Prev. **33**(1), 89–97 (2001)
7. van Lint, J., Hoogendoorn, S., van Zuylen, H.: Accurate freeway travel time prediction with state-space neural networks under missing data. Transp. Res. Part C: Emerg. Technol. **13**(5), 347–369 (2005)

8. Chang, G.-L., Mahmassani, H.S.: Travel time prediction and departure time adjustment behavior dynamics in a congested traffic system. Transp. Res. Part C: Emerg. Technol. **22**(3), 217–232 (1988)

9. Gipps, P.G.: A behavioural car-following model for computer simulation. Transp. Res. Part B **15**(2), 105–111 (1981)

10. Treiber, M., Kesting, A.: Elementary car-following models. In: Treiber, M., Kesting, A. (eds.) Traffic Flow Dynamics. Springer, Heidelberg (2013). https://doi.org/10.1007/978-3-642-32460-4_10

11. Zhang, S., Deng, W., Zhao, Q., Sun, H., Litkouhi, B.: Dynamic trajectory planning for vehicle autonomous driving. In: Proceedings - 2013 IEEE International Conference on Systems, Man, and Cybernetics, SMC 2013, pp. 4161–4166 (2013)

12. Bai, F., Krishnan, H.: Reliability analysis of DSRC wireless communication for vehicle safety applications. In: IEEE Intelligent Transportation Systems Conference (ITSC), pp. 355–362 (2006)

13. Treiber, M., Kesting, A.: Traffic Flow Dynamics. Springer, Heidelberg (2013). https://doi.org/10.1007/978-3-642-32460-4

14. Kesting, A., Treiber, M., Helbing, D.: General lane-changing model MOBIL for car-following models. Transp. Res. Rec.: J. Transp. Res. Board **1999**(1), 86–94 (2007)

15. Ferber, J.: Multi-Agent Systems: An Introduction to Distributed Artificial Intelligence, vol. 222. Addison-Wesley, Boston (1999)

16. Taillandier, P., Vo, D.-A., Amouroux, E., Drogoul, A.: GAMA: a simulation platform that integrates geographical information data, agent-based modeling and multi-scale control. In: Desai, N., Liu, A., Winikoff, M. (eds.) PRIMA 2010. LNCS (LNAI), vol. 7057, pp. 242–258. Springer, Heidelberg (2012). https://doi.org/10.1007/978-3-642-25920-3_17

17. Arcile, J., Devillers, R., Klaudel, H., Klaudel, W., Woźna-Szcześniak, B.: Modeling and checking robustness of communicating autonomous vehicles. Distributed Computing and Artificial Intelligence, 14th International Conference. AISC, vol. 620, pp. 173–180. Springer, Cham (2018). https://doi.org/10.1007/978-3-319-62410-5_21

18. UPPAAL. http://www.uppaal.org/

19. Larsen, K.G., Pettersson, P., Yi, W.: UPPAAL in a nutshell. Int. J. Softw. Tools Technol. Transfer (STTT) **1**, 134–152 (1997)

20. Emerson, E.A., Halpern, J.Y.: "Sometimes" and "not never" revisited: on branching versus linear time temporal logic. J. ACM **1**(33), 151–178 (1986)

EUMAS 2017: Games

How Game Complexity Affects
the Playing Behavior of Synthetic Agents

Chairi Kiourt[1]([⊠])⑩, Dimitris Kalles[1]⑩, and Panagiotis Kanellopoulos[2]⑩

[1] School of Science and Technology, Hellenic Open University, Patras, Greece
{chairik,kalles}@eap.gr
[2] CTI "Diophantus" and University of Patras, Rion, Greece
kanellop@ceid.upatras.gr

Abstract. Agent based simulation of social organizations, via the investigation of agents' training and learning tactics and strategies, has been inspired by the ability of humans to learn from social environments which are rich in agents, interactions and partial or hidden information. Such richness is a source of complexity that an effective learner has to be able to navigate. This paper focuses on the investigation of the impact of the environmental complexity on the game playing-and-learning behavior of synthetic agents. We demonstrate our approach using two independent turn-based zero-sum games as the basis of forming social events which are characterized both by competition and cooperation. The paper's key highlight is that as the complexity of a social environment changes, an effective player has to adapt its learning and playing profile to maintain a given performance profile.

Keywords: Board games · Playing behaviors
Multi-agent systems · Game complexity · Social events

1 Introduction

Turn-based zero-sum games are most popular when it comes to studying social environments and multi-agent systems [1–3]. For a game agent, the social environment is represented by a game with all its agents, components and entities, such as rules, pay-offs and penalties, amongst others [2,4,5], while learning in a game is said to occur when an agent changes a strategy or a tactic in response to new information [5–8]. Social simulation involves artificial agents with different characteristics (synthetic agents), which interact with other agents, possibly employing a mix of cooperative and competitive attitudes, towards the investigation of social learning phenomena [4,5,9].

The mimicking of human playing behaviors by synthetic agents is a realistic method for simulating game-play social events [5], where the social environment (games) as well as the other agents (opponents) [10,11] are among the key factors which affect the playing behavior of the agents.

© Springer Nature Switzerland AG 2018
F. Belardinelli and E. Argente (Eds.): EUMAS 2017/AT 2017, LNAI 10767, pp. 307–322, 2018.
https://doi.org/10.1007/978-3-030-01713-2_22

The solvability of board games is being investigated for over 25 years [12–15]. Several studies focusing on board game complexity have shown that board games vary from low to high complexity levels [13–15], which are mainly based on the game configuration and the state space of the game, with more complex games having larger rule set and more detailed game mechanics. In general, solvability is related to the *state-space complexity* and *game-tree complexity* of games [14,15]. The *state-space complexity* is defined as the number of legal game positions obtainable from the initial position of the game. The *game-tree complexity* is defined as the number of leaf nodes in the solution search tree of the initial position of the game. In our investigation, we adopted the *state-space complexity* approach, which is the most-known and widely used [13–15].

The complexity of a large set of well-known games has been calculated [14,15] at various levels, but their usability in multi-agent systems as regards the impact on the agents' learning/playing progress is still a flourishing research field.

In this article, we study the game complexity impact on the learning/training progress of synthetic agents, as well as on their playing behaviors, by adopting two different board games. Different playing behaviors [5] are adopted for the agents' playing and learning progress. We experiment with varying complexity levels of *Connect-4* (a medium complexity game) and *RLGame* (an adaptable complexity game). These two different games cover an important range of diverse social environments, as we are able to experiment at multiple complexity levels, as determined by a legality-based model for calculating state-space complexity. Our experiments indicate that synthetic agents mimic quite well some human-like playing behaviors in board games. Additionally, we demonstrate that key learning parameters, such as exploitation-vs-exploration trade-off, learning backup and discount rates, and speed of learning are important elements for developing human-like playing behaviors for strategy board games. Furthermore, we highlight that, as the complexity of a social environment changes, the playing behavior (essentially, the learning parameters set-up) of a synthetic agent has to adapt to maintain a given performance profile.

2   Background Knowledge

In this section, we describe the games adopted for the experimental sessions, the structure of the synthetic agents' learning mechanisms and the development of the social environments.

Connect-4 is a relatively recent game, fairly similar to *tic-tac-toe*, but uses a 6 × 7 board with gravity. Both agents have 21 identical 'coins', and each agent may only place its coins in the lowest available slot in a selected column (essentially, by inserting a coin at the free top of the column and allowing it to "fall"). The goal of the game is to connect four of one's own coins of the same color next to each other vertically, horizontally or diagonally before the opponent reaches that goal. If all of both agents' coins are placed and no agent has achieved this goal, the game is a draw. *Connect-4* is a turn-based game and each agent has exactly one move per turn. It has a medium state space complexity of 4.5×10^{12} board positions [16]. Figure 1 depicts an example of the *Connect-4* game, in which agent B wins the game.

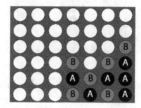

Fig. 1. A *Connect-4* game in which player B wins.

RLGame is a board game [17] involving two agents and their pawns, played on a square board. Two $\alpha \times \alpha$ square bases are on opposite board corners; these are initially populated by β pawns for each agent, with the white agent starting from the lower left base and the black agent starting from the upper right one. The possible configurations of the *RLGame* are presented in Table 1. The goal for each agent is to move a pawn into the opponent's base or to force all opponent pawns out of the board (it is the player not the pawn who acts as an agent, in our scenario). The base is considered as a single square, therefore a pawn can move out of the base to any adjacent free square. Agents take turns and pawns move one at a time, with the white agent moving first. A pawn can move vertically or horizontally to an adjacent free square, provided that the maximum distance from its base is not decreased (so, backward moves are not allowed). A pawn that cannot move is lost (more than one pawn may be lost in one move). An agent also loses by running out of pawns.

Table 1. A description of game configurations

Board size (n)	5, 6, 7, 8, 9, 10
Base size (α)	2, 3, 4
Number of pawns (β)	1, 2, 3, 4, 5, 6, 7, 8, 9, 10

The implementation of some of the most important rules is depicted in Fig. 2. In the leftmost board the pawn indicated by the arrow demonstrates a legal ("tick") and an illegal ("cross") move, the illegal move being due to the rule that does not allow decreasing the distance from the home (black) base. The rightmost boards demonstrate the loss of pawns, with arrows showing pawn casualties. A "trapped" pawn, either in the middle of the board or when there is no free square next to its base, automatically draws away from the game.

For our study, in both games, each agent is an autonomous system that acts according to its characteristics and knowledge. The learning mechanism used

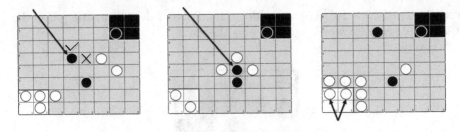

Fig. 2. Example of *RLGame* rules into action.

(Fig. 3) is based on reinforcement learning, by approximating the value function with a neural network [2,4], as already documented in similar studies [18,19]. Each autonomous (back propagation) neural network [20] is trained after each player makes a move. The board positions for the next possible move are used as input-layer nodes, along with flags regarding the overall board coverage. The hidden layer consists of half as many hidden nodes. A single node in the output layer denotes the extent of the expectation to win when one starts from a specific game-board configuration and then makes a specific move. After each move the values of the neural network are updated through the *temporal difference learning method*, which is a combination of Monte Carlo and dynamic programming [20]. As a result, collective training is accomplished by putting an agent against other agents so that knowledge (experience) is accumulated.

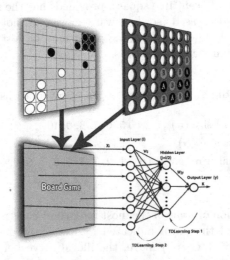

Fig. 3. Learning mechanism of *RLGame* and *Connect-4*

For both games, the agent's goal is to learn an optimal strategy that will maximize the expected sum of rewards within a specific amount of time, determining which action should be taken next, given the current state of the environment. The strategy to select between moves is ϵ-Greedy (ϵ), with ϵ denoting the probability to select the best move (exploitation), according to present knowledge, and $1 - \epsilon$ denoting a random move (exploration) [21]. The learning mechanism is associated with two additional learning parameters, Gamma (γ) and Lambda (λ). A risky or a conservative agent behavior is determined by the parameter, which specifies the learning strategy of the agent and determines the values of future payoffs, with values in $[0,1]$; effectively, *large values are associated with long-term strategies*. The speed and quality of agent learning is associated with λ, which is the learning rate of the neural network, also in $[0,1]$. *Small values of λ can result in slow, smooth learning; large values could lead to accelerated, unstable learning*. These properties are what we, henceforth, term as "characteristic values" for the playing agents.

RLGame and *Connect-4*, in their tournament versions [5], both fit the description of an autonomous organization and of a social environment, as defined by Ferber et al. [1,4]. Depending on the number of agents, social categories can be split into sub-categories of *micro-social environments, environments composed of agent groups* and global societies, which are the next level of the cooperation and competition extremes of social organizations [2,4].

On one hand, *RLGame* was chosen because it is a fairly complex game for studying learning mechanism and developing new algorithms, because all the pawns of the game have the same playing attributes. It is not as complicated as *Chess*, where almost all pieces have their own playing attributes, or *Go*, which would make it difficult to study in detail the new learning algorithms. Furthermore, its complexity scales with the number of pawns and board dimensions, which allows for fewer non-linear phenomena that are endemic in games like *Chess*, *Go*, or *Othello* (for example, knight movement in *Chess* or column color inversion in *Othello*, are both instances of such phenomena). We view this as a key facilitator in our quest for opponent modelling (but acknowledge the importance and the interestingness of non-linear aspects of game play). On the other hand, *Connect-4* was chosen due to its low complexity. With these two different games, we believe that we cover a quite important range of diverse environments, as we can accommodate several levels of complexity in *RLGame* and pretty low complexity in *Connect-4*.

3   Game Complexity

Combinatorial game theory provides several ways to measure the game complexity of two-person zero-sum games with perfect information [13,14], such as: *state-space complexity, game tree size, decision complexity, game-tree complexity* and *computational complexity*. In this study, we use the *state-space complexity* approach, which is the most known and widely used [13–15]. Nowadays, dozens of games are solved by many different algorithms [14,15].

Connect-4 is one of the first turn-based zero-sum games solved by computer [12]. It has a medium state space complexity of 4.5×10^{12} board positions in

6 × 7 board size [16]. Tromp [22] presented some game theoretical values of *Connect-4* on medium board sizes up to $width + height = 15$, some of which are presented in Table 2 [23].

Table 2. *Connect-4*, game configurations associated to their state-space sizes.

Height, Width (size)	State space complexity	β (coins per player)
8,2	1.33×10^4	8
8,3	8.42×10^6	12
8,4	1.10×10^9	16
7,4	1.35×10^8	14
7,5	1.42×10^{10}	17.5
6,5	1.04×10^9	15
6,6	6.92×10^{10}	18
6,7	4.53×10^{12}	21
5,5	6.98×10^7	12.5
5,6	2.82×10^9	15
5,7	1.13×10^{10}	17

The complexity of the *RLGame* depends mainly on the value of parameters n, α, and β. The number of the various positions that might occur is bounded from above by:

$$\sum_{i=1}^{\beta}\sum_{j=1}^{\beta} \binom{n^2 - 2\alpha^2}{i+j}\binom{i+j}{i}(1 + 2(\beta - i))(1 + 2(\beta - j)). \tag{1}$$

The first (leftmost) term denotes the number of ways to place $i+j$ pawns in the playing field (on the board but outside the bases) and the second term denotes the number of ways to partition these $i+j$ pawns into i white and j black pawns. The two rightmost terms intend to capture, for each given configuration of i white and j black pawns in the playing field, the additional number of positions that may occur because each player might have pawns in its own base and no pawn in the enemy base (there are $\beta - i$ such configurations for the white player) or a single pawn in the enemy base and possibly some pawns in its own base (again, there are $\beta - i$ such configurations for the white player).

Naturally, the above formula overestimates the number of possible states since it also includes illegal states, so we devised a simple simulation with the following steps to derive a better estimate.

- Given n, α, and β, we examine all valid configuration profiles (n, α, β, i, j) where i, j denote the number of white and black pawns in the playing field.
- We generated 1000 random positions per valid profile and tested whether some of them contained dead pawns (e.g., pawns with no legal moves).

- For each configuration profile, we multiplied the fraction of such "legit" positions (we did not check whether a position without dead pawns can actually arise in a real game) with $[1 + 2(\beta - i)][1 + 2(\beta - j)]$ to take into account the $\beta - i$ (respectively, $\beta - j$) white (respectively, black) pawns that are not in the playing field for each configuration profile.
- We summed the number of "legit" positions over all configuration profiles for the given values of n, α and β and calculated the ratio of "apparently legit states" provided by this simulation over the "theoretical estimation" provided by the formula.

Table 1 reviews the (n, α, β) configurations we used; since bases should be at least one square apart in any given board, we eventually end-up with fewer valid (n, α) combinations (shown alongside the results in Table 3). Additionally, for valid configurations we demand that $0 < i \leq \beta$ and $0 < j \leq \beta$.

Table 3. RLGame, games' extreme configurations associated to their state-space sizes. We state the theoretical upper bound and the ratio of "legit" positions that arose in simulations.

Board, Base (size)	$\beta = 1$		$\beta = 10$	
	Formula	Ratio	Formula	Ratio
5,2	3.83×10^2	.991	1.11×10^{10}	.127
6,2	9.33×10^2	.997	1.50×10^{14}	.088
7,2	1.89×10^3	.999	6.93×10^{17}	.177
7,3	1.12×10^3	.994	1.37×10^{15}	.113
8,2	3.43×10^3	.998	7.21×10^{20}	.373
8,3	2.36×10^3	1.	9.10×10^{18}	.254
9,2	5.70×10^3	.996	2.40×10^{23}	.562
9,3	4.29×10^3	.997	9.64×10^{21}	.486
9,4	2.66×10^3	1.	3.72×10^{19}	.315
10,2	8.93×10^3	1.	3.50×10^{25}	.712
10,3	7.14×10^3	1.	2.96×10^{24}	.645
10,4	4.97×10^3	.998	5.12×10^{22}	.530

We only report the state-space size for the extreme cases of $\beta = 1$ and $\beta = 10$ for each (n, α) configuration used, since we observed that the approximation ratios strictly decrease with increasing values of β (thus creating more room for pawn interdependencies which lead to illegal moves). These results are shown in Table 3 and confirm that, even for relatively small dimensions, state space complexity is well over 10^{10}.

4   Experimental Sessions

In order to study the game complexity effect in synthetic agents' learning/training process as well as in their playing behaviors, in multi-agent social environments, three independent tournament sessions (experiments) with the same pre-configurations were designed and run for both *RLGame* and *Connect-4*; for simplicity, we will name these tournament sessions as $RL - R(x \times y)$ for *RLGame* and $C4 - R(x \times y)$ for *Connect-4*, where $(x \times y)$ presents the game configuration. Table 4 presents the game configurations selected for the tournament sessions (experiments). We chose three different game configurations for each game, in order to study three different complexity level of each game. We remark that in the following we only compare agents playing the same game; we never compare an agent from *RLGame* to an agent from *Connect-4*.

Table 4. Selected game configurations for the tournament sessions (experiments).

Connect-4			RLGame		
Experiment (Tournament) name	Size (Height, Width)	State space complexity	Experiment (Tournament) name	Size (Board, Base)	State space complexity ($\beta = 10$)
$C4 - R(8 \times 3)$	8,3	8.42×10^6	$RL - R(5 \times 2)$	5,2	1.11×10^{10}
$C4 - R(7 \times 4)$	7,4	1.35×10^8	$RL - R(7 \times 2)$	7,2	6.93×10^{17}
$C4 - R(6 \times 7)$	6,7	4.53×10^{12}	$RL - R(10 \times 2)$	10,2	3.50×10^{25}

According to the scenario of these tournaments sessions, we initiated 64 agents in a *Round Robin* tournament with 10 games per match. All agents had different characteristic value configurations for ϵ, γ and λ, with values ranging from 0.6 to 0.9, with an increment step of 0.1. Four different values for each characteristic value (ϵ-γ-λ), implies $4^3 = 64$ agents with different playing behaviors (different characteristic values). Each agent played 63 matches against different agents, resulting in a total number of $\binom{64}{1} \times 10 = 200,160$ games, for each tournament session. All tournament sessions were identical in terms of agent configurations and flow of execution.

The ranges of the characteristic values (ϵ-γ-λ) are selected, because of their association with the playing behaviors of the agent [5]. For example, if we had an agent that exploits 5% of its knowledge (ϵ), then it almost always learn something new and would only rarely demonstrate what it learned [20,24]. Also, if we set $\lambda = 0.05$, the agent would learn very slow, which is not effective in case the opponent opts to play head-on attack (one pawn moving directly to the opponent base for *RLGame*), as an agent with a low λ may be less interested to learn a more structured strategy by using many pawns that may defend its base or to force opponent pawns out of the board. Wiering et al. [25] suggested that λ values larger than 0.6 perform best. The discount rate parameter, γ, as reported by Sutton and Barton [20], tilts the agent towards being myopic and only concerned with maximizing immediate rewards when $\gamma = 0$, while it allows the agent to become more farsighted and take future rewards into account more strongly when $\gamma = 1$. For this reason, on one hand, by setting the γ values roughly to 0.6, we may say that the agent adopts short term strategies (risky), on the other hand, by setting the γ values to 0.9 we represent the agents with long term strategies (conservative agents). With the characteristic values ϵ-γ-λ ranging between 0.6 and 0.9, we kept a balance.

Based on the agents' characteristic values (ϵ-γ-λ) and their performance, we developed a set of playing behavior descriptors [5], see Table 5.

Table 5. Agents playing behavior descriptors based on their characteristic values and their performance

Characteristic Values	Key parameters (Playing behavior descriptors)
$0.6 \leq \epsilon \leq 0.9$	*Exploration, exploitation tradeoff* (*knowledge explorer to exploiter*)
$0.6 \leq \gamma \leq 0.9$	*Learning back-up and discount rates* (*risky to conservative, short to long term strategies*)
$0.6 \leq \lambda \leq 0.9$	*Speed & stability of learning* (*slow smooth to fast and unstable learning*)
$1 \leq r \leq 64$	*Agents' rankings, performance* (*good playing to bad playing agents*)

The first three descriptors are composed from the characteristic values derived from previous experiments [5]. Those three descriptors define the characteristics limits, which determine playing behaviors depending on their preferred strategies. Simply put, every descriptor may represent a synthetic agent's playing behavior in the experimental social environment. An example of synthetic agent's playing behavior is that a 'Knowledge Exploiter' (high ϵ value) and 'Conservative' (high γ value) and 'Fast, Unstable Learner' (high λ values) agent tends to be 'Bad playing' (high r value), which we do not consider positive for a game-playing agent.

The agents are rated by using the *ReSkill* tool [26]. All the last ratings of tournament sessions are converted to rankings (r), in order to compare more effectively the experiments by using statistical methods, such as the *Spearman's rank correlation coefficient* (ρ) [27], which measures the statistical dependence between two variables, and is specifically efficient at capturing the monotonic (non-linear, in general) correlation on ranks and the *Kendall rank correlation coefficient* (τ) [28], which measures the ordinal association between two measured quantities, both considered as adequate statistical measures to compare ranking lists quantitatively [29]. As known, the range of both coefficients falls within $[-1, 1]$, with high negative values representing strong negative correlation, low absolute values representing small or no correlation and high positive values representing strong positive correlation. Table 6 shows a *Spearman's* and *Kendall's* correlation coefficients distance heat-map, for the tournament sessions introduced in Table 4. The top value of each cell shows the ρ correlation coefficient while the bottom value of each cell the correlation coefficient. Darker gray cells indicate a high correlation between two tournament sessions (agent rankings), while lighter gray cells indicate a strong negative correlation. Table 6 also represents an indicative correlation between the state-space complexities of the social environments.

Table 6. *Spearman's* and *Kendall's* correlation coefficients comparison of each tournament session, presented as a distance heat-map, where high distances are presented with light gray and smaller distances with darker gray

	$C4 - R(8 \times 3)$ 8.42×10^6	$C4 - R(7 \times 4)$ 1.35×10^8	$C4 - R(6 \times 7)$ 4.53×10^{12}	$RL - R(5 \times 2)$ 1.11×10^{10}	$RL - R(7 \times 2)$ 6.93×10^{17}	$RL - R(10 \times 2)$ 3.50×10^{25}
$C4 - R(8 \times 3)$ 8.42×10^6	1	0.340 0.237	-0.043 -0.019	-0.340 -0.212	-0.274 -0.186	-0.192 -0.134
$C4 - R(7 \times 4)$ 1.35×10^8	0.340 0.237	1	0.090 0.064	-0.477 -0.332	-0,5 0.362	-0.518 -0.362
$C4 - R(6 \times 7)$ 4.53×10^{12}	-0.043 -0.019	0.090 0.064	1	-0.179 -0.127	-0.167 -0.121	-0.229 -0.138
$RL - R(5 \times 2)$ 1.11×10^{10}	-0.340 -0.212	-0.477 -0.332	-0.179 -0.127	1	0.673 0.482	0.720 0.519
$RL - R(7 \times 2)$ 6.93×10^{17}	-0.274 -0.186	-0.500 -0.362	-0.167 -0.121	0.673 0.482	1	0.740 0.561
$RL - R(10 \times 2)$ 3.50×10^{25}	-0.192 -0.134	-0.518 -0.362	-0.229 -0.138	0.720 0.519	0.740 0.561	1

In order to verify the tournament sessions' correlations, we applied a *k-means* clustering for all tournament sessions and we developed the heat-maps of Fig. 4. We set the number of the *k-means* clusters fixed to 3 (C1, C2 and C3), to build three clusters based on the agents' performance (by using the agents' rankings from each tournament sessions). Also, we set the re-runs of the *k-means* algorithm to 100 and the *maximal iterations* within each algorithm run to 300. Due to the number of the agents (64) and the number of the tournament sessions (3 for each game), the *k-means* configuration was good enough to show the best correlation between the agents' performances associated to the tournament sessions. We tested the *k-means* algorithm with larger number of *re-runs* and *maximal iteration* but there was no difference in the result. Figure 4 presents three rows for each game (one for each tournament session) and 64 columns (one for each agent). The columns are separated in three clusters for each game. Each cluster (C1, C2 and C3) depicts the association of the agents, based on their rankings in the three tournament sessions. Each agent (rows in the graphs) is composed from three colored cells, where each cell depicts the performance of the agent in the corresponding tournament session. The colored bars, from light grey to dark grey, at the right of each graph, depict the ranking positions. In example, each dark gray cell depicts a bad playing agent in the corresponding tournament (row), the darkest cell of the C3 cluster, tournament session $C4 - R(8 \times 3)$, shows the worst playing agent of that experimental session, which was ranked in the 64th position in the last round of the tournament. The correlation between the agents of each cluster (C1, C2 and C3), of each game, is depicted by a tree graph (dendrogram) in the top of each cluster. Each row (tournament session) and column (agents) are clustered by leaf ordering. As leaves we mean the lines (leaf of the dendrogram) that show the correlation between two variables (agents or tournament sessions). For example, the leaves: $C4 - R(8 \times 3)$ and $C4 - R(7 \times 4)$ are higher related (rows of *Connect-4* game), than the leaf $C4 - R(6 \times 7)$, which differs more than the two other leaves. This can be confirmed if one checks the color shades of the cells (agent) in the three tournaments (three cells in a row). If an agent has similar color shades in the three cells, it means that the agent performs the same in the three tournament sessions of the game. For example, the top performer agent of C1 cluster in *Connect-4* game is *Agt_48*, each cell of each tournament session has intense light gray color.

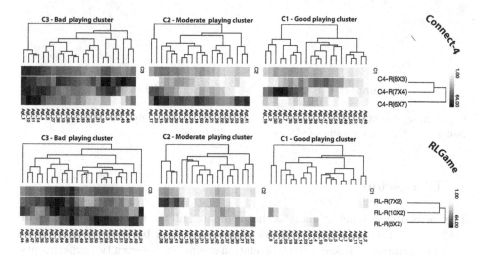

Fig. 4. *K-means* clustering for each tournament session of both games and a dendrogram representing the correlation of agents and tournament sessions

Figure 5 depicts the spatial allocation of each cluster, resulting from the *k-means* clustering (Fig. 4), associated to the average number of the agents' characteristic values (ϵ-γ-λ), respectively for each game (*Connect-4* and *RLGame*). The shapes in the graphs in Fig. 5 indicate the state-space complexity of the different tournament sessions of each game. The circles represent the high state-space complexities, triangles represent the medium state-space complexities and the squares represent the low state-space complexities respectively for each game. The colors of the shapes represent the C1, C2 and C3 clusters. In example, the black square in the left graph depicts the C3 cluster (bad playing agents) of the *Connect-4*'s lowest state space complexity, in a special allocation of the characteristic values (ϵ-γ-λ). This means that the bad playing agents of the *Connect-4*'s lowest complexity, seem to have low ϵ-greedy ($\epsilon \approx 0.68$), high lambda ($\lambda \approx 0.85$)

and medium gamma ($\gamma \approx 0.72$). If we associate these characteristic values with the playing behaviour descriptors of Table 5, we can say that a bad playing agent in a low complexity environment of the *Connect-4* game, seems to be an "exploiter", a "fast, unstable learner", which takes into account "medium-term strategies".

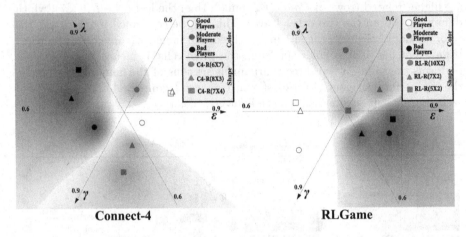

Connect-4   **RLGame**

Fig. 5. Spatial allocation of the cluster (C1, C2 and C3), associated to the characteristic values (ϵ-γ-λ), of both games (*Connect-4* and *RLGame*).

5   Discussion

The correlation coefficient analysis that compared all the tournament sessions of both games (Table 6) shows a high correlation coefficient between the three tournament sessions of *RLGame*. The correlation coefficient between two experiments (two different tournament sessions) presents the similarity or the differentiation of the agents' performances (agents with the same playing profile) in the studied experimental state spaces. *Connect-4's* tournament sessions show a quite good correlation between the two lower complexity state-spaces ($C4 - R(8 \times 3)$ and $C4 - R(7 \times 4)$), while the correlation of the higher complexity state space compared to the two lower complexity state-spaces of the Connect-4 appears to be neutral, with about 0 correlation coefficient ($C4 - R(8 \times 3)$ and $C4 - R(7 \times 4)$ correlation compared to $C4 - R(6 \times 7)$). An important highlight is that while the complexity of the *Connect-4* increases, the negative correlation between the *Connect-4's* and *RLGame's* tournament sessions decreases (third column and last three rows of Table 6). For example, the correlation between $C4-R(8\times3)$ and all *RLGame* tournament sessions show an average $\rho \approx -0.268$ and $\tau \approx -0.177$, while the correlation between the $C4 - R(6 \times 7)$ and all *RLGame* tournament sessions, shows an average $\rho \approx -0.191$ and $\tau \approx -0.128$, which is an increase of 4% for and 3% for correlations. This highlights that as the complexity level of *Connect-4* increases (referring to the $C4 - R(6 \times 7)$ variant), stronger positive correlation with all the tournament session of *RLGame* is observed, as both ρ and τ values increase from negative to 0. Generally in *RLGame*, agents with similar playing profiles behave in the same way as the state complexity of *RLGame* changes, while this is not the case for agents in *Connect-4*. We had originally reported that we attributed the differences in performance of agents of the same set-up to the different complexity of the *Connect-4* and *RLGame* games. This is further strengthened by the finding that a *Connect-4* variant of higher complexity is closer to *RLGame*.

The *k-means* clustering shows a higher correlation between the *RLGame* tournament sessions than the corresponding *Connect-4*'s tournament sessions, which is depicted by the heat-maps of Fig. 4 and supports the results of correlation coefficient analysis. The color shades (heat-maps) of the *RLGame* tournament sessions are more evenly allocated compared to the heat-maps of the *Connect-4* tournament sessions. The single most uneven color allocation of the *Connect-4*'s heat-maps appears in the C2 cluster, where one mostly finds moderate playing agents and highlights that almost all agents of this cluster played better in the two lower levels the *Connect-4* state-space complexity variants.

The special allocations of the clusters C1, C2 and C3 (for both games), associated with the characteristic values (ϵ-γ-λ) and the performance of the cluster, highlight an estimation of the synthetic agents' playing behaviors of each cluster, as shown in Fig. 5. For example, the good playing agents of the two lowest state-space complexities configurations of *Connect-4* game (C1 clusters of $C4 - R(8 \times 3)$ and $C4 - R(7 \times 4)$), tend to have high ϵ-greedy ($\epsilon \approx 0.81 \implies$ *knowledge exploiters*), medium lambda ($\lambda \approx 0.76 \implies$ *medium speed learner*) and small gamma ($\gamma \approx 0.69 \implies$ *risky (short term strategy selection)*). The two graphs of Fig. 5 highlight important differences in the agents' performance and playing behaviors based on the games and their complexity variations, such as:

- Good playing agents tend to be exploiters (high ϵ value) in *Connect-4*, in contrast to *RLGame*, where good playing agents tend to be explorers (low ϵ value), which is reasonable since *RLGame* is much more complex than *Connect-4* and the good playing agents respond to the environment, thus shifting towards becoming knowledge explorers.
- Bad playing agents are associated with low ϵ values in *Connect-4* and high ϵ values in *RLGame*, which is exactly the opposite to the good playing agents in both games.
- Moderate playing agents are scattered in both graphs (both games) and their playing behaviors is not clear.

It is clear that the performance of the agents depends on the game and on its complexity level. Due to the higher complexity level of the *RLGame*, the good playing agents need to be more sophisticated (more knowledge explorers, slow and smooth learners and focusing on longer term strategies), which is not surprising if one aims at a more realistic simulation of playing behavior.

Each good playing agents' cluster changes its characteristic values (ϵ-γ-λ), only by slight shifting (as in Fig. 5), as the complexity of the game increases.

By observing the C1 clusters of the two lower complexity tournament sessions of both games ($C4 - R(8 \times 3)$ and $C4 - R(7 \times 4)$ for *Connect-4*, $RL - R(5 \times 2)$ and $RL - R(7 \times 2)$ for *RLGame*), we highlight that they have similar playing characteristic (ϵ-γ-λ) values (the white triangles and squares are allocated to almost the same part, respectively, of each graph in Fig. 5). The C1 cluster (white circle in left graph of Fig. 5) of *Connect-4*'s highest complexity tournament session ($C4 - R(6 \times 7)$) shows a slight shifting in comparison to the C1 clusters of the lower complexity tournament sessions ($C4 - R(8 \times 3)$ and $C4 - R(7 \times 4)$). We observe a shifting of about -12% for ϵ, -2% for λ and +8% for γ.

The C1 cluster (white circle in right graph of Fig. 5) of the *RLGame*'s highest complexity tournament session ($RL - R(10 \times 2)$), shows a similar slight sifting, in comparison to the C1 clusters of the lower complexity tournament sessions ($RL - R(5 \times 2)$ and $RL - R(7 \times 2)$). A shifting of about -2% for ϵ, -7% for λ and $+3\%$ for γ is observed.

Such shifting of the ϵ, γ and λ values indicates that as the complexity of the environment increases (environments of *Connect-4* and *RLGame*), good playing agents tend to become more sophisticated (*more knowledge explorers, more slow and smoother learners and focused in longer-term strategies*). The largest shifting appears in the C2 clusters (moderate playing agents) of both games' all complexity levels, which indicates that the moderate playing agents are hard to classify based on their characteristic values (ϵ-γ-λ). The C3 clusters of the *Connect-4* seem to be more affected by low ϵ values, while the C3 clusters of the *RLGame* seem to be more affected by high ϵ values.

6   Conclusion and Future Directions

Based on the outcomes of the experimental tournament sessions, which spanned three different complexity levels for each game, *Connect-4* and *RLGame*, where we used the same agents' playing profile setups (same characteristic values ϵ-γ-λ), we highlighted that an agents' playing profile does not readily lead to a comparable performance when the complexity of the environment (game) changes.

If an agent focuses on a specific performance level, in environments of varying complexity, its playing profile (characteristic values ϵ-γ-λ) has to be re-adapted along specific directions based on the environment complexity. Our findings suggest that, as complexity increases (from *Connect-4* to *RLGame* and from a low-complexity *RLGame* variant to a higher complexity one), an agent stands a better chance of maintaining its performance profile (as indicated by its ranking), by decreasing its ϵ and λ values and increasing its γ one (though, of course, the exact change ratios may be too elusive to define). For this reason, we state that the re-adaptation of the agents' characteristic values depends on the game and its complexity but, broadly speaking, we note that as the complexity of the environment increases, good playing agents have to be more sophisticated: increasing their knowledge exploration bias (lower ϵ values), becoming slower and smoother learners (lower λ values) and focusing on longer term strategies (higher γ values). These findings are corroborated by the experimental sessions of both games, *Connect-4* and *RLGame* and it appears that an agent with a given ϵ-γ-λ profile cannot expect to maintain its performance profile if the environment changes with respect to the underlying complexity. Experimenting with a *Connect-4* variant of large $n \times m$ dimensions and maybe extending *Connect-4* to *Connect-k* could eventually shift the association with *RLGame* to larger positive values, thus further strengthening the validity of our findings.

The experimental results of this paper highlight that synthetic agents are important elements of the simulation of realistic social environments and that just a handful of characteristic values (ϵ-γ-λ), namely, the exploitation-vs-exploration trade-off, learning backup and discount rates, and speed of learning, can synthesize a diverse population of agents with starkly different learning and playing behaviors.

An apparently promising and interesting investigation direction concerns the synthetic agents' application to other games (better known ones) and other complexity levels, such as checkers, chess etc., to investigate the learning progress of the synthetic agents' and the adjustability of their playing behaviors in diverse social environments. Additionally, as we highlighted that a synthetic agent's playing behavior may have to change in response to a change in the environment's complexity, this raises the generic question of how to modify one's characteristic values (ϵ-γ-λ) based on an assessment of the surrounding environment. Such an assessment could be based either on the complexity of the environment or on the level of the opponent but both approaches involve making an estimation based on limited information (for example, a limited number of games against some opponents should be able to help an agent to gauge whether it operates in a complex or simple environment or where its opponents might be situated in terms of their values in the ϵ-γ-λ parameters). Thus, adapting oneself based on incomplete and possibly partially accurate information is a huge challenge.

References

1. Ferber, J., Gutknecht, O., Michel, F.: From agents to organizations: an organizational view of multi-agent systems. In: Giorgini, P., Müller, J.P., Odell, J. (eds.) AOSE 2003. LNCS, vol. 2935, pp. 214–230. Springer, Heidelberg (2004). https://doi.org/10.1007/978-3-540-24620-6_15
2. Shoham, Y., Leyton-Brown, K.: Multiagent Systems: Algorithmic, Game-Theoretic, and Logical Foundations. Cambridge University Press, Cambridge (2008)
3. Wooldridge, M.: An Introduction to MultiAgent Systems, 2nd edn. Wiley Publishing, Hoboken (2009)
4. Ferber, J.: Multi-Agent Systems: An Introduction to Distributed Artificial Intelligence. Addison-Wesley/Longman Publishing, Boston/Harlow (1999)
5. Kiourt, C., Kalles, D.: Synthetic learning agents in game-playing social environments. Adapt. Behav. **24**(6), 411–427 (2016)
6. Marom, Y., Maistros, G., Hayes, G.: Experiments with a social learning model. Adapt. Behav. **9**(3–4), 209–240 (2001)
7. Al-Khateeb, B., Kendall, G.: Introducing a round robin tournament into evolutionary individual and social learning checkers. In: Proceedings of the Developments in E-systems Engineering (DeSE), pp. 294–299 (2011)

8. Caballero, A., Botía, J., Gómez-Skarmeta, A.: Using cognitive agents in social simulations. Eng. Appl. Artif. Intell. **24**, 1098–1109 (2011)
9. Gilbert, N., Troitzsch, K.G.: Simulation for the Social Scientist. Open University Press, Buckingham (2005)
10. Kiourt, C., Kalles, D.: Using opponent models to train inexperienced synthetic agents in social environments. In: Proceedings of the 2016 IEEE Conference on Computational Intelligence and Games (CIG), pp. 1–4 (2016)
11. Kiourt, C., Kalles, D.: Learning in multi agent social environments with opponent models. In: Rovatsos, M., Vouros, G., Julian, V. (eds.) EUMAS/AT -2015. LNCS (LNAI), vol. 9571, pp. 137–144. Springer, Cham (2016). https://doi.org/10.1007/978-3-319-33509-4_12
12. Allis, L. V.: Knowledge-based approach of connect four: The game is over, white to move wins. Master's thesis, Vrije Universiteit (1988)
13. Allis, L. V.: Searching for Solutions in Games and Artificial Intelligence. PhD thesis, Maastricht University (1994)
14. van den Herik, H., Uiterwijk, J.W., van Rijswijck, J.: Games solved: now and in the future. Artif. Intell. **134**(1), 277–311 (2002)
15. Heule, M., Rothkrantz, L.: Solving games. Sci. Comput. Program. **67**(1), 105–124 (2007)
16. Edelkamp, S., Kissmann, P.: Symbolic classification of general two-player games. In: Dengel, A.R., Berns, K., Breuel, T.M., Bomarius, F., Roth-Berghofer, T.R. (eds.) KI 2008. LNCS (LNAI), vol. 5243, pp. 185–192. Springer, Heidelberg (2008). https://doi.org/10.1007/978-3-540-85845-4_23
17. Kalles, D., Kanellopoulos, P.: On verifying game designs and playing strategies using reinforcement learning. In: Proceedings of the 2001 ACM Symposium on Applied Computing (SAC), pp. 6–11 (2001)
18. Tesauro, G.: Practical issues in temporal difference learning. Mach. Learn. **8**, 257–277 (1992)
19. Tesauro, G.: Temporal difference learning and TD-Gammon. Commun. ACM **38**, 58–68 (1995)
20. Sutton, R.S., Barto, A.G.: Introduction to Reinforcement Learning. MIT Press, Cambridge (1998)
21. March, J.G.: Exploration and exploitation in organizational learning. Organ. Sci. **2**, 71–87 (1991)
22. Tromp, J.: Solving connect-4 on medium board sizes. ICGA J. **31**(1), 110–112 (2008)
23. Tromp, J.: John's connect four playground. https://tromp.github.io/c4/c4.html. Accessed 27 Oct 2017
24. Sutton, R.S.: Learning to predict by the methods of temporal differences. Mach. Learn. **3**, 9–44 (1988)
25. Wiering, M. A., Patist, J. P., Mannen, H.: Learning to play board games using temporal difference methods. Technical report: UU-CS-2005-048 (2005)
26. Kiourt, C., Pavlidis, G., Kalles, D.: Reskill: relative skill-level calculation system. In: Proceedings of the 9th Hellenic Conference on Artificial Intelligence (SETN), pp. 39:1–39:4 (2016)
27. Spearman, C.: The proof and measurement of association between two things. Am. J. Psychol. **15**(1), 70–101 (1904)
28. Kendall, M.: A new measure of rank correlation. Biometrica **30**(1–2), 81–93 (1936)
29. Langville, N., Meyer, C.: Who's #1?: The Science of Rating and Ranking. Princeton University Press, Princeton (2012)

Rational Coordination in Games with Enriched Representations

Valentin Goranko[1,2(✉)], Antti Kuusisto[3], and Raine Rönnholm[4(✉)]

[1] Stockholm University, Stockholm, Sweden
valentin.goranko@philosophy.su.se
[2] University of Johannesburg, Johannesburg, South Africa
[3] University of Bremen, Bremen, Germany
kuusisto@uni-bremen.de
[4] University of Tampere, Tampere, Finland
raine.ronnholm@uta.fi

Abstract. We consider pure win-lose coordination games where the representation of the game structure has additional features that are commonly known to the players, such as colouring, naming, or ordering of the available choices or of the players. We study how the information provided by such enriched representations affects the solvability of these games by means of principles of rational reasoning in coordination scenarios with no prior communication or conventions.

1 Introduction

Pure win-lose coordination games (WLC games) ([2]) are strategic form games in which all players receive the same payoffs, either 1 (*win*) or 0 (*lose*), and thus all players have the same preference, viz. to coordinate on any winning outcome.

This paper is a sequel to [2] (see also the extended version [3]), where we identified a hierarchy of principles of reasoning that rational players may apply in WLC games when they cannot use preplay communication and do not share any previously agreed-upon conventions. Additionally, [2] also provides a comparative analysis of the classes of WLC games that can be solved by applying such rational principles.

Here we consider WLC games with representation models enriched with additional relations on the choices or players. The additional structure is assumed to be commonly known by the players. For example, unary relations over the choices—interpreted as a labelling or colouring—can be used by the players to select choices. Also, an ordering (partial or total) is a natural example of a binary relation over the choices of players that can provide information which the players can use for their common benefit. We also consider representations with orderings of the *players* which intuitively correspond to priority orders in hierarchical systems of agents. The main research question of this study is to analyse

---

[2]Valentin Goranko—Visiting Professorship

F. Belardinelli and E. Argente (Eds.): EUMAS 2017/AT 2017, LNAI 10767, pp. 323–338, 2018.
https://doi.org/10.1007/978-3-030-01713-2_23

how the additional information provided by such enriched representations affects the solvability of these games by means of rational reasoning only.

As in [2], we assume that the players are rational and commonly believe to pursue the same goal (to coordinate). Futhermore, we assume that the full structure of the game is represented to all the players and is commonly known to them. As we will show in Sect. 4.5, the extra information provided by the additional relations can be either useful or detrimental for the players, and this depends not only on the content of that information but also on the reasoning principles which we assume the players to follow.

Typically, the additional representation structure can be useful to the players by creating *salient features* of the game and *focal points* amongst the winning profiles, or it can gradually establish *conventions* amongst the players. Thus, the present work is related, at least in spirit, to previous studies on focal points and conventions, originating from Schelling [6] and Lewis [4] and further developed in the context of coordination games in, e.g., [5,7,8]. However, the relation with that (and other) previous work on coordination and conventions is mainly conceptual, whereas both the technical framework introduced in [2] and expanded here, and the study of the effect of enriched representations of coordination games in that framework are, to the best of our knowledge, our original contributions. Some related considerations regarding symmetries in coordination games, in a technically different framework have been investigated in [1].

In the present work we only consider single-round coordination games and do not assume any preplay communication. Repeated coordination games are studied in a follow-up work. We do not discuss the use of *conventions*, either, which is a topic of another follow-up work. We only note that, in the context of single-round coordination games studied here, we regard conventions as principles of coordination that are not likely to be adopted by all players through their individual rational reasoning only, but can be explicitly agreed upon in preplay communication. Lewis [4] is a seminal study of a somewhat different concept of conventions that are gradually emerging principles of coordination adopted by the players in the process of repeated coordination attempts.

2   Preliminaries

2.1   Basic Definitions and Notation

We begin with the definition of win-lose coordination games. As in [2] we define them as *relational structures*, which is technically convenient for our study.

Definition 1 ([2]). *An n-player **win-lose coordination game** (WLC game) is a relational structure $G = (A, C_1, \ldots, C_n, W_G)$ where A is a finite domain of **choices**, each $C_i \neq \emptyset$ is a unary predicate, representing the choices of player i, $C_1 \cup \cdots \cup C_n = A$, and W_G is an n-ary relation such that $W_G \subseteq C_1 \times \cdots \times C_n$. Here we also assume, for technical convenience, that the players have pairwise disjoint choice sets, i.e., $C_i \cap C_j = \emptyset$ for every $i, j \leq n$ such that $i \neq j$. A tuple $\sigma \in C_1 \times \cdots \times C_n$ is called a **choice profile** for G and the choice profiles in W_G are called **winning profiles**.*

We use the following terminology for a WLC game $G = (A, C_1, \ldots, C_n, W_G)$.

- For every choice $c \in C_i$ of a player i, the **winning extension of** c **in** G is the set $W_G^i(c)$ of all tuples $\tau \in C_1 \times \cdots \times C_{i-1} \times C_{i+1} \times \cdots \times C_n$ such that the choice profile obtained from τ by adding c to the i-th position is winning.
- A choice $c \in C_i$ of a player i is **(surely) winning** /respectively **(surely) losing**/ if it is guaranteed to produce a winning /respectively losing/ choice profile regardless of what choices the other player(s) make.

The n-ary winning relation W_G of an n-player WLC game G defines a *hypergraph* on the set of all choices. We give visual presentations of hypergraphs corresponding to WLC games as follows. The choices of each player are displayed as columns of nodes, starting from the choices of player 1 on the left and ending with the column with choices of player n. The winning relation consists of lines that represent the winning profiles. This kind of graphical presentation of a WLC game G will be called a *game graph (drawing) of* G.

Example 1. *([2]).* Here are two examples of WLC games: a 2-player game G_Σ with 2 choices for player 1 (left) and 3 choices for player 2 (right), and a total of 4 winning profiles; and a 3-player WLC game G^* also with 4 winning profiles, each represented as a triple of choices connected by (solid or dotted) lines.

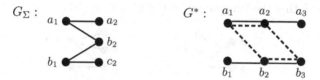

We now introduce a uniform notation for certain classes of WLC games. See the picture below for examples (and [2] for more of them). Let $k_1, \ldots, k_n \in \mathbb{N}$.

- $G(k_1 \times \cdots \times k_n)$ is the n-player WLC game where the player i has k_i choices and the winning relation is the *universal relation* $C_1 \times \cdots \times C_n$.
- Suppose that $G(A)$ and $G(B)$ have been defined and both have the same number of players. Then $G(A + B)$ is the *disjoint union* of $G(A)$ and $G(B)$, i.e., the game obtained by assigning to each player a disjoint union of her/his choices in $G(A)$ and $G(B)$, and where the winning relation for $G(A + B)$ is the union of the winning relations in $G(A)$ and $G(B)$.
- Let $m \in \mathbb{N}$. Then $G(mA) := G(A + \cdots + A)$ (m times).

$$G(2 \times 3) \qquad G(1 \times 1 + 2 \times 2) \qquad G(3(1 \times 1 \times 1))$$

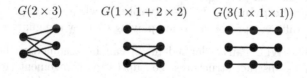

2.2 Symmetries of WLC Games and Structural Principles

As discussed in [2], in the case of no preplay communication and no conventions the choices of rational players should be independent of the names of the choices in the game and of any ordering (or naming) of the players. That is, rational principles of reasoning and choice in that setup should only take the 'structural properties' of the game into account. For defining this more precisely, we introduce the following notions:

- A **choice renaming** between G and G' is an isomorphism $G \to G'$.
- A **player renaming** between G and G' is any permutation β of the players names (indices) such that G' is obtained by applying β to the components of the winning relation of G.
- A **full renaming** between G and G' is a combination of choice renaming and player renaming. We say that G and G' are **structurally equivalent** if there is a full renaming between them.

For formal definition of these notions, see [2]. However, the following example should suffice for understanding the intuition behind these notions.

Example 2. The following WLC games G and G' are structurally equivalent. Indeed, the game G' is obtained from G by renaming (swapping) the players and then permuting the two choices of the player on the left.

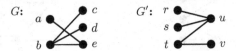

A **protocol** is a mapping Σ that assigns to every pair (G, i), where G is a WLC game and i is a player in G, a nonempty set $\Sigma(G, i) \subseteq C_i$ of choices of i. Thus, a protocol gives a global nondeterministic strategy for playing any WLC game in the role of any player. Intuitively, a protocol represents a global mode of acting in any situation that involves playing WLC games. Hence, protocols can be informally regarded as global "reasoning styles" or "behaviour modes". We say that a protocol Σ is **structural** if it is "indifferent with respect to full renamings" (see [2] for the formal definition). Clearly, structural protocols must be generally non-deterministic in order to treat symmetric choices equally.

A **(structural) principle** of reasoning in WLC games is a set of (structural) protocols and therefore principles can be seen as properties of protocols. We say that a player **follows a principle P** if she uses a protocol from P. A WLC game G is **solved by the principle P** (**P-solvable**) if, whenever all players follow P (with possibly different protocols) when playing G, they are guaranteed to win.

Remark. The WLC games defined in [2] can be assumed to be presented to each player as abstract structures, i.e., up to re-arrangement (renaming) of the players and their choices. Thus, the names and the possible ordering of the choices and players are only known and used by each player privately, but are not shared amongst the players, so common knowledge of the names (or ordering) cannot be used in the players' reasoning. One main objective of the present work is to investigate the effect of having some of these features commonly known to the players.

3   WLC Games with Enriched Representations

Now we will consider WLC games with representations enriched with additional relations on choices and players.

3.1   Enriched WLC Games with Choice Colouring and Ordering

Definition 2. *An **enriched** WLCgame is any WLC game G (defined as in Definition 1) expanded with interpretations of some additional relational symbols in the domain of choices of G. More precisely, if G is a WLC game and $\Phi = \{R_1, \ldots, R_k\}$ is a set of relation symbols, a Φ-**enrichment** of G is any enriched WLC game G^Φ, defined exactly as G except that all symbols in Φ are assigned interpretations (relations with matching arities) in the domain of choices of G. Formally, if $G = (A, C_1, \ldots, C_n, W_G)$, then G^Φ is of the type $(A, C_1, \ldots, C_n, R_1^A, \ldots, R_k^A, W_G)$, where $R_1^A, \ldots, R_k^A$ are relations on A assigned as respective interpretations of the symbols $R_1, \ldots, R_k$.*

Note that the enrichment of a WLC game affects only the (commonly given) representation of the game, not the underlying structure involving the winning relation and the choice sets C_i.

The notions of renaming from the previous section can be defined likewise for enriched WLC games. The additional structure given by the relations interpreting Φ adds extra requirements for the isomorphisms (in particular, automorphisms) on enriched WLC games, thus making these games 'more rigid' and therefore eliminates some choice and player renamings. This could be seen as an advantage for the players, since it enables more structural principles which they can use. However, as we will show further, the enrichment of the game model can also be disadvantageous for the players depending, inter alia, on the (rational) principles of reasoning they are following.

A unary relation $R \in \Phi$ can be regarded as a **colouring** on the set of choices of each player, thus splitting the choice of the game into R-*coloured choices* and *non-R-coloured choices*. WLC games enriched with one or more colours will be called **coloured WLC games**[1]. As a simple example, consider a scenario where each of several people is going to buy a piece of clothing as a present for a common friend (say, who just lost all her clothes in a fire). Suppose they do not know what the others will buy and cannot communicate on that before they

---

[1] Note that the notion of 'colour' is used metaphorically, rather than literally here, because we assume that a choice may have several colours, or none at all. Thus, the notion of colour used here is more in line with its traditional use in logic, not in graph theory. In particular, every choice of every player is associated with a (possibly empty) set of colours, called further 'colour type', rather than a single colour.

make their choices. Then, it would be natural that each person chooses an item in a neutral colour, say black or white, which is more likely to match the choices of the others. On the other hand, if they would have had the knowledge that their friend has a clear colour preference, say for purple clothes, then each of them would naturally choose something in purple – which could have a good or bad overall effect, depending on the concrete choices, but would at least ensure colour matching of the presents.

A special case of a colouring is **naming** of choices, when (formally) the interpretation of the unary relation R intersects each player's choice set in at most a singleton, and thus R serves as a name of that single choice (if any) of each player. We assume the names are commonly known and can be used by the players for coordination. For instance, consider the coordination problem of several people who are to meet somewhere in a completely unknown to them city without being able to communicate before the meeting, but each of them is given a map (the same for all) on which several possible meeting places are indicated, but only one of them – say the central square – is named on the map. That would immediately create a unique *focal point* that would naturally be chosen by all as the expected meeting place. Or, consider the common situation of two cars approaching each other on a narrow road. Using a simple convention or preplay communication, they can easily coordinate by each using an action choice with a commonly shared name, like '(swerve to the) Right' or '(swerve to the) Left'. On the other hand, if all players have to coordinate by choosing the same choice but they cannot refer by (commonly known) names to their choices, and if some players have two or more commonly available choices that create a 'bad symmetry', then the players will not be able to reach a guaranteed coordination, even with preplay communication.

An important particular case is when all players have the same number of choices, which are named by the same set of names (unary symbols). Then one can think that all players share the same set of choices[2]. The class of so enriched WLC games will be called WLC **games with shared choices**. Many 'real life' coordination games fall in this class. A typical example is when two or more persons are to meet somewhere in the city, and they have several commonly known to them choices of places but have not been able to communicate and decide on any of them. A variant of that is the coordination problem of meeting of all persons at a given place but at a time (hour or day) which has not been agreed upon in advance.

Another natural enrichment of WLC games is provided by a binary relation $R \in \Phi$ that defines a partial (pre-)order on the set of choices of each player. Such games are called WLC **games with partial choice (pre-)ordering**; when the (pre-)order is total (linear), we call them WLC **games with (total) choice (pre-)ordering**. Note, that WLC games with choice ordering and the same number of choices for each player could also be interpreted as games with shared

---

[2] Even though the sets of players' choices are formally pairwise disjoint by definition, common names for all choices would establish a natural 1-1 correspondence between the choices in the different players' sets.

choices, as in this case the ordinal numbers of each player's choices in the ordering can serve as shared names of these choices ('1st choice', '2nd choice', etc.).

When considering 'real life' coordination scenarios, there are several ways how a natural ordering of choices can arise, for instance:

(1) Certain choices can be easier to execute than others (taking more time or effort) or otherwise preferable by the players.
(2) An ordering can arise from spacial or otherwise comparable properties of different choices, e.g. by them being displayed in an order from left to right, or by physical size, weight, distance, etc.

In a setting similar to scenario (1) above, it is quite natural to assume that players would prefer the first choices in the ordering when trying to coordinate. However, in a setting similar to (2), it is not so clear whether players would prefer the first or last choices in the ordering. In reality that may depend, for instance, on whether the agent's native language uses left-to-right or right-to-left writing. We will get back to this point in the next section where we consider rational principles in enriched WLC games.

We will use a graphical presentation for game graphs of enriched WLC games with colouring(s) and/or an ordering of choices as follows.

– Each unary relation symbol is associated with a colour (or a pattern). The nodes in the game graph are then displayed with the corresponding colours.
– When there is an ordering of choices, each player's choices are displayed in ascending order from top to bottom. We may also display a numbering on the side of the game graph to indicate that the choices in the game are ordered.

3.2 WLC Games with Ordering of Players

In many real agents' groups there is a natural hierarchy or priority order amongst the agents, which gives higher priority to the choices of the 'superior' agents over those of her 'inferior' ones. A typical example is a coordination problem in a military or other hierarchical organisation. When solving such coordination problems the agents are naturally assumed to respect that hierarchy in their considerations and decisions. For instance, if an employee and his boss are supposed to meet at a given time, but the place is not specified in advance, then the boss' office would be the natural common choice.

Formally, WLC games can be enriched with a commonly known (linear) ordering of the players, which can be used by them for coordination. The enrichments of WLC games with ordering of the players will be called WLC **games with player ordering**. This could be further generalized to partial orderings or pre-orderings of players, but we leave the analysis of these for a future work.

Remark. The ordering of the players is, in fact, implicitly included in the definition of standard WLC games in [2], but that is only for the sake of the formal definition. In that basic setup we do not assume this ordering to be common knowledge amongst the players and thus they cannot use it in their reasoning. Thus, in the setup of [2], when players are using structural protocols they cannot use that ordering, and that is why these protocols must prescribe sets of choices that are invariant under player renamings.

Now, an enrichment of a WLC game G with players ordering can be practically obtained simply by making the players ordering from its definition commonly accessible to the players, and therefore by relaxing the condition prescribing that structural protocols must be invariant under player renamings. More precisely, let P be a structural principle (cf. [2]). If we want to consider P in a setting where the ordering of the players is commonly known and can be used by the players, we can do that technically as follows: we consider a principle P' which is defined exactly as P, with the only difference being that P' may contain protocols which are not invariant under player renamings.

4   Principles of Rational Choice in Enriched WLC Games

In [2] we define and study a hierarchy of rational principles of reasoning in WLC games, some of which we discuss and list briefly here for the reader's convenience (see the precise definitions in [2]). First, some principles of basic rationality:

Non-losing principle (NL): Never play a losing choice, if possible.
Sure winning principle (SW): Always play a winning choice, if possible.
Individually rational choices (IRC): Never play a weakly dominated choice.
Collective rational choices (CRC): Assume that everyone follows IRC.

In [2] we have also defined *symmetry based principles* which use the renamings defined in Sect. 2.2. for lack of space, we only give here the intuition behind these principles via examples. First, consider the game $G(2(1 \times 2) + (1 \times 1))$. Here the choices with out-degree 2 are automorphic, so Player 1 should be 'indifferent' between them. Likewise, Player 2 should be indifferent between all of her choices in the subgames $G(1 \times 2)$. If players select their choices from these subgames, winning is not guaranteed and we say that these choices generate a *bad choice symmetry*. The principle of **Elimination of bad choice symmetries (ECS)** prescribes such choices to be avoided, if possible. Hence, following ECS, both players select from within the subgame $G(1 \times 1)$ and thus successfully coordinate.

Now, consider the game $G(1 \times 2 + 2 \times 1 + 1 \times 1)$. Here there is a full renaming of the game which relates the choices of players between $G(1 \times 2)$ and $G(2 \times 1)$. Therefore, if Player 1 has some (rational) reason to select a choice with out-degree 2, then Player 2 should have the same reason to select the choice with in-degree 2. Since they would fail to coordinate this way, we say that these choices generate a *bad player symmetry*. The same holds for the two other choices in these subgames. The principle of **Elimination of bad player symmetries (EPS)** prescribes to the players to avoid such choices, if possible. The principle of **Elimination of bad symmetries (ES)** combines EPS and EPS.

We now look at the applications of those principles in enriched WLC games, beginning with the following observation which follows directly from definitions.

Proposition 1. *Every rationality principle* P *presented in [2], except for the symmetry principles (ECS, EPS and ES), has the same strength with respect to enriched* WLC *games. That is, any* WLC *game* G *is solved by* P *iff any enriched game* G^Φ *is solved by* P, *for any* Φ. *Furthermore, adding the ordering of players to* G^Φ *does not affect the strength of these principles.*

In particular, the rationality principle from standard game theory, prescribing iterated elimination of dominated choices (using CRC), does not give anything more—or less—for enriched games, unless combined with other principles which we discuss further. Let us now consider the extensions of the symmetry principles. For any P $\in$ {ECS, EPS, ES} we make the following observations:

- P can be used in enriched WLC games, just like in the standard WLC games, but the actual definition of P depends on the definitions of renamings.
- Some P-unsolvable WLC games become P-solvable when the game is suitably enriched. For example, the game $G(3(1 \times 1))$ becomes P-solvable when a same color is given for a single pair of choices that are winning. (Recall the example with the map of possible meeting places, of which only one is named.) This is because then the uncoloured subgame $G(2(1 \times 1))$ becomes eliminated due to a bad symmetry (so, the players do not consider anymore playing there).
- For any nontrivial (e.g., not solvable by NL) WLC game G that is P-solvable, there is an enriched game G^Φ which is not P-solvable, obtained by adding colouring in a such way as to eliminate any non-trivial renamings.
- We also note that the ordering of players makes EPS completely unusable, but does not effect ECS, so the principle ES becomes equivalent with ECS.

4.1   Principles of Rational Choice in Coloured WLC Games

Enrichments of WLC games give rise to a range of new principles, with varying degrees of rationality. We give here a representative selection.

Let G^Φ be a coloured WLC game and let $\Psi \subseteq \Phi$ be the set of all *unary* predicate symbols ('colours') in Φ. Now every subset of Ψ (incl. $\emptyset$) forms a **colour type** in G^Φ and two choices c and c' are said to have the same colour type if the same predicates from Ψ hold of each of them. Thus, colour types form a partition on the choices in G^Φ, generating a respective equivalence relation there (and play the same role as vertex colours in graph theory). If $|\Psi| = n$, there are *at most* 2^n different colour types, and corresponding equivalence classes, in G^Φ.

The following principle can be naturally applied to coloured WLC games.

Colour matching principle (CM): If there is a unique colour type whose choices guarantee a win, choose from that colour type.

To 'guarantee a win' here means that if all players pick, no matter how, their choices from that colour type, they will win.

For example, *structurally unsolvable*[3] WLC games like $G(3(1 \times 1 \times 1))$, G_O and $G(2(2 \times 2))$ can become CM-solvable by adding a suitable colourings using

---

[3] Intuitively, structurally unsolvable WLC games are those that cannot solved by *any* structural principle. For a precise definition, see [2] where we give a complete characterisation of such games.

a single colour, 'white' (the non-coloured choices are indicated in black and the superscript[1] indicates an enrichment with one colour). See these coloured versions on Fig. 1.

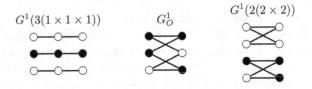

$G^1(3(1 \times 1 \times 1))$ G_O^1 $G^1(2(2 \times 2))$

Fig. 1. Some examples of CM-solvable coloured WLC games.

Note that *almost every* WLC game with a non-empty winning relation can become CM-solvable by adding just one colour and colouring a suitable single winning tuple. However, this does not work with the game $G(2(1 \times 1))$, because any such colouring here creates a complete symmetry between the coloured and the un-coloured winning pair. (But one could argue that a single colour would still suffice, as colouring just 1 (or 3) of the 4 choices would break this symmetry. See further an extension of the principle CM that covers this case.)

The principle CM is a particular case of a more general type of rational reasoning, as follows. Given a coloured WLC game G, consider each colour – or, more generally, each colour type C – as defining a subgame, denoted $G_{|C}$, of G, obtained as a restriction of G to the choices having the colour type C. Thus, a family of at most 2^n such subgames, hereafter called for short **monochrome subgames**, arises in a coloured WLC game with n colours. Now, the players can naturally consider each of these monochrome subgames on their own and try to coordinate on it. If they can coordinate in *exactly one* of these subgames by applying some (rational) principle P (e.g. the ones described in [2]), then they could focus on that subgame and use that solution for the entire game. Thus, a natural generalisation of CM (in which exactly one monochrome subgame has a complete winning relation), parameterised with a given underlying (rational) principle P, can be formulated as follows.

Generalised colour matching principle (GCM^P):
If there is a unique colour type C in the game G such that the monochrome subgame $G_{|C}$ is P-solvable, then select a choice according to the principle P applied to $G_{|C}$.

What if the players can coordinate by applying P in *more than one* of the monochrome subgames of G? It is then possible (but not necessary) that the choices prescribed by P in these subgames of G can be combined in a surely winning way. This leads to a further generalisation of GCM^P formulated as follows. Let G^P be the union of all monochromatic games which P solves. If P also solves G^P, then the players make their choices by applying P in G^P.

For example, consider the coloured games on Fig. 2. (For technical reasons, we represent the different colour types here by white, black, and different shades of grey.) In the game G_1^1, only the 'white' monochrome game is solvable by applying NL and thus G_1^1 is GCM^{NL}-solvable. Likewise G_2^1 is GCM^{SW}-solvable as only the 'black' monochrome game is SW-solvable. In the 2-coloured game G_3^2, the only (rationally) solvable monochrome subgame, again by applying SW, is the one indicated in dark grey. In G_4^2, by applying the Basic individual rationality principle BIR (the combination of SW and NL), there are two solvable monochrome subgames, the 'black' one and the 'grey' one, so the principle GCM^{BIR} does not solve the game. But note that there is a solution by applying BIR for the generalised colour type combining both, i.e. in the subgame $G_4^2 \,|_{bg}$ restricted to the black and grey colour types, pictured to the right of G_4^2. Thus, one can argue that G_4^2 is solvable by the generalised version of GCM^{BIR}, as described above. Note also that the colourless versions of G_1^1, G_2^1, G_3^2 and G_4^2 are not solvable by any of the principles defined in [2].

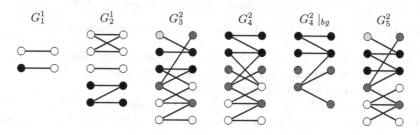

Fig. 2. Some examples of GCM^{P}-solvable coloured WLC games.

In the game G_5^2 (Fig. 2), each of the 'black', 'white' and 'dark grey' subgames are all SW-solvable. But since their solutions are not pairwise compatible, it is not clear which of them should be preferred by the players in order to coordinate. There is also a different type of coordination problem related to the principle GCM^{P}: Since GCM^{P} is defined with respect to some (rational) principle P, it is possible that a WLC game G is solvable with both GCM$^{\mathrm{P_1}}$ and GCM$^{\mathrm{P_2}}$, but these solutions are not compatible. This creates a *higher-order coordination* problem about making the choice between the principles P_1 and P_2. (The same problem arises even in WLC games with plain representation, studied in [2].)

The coordination principles based on colourings presented so far can be extended even further. Consider, e.g., coloured versions of the game $G(3(1 \times 1))$ with the following colourings of the pairs of winning choices:

(1) (red, red), $(red, blue)$, $(blue, blue)$;
(2) $(red, blue)$, $(green, green)$, $(green, green)$.

Neither of these games can be solved with the principles presented in this Subsect. 4.1, but they clearly suggest new principles that consider not just monochrome subgames, but also subgames with different colouring patterns (like, the 'red-blue' subgame). Since such new principles are generally not compatible with the ones we have presented here, further higher-order coordination prob-

lems amongst them arise. These issues we will be consider further in an extended
version of this paper.

4.2   Principles of Rational Choice in WLC Games with Choice Ordering

When considering WLC games with choice ordering, one can talk about **order-matching choice profiles**, each consisting of choices that have the same ordinal
position in each player's ordering. Thus, the matching choice profiles can natu-
rally be ordered with orderings of the choices of each player (the first one being
the choice profile which has the first choice in the ordering of each player).

The following principle naturally arises in WLC games with a choice ordering.

Choice order-matching principle (COM):
Play the least order-matching choice profile that is winning, if there is any.

For example, consider the WLC games with choice ordering on Fig. 3.

- The WLC game G_1, enriching the structurally unsolvable game $G(3(1 \times 1 \times 1))$ with choice ordering, is COM-solvable and the least winning choice is 1
  because (1,1,1) is a winning choice profile.
- The WLC game with choice ordering G_2 is COM-solvable, prescribing to both
  players the least winning choice 3, because (3,3) is a winning choice profile,
  while (1,1) and (2,2) are not.
- The WLC game with choice ordering G_3 is not COM-solvable, though it is
  solvable by the principle of Collective Rational Choices (CRC).

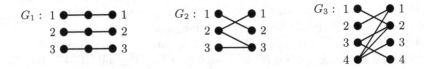

Fig. 3. Some examples of COM-solvable WLC games with choice ordering.

As we have noted at the end of Sect. 3.1, the ordering of choices can arise in
different ways. In the coordination scenario of type (1), described there, COM
seems a rather rational principle to follow. If the ordering presents players' preferences then, by following COM, players are looking for a winning choice profile
which is "equally preferable to all players" and, under this condition, "as preferable for everyone as it can be".

However, in a scenario of type (2) (in Sect. 3.1) it is harder to justify why the
first choices in the ordering should be preferred over the last ones in the ordering.
If, for instance, the ordering arises from a linear ordering of choices from left to
right, then (assuming no conventions) there is no clear reason to prefer either

the leftmost or the rightmost choice. And, in a situation where choosing the first or the last choice in the ordering could be considered *equally rational*, one could even argue that the most rational compromise would be to select the middle choice in the ordering, if there is a winning middle choice.

4.3 Principles of Rational Choice in WLC Games with Player Ordering

If a WLC game is enriched with a commonly known ordering of players, then players can use this order in their reasoning. One possible interpretation here is that players select their choices as if they play *not simultaneously, but consecutively*, following that order (hierarchy), but *without the choices being announced* to the other players. Therefore, if the players follow a (rational) principle P, they may apply the *iterated reasoning* of P according to their hierarchical order. We call this **Hierarchical reasoning with respect to P** (HR^P).

We present here two examples where a structurally unsolvable game G becomes solvable with HR^P when we add player ordering to G. Consider first the game $G(1 \times 2 + 2 \times 1)$ and the principle of **Probabilistically optimal reasoning (PR)** (see [2]). By following PR, a player simply selects a choice with the largest winning extension. Clearly if players follow PR in $G(1 \times 2 + 2 \times 1)$, then they both will select a choice with out-degree of 2 and lose. But if Player 2 assumes Player 1 to follow PR, then Player 2 can coordinate with her/him. Therefore this game is HR^{PR}-solvable with the player ordering $(1, 2)$.

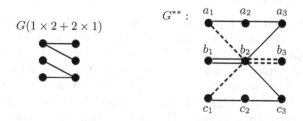

Fig. 4. Some examples of solvable WLC games with players ordering.

Consider then the game G^{**} in Fig. 4, where the winning triples are indicated by either solid or dashed line segments. Here the choices a_1 and c_1 of Player 1 generate (cf. ECS) a bad choice symmetry. Thus if Players 2 and 3 assume Player 1 to follow ECS, then they can coordinate with her by selecting their choices on a winning choice profile (b_1, b_2, a_3) or (b_1, b_2, c_3). Note that the choice b_1 generates (cf. ECS) a bad player symmetry and thus it is easy to see that this game is structurally unsolvable without the player ordering. However, the ordering of the players breaks this symmetry, and thus EPS arguably does not apply.

4.4 Principles Combining Orderings of Choices and Players

If a WLC game is enriched with both choice-ordering and players-ordering, then the players can naturally use the *lexicographic order* of all choice profiles determined by both the ordering of players and the ordering of choices. So, here is a natural alternative to COM:

Least Lexicographic Order principle (LLO): Play the least winning choice profile in the lexicographic order of all choice profiles, if there is one.

Clearly, *every* WLC game with commonly known orderings of choices and players and non-empty winning relation can be solved by applying (LLO). For illustration, consider the application of LLO in a scenario where the orderings of choices are made according to the players' preferences and there is a hierarchical order of the players. Now, following LLO can be interpreted as follows:

"Players select a winning choice profile in such a way as if all players get to choose consecutively, following the hierarchy from top to bottom, and each of the players makes their most preferred choice that can coordinate (win) with the choices already made by all previously choosing (i.e., superior) players."

For example, consider the game G^* from Example 1. Suppose an ordering of choices such that Player 1 "prefers" a_1 to b_1, Player 2 prefers b_2 to a_2 and Player 3 prefers a_3 to b_3. By following the player ordering $(1, 2, 3)$, the LLO-prescribed solution would now be (a_1, b_2, b_3).

4.5 On the Compatibility of the New and Old Principles

Both CM and COM are incompatible with most of the rationality principles presented in [2]. Thus, one may ask how rational players would (and should) behave in a game which is solvable by some (purely) rational principle, but some additional feature in the game creates an alternative focal point conflicting with the prescribed choices of that principle. For instance, consider the game $G^1(2(2 \times 2) + (1 \times 1))$ in Fig. 5. On the one hand, the symmetry principle ECS applied to the plain game $G(2(2 \times 2) + (1 \times 1))$ prescribes playing the pair in the subgame $G(1 \times 1)$, whereas the principle CM applied to the coloured version $G^1(2(2 \times 2) + (1 \times 1))$ prescribes playing in the 'black' subgame, which is readily solved. (Note that there are no bad choice symmetries in $G^1(2(2 \times 2) + (1 \times 1))$, as the added colouring breaks the corresponding automorphisms.)

Now, consider the 1-coloured game G_Z^1 on the right, also enriched with choice ordering. Note first that its plain version G_Z is solvable by the principle of Collective Rational Choices (CRC), which prescribes playing the middle choice profile $(3,2)$. On the other hand, G_Z with the given colouring is solvable by CM, which prescribes playing either of the choice profiles $(4,3)$ or $(4,4)$. Clearly, if the two players apply different principles amongst these, they lose. Note also that G_Z with the ordering of choices is solvable with COM which prescribes playing the choice profile $(1,1)$. So the game G_Z^1 has three different incompatible solutions, depending on if players follow CRC, CM or COM.

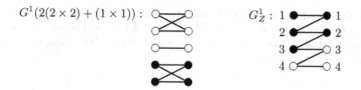

Fig. 5. Examples on incompatibility of some principles.

Furthermore, the generalised principle GCM^P applied to colourless WLC games obviously coincides with the respective underlying principle P applied to them. However, as the examples above show, on coloured games GCM^P may become incompatible with some rationality principles for plain WLC games with which P itself is compatible, or even with P itself! Indeed, the coloured game G^1_Z is not solvable by GCM^{CRC} because each of the two monochrome subgames is solvable by CRC—respectively with any of the choice profiles (4,3) or (4,4) for the 'white' subgame, and any of the choice profiles (2,1) or (2,2) for the 'black' subgame. But these solutions are not mutually compatible and thus the principle GCM^{CRC} fails on the entire game. Hence we also see that GCM^P may turn out to be disadvantageous as compared to CM, too.

Lastly, a few words on further enrichments. Besides total (linear) orderings of choices, WLC games can also be enriched with *partial orderings*, *preorderings*, *matchings* and other natural binary relations. For such games, one could define natural variants of the principles formulated above. For instance, note that a (partial) preorder on choices can also be seen as a (partial) ordering of colours. Thus, COM can be naturally generalised and can also be combined with GCM^P. For lack of space, we leave out the details here. Formal definitions and further study of these principles will be included in an extended version of this paper.

5   Concluding Remarks

In this work we have studied how additional features of the representation of coordination scenarios (games), that are commonly known amongst the players, can be used by rational players in order to achieve coordination. We have shown that in the enriched games one cannot achieve much more with the principles presented in [2], but a variety of new principles emerges which still seem rational, and certainly reasonable. However, like in [2], it seems very difficult to determine which of the reasoning principles stated here can be qualified as (purely) rational and which not.

There are many natural further extensions of this work, such as adding imperfect information or considering repeated coordination games or dis-coordination games. Also, some more technical issues—such as precise characterisations of the solving powers of various principles, and computational complexities of solving coordination games with them—could be pursued further. Lastly, it would be very interesting to see how real agents (people) actually behave in coordination scenarios studied here, by setting up concrete (live or web-based) experiments.

Acknowledgements. The work of Valentin Goranko was partly supported by a research grant 2015-04388 of the Swedish Research Council. The work of Antti Kuusisto was supported by the ERC grant 647289 "CODA". We thank the anonymous referees for valuable comments.

References

1. Alós-Ferrer, C., Kuzmics, C.: Hidden symmetries and focal points. J. Econ. Theory **148**(1), 226–258 (2013)
2. Goranko, V., Kuusisto, A., Rönnholm, R.: Rational coordination with no communication or conventions. In: Baltag, A., Seligman, J., Yamada, T. (eds.) LORI 2017. LNCS, vol. 10455, pp. 33–48. Springer, Heidelberg (2017). https://doi.org/10.1007/978-3-662-55665-8_3
3. Goranko, V., Kuusisto, A., Rönnholm, R.: Rational coordination with no communication or conventions. Technical report (2017). arXiv:1706.07412
4. Lewis, D.: Convention, A Philosophical Study. Harvard University Press, Cambridge (1969)
5. Mehta, J., Starmer, C., Sugden, R.: Focal points in pure coordination games: an experimental investigation. Theory Decis. **36**(2), 163–185 (1994)
6. Schelling, T.C.: The Strategy of Conflict. Harvard University Press, Cambridge (1960)
7. Sugden, R.: Spontaneous order. J. Econ. Perspect. **3**(4), 85–97 (1989)
8. Sugden, R.: A theory of focal points. Econ. J., 533–550 (1995)

On Cooperative Connection Situations Where the Players Are Located at the Edges

Stefano Moretti[⊠]

Université Paris-Dauphine, PSL Research University, CNRS, UMR [7243],
75016 Paris, France
stefano.moretti@dauphine.fr

Abstract. In classical cooperative connection situations, the agents are located at some nodes of a network and the cost of a coalition is based on the problem of finding a network of minimum cost connecting all the members of the coalition to a source.

In this paper we study a different connection situation with no source and where the agents are the edges, and yet the optimal network associated to each coalition (of edges) is not fixed and follows a cost-optimization procedure. The proposed model shares some similarities with classical minimum cost spanning tree games, but also substantial differences, specifically on the appropriate way to share the costs among the agents located at the edges. We show that the core of these particular cooperative games is always non-empty and some core allocations can be easily computed.

Keywords: Coalitional games · Connection situations
Cost allocation protocols · Core

1 Introduction

This paper deals with an alternative class of cooperative cost games defined on *minimum cost spanning tree (mcst)* situations. A (classical) mcst situation arises in the presence of a group of agents that are willing to be connected as cheap as possible to a source (e.g., a supplier of a service, if the agents are computers, or a water purifier, if the agents represent farms in a drainage system). Since links are costly, agents evaluate the opportunity of cooperating in order to reduce costs: if a group of agents decides to cooperate, a spanning network minimizing the total cost of connection of all the agents in the group with the source (i.e., a mcst) is constructed, and the total cost of the mcst must be shared among the agents of the group. The problem of finding an mcst can be easily solved

S. Moretti—This work benefited from the support of the French National Research Agency (ANR) projects NETLEARN (grant no. ANR-13-INFR-004) and CoCoRICo-CoDec (grant no. ANR-14-CE24-0007).

F. Belardinelli and E. Argente (Eds.): EUMAS 2017/AT 2017, LNAI 10767, pp. 339–353, 2018.
https://doi.org/10.1007/978-3-030-01713-2_24

by means of alternative algorithms proposed in the literature (*e.g.*, the Kruskal algorithm [9] or the Prim algorithm [14]). However, finding an mcst does not guarantee that it is going to be really implemented: the agents must agree on the way the cost of the mcst must be shared, and then a cost allocation problem must be addressed. This cost allocation problem was introduced in [5] and has been studied with the aid of cooperative game theory since the basic paper [3]. After this seminal paper, many cost allocation methods have been proposed in the literature on *mcst games* (see, for instance, [2,4,6,7,10,18]).

More recently, alternative connection situations have been introduced where the focus of interest of rational agents are the edges of a network. For instance, in [8], the agents demand a connection between certain nodes of a network, using a single link or via longer paths, and it is assumed that the set of implemented edges is exogenously fixed and may be "redundant" (see also [11] for an alternative approach considering redundant links). A still different class of games has been studied in [1], where the players are the edges of a graph and a coalition of edges gets value one if it is a connected component in the graph, and zero otherwise. All the aforementioned models deal with coalitional games where the cost of a coalition is fixed, or its computation is based on a structural property of the graph. In this paper, we investigate a particular subclass of the family of games introduced in [12], where the complexity of solutions for cooperative games defined on matroids has been extensively investigated. In our framework, the players are the edges of a weighted undirected graph, and the cost associated to each coalition (of edges) is the one of an optimal network connecting the endpoints of the edges in the coalition. The model we study in this paper is quite natural in a context where different service providers wish to satisfy a demand of economic exchange between pairs of nodes of a network (*e.g.*, an airline network, a content delivery network on the web, a telecommunication network, etc.). For example, a very common strategic problem for airlines participating in pooled flights is to decide how to allocate joint revenues and costs. Consider, for instance, three airports 1, 2 and 3 which are connected to each other by three different flight operators, each providing an air transport service on a different single connection between two airports: an operator over the link $1-2$, another one over the link $1-3$ and a still different one over $2-3$ (see Fig. 1 for a graphical representation of this connection situation). Clearly, implementing each flight connection between two airports need not be the best strategy. In fact, the implementation of only two links would be sufficient to guarantee the connection among the three airports at a lower cost (provided that the capacity constraints imposed by the flight vectors satisfy the demand for the service). Consequently, the decision of the flight operators on whether to cooperate for the implementation of an optimal airline network, also depends on the allocation method used to share the monetary savings generated by this cooperation.

The structure of the paper is as follows. We start in the next section with some basic definitions on cooperative games and graphs. Then, in Sect. 3 we introduce the proposed model, namely, a *Link Connection (LC) situation*, and the associated (coalitional) LC game, and we study their properties. In Sect. 4 we study a procedure to decompose an LC game as a positive linear combination of "simple" LC games, which are defined on weighted networks with weights equal to 0 or 1. Section 5 deals with the problem of finding allocations in the core of an LC game. Section 6 concludes with some research directions.

2   Preliminaries and Notations

A *coalitional cost game* (or, shortly, a *cost game*) is a pair (N, c), where $N = \{1, \ldots, n\}$ denotes the set of players and $c : 2^N \to \mathbb{R}$ is the *characteristic function*, (by convention, $c(\emptyset) = 0$). A group of players $S \subseteq N$ is called *coalition* and $c(S)$ is the *cost* incurred by coalition S. If the set N of players is fixed, we identify a cost game (N, c) with its characteristic function c and we denote as $\mathcal{CG}^N$ the class of all cost games with N as the set of players. For a coalition $S \subseteq N$, we shall denote by s or $|S|$ its cardinality.

A cost game (N, c) is said to be *subadditive* if it holds that $c(S \cup T) \leq c(S) + c(T)$ for all $S, T \subseteq N$ such that $S \cap T = \emptyset$. Moreover, a game (N, c) is said to be *concave* or *submodular* if it holds that $c(S \cup T) + c(S \cap T) \leq c(S) + c(T)$ for all $S, T \subseteq N$. Equivalently, a game (N, c) is said to be concave if it holds that $m_i^c(S) \geq m_i^c(T)$ for all $i \in N$ and all $S \subseteq T \subseteq N \setminus \{i\}$, and where $m_i^c(S) = c(S \cup \{i\}) - c(S)$ is the *marginal contribution* of player i to $S \cup \{i\}$. Given a cost game c, an *allocation* is a vector $x \in \mathbb{R}^N$ such that the *efficiency* condition $\sum_{i \in N} x_i = c(N)$ is satisfied.

An important subset of allocations is the *core*, which represents a classical "solution set" for TU-games. The core of game (N, c) is defined as the set of allocation vectors for which no coalition has an incentive to leave the grand coalition N, precisely,

$$Core(c) = \{x \in \mathbb{R}^N : \sum_{i \in N} x_i = c(N), \sum_{i \in S} x_i \leq c(S) \quad \forall S \subset N\}.$$

A (one-point) *solution* for cost games in $\mathcal{CG}^N$ is a map $\psi : \mathcal{CG}^N \to \mathbb{R}^N$ assigning to each cost game c in $\mathcal{CG}^N$ an $|N|$-vector of real numbers. The Shapley value [15] ϕ is a special solution assigning to each cost game (N, c) an $|N|$-vector computed according to the following formula:

$$\phi_i(c) = \sum_{S \in 2^{N \setminus \{i\}}} p_s m_i^c(S) \tag{1}$$

for each $i \in N$ and with $p_s = \frac{1}{n\binom{n-1}{s}}$ for each $s = 0, \ldots, |N| - 1$.

We provide now some notations about graphs. An undirected *graph* or *network* is a pair $\langle V, E \rangle$, where V is a finite set of vertices or nodes and E is a set of edges e of the form $\{i, j\}$ with $i, j \in V$, $i \neq j$. Given a graph $\langle V, E \rangle$, let $V(E) = \bigcup_{\{i,j\} \subseteq E} \{i, j\}$ be the set of vertices (of the edges) in E. A *path* between i and j in a graph $\langle V, E \rangle$ is a sequence of nodes $(i_0, i_1, \ldots, i_k)$, where $i = i_0$ and $j = i_k$, $k \geq 1$, such that $\{i_t, i_{t+1}\} \in E$ for each $t \in \{0, \ldots, k-1\}$ and such that all these edges are distinct. Two nodes $i, j \in V$ are said to be *connected* in $\langle V, E \rangle$ if $i = j$ or there exists a path between i and j in $\langle V, E \rangle$. A *component* of $\langle V, E \rangle$ is a maximal subset of V with the property that any two nodes in this subset are connected. The set $\mathcal{P}_E$ of all components in $\langle V, E \rangle$ is a partition of V. A graph $\langle V, E \rangle$ is *connected* if for each $i, j \in V$ with $i \neq j$ there exists a path between i and j in $\langle V, E \rangle$. A *cycle* in $\langle V, E \rangle$ is a path from i to i for some $i \in V$. A path $(i_0, i_1, \ldots, i_k)$ is *without cycles* if there do not exist $a, b \in \{0, 1, \ldots, k\}$, $a \neq b$, such that $i_a = i_b$. A graph where all paths are without cycles is called *forest*, and a forest that is also connected is called *tree*.

3   Link Connection Games

A *link connection (LC) situation* is defined as a triple $\mathcal{L} = \langle V, E, w \rangle$, where $\langle V, E \rangle$ is an undirected graph and $w : E \to [0, \infty)$ is a *weight function*, that is a map assigning to each edge $\{i, j\} \in E$ a non-negative number $w(\{i, j\})$ (in order to simplify our notation, an edge $\{i, j\}$ will be also denoted as ij, whenever no confusion can arise). Each edge $\{i, j\} \in E$ identifies an economic entity (*e.g.*, a service provider) aimed to satisfy a demand of connection between nodes i and j for the fruition of a service (*e.g.*, a communication channel in a telecommunication network, an on-line service on the web, a flight in an airlines network, etc.). A service connection between i and j can be implemented directly at a cost $w(\{i, j\})$, or indirectly, via a path between i and j in $\langle V, E \rangle$ using edges whose connection is already activated. Differently stated, once a connection between two nodes $\{i, j\} \in E$ is activated (at a cost $w(\{i, j\})$), the same connection can be exploited to implement the delivery of other services with no extra-costs. Each service provider $\{i, j\} \in E$ may decide whether to directly satisfy the request between i and j (at the cost $w(\{i, j\})$) or, in alternative, to cooperate with other service providers in order to exploit the connection already implemented.

In the following, the cost of a *network* $\langle V, L \rangle$ in an LC situation $\mathcal{L} = \langle V, E, w \rangle$ and with $L \subseteq E$ is denoted by $w(L) = \sum_{e \in L} w(e)$. Given an LC situation $\mathcal{L} = \langle V, E, w \rangle$, it is possible to determine at least one *minimum cost spanning forest (mcsf)* $\langle V, \Gamma \rangle$ for $\mathcal{L}$, *i.e.* a network without cycles of minimum cost with $\Gamma \subseteq E$ and such that i and j are connected in $\langle V, E \rangle$ if and only if they are connected in $\langle V, \Gamma \rangle$, for each $i, j \in V$. So, the set of components $\mathcal{P}_\Gamma$ in $\langle V, \Gamma \rangle$ coincides with the set of components $\mathcal{P}_E$ in $\langle V, E \rangle$. If $\langle V, E \rangle$ is a connected graph, then a mcsf $\langle V, \Gamma \rangle$ for $\mathcal{L}$ is a tree and it is called *minimum cost spanning tree (mcst)* for $\mathcal{L}$. In the following we will also use the notation $\mathcal{L}_{|S} = \langle V(S), S, w_{|S} \rangle$ to denote the (sub-) LC situation such that $w_{|S} : S \to \mathbb{R}$ with $w_{|S}(e) = w(e)$ for each $e \in S$ (here $V(S) := \bigcup_{e \in S} e$ is the set of vertices of the edges belonging to S).

Definition 1. Given an LC situation $\mathcal{L} = \langle V, E, w \rangle$, the corresponding *LC game* is defined as the cost game (E, c), where E is the set of players (service providers, located at the edges of the network) and the cost $c(S)$ of each coalition $S \in 2^N \setminus \{\emptyset\}$, is as follows:

$$c(S) = \min\{w(\Gamma) | \langle V(S), \Gamma \rangle \text{ is a spanning forest for } \langle V(S), S, w_{|S} \rangle\}.$$

Remark 1. In Definition 1, and in the remaining of this paper, we are motivated to study a cooperative situation where the cost of coalition $S \subseteq N$ does not depend on the actions adopted by service providers in $N \setminus S$. Therefore we make the assumption that the service providers of a coalition S can only implement the services over the edges in S, and are not allowed to use connections in the complementary coalition.

Example 1. Consider the LC situation depicted in Fig. 1. The corresponding LC game $(E = \{12, 13, 23\}, c)$ is such that $c(\{12\}) = 4$, $c(\{13\}) = 2$, $c(\{23\}) = 3$, $c(\{12, 23\}) = 7$, $c(\{12, 13\}) = 6$, $c(\{13, 23\}) = 5$ and $c(\{12, 13, 23\}) = 5$. Notice that the core of the game (E, c) is $Core(c) = \{x \in \mathbb{R}^E : \sum_{i \in E} x_i = 5, 4 \geq x_{12} \geq 0, 2 \geq x_{13} \geq -2, 3 \geq x_{23} \geq -1\}$.

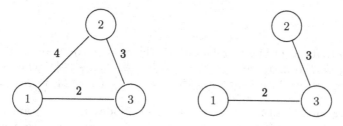

Fig. 1. An LC situation $\mathcal{L} = \langle V, E, w \rangle$, with $V = \{1, 2, 3\}$, $E = \{\{1, 2\}, \{1, 3\}, \{2, 3\}\}$, $w(1, 2) = 4$, $w(1, 3) = 2$, $w(2, 3) = 3$ (left side) and the corresponding mcst (right side).

Proposition 1. *Let $\mathcal{L} = \langle V, E, w \rangle$ be an LC situation. The corresponding LC game (E, c) is subadditive.*

Proof. The proof is straightforward and therefore is omitted.   □

It is well known that concave games have a non-empty core, which also contains the Shapley value [16]. The following example shows that, in general, LC games are not concave, so we cannot use the concavity argument to guarantee that the core of LC games is non-empty.

Example 2 (LC games are not necessarily concave). Consider the LC situation $\mathcal{L} = \langle V, E, w \rangle$ depicted in Fig. 2, with $E = \{12, 13, 23, 24, 34\}$. Clearly, the cost of many coalitions of edges is simply the sum of the costs of the individual edges (*e.g.*, $c(13, 24) = 3$). For other coalitions, the construction of spanning forests determine some extra monetary savings (*e.g.*, the spanning tree $\Gamma = \{12, 13, 24\}$ is the optimal configuration which guarantees the connection of the adjacent nodes of all possible links in the graph at a total cost of 4). Notice that the corresponding LC game is not concave. Consider the coalitions $S = \{23, 34\}$ and $T = \{12, 13, 23, 34\}$. Then, $c(S \cup 24) = 6$, $c(T \cup 24) = 4$, and $c(S) = 12$, $c(T) = 6$. So, $m_{24}^c(S) = -6$ and $m_{24}^c(T) = -2$.

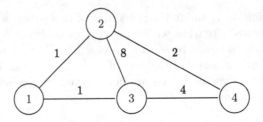

Fig. 2. An LC situation whose corresponding LC game is not concave.

Table 1. The LC game corresponding to the LC situation of Fig. 2. All omitted coalitions have an additive cost, that is $c(S) = \sum_{e \in S} w(e)$.

S	12,13,23	23,24,34	12,13,24,24	12,13,23,34	12,13,23,24	23,24,34,13	23,24,34,12	E
$c(S)$	2	6	4	6	4	7	7	4

Notice also that, according to relation (1), the Shapley value of game (E, c) is $(\phi_{12}(c), \phi_{13}(c), \phi_{24}(c), \phi_{34}(c), \phi_{23}(c)) = (-\frac{16}{15}, -\frac{16}{15}, -\frac{1}{15}, \frac{29}{15}, \frac{64}{15})$, which is not an element of $Core(c)$, since $\phi_{24}(c) + \phi_{34}(c) + \phi_{23}(c) > 6 = c(24, 34, 23)$.

Consider an LC situation $\mathcal{L} = \langle V, E, w \rangle$. Nodes $i, j \in V$ are called $\mathcal{L}$-*connected* if $i = j$ or if there exists a path $(i_0, \ldots, i_k)$ from i to j in $\langle V, E \rangle$, with $w(\{i_s, i_{s+1}\}) = 0$ for every $s \in \{0, \ldots, k-1\}$. A $\mathcal{L}$-*component* of $\mathcal{L}$ is a maximal subset of V with the property that any two nodes in this subset are $\mathcal{L}$-connected. We denote by $\mathcal{C}(\mathcal{L})$ the set of all the $\mathcal{L}$-components. Given a component T in $\langle V, E \rangle$, let $\mathcal{C}_T(\mathcal{L}) = \{C \subseteq T : C \text{ is a } \mathcal{L}\text{-component}\}$ be the set of all $\mathcal{L}$-components contained in T (notice that $\mathcal{C}_T(\mathcal{L})$ forms a partition of T and that $\mathcal{C}_E(\mathcal{L}) = \mathcal{C}(\mathcal{L})$). Similarly, for each non-empty coalition $S \subseteq E$, $\mathcal{C}_T(\mathcal{L}_{|S}) = \{C \subseteq T : C \text{ is a } \mathcal{L}\text{-component}\}$ denotes the set of all $\mathcal{L}_{|S}$-components (i.e., in the restriction $\mathcal{L}_{|S} = \langle V(S), S, w_{|S} \rangle$) contained in T.

An LC situation $\mathcal{L}' = \langle V, E, w' \rangle$ such that $w'(e) \in \{0, 1\}$ for each $e \in E$ is said to be *simple*. Following the decomposition in [4] for classical connection situations, the next lemma shows that an LC situation can be decomposed as a sum of simple LC situations. We first need some further notations. Let $\mathcal{L} = \langle V, E, w \rangle$ be an LC situation. We define the set Σ_E of *linear orders* on E as the set of all bijections $\sigma : \{1, \ldots, |E|\} \to E$. For each $\sigma \in \Sigma_E$ define the simple LC situation $\mathcal{L}^{\sigma,k} = \langle V, E, e^{\sigma,k} \rangle$, for each $k \in \{1, 2, \ldots, |E|\}$, where the vector $e^{\sigma,k} \in \{0, 1\}^E$, is such that $e^{\sigma,1}(\sigma(j)) = 1$ for all $j \in \{1, 2, \ldots, |E|\}$, and for each $k \in \{2, \ldots, |E|\}$

$$e^{\sigma,k}(\sigma(1)) = e^{\sigma,k}(\sigma(2)) = \ldots = e^{\sigma,k}(\sigma(k-1)) = 0$$
$$\text{and}$$
$$e^{\sigma,k}(\sigma(k)) = e^{\sigma,k}(\sigma(k+1)) = \ldots = e^{\sigma,k}(\sigma(|E|)) = 1. \quad (2)$$

Lemma 1. Let $\mathcal{L} = \langle V, E, w \rangle$ be an LC situation. Let $\sigma \in \Sigma_E$ be such that $w(\sigma(1)) \leq w(\sigma(2)) \leq \ldots \leq w(\sigma(|E|))$. Then we have that

$$w = w(\sigma(1))e^{\sigma,1} + \sum_{k=2}^{|E|} \left(w(\sigma(k)) - w(\sigma(k-1)) \right) e^{\sigma,k}. \tag{3}$$

Proof. The proof is very similar to the decomposition procedure introduced in [4]. □

Example 3 (follows Example 2). Consider the LC situation of Example 2 and the ordering $\sigma = (\{1,2\}, \{1,3\}, \{2,4\}, \{3,4\}, \{2,3\})$. Notice that $w(\sigma(1)) \leq \ldots \leq w(\sigma(5))$. According to Lemma 1 we have that

$$w = e^{\sigma,1} + 0e^{\sigma,2} + e^{\sigma,3} + 2e^{\sigma,4} + 4e^{\sigma,5}$$

where the weight vectors $e^{\sigma,1}, \ldots, e^{\sigma,5}$ are such that $e^{\sigma,1} = (1,1,1,1,1)$, $e^{\sigma,2} = (0,1,1,1,1)$, $e^{\sigma,3} = (0,0,1,1,1)$, $e^{\sigma,4} = (0,0,0,1,1)$ and $e^{\sigma,5} = (0,0,0,0,1)$.

4 A Decomposition Theorem

It is easy to check that for a simple LC situation $\mathcal{L}' = \langle V, E, w' \rangle$ and a component T in $\langle V, E \rangle$, the total cost of a tree spanning all nodes in T at the minimum cost is equal to the the number of elements in $\mathcal{C}_T(\mathcal{L}')$ minus one, which is precisely the minimum number of edges of cost 1 that are needed to connect all $\mathcal{L}'$-components. So, for a simple LC situation $\mathcal{L}' = \langle V, E, w' \rangle$ it holds that the corresponding LC game (E, c') can be rewritten as

$$c'(S) = \sum_{T \text{ is a component in } \langle V(S), S \rangle} \left(|\mathcal{C}_T(\mathcal{L}'_{|S})| - 1 \right) \tag{4}$$

for each $S \in 2^E \setminus \{\emptyset\}$. In other terms, the cost of a coalition S is given by the sum, over all the components T in the sub-graph $\langle V(S), S \rangle$, of the minimum number of links of cost 1 needed to connect all the $\mathcal{L}'_{|S}$-components contained in T.

Example 4 (follows Example 2). Consider the simple LC situation $\mathcal{L}' = \langle V, E, w' \rangle$ with $\langle V, E \rangle$ of Example 2 and w' such that $w'(2,3) = w'(2,4) = w'(3,4) = 1$ and $w'(1,2) = w'(1,3) = 0$, as depicted in Fig. 3. We have $\mathcal{C}(\mathcal{L}') = \{\{1,2,3\}, \{4\}\}$ and, by relation (4), $c(E) = |\mathcal{C}(\mathcal{L}')| - 1 = 1$.

Now, let $S = \{13, 24\}$. The LC situation $\mathcal{L}'_{|S} = \langle V(S), S, w'_{|S} \rangle$ is such that there are two components in $\langle V(S), S \rangle$, precisely, $\{1,3\}$ and $\{2,4\}$. Component $\{1,3\}$ contains only one $\mathcal{L}'_{|S}$-component, i.e., $\mathcal{C}_{\{1,3\}}(\mathcal{L}'_{|S}) = \{\{1,3\}\}$, whereas component $\{2,4\}$ contains two $\mathcal{L}'_{|S}$-components, i.e., $\mathcal{C}_{\{2,4\}}(\mathcal{L}'_{|S}) = \{\{2\}, \{4\}\}$. So, according to relation (4), $c'(S) = |\mathcal{C}_{\{1,3\}}(\mathcal{L}'_{|S})| - 1 + |\mathcal{C}_{\{2,4\}}(\mathcal{L}'_{|S})| - 1 = 1$. Differently, if $S = \{13, 12, 23, 24\}$, then $\langle V(S), S \rangle$ is connected, and, again, we have $\mathcal{C}_{\{1,2,3,4\}}(\mathcal{L}'_{|S}) = \{\{1,2,3\}, \{4\}\}$ and $c(S) = 1$.

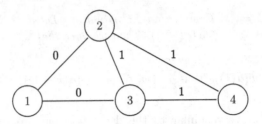

Fig. 3. A simple LC situation.

Following the approach introduced in [13] to decompose mcst games, we can now prove the following lemma.

Lemma 2. *Let $\mathcal{L} = \langle V, E, w \rangle$ be an LC situation with at least one edge $e \in E$ such that $w(e) > 0$, and let $\alpha = \min\{w(e) : w(e) > 0\}$ be its minimum weight. Let $\mathcal{L}' = \langle V, E, w' \rangle$ be the simple LC situation defined by $w'(e) = 1$ if $w(e) > 0$ and $w'(e) = 0$, otherwise, for each $e \in E$, and let $\mathcal{L}'' = \langle V, E, w'' \rangle$ be the LC situation with $w'' = w - \alpha w'$. Finally, let c, c' and c'' be the LC games corresponding to $\mathcal{L}$, $\mathcal{L}'$ and $\mathcal{L}''$ respectively. Then, $c = \alpha c' + c''$.*

Proof. Clearly, by definition we have $w = \alpha w' + w''$. Let $S \in 2^E \setminus \{\emptyset\}$ and let $\langle V(S), \Gamma' \rangle$ be a mcsf for $\langle V(S), S, w'_{|S} \rangle$. Write $\Gamma' = L^0 \cup L^1$ where $L^0 := \{l \in \Gamma' : w'(l) = 0\}$ and $L^1 := \{l \in \Gamma' : w'(l) = 1\}$. The cost of Γ' is:

$$c'(S) = w'(\Gamma') = |L^1| = \sum_{T \text{ is a component in } \langle V(S), S \rangle} (|\mathcal{C}_T(\mathcal{L}'_{|S})| - 1) \tag{5}$$
$$= \sum_{T \text{ is a component in } \langle V(\Gamma'), \Gamma' \rangle} (|\mathcal{C}_T(\mathcal{L}'_{|\Gamma'})| - 1),$$

where the first equality follows from relation (4) and the second one from the fact that Γ' is a spanning forest in $\langle V(S), S \rangle$, which means that $\mathcal{P}_{\Gamma'} \equiv \mathcal{P}_S$.

We first show that there exists a mcsf Γ'' for $\langle V(S), S, w'' \rangle$ with $L^0 \subseteq \Gamma''$. Take an arbitrary mcsf Γ for S in $\langle V(S), S, w'' \rangle$. If $L^0 \not\subseteq \Gamma$ choose an $l \in L^0 \setminus \Gamma$. Since $\Gamma \cup \{l\}$ contains a cycle R, whereas Γ', and hence L^0, do not contain cycles, we can find an edge $l' \in R$ with $l' \notin L^0$. Define $\tilde{\Gamma} := (\Gamma \cup \{l\}) \setminus \{l'\}$. Since $w''(l) = 0$ and $w''(l') \geq 0$ we find that also $\tilde{\Gamma}$ is a mcsf for $\langle V(S), S, w'' \rangle$. Moreover $|\tilde{\Gamma} \cap L^0| = |\Gamma \cap L^0| + 1$. Repeating this argument results in the tree Γ'' with $L^0 \subseteq \Gamma''$.

Note that the set $\mathcal{P}_{\Gamma'}$ of all components in $\langle V(\Gamma'), \Gamma' \rangle$ coincides with the one $\mathcal{P}_{\Gamma''}$ in $\langle V(\Gamma''), \Gamma'' \rangle$. Moreover, since $L^0 \subseteq \Gamma''$, then for each component $T \in \mathcal{P}_{\Gamma'}$ (or, equivalently, in $\mathcal{P}_{\Gamma''}$), the number of $\mathcal{L}'_{|\Gamma''}$-components contained in T must be at most the corresponding number of $\mathcal{L}'_{|\Gamma'}$-components. Consequently, we have that

$$w'(\Gamma'') = \sum_{T \text{ is a component in } \langle V(\Gamma''), \Gamma'' \rangle} (|\mathcal{C}_T(\mathcal{L}'_{|\Gamma''})| - 1)$$
$$\leq \sum_{T \text{ is a component in } \langle V(\Gamma'), \Gamma' \rangle} (|\mathcal{C}_T(\mathcal{L}'_{|\Gamma'})| - 1) = w'(\Gamma'). \tag{6}$$

Therefore, Γ'' is also a mcsf for $\langle V(S), S, w' \rangle$. Having $w = \alpha w' + w''$ and the fact that Γ'' is a mcsf for S in both $\langle V(S), S, w' \rangle$ and $\langle V(S), S, w'' \rangle$ we may conclude that Γ'' is also a mcsf for S in $\langle V(S), S, w \rangle$. So, $c(S) = w(\Gamma'') = \alpha w'(\Gamma'') + w''(\Gamma'') = \alpha c'(S) + c''(S)$.   □

The following decomposition theorem shows that every link game can be written as a non-negative combination of LC games corresponding to simple LC situations.

Theorem 1. *Let $\mathcal{L} = \langle V, E, w \rangle$ be an LC situation and let (E, c) be its corresponding LC game. Let $\sigma \in \Sigma_E$ be such that $w(\sigma(1)) \le w(\sigma(2)) \le \dots \le w(\sigma(|E|))$. Define the LC game $(E, c^{\sigma,k})$ corresponding to the simple LC situation $\mathcal{L}^{\sigma,k} = \langle V, E, e^{\sigma,k} \rangle$, for each $k \in \{1, \dots, |E|\}$. Then,*

$$c = w(\sigma(1))c^{\sigma,1} + \sum_{k=2}^{|E|} \big(w(\sigma(k)) - w(\sigma(k-1)) \big)\, c^{\sigma,k}. \tag{7}$$

Proof. The proof follows directly by Lemma 1 and the recursive application of Lemma 2, using $e^{\sigma,j}$ in the role of w', $w(\sigma(j)) - w(\sigma(j-1))$ in the role of α, and $\sum_{k=j+1}^{|E|} \big(w(\sigma(k)) - w(\sigma(k-1)) \big)\, e^{\sigma,k}$ in the role of w'' at each recursive call $j \in \{1, \dots, |E| - 1\}$ (and setting, by convention, $w(\sigma(0)) = 0$).   □

Example 5 (follows Examples 2 and 3). Consider again the LC situation of Examples 2 and 3, with $\sigma = (\{1,2\}, \{1,3\}, \{2,4\}, \{3,4\}, \{2,3\})$. According to Theorem 1 we have $c = c^{\sigma,1} + 0c^{\sigma,2} + c^{\sigma,3} + 2c^{\sigma,4} + 4c^{\sigma,5}$, where the LC games $c^{\sigma,1}, \dots, c^{\sigma,5}$ corresponding to the simple LC situations $e^{\sigma,1}, \dots, e^{\sigma,5}$ are those shown in Table 2. One can easily verify that the last row of Table 2 coincides with the LC game c, as computed in Example 2 (see Table 1).

Table 2. Decomposition of the LC game corresponding to the LC situation of Fig. 2.

S	$\{12, 13, 23\}$	$\{23, 24, 34\}$	$\{12, 13, 23, 34\}$	$\{12, 13, 23, 24\}$	$\{23, 24, 34, 13\}$	$\{23, 24, 34, 12\}$	E
$c^{\sigma,1}(S)$	2	2	3	3	3	3	3
$c^{\sigma,2}(S)$	2	2	3	3	3	3	3
$c^{\sigma,3}(S)$	0	2	1	1	2	2	1
$c^{\sigma,4}(S)$	0	1	1	0	1	1	0
$c^{\sigma,5}(S)$	0	0	0	0	0	0	0
Sum	2	6	6	4	7	7	4

5   The Core of an LC Game

In this section we prove that LC games have a non-empty core and that core allocations can be efficiently computed, even if, as we have shown in the previous section, LC games are not necessarily concave. One could argue that the savings due to cooperation in an LC situation originate from the possibility to break cycles without destroying the connectivity of the network. On the other hand, it is not immediately clear how those savings should be shared among the links involved in the cycle in order to obtain a core allocation. Next example shows that trivial allocation protocols, to be more specific, the equal sharing rule applied to the edges involved in the cycles, in general does not provide a core allocation.

Example 6. Consider the simple LC situation $\mathcal{L}' = \langle V, E, w' \rangle$ depicted in Fig. 4, with the set E composed by the 15 edges depicted in Fig. 4 and where the cost $w'(e)$ of each edge $e \in E$ is equal to 1. In order to obtain a mcsf on $\mathcal{L}'$ it suffices to eliminate four edges such that no cycles appear and the network remains connected (*e.g.*, deleting edges $\{1,2\}, \{4,5\}, \{7,8\}$ and $\{10,11\}$), therefore leading to an optimal network of cost 11. On the other hand, if we split equally the total cost 11 (or the total saving 4) among the edges of the network we obtain that each link in E should pay $\frac{11}{15}$ which is not in the core of the corresponding LC game, since $c(12, 13, 23) = 2 < 3\frac{11}{15} = x_{12} + x_{13} + x_{23}$.

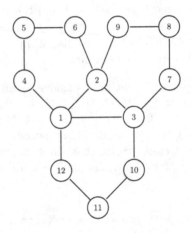

Fig. 4. A simple LC situation where the equal sharing allocation does not belong to the core (the cost of each edge is 1).

Even if the cycles play a central role in the determination of the savings (as illustrated in the previous example), defining an allocation rule based on the analysis of the cycles of a graph could be computationally very hard (one edge may belong to several cycles). In the following, our objective is to prove that LC games have a non-empty core and core allocations can be easily computed without looking at the cycles of a graph.

Let $\mathcal{L}' = \langle V, E, w' \rangle$ be a simple LC situation (with $w'(e) \in \{0, 1\}$). For each $i \in V$, let $C_i(\mathcal{L}')$ be the $\mathcal{L}'$-component to which i belongs. We denote by $B_{ij}^{\Gamma} = \{\{k, l\} \in E : k \in C_i(\mathcal{L}') \text{ and } l \in C_j(\mathcal{L}')\}$ the *bridge* set of all edges connecting the two $\mathcal{L}'$-components $C_i(\mathcal{L}')$ and $C_j(\mathcal{L}')$ (clearly, $\{i, j\} \in B_{ij}^{\Gamma}$ and $w(k, l) = 1$ for each $\{k, l\} \in B_{ij}^{\Gamma}$). Moreover, let $\bar{E}^{\Gamma} = E \setminus \bigcup_{e \in \Gamma : w'(e)=1} B_{ij}^{\Gamma}$ be the set of edges in E that do not belong to any set B_{ij}^{Γ} with $\{i, j\} \in \Gamma$ and $w'(i, j) = 1$.

Remark 2. Let $\langle V, \Gamma \rangle$ be a mcsf for the simple LC situation $\mathcal{L}' = \langle V, E, w' \rangle$. Note that for $\{i, j\}, \{k, l\} \in \Gamma$ with $\{i, j\} \neq \{k, l\}$ and $w'(i, j) = w'(k, l) = 1$, we have $B_{ij}^{\Gamma} \cap B_{kl}^{\Gamma} = \emptyset$, since each edge of cost 1 in Γ connects two disjoint $\mathcal{L}'$-components.

Example 7 (follows Example 4). Consider again the simple LC situation $\mathcal{L}' = \langle V, E, w' \rangle$ of Example 4. Let the tree $\Gamma = \{\{1, 2\}, \{1, 3\}, \{2, 4\}\}$ be a mcst in $\mathcal{L}'$. Then, we have that $B_{24}^{\Gamma} = \{\{2, 4\}, \{3, 4\}\}$ and $\bar{E}^{\Gamma} = \{\{1, 2\}, \{1, 3\}, \{2, 3\}\}$.

Now, we can introduce a family of cost sharing vectors for simple LC games.

Definition 2. *Let $\mathcal{L}' = \langle V, E, w' \rangle$ be a simple LC situation and let $\langle V, \Gamma \rangle$ be a mcsf for $\mathcal{L}' = \langle V, E, w' \rangle$. We denote by $\mathcal{X}(\mathcal{L}', \Gamma)$ the set of (positive) vectors $x \in \mathbb{R}_+^E$ satisfying the following two conditions:*

(i) $\sum_{e \in B_{ij}^{\Gamma}} x_e = 1$ *for all $\{i, j\} \in \Gamma$ such that $w'(i, j) = 1$;*

(ii) $x_e = 0$ *for all $e \in \bar{E}$,*

where $\langle V, \Gamma \rangle$ is a mcsf for the simple LC situation $\mathcal{L}'$.

In other words, $\mathcal{X}(\mathcal{L}', \Gamma)$ is the set of positive allocation vectors such that the service providers located over the edges in $\bar{E}^{\Gamma}$ pay nothing and those over the edges in B_{ij}^{Γ}, for each $\{i, j\} \in \Gamma$ with $w'(i, j) = 1$, share the cost to connect $C_i(\mathcal{L}')$ and $C_j(\mathcal{L}')$.

Lemma 3. *Let $\mathcal{L}' = \langle V, E, w' \rangle$ be a simple LC situation (with $w'(e) \in \{0, 1\}$) and let $\langle V, \Gamma \rangle$ be a mcsf for $\mathcal{L}'$. Then $\mathcal{X}(\mathcal{L}', \Gamma) \neq \emptyset$ and $\sum_{e \in E} x_e = w'(\Gamma)$.*

Proof. To prove that $\mathcal{X}(\mathcal{L}', \Gamma) \neq \emptyset$, simply take the vector $x \in \mathbb{R}_+^E$ such that

$$x_e = \begin{cases} \frac{1}{|B_{ij}^{\Gamma}|} & \text{if } \exists \{i, j\} \in \Gamma \text{ with } w'(i, j) = 1 \text{ and } e \in B_{ij}^{\Gamma}, \\ 0 & \text{otherwise,} \end{cases} \quad (8)$$

for each $e \in E$. It is immediate to check that the vector x defined according to relation (8) satisfies conditions (i) and (ii) in Definition 2. To see that every vector $x \in \mathcal{X}(\mathcal{L}', \Gamma)$ is efficient, simply notice that

$$\sum_{e \in E} x_e = \sum_{\{i, j\} \in \Gamma : w'(i, j) = 1} \sum_{e \in B_{ij}^{\Gamma}} x_e = \sum_{\{i, j\} \in \Gamma : w'(i, j) = 1} 1 = w'(\Gamma),$$

where the first equality follows from condition (ii) in Definition 2, and the second equality from condition (i). $\square$

Example 8 (follows Examples 4 and 7). The allocation vectors in $\mathcal{X}(\mathcal{L}', \Gamma)$, whatever mcsf Γ for $\mathcal{L}'$ is constructed, is such that the edges $\{2, 4\}$ and $\{3, 4\}$ share the cost of connecting the $\mathcal{L}'$-components $\{1, 2, 3\}$ and $\{4\}$. We have that

$$\mathcal{X}(\mathcal{L}', \Gamma) = \{x \in \mathbb{R}_+^E : x_{12} = x_{13} = x_{23} = 0 \text{ and } x_{24} + x_{34} = 1\}.$$

Next lemma, that holds for general LC situations, is useful to prove the non-emptiness of the core of simple LC games, as shown by Proposition 2.

Lemma 4. Let $\mathcal{L} = \langle V, E, w \rangle$ be an LC situation, let $\langle V, \Gamma \rangle$ be a mcsf for $\mathcal{L}$ and let c be the corresponding LC game. For each $S \subseteq E$. Then,

$$c(S) \geq w(\Gamma \cap S), \tag{9}$$

Proof. Recall that $c(S) = w(\Gamma_S) = \sum_{e \in \Gamma_S} w(e)$, where Γ_S is a mcsf for the restriction $\mathcal{L}_S = \langle V(S), S, w_{|S} \rangle$, and $w(\Gamma \cap S) = \sum_{e \in \Gamma \cap S} w(e)$.

First note that each component T in $\langle V(\Gamma \cap S), \Gamma \cap S \rangle$ is also a connected set of nodes in the network $\langle V(S), \Gamma_S \rangle$. So, if two nodes $i, j \in V$ are connected in the network $\langle V, \Gamma \rangle$ they must be connected also in the network $\langle V, (\Gamma \setminus S) \cup \Gamma_S \rangle$ (i.e., $\langle V, (\Gamma \setminus S) \cup \Gamma_S \rangle$ is a spanning network for $\langle V, E \rangle$, meaning that $\mathcal{P}_{(\Gamma \setminus S) \cup \Gamma_S} \equiv \mathcal{P}_E$), and this directly implies relation (9). Suppose, on the contrary, that $w(\Gamma \cap S) > c(S) = w(\Gamma_S)$. By simple considerations on the sets of edges Γ, S and Γ_S we obtain that

$$w(\Gamma) = w((\Gamma \cap S) \cup (\Gamma \setminus S)) = w(\Gamma \cap S) + w(\Gamma \setminus S) > w(\Gamma_S) + w(\Gamma \setminus S) \geq w(\Gamma_S \cup (\Gamma \setminus S)),$$

which yields a contradiction with the fact that Γ is a mcsf for $\langle V, E \rangle$ (notice that the second equality follows from the fact that $(\Gamma \cap S) \cap (\Gamma \setminus S) = \emptyset$ and the last inequality from the fact that $\Gamma_S \cap (\Gamma \setminus S)$ is not necessarily empty). $\square$

Proposition 2. Let $\mathcal{L}' = \langle V, E, w' \rangle$ be a simple LC situation (with $w'(e) \in \{0, 1\}$) and let (E, c') be the corresponding LC game. Then, $\mathcal{X}(\mathcal{L}', \Gamma) \subseteq Core(c') \neq \emptyset$.

Proof. By Lemma 3 we know that $\mathcal{X}(\mathcal{L}', \Gamma) \neq \emptyset$ and that each element $x \in \mathcal{X}(\mathcal{L}', \Gamma)$ is an efficient allocation. Now, in order to prove that $x \in \mathcal{X}(\mathcal{L}', \Gamma)$ is in $Core(c')$ we need to prove that $\sum_{e \in S} x_e \leq c'(S)$ for all $S \subseteq E$. Notice that

$$\sum_{e \in S} x_e = \sum_{\{i,j\} \in S \cap \Gamma : w'(i,j) = 1} \sum_{e \in S \cap B_{ij}^\Gamma} x_e \leq \sum_{e \in S \cap \Gamma : w'(i,j) = 1} 1 = \sum_{e \in S \cap \Gamma} w'(e) \leq c'(S), \tag{10}$$

for each $S \subseteq E$, where the first equality follows from condition (ii) in Definition 2, the first inequality from condition (i) in Definition 2, the second equality from the fact that w' is a simple LC situation and the second inequality from Lemma 4. $\square$

We can finally prove that LC games have a non-empty core.

Theorem 2. Let $\mathcal{L} = \langle V, E, w \rangle$ be an LC situation and let (E, c) be the corresponding LC game. Then, $Core(c) \neq \emptyset$.

Proof. Let $\sigma \in \Sigma_E$ be such that $w(\sigma(1)) \leq w(\sigma(2)) \leq \ldots \leq w(\sigma(|E|))$. For each $k \in \{1, \ldots, |E|\}$, take $x^k \in \mathcal{X}(\mathcal{L}^{\sigma,k}, \Gamma^k)$, where $\langle V, \Gamma^k \rangle$ is a mcsf for $\mathcal{L}^{\sigma,k}$ and

$c^{\sigma,k}$ is the LC game corresponding to the simple LC situation $e^{\sigma,k}$. Define the vector $x \in \mathbb{R}^E$ such that

$$x = w(\sigma(1))x^k + \sum_{k=2}^{|E|} \left(w(\sigma(k)) - w(\sigma(k-1))\right)x^k.$$

For each $S \subseteq E$ with $S \neq \emptyset$ we have that

$$\sum_{e \in S} x_e \leq w(\sigma(1))c^{\sigma,1}(S) + \sum_{k=2}^{|E|} \left(w(\sigma(k)) - w(\sigma(k-1))\right) c^{\sigma,k}(S) = c(S), \quad (11)$$

where the inequality follows from the fact that, by Proposition 2, $x^k \in Core(c^{\sigma,k})$ and the fact that $w(\sigma(1)) \geq 0$ and $w(\sigma(k)) - w(\sigma(k-1)) \geq 0$ for each $k \in \{1, \ldots, |E|\}$, and the second equality follows directly from Theorem 1; similarly, for the efficiency condition of core allocations in $\mathcal{X}(\mathcal{L}^{\sigma,k}, \Gamma^k)$ we have

$$\sum_{e \in N} x_e = w(\sigma(1))c^{\sigma,1}(E) + \sum_{k=2}^{|E|} \left(w(\sigma(k)) - w(\sigma(k-1))\right) c^{\sigma,k}(E) = c(E) = w(\Gamma).$$

Then it has been established that $x \in Core(c)$.   □

Example 9 (follows Examples 2, 3 and 5). Let $\Gamma^k = \Gamma = \{\{1,2\}, \{1,3\}, \{2,4\}\}$ for each $k \in \{1, \ldots, 5\}$ (notice that this is a mcsf obtained using the Kruskal algorithm [9] on the ordering of the edges σ). It is easy to check that $\mathcal{X}(\mathcal{L}^{\sigma,1}, \Gamma) = \{(x_{12}, x_{13}, x_{24}, x_{34}, x_{23}) = (1,1,1,0,0)\}$, $\mathcal{X}(\mathcal{L}^{\sigma,2}, \Gamma) = \{x \in \mathbb{R}_+^E : x_{13} + x_{23} = x_{24} = 1 \text{ and } x_{12} = x_{34} = 0\}$, $\mathcal{X}(\mathcal{L}^{\sigma,3}, \Gamma) = \{x \in \mathbb{R}_+^E : x_{12} = x_{13} = x_{23} = 0 \text{ and } x_{24} + x_{34} = 1\}$ and $\mathcal{X}(\mathcal{L}^{\sigma,4}, \Gamma) = \mathcal{X}(\mathcal{L}^{\sigma,5}, \Gamma) = \{(x_{12}, x_{13}, x_{24}, x_{34}, x_{23}) = (0,0,0,0,0)\}$. Consider for instance the core allocations $x^k \in \mathcal{X}(\mathcal{L}^{\sigma,k}, \Gamma)$ computed according to relation (8) as follows:

	$\{1,2\}$	$\{1,3\}$	$\{2,4\}$	$\{3,4\}$	$\{2,3\}$
x^1	1	1	1	0	0
x^2	0	$\frac{1}{2}$	1	0	$\frac{1}{2}$
x^3	0	0	$\frac{1}{2}$	$\frac{1}{2}$	0
x^4	0	0	0	0	0
x^5	0	0	0	0	0
$x = x^1 + 0x^2 + x^3 + 2x^4 + 4x^5$	1	1	$\frac{3}{2}$	$\frac{1}{2}$	0

One can easily verify that $x \in Core(c)$, as immediately suggested by Theorem 2.

6   Concluding Remarks

In this paper we studied a class of cooperative games where the players are the edges of a weighted graph and the goal of a coalition of edges is to connect the adjacent nodes at a minimum cost. We also provided a procedure based on a decomposition theorem to easily generate allocation vectors in the core of an LC game. An interesting research direction is related to the property-driven analysis of particular one-point solutions for LC situations, *i.e.* maps that associate to each LC situation a particular allocation vector, independently from the selected mcsf and, possibly, in the core of the corresponding LC game. Alternative cost allocation protocols keeping into account the role of edges in maintaining the connectivity of the network should be further investigated.

As shortly suggested in Example 9, the procedure to find core allocations used in the proof of Theorem 2 is strongly related to the Kruskal algorithm for finding a spanning network of minimum cost on weighted graphs [9]. In general, it is possible to define a procedure aimed at computing vectors in $\mathcal{X}(\mathcal{L}^{\sigma,k}, \Gamma^k)$ at each k-th step of the Kruskal algorithm, and obtain, after precisely n-steps (where n is the number of nodes, if the graph is connected) both an optimal network and an allocation in the core of the LC game. On the other hand, the procedure used in Theorem 2 selects the elements of a particular subset of the core, and the issue of how to efficiently generate all the allocations in the core of an LC game (or other specific subsets of stable allocations) is still an open problem. Notice that the non-emptiness of the core for LC games can be also proved using the results in [12] for games on matroids (LC games being a special case of games on matroids), and an interesting related question is whether the procedure used in Theorem 2 can be generalized to the more general framework of matroids.

Another open question concerns the existence of solutions for LC games that are *cost monotonic* (*i.e.*, such that if some connection costs go down, then no edges will pay more) and, in addition, that can be extended to a *population monotonic allocation scheme* (pmas) [17] (roughly speaking, an allocation method is pmas extendible if it assigns an allocation vector to every coalition in a monotonic way and such that the cost allocated to some edge does not increase if the coalition of edges to which it belongs becomes larger). It would be interesting to analyse whether the core allocations computed according to the procedure used in Theorem 2 satisfy these properties.

Finally, as an alternative framework, one could imagine a version of a (monotonic) LC game where each service provider has the power, alone or in cooperation, to control the implementation of the services over the entire network, and not only those using the connections within a given coalition, like in the current version of the model.

References

1. Aziz, H., Lachish, O., Paterson, M., Savani, R.: Wiretapping a hidden network. In: Leonardi, S. (ed.) WINE 2009. LNCS, vol. 5929, pp. 438–446. Springer, Heidelberg (2009). https://doi.org/10.1007/978-3-642-10841-9_40
2. Bergañtinos, G., Lorenzo, L., Lorenzo-Freire, S.: A generalization of obligation rules for minimum cost spanning tree problems. Eur. J. Oper. Res. **211**, 122–129 (2011)
3. Bird, C.: On cost allocation for a spanning tree: a game theoretic approach. Networks **6**, 335–350 (1976)
4. Branzei, R., Moretti, S., Norde, H., Tijs, S.: The P-value for cost sharing in minimum cost spanning tree situations. Theory Decis. **56**, 47–61 (2004)

5. Claus, A., Kleitman, D.J.: Cost allocation for a spanning tree. Networks **3**, 289–304 (1973)
6. Feltkamp, V.: Cooperation in controlled network structures, PhD Dissertation, Tilburg University, The Netherlands (1995)
7. Granot, D., Huberman, G.: On minimum cost spanning tree games. Math. Prog. **21**, 1–18 (1981)
8. Hougaard, J.L., Moulin, H.: Sharing the cost of redundant items. Games Econ. Behav. **87**, 339–352 (2014)
9. Kruskal, J.B.: On the shortest spanning subtree of a graph and the traveling salesman problem. Proc. Amer. Math. Soc. **7**, 48–50 (1956)
10. Moretti, S., Tijs, S., Branzei, R., Norde, H.: Cost allocation protocols for supply contract design in network situations. Math. Meth. Oper. Res. **69**(1), 181–202 (2009)
11. Moulin, H., Laigret, F.: Equal-need sharing of a network under connectivity constraints. Games Econ. Behav. **72**(1), 314–320 (2011)
12. Nagamochi, H., Zeng, D.Z., Kabutoya, N., Ibaraki, T.: Complexity of the minimum base game on matroids. Math. Oper. Res. **22**(1), 146–164 (1997)
13. Norde, H., Moretti, S., Tijs, S.: Minimum cost spanning tree games and population monotonic allocation schemes. Eur. J. Oper. Res. **154**(1), 84–97 (2004)
14. Prim, R.C.: Shortest connection networks and some generalizations. Bell Syst. Tech. J. **36**, 1389–1401 (1957)
15. Shapley, L.S.: A Value for n-Person Games. In: Kuhn, H.W., Tucker, A.W. (ed.) Contributions to the Theory of Games II, Ann. Math. Studies 28, 307–317, Princeton University Press (1953)
16. Shapley, L.S.: Cores and convex games. Int. J. Game Theory **1**, 1–26 (1971)
17. Sprumont, Y.: Population monotonic allocation schemes for cooperative games with transferable utility. Games Econ. Behav. **2**, 378–394 (1990)
18. Tijs, S., Branzei, R., Moretti, S., Norde, H.: Obligation rules for minimum cost spanning tree situations and their monotonicity properties. Eur. J. Oper. Res. **175**, 121–134 (2006)

EUMAS 2017: Negotiation, Planning and Coalitions

On Decentralized Implicit Negotiation in Modified Ultimatum Game

Jitka Homolová[✉], Eliška Zugarová, Miroslav Kárný,
and Tatiana Valentine Guy

Department of Adaptive Systems, The Czech Academy of Sciences,
Institute of Information Theory and Automation,
P.O. Box 18, 182 08 Prague 8, Czech Republic
{jkratoch,school,guy}@utia.cas.cz, eliska.zugarova@gmail.com

Abstract. Cooperation and negotiation are important elements of human interaction within extensive, flatly organized, mixed human-machine societies. Any sophisticated artificial intelligence cannot be complete without them. Multi-agent system with dynamic locally independent agents, that interact in a distributed way is inevitable in majority of modern applications. Here we consider a *modified* Ultimatum game (UG) for studying negotiation and cooperation aspects of decision making. The manuscript proposes agent's optimizing policy using Markov decision process (MDP) framework, which covers *implicit* negotiation (in contrast with explicit schemes as in [5]). The proposed solution replaces the classical game-theoretical design of agents' policies by an adaptive MDP that is: (i) more realistic with respect to the knowledge available to individual players; (ii) provides a first step towards solving negotiation essential in conflict situations.

Keywords: Cooperation · Negotiation · Economic game
Ultimatum game · Markov decision process

1 Introduction

Human intelligence develops in a context of different social interactions (within family, school, etc.) and their importance can hardly be overestimated. Artificial intelligence cannot be complete without supporting cooperation and negotiation as the basics of any dynamic decision making (repetitive, history-dependent). Many applications in the fields of Artificial Intelligence, Computer Science and Economics (cooperative control, flocking, distributed sensor networks, communication networks, transportation) represent multi-agent systems with dynamic locally independent agents that need to coordinate to reach certain quantities of interest for mutual satisfaction. Dynamics, i.e. significant dependence of the actual decision-making task on the past history of agents' interactions is one of the important characteristics of these systems. Studying cooperation without a facilitator can bring us a better understanding of human behavior [3,9] as well as an improving of overall performance of distributed computer systems [12,21].

© Springer Nature Switzerland AG 2018
F. Belardinelli and E. Argente (Eds.): EUMAS 2017/AT 2017, LNAI 10767, pp. 357–369, 2018.
https://doi.org/10.1007/978-3-030-01713-2_25

Cooperative aspects can be well studied using economic games [9,19]. Here we consider a modification of the Ultimatum game (UG) [10], which is an economic game with simple rules. Two players (hereinafter agents) are to decide how to divide some goods between themselves. In the standard UG roles of agents are asymmetric: one agent proposes a division and the second one either accepts it or decides that none of agents gets anything.

It has been reported [6] that human-players do not behave rationally and their decisions do not follow the normative strategy implied by game theory [18]. The irrationality of a human-player in the Ultimatum Game has been already discussed. The paper [7] suggests that the human is also driven by the sense for fairness. The paper further introduces three models of player's distinguishing of an affection degree with which the player is under influence of his individual tendency to consider a social profit (fairness) or an economic profit. The experimental results [7] have shown people do behave rationally with the reward that respected fairness.

The considered modification of UG balances the roles of both agents. The good division then can be interpreted as cake splitting. Both agents make a request for a certain number of pieces of the cake. In case of the demands compatibility, the cake is divided accordingly and they both get what they asked for. Oppositely, in case of the number of pieces of the cake exceeding, they both get nothing. This modification is close to the Nash's bargaining game [13].

There are some examples illustrating the real-life use of bargaining in human decision making: negotiating over a price by a seller and a buyer, bargaining over a trade agreement by two companies, finding a balance between the needs of employees and the interests of the employer by a company and a labor union or immigration quotas debating by European countries. In all of these examples, the common objective of all parties is reaching a consensus.

There is a number of studies focused on cooperation in decision making [11,14,20]. However, a reliable solution, applicable to distributed facilitator-free scenario and especially to the problem of human decision-making, still does not exist. *The main goal of this paper is to make a step towards distributed negotiation allowing cooperation within a flatly organized, dynamic human-machine society.* This goal can be reached if the policy of each individual agent is designed from the agent's perspective only. This justifies a formulation when the co-players are taken as a part of the agent's environment modeled in a feasible way. The theory of Markov decision processes (MDP) provides such a feasible approach. The intention to reach unlimited scalability excludes the (otherwise relevant) framework of Bayesian games [8]. It should be emphasized that the article does not aim to challenge existing solutions of UG, but uses modified version of UG for studying negotiation aspects.

Section 2 introduces necessary notations, recalls Markov Decision Process (MDP) and outlines a solution concept. Section 3 introduces modified UG and formulates it in terms of MDP. The key step is defining reward function that *implicitly* motivates negotiation. Section 4 describes two different models of a non-optimizing agent. Section 5 describes simulation experiments and Sect. 6 summarizes the results and adds some remarks on future research directions.

2   Preliminaries

This section introduces notations and recalls necessary notions.

$\mathbb{N}, \mathbb{R}$ set of natural numbers, set of real numbers
$x \in \mathbf{X}$ value x from the set of values $\mathbf{X}$
x_t value of x at discrete time t
$p(x|y)$ conditional probability of random variable x conditioned on random variable y
$E[x]$ expectation of random variable x
$E[x|y]$ conditional expectation of random variable x conditioned on random variable y

2.1   Markov Decision Process

The addressed problem is formulated as a discrete-time discrete-valued *Markov Decision Process* (MDP). Let us remind a single-agent MDP (a detailed description can be found in [17]).

Definition 1 (MDP). *The fully observable MDP is characterized by* $\{\mathbf{T}, \mathbf{S}, \mathbf{A}, p, R\}$, *where* $\mathbf{T} = \{1, 2, ..., N\}, N \in \mathbb{N}$, *is a set of decision epochs;* $\mathbf{S}$ *is a set of all possible system states and* $\mathbf{A}$ *denotes a set of all actions available to the agent. Function* $p : \mathbf{S} \times \mathbf{A} \times \mathbf{S} \mapsto [0,1]$ *expresses the transition probability* $p_t(s_{t+1}|s_t, a_t)$ *that moves the system from state* $s_t \in \mathbf{S}$ *to state* $s_{t+1} \in \mathbf{S}$ *after an agent chooses action* $a_t \in \mathbf{A}$; $R : \mathbf{S} \times \mathbf{A} \times \mathbf{S} \mapsto \mathbb{R}$ *is a real-valued function representing the agent's reward* $r_t(s_{t+1}, s_t, a_t)$ *after taking action* $a_t \in \mathbf{A}$ *in state* $s_t \in \mathbf{S}$ *stimulating the transition to state* s_{t+1}.

The full observability means that the agent observes *precise* state s_{t+1} reached *after* action a_t is taken. This does not imply however that the agent is able to precisely predict future states.

In each decision epoch $t \in \mathbf{T}$, the agent chooses the action $a_t \in \mathbf{A}$ based on the *randomized DM rule* $p_t(a_t|s_t)$, which is a non-negative function representing a probability of the action a_t in the given state $s_t \in \mathbf{S}$. The agent's goal is to find an optimal *DM policy* π_t, that is a sequence of DM rules mapping states to actions to maximize expected reward over some horizon $h \in \{1, 2, ..., N - t\}$:

$$\pi_{t,h} = \left\{ p_\tau(a_\tau|s_\tau) \Big| s_\tau \in \mathbf{S}_\tau, a_\tau \in \mathbf{A}_\tau, \sum_{a_\tau \in \mathbf{A}_\tau} p_\tau(a_\tau|s_\tau) = 1, \forall s_\tau \in \mathbf{S}_\tau \right\}_{\tau=t}^{t+h}. \quad (1)$$

MDP with finite horizon h evaluates quality of the DM policy by an *expected total reward* $E\left[\sum_{\tau=t}^{t+h} r_\tau(s_{\tau+1}, s_\tau, a_\tau)|s_t \right]$.

In game round $t \in \mathbf{T}$ and state $s_t \in \mathbf{S}$, the *expected reward function* is defined as:

$$E_t\big[r_t(s_{t+1}, s_t, a_t)|s_t\big] = \sum_{s_{t+1}\in\mathbf{S}_{t+1} a_t\in\mathbf{A}_t} r_t(s_{t+1}, s_t, a_t)p_t(s_{t+1}, a_t|s_t), \qquad (2)$$

where $p_t(s_{t+1}, a_t|s_t) = p_t(s_{t+1}|a_t, s_t)p_t(a_t|s_t)$.

The solution to MDP [17] is a sequence of functions $\left\{p_\tau^{opt}(a_\tau|s_\tau)\right\}_{\tau=t}^{t+h}$ that maximizes the expected reward and forms the optimal decision policy:

$$\pi_{t,h}^{opt} = \arg\max_{\{\pi_{t,h}\}} E\left[\sum_{\tau=t}^{t+h} r_\tau(s_{\tau+1}, s_\tau, a_\tau)|s_t\right]. \qquad (3)$$

3   Modified Ultimatum Game

We use a modified version of the UG, a so-called cooperative UG scenario considering two agents $\mathcal{A}$ and $\mathcal{B}$ and an available amount of money (goods) q to split. Unlike the classical UG [18] roles of both players are the same. In the considered modification of the UG each round is treated as a round of an N-round repeated game. In the round, there is an action stage and a reward stage. During the *action* stage, each agent decides on own demand without knowing that of the co-player. Note that their interests are competitive. At the *reward* stage both agents get their rewards depending on whether amount q can cover the sum of their demands. In addition to plausibility for modeling cooperation and negotiation, the modified UG allows to adjust the amount of information the agents obtain (the degree of uncertainty), which is obviously an important aspect of the policy choice.

The overall scenario is as follows. At the beginning of the round $t \in \mathbf{T}$, each agent $k \in \{\mathcal{A}, \mathcal{B}\}$ chooses action $a_t^k \in \mathbf{A}^k$ that is a portion of q he wants to receive in this round. In case that demands sum up to less than q, both agents receive what they had asked for, otherwise, neither of the agents gets anything. Thus, the pure economic profit of agent $\mathcal{A}$ in round $t \in \mathbf{T}$ equals:

$$z_t^{\mathcal{A}} = a_t^{\mathcal{A}}\chi(a_t^{\mathcal{A}}, a_t^{\mathcal{B}}), \quad z_t^{\mathcal{A}} \in \mathbf{Z}_{\mathcal{A}} \qquad (4)$$

where $\mathbf{Z}_{\mathcal{A}} = \{0, 1, 2, ..., q-1\}$ is a set of all possible profits of agent $\mathcal{A}$ in one game round, and

$$\chi(a_t^{\mathcal{A}}, a_t^{\mathcal{B}}) = \begin{cases} 1 & \text{if } a_t^{\mathcal{A}} + a_t^{\mathcal{B}} \leq q, \\ 0 & \text{if } a_t^{\mathcal{A}} + a_t^{\mathcal{B}} > q. \end{cases} \qquad (5)$$

3.1   Modified UG as MDP

Interactive nature of the game implies that effect of the agent's individual actions depends on actions of the opponent. They are perceived and also modified in dependence on the game history, here, for simplicity restricted to Markovian case. We are interested in a *distributed* solution of the cooperation and consider the game from a point of view of a single agent $\mathcal{A}$. Generally the whole approach can be applied to agent $\mathcal{B}$ too as the process is fully observable to each of them and they may work with the structurally same reward function.

Definition 2 (Modified UG as MDP of the Agent $\mathcal{A}$). *The modified UG is modeled by* $\{\mathbf{T}, \mathbf{S}, \mathbf{A}, p, R\}$, *Definition 1, where*

- $\mathbf{A} = \mathbf{A}^{\mathcal{A}} = \{1, 2, ..., q - 1\}$ *is a set of all possible actions;* $a_t^{\mathcal{A}} \in \mathbf{A}^{\mathcal{A}}$
- $s_t = (a_{t-1}^{\mathcal{A}}, a_{t-1}^{\mathcal{B}}) \in \mathbf{S}$, *where* $a_t^{\mathcal{B}} \in \mathbf{A}^{\mathcal{B}}$ *is a portion of* q *demanded by agent* $\mathcal{B}$ *at* $t \in \mathbf{T}$, $\mathbf{A}^{\mathcal{B}} = \{1, 2, ..., q - 1\}$
- *initial state* $s_1 = (a_0^{\mathcal{A}}, a_0^{\mathcal{B}})$ *is preset to a fair offer corresponding to half of* q, *i.e.* $a_0^{\mathcal{A}} = a_0^{\mathcal{B}} = \frac{q}{2}$
- *reward of agent* $\mathcal{A}$ *is defined by* $r_t = a_t^{\mathcal{A}} \chi(a_t^{\mathcal{A}}, a_t^{\mathcal{B}}) - \omega^{\mathcal{A}} \mid q - (a_t^{\mathcal{A}} + a_t^{\mathcal{B}}) \mid$, *where* $\omega^{\mathcal{A}} \in [0, 1]$ *is a weight reflecting the degree of cooperation of the agent* $\mathcal{A}$.

In the definition of the reward function, the first term represents pure economical profit, cf. (4). The second term expresses "unused potential" if some monetary amount left after division; and "overshoot" in case when sum of demands being greater than q. The reward thus equals $a_t^{\mathcal{A}} - \omega^{\mathcal{A}} \cdot \mid q - (a_t^{\mathcal{A}} + a_t^{\mathcal{B}}) \mid$ if $\chi(a_t^{\mathcal{A}}, a_t^{\mathcal{B}}) = 1$ and $-\omega^{\mathcal{A}} \cdot \mid q - (a_t^{\mathcal{A}} + a_t^{\mathcal{B}}) \mid$ when no consensus has been reached.

The cooperativeness weight $\omega^{\mathcal{A}}$ depends on the personality traits of an agent and reflects importance of the second term in the agent's reward definition. Thus, $\omega^{\mathcal{A}}$ is specific and private for each agent working with it. Value $\omega^{\mathcal{A}} = 0$ implies reward depending on pure economical profit, while $\omega^{\mathcal{A}} > 0$ makes the designed strategy to be respecting the degree of influence of "overshoot" as well as "unused potential" on the agent. This weight reflects the human style of playing and therefore the optimal policy is implicitly forced by the discussed summand to take into account actions of the co-player, i.e. to cooperate.

The optimal policy, see Definition 2, can be computed by solving classical MDP using a dynamic programming algorithm [2,16]. It needs the transition probability $p(s_{t+1} | a_t^{\mathcal{A}}, s_t)$. Conditional independence of agents' actions and the definition of the state imply

$$p(s_{t+1} | a_t^{\mathcal{A}}, s_t) = p(a_{t+1}^{\mathcal{A}} | a_t^{\mathcal{A}}, a_t^{\mathcal{B}}) p(a_{t+1}^{\mathcal{B}} | a_t^{\mathcal{A}}, a_t^{\mathcal{B}}). \qquad (6)$$

The first factor is a part of the optimized policy. The second factor models agent $\mathcal{B}$ and can be recursively estimated using Bayesian paradigm [15]. To simplify explanation, it is assumed to be given. Its considered forms are discussed below.

4   Models of the Agent $\mathcal{B}$

To bring better understanding of the role and the effect of the introduced reward (see Definition 2), two different models of the non-optimizing agent $\mathcal{B}$ are presented and further studied. Studies of learning and optimizing agents with different prior knowledge and different cooperativeness degrees are straightforward natural extensions of the current work and are supposed to be reported in the future. The goal is to verify whether considering or conforming the second agent's actions leads to a higher profit and a higher number of successful rounds comparing to a non-cooperative strategy.

In each round, *the non-optimizing agent* $\mathcal{B}$ heuristically adjusts demands according to the results of the previous round. Generally, if the sum of both agents' demands is greater than available amount q, the agent $\mathcal{B}$ lowers the demand by a portion of the excess to avoid repeating the failure. Oppositely, if q is not used up and some amount left, the agent $\mathcal{B}$ raises the demand by a portion of the amount left to increase the chance of distributing of the whole amount q in the current round.

The proposed models of the non-optimizing agent $\mathcal{B}$ differ in the degree of an aggression of the agent or, in other words, in the extent to which the demand changes. In both models, we assume that the transition probabilities do not change during the whole game.

4.1   Type B1

The non-optimizing agent $\mathcal{B}$ of type B1 represents the basic concept of the agent $\mathcal{B}$. This type of the agent is less aggressive and more fair. The DM aim of this agent's type is to reduce the difference between q and the sum of demands from the previous round by roughly one half. This means that in the round t, the agent $\mathcal{B}$ increases or decreases next demand by $\frac{1}{2}[q - (a^{\mathcal{A}}_{t-1} + a^{\mathcal{B}}_{t-1})]$ accordingly to the "unused potential" or the "overshoot" of the available amount q.

The transition probability used for the model of the agent $\mathcal{B}$ of the type B1 can be modeled by the discretized Gaussian probability distribution with the corresponding expected mode $\frac{1}{2}(q - a^{\mathcal{A}}_{t-1} + a^{\mathcal{B}}_{t-1})$:

$$p_t(a^{\mathcal{B}}_t | a^{\mathcal{A}}_{t-1}, a^{\mathcal{B}}_{t-1}) \propto \exp\left(-\frac{\left(a^{\mathcal{B}}_t - \frac{1}{2}(q - a^{\mathcal{A}}_{t-1} + a^{\mathcal{B}}_{t-1})\right)^2}{2\sigma^2}\right), \qquad (7)$$

where $a^{\mathcal{A}}_{t-1}, a^{\mathcal{B}}_{t-1} \in \mathbf{A}$ are the demands of the agents at round $(t-1) \in \mathbf{T}$, and σ^2 is the variance of the discrete Gaussian distribution.

Such behavior can be explained by an effort to act fairly in terms of utilizing the whole amount q. The type B1 agent anticipates that the agent $\mathcal{A}$ step back by a half of an excess or raise their demands by a half of the remained part of the available amount q. However, the agent $\mathcal{B}$ does not take into consideration the difference between the individual demands. In case of the large difference, the split then becomes unfair.

Even though the model (7) serves the creation of an active opponent of the agent $\mathcal{A}$, the agent's strategy does not correspond well to human thinking [3].

4.2   Type B2

Proposed type B2 is more complex and efficient variant of the non-optimizing agent $\mathcal{B}$. It reflects human style of playing. As described in the previous subsection, the type B1 agent adapts the actions in dependence on the difference between the sum of demands and the available amount q. For the type B2 agent, change of demand depends on the agent $\mathcal{A}$ action from the previous round. The action range of the agent $\mathcal{A}$ is divided into three regions for which the offset of the new demand of the agent $\mathcal{B}$ is set differently.

Let $q = 10$, $t \in \mathbf{T}$ be the current game round and $a_{t-1}^{\mathcal{A}}$, $a_{t-1}^{\mathcal{B}} \in \mathbf{A}$ be the demands from the previous game round. Then demand $a_{t-1}^{\mathcal{A}}$ can belong to the following sets: $\{1, 2, 3\}$, $\{3, 4, 5\}$ and $\{6, 7, 9\}$. Transition probabilities related to the type B2 are set for each set as follows.

Case 1: The demand of the agent $\mathcal{A}$ when $a_{t-1}^{\mathcal{A}} \in \{1, 2, 3\}$.

1. If $q - (a_{t-1}^{\mathcal{A}} + a_{t-1}^{\mathcal{B}}) \geq 0$, i.e. some amount of q is left in the previous round, then the agent of the type B2 increases the demand by one third of the part of q lost in round $(t - 1)$:

$$p_t(a_t^{\mathcal{B}} | a_{t-1}^{\mathcal{A}}, a_{t-1}^{\mathcal{B}}) \propto \exp\left(-\frac{\left(a_t^{\mathcal{B}} - \frac{1}{3}(q - a_{t-1}^{\mathcal{A}} + 2a_{t-1}^{\mathcal{B}})\right)^2}{2\sigma^2} \right).$$

2. If $q - (a_{t-1}^{\mathcal{A}} + a_{t-1}^{\mathcal{B}}) < 0$, i.e. the agents' demands exceed amount q in the previous round, the agent of the type B2 decreases the demand by two thirds of the amount that exceeded q:

$$p_t(a_t^{\mathcal{B}} | a_{t-1}^{\mathcal{A}}, a_{t-1}^{\mathcal{B}}) \propto \exp\left(-\frac{\left(a_t^{\mathcal{B}} - \frac{2}{3}(q - a_{t-1}^{\mathcal{A}} + \frac{1}{2}a_{t-1}^{\mathcal{B}})\right)^2}{2\sigma^2} \right).$$

Case 2: The demand of the agent $\mathcal{A}$ when $a_{t-1}^{\mathcal{A}} \in \{4, 5, 6\}$.

1. The agent of the type B2 behaves identically to the type B1 (7):

$$p_t(a_t^{\mathcal{B}} | a_{t-1}^{\mathcal{A}}, a_{t-1}^{\mathcal{B}}) \propto \exp\left(-\frac{\left(a_t^{\mathcal{B}} - \frac{1}{2}(q - a_{t-1}^{\mathcal{A}} + a_{t-1}^{\mathcal{B}})\right)^2}{2\sigma^2} \right).$$

Case 3: The demand of the agent $\mathcal{A}$ when $a_{t-1}^{\mathcal{A}} \in \{7, 8, 9\}$.

1. If $q - (a_{t-1}^{\mathcal{A}} + a_{t-1}^{\mathcal{B}}) \geq 0$, the agent of the type B2 raises the demand by two thirds of the amount not distributed in round $(t - 1)$:

$$p_t(a_t^{\mathcal{B}} | a_{t-1}^{\mathcal{A}}, a_{t-1}^{\mathcal{B}}) \propto \exp\left(-\frac{\left(a_t^{\mathcal{B}} - \frac{2}{3}(q - a_{t-1}^{\mathcal{A}} + \frac{1}{2}a_{t-1}^{\mathcal{B}})\right)^2}{2\sigma^2} \right).$$

2. If $q - a_{t-1}^{\mathcal{A}} - a_{t-1}^{\mathcal{B}} < 0$, then the agent of the type B2 lowers the demand by one third of the exceeded amount:

$$p_t(a_t^{\mathcal{B}} | a_{t-1}^{\mathcal{A}}, a_{t-1}^{\mathcal{B}}) \propto \exp\left(-\frac{\left(a_t^{\mathcal{B}} - \frac{1}{3}(q - a_{t-1}^{\mathcal{A}} + 2a_{t-1}^{\mathcal{B}})\right)^2}{2\sigma^2} \right).$$

Case 1 can be interpreted as the type B2 agent either decreases the demand in case of an excess to prevent it happening again, or the agent increases the demand by a smaller amount in case of not spending the full amount q because of the tolerance assumption of the agent $\mathcal{A}$.

In Case 2, the type B2 agent expects the fairness of the agent $\mathcal{A}$, which means that such agent anticipates from the agent $\mathcal{A}$ to ask for only a half of the amount left or to drop a half of the excess.

In Case 3, the type B2 agent tries to stop the agent $\mathcal{A}$ from continuing to take actions of the high value (the actions from the region $\{7, 8, 9\}$), because these actions lead to an unfair splitting of the amount q. By this reason, the agent asks for the larger portion of the amount lost and is willing to retreat less in case of the excess.

Such model of the agent $\mathcal{B}$ better corresponds to the anticipated behavior of a human [7,9].

5   Illustrative Experiments

The proposed approach is illustrated on several simulated examples ran in Matlab environment. Each game had $N = 30$ rounds. The available amount to split was $q = 10 \mathrm{CZK}$[1] in each round. The simulation ran for five different values of the cooperativeness weight $w^{\mathcal{A}} \in \{0, 0.25, 0.5, 0.75, 1\}$. The reward (see Definition 2) used the design of the optimal policy of the agent $\mathcal{A}$ that was found by the dynamic programming [2]. The weight $w^{\mathcal{A}}$ reflected individual tendency of the agent $\mathcal{A}$ to consider negotiations $(0 < w^{\mathcal{A}} \leq 1)$ or not $(w^{\mathcal{A}} = 0)$.

In case of $w^{\mathcal{A}} = 0$, the agent $\mathcal{A}$ is interested only in the monetary profit and does not cooperate. In case of $0 < w^{\mathcal{A}} \leq 1$, the agent is also, to some degree, committed to use the potential of each round. It means that the agent tries do not exceed the available amount q and to split it fully. This weight $w^{\mathcal{A}}$ does *not* express a balance between the importance of the economic profit and the cooperation.

The first example is a game of two non-optimising agents (so-called type $\mathcal{B}$ agents, see Sect. 4). We need it for the later comparison with a game when one of the players cooperates and optimizes.

In the current example, one agent was of the type B1 (see Sect. 4.1) while another of the type B2 (see Sect. 4.2), so the transition probabilities of both models were proportional to the Gaussian distribution. Let's recall the agent of the type B2 is more complex version of the agent of the type B1 whose demand depends on the previous action of the opponent. The standard deviation of $\sigma = 3$ was chosen and the seed parameter for the reproducibility was set to the value of 90 during the simulation. The numerical results are summarized in the Table 1. Plots of the cumulative profits of the agents and their corresponding actions are shown in Figs. 1 and 2.

As it can be seen from the results, the higher flexibility to the actual situation of the agent $\mathcal{B}$ of the type B2 causes the better choice of actions and so the reaching the higher total profit of such agent type.

---

[1] Czech crowns.

Table 1. Game of type B1 agent and type B2 agent

Standard deviation $\sigma = 3$	
Percentage of the successful rounds (%)	63.3
Total profit of the agent $\mathcal{B}$ of the type B1 (CZK)	71
Total profit of the agent $\mathcal{B}$ of the type B2 (CZK)	85

Table 2. Game with the optimizing agent $\mathcal{A}$ and the agent $\mathcal{B}$ of the type B1.

Standard deviation $\sigma = 3$					
Weight $\omega^{\mathcal{A}}$	0.00	0.25	0.50	0.75	1.00
Percentage of the successful rounds (%)	70.0	76.7	70.0	70.0	66.7
Total profit of the agent $\mathcal{A}$ (CZK)	126	137	129	131	121
Total profit of the agent $\mathcal{B}$ (CZK)	61	68	64	62	56
Standard deviation $\sigma = 4$					
Weight $\omega^{\mathcal{A}}$	0.00	0.25	0.50	0.75	1.00
Percentage of the successful rounds (%)	70.0	76.7	70.0	76.7	76.7
Total profit of the agent $\mathcal{A}$ (CZK)	119	133	126	126	128
Total profit of the agent $\mathcal{B}$ (CZK)	66	75	75	75	75
Standard deviation $\sigma = 5$					
Weight $\omega^{\mathcal{A}}$	0.00	0.25	0.50	0.75	1.00
Percentage of the successful rounds (%)	76.7	73.3	73.3	73.3	73.3
Total profit of the agent $\mathcal{A}$ (CZK)	122	116	121	123	119
Total profit of the agent $\mathcal{B}$ (CZK)	78	73	70	70	71

The second example represents a set of the games with the optimizing agent $\mathcal{A}$ and the non-optimizing agent $\mathcal{B}$ of the type B1 (see Sect. 4.1). The simulation ran with five values of the cooperativeness weight $\omega^{\mathcal{A}}$ and three different values of the standard deviation $\sigma \in \{3, 4, 5\}$ in the model of the agent $\mathcal{B}$. The seed parameter was set to 13. The numerical results can be seen in Table 2. The progress of the cumulative profits of the agents for $\omega^{\mathcal{A}} = 0.25$ and $\sigma = 3$ is plotted in Fig. 3 and the corresponding actions in Fig. 4.

The last example focuses on a set of the games with the optimizing agent $\mathcal{A}$ and the non-optimizing agent $\mathcal{B}$ of the type B2 (see Sect. 4.2). The simulation also ran for five values of the cooperativeness weight $\omega^{\mathcal{A}}$ and three values of the standard deviation $\sigma \in \{3, 4, 5\}$. The seed parameter for the reproducibility was set to the value of 20. The numerical results are presented in Table 3. The course of the cumulative profits of the agents, using $\omega^{\mathcal{A}} = 0.25$ and $\sigma = 3$, are plotted in Fig. 5. The actions of the agents can be seen in Fig. 6.

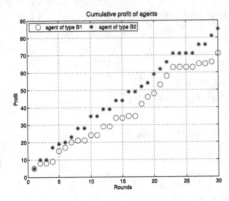

Fig. 1. Cumulative profits: non-optimizing agents, player 1 is of the type B1 and player 2 is of the type B2.

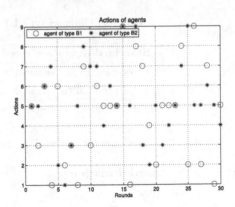

Fig. 2. Actions: non-optimizing agents, player 1 is of the type B1 and player 2 is of the type B2.

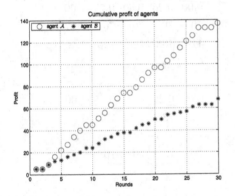

Fig. 3. Cumulative profits: player 1 is the optimizing agent $\mathcal{A}$ and player 2 is the non-optimizing agent $\mathcal{B}$ of the type B1.

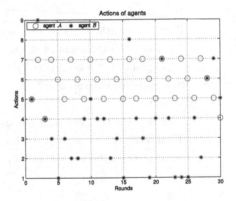

Fig. 4. Actions: player 1 is the optimizing agent $\mathcal{A}$ and player 2 is the non-optimizing agent $\mathcal{B}$ of the type B1.

The results show that the optimization positively leads to the higher profit independently of the cooperativeness weight. Once again, the higher flexibility to the actual situation of the agent $\mathcal{B}$ of the type B2 brings the possibility to assert at the expense of the agent $\mathcal{A}$. Another interesting point is that too much effort to maximize the potential of each game round leads to a worsening of overall results that can be seen mainly from the percentage of the successful rounds.

Table 3. Game with the optimizing agent $\mathcal{A}$ and the agent $\mathcal{B}$ of the type B2.

Standard deviation $\sigma = 3$					
Weight $\omega^{\mathcal{A}}$	0.00	0.25	0.50	0.75	1.00
Percentage of the successful rounds (%)	53.3	60.0	60.0	50.0	50.0
Total profit of the agent $\mathcal{A}$ (CZK)	88	102	100	87	86
Total profit of the agent $\mathcal{B}$ (CZK)	61	67	67	53	53
Standard deviation $\sigma = 4$					
Weight $\omega^{\mathcal{A}}$	0.00	0.25	0.50	0.75	1.00
Percentage of the successful rounds (%)	63.3	60.0	56.7	56.7	53.3
Total profit of the agent $\mathcal{A}$ (CZK)	99	94	92	91	88
Total profit of the agent $\mathcal{B}$ (CZK)	76	71	62	64	58
Standard deviation $\sigma = 5$					
Weight $\omega^{\mathcal{A}}$	0.00	0.25	0.50	0.75	1.00
Percentage of the successful rounds (%)	73.3	56.7	56.7	56.7	56.7
Total profit of the agent $\mathcal{A}$ (CZK)	111	88	89	91	91
Total profit of the agent $\mathcal{B}$ (CZK)	91	62	62	62	61

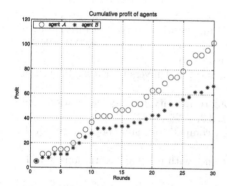

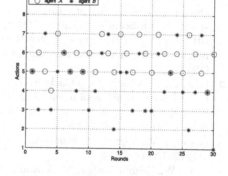

Fig. 5. Cumulative profits: player 1 is the optimizing agent $\mathcal{A}$ and player 2 is the non-optimizing agent $\mathcal{B}$ of the type B2.

Fig. 6. Actions: player 1 is the optimizing agent $\mathcal{A}$ and player 2 is the non-optimizing agent $\mathcal{B}$ of the type B2.

6 Concluding Remarks

The paper introduces an innovative approach to the implicit cooperation in the modified UG. The optimizing agent is modeled via Markov decision process. The key step of the proposed approach is the special reward function (see Definition 2) respecting not only the economic profit of the agent but also reflecting the agent's willingness for the cooperation. Such a reward function implicitly forces the agent to negotiate. By optimizing overall behavior of the agents their optimal degree of cooperation can be searched for.

The adopted approach was driven by our main concern: the search for a *feasible, fully scalable,* design of approximately optimal DM policy under the need for a cooperation. The inspected framework also allows respecting the influence of such subtle phenomena as emotions in decision making [1]. In this respect, the gained results are the first promising step in creating the applicable DM strategies allowing for the *fully scalable* distributed cooperation and negotiation in the extensive *mixed human-machine* societies.

The foreseen research will consider: (i) different types of the agents (learning, optimizing ones, differing in cooperativeness degree, using more realistic non-symmetric reward [4] and others); (ii) including the fairness aspects into the reward function [7]; (iii) dependence of economic profit on the cooperativeness weight; (iv) learning the co-player's model and its cooperativeness weights.

Acknowledgement. The research has been supported by the project GA16-09848S, LTC 18075 and EU-Cost Action 16228.

References

1. Avanesyan, G., Kárný, M., Knejflová, Z., Guy, T.V.: Demo: What lies beneath players' non-rationality in ultimatum game? In: Preprints of the 3rd International Workshop on Scalable Decision Making held in conjunction with ECML-PKDD 2013. ÚTIA AVČR, Prague, Czech Republic (2013)
2. Bellman, R.E.: Dynamic Programming. Princeton University Press, Princeton (1957)
3. Fehr, E., Fischbacher, U., Gächter, S.: Strong reciprocity, human cooperation, and the enforcement of social norms. Hum. Nat. **13**, 1–25 (2002)
4. Fehr, E., Schmidt, K.: A theory of fairness, competition, and cooperation. Q. J. Econ. **114**(3), 817–868 (1999)
5. Goranko, V., Turrini, P.: Non-cooperative games with preplay negotiations. CoRR abs/1208.1718 (2012)
6. Güth, W., Schmittberger, R., Schwarze, B.: An experimental analysis of ultimatum bargaining. J. Econ. Behav. Organ. **3**(4), 367–388 (1982)
7. Guy, T.V., Kárný, M., Lintas, A., Villa, A.: Theoretical Models of Decision-making in the Ultimatum Game: Fairness vs. Reason, pp. 185–191. Springer, Singapore (2016). https://doi.org/10.1007/978-981-10-0207-6_26
8. Harsanyi, J.: Games with incomplete information played by Bayesian players I-III. Manag. Sci. **50**(12 Supplement), 1818–1824 (2004)
9. Haselhuhn, M.P., Mellers, B.A.: Emotions and cooperation in economic games. Cogn. Brain Res. **23**, 24–33 (2005)
10. Hůla, F., Ruman, M., Kárný, M.: Adaptive proposer for ultimatum game. In: Villa, A.E.P., Masulli, P., Pons Rivero, A.J. (eds.) ICANN 2016. LNCS, vol. 9886, pp. 330–338. Springer, Cham (2016). https://doi.org/10.1007/978-3-319-44778-0_39
11. Johansson, B., Speranzon, A., Johansson, M., Johansson, K.H.: On decentralized negotiation of optimal consensus. Automatica **44**(4), 1175–1179 (2008)
12. Kraus, S.: Negotiation and cooperation in multi-agent environments. Artif. Intell. **94**(1–2), 79–97 (1997)

13. Nash, J.F.: The bargaining problem. Econometrica **18**(2), 155–162 (1950)
14. Olfati-Saber, R., Fax, J., Murray, R.: Consensus and cooperation in networked multi-agent systems. Proc. IEEE **95**(1), 215–233 (2007)
15. Peterka, V.: Bayesian approach to system identification. In: Eykhoff, P. (ed.) In Trends and Progress in System Identification, pp. 239–304. Pergamon Press, Netherlands (1981)
16. Powell, W.B.: Approximate Dynamic Programming, 2nd edn. Wiley, Hoboken (2011)
17. Puterman, M.L.: Markov Decission Processes. Wiley, Hoboken (1994)
18. Rubinstein, A.: Perfect equilibrium in a bargaining model. Econometrica **50**(1), 97–109 (1982)
19. Sanfey, A.G.: Social decision-making: insights from game theory and neuroscience. Science **318**, 598–602 (2007)
20. Semsar-Kazerooni, E., Khorasani, K.: Multi-agent team cooperation: a game theory approach. Automatica **45**(10), 2205–2213 (2009)
21. Xuan, P., Lesser, V., Zilberstein, S.: Communication decisions in multiagent cooperation: model and experiments. In: Proceedings of the Fifth International Conference on Autonomous Agents, Montreal, Canada, pp. 616–623 (2001). http://rbr.cs.umass.edu/shlomo/papers/XLZagents01.html

Negotiation Strategy of Divisible Tasks for Large Dataset Processing

Quentin Baert[(✉)], Anne-Cécile Caron, Maxime Morge,
and Jean-Christophe Routier

Univ. Lille, CNRS, Centrale Lille, UMR 9189 - CRIStAL - Centre de Recherche en
Informatique Signal et Automatique de Lille, 59000 Lille, France
{quentin.baert,anne-cecile.caron,maxime.morge,
jean-christophe.routier}@univ-lille.fr

Abstract. MapReduce is a design pattern for processing large datasets on a cluster. Its performances depend on some data skews and on the runtime environment. In order to tackle these problems, we propose an adaptive multiagent system. The agents interact during the data processing and the dynamic task allocation is the outcome of negotiations. These negotiations aim at improving the workload partition among the nodes within a cluster and so decrease the runtime of the whole process. Moreover, since the negotiations are iterative the system is responsive in case of node performance variations. In this paper, we show how, when a task is divisible, an agent may split it in order to negotiate its subtasks.

Keywords: Application of mas · Automated negotiation · Adaptation

1 Introduction

The processing of large datasets requires to distribute data on multiple machines, typically a cluster of PC. Processing such distributed data is the purpose of the MapReduce design pattern [1]. A MapReduce application is composed of a map function which filters the data in order to build key-value couples and a reduce function which aggregates them. Many implementations of MapReduce exist, but the most popular is the open-source implementation Hadoop.

The user of a distributed application based on the MapReduce design pattern (e.g. Hadoop) must know its implementation, the input data and the runtime environment in order to configure beforehand the job. Nevertheless, even with a finely tuned configuration, data skews and heterogeneous runtime environments challenge the implementation choices.

In [2], the authors identify two common data skews during the reduce phase: (i) the partitioning skew occurs when a reducer processes a larger number of keys than others; (ii) the expensive key groups occurs when few keys are associated with a large number of values. As stated in [3], these two skews are widespread

This project is supported by the CNRS Challenge Mastodons.

F. Belardinelli and E. Argente (Eds.): EUMAS 2017/AT 2017, LNAI 10767, pp. 370–384, 2018.
https://doi.org/10.1007/978-3-030-01713-2_26

in today's applications and, they lead to an unbalanced workload of the reducers. Since the job ends when all the reducers have finished their work, the process is penalized by the most loaded reducer or (the slowest one). In this paper, we propose a multiagent system which implements the distributed MapReduce pattern where reducer agents negotiate divisible tasks while they process a job in order to improve the workload partition and so the runtime. The adaptivity of the MAS allows us to tackle both the reduce phase data skews and a heterogeneous runtime environment without data preprocessing. In [4], we have discussed the formal properties of our MAS and we have shown the advantages of a MAS architecture. Moreover, we have addressed the partitioning skew thanks to negotiations between reducers. Here, we address the expensive key groups skew with a negotiation strategy of divisible tasks. When the task delegation is socially irrational, our agents may split that task and negotiate the subtasks in order to reach a fairer task allocation. A reducer negotiates and splits tasks using its local beliefs about its peers workloads. These beliefs are updated during the reduce phase using the informations exchanged through the negotiations. Since the nodes may have heterogeneous performances, the process constantly adapts the distribution of the computations to the dynamics of the job processing. Furthermore, in order to improve the responsiveness of the MAS, we extend the negotiation process such that the agents can simultaneously bid in concurrent auctions. Finally, we show through several experiments that the workload balancing speeds up the data processing.

Section 2 presents the MapReduce design pattern and the related works. In Sect. 3, we shortly present our negotiation process with an illustrative example and we present our negotiation strategy of divisible task. Section 4 presents our experiments which highlight the added value of our adaptive multiagent system. Finally, Sect. 5 concludes and presents future works.

2   Motivation

MapReduce jobs consist of two sets of tasks, i.e. the *map* tasks and the *reduce* tasks, which are distributed among nodes within a cluster. A node which performs a map task (resp. a reduce task) is called a mapper (resp. a reducer). In order to perform such tasks, the nodes need these two functions given by the user:

$$map: (K1, V1) \rightarrow list[(K2, V2)]$$
$$reduce: (K2, list[V2]) \rightarrow list[(K3, V3)]$$

Figure 1 illustrates the MapReduce data flow as implemented in Hadoop:

1. the supervisor shares input data by giving a slot to each mapper;
2. the mappers apply the map function over their slots and build the intermediate key-value pairs $(key : K2, value : V2)$;
3. a partitioning function is applied over the output of the mappers in order to split them in subsets, i.e. one subset per reducer such that the couples with the same key are sent to the same reducer. In this way, a reducer process all the values of the same key (for data consistency);

4. the reducers aggregate the intermediate key-value to build the couples $(K2, list[V2])$. They apply the reduce function over the groups of values associated to each key;
5. the final key-value couples $(K3, V3)$ are written in the distributed file system.

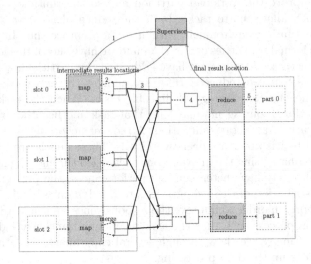

Fig. 1. MapReduce data flow.

Several criteria must be considered to compare our proposal to others[1]:

1. Prior knowledge about the data. Since the datasets are large, analyzing data beforehand is not realistic;
2. Data skew. We aim at addressing the data skews which lead to an unbalanced workload;
3. Self-adaptivity. We want the system to autonomously and constantly balance the workload.
4. Decentralization. A decentralized process is more responsive, robust and efficient than a centralized one.
5. Weak parametrization. Setting the parameters of a job requires to know the input data, the runtime environment and the MapReduce implementation. We aim at providing a solution which adapts the task allocation without expertise about the data and the computation environment.

The distribution of the MapReduce pattern needs to tackle the data skews which penalize the efficiency of the computation. [5] and [6] predict the performance with job profiling by collecting data during the previous runs. We do not want to preprocess data due to its computational cost, in particular for large datasets.

---

[1] Fault tolerance is out of the scope of our study.

The partitioning skew leads to an unbalanced key allocation to the reducers. Without any prior knowledge about the data, the partitioning function cannot warrant a fair key allocation, and so a fair task allocation among the reducers. This data skew is tackled in [2, 7, 8] using centralized solutions with prior knowledge about the data and the environment or parametrized system. In [4], we also address it with a dynamic task allocation which is the outcome of concurrent negotiations between reducer agents all along the reduce phase. Unlike the other works, our proposal is decentralized and it does not require any configuration.

The data skew of expensive key groups is due to the fact that few keys are associated with a large number of values. For instance, it happens when the data can be approximated with a Zipfian distribution [9], i.e. the number of values for a key is inversely proportional to its rank in the frequency table. The consequent congestion phenomenon in the reduce phase is studied in [10]. Most of the time, this problem cannot be solved by a different key allocation to the reducers since a reducer is overloaded as soon as it is responsible for an expensive task. Even if this data skew is raised in [2], no solution is given. In [11], the authors also highlight this data skew. Since they claim that MapReduce requires that each key must be processed by a single reducer, they consider that the possibilities of fitting the system for this skew are very small. Then, their proposal is restricted to a user alert and ad-hoc solutions. In [8], the authors concretely tackle this issue. They propose to split the outputs of the mappers into blocks whose size must be *a priori* set up by the user. Thus, the values associated with the same key can be distributed in several blocks. The authors introduce the notion of *intermediate reduce* tasks which are applied to a subset of the values to produce *intermediate results*. Since the size of these tasks are parameterized, it is easier to balance the workload. The intermediate results for the same key are aggregated during the *final reduce phase*. This approach is centralized since the master node gathers all the information about the intermediate tasks and it orchestrates the reduce tasks allocation. Moreover, this proposal is based on some parameters which must be defined *a priori* (e.g. the size of non-divisible tasks). Finally, the task split is systematic. In this paper, we adopt a similar approach by splitting the tasks corresponding to the keys with a large number of values. The resulting subtasks can be negotiated and so dynamically allocated to the reducers in order to reach a balanced workload. However, unlike [8], the task split is only performed if necessary. Moreover, this mechanism does not require any predefined parameter to setup the size of the subtasks.

More generally, the multiagent approach for distributed problem solving, which encompasses distributed constraint solving [12] and negotiation [13], is suitable for adapting to unknown data and dynamic computing environments. It is worth noticing that, in most of the works on negotiation, agents give priority to their own goals. Conversely, in our context of distributed problem solving, agents have a common goal which has the priority over the individual ones. Contrary to [13], our mechanism does not allocate resources based on agents' preferences once for all, but it iterates several task negotiations based on a local estimation of the remaining tasks to perform. In [12], the authors consider the problem of parallelizing heterogeneous computational tasks where each agent may not be able to perform all the tasks and may have different computational speeds. Let us note that this work addresses problems where the interactions between the tasks and machines are sparse, i.e. each agent can execute a small number of tasks and each task can be executed by a small number of agents. This is not the case in MapReduce applications. To our best knowledge, there are few works linking MAS and MapReduce frameworks. [14] presents a MapReduce pattern implementation based on mobile agents to replicate code and data for fault tolerance. However, this work does not apply self-organization techniques in order to adapt the MAS to the input data or the runtime environment. For this purpose, we adopt multiagent negotiation techniques.

3   Proposal

Our MAS addresses the two following data skews: the partitioning skew and the expensive key groups.

In order to address the partitioning skew, our reducers negotiate tasks using the Contract Net protocol. Doing so, they balance their workloads (called contributions) while they perform tasks during the reduce phase. It is important to note that task processing and negotiations simultaneously occur. Adaptation of the workload is then continuous. This process was presented in [4]. Here we extend it in order to allow agents to simultaneously bid in concurrent auctions, then to address the data skew of expensive key groups, we introduce a task split mechanism which allows reducers to partially process a task. This process leads to subtasks negotiations which refine the workload balancing.

3.1   Negotiation Process

Let us recall the basic principles of the negotiation process through an example. We consider here a particular auction for a single MapReduce job.

A reduce task represents a key and all its associated values. The cost of a task is defined by the number of values it contains. Thereby a task has the same cost for all the reducers of the system. We call *contribution* of a reducer the sum of costs for the remaining tasks it must perform.

In our example, we assume that the mapper phase has been completed and that the reduce tasks are initially allocated to four reducers, $\Omega = \{1, 2, 3, 4\}$. We focus on the task allocation at time t such that the individual contributions are $c_1(t) = 10$, $c_2(t) = 8$, $c_3(t) = 3$ and $c_4(t) = 5$ where $c_i(t)$ is the contribution of the agent i at time t (see Fig. 2a). Each reducer has beliefs concerning the contributions of others. These beliefs are updated through information carried by the negotiation messages.

In order to decrease their contribution all the reducers initiate auctions. In particular, reducer #1 initiates an auction about the task τ with $c_\tau = 3$ through a call for proposal (cfp) sent to the peers (see Fig. 2b). A cfp contains the contribution of the initiator $(c_1(t))$ and the cost of the task to negotiate (c_τ).

In order to decide if it can manage the task τ at time $t+1$, reducer i ($i \in \Omega \backslash \{1\}$) must satisfy the following acceptability criterion: $c_i(t) + c_\tau < c_1(t)$. The reducers which satisfy this criterion will improve the workload partition since they may take the responsibility of the task τ. Therefore, they make a proposal for τ while the others refuse the task delegation. For instance, reducer #2 does not take the responsibility of τ. Otherwise, its contribution $c_2(t) + c_\tau$ would be higher than $c_1(t)$. Meanwhile, reducer #3 and reducer #4 make some proposals for τ by sending their contributions to reducer #1 (see Fig. 2c).

Reducer #1 receives the proposals of the agents $\Omega' = \{3, 4\}$. It updates its belief contributions about the other for future decisions. Then, it chooses to delegate τ to the least loaded bidder by applying the following selection criterion: $\underset{j \in \Omega'}{\operatorname{argmin}}(c_j(t))$. In this way, reducer #1 accepts the proposal of reducer #3 and it rejects the one of reducer #4 (see Fig. 2d).

After the negotiation (at time $t+1$), we observe that the task τ belongs to reducer #3. The new contributions are $c_1(t+1) = 7$, $c_2(t+1) = 8$, $c_3(t+1) = 6$ and $c_4(t+1) = 5$. Negotiation leads to a more efficient configuration, i.e. a fairer task allocation (see Fig. 2e).

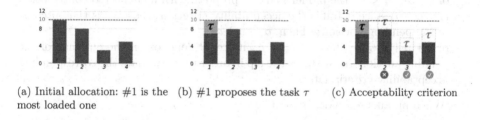

(a) Initial allocation: #1 is the most loaded one   (b) #1 proposes the task τ (c) Acceptability criterion

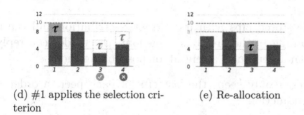

(d) #1 applies the selection criterion   (e) Re-allocation

Fig. 2. Step-by-step negotiation process: reducer #1 delegates the task τ.

As it will be illustrated in our experiments (cf. Sect. 4), the task allocation is dynamic and adaptive since negotiations are repeated. For instance, if a reducer is slowed down for some reasons, then an unbalanced allocation will appear, and so a negotiation will be triggered in order to delegate another task and decrease the current contribution of the delayed reducer.

Several reducers can simultaneously initiate negotiations but a reducer is either initiator or bidder at time t. In the following section, we will allow a bidder to be involved in more than one auction at a time.

3.2   Multi-auctions

We consider here a concurrent multi-auction process which allows agent to bid in several simultaneous auctions. In this way, the gap between the most loaded reducer and the least loaded one is filled faster and so, the responsiveness of the MAS is improved.

In order to manage several concurrent auctions, a bidder maintains an overhead of its current contribution. This overhead is the sum of all the task costs for which the bidder has made a proposal. In other words, a bidder records the overhead corresponding to the win of all the auctions in which it is involved. In this way, a bidder can make relevant proposals in several auctions and bids only if it may fulfill the acceptability criterion with its expected contribution (which includes its current contribution and its overhead).

Let c be the contribution of the reducer and o its current overhead. Initially, $o = 0$. When the reducer receives a cfp about a task τ with the cost c_τ from an initiator i with the contribution c_i, the bidder adopts the following behaviour:

- either $c + c_\tau \geq c_i$, the bidder does not fulfill the acceptability criterion and it declines the cfp;
- or $c + o + c_\tau < c_i$, the bidder makes a proposal with its expected contribution (i.e. $c + o$) since it fulfils the acceptability criterion whatever is the outcome of the pending auctions. Then, $o \leftarrow o + c_\tau$;
- or $c + o + c_\tau \geq c_i$ and $c + c_\tau < c_i$, its reply depends on the outcome of the pending auctions, so it stores the cfp in order to re-evaluate the corresponding acceptability criteria later.

When an auction ends, the bidder:

1. updates the overhead, i.e. $o \leftarrow o - c_\tau$, and possibly its contribution $c \leftarrow c + c_\tau$ if it wins the bid;
2. re-evaluates the stored cfps with its current contribution and the updated overhead. According to the previous behaviour, the bidder can reply to the stored cfps by an acceptance, a refusal, or postponing them.

Finally, the bidder only keeps the last cfp for each peer in order to avoid replying to a closed auction.

3.3   Task Split: Principle and Bootstrapping

The skew of expensive key groups can be tackled neither with a static partition nor with our negotiation process. In order to allow reducers with expensive tasks to decrease their contributions by negotiation, we consider that the tasks are divisible. Therefore, we propose to split the expensive tasks into cheaper subtasks which are negotiable. In order to decrease the communicational and computational overhead of negotiations, tasks are split only if required.

As explained in Sect. 2, the tasks split requires to slightly modify the design pattern by introducing an intermediate reduce phase and a final reduce phase. Similarly to [8], we define the three following functions:

$$map: (K1, V1) \rightarrow list[(K2, V2)]$$
$$IR: (K2, list[V2]) \rightarrow (K2, list[V2])$$
$$FR: (K2, list[V2]) \rightarrow list[(K3, V3)]$$

The user must decompose the reduce function R in an *intermediate reduce* function (IR) and a *final reduce* function (FR) such that for each key k and its values S, $R(k, S) = FR(k, < IR(k, S_1); \cdots ; IR(k, S_n) >)$ whatever is the partitioning of the values $S = S_1 \cup \cdots \cup S_n$.

The reduce function is an aggregation function. In [15], the authors identify three families of those functions: (i) the distributive functions where the reduce, the intermediate reduce and the final reduce are the same function (e.g. sum, min, max, count); (ii) the algebraic functions which can be decomposed using a bounded number of distributive functions (e.g. avg is decomposed by using an intermediate reduce function computing a sum and count the number of values, the division of the sum by the number of values is performed by the final reduce); and (iii) the holistic functions which are neither distributive nor algebraic (such as the median). It is difficult to find a relavante (IR, FR) decomposition for such functions since it may require too much intermediate data.

When a task is split into subtasks, IR is applied on each sub-task, producing an intermediate result, and FR is applied on all these intermediate results to produce the final result. Subtasks are considered as any other tasks, so they can be split and negotiated. The intermediate results have to be processed by the same reducer to compute the final result. So when a reducer initially splits a task, it collects the intermediate results and apply the final reduce function.

Let us study an example. The task τ is allocated to reducer i. This reducer splits τ in $\{\tau_1, \tau_2, \tau_3\}$. It processes τ_1 with IR function and it delegates τ_2 and τ_3 to reducers j and l, respectively. Reducer j splits τ_2 in τ_{21} and τ_{22} in order to delegate τ_{22} to a fourth reducer. The results of the application of IR on $\{\tau_1, \tau_{21}, \tau_{22}, \tau_3\}$ are sent to reducer i, i.e. the reducer which has split the initial task τ. Thereafter, i applies the final reduce function FR on these intermediates results.

In order to illustrate the negotiation strategy of subtasks, let us consider a population of n reducers. In order to bootstrap a task split, reducer i must fulfill the following split conditions:

1. there exist m reducers ($1 \leq m \leq n-1$) which are less loaded than i according to its beliefs;
2. i cannot delegate any task according to its beliefs;

Reducer i aims at decreasing its contribution. For this purpose, it splits its most expensive task in $k + 1$ subtasks of the same cost with $1 \leq k \leq m$. The allocation of the k subtasks is conventionally negotiated with the peers.

3.4   Task Split Process

The task split heuristic is based on the beliefs of the reducer about the other reducers contributions. Let's remember that each reducer receives call for proposal from its pairs during negotiations. These messages contain the contributions of the auctioneers and allow the initiator to keep its beliefs up to date.

Definition 1 (Delta of contribution). *Let $\Omega = \{1,\ldots,n\}$ be a population of n reducers. At time t, each reducer i with the contribution $c_i(t)$ has a vector $r_i = \, <r_{i_1},\ldots,r_{i_{n-1}}> \, \in \Omega^{n-1}$ of its peers by increasing order of contributions. Let $c_{i_k}(t)$ be the estimated contribution of reducer r_{i_k} (i.e. the belief of reducer i about the contribution of the kth reducer in r_i). For each $r_{i_k} \in r_i$, we define the delta of contributions as:*

$$\Delta_i^k = c_i(t) - c_{i_k}(t)$$

According to the split conditions, if agent i can split a task, then there are m reducers which are less loaded than i. None of its tasks are negotiable, especially its biggest task τ and so we have: $\forall k \in [1;m]$, $c_\tau \geq \Delta_i^k$. Thus, the split of the task τ aims at delegating k subtasks with the same cost. This delegation allows the reducers to decrease its contribution as much as possible.

Reducer i computes k such that:

$$k = \underset{k \in [1;m]}{\mathrm{argmin}}(c_i(t) - \frac{k\Delta_i^k}{k+1})$$

This leads to the building of $k+1$ subtasks $\tau_1, \ldots, \tau_{k+1}$ with $c_{\tau_1} = \ldots = c_{\tau_k} = \frac{\Delta_i^k}{k+1}$ and $c_{\tau_{k+1}} = c_\tau - \frac{k\Delta_i^k}{k+1}$.

The following example illustrates how k is chosen and the impact it has on the contributions after negotiations.

Example. Let $\Omega = \{1,2,3,4\}$ be a set of four reducers with the contributions $c_1(t) = 80$, $c_2(t) = 20$, $c_3(t) = 40$ and $c_4(t) = 30$. Reducer #1 has two tasks: τ and μ. Since μ is the current running task, reducer #1 can only initiate an auction about the task τ which is not negotiable (see Fig. 3). Therefore, there exist $m = 3$ reducers which are less loaded than reducer #1. The latter can split the task τ to decrease its contribution. We observe:

- $r_1 =\, < 2,4,3 >$ (i.e. the peers by increasing order of contributions);
- $\Delta_1^1 = c_1(t) - c_2(t) = 60$, $\Delta_1^2 = c_1(t) - c_4(t) = 50$, $\Delta_1^3 = c_1(t) - c_3(t) = 40$.

The number of subtasks modifies the resulting contributions. It is not always the case that $k = m$ gives the lowest contribution among the peers to the initiator.

If reducer #1 shares the task τ with a single reducer ($k = 1$), it builds the subtasks in order to balance its contribution with the peers. The best split to balance c_1 and c_2 consists in only considering Δ_1^1 and splitting it into two subtasks with the same cost. Therefore, the subtasks τ_1 and τ_2 are built from τ such that $c_{\tau_1} = \frac{\Delta_1^1}{2}$ and $c_{\tau_2} = c_\tau - c_{\tau_1} = c_\tau - \frac{\Delta_1^1}{2}$. In this way, reducer #2 may accept the task τ_1 which leads to a configuration where $c_1(t+1) = c_2(t+1) = 50$ (see Fig. 4).

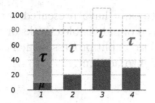

Fig. 3. Initial configuration where reducer #1 cannot negotiate the task τ.

In the same way, the configurations with $k = 2$ (see Fig. 4) is such that $c_1(t+1) = c_4(t+1) = 46$ and $c_1(t+1) = c_3(t+1) = 50$ in the configuration with $k = 3$ (see Fig. 4).

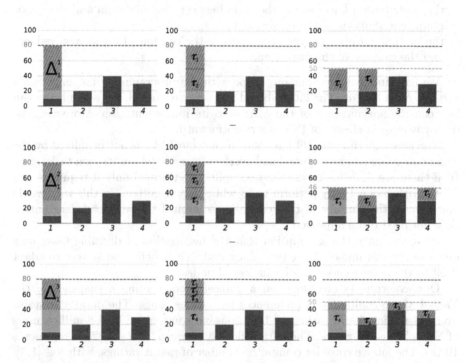

Fig. 4. Split of the task τ between reducers #1 and #2 (top), between reducers #1, #2 and #4 (center) and between reducers #1, #2, #3 and #4 (bottom).

More generally, if reducer #1 delegates k subtasks with the cost $\frac{\Delta_1^k}{k+1}$, its new contribution is $c_1(t+1) = c_1(t) - \frac{k\Delta_1^k}{k+1}$. We can observe that there is a value for k (here $k = 2$) which minimizes $c_1(t+1)$:

$$k = \underset{k \in [1;3]}{\operatorname{argmin}}(c_1(t) - \frac{k\Delta_1^k}{k+1}).$$

Due to lack of place, we only have presented a continuous tasks split. In reality, the tasks are composed of indivisible chunks of data (previously produced by the mappers). The actual task split process, which is similar to this continuous heuristic, take these chunks into account.

4   Experiments

Our experiments compare our proposal to the classical MapReduce distribution. Moreover, they evaluate the added-value of the negotiation of divisible tasks and of the multi-auction process. In other words, we compare our MAS with the one previously proposed in [4] using these metrics:

- the runtime of the reduce phase;
- the contribution fairness, i.e. the ratio between the minimum and the maximum contributions of the system at time t;
- the runtime fairness, i.e. the ratio between the runtime of the slowest reducer and the runtime of the fastest one.

We have implemented our prototype with the programming language Scala and the Akka toolkit. The latter, based on the actor model, helps to fill the gap between the specification of the MAS and its implementation. Moreover, the deployment on a cluster of PCs is straightforward.

Previous experiments [16] have shown that our MAS is not penalized by the communicational and computational overhead due to the negotiation tasks since (i) if there are divisible tasks, the task split is performed only if required; and (ii) the reducers actually perform tasks while they negotiate. In this way, we do not increase the runtime of the reduce phase even if the workload distribution does not need to be improved.

Here, we make the assumption that the negotiation of divisible tasks may decrease the runtime of the reduce phase and that it helps the system to adapt itself to the heterogeneous performances of nodes.

Our experiments are based on a dataset[2] representing a snapshot of the Yahoo! Music community's preferences for various songs. The dataset contains over 717 million 5-star ratings of 136 thousand songs given by 1.8 million users of Yahoo! Music services. The data collected between 2002 and 2006 represents 10 Go. The job we consider counts the number of n-star ratings, with $n \in [1, 5]$. This dataset contains 4 "expensive" keys and 1 "cheap" one.

We compare the runtime of the reduce phase in the classical distribution of MapReduce with the MAS proposed in [4] and with our MAS which split tasks. We perform the job with one reducer per node. Since a reducer can process data from a mapper on another machine, the reduce phase is penalized by the non-locality of the data. This is the reason why we deploy the mappers on different machines than reducers in our experiments.

Figure 5 shows the runtimes according to the number of machines used, i.e. Intel (R) Core (TM) i5 3.30 GHz PCs with 4 cores and 8 GB of RAM. For each

---

[2] http://webscope.sandbox.yahoo.com/.

set of parameters, we perform 5 runs. Since the standard deviation due to the non-determinism of the scheduler is weak, we only show the averages on the different runs. The classical approach and the negotiation of indivisible tasks have the same performance since the 5 keys are not negotiable. They are not suitable for expensive key groups and so they are penalized by this data skew. By contrast, the negotiation of divisible tasks ends earlier since the available resources are better used. The runtime fairness reached by the negotiation of divisible tasks is about 0.99 while the runtime fairness of the classical approach is closed to 0 when at least one reducer does not perform any task and 0.36 with 5 reducers.

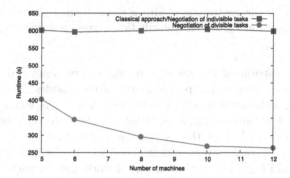

Fig. 5. Runtimes of the reduce phases

Figure 6 illustrates the dynamic of the contributions during the reduce phase due to the negotiation of divisible tasks between 12 agents. This mechanism quickly fills the gap between the most loaded reducer and the least loaded one during the whole process. Indeed, the negotiation of divisible tasks occurs simultaneously to task processing, this makes it possible to dynamically and continuously allocate the tasks to the least loaded reducers. Additionally, we compare the concurrent multi-auction process which allows agent to bid in several simultaneous auctions to a single auction process where each reducer can be involved as an auctioneer in at most one auction at a time. While the single-auction process requires 58s to reach a contribution fairness greater than 0.70, the multi-auction process only needs 3s[3]. Since the multi-auction process improves the responsiveness, the reduce phase with a multi-auction process is faster by 33s (around 12 %).

Finally, we have performed the same job on 7 machines. The first 6 reducers run alone on one computer and the 6 other reducers run together on a single computer and are then penalized. In our approach, the task allocation is adapted to the heterogeneous performance of nodes (cf. right of Fig. 7). We can see that

---

[3] It is worth noticing that the negotiations and the data processing are not sequential but concurrent.

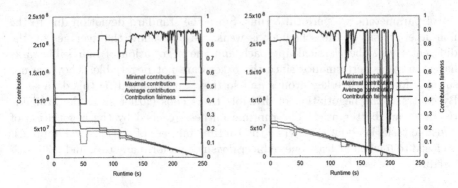

Fig. 6. Evolution of the contributions with a single-auction process (at left) and a multi-auction process (at right). The contribution fairness is defined in $[0; 1]$.

the system has distributed the tasks such that the reducers end their work at the same time according to the performances of their nodes. The dynamic and continuous task reallocation loads more the first 6 reducers which run alone on a computer until a runtime fairness of 0.99, i.e. the reducers finish their work almost simultaneously. Indeed, the negotiation of divisible tasks makes it possible to dynamically and continuously allocate the tasks to the fastest reducers. For comparison, left of Fig. 7 shows the amount of work done by each reducer at the end of the job with an homogeneous environment.

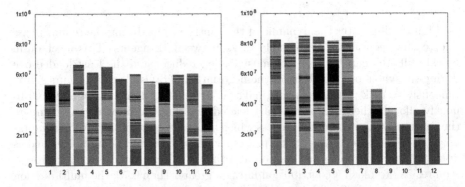

Fig. 7. The amount of work done by each reducer at the end of the job in a homogeneous runtime environment (at left) and in an heterogeneous runtime environment (at right).

These experiments show that our MAS benefits from the parallelism more than the other implementations. In particular, the negotiation of divisible tasks decreases the runtime of the reduce phase by improving the workload partition. Moreover, the multi-auction process improve the responsiveness.

5   Conclusion

In this paper we have shown how the deployment of the MapReduce design pattern using a MAS can address the data skews which penalize the reduce phase, in particular the expensive key groups. Our system requires neither pre-processing nor parametrization depending on the data but it addresses most of the practical applications. In our MAS implementation, the reducer agents split "non-negotiable" tasks and negotiate the task allocation while they process the data. Their decisions are based on the remaining data to process, i.e. their contributions. This continuous decision-making process is local and it requires no centralization of information. In order to improve the responsiveness, we have proposed a multi-auction process which allows agent to bid in several simultaneous auctions. It is worth noticing that if the runtime environment is heterogeneous, the system is self-adaptive. Our experiments have shown that the negotiation of divisible tasks can decrease the runtime of the reduce phase by iteratively relieving the most loaded (or slowest) reducers.

In future works, we will integrate a data locality criterion in the collective decision-making process in order to limit the data transfer cost. For this purpose, we plan to abstract away from our practical application to consider the general problem of dynamic task re-allocation between heterogeneous machines.

References

1. Dean, J., Ghemawat, S.: MapReduce: simplified data processing on large clusters. In: SOSDI, pp. 137–150 (2004)
2. Kwon, Y., Balazinska, M., Howe, B., Rolia, J.: Skewtune: mitigating skew in MapReduce applications. In: ACM SIGMOD ICMD, pp. 25–36 (2012)
3. Kwon, Y., Ren, K., Balazinska, M., Howe, B.: Managing skew in Hadoop. IEEE Data Eng. Bull. **36**(1), 24–33 (2013)
4. Baert, Q., Caron, A.C., Morge, M., Routier, J.C.: Fair multi-agent task allocation for large datasets analysis. KAIS (2017). https://doi.org/10.1007/s10115-017-1087-4
5. Lama, P., Zhou, X.: Aroma: automated resource allocation and configuration of MapReduce environment in the cloud. In: ICAC, pp. 63–72 (2012)
6. Verma, A., Cherkasova, L., Campbell, R.: Aria: automatic resource inference and allocation for MapReduce environments. In: ICAC, pp. 235–244 (2011)
7. Chen, Q., Zhang, D., Guo, M., Deng, Q., Guo, S.: SAMR: a self-adaptive MapReduce scheduling algorithm in heterogeneous environment. In: ICCIT, pp. 2736–2743. IEEE (2010)
8. Liroz-Gistau, M., Akbarinia, R., Valduriez, P.: FP-Hadoop: efficient execution of parallel jobs over skewed data. VLDB Endow. **8**(12), 1856–1859 (2015)
9. Li, W.: Random texts exhibit Zipf's-law-like word frequency distribution. IEEE Trans. Inf. Theory **38**(6), 1842–1845 (1992)
10. Lin, J.: The curse of Zipf and limits to parallelization: a look at the stragglers problem in MapReduce. In: Workshop on Large-Scale Distributed Systems for Information Retrieval (2009)
11. Gufler, B., Augsten, N., Reiser, A., Kemper, A.: Handling data skew in MapReduce. In: ICCCSS, pp. 574–583 (2011)

12. Vinyals, M., Macarthur, K.S., Farinelli, A., Ramchurn, S.D., Jennings, N.R.: A message-passing approach to decentralized parallel machine scheduling. Comput. J. **57**(6), 856–874 (2014)
13. Nongaillard, A., Mathieu, P.: Egalitarian negotiations in agent societies. AAI **25**(9), 799–821 (2011)
14. Essa, Y.M., Attiya, G., El-Sayed, A.: Mobile agent based new framework for improving big data analysis. IJACSA **5**(3), 25–32 (2014)
15. Gray, J., et al.: Data cube: a relational aggregation operator generalizing group-by, cross-tab, and sub-totals. Data Mining Knowl. Discov. **1**(1), 29–53 (1997)
16. Baert, Q., Caron, A.C., Morge, M., Routier, J.C.: Stratégie de découpe de tâche pour le traitement de données massives. In: Garbay, C., Bonnet, G., (eds.) Journées Francophones sur les Systèmes Multi-Agents. Cohésion: fondement ou propriété émergente, Caen, France, Cépaudès édition, pp. 65–75, July 2017

Combining Self-Organisation with Decision-Making and Planning

Christopher-Eyk Hrabia$^{(\boxtimes)}$, Tanja Katharina Kaiser, and Sahin Albayrak

Technische Universität Berlin, DAI-Lab,
Ernst-Reuter-Platz 7, 10587 Berlin, Germany
christopher-eyk.hrabia@dai-labor.de

Abstract. Coordination of mobile multi-robot systems in a self-organised manner is in the first place beneficial for simple robots in common swarm robotics scenarios. Moreover, sophisticated robot systems as for instance in disaster rescue teams, service robotics and robot soccer can also benefit from a decentralised coordination while performing complex tasks. In order to facilitate self-organised sophisticated multi-robot applications a suitable approach is to combine individual decision-making and planning with self-organization. We introduce a framework for the implementation and application of self-organization mechanisms in multi-robot scenarios. Furthermore, the integration into the hybrid behaviour planning framework ROS Hybrid Behaviour Planner is presented. This combined approach allows for a goal-directed application of self-organisation and provides a foundation for an automated selection of suitable mechanisms.

Keywords: Self-organization · Behaviour-based planning
Behaviour networks · Hybrid planning · Decision-making
Multi-robot systems

1 Introduction

An increasing application of mobile, autonomous, and intelligent multi-robot systems in various scenarios can be expected in the near future. Possible application domains range from space exploration, disaster rescue operations with aerial and ground robots to more industrial applications as warehouse logistics or heterogeneous service robots operating as a team in future smart-building environments. To address more complex problems or tasks that need to be distributed amongst several robots, it is necessary to coordinate robots to achieve a collaborative behaviour. An intuitive approach for such collaborative behaviour is the control and coordination of multi-robot systems by a centralised instance. Although, this has disadvantages, like having a single point of failure, a required persistent communication connection and limitations for the number of robots.

This work was partially supported by the German Federal Ministry of Education and Research (BMBF grants 13N14093, project EffFeu).

F. Belardinelli and E. Argente (Eds.): EUMAS 2017/AT 2017, LNAI 10767, pp. 385–399, 2018.
https://doi.org/10.1007/978-3-030-01713-2_27

An alternative might be considering decentralised coordination algorithms that allow to coordinate individual robots, e.g. by applying certain rules on the micro level, which leads to a desired behaviour on the macro level of the system. How to develop and engineer such self-organised systems is commonly researched in the field of self-organisation [5] in general, and in other more specific fields like swarm robotics [7], and swarm engineering [17]. However, most research applying such decentralised approaches in robotics is studying these concepts with very simple robots inspired by social insects without having more sophisticated capabilities or tasks for the individual systems [3].

More sophisticated robots, like service robots or autonomous drones, are using decision-making algorithms or even task-level planning for a more goal-oriented mission control. Decision-making applies methods, like hierarchical state machines [2] or behaviour trees [4]. Task-level planning, for instance applies STRIPS-like planners using the PDDL language [12] or hierarchical task networks (HTN) as used by the well-known SHOP planner [20]. Such approaches are also suitable for centralised multi-robot planning and coordination.

Coordination of mobile multi-robot systems in a self-organised manner is not only beneficial for simple robots in common swarm robotics scenarios. More sophisticated robot systems, for instance in disaster rescue teams, can benefit from decentralised coordination while operating complex tasks. An example would be rescue robots using a self-organised exploration strategy while applying a certain rescue procedure with several dependent tasks to help individual victims once they are found. However, there is a gap in between these worlds of individual or centralised decision-making and planning of robots and self-organised coordination of many simple robots. We are not aware of a system that allows the modelling and implementation of the robot behaviour exhibiting both self-organised coordination as well as task-level decision-making and planning in a common approach. To facilitate the idea of self-organised sophisticated multi-robot systems it is desirable to combine decision-making and planning with self-organisation.

In this paper, we address this problem by first discussing background and related work in Sect. 2. In Sect. 3, we introduce a common framework for the implementation of self-organisation mechanisms in multi-robot scenarios. Furthermore, we show how this framework can be integrated into the hybrid behaviour planning framework – ROS Hybrid Behaviour Planner [16] – in Sect. 4. This combined approach allows for a goal-directed application of self-organisation and provides a foundation for an automated selection of suitable self-organisation mechanisms and configurations. Section 5 introduces a first semi-automated mechanisms selection that can relieve a designer of self-organised multi-robot systems from tedious application-dependent engineering of mechanisms. Finally, we show an experiment as a proof-of-concept in Sect. 6 and summarise our contribution as well as future steps in Sect. 7.

2   Related Work

In the introduction we have already mentioned some popular solutions that have been developed to address well-known challenges in the robotics domain, such as decision making [2,4] and planning [12,20]. In the field of self-organisation much attention is spend on the development of certain mechanisms as surveyed in [24]. Moreover, the development of frameworks that allow for a simplified engineering of multi-robot and self-organised systems is as well in focus. For instance the middleware jSwarm [15] allows for centralized sequential programming with spatial-temporal constraints with concentration on the motion in space of swarm robot systems. jSwarm provides an abstract infrastructure for a centralized controlled distributed swarm robot system. The focus of jSwarm is more on performance optimization with software migration and less on enabling more robust and self-organised distributed systems.

Buzz is a domain specific language that provides a middleware for simplified implementations of swarm robot applications [22]. In Buzz a set of robots (swarm) is a first level object that can be used for group task assignment and set operations (intersection, union, difference, and negation). Furthermore, Buzz has capabilities for neighbourhood operations (queries, filtering, and virtual stigmergy) and information sharing. Nevertheless, the implemented approach does only provide an environment for developers wherein self-organization and cognitive algorithms can be implemented, but neither does it support the selection or evaluation of available algorithms nor the combination with individual decision making and planning.

Fernandez-Marquez et al. [9] analyse, classify and describe a set of bio-inspired self-organizing mechanisms in a domain independent manner. The authors classify mechanisms and their relations into three layers of basic, composed and higher-level patterns. In that sense, the composed layer is created by a combination of basic mechanisms and the higher-level patterns show different options of exploiting the basic and composed mechanisms. On the basic level they identified some basic patterns, such as spreading, aggregation, evaporation, and repulsion forming the foundation for a realization of all composed and higher-level mechanisms. The created catalogue of patterns is intended to be used as a base for modular design and implementation of self-organizing systems. A subset of these described patterns is implemented in the execution model BIO-CORE [10], which provides basic bio-inspired services, namely the basic patterns evaporation, aggregation and spreading as well as the gradient pattern. BIO-CORE consists of three main parts: a shared data space which allows to exchange data, basic bio-inspired services that implement basic bio-inspired mechanisms and interfaces that provide primitives for the agents to interact with the core.

The mentioned frameworks illustrate common research directions in the related fields that focus either on specific self-organisation capabilities, mechanism engineering or providing a common infrastructure for developing self-organised systems. To our best knowledge, there are no approaches that try to combine concepts from decision-making and planning with a general purpose self-organisation framework as BIO-CORE. In order to provide a foundation for the combination of these two research areas in the domain of multi-robot system we have developed a decision-making and planning framework for the popular Robot Operating System (ROS).[1] The framework ROS Hybrid Behaviour Planner (RHBP) combines the advantages of reactive opportunistic decision-making and goal-oriented deliberative planning in a hybrid architecture [16]. The decision-making layer is based on the idea of behaviour networks that allow for dynamic state transitions and simplify the integration of self-organisation due the heuristic nature of the applied utility-function-based action selection algorithm. The deliberative layer makes use of state-of-the-art planners through its PDDL interface. In RHBP a problem is modelled with behaviours, preconditions, effects and goals, whereby conditions are expressed as a combination of virtual sensors and activation functions. The combined condition objects allow to normalize arbitrary sensor information to create an activation value that is applied in the decision-making process. Here, the decision-making considers the relationship between preconditions and effects as well as the results of the interfaced PDDL-planner. RHBP is the foundation for our work presented in the following sections.

3   Self-organisation Framework

The first contribution of this work is the realisation of a modular and reusable framework for self-organisation. This part of the implementation is completely independent from the RHBP and can be used generally.

A modified version of the bio-inspired design patterns of self-organisation mechanisms presented in [9] constitutes the basis of our self-organisation framework. An advantage of both the original design patterns and our adapted version is their modular character and the modelled relationships between the patterns. Thus, existing patterns can be used as the basis for the realisation of new ones. In contrast to the design patterns presented in [9], our adapted version bases all advanced patterns on the gradient pattern, which allows for a simplified and more general implementation. Furthermore, the patterns were regrouped to categorise them on their purpose instead of their complexity as shown in Fig. 1.

The bio-inspired design patterns are categorised in three groups, namely *Basic Functionality Patterns*, *Movement Patterns* and *Decision Patterns*. Basic Functionality Patterns provide required functionalities for the other pattern categories. Apart from spreading, these patterns do not lead to actions that are executed by the agents themselves. Movement Patterns lead to the movement of the agents, e.g. enabling robots to base their movement on a potential field. Finally, Decision Patterns enable collective decisions.

The central *Basic Functionality Pattern* is the *Gradients* pattern as all *Movement Patterns* and *Decision Patterns* are built on it. Gradients are information which are subject to *Spreading*, *Aggregation* and possibly *Evaporation*. In addition to including all data points required for the advanced patterns, gradients

---

[1] https://github.com/DAInamite/rhbp.

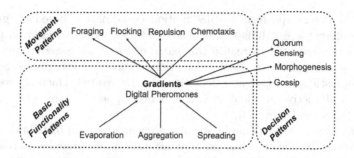

Fig. 1. Bio-inspired self-organisation design patterns. Arrows indicate relationships.

contain a pose indicating where the data is located. Gradients can either be deposited in the environment or be attached to a moving entity like an agent. Moreover, gradients are either spread by agents or present in the environment.

Spread gradient data (*SoMessage*) is stored and manipulated by a library we have named self-organisation buffer (*SoBuffer*). Both Aggregation, or information fusion, and Evaporation, which reduces the relevance of information over time, are applied on the gradient data by the SoBuffer. Each gradient has individual evaporation attributes, namely frequency and strength, attached to it, which specify the rate at which evaporation is executed over the data point by the SoBuffer. In addition, the SoBuffer can aggregate the received gradient data based on their purpose. Hence, gradients which are used for different tasks can be aggregated differently or used without aggregation. For example, gradient data can be aggregated based on its location or its sender. The implementation applies the publish-subscribe design pattern, whereby spread gradient information (*SoMessage*) is received, collected and filtered on the receiver-side (*SoBuffer*). This enables the combination of individual and decentralised mechanisms within one information space. In the following, we consider a self-organisation mechanism as an implementation of an abstract self-organisation pattern.

The *Digital Pheromone* pattern is a special case of the Gradients pattern. Digital Pheromones are evaporating gradients which are deposited in the environment [9]. All Basic Functionality Patterns were realised based on [9].

Advanced patterns can request different subsets of the stored gradient data from the SoBuffer to base their calculations on those. Movement Patterns and Decision Patterns are integrated as mechanisms in the self-organisation framework. Both are based on abstract classes which provide a common basis for the mechanism implementations. Therewith, new mechanisms can be straightforwardly implemented using these blueprints.

Each movement mechanism determines a movement vector an agent can follow. All four Movement Patterns depicted in Fig. 1 are integrated in the self-organisation framework. For each Movement Pattern one or more mechanisms are realised which allow to employ the pattern in different scenarios.

The *Chemotaxis* pattern enables motion coordination based on gradients [9]. Two different algorithms to calculate movement vectors based on gradient fields were implemented to realise this pattern. Firstly, a general approach for attractive and repulsive gradient calculations as in [1] is integrated. Secondly, a more sophisticated gradient calculation was integrated which allows agents to reach an attractive gradient even if it is overlapped by a repulsive gradient following the formulas by [14].

The *Repulsion* pattern enables agents to reach a uniform distribution and to avoid collisions [9]. Two mechanism implementations are provided to realise this pattern. In one mechanism, the repulsive gradient formula of [1] is utilised while the second mechanism applies the repulsion formula presented in [9].

Flocking allows motion coordination and pattern formation in swarms [9]. A mechanism based on [23] is provided and also a more complex version applying the gradient-based formulas of [21] is integrated in the framework.

Moreover, the *Ant Foraging* pattern is part of the presented self-organisation framework. Foraging is a pattern for collaborative search which allows to explore and exploit an environment [9]. The pattern requires several mechanisms to be realised which are based on [9] as well as on [6].

The abstract class for decision mechanisms, which implement the Decision Patterns, includes two common methods. One method determines the current value and state of an agent and depends on the pattern. The other method spreads these values as a gradient message and is universal for all patterns.

Quorum Sensing allows collective decision making based on a required threshold number of agents. It can be implemented in a general way following [9].

The other two Decision Patterns, namely *Morphogenesis* and *Gossip*, are highly dependent on the use case. The Morphogenesis pattern allows to determine the agent's behaviour based on its spatial position [9]. Gossip enables to obtain shared agreements between all agents [9]. For both patterns, sample mechanisms are implemented to exemplify their feasibility. The sample Gossip mechanism determines the maximum spread value while the sample Morphogenesis mechanism determines the barycentre of a group of agents using the algorithm proposed in [18].

The self-organisation framework was realised completely within the Robot Operating System (ROS). Next to being easy to extend and to apply, it provides hardware abstraction and an established messaging communication infrastructure. The latter aspect is useful in particular to realise Spreading. As already mentioned above, the implementation relies on the publisher-subscribe design pattern, which is a core concept of ROS, and it is inspired by the information sharing and filtering architecture of the popular tf package [11].

4   Combining Decision-Making, Planning and Self-organisation

The combination of decision-making, planning and self-organisation is realised by integrating the self-organisation framework presented in Sect. 3 into the RHBP that is recapped in Sect. 2. The following introduced extension provides necessary components to use the presented self-organisation mechanisms within the hybrid planning structure of the RHBP. The behaviour network layer of the RHBP is based on the dependencies of behaviour preconditions, effects and desired world changes. These dependencies are used for the activation calculation within the RHBP, serving as a heuristic estimation for decision-making and providing a well-matching foundation for the integration of self-organisation. This is because the normalisation of conditions through the application of different utility functions (activation functions) enables the straightforward integration of non-discrete relationships as we find them in self-organisation mechanisms.

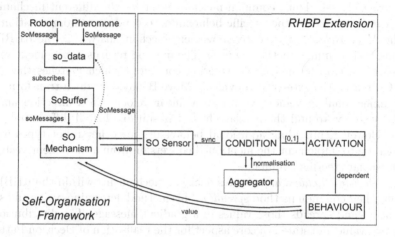

Fig. 2. Architecture for the integration of self-organisation into the RHBP

Figure 2 illustrates both the self-organisation framework presented in Sect. 3 and the integration into the RHBP using components provided by the extension. Three extended component types have been implemented to enable the use of self-organisation mechanisms, namely *sensor*, *condition* and *behaviour*.

The *Self-Organisation Sensor* (*SO Sensor*) is a central component to enable the integration of self-organisation into the RHBP. It is a complex sensor type which senses gradient-based information provided by the self-organisation framework by invoking their common methods. Specifically, it provides access to our SoBuffer and thereby allows to sense movement vectors, gradient values and agent states. Movement vectors are calculated by the movement mechanisms. For some mechanism implementations, it is possible to sense a vector leading to the goal gradient, too. The sensing of values and states of agents are related to the decision mechanisms.

Figure 2 illustrates the usage of the Self-Organisation Sensor in a *Condition*, which normalises the sensor values and maps them to activation levels using the standard activators provided by the RHBP core implementation, for instance

Boolean, threshold and linear functions. Several special self-organisation conditions are provided by the extension to allow the modelling of different application scenarios. For example, conditions related to movement mechanisms determine activation levels based on the presence of a potential field or the length of the movement vector. Sample conditions for mechanisms related to Decision Patterns lead to activation when the state or value of the robot has changed. The provided conditions are not exhaustive and can be extended as required.

The main components for the execution of self-organisation within the RHBP are behaviours. Several behaviours that execute the self-organisation mechanisms provided by the framework are part of the RHBP self-organisation extension. Both movement mechanisms and decision mechanisms are implemented based on abstract classes. Thus, common methods exist for the different mechanisms which can be reused by the specific behaviours to conduct self-organisation.

The *Move Behaviour* executes movement mechanisms within the RHBP by invoking their common method *move()*. The method returns a movement vector which will be transformed into a steering command which matches the robot type. Currently, the extension provides a Move Behaviour which transforms the three dimensional movement vector to a linear velocity in x-direction and an angular velocity around the z-axis. Thus, it is suitable for all differential drive robots. However, providing additional behaviours for other robot types would only require to implement the mentioned conversion from a movement vector to the particular steering command.

The *Decision Behaviour* executes decision mechanisms within the RHBP by invoking their common method *spread()*. This method determines value and state of an agent and spreads those values in a gradient message. The distribution of an agent's value and state is a core aspect for the realisation of Decision Patterns as each agent determines its own value and state based on its neighbours' data.

Several additional behaviours were integrated in the extension to realise behaviours which are not common for all mechanisms. For example, the Ant Foraging Pattern requires that the state of the agents is set to specific values in several cases. Hence, a special RHBP behaviour allows to set the state related to a mechanism to a predefined value.

5   Selecting Self-organisation Mechanisms

Selecting an appropriate self-organisation mechanism for the intended system behaviour is a challenging task. Usually system designers have to choose a suitable coordination mechanism during design time to let multi-robot systems collaborate in the desired fashion to fulfil an intended task. But the suitability of a chosen coordination mechanism might change during task execution as the environment or system capabilities might change. Hence, the *Coordination Mechanism Selector (CMS)* was realised, which provides a foundation to determine the most suitable self-organisation mechanism in a given situation based on expert knowledge or experience and a self-organisation goal that indicates the task of the agent. Thus, system designers are relieved from the task to select a self-organisation mechanism during design time and it is possible to improve the adaptation capabilities of the resulting system.

The *Self-Organisation Coordinator (SO Coordinator)* consists of two components, namely its own RHBP instance and the Coordination Mechanism Selector, as illustrated in Fig. 3. Self-organisation mechanisms can be encapsulated by the Self-Organisation Coordinator as all components required for the realisation of a self-organisation mechanism, e.g. behaviours and goals, are assigned to its own RHBP instance. Thus, a higher-level RHBP instance can treat the self-organisation mechanism as one behaviour, in the form of the Self-Organisation Coordinator, no matter how many components are required for its realisation. Hence, its own RHBP instance is used to monitor and control the particular self-organisation mechanism realised within our framework. It is also possible to integrate or combine several self-organisation mechanisms by using multiple Self-Organisation Coordinator instances per Behaviour Network. This architecture helps to separate the application specific modelling using the RHBP from a generic self-organisation mechanism implementation and makes the mechanism implementation exchangeable.

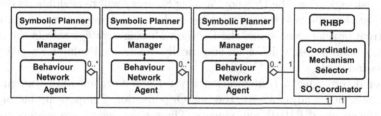

Fig. 3. Integration of the Coordination Mechanism Selector in the structure of the RHBP. A SO Coordinator is always bound to an individual agent in a decentralised fashion.

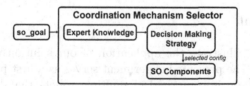

Fig. 4. Architecture of the Coordination Mechanism Selector

As illustrated in Fig. 4, the Coordination Mechanism Selector consists of three layers, namely *Expert Knowledge, Decision Making Strategy* and *Self-Organisation Components (SO Components)*. Additionally, each Self-Organisation Coordinator requires a self-organisation goal, which indicates the task of the multi-robot system, as input.

The Expert Knowledge maps self-organisation goals to a list of suitable mechanism options. Each option consists of a *configuration key*, a *score* and *parameters*. The configuration key is an indicator for a self-organisation configuration that can be used to fulfil a self-organisation goal. The indicated self-organisation configurations are specified in a reusable configuration library. Each configuration includes RHBP components and parameters as presented in Sects. 3 and 4. The parameters of the configuration will be replaced with the parameters included in the option to adjust the setting based on the self-organisation goal. The score specified in each option rates the feasibility of the self-organisation goal using the specified self-organisation configuration. This allows to create a repository of suitable self-organisation configurations that have been evaluated in respect to a given system goal. This concept is inspired by the proposed hypothesis database of Edmonds et al. [8].

The Decision Making Strategy is the central component of the Coordination Mechanism Selector. Its aim is to determine a suitable self-organisation configuration based on a self-organisation goal and the provided Expert Knowledge. Moreover, it might be used to adjust the score included in the options of the Expert Knowledge, e.g., using online learning [19] or evolutionary approaches [13]. Therewith, the decision making process can incorporate experience, which is essential to determine the most suitable self-organisation mechanism in a dynamic environment. As the environmental conditions might change during task execution, the Decision Making Strategy will re-evaluate its decision and adjust the self-organisation mechanism during task execution if required. In the current development stage, the Decision Making Strategy selects the option with maximum score, which is an empirically determined value for a given self-organisation goal.

After determining a configuration key for a self-organisation configuration and its parameter adjustments, the Self-Organisation Components factory will create the specified RHBP components. These components are associated with the RHBP instance being part of the Self-Organisation Coordinator and are therewith encapsulated. All three layers of the Coordination Mechanism Selector can be replaced or enhanced straightforwardly due to its modular structure.

6   Experiment

In this section, we illustrate the application of our solution with a simulated example scenario. The presented experiment serves as a first proof of our work. The example scenario is comprised of multiple robots that have to maintain an open unknown space by keeping it clean and managing the recycling and dumping process of found garbage items. The recycling and dumping process requires that once garbage is found, first it needs to be transported to a recycling station, before all leftovers are transported to the dump station. The robots have to patrol the environment repeatedly over time. Moreover, the robots have to make sure that they avoid collisions with each other.

The cleaning process with several dependent stages is different to common swarm robot experiments that focus on achieving one certain stable state in a decentralised manner. We have integrated this additional complexity in order to illustrate the beneficial combination of self-organisation with more complex decision-making and planning. However, we still keep this simulated experiment comparably simple to improve the transparency.

For the simulation, we use an extended version of the basic turtlesim simulation, commonly known from the ROS beginner tutorials. This simulation allows to control multiple differential wheeled robots in an empty space. Our version[2] extends the original implementation with capabilities of sensing other robots, allowing to configure a torus environment without borders, adding various visualization options to draw additional elements into the world and replacing the turtle robots with cleaning robots. To simulate the garbage items and their detection we make also use of our SoBuffer implementation to randomly spread garbage gradients with a special identifier in the environment, which then can be sensed with the corresponding gradient sensors. The simulation environment in a particular start configuration and during execution is shown in Fig. 5.

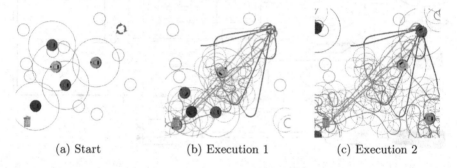

    (a) Start   (b) Execution 1   (c) Execution 2

Fig. 5. Visualised simulation scenario. Green circles are garbage items; Red solid circles around robots denote the sensor range. Red dotted cycles show virtual pheromones, the size corresponds to the evaporation stage (smaller=older). Garbage bin and recycling symbol visualize dump and recycling station. Grey lines mark robot trajectories; Purple lines mark trajectories after garbage was collected; Orange lines mark trajectories after garbage was recycled. (Color figure online)

The modelled RHBP solution with behaviours, goals and corresponding preconditions and effects is visualised in Fig. 6. Each robot instantiates this model independently resulting in a decentralised solution with coordination and interaction amongst the robots only carried out through the simulation environment by sensing each other as well as exchanging information through the virtual gradient space of the SoBuffers. Three goals formulate the target conditions for the robots, *PatrolEnvironment* expressing the need for a repeated cleaning process in the environment, *GarbageCleaned* modelling the need to clean garbage items once they are found, and *AvoidCollision* to keep the robots in a safe distance of each other. The garbage recycling and dumping state is tracked by influencing special ROS topics in the related behaviours and accessing them through so

---

[2] https://github.com/cehberlin/ros_tutorials/tree/clean_robots.

called *KnowledgeSensors*. The picking of garbage is implemented by sending gradient information that result in the deletion of garbage gradients at this position. The behaviours *MoveToDump* and *MoveToRecycling* are using distance conditions formulated with *LinearActivators*, which provide higher activation for a larger distance to target, and *Pose* sensors for the current robot position.

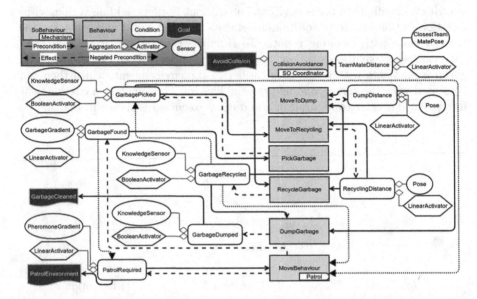

Fig. 6. Model of the RHBP solution for an individual robot of the experiment illustrating the relationships with preconditions, behaviours and effects.

So far this part of the model is expressed with RHBP core components. Nevertheless, the exploration and patrolling applies self-organisation with a patrol mechanism that is based on the virtual pheromone pattern. In our implementation each robot spreads evaporating gradients at its current position while moving through the environment and calculates the movement vector using a repulsion pattern to push itself away from the gradient field. Both together results in robot motion that prefers the motion into unknown space or space that has not been visited for a longer time period. All robots share these virtual pheromones through the SoBuffer library communication infrastructure, thus they are able to coordinate in a self-organised manner.

In the shown model, we have two self-organisation mechanisms for combined exploration-patrol and collision avoidance. For collision avoidance we apply the *So Coordinator* that automatically selects a suitable mechanism based on the given self-organisation goal *AvoidCollision* and the available scores in our database. The different characteristic of the goal is also indicated by the visualised aggregation relationship instead of a link to a condition. In contrast to collision avoidance, patrolling is manually selected by integrating directly the

Patrol mechanism. The direct selection of a mechanism has the disadvantage of making a later exchange of the mechanism more difficult. However, we have taken this approach here to illustrate different possible usage styles of our framework, although the specific *Patrol* mechanisms could be replaced easily by an *SO Coordinator* instance with a corresponding self-organisation goal.

The scenario visualised in Fig. 5 with the model of Fig. 6 has been tested with 5 robots and 10 garbage items randomly positioned in 5 different start configurations (scenarios). The positions of recycling and dump station have not been altered between the trials. Moreover, we have manually manipulated the expert knowledge scores to force the *SO Coordinator* to run all 5 scenarios once with the collision avoidance mechanisms based on the repulsion pattern from Fernandez-Marquez et al. [9] and once with the algorithm from Balch and Hybinette [1]. Both patterns rely on robot pose gradients to allow the robots to determine the repulsive forces from each other.

Table 1. Experiment results of a comparison between different available self-organisation patterns for collision avoidance

Scenario	Fernandez-Marquez		Balch/Hybinette	
	Duration in s	Collisions/s	Duration in s	Collisions/s
1	270.39	2.02	89.84	2.65
2	1484.70	1.42	177.26	1.42
3	1162.18	1.60	471.90	1.55
4	952.40	1.22	326.14	2.08
5	363.93	2.25	267.02	3.11
Mean	846.72	1.70	266.43	2.16
Median	952.40	1.60	267.02	2.08
STD	465.39	0.38	130.32	0.64

The experiment results are listed in Table 1 and show different characteristics for both applied mechanisms. We see that the runs with Balch and Hybinette mechanism clearly outperform runs with the Fernandez-Marquez mechanism in terms of execution time (duration) for completing the mission. However, runs with Fernandez-Marquez mechanism are having fewer collisions per time. For the number of collisions over time, it has to be considered that one collision might be counted several times, depending on the sensor frequency of the simulation, if the robots stay for a moment in the collision pose.

The obtained results of this experiment could now be used to create a score for the mechanism configurations in our expert knowledge library. However, we have not yet fine-tuned the parameters of the mechanisms, which might influence the results. Thus it would be useful to repeat the experiment with other parameter configurations. Nevertheless, the presented results illustrate the application of our work and highlight the importance of an inexpensive exchange of self-organisation mechanisms and their configuration within a decision-making and planning framework. However, it also indicates that our SO coordinator concept is providing a suitable foundation for the integration of experience and expert knowledge with self-organisation pattern, but a system designer needs further support on an automatic determination of the mechanisms scores.

7   Conclusion

In this paper, we have presented a general purpose self-organisation library for the multi-robot domain and how this framework can be combined with our decision-making and planning framework RHBP. The self-organisation library (SoBuffer) already provides a wide range of mechanisms and allows for additional extensions due to its modular and generic architecture. The further introduced integration of the library into the RHBP closes a gap between the research fields of decision-making, planning and self-organisation. It enables the development of autonomous robots resolving tasks with complex dependencies while allowing for self-organised coordination and problem resolving within one framework. Both worlds can directly interact with each other by making use of the same domain model, information sources and abstract system capabilities. The integration into the popular ROS framework does also guarantee a fast adoption and integration into existing solutions and software ecosystems.

Furthermore, we have extended our self-organisation library with the concept and an initial implementation of SO Coordinator components that help to abstract the actual self-organisation mechanisms from the intentions of a system designer. Moreover, this approach provides the necessary infrastructure to collect abstract self-organisation mechanisms and their configuration in a common database. While the current determination of the mechanism scores is only making use of expert experience, it already includes infrastructure to enable more sophisticated approaches in the near future, like online and offline machine learning or applying evolutionary strategies. Besides proceeding towards this direction, we plan to further evaluate our solution in real life experiments using multi-robot systems.

References

1. Balch, T., Hybinette, M.: Social potentials for scalable multi-robot formations. In: Proceedings of the IEEE International Conference on Robotics and Automation, ICRA 2000, vol. 1, pp. 73–80. IEEE (2000)
2. Bohren, J., Cousins, S.: The SMACH high-level executive [ROS news]. IEEE Robot. Autom. Mag. **17**(4), 18–20 (2010)
3. Brambilla, M., Ferrante, E., Birattari, M., Dorigo, M.: Swarm robotics: a review from the swarm engineering perspective. Swarm Intell. **7**(1), 1–41 (2013)
4. Colledanchise, M., Ögren, P.: How behavior trees modularize hybrid control systems and generalize sequential behavior compositions, the subsumption architecture, and decision trees. IEEE Trans. Robot. **33**(2), 372–389 (2017)

5. De Wolf, T., Holvoet, T.: Emergence versus self-organisation: different concepts but promising when combined. In: Brueckner, S.A., Di Marzo Serugendo, G., Karageorgos, A., Nagpal, R. (eds.) ESOA 2004. LNCS (LNAI), vol. 3464, pp. 1–15. Springer, Heidelberg (2005). https://doi.org/10.1007/11494676_1

6. Deneubourg, J.-L., Aron, S., Goss, S., Pasteels, J.M.: The self-organizing exploratory pattern of the argentine ant. J. Insect Behav. **3**(2), 159–168 (1990)

7. Dorigo, M., et al.: Evolving self-organizing behaviors for a swarm-bot. Auton. Robot. **17**(2–3), 223–245 (2004)

8. Edmonds, B.: Using the experimental method to produce reliable self-organised systems. In: Brueckner, S.A., Di Marzo Serugendo, G., Karageorgos, A., Nagpal, R. (eds.) ESOA 2004. LNCS (LNAI), vol. 3464, pp. 84–99. Springer, Heidelberg (2005). https://doi.org/10.1007/11494676_6

9. Fernandez-Marquez, J.L., Di Marzo Serugendo, G., Montagna, S., Viroli, M., Arcos, J.L., Arcos, J.L.: Description and composition of bio-inspired design patterns: a complete overview. Natural Comput. **12**(1), 43–67 (2013)

10. Fernandez-Marquez, J.L., Serugendo, G.D.M., Montagna, S.: BIO-CORE: bio-inspired self-organising mechanisms core. In: Hart, E., Timmis, J., Mitchell, P., Nakamo, T., Dabiri, F. (eds.) BIONETICS 2011. LNICST, vol. 103, pp. 59–72. Springer, Heidelberg (2012). https://doi.org/10.1007/978-3-642-32711-7_5

11. Foote, T.: tf: the transform library. In: 2013 IEEE International Conference on Technologies for Practical Robot Applications (TePRA), Open-Source Software Workshop, pp. 1–6, April 2013

12. Fox, M., Long, D.: PDDL2.1: an Extension to PDDL for expressing temporal planning domains. J. Artif. Int. Res. **20**(1), 61–124 (2003)

13. Francesca, G., et al.: AutoMoDe-Chocolate: automatic design of control software for robot swarms. Swarm Intell. **9**(2–3), 125–152 (2015)

14. Ge, S.S., Cui, Y.J.: New potential functions for mobile robot path planning. In: Proceedings of the 14th IFAC World Congres, pp. 509–514 (1999)

15. Graff, D., Richling, J., Werner, M.: jSwarm: distributed coordination in robot swarms. In: Robotic Sensor Networks (RSN) (2014)

16. Hrabia, C.-E., Wypler, S., Albayrak, S.: Towards goal-driven behaviour control of multi-robot systems. In: 2017 3nd International Conference on Control, Automation and Robotics (ICCAR), pp. 166–173, April 2017

17. Kazadi, S.T.: Swarm engineering. phd, California Institute of Technology (2000)

18. Mamei, M., Vasirani, M., Zambonelli, F.: Experiments of morphogenesis in swarms of simple mobile robots. Appl. Artif. Intell. **18**, 903–919 (2004)

19. Matarić, M.J.: Issues and approaches in the design of collective autonomous agents. Robot. Auton. Syst. **16**(2–4), 321–331 (1995)

20. Nau, D.S., et al.: Shop2: an HTN planning system. J. Artif. Intell. Res. **20**, 379–404 (2003)

21. Olfati-Saber, R.: Flocking for multi-agent dynamic systems: algorithms and theory. IEEE Trans. Autom. Control. **51**(3), 401–420 (2006)

22. Pinciroli, C., Beltrame, G.: Buzz: an extensible programming language for heterogeneous swarm robotics. In: 2016 IEEE/RSJ International Conference on Intelligent Robots and Systems (IROS), pp. 3794–3800. IEEE (2016)

23. Reynolds, C.W.: Steering behaviors for autonomous characters. In: Game Developers Conference 1999, pp. 763–782 (1999)

24. Serugendo, G.D.M., Gleizes, M.P., Karageorgos, A.: Self-organisation and emergence in MAS: an overview. Informatica (Slovenia) **30**(1), 45–54 (2006)

Towards Dynamic Coalition Formation for Intelligent Traffic Management

Jeffery Raphael[✉] and Elizabeth I. Sklar

Department of Informatics, King's College London, London, UK
{jeffery.raphael,elizabeth.sklar}@kcl.ac.uk

Abstract. Adaptive traffic management aims to adjust the timing of signals at road intersections to ensure smooth travel of vehicles through urban environments. A popular commercial system for handling traffic in this way is SCOOT (Split, Cycle and Offset Optimisation Technique), which involves reading data from sensors embedded in roadways to capture real-time information about traffic volume and making small changes to traffic signal timing in response. SCOOT operates in regions of connected intersections, but the sets of intersections in a region are fixed and the intersections do not communicate with each other. The research presented here takes a multi-agent approach whereby intersections work together in "coalitions" to improve traffic flow, using a market-based mechanism and forming coalitions dynamically as traffic conditions change over time. Experimental results show that this dynamic coalition approach performs better than SCOOT in several types of traffic conditions.

Keywords: Multi-agent simulation · Traffic management
Mechanism design

1 Introduction

Modern approaches to traffic control systems rely on mathematical models of traffic and/or optimisation algorithms [20] (e.g., OPAC, RHODES, SCAT and SCOOT). However, these methods are difficult to configure and maintain, and they do not scale well [20]. The *multi-agent systems (MAS)* paradigm offers a more flexible approach for traffic management [20] because MAS can model complex systems that are dynamic and distributed [3,4] and because the different elements of traffic can be viewed as a large collection of autonomous agents [21]. This allows us to apply a wide range of methodologies for defining the relationships between these elements.

In the approach presented here, we utilise market-based mechanisms, specifically *auctions*, as a framework for coordinating agent interaction. Unlike many other auction-based traffic control systems [2,12,19] which rely on *vehicle agents* to represent individual vehicles, our method uses traffic signals and other transportation infrastructure that is currently available. Our multi-agent traffic control system is comprised of two agents: *intersection agents* and *traffic signal*

© Springer Nature Switzerland AG 2018
F. Belardinelli and E. Argente (Eds.): EUMAS 2017/AT 2017, LNAI 10767, pp. 400–414, 2018.
https://doi.org/10.1007/978-3-030-01713-2_28

agents. Intersection agents act as auction managers and periodically execute a first-price, single-item auction. The *traffic signal agents* represent *phases*, where a phase is the segment of a traffic signal timing allotted to a set of vehicle movements. *Traffic signal agents* participate in the auction and bid against one another to adjust traffic signal timing. Similar to SCOOT, our approach relies on the manipulation of traffic signal parameters with the aid of information from in-ground vehicle detectors. The operation of SCOOT [6] (and hence its name) centres around making small adjustments to three parameters: *split*—the amount of time within a phase that a traffic signal is green (also referred to as *green time*); *cycle*—the total amount of time it takes for all phases in an intersection to receive their allocated green time; and *offset*—the difference in starting times of two consecutive traffic signals along a roadway. In SCOOT, *offsets* are adjusted in relation to the intersections that belong to a *region* (a pre-defined set of connected intersections). In the work presented here, we do not have pre-defined fixed regions, like those relied on by SCOOT. Instead, we define regions dynamically as traffic conditions change.

This paper is structured as follows. Section 2 describes the approach we have taken to explore the impact of dynamically assigning regions as traffic flows. Section 3 explains a series of experiments we ran in order to evaluate the efficacy of our approach. Section 4 presents the results of our experiments. Section 5 discusses our approach within the context of related work at the intersection of MAS and traffic control. Finally, in Sect. 6, we summarise and outline steps for future work.

2 Approach

Our previous work [13,14] on multi-agent auction-based traffic control systems experimented with different bidding rules to adjust the same three parameters employed by SCOOT. In GRACE [14], *traffic signal agents* have the ability to adjust either *split*, *cycle* or *offset* or some combination of all three. However, the traffic signal agents are greedy and work to improve only traffic flow for their respective phase. In this paper, we present DC2, a variant of GRACE where dynamic coalitions are formed to allow intersections to coordinate signal timing adjustments. Here, a *coalition* is a temporary pairing of intersections for coordination via *offset* adjustments. Furthermore, in DC2 traffic signal agents are influenced by their neighbours. More specifically, the preferred *offset* of a traffic signal agent is subject to upstream traffic conditions.

In SCOOT, *offset* adjustments are employed for intersection coordination, but the intersections that are coordinated lie along fixed radial (linear path) road networks. In DC2, the coalitions are dynamically formed and dissolved once they are no longer of value. Additionally, using *offset* adjustments for junction coordination sets DC2 apart from other market-based traffic systems. In many market-based traffic systems, traffic signals are either removed from the traffic control system (e.g., [2,17]) or *offset* adjustments are ignored (e.g., [7,12]).

In DC2, traffic signal agents have two key components: a *utility function* which returns the utility of traffic signal timing adjustments and a *bidding rule*, which allows traffic signal agents to express a preference for particular timing adjustments.

The **utility function** used in DC2 is:

$$U(\Delta split, \Delta cycle, \Delta offset) = -X + D^I(\Delta split, \Delta cycle, \Delta offset) \qquad (1)$$

where the tuple $\langle \Delta split, \Delta cycle, \Delta offset \rangle$ is a collection of adjustments to *split*, *cycle* and *offset*. Adjustments are made in discrete steps measured in seconds. For example, given $\langle 2, -10, 4 \rangle$, green time would be increased by 2 s, cycle length reduced by 10 s and *offset* increased by 4 s.

The function $D^I(\Delta split, \Delta cycle, \Delta offset)$ returns the estimated number of stopped vehicles if adjustments $\langle \Delta split, \Delta cycle, \Delta offset \rangle$ were adopted—but in relation to the intersection, that is, if intersection I were allowed to apply the *offset* in the manner it chooses. This allows junctions to form *coalitions*, more specifically, coordinate signal timing changes with any neighbouring junction depending on traffic conditions.

The variable X is the current level of use for each link under the agent's control, or *degree of saturation* [11,15], defined as:

$$X = \frac{v}{c} * \frac{L}{g} \qquad (2)$$

where v is the volume of traffic read by the traffic signal agent[1]; c is the maximum possible volume of traffic (in vehicles per hour); L is cycle length; and g is green time.

The **bidding rule** for DC2 is:

$$b = \sum_i^n X_i \qquad (3)$$

where each X_i is the current level of use for each link under the bidding agent's control.

The possible adjustment values for DC2 are:

$$\Delta split = \{0, 1, 2, 3, 4, 5\}$$
$$\Delta offset = \{-4, -3, -2, -1, 0, 1, 2, 3, 4\}$$
$$\Delta cycle = \{\emptyset\}$$

In DC2, the agent framework remains the same as in our previous work [13,14]. At every junction there is an intersection agent (the auction manager) and two traffic signal agents. At the beginning of each auction, traffic signal agents generate a set of possible adjustments to traffic signal timing using the sets $\Delta split$ and $\Delta offset$. The $\Delta cycle$ is an empty set because in DC2, traffic signal agents do not make changes to the cycle length (this is a requirement

---

[1] In SCOOT, traffic volume is measured through induction loop sensors buried in the road. We assume the existence of these sensors in our method.

needed to form green waves). Traffic signal agents select their preferred signal timing adjustments using Eq. (1), i.e., the signal timing adjustment with the highest utility is preferred. Thus, in DC2 the single item up for auction is the authority to implement changes to the traffic signal timing. In other words, the intersection adopts the preferred signal timing adjustments of the traffic signal agent that wins the auction. Furthermore, traffic signal agents utilise Eq. (3) to generated bids. In DC2, *intersection agents* execute an auction every 300 s.

3 Experiments

We evaluated our auction-based methods experimentally using the *Simulation of Urban MObility (SUMO)* traffic simulator [10]. SUMO is an open source microscopic traffic simulator and is often used in research concerning vehicular communication (either vehicle-to-vehicle or vehicle-to-infrastructure), but it is also used to study route choice and traffic control algorithms [10]. Although it has a GUI front-end, for our experiments we treated it as a back-end server, and we developed a client application to control the simulation using SUMO's Traffic Control Interface (TraCI) through a TCP socket to facilitate batch processing of experimental runs.

We utilised three benchmarks for evaluating the effectiveness of our auction-based methods: FIXED, SUPRL and SCOOT. First, we tested a FIXED method of controlling traffic signals, which represents traditional, non-adaptive, traffic lights that execute the same light sequence timings in every cycle. In addition, for comparison we implemented the reinforcement-learning traffic control system described by Bazzan *et al.* [1], which we label SUPRL. Bazzan *et al.* [1] utilised *supervisors* as high-level agents that observed small groups of intersection-level agents. The high-level agents are concerned with the joint-action space of the subordinate agents while the intersection-level agents act locally. More specifically, the high-level agents keep track of the average reward earned by their subordinates and use this information to suggest actions (intersection-level agents are not forced to take the actions suggested by its supervisor). Intersection-level agents can perform three actions; each action is a complete traffic signal timing plan. The first action is a neutral traffic signal setting, i.e., the green time is evenly divided amongst the two phases. The second favours the phase that services the north/south bound lanes (by allotting more green time to the phase). The third favours the west/east bound lanes. Lastly, in SUPRL each supervisor has three subordinate agents. Our third benchmark is an implementation of SCOOT. A description of our SCOOT implementation on SUMO is given in [14].

We employed two different road networks for our experiments, based on the US cities of Portland and Phoenix. The **Portland** map (Fig. 1a) has two-way, single lane, streets running East/West and North/South. However, it also has a large avenue running along its perimeter which is two-way with four lanes. Traffic signals use a two-phase signal plan: during one phase, North/South bound traffic passes through the intersection, while West/East bound traffic passes in the other phase. Additionally, roadways do not include dedicated turning (right or left)

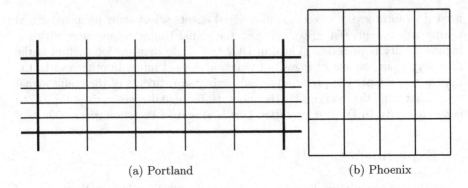

(a) Portland   (b) Phoenix

Fig. 1. Road networks used for experiments (not to scale).

phases; therefore left and right turns were given lower priority than through movements, i.e., vehicles turning left or right waited until it was safe to do so.

The **Phoenix** map (Fig. 1b) is a grid-based city organised in square *blocks*. The four traffic signals in the corners of the network are deactivated because these four traffic signals control streams that run without conflicts (i.e., vehicles traversing these intersections will never have to yield to one another). The roadways on the Phoenix map are all one-way and do not have a dedicated turning lane. All traffic signals use a two-phase signal plan: during one phase, North/South bound traffic passes through the intersection, while West/East bound traffic passes in the other phase. For our experiments, the signal plan did not include dedicated turning (right or left) phases; therefore left and right turns were given lower priority than through movements.

We utilised three different traffic patterns to conduct our experiments: **structured**—a traffic flow through the network with an identifiable (e.g., commuter) path with heavy volume; **unstructured**—a traffic flow with no identifiable path with heavy volume; and **football**—a traffic flow that emulates road conditions before, during and after a special event, like a football match. In all three patterns, a *disruption* is injected into the system about an hour into the simulation (e.g., where there is a traffic accident or a sudden increase in traffic volume and then is cleared some period later). For the *football* traffic pattern, two disruptions occur: one before the game starts and one after it is over.

Each set of experimental conditions (2 maps × 3 traffic patterns) was repeated 30 times ("runs") to attain suitable statistics. Each simulation run lasted a maximum of 15,000 s (4 h and 10 min); simulations could terminate early if all vehicles reached their destination before the maximum time had passed. Data for the cumulative averages is not collected until after the $1,000^{th}$ s. This allows traffic flow to level off, so that averages more accurately reflect actual performance when the network is "full".

We evaluated the performance of the traffic controllers using two categories of metrics: *Travel Time* and *Number Stopped*. Travel time is by far the most common way of measuring the effectiveness of traffic controllers and is computed for an individual vehicle as the amount of time it takes for the vehicle to complete its journey; lower travel times are better. *Number Stopped* is a measure of how the traffic is flowing and is computed as the number of vehicles that are not moving at any given time step: if more vehicles are moving—hence lower numbers of vehicles stopped—then the whole traffic system is operating more smoothly.

We examined *Travel Time* and *Number Stopped* in several different forms: *Average Travel Time* (ATT) of all the vehicles across the 30 simulations, which gives an overall measure of the effectiveness of the traffic control system; *Cumulative Average Travel Time* (CATT) as the simulation executes, which gives a measure of how the traffic control system performs over time particularly as traffic conditions change; *Average Travel Time on Arrival* (ATTA) for the group of vehicles that have finished their trip at each time step, which gives a measure of how well the traffic control system responds to disruptions in the system, both with respect to the moment after the disruption as well as how well the system recovers after the disruption has passed; *Average Number Stopped* (ANS) across the 30 simulations, which gives the average number of stopped vehicles in the network (per time step); and *Cumulative Average Number Stopped* (CANS) as the simulation executes, which gives a measure of the number of stopped vehicles in the network at each time step.

4 Results

This section presents and analyses the results for each map, Phoenix (Sect. 4.1) and Portland (Sect. 4.2). On each map we simulated three traffic scenarios: *structured*, *unstructured* and *football* traffic. Additionally, we measure performance using *travel time* and *number stopped*.

4.1 Phoenix Map

Average Travel Time (ATT). In *unstructured* traffic, DC2 has lower ATT than all three benchmarks, Table 1. Also, in the *football* scenario, DC2 has lower ATT than FIXED and SCOOT. Lastly, in *structured* traffic, DC2 has lower ATT than FIXED and SUPRL.

Table 1. Average travel times (ATT) for each mechanism and traffic scenario on the Phoenix map.

Average travel time (ATT) (*std.*)		
Traffic pattern		
Mechanism	*Structured*	*Unstructured*	*Football*
DC2	*147.47* (0.78)	**515.55** (10.97)	*157.34* (4.6)
FIXED	166.11 (1.09)	1108.81 (168.99)	190.89 (12.8)
SCOOT	**144.8** (3.44)	1231.36 (369.63)	184.81 (7.66)
SUPRL	159.48 (1.3)	855.66 (78.43)	**142.76** (4.05)

Table 2. Average number of stopped vehicles (ANS) for each mechanism and traffic scenario on the Phoenix map.

Average number of stopped vehicles (ANS) (*std.*)		
	Traffic pattern		
Mechanism	*Structured*	*Unstructured*	*Football*
DC2	**58.27** (1.08)	**19.53** (1.5)	38.9 (2.54)
FIXED	70.23 (1.33)	68.33 (16.6)	50.27 (5.01)
SCOOT	60.17 (2.18)	89.97 (52.73)	38.5 (3.14)
SUPRL	66.63 (1.4)	46.6 (7.83)	**30.13** (1.81)

Cumulative Average Travel Time (CATT). On the Phoenix map in the *unstructured* traffic scenario, DC2 has the lowest CATT, Fig. 2a. Figure 2a shows that in comparison to the other mechanisms, DC2 shows little change in CATT during the *unstructured* traffic disruption. In the *football* scenario, prior to the first disruption, DC2 have the lowest CATT, Fig. 2b. However, during the first disruption, DC2 has a sharp increase in CATT but begins to recover sooner than SCOOT during the football match. Figure 2b shows that during the football match, the CATT of DC2 decreases and remains lower than the CATT of SCOOT during the second disruption. After the second disruption, the CATT of DC2 is lower than the CATT of SCOOT and FIXED but higher than the CATT of SUPRL. In *structured* traffic, DC2 has lower CATT than FIXED and SUPRL but not SCOOT, Figs. 2b.

Average Number of Stopped vehicles (ANS). Table 2 shows that in *unstructured* traffic, DC2 has a lower ANS than the benchmarks in *structured* and *unstructured* traffic. In the *unstructured* traffic scenario, DC2 halves the ANS compared with SUPRL. In *football* traffic, DC2 and SCOOT have similar ANS; both mechanisms have lower ANS than FIXED but not SUPRL. DC2 also has lower ANS than the benchmarks in *structured* traffic.

Cumulative Average Number of Stopped Vehicles (CANS). In the *unstructured* traffic scenario, DC2 has the lowest CANS throughout the entire scenario, Fig. 3a. The CANS of DC2 quickly reaches its peak during the disruption, unlike the other mechanisms. In the *football* scenario, Fig. 3c, during the first disruption DC2 performs similar to SCOOT. However, after the first disruption has ended, DC2 recovers sooner than SCOOT, i.e., DC2 returns to pre-disruption levels of CANS first. During the football match DC2 has lower CANS than SUPRL and FIXED but does not outperform SCOOT.

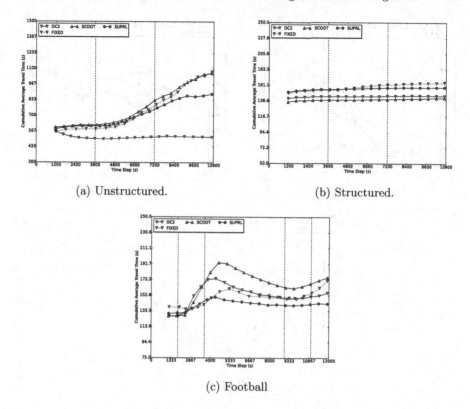

(a) Unstructured.

(b) Structured.

(c) Football

Fig. 2. Cumulative average travel times (CATT) on the Phoenix map (over 30 simulations). Beginning and ending of disruptions are marked by dotted lines.

4.2 Portland Map

Average Travel Time (ATT). In *structured* and *unstructured* traffic, DC2 has lower ATT than FIXED, SCOOT and SUPRL, Table 3. In the *football* scenario, DC2 has lower ATT than SCOOT (and slightly lower than FIXED) but DC2 does not outperform SUPRL. However, in some scenarios, the magnitude of the difference is small. For example, in *structured* traffic, the difference in ATT between DC2 and FIXED is approximately 2.44 s.

Cumulative Average Travel Time (CATT). In the *unstructured* traffic scenario, initially, the CATT of DC2 is greater than the CATT of SCOOT, however, during the *unstructured* traffic disruption, DC2 maintain CATT lower than SCOOT, Fig. 4a. Figure 4a also shows that DC2 has lower CATT than all the other mechanisms after the disruption ends. DC2 performs well in terms of CATT in *unstrctured* traffic on the Phoenix map as well. In the *football* scenario, DC2 performs as well as SUPRL, Fig. 4c. During the first disruption all the mechanisms have a similar rate of increase in CATT. However, during the football match, travel times with SCOOT continue to increase beyond DC2 and SUPRL.

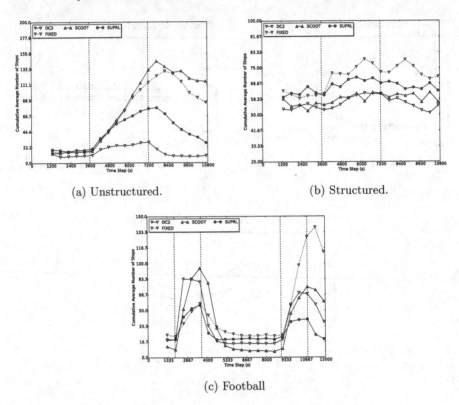

(a) Unstructured. (b) Structured.

(c) Football

Fig. 3. Cumulative average number of stops (CANS) on the Phoenix map (over 30 simulations). Beginning and ending of disruptions are marked by dotted lines.

The CATT of DC2 and SUPRL plateaus sooner than SCOOT during the football match. Additionally, DC2 and SUPRL show signs of recovery during the match and no adverse effects during the second *football* disruption. However, in the *football* scenario, FIXED has the lowest CATT from beginning of the football match and onward, in comparison to the other mechanisms. In *structured* traffic, DC2 has the lowest CATT, Fig. 4b. However, in *structured* traffic, the CATT of FIXED is nearly identical to DC2.

Average Number of Stopped Vehicles (ANS). Overall the *unstructured* traffic scenario has fewer stops in comparison to the other scenarios, Table 4. DC2 has lower ANS than FIXED and SUPRL in the *unstructured* traffic scenario. However, in *unstructured* traffic on the Portland map, SCOOT has the lowest ANS, this is not the case on the Phoenix map. In the *football* scenario, DC2 has lower ANS than FIXED and SCOOT but not SUPRL. In *structured* traffic, DC2 has lower ANS to SCOOT and SUPRL only.

Table 3. Average travel times (ATT) for each mechanism and traffic scenario on the Portland map.

Average travel time (ATT) (*std.*)		
	Traffic pattern		
Mechanism	*Structured*	*Unstructured*	*Football*
DC2	**226.94** (1.3)	**483.85** (12.36)	298.51 (9.42)
FIXED	229.38 (0.88)	569.87 (18.05)	299.6 (5.09)
SCOOT	360.86 (11)	510.6 (26.52)	392.73 (23.55)
SUPRL	244.13 (1.17)	577.7 (10)	**271.56** (5.62)

Table 4. Average number of stopped vehicles (ANS) for each mechanism and traffic scenario on the Portland map.

Average number stopped (ANS) (*std.*)		
	Traffic pattern		
Mechanism	*Structured*	*Unstructured*	*Football*
DC2	*170* (2.49)	*22.13* (1.59)	*131.07* (5.68)
FIXED	**161.13** (2.71)	28.83 (2.45)	143.4 (3.61)
SCOOT	319.8 (13.78)	**19.27** (2.27)	153.77 (13.37)
SUPRL	185.33 (3.18)	29.63 (1.52)	**122.73** (4.89)

Cumulative Average Number of Stopped Vehicles (CANS). In *unstructured* traffic, DC2 have lower CANS than SUPRL and FIXED, even during the disruption, Fig. 5a. However, in *unstructured* traffic, SCOOT has the lowest CANS during the entire scenario. On the Portland map, the *unstructured* traffic disruption does not affect the mechanisms in the same manner as it does on the Phoenix map. In *unstructured* traffic on the Portland map, during the disruption, the increase in CANS displayed by DC2, FIXED, SCOOT, and SUPRL is not as sharp as it is on the Phoenix map. In the first disruption of the *football* scenario, all the mechanisms have similar rates of increase in CANS, Fig. 5c. DC2, FIXED and SUPRL have a much sharper decline in CANS during the match than SCOOT. Additionally, during the same period, DC2 performs similar to SUPRL in terms of CANS. Although at the beginning of the football match the CANS of DC2 is similar to SCOOT's CANS, by the end of the football match the CANS of DC2 is much lower than the CANS of SCOOT. Also, during the second disruption, DC2 and SUPRL are able to maintain lower numbers of stopped vehicles compared to SCOOT and FIXED. In *structured* traffic, DC2 outperforms SCOOT and SUPRL in maintaining low CANS, Fig. 5b. DC2 does not display a substantial increase in CANS during the disruptions. However, in *structured* traffic, the CANS of DC2 is similar to FIXED.

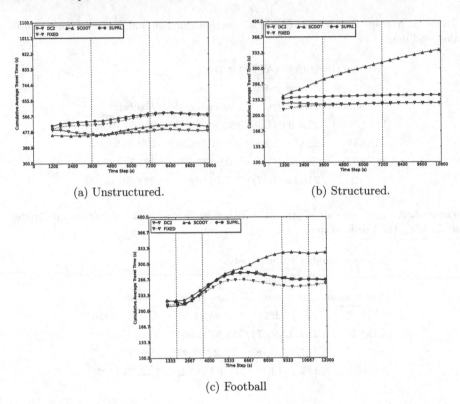

(a) Unstructured.

(b) Structured.

(c) Football

Fig. 4. Cumulative average travel times (CATT) on the Portland map (over 30 simulations). Beginning and ending of disruptions are marked by dotted lines.

4.3 Summary

While DC2 does not perform best for all metrics under all experimental conditions, it exhibits lower ATT and ANS in *unstructured* traffic and similar (though second-best) results to SCOOT in *structured* traffic, for both maps—except for ANS on the Portland map. Surprisingly, FIXED performs best under this condition, and SCOOT is markedly the worst performer.

5 Related Work

The use of economic principles in traffic management and control is nothing new, e.g., tolling systems have been in use for hundreds of years. Market-based traffic controllers (and traffic management systems) employ a variety of auctions, e.g., second price sealed bid [2], or combinatorial auctions [19] and walrasian auction [18]. Auctions are a versatile framework for agent interaction and have woven their way into the traffic domain through a variety of approaches. Many market-based traffic systems treat roadways and/or the intersections as a commodity where drivers participate in a market to gain access to said commodity.

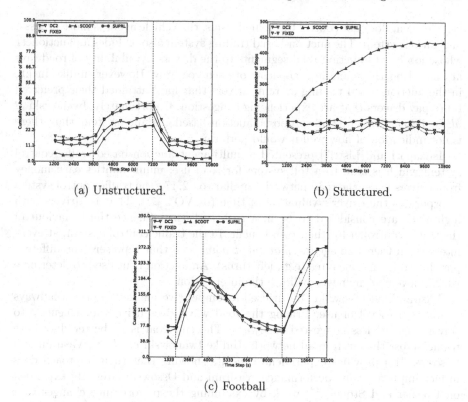

(a) Unstructured.   (b) Structured.

(c) Football

Fig. 5. Cumulative average number of stops (CANS) on the Portland map (over 30 simulations). Beginning and ending of disruptions are marked by dotted lines.

For example, Carlino *et al.* [2] implemented a traffic control system where vehicles bid on traffic signal phases. Schepperle and Böhm [17] employed a similar strategy except vehicles are bidding on periods of time when it is safe to traverse the intersection. While Carlino *et al.* [2] and Schepperle and Böhm [17] used the intersection as a commodity, Vasirani and Ossowski [19] presented a system for traffic assignment where an auction is used for route selection. One of the more interesting properties of auction-based traffic control systems is their ability to seamlessly incorporate individual valuations of time [2,7,16,17].

Iwanowski [9] proposed a multi-agent market-based traffic management system to balance road use. The traffic management system provides route guidance for drivers in order to reduce traffic congestion. The aim of [9] is to coordinate drivers via a central unit (the road network operator) and distribute the drivers across the network while taking into consideration individual route preferences. This work is further developed in [8] where Iwanowski *et al.* describes the *auction-based trading* traffic control system. In auction-based trading, the vehicle agent (referred to as *vehicle/driver units* in [8]) plays a similar role to vehicle agents in [9], that is, vehicle agents bid for routes on behalf of the driver. The vehicle agent does not control the vehicle, thus, the vehicle agent is more or less a navigation system. The auction-based trading system also includes an auctioneer whose job it is to auction road segments to the drivers. Availability of roadways are based on the maximum capacity of each roadway. However, unlike in [9], in the auction-based trading system, drivers that have attained their preferred route pay drivers that are experiencing congestion. Unfortunately, Iwanowski *et al.* [8] did not evaluate their proposed auction-based guidance system, thus, there is not indication of how well it would perform.

Isukapati and List [7] presented a multi-agent auction-based traffic control system which is akin to a toll system for road use; municipalities earn money from drivers using the road network. Similar to [2,17], the traffic control system incorporates the driver's valuation of time (or VOT [7]). That is, drivers with high VOT are considered to be in a rush and can influence the behaviour of the traffic controller for their own benefit. In the traffic control system, at every intersection there are agents, *movement managers*, that represent the different possible traffic manoeuvres (e.g., left turns). An auction is utilised to determine which movement manager will use the intersection.

Vasirani and Ossowski [18] utilised a competitive market to price roadways according to level of use. Pricing the road ways gives drivers an incentive to travel cheaper, less congested roadways. The end goal is to better distribute traffic across the entire road network. Unlike Iwanowski *et al.* [8], Vasirani and Ossowski [18] provides experimental results showing that their approach does in fact improve traffic performance. Vasirani and Ossowski later [19] expanded on Dresner and Stone's [5] work by examining the performance changes to a reservation-based system where time slots were allocated using a *combinatorial auction (CA)*. The authors tackled both the traffic control problem (at a single intersection) and traffic assignment problem (in a road network) with their market-based approach. As drivers approached the intersection, reservations were awarded through the auction, instead of *first-come, first-served* (FCFS) which Dresner and Stone [5] employed in their work. In this way, drivers express their true valuation for a contested reservation. As stated earlier, Dresner and Stone's [5] traffic control systems relies on vehicle agents running on autonomous vehicles, thus, Vasirani and Ossowski's [19] this approach requires both as well. However, in Vasirani and Ossowski's [19] system, the vehicle agents are responsible for participating in the auction as well as controlling the vehicle. In a network with a single intersection, the authors looked at the delay experienced by drivers based on the amount they were willing to "pay" to use the intersection. They found that initially, having a willingness to pay does decrease delay, but eventually this levels off. However, CA was found to increase overall delay. As the intensity of traffic increased, CA experienced far more delays and rejected reservations than the FCFS approach.

6 Summary

We have presented an auction-based multi-agent traffic control system which forms dynamic regions or coalitions. The coalitions improve traffic flow through a series of city blocks that may not always form a linear path. Additionally, our approach relies on local traffic state information from in-ground vehicle detectors, thus, omitting the need for more advanced communication capabilities such as vehicle-to-vehicle or vehicle-to-infrastructure communication devices. We evaluated our approach on two grid-based maps under three traffic conditions and examined the travel time and number of stops. Experimental results have demonstrated the efficacy of our approach in comparison with others. The next steps in this line of inquiry involve increasing the size of a coalition in order to prove the scalability of our method.

References

1. Bazzan, A.L.C., de Oliveira, D., da Silva, B.C.: Learning in groups of traffic signals. Eng. Appl. Artif. Intell. **23**(4), 560–568 (2010)
2. Carlino, D., Boyles, S.D., Stone, P.: Auction-based autonomous intersection management. In: Proceedings of the 16th IEEE Intelligent Transportation Systems Conference (ITSC) (2013)
3. Chen, B., Cheng, H.H.: A review of the applications of agent technology in traffic and transportation systems. IEEE Trans. Intell. Transp. Syst. **11**(2), 485–497 (2010)
4. Chen, B., Cheng, H.H., Palen, J.: Integrating mobile agent technology with multi-agent systems for distributed traffic detection and management systems. Transp. Res. Part C Emerg. Technol. **17**(1), 1–10 (2009)
5. Dresner, K.M., Stone, P.: Multiagent traffic management: a reservation-based intersection control mechanism. In: Proceedings of the Third International Joint Conference on AAMAS, pp. 530–537. IEEE Computer Society (2004)
6. Hunt, P.B., Robertson, D.I., Bretherton, R.D., Winton, R.I.: SCOOT - a traffic responsive method of coordinating signals. Technical report 1014, Transport and Road Research Laboratory (1981)
7. Isukapati, I.K., List, G.F.: Agent based framework for modeling operations at isolated signalized intersections. In: Proceedings of the 18th IEEE International Conference on Intelligent Transportation Systems, pp. 2900–2906. IEEE (September 2015)
8. Iwanowski, S., Spering, W., Coughlin, W.: Road traffic coordination by electronic trading. Transp. Res. Part C Emerg. Technol. **11**(5), 405–422 (2003)
9. Iwanowski, S.: Auction-based traffic control on roads. In: Proceedings of the 7th World Congress on Intelligent Systems (2000)
10. Krajzewicz, D., Erdmann, J., Behrisch, M., Bieker, L.: recent development and applications of SUMO - Simulation of Urban MObility. Int. J. Adv. Syst. Meas. **5**(3&4), 128–138 (2012)
11. Lee, S.S., Lee, S.H., Oh, Y.T., Choi, K.C.: Development of degree of saturation estimation models for adaptive signal systems. RSCE J. Civ. Eng. **6**(3), 337–345 (2002)
12. Mashayekhi, M., List, G.: A Multi-agent auction-based approach for modeling of signalized intersections. In: Second Workshop on Synergies Between Multiagent Systems, Machine Learning and Complex Systems (TRI 2015), Buenos Aires, Argentina (July 2015)

13. Raphael, J., Maskell, S., Sklar, E.: From goods to traffic: first steps toward an auction-based traffic signal controller. In: Demazeau, Y., Decker, K.S., Bajo Pérez, J., de la Prieta, F. (eds.) PAAMS 2015. LNCS (LNAI), vol. 9086, pp. 187–198. Springer, Cham (2015). https://doi.org/10.1007/978-3-319-18944-4_16

14. Raphael, J., Maskell, S., Sklar, E.: An empirical investigation of adaptive traffic control parameters. In: Proceedings of the Workshop on Agents in Traffic and Transportation at IJCAI 2016. CEUR-WS.org (2016)

15. Roess, R.P., Prasas, E., McShane, W.R.: Traffic Engineering: International Edition, 4th edn. Pearson Education Inc., London (2009)

16. Schepperle, H., Böhm, K.: Agent-based traffic control using auctions. In: Klusch, M., Hindriks, K.V., Papazoglou, M.P., Sterling, L. (eds.) CIA 2007. LNCS (LNAI), vol. 4676, pp. 119–133. Springer, Heidelberg (2007). https://doi.org/10.1007/978-3-540-75119-9_9

17. Schepperle, H., Böhm, K.: Auction-based traffic management: towards effective concurrent utilization of road intersections. In: 10th IEEE International Conference on E-Commerce Technology (CEC)/5th IEEE International Conference on Enterprise Computing. E-Commerce and E-Services (EEE), pp. 105–112. IEEE, Washington, D.C. (2008)

18. Vasirani, M., Ossowski, S.: A computational market for distributed control of urban road traffic systems. IEEE Trans. Intell. Transp. Syst. **12**(2), 313–321 (2011)

19. Vasirani, M., Ossowski, S.: A market-inspired approach for intersection management in urban road traffic networks. J. Artif. Intell. Res. **43**, 621–659 (2012)

20. Wang, F.Y.: Agent-based control for networked traffic management systems. IEEE Intell. Syst. **20**(5), 92–96 (2005)

21. Weiss, G. (ed.): Multiagent Systems: A Modern Approach to Distributed Artificial Intelligence. MIT Press, Cambridge (1999)

AT 2017: Algorithms and Frameworks

A Multi-agent Approach for Composing Negotiation Items in a Reverse Logistic Virtual Market

Adriana Giret(✉)[iD], Adrian Martinez, and Vicente Botti[iD]

Dpto. Sistemas Informáticos y Computación, Universitat Politècnica de València,
Camino de Vera s/n, 46022 Valencia, Spain
agiret@dsic.upv.es

Abstract. In this work a reverse production process is conceived as a service-based manufacturing network (ecosystem), in which the manufacturing companies "play" in the ecosystem by means of market services. One complex problem in a reverse logistic virtual market is the efficient composition and decomposition of the negotiation items. A negotiation item is defined as an item subject to be recycled: used products/scraps/wastes, a sub-part of a used product/scrap/waste, or the materials that are contained in the used product/scrap/waste. In this work we present a Multi-agent approach in order to compose the last two types of negotiation items from an orchestration of negotiation processes among the different stakeholders of the reverse logistic process (i.e. collecting points, recycling plants, disassembly plants, secondary material markets). In this way a call for buying, for example 10 tons of steel, can be handle in the virtual market as a complex process of buying and selling used products/scraps/wastes, or their sub-parts, in order to decompose and pre-process them (by recycling and/or disassembly plants) for extracting the steel contained in those items.

1 Introduction

Many research works have demonstrated the positive effects of internal measures towards sustainability in manufacturing systems [7]. Lately the goal has begun to shift to integrating all of the business value-adding operations, including purchasing and in-bound logistics, production and manufacturing, distribution and out-bound logistics, in such a way that activities associated with these functions have the least harmful environmental impact [14]. Greening the supply chain is one such innovative idea [3].

A green supply chain can be conceived as something as small as buying green products from a supplier to the much broader context of an industrial ecosystem [4]. Sustainable supply chain is an active research field in which new techniques are continuously proposed to reduce negative environmental impacts while pursuing production economy [14]. Sustainable supply chain network consists of forward production processes and reverse (recycling) production processes (reverse

© Springer Nature Switzerland AG 2018
F. Belardinelli and E. Argente (Eds.): EUMAS 2017/AT 2017, LNAI 10767, pp. 417–430, 2018.
https://doi.org/10.1007/978-3-030-01713-2_29

logistics). Nevertheless, most of the research and development attention is targeted to the forward action of the supply chain [4], whereas few research works have considered how this supply chain can or should work in reverse to reclaim products at the end of their life-cycle and return them through the supply chain for decomposition, disposal or re-use of key components. Systems in which the two approaches (forward and reverse) are combined can drastically reduce the negative impacts to the environment [18]. These systems are called closed-loop production systems[1].

In [5] an intelligent approach for reverse production ecosystems is tackle by means of a Multi-agent supported Virtual Market. In that work the reverse production process is conceived as a service-based manufacturing network [6], in which all the activities are outsourced and the stakeholders (i.e. manufacturing companies, collecting points, recycling plants and disassembly plants) use agents that provide interfaces/services to "play" in that ecosystem. In [5] the backbone structure of the virtual market is presented. In order to complete the Multi-agent structure defined for the virtual market in this paper we focus on the complex problem of composing negotiation items. A negotiation item is defined as an item subject to be recycled: used products/scraps/wastes, a sub-part of a used product/scrap/waste, or the materials that are contained in the used product/scrap/waste. The approach we follow in order to compose the last two types of negotiation items is an orchestration of negotiation processes among the different stakeholders.

2   Green Supply Chains and Intelligent Manufacturing Systems

The US Department of Commerce [12] defines sustainable manufacturing as: "the creation of manufactured products that use processes that minimize negative environmental impacts, conserve energy and natural resources, are safe for employees, communities, and consumers and are economically sound".

A consensus definition of green and sustainable supply chains does not exist (for a large review on definitions see [1]). It is identified as a sub-discipline of supply chain managing expanding the work in a variety of areas. An in-depth state-of-the-art review on green supply chains can be found in [4]. In this work we consider a manufacturing supply chain as a system that consists of 5 layers, including raw material supply, manufacturing, wholesaling, retailing, and end-customers. Whereas, a used-product and/or waste materials reverse logistics chain includes collecting points, recycling plants, disassembly plants, secondary material markets, and final disposal locations of wastes. All these activities are

---

[1] A closed-loop production system is defined as the "taking back of products from customers and recovering added value by reusing the entire product, and/or some of its modules, components and parts" [17]. The closed-loop construct consists of the common forward supply chain and the so-called reverse supply chain which closes the loop. In summary, there exist three different options to close the loop: reusing the product as a whole, reusing the components or reusing the materials.

executed with the purpose of capturing value, or proper disposal. The keys to the successful design and use of reverse logistics systems include costs, overall quality, customer service, environmental concerns and legislative concerns. Other factors to consider are: cost-benefit analysis, transportation, warehousing, supply management, remanufacturing and recycling, and packaging.

Initiatives such as Industrie 4.0, Smart Industry, Industrie du Futur, among others from Europe; Industrial Internet Consortium from USA; Industrial Value Chain Initiative from Japan; Made in China 2025 from China, are trying to integrate Internet and manufacturing systems in order to fully digitalize the factories of the future. This new production paradigm is based on concepts as autonomy and co-operation because both are necessary to create flexible behavior and thus to adapt to the changing production conditions. One such approach is the Intelligent Manufacturing Systems (IMS) paradigm. In IMS the manufacturing system is conceived as a distributed system in which its constituent components, such as machines, resources, products, and staff, have intelligent capabilities for acting in its environment pursuing global system goals; and have autonomous execution for decision making, social interaction with other intelligent entities, and collaboration for achieving the system goals.

Agent based Manufacturing Systems, are based on Multi-Agent System (MAS) technology [2]. The specialized literature in IMS, focused on MAS, offers successful approaches for achieving sustainability in manufacturing systems. The concept of Go-green Holon proposed in [16], is a pre-built development artifact that includes efficiency-oriented mechanisms (optimizing sustainability means), in addition to classical effectiveness-oriented mechanisms, to make a decision and/or execute an operation in IMS. Go-green ANEMONA [8] is a complete software engineering method for developing sustainable IMS. The method helps the designer to specify and implement sustainable optimization functions in IMS providing development guidelines and modeling templates. On the other hand, in [9] it is proposed the application of agent-based systems for supply-chain synchronized production planning including management of raw materials flow as well as flow of returned by customer obsolete products and defected semi-products and products that are refused by quality control within the factory. In [13] a multi-agent architecture is proposed to address waste classification, recycling, logistics, and reuse of products. Whereas, in [11] a multi-agent system framework to achieve coherent and consistent workflows that can meet order requirements is proposed. Finally, [5] presents an abstract definition of a virtual market for reverse production process that specify the roles and services required in order to implement it, but leaving open the issue of autonomously composing and decomposing negotiation items considering economic and environmental costs. The following sections introduce our approach that intends to solve it.

3   A Virtual Market Approach for Reverse Production Systems

In this work we will use the Agent-based Virtual Market approach for Reverse Production Systems proposed in [5]. The overall idea behind the Virtual Market

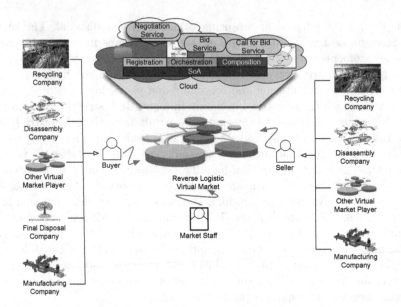

Fig. 1. Reverse logistic virtual market ecosystem

is to facilitate the participation of stakeholders in the activities of green supply chains by means of Service Oriented Manufacturing Systems [6], providing an easy to use interface for the players of a wider reverse logistic ecosystem as a step towards virtual outsourcing of reverse manufacturing processes. Figure 1 shows the structure of the virtual market. The framework provides the definition of the agent roles and the services supported and provided for playing in the market, such as: QueryNegotiation, QueryAgreement, CallForBid, CreateNegotiationDialog, EnterNegotiationDialog, LeaveNegotiationDialog, Bid, AcceptAgreement, RejectAgreement, etc.

Taking into account the features of a virtual market for reverse production systems it is very common to have a CallForBid, let's say to buy a given item (for example a given amount of recycled material) that is not available in the market as such because there is no corresponding CallForBid to sell the requested item due to: (i) the amount of material does not mach the requested amount, or (ii) the material is available but as a part/component material of offered products/wastes/sub-parts in the market, that requires a transformation and/or decomposition process in order to extract the material.

In this work we call this problem a composition of negotiation items (the complementary problem of decomposing or dividing a negotiation item in order to get a lower amount of the item is not tackled in this paper), and try to solve it providing a special service that arranges and orchestrates a set/sequence of different negotiation interactions in order to get the negotiation item required by the given CallForBid. In the following sections we present our approach to solve the problem outlining first the key roles of the virtual market that interact in the composition of negotiation items, the algorithms designed to arrange and orchestrate the sequence of negotiation protocols to compose the item, illustrating our approach with examples.

3.1 Roles in the Market

The key roles of the reverse logistic virtual market for solving the composition of negotiation items are the following four (the complete description of all the roles can be found in [5]):

- Seller: plays the role of a company (i.e. manufacturing plant, collecting points, recycling plants, disassembly plants, secondary material markets) that wants to get rid of its used products/scraps/wastes, or their sub-parts while earning some money and/or trying to reduce its environmental cuota (since a correct disposal of these items, or a re-use of them into other production proceses, can contribute to lower their hazardous environmental impact).
- Buyer: this role represents a company that wants to buy some used products/scraps/wastes, or their sub-parts with the purpose of resell them, recycle and then sell them, or recycle and introducing the new obtained products to its production chain instead of buying new unprocessed items.
- Manager: this role has brokering and supporting responsibilities in the market, being a crucial role in order to arrange and orchestrate the sequence of negotiation protocols to compose the negotiation item.
- Processor: this role is a specialization of the role company with the main capability of processing items subject to be recycled in order to obtain raw materials or sub-parts from them. A Processor is a company and as such can play in the market as a Seller and/or Buyer depending on the purpose of the negotiation protocol and the item being negotiated. This role is key in the orchestration of the sequence of negotiation interactions since a transformation process must be executed in order to process and/or extract the item that is contained in the used products/scraps/wastes, or their sub-parts.

3.2 Negotiation Items

A negotiation **item** is defined as $\iota = \langle \tau_\iota, O, \rho_\iota \rangle$, where τ_ι is the item type, O is the ontology where the item ι is defined, and ρ_ι is a set of property values that define the particular attributes that characterize the item itself. The list ρ_ι is domain-dependent, and is defined using the approach presented in [15]. For example the following is a fragment description of a waste *ItemX* that also specifies its component materials.

```
Individual: ItemX
Types: GenericProducts, Waste
and (weights weight((weight-value 10) and (weight-unit Kilogram)))
and (contains some((material-value some Glass) and (material-percentage value 35))
and (contains some((material-value some Plastic) and (material-percentage value 32)))
```

```
and (contains some((material-value some Steel) and (material-percentage value 20)))
and (has price((price-value 40) and (price-currency Euros))) ...
```

A CallForBid is defined as

$$CallForBid(m, Access_{type}, recipient_{List}, dialog_{ID}, protocol, \delta, C),$$

where m is the Manager ID in charge of the market, $Access_{type}$ specifies the type of access and can get a value from $\{Public, Private\}$ if it is $Public$ then all the players in the market could participate and $recipient_{List}$ is an empty list, whereas if the value is $Private$ only the agents that appear in the $recipient_{List}$ can be informed and allowed in the corresponding negotiation interaction. $dialog_{ID}$ is the negotiation dialog/interaction that is receiving players; the negotiation protocol $protocol$ used in that dialog; the set of items, δ, that is being negotiated; and the set of constraints, C, to participate in are also made public. In order to simplify the composition of the negotiation items that are requested by any CallForBid in this paper we assume that δ has only one element.

This ontology description is used by the Buyers and Sellers to reason about the items and evaluate the profit they can get from the item negotiation. On the other hand the Manager uses the ontology in order to support and facilitate the interaction of the market players by means of negotiation functions. More details on the ontology description can be found in [5].

3.3   Market Behavior for Solving the Composition of Negotiation Items

In order to get a proper understanding of the dynamics of the market let's describe the market behavior with the following simplified phases:

Inform Manager. First of all, the agents (Buyers and Sellers) reason about their knowledge base in order to decide what they are willing to buy or sell. The decision will depend on their goals (e.g. "increase economic profit", "reduce CO2/pollutant cuota", "reduce waste/scraps/sub-parts items from the warehouse", etc.), the current state of the market in terms of negotiation items that are currently offered (Set-of-ItemsOffered), and the recommendations received from the Manager (Set-of-NegotiationInvite, invitations to play as buyer/seller in negotiation interactions created by the Manager). The agents inform the Manager about their decision on those items issuing CallForBids when the decision is positive (buying or selling a given item).

Receive CallForBids. In this phase the Manager processes the received CallForBids in order to search the market for possible matching items subject to be negotiated and support the Buyers and Sellers interested in the items. The function GetMatchFromCallForBid allows the Manager to search in the market for possible matching items subject to be negotiated. This function looks into two knowledge bases: (i) the Set-of-ItemsOffered and (ii) the complete List-of-CallForBids. In the searching process the Manager not only tries to find the exact item looked for but also looks into the item description in terms of parts and components (see the ontology description for items) in order to mark the possible matching item when there is a possibility to obtain the item looked for by means of a transformation process from the matching item. The output from GetMatchFromCallForBid is a list of all possible matching items found. If the list is empty the CallForBids are kept in the market for later processing waiting for changes in the List-of-CallForBids and the Set-of-ItemsOffered. If the list is not empty, every match could state three possible situations: (i) there are one or more items in the Set-of-ItemsOffered that match the item and the amount looked for, or (ii) there are one or more items in the Set-of-ItemsOffered that match the item but not the amount looked for, or (iii) the item looked for (and the amount requested) is available but as a part/component item/material of offered matching items in the market, that requires a transformation and/or decomposition process in order to extract the item/material.

For every match found by GetMatchFromCallForBid and according to the situation identified by the Manager proceeds as following

1. Situation (i) - a match (or a set of them) is found. The Manager acts as a broker among the Buyer/s and Seller/s interested in the CallForBid and sends invitations to those agents. The agents receive the invitations and save them into their individual Set-of-NegotiationInvite. The next steps are executed in the Negotiation phase of the market.
2. Situation (ii) - the type of item requested is offered in the market but the amount of it does not match the request. The Manager solves this situation by a sequence of two orchestrated negotiation sequences.
   - In the first sequence a team formation process is executed among the CallForBids initiators (buyers or sellers) of the matching items marked by the function GetMatchFromCallForBid. This negotiation interaction aims to form a coalition among the sellers (or buyers) in order for them to agree to sell (or buy) a composition/lot of items instead of selling (or buying) them individually and to agree on the terms of the composed negotiation item (i.e. who will act as representative of the composed item in the subsequent negotiations, how the profit will be distributed among the coalition members, which coalition constraints will rule the process, etc.). For the coalition formation we follow the work presented in [10], defining an utility function for each item based on the preferences of the agent that is trying to sell or buy the item in a coalition instead of individually. The list of possible members of the coalition is used in order to start a negotiation interaction that arranges the coalition itself. In this process the different possible candidates are contacted one by one querying the willingness to take part in the coalition and its reserve price for the given item (this price defines the member's percentage share in the negotiation of the composed item). Different negotiation protocols can be used for defining the members and their percentage share, in the current

implementation we use a single step Face-to-Face protocol. The Manager uses the output of the utility function and the result from the members percentage share to arrange a proposal for the profit distribution and the coalition constraints, sending the proposal to the coalition members in order to agree on them. In the current implementation of the market we have simplified this process as: the Manager acts as the representative of the coalition, the profit distribution and coalition constraints agreement is negotiated following a simple Face-to-Face protocol in which the Manager proposes and each individual coalition member accepts or rejects in a single step. More complex approaches will be examined in future versions of our work.

- Finally for the negotiation of the composed item (agreed by the coalition) a Manager represents them in the interaction, following the coalition rules, and the interaction is executed following the negotiation protocol stated in the initial CallForBid. In order to coupe with the situation of two or more coalitions with conflicting goals, a new Manager is instantiated for every coalition during the Negotiation phase. The concrete negotiation interaction for this sequence is executed in the Negotiation phase of the market. At the end of the negotiation interaction the coalition agreement is executed distributing the profits among the members.

3. Situation (iii) - the type of item requested is found as part or component of other items offered in the market. The Manager solves this situation trying to orchestrate a feasible sequence of possible negotiation interactions that will allow to obtain the requested composed item that, in general, will require at least one transformation process executed by a Processor role. For this situation the Manager must find out a plan (or list of possible plans) for composing the requested item. For example, a given CallForBid for buying item Z, let's say 10 tons of steel, by Buyer A is received by the Manager and it is marked as situation (iii). Function GetMatchFromCallForBid tells the Manager that in Set-of-ItemsOffered the items X offered by Seller AX, Y offered by Seller AY and W offered by Seller AW (the type of item W is steel and the amount is 2 tons) can be used to compose item Z and items X and Y requires a transformation process before the item composition (both items contain steel as internal material and adding the amount present in the two items the total is 8 tons). The Manager starts a planning process in order to orchestrate the negotiations required to transform items X and Y. To do so function FindProcessors(input-item, output-item) is executed (for this particular example the calls look like FindProcessors(X, Z) and FindProcessors(Y, Z)) by the Manager getting the list of Processor agents, let's say Processor P1 for transforming X and Processor P3 for transforming Y, that can perform the transformation process of the given items into the type of Z (steel). As next step the Manager sends two separate negotiation invitations creating a negotiation dialog to Seller AX and Buyer P1 and a negotiation dialog to Seller AY and Buyer P3. If the invitations succeed, which means the items X and Y where sold to the corresponding Processors and were transformed to the type of Z, new CallsForBids are created by P1 and P3 offering

new processed items W1 and W2 with their corresponding amount. At this point the market is in Situation (ii) and the Manager solves it following the procedure described above. It is important to point out that in the current implementation of this algorithm we still do not solve the error situations, for example what happens if not all the negotiations for selling to the Processors are successful, or the error situation in which a given Processor refuses to offer the processed item into the market, or what happens when more items are processed that required. In order to solve them the Manager would need re-planning capabilities that currently are not implemented in the proposed virtual market.

Negotiation. When a Buyer and/or Seller receives a negotiation invitation from the Manager and decides to play in the given negotiation interaction it informs the Manager of its decision. In order to start the negotiation interaction the Manager waits for all the players (the number and features of the players are defined by the constraint C in the corresponding CallForBid) to accept the invitation. The negotiation interaction is executed using the negotiation *protocol* stated in the corresponding CallForBid, which can be any of the negotiation protocols provided by the framework (i.e. normal purchase, first-price auction, english auction, dutch auction, etc.). The Buyers and Sellers build their individual bids in order to play in the interaction using their own decision functions. One example function is described in the following section, called WorthyItem that was implemented for evaluating the approach.

Removing the Offered Item. When the negotiation interaction succeeds, which means a buyer and seller reached an agreement, the Manager deletes the sold item from the Set-of-ItemsOffered, marks the CallForBid as done and creates a new entry in the Set-of-Agreements.

3.4   Agent's Decision Function: WorthyItem

The agents playing in a negotiation interaction to buy or sell an item must have reasoning mechanisms to evaluate which item offered in CallForBids and NegotiationInvites are worth to bid for. The embedded reasoning mechanism can be any and the agents might have different functions to implement it. In this section we specify two decision functions that were implemented in order to test the framework.

The first proposed function can be labeled as *"the greener the better"* in which the worthiness of the item is heavily determined by its eco-worthiness and less on the item economic profit. It is evaluated in terms of the items price, the footprint of the items needing recycling if any and the transportation cost. The variable $eco\text{-}worth_\iota$ marks the quality of environmental impact of the item ι taking values from $[0, 1]$. The following rules are applied by the *WorthyItem* to define the value of *eco-worth*:

- Raw materials on destination are worthier than unprocessed components due to their footprint is zero (since no new transformation processes to recycle them are required). $eco\text{-}worth_\iota = 1$. Raw materials that need transportation to destination are marked as $eco\text{-}worth_\iota = 1 - K * (ItemWeight * TravelDistance)$. Where K is a constant of the transportation method used (train, truck, etc.) defining its emissions.
- Ready to use sub-parts on destination are market as $eco\text{-}worth_\iota = 1$. Used sub-parts that need transportation to destination are marked as $eco\text{-}worth_\iota = 1 - K * (ItemWeight * TravelDistance)$. Where K is a constant of the transportation method used (train, truck, etc.) defining its emissions.
- Unprocessed components requiring a transformation process are marked with $eco\text{-}worth_\iota = 0,5 - fp$, where fp is a value that states how environmental hazardous is the transformation process required to recycle it. Unprocessed components that need transportation to destination are marked as $eco\text{-}worth_\iota = 0,5 - fp - K * (ItemWeight * TravelDistance)$. Where K is a constant of the transportation method used (train, truck, etc.) defining its emissions.

Then the *WorthyItem* function is defined as:

$WorthyItem(\iota) =$
$(EstimatedProfitFromItem(\iota) -$
$(ItemPrice(\iota) + ItemTransportationCost(\iota) + ItemProcessingCost(\iota))) *$
$eco\text{-}worth_\iota$

The agent searches its lists of NegotiationInvites and CallForBids. For every element ι in those lists executes the $WrothyItem(\iota)$ function in order to sort the list of items in terms of their worthiness (in a priority order, the worthiest items are at the top of the list). The next step for the agent is to start bidding for the bids in the list in decreasing order whenever its budget allows it. In the current implementation of the function dynamic modifications of the worthiness list are not taken into account. Nevertheless, future versions of the function will tackle it.

Let's sort 2 items: Item A is a package with 10 kg of steel for a price of 200 Euros and Item B is an old car that requires transformation in order to obtain also 10 kg of steel, this product cost 100 Euros. The buyer that has received these items through CallForBids is only interested in buying 10 kg of steel, but must decide which item is worthier. This buyer is concerned about the carbon footprint.

For Item A the buyer estimates a profit of 300 Euros, the item price is 200 Euros, the transportation cost is 20 Euros and there is no transformation processing cost. On the other hand the transportation of the material to the destination has an environmental cost of 57 kg of C02 emission. So WorthyItem(A) $= (300 - (200 + 20 + 0)) * (1 - 57) = -3680$.

On the other hand, Item B which requires transformation to obtain the steel needed, has a profit estimated of 300 Euros, price of 100 Euros, transformation cost of 60 Euros, the transformation environmental cost fp is 23 kg CO2.

The transportation cost is 15 Euros, and the transportation of the material to the destination has a total environmental cost of $40\,kg$ of C02 emission. Then WorthyItem(B) $= (300 - (100 + 15 + 60)) * (0, 5 - 23 - 40) = -7812,5$.

Then Item A is worthier than Item B for the given buyer.

The second proposed function is labelled as **"Carbon Offset"**. A carbon offset is a reduction in emissions of carbon dioxide or greenhouse gases made in order to compensate for or to offset an emission made elsewhere. Carbon offset is a quantity of money that should be paid to compensate the emissions. This quantity depends on the amount of gases emitted and its type, and is used to promote hydroelectric power plants, wind and solar parks or planting trees. In this version of the *WorthyItem* function we include carbon offsets as the compensation cost that the buyer must add to the item price when calculating the item economic cost. The compensation cost does not go to the seller, but to the managing entity in charge of wind plants, solar parks, etc.

In this way *WorthyItem* function is defined as:

$WorthyItem(\iota) =$
$ItemPrice(\iota)+$
$ItemTransportationCost(\iota)+$
$K * ItemTransportationEmissions(\iota)+$
$ItemProcessingCost(\iota)+$
$K * ItemProcessingEmission(\iota)$

When the items do not require processing its *ItemProcessingCost* and *ItemProcessingEmission* are zero.

Transportation emission and processing emission are measured in Kg of CO2 and K is measured in Euro/Kg, that is the quantity of money needed to compensate $1\,kg$ of CO2. In future versions other gases will be considered, for instance N2O, CH4. In that case, the functions *ItemTransportationEmissions* and *ItemProcessingEmissions* will return an array and K will be an array in which every element will be the quantity needed to compensate $1\,kg$ of each gas.

In order to improve the decision function we have defined $EstimatedProfit FromItem(\iota)$. This function estimates the economic profit for the buyer from getting the item. In this case, only if
$EstimatedProfitFromItem(\iota) > WorthyItem(\iota),$
The match will be processed and the higher this different is, the more interested will be the agent in trading the given item.

Let's suppose K $= 0.06$ Euros and two items to evaluate. Item A, $10\,kg$ of steel with a price of 200 Euros, and; Item B, a car, with a price of 100 Euros that can be processed to obtain also $10\,kg$ of steel. The buyer estimates a profit of 300 Euros from $10\,kg$ of steel. Item A has a transportation cost of 20 Euros and transportation emission of $57\,kg$ of CO2, then $300 - (200 + 20 + 0.06 * 57 + 0 + 0) = 76.58$ Euros.

On the other hand item B, has a transportation cost of 60 Euros and $23\,kg$ of CO2 transportation emission. This item needs processing and its associated cost is 15 Euros and CO2 processing emission of 40 kg. Then $300 - (100 + 60 + 23 * 0.06 + 15 + 40 * 0.06) = 121.22$ Euros.

In this way the buyer will select item B because this is the item that has the higher difference between *EstimatedProfitFromItem* and *WorthyItem*. However, it will pollute more, this is compensated by paying $23 * 0.06 + 40 * 0.06 = 3.78$ Euros to build renewable energy sources.

The same reasoning mechanism on items worthiness is applied when the agent is trying to agree to take part into a coalition. Worthier items are prioritized.

4   Discussion

The prototype implementation of the approach described in this paper is implemented in Magentix2 (http://www.gti-ia.upv.es/sma/tools/magentix2/index.php). In this prototype Buyers and Sellers use the same decision algorithms and the negotiation protocols currently supported are: Face-to-Face, English Auction and Dutch Auction. Such configuration helped us to undergo prototype tests in order to measure its correctness. The performed tests are lab tests in which the data base of offered items and initial CallForBids are manually loaded. The results from those tests proved that the prototype is correct with respect to its specification, but we still are working on completing the prototype in order to undergo a verification with respect to a real industrial scenario.

The simplifications made to the current specification needs revision in order to support complex situations of real industrial scenarios, such as: the set of items called for in a CallForBid must have more than one element, the coalition intermediate negotiation protocols requires more complete approaches in which the possible members are allowed to make counter offers, dynamic modifications of the worthiness list of items must be taken into account in order to reflex new offers appearing in the market during runtime, more negotiation protocols must be supported, the value tuning of variable *eco-worth* must be verified with real industrial data, etc.

5   Conclusion and Future Works

A MAS approach for composition of negotiation items was presented in this paper. The items can represent used-products/scraps/waste and recycle materials that are offered in a virtual market of reverse production processes. The approach described is based on three different roles in the market representing the stakeholders in a green supply chain. One of the key roles in the proposed approach is the Manager that provides to Buyers and Sellers in the market supporting functions in order to compose negotiation items that commonly appear in a reverse production market. The three situations that might appear in such markets were identified and a distributed solving process was described. The proposed approach was implemented as a prototype with simplified negotiations and decision functions that allowed to test the proposal.

As ongoing works we are enhancing and completing the definition of the composition steps of the proposed distributed solving process already identified as weaknesses. Moreover we plan to distribute the search process to find possible items match from the Manager to the Buyer and Sellers of the market in order to lower down the computational load of the Manager.

Acknowledgement. This work is supported by research project TIN2015-65515-C4-1-R from the Spanish government.

References

1. Ahi, P., Searcy, C.: A comparative literature analysis of definitions for green and sustainable supply chain management. J. Clean. Prod. **52**, 329–341 (2013)
2. Castelfranchi, C., Lespérance, Y. (eds.): ATAL 2000. LNCS (LNAI), vol. 1986. Springer, Heidelberg (2001). https://doi.org/10.1007/3-540-44631-1
3. Ebinger, F., Goldbach, M., Schneidewind, U.: Greening supply chains: a competence-based perspective. In: Sarkis, J. (ed.) Greening the Supply Chain, pp. 251–269. Springer, London (2006). https://doi.org/10.1007/1-84628-299-3_14
4. Fahimnia, B., Sarkis, J., Davarzani, H.: Green supply chain management: a review and bibliometric analysis. Int. J. Prod. Econ. **162**, 101–114 (2015)
5. Giret, A., Salido, M.A.: A multi-agent approach to implement a reverse production virtual market in green supply chains. In: Lödding, H., Riedel, R., Thoben, K.-D., von Cieminski, G., Kiritsis, D. (eds.) APMS 2017. IAICT, vol. 514, pp. 399–407. Springer, Cham (2017). https://doi.org/10.1007/978-3-319-66926-7_46
6. Giret, A., Garcia, E., Botti, V.: An engineering framework for service-oriented intelligent manufacturing systems. Comput. Ind. **81**, 116–127 (2016)
7. Giret, A., Trentesaux, D., Prabhu, V.: Sustainability in manufacturing operations scheduling: a state of the art review. J. Manuf. Syst. **37**(Part 1), 126–140 (2015)
8. Giret, A., Trentesaux, D., Salido, M.A., Garcia, E., Adam, E.: A holonic multi-agent methodology to design sustainable intelligent manufacturing control systems. J. Clean. Prod. **167**, 1370–1386 (2017)
9. Golinska, P., Fertsch, M., Gómez, J.M., Oleskow, J.: The concept of closed-loop supply chain integration through agents-based system. In: Gómez, J.M., Sonnenschein, M., Müller, M., Welsch, H., Rautenstrauch, C. (eds.) Information Technologies in Environmental Engineering. Environmental Science and Engineering (Environmental Engineering), pp. 189–202. Springer, Heidelber (2007). https://doi.org/10.1007/978-3-540-71335-7_20
10. Greco, G., Guzzo, A.: Coalition formation with logic-based agents. In: Criado Pacheco, N., Carrascosa, C., Osman, N., Julián Inglada, V. (eds.) EUMAS/AT-2016. LNCS (LNAI), vol. 10207, pp. 455–469. Springer, Cham (2017). https://doi.org/10.1007/978-3-319-59294-7_37
11. Hsieh, F.S.: Scheduling sustainable supply chains based on multi-agent systems and workflow models. In: 2015 10th International Conference on Intelligent Systems and Knowledge Engineering (ISKE), pp. 252–259, November 2015
12. International Trade Administration: How does Commerce define Sustainable Manufacturing? US Department of Commerce (2007)
13. Mishra, N., Kumar, V., Chan, F.T.S.: A multi-agent architecture for reverse logistics in a green supply chain. Int. J. Prod. Res. **50**(9), 2396–2406 (2012)

14. Sarkis, J.: A strategic decision framework for green supply chain management. J. Clean. Prod. **11**(4), 397–409 (2003)
15. Sinha, A., Couderc, P.: Using OWL ontologies for selective waste sorting and recycling. In: OWLED. CEUR Workshop Proceedings, vol. 849 (2012)
16. Trentesaux, D., Giret, A.: Go-green manufacturing holons: a step towards sustainable manufacturing operations control. Manuf. Lett. **5**, 29–33 (2015)
17. Daniel, V., Guide, R.: OR forum—the evolution of closed-loop supply chain research. Oper. Res. **57**(1), 10–18 (2009)
18. Winkler, H.: Closed-loop production systems—a sustainable supply chain approach. CIRP J. Manuf. Sci. Technol. **4**(3), 243–246 (2011)

Two Prediction Methods
for Intention-Aware Online Routing
Games

László Z. Varga^(✉) ⓘ

Faculty of Informatics, ELTE Eötvös Loránd University, Budapest 1117, Hungary
lzvarga@inf.elte.hu

Abstract. Intention-aware prediction is regarded as an important agreement technology to help large amount of agents in aligning their activities towards an equilibrium. If the agents do not align their activities in online routing games, then the multi-agent system is not guaranteed to get to a stable equilibrium. We formally define two intention-aware prediction methods for online routing games and empirically evaluate them in a real-world scenario. The experiments confirm that the defined intention-aware routing strategies limit the fluctuation in this online routing game scenario and make the system more or less converge to the equilibrium.

1 Introduction

One of the most interesting challenge of information technology is to build applications where autonomous agents make decentralised decisions. Designers want to create optimal systems, therefore they need formal models to be able to define and measure design criteria. Currently the best model of multi-agent decision making is founded in game theory. Designers prefer systems with equilibrium, because if equilibrium cannot be reached, then the system may continuously change, and unwanted conditions may occur. If there is at least one equilibrium, then it is assumed that the system stays in the equilibrium state. However, the equilibrium may not be optimal. This inefficiency is measured with the *price of anarchy* which is the ratio between the efficiency measure of the equilibrium and the optimum. There are games with many equilibria. In this case, if there is no coordination, then agents do not know which equilibrium is the goal of the collective. Even if the agents know which equilibrium is the goal of the collective, then all agents must have complete knowledge about the game, and the agents must come to the equilibrium with full rationality. For example if half of the agents have to select action a_1 and half of the agents have to select action a_2, then agents should agree on which agent is in which half. If the agent collective has a large amount of members, then it is not realistic that the agents directly negotiate their roles. *Agreement technology* is needed to align the agents' actions towards the optimum, or at least towards a common equilibrium.

ⓒ Springer Nature Switzerland AG 2018
F. Belardinelli and E. Argente (Eds.): EUMAS 2017/AT 2017, LNAI 10767, pp. 431–445, 2018.
https://doi.org/10.1007/978-3-030-01713-2_30

A typical application area where large amount of autonomous actors have to align their actions is urban traffic. Traffic engineers assume that the traffic is always assigned in accordance with the equilibrium. However, with the advent of navigation software with real-time traffic information, this assumption may not be valid. This issue will be more critical when the traffic will be driven by autonomous cars, because autonomous cars will make *informed and rational* decisions. Autonomous cars can use telecommunication technologies to "see" beyond objects (e.g. the car behind the corner) and to "see" much farther away (e.g. congestion along the planned route on the other side of the city). As more and more information services are deployed to provide real-time traffic information to traffic participants, autonomous cars will have real-time, and more precise information than humans. If decentralised adaptation is based on real-time information, then the equilibrium assumption of traffic engineers may not hold, and the classical game theory models may not describe the system well, because the decision making strategy of the subsequent agents of the same traffic flow may vary. This is modelled with the online routing game model. Investigations with the online routing game model revealed that equilibrium cannot be guaranteed, if the agents continuously and selfishly adapt to the real-time information. In order to alleviate this problem, the agents have to coordinate their activities through agreement technologies. If there are large amount of agents in the system, then direct communication among the agents is not realistic, and the indirect communication through intention sharing (or intention-awareness) is used. There are already a few analytic and empirical investigations of the power of intention-awareness, however the intention-aware prediction methods have not been fully defined and investigated. This paper contributes to the state of the art by formally defining two intention-aware prediction methods, and evaluating them in a real-world scenario.

In Sect. 2 we overview the previous work that lead to this research. In Sect. 3 we formally define two intention-aware prediction methods for online routing games. In Sect. 4 we describe the real world scenario where the methods are evaluated. In Sect. 5 we evaluate the methods, and finally in Sect. 6 we conclude the paper.

2   Previous Work (Based on [16])

Game theory, currently considered as the best model of multi-agent decision making [7], is concerned with the equilibrium. This is in line with the assumption of traffic engineers, who assume that the traffic is always assigned in accordance with the equilibrium [1,17]. Game theory [6] proved that in some routing problems there is always a unique equilibrium, and the price of anarchy has an upper limit. The routing problem is a network with source routing, where end users simultaneously choose a full route to their destination, and the traffic is routed in a congestion sensitive manner. If the cost functions are linear functions of the traffic flow, then the price of anarchy is at most $4 \div 3$ [8], i.e. this is how bad the overall traffic is when decentralised autonomous decision making is applied by the traffic flows.

The equilibrium is an important concept, because none of the agents has an incentive to deviate from the equilibrium, therefore the equilibrium seems to be a stable state of the system. However the classic game theory models assume an idealistic situation: all the agents know what the equilibrium is, all the agents know what other agents are doing, and all the agents know what their role is in the equilibrium. However the classic game theory does not investigate how this idealistic situation emerges. In accordance with the basic theory of multi-agent systems [19], the agent behaviour goes in cycles: the agents perceive their environment (possibly communicating with other agents), decide what action to perform, and then perform the action. Can multi-agent systems get to the equilibrium through these feedback cycles, and do they stay in the equilibrium?

In order to answer this question, game theory investigated the *evolutionary dynamics* where the agents receive feedback by observing their own and other agents' actions and utility, and change their own actions based on these observations. It is proved that with this feedback assumption, the above mentioned routing game converges to the equilibrium [5,9]. Another type of feedback is used in *regret minimisation*, where agents compare their actually experienced utility with the best possible utility in retrospect. It is proved that if the agents of the routing game select actions to minimize their regret, then their behaviour will converge to the equilibrium [2]. Even if we ignore the problem of knowing all other agents' actions and utility, or the problem of computing the best possible utility in retrospect, we still have other problems. The investigations of game dynamics have the following assumptions: the decision is on the flow level; the game is repeated; and the decision is based on experiences from the previous games. These assumptions may be valid for telecommunication networks, but in many other applications, like autonomous cars in traffic networks, the flow is made up of individual agents who follow each other, and the agents decide individually on their actions based on the real-time situation. The decisions of the agents are not coordinated on the flow level.

The *online routing game* model (developed in [11], and refined in [10]) models the online routing game problem where each subsequent agent of the traffic flow may select different route based on real-time information. In order to measure the efficiency of real-time data usage, the *benefit of online real-time data* concept was defined [11]. The benefit of online real-time data is the ratio between the travel time with real-time data based planning and the travel time without real-time data based planning. The agents are happy with real-time data, if the benefit value is below 1. Three types (worst/average/best) of benefit of online real-time data are needed in case an equilibrium cannot be achieved. It is proved [11], that if the agents try to maximise their utility, then the following properties are true: equilibrium is not guaranteed; "single flow intensification" is possible; and the worst case benefit value of online real-time data is not guaranteed to be below 1. Equilibrium may not be reached, because the traffic may fluctuate. "Single flow intensification" happens when vehicles entering the road network later may select alternative faster routes, and they may catch up with the vehicles already on the road, and this way they cause congestion. All-in-all, sometimes the traffic may produce strange behaviour [12] and the collective of agents may be worse off by exploiting real-time information than without exploiting real-time information. This means that if the agents selfishly optimise their action in the online routing problem, then they are not guaranteed to reach an equilibrium, although the (non-online) routing game model says that there is an equilibrium.

In order to coordinate the actions of the agents, intention-aware agreement technology is proposed. The agents do not communicate directly with each other, but they communicate their intentions to a central service. The central service aggregates the data about the agent collective and sends feedback to the agents [3]. The *intention-aware* [18] and the *intention propagation* [4] approaches are based on this scheme. In this paper we call both of them intention-aware prediction method. When an agent has made a decision on its planned route, then it sends its selected intention to the central service. The central service is able to make a forecast of the future traffic situation, based on the current traffic state and the communicated intentions of the agents. The central service provides the traffic forecast back to those agents who are still planning their trips, and these agents use this information to plan their trip, and when they have made a decision, then they also communicate their intentions to the central service. In theory, the online navigation software like Google Maps and Waze know the intentions of the agents, and they could use this information to make predictions.

The online routing game model was used to prove [10] that there is no guarantee on the value of the worst case benefit of online data, and there is no guarantee on the equilibrium, even if intention-aware prediction is applied. This means that if the agents selfishly exploit intention-aware prediction, then in some networks and in some cases the traffic may be worse off by exploiting real-time information and prediction than without. This is mainly because the prediction of the central service does not take into account the decisions of those agents who base their decision on the current prediction. However, it is proved [13] that in a small but complex enough network, where there is only one traffic flow, and there is no simultaneous decision making, there is a guarantee on the value of the worst case benefit of online real-time data with prediction. In that network, the agents might just slightly be worse off with real-time data and prediction in some cases. It is also proved [15] that in the network of [13], the system converges to the equilibrium, which means that the intention-aware prediction establishes enough coordination among the agents in that network.

According to the conjecture of [14], if simultaneous decision making among the agents is prevented, then intention-aware prediction can limit the fluctuation in the multi-agent system, and the traffic converges to the equilibrium in bigger networks as well. This conjecture neither has been proved nor refuted analytically. The main contribution of this paper is the empirical investigation of this conjecture in a simulation environment of a real-world setting.

3   The Intention-Aware Prediction Methods

The prediction method is a critical point of those online routing games that exploit intention-aware prediction. In this paper we formalise two prediction methods: the detailed prediction method and the simple prediction method.

The *detailed prediction method* takes into account all the intentions already submitted to the central service, then it computes what will happen in the future if the agents execute the plans assigned by these intentions, and then it computes for each route in the network the predicted travel time by taking into account the predicted travel conditions. The prediction algorithm used in [18] is close to this detailed prediction method, the main difference is that the prediction algorithm of [18] uses probabilistic values, while the method in this paper is deterministic.

The *simple prediction method* also takes into account all the intentions already submitted to the central service, and then it computes what will happen in the future if the agents execute the plans assigned by these intentions. However when the simple prediction method computes for each route in the network the predicted travel time, then it takes into account only the latest predictions for each road. This way, the simple prediction method needs a little bit less computation, and the simple prediction method kind of brings forward the predictions. The simple prediction method is an approximation and does not try to be exact. As time goes by, if no new prediction is generated for a road, then the simple prediction method "evaporates" the prediction for that road, like the bio-inspired technique of [4].

3.1   The Detailed Prediction Method

There are three algorithms in the core of the detailed prediction method: Algorithm 1 is the intention propagation, Algorithm 2 is the prediction for the roads, and Algorithm 3 is the prediction for the routes. The main data structure to keep track of future states is the *ArrivalsList* for each road. The *ArrivalsList* contains a list of (t, tt) tuples where a tuple means that an agent is predicted to enter the given road at time t and the predicted travel time of this agent on the road is tt.

Algorithm 1 is invoked when an agent decides to go on *GivenRoute* and submits its intention. This algorithm invokes the *PredictedRoadTravelTime* function of Algorithm 2 for each road of *GivenRoute* to predict the arrival time and travel time on each road. The predicted values are stored in the *ArrivalsList* of each road of *GivenRoute*.

The *PredictedRoadTravelTime* function of Algorithm 2 first finds out if agents are already predicted to travel on *GivenRoad* at *GivenTime*, and then computes the predicted remaining travel time of the agent in *ArrivalsList* of the road just before *GivenTime*, because this agent cannot be overtaken if an agent enters the road at *GivenTime*, in accordance with the online routing game model. Then the function computes the travel time computed from the road characteristic using the number of agents in *ArrivalsList* of the road in the last time unit before *GivenTime*. The bigger computed value is returned.

Algorithm 3 is invoked to update the predicted travel times on all routes when an agent asks for predictions to select its route, because the route selection is based on the predicted route travel times. The travel times of the roads of the route are predicted using the *PredictedRoadTravelTime* function of Algorithm 2 and taking into account the predicted arrival time at each road.

Algorithm 1. Intention propagation in case of detailed prediction

---

Data: GivenRoute

Result: predicted arrivals are recorded at each road of GivenRoute

1 **begin**

2   TravelTime ⟵ 0

3   RoadTravelTime ⟵ 0

4   Time ⟵ *CurrentTime*

5   **for** Road ∈ GivenRoute **do**

6   RoadTravelTime ⟵

            PredictedRoadTravelTime(Road, Time + TravelTime)

7   Append(ArrivalsList of Road, (Time + TravelTime, RoadTravelTime))

8   TravelTime ⟵ TravelTime + RoadTravelTime

Algorithm 2. Compute the predicted travel time on a road at a given time

---

Data: GivenRoad, GivenTime

Result: PredictedRoadTravelTime (GivenRoad,GivenTime) returns the predicted travel time on GivenRoad at GivenTime

1 **begin**

2   // the longest predicted remaining travel time of cars

3   **if** ArrivalsList *of* GivenRoad *is empty* **then**

4   TravelTimeAlready ⟵ 0

5   **else**

6   TravelTimeAlready ⟵ the remaining travel time of the car in ArrivalsList of GivenRoad before GivenTime

7   // the predicted travel time from road characteristic

8   TravelTime ⟵ the travel time computed from road characteristic using the car flow in ArrivalsList of GivenRoad in the last time unit before GivenTime

9   **if** TravelTimeAlready > TravelTime **then**

10   **return** TravelTimeAlready

11   **else**

12   **return** TravelTime

3.2 The Simple Prediction Method

The core of the simple prediction method has three algorithms: Algorithm 4 is the intention propagation, Algorithm 5 is the prediction update for the roads to "evaporate" predictions, and Algorithm 6 is the prediction for the routes. The simple prediction method also has the *ArrivalsList* for each road. In addition, each road has a *PredictedTravelTime* property which stores the travel time predicted by the simple prediction method. The *PredictedTravelTime* property always stores the predicted travel time which was computed for the involved roads during the last intention submission.

Algorithm 3. Update the predicted travel time for all routes in case of detailed prediction

---

Data:
Result: PredictedRouteTravelTime of each Route is updated

1 begin
2   for Route ∈ *all routes* do
3   TravelTime ⟵ 0
4   Time ⟵ *CurrentTime*
5   for Road ∈ Route do
6   TravelTime ⟵
            TravelTime + `PredictedRoadTravelTime`(Road, Time + TravelTime)
7   PredictedRouteTravelTime of Route ⟵ TravelTime

Algorithm 4 is similar to the intention submission of the detailed prediction method, the difference is that the predicted travel time of each road is stored immediately in the *PredictedTravelTime* property of the road (lines 7–8 of the algorithm).

Algorithm 4. Intention propagation in case of simple prediction

---

Data: GivenRoute
Result: predicted arrivals are recorded at each road of GivenRoute and the predicted travel time for each road of GivenRoute is recorded

1 begin
2   TravelTime ⟵ 0
3   RoadTravelTime ⟵ 0
4   Time ⟵ *CurrentTime*
5   for Road ∈ GivenRoute do
6   RoadTravelTime ⟵
         `PredictedRoadTravelTime`(Road, Time + TravelTime)
7   // time independent prediction
8   PredictedTravelTime of Road ⟵ RoadTravelTime
9   Append(ArrivalsList of Road, (Time + TravelTime, RoadTravelTime))
10   TravelTime ⟵ TravelTime + RoadTravelTime

Algorithm 5 is invoked to "evaporate" the prediction of each road after an elapsed time (for example in every simulation step of the simulation program). The algorithm deduces the elapsed time from each prediction until the minimum travel time of the road is reached. The idea is that, as time goes by, the agents travel on the roads and their remaining travel time decreases, and so does the predicted travel time.

Algorithm 5. Update the predicted travel time of each road with the elapsed time in case of simple prediction

---

Data: elapsed time of the simulation step
Result: PredictedTravelTime of each Road is reduced with the elapsed time
1 **begin**
2   **for** Road ∈ *all roads* **do**
3   PredictedTravelTime of Road ⟵ PredictedTravelTime of Road decreased with the elapsed time
4   **if** PredictedTravelTime *of* Road < *minimum travel time on* Road **then**
5   PredictedTravelTime of Road ⟵ minimum travel time on Road

---

Algorithm 6 is invoked to update the predicted travel times on all routes when an agent asks for predictions to select its route. The travel times of the roads of the route are predicted using the *PredictedTravelTime* property of each road.

Algorithm 6. Update the predicted travel time for all routes in case of simple prediction

---

Data:
Result: PredictedTravelTime of each Route is updated
1 **begin**
2   **for** Route ∈ *all routes* **do**
3   TravelTime ⟵ 0
4   **for** Road ∈ Route **do**
5   TravelTime ⟵ TravelTime + PredictedTravelTime of Road)
6   PredictedTravelTime of Route ⟵ TravelTime

---

4 Experimental Set-Up

The above defined prediction methods were evaluated in a simulation environment of a real-world scenario. A critical region of Budapest (shown in Fig. 1) was modelled in the online routing game simulation software of [11]. This region is heavily loaded in the morning rush hours, because commuter cars enter the town at point A (red in the figure), and basically all of them must go through point E.

The commuters have three choices: $route_1 = (A, C, E)$, $route_2 = (A, B, C, E)$, and $route_3 = (A, B, E)$. The road lengths are: $(A, B) = 2.5\,\text{km}$, $(A, C) = 3.1\,\text{km}$, $(B, C) = 0.8\,\text{km}$, $(B, E) = 2.2\,\text{km}$, and $(C, E) = 1.1\,\text{km}$. Assuming that on an empty road the cars can travel at speed $40\,\text{km/h}$, the minimum travel time in minutes (fixed part of the cost function) for the roads

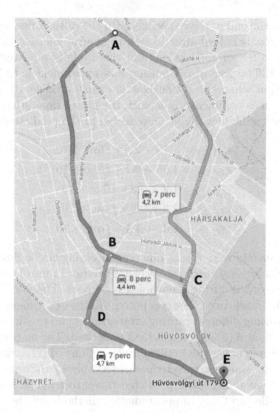

Fig. 1. Google Map extract showing the real-world scenario of the experiment in a tranquil period of a summer vacation day (Color figure online)

is: $(A, B) = 3.75$, $(A, C) = 4.65$, $(B, C) = 1.2$, $(B, E) = 3.3$, and $(C, E) = 1.65$. This is more or less in line with the times indicated in Fig. 1.

Information on the traffic flow going into the town on this road can be obtained from the web site[1] of the Hungarian Public Road Non-profit PLC. The measured yearly average traffic flow is about 12 $car \div minute$. In accordance with the own observation of the author, the estimated highest traffic flow into the town is 50 $car \div minute$. Also author's observation is that the variable part of the travel time is about $roadlength * flow \div 10$. The cost functions of the roads are shown in Eq. 1, where the cost is in $minute$ and the traffic flow is in $car \div minute$.

The experiment simulates a 90 min long rush hour period. Because the experiment starts with an empty road network, a 17 min long initial period is added to populate the road network, so the experiment is run for 107 min. Two types of experiments were run: a steady flow experiment and a pulsing flow experiment. In the steady flow experiment, the incoming traffic flow remains constant from

---

[1] http://internet.kozut.hu/Lapok/forgalomszamlalas.aspx.

the beginning till the end of the experiment. In the pulsing flow experiment, the incoming traffic flow is halved after 10 min, then after another 10 min the traffic flow is returned to the original value, and this cycle is repeated until the end of the experiment. The goal of the pulsing flow experiment is to investigate the power of prediction when the traffic flow is changing. The 10 min period was selected, because it is commensurable with the travel time in the network, and the change in the traffic flow might be reflected in the predictions.

$$c_{(A,B)} = 3.75 + 2.5 * flow \div 10$$
$$c_{(A,C)} = 4.65 + 3.1 * flow \div 10$$
$$c_{(B,C)} = 1.2 + 0.8 * flow \div 10 \tag{1}$$
$$c_{(B,E)} = 3.3 + 2.2 * flow \div 10$$
$$c_{(C,E)} = 1.65 + 1.1 * flow \div 10$$

Several experiments were run at different incoming traffic flow values from 5 $car \div minute$ to 50 $car \div minute$ in steps of 5. The travel time of cars from point A to point E was recorded during the whole experiment. The maximum value and the average of the travel times were computed. All the experiments were executed in three versions using different routing strategies: (1) no prediction, (2) detailed prediction method, and (3) simple prediction method. The no prediction routing strategy is the simple naive (SN) online routing game of [11], where the routing strategy selects the shortest travel time observable in the real-time status of the network (and not the shortest predicted travel time). The routing strategies based on the detailed and the simple prediction methods are the intention-aware routing strategies described in this paper. The summary of the measured values are shown in Table 1.

Table 1. The measured maximum and average travel times in minutes

Flow	Steady flow						Pulsing flow					
	No pred.		Det. pred.		Simple pred.		No pred.		Det. pred.		Simple pred.	
	Max.	Avg.	Max.	Avg.	Max.	Avg.	Max.	Avg.	Max.	Avg.	Max.	Avg.
5	9.40	8.40	7.73	7.41	7.98	7.58	9.02	8.00	7.73	7.23	7.98	7.41
10	11.75	10.35	9.14	8.56	9.08	8.60	11.44	9.81	9.16	8.17	9.08	8.25
15	14.10	12.40	10.87	9.81	10.43	9.75	14.10	11.44	10.68	9.13	10.49	9.15
20	16.45	14.44	13.38	11.63	11.71	10.87	16.51	13.46	12.77	10.39	11.97	10.15
25	18.80	16.62	17.12	14.10	13.45	12.18	18.80	15.24	16.14	11.98	13.45	11.20
30	21.15	18.75	21.48	16.11	16.21	13.88	21.61	17.40	18.93	13.69	15.75	12.57
35	23.50	20.90	23.08	18.35	19.00	16.50	23.78	19.30	21.11	15.17	17.94	14.13
40	25.85	23.01	25.24	19.83	20.96	18.21	30.71	22.35	22.80	16.96	19.35	15.50
45	28.20	25.15	26.80	21.48	22.30	19.73	30.25	24.22	26.20	18.75	22.08	17.47
50	30.55	27.40	28.87	23.32	23.69	21.28	30.55	25.48	27.61	20.34	23.36	18.95

5 Evaluation

The goal of the experiments was to test the following hypotheses:

H1: Any of the above intention-aware predictive routing performs better than the non predictive routing.
H2: The detailed prediction method performs better than the simple prediction method, because the detailed method gives more precise predictions.
H3: The intention-aware prediction methods limit the fluctuation of the congestions in the multi-agent system.
H4: The traffic converges to the equilibrium with the intention-aware prediction methods.

In order to compare the different routing methods, the diagram of maximum and average travel times was drawn. Figure 2 shows the maximum travel times and Fig. 3 shows the average travel times for different traffic flow values in the steady flow experiments. The diagrams for the pulsing flow experiments are similar to these diagrams, and they are not included in this paper to spare space.

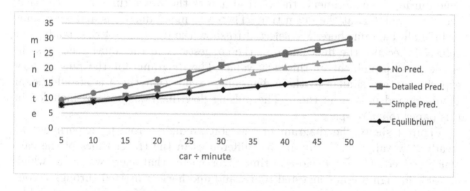

Fig. 2. Maximum travel times in the steady flow experiment

The diagrams also contain the computed equilibrium travel time. The equilibrium travel time can be computed by making the costs of all routes equal (using the cost functions of Eq. 1) and then solving the equations. The computation is not detailed here.

As we can see from the diagrams, the travel time with the non predictive routing is the longest in all measured cases (except at 30 where the maximum is a bit less than the maximum of the detailed prediction), so **hypothesis H1 was confirmed** in the experiment.

We can also see in the diagrams, that the travel time with the detailed predictive routing is longer than the travel time with the simple predictive routing if the traffic flow is above 20, so **hypothesis H2 was refuted** in the experiment.

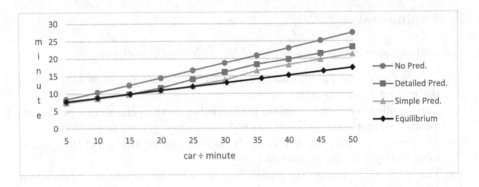

Fig. 3. Average travel times in the steady flow experiment

This is a bit unexpected and raises new questions. Is it better not to give more detailed predictions, or the detailed prediction method may be a bit misleading?

In order to visualise the fluctuation aspect in the multi-agent system, the diagram that shows the travel time of cars from point A to point E during the whole experiment was drawn. In this diagram the horizontal axis is the elapsed time during the experiment, the vertical axis is the travel time of the car that arrived at point E at the given time. There are many diagrams and we cannot include all diagrams here. We selected to show the diagrams of the steady flow value 50, because the fluctuation of the congestions in the multi-agent system is the most prominent at this flow value. The diagrams for the pulsing flow experiments are similar to these diagrams, except that there is an additional 10 min period pulsing in them. The pulsing flow diagrams are not included in this paper to spare space.

Figure 4 shows the diagram of the non predictive routing experiment at steady flow value 50. There are big differences in the travel times of the cars which arrived at point E close in time. This means that there was a car which arrived through a non congested route, and another car arrived through a congested route, and the travel times of the routes were far from equilibrium. The average travel time in this non predictive experiment is about 58% higher than the equilibrium value.

Figure 5 shows the diagram of the detailed prediction routing experiment at steady flow value 50. As we can see, the differences in the travel times of the cars which arrived at point E close in time are smaller than on Fig. 4. This means that the travel times of the routes were somewhat closer to a kind of equilibrium during the whole experiment. The average travel time in this detailed prediction experiment is about 34% higher than the equilibrium value.

Figure 6 shows the diagram of the simple prediction routing experiment at steady flow value 50. As we can see, there are no big differences in the travel times of the cars which arrived at point E close in time. This means that the travel times of the routes were close to a kind of equilibrium during the whole experiment, although this kind of equilibrium was a little bit pulsing. The average

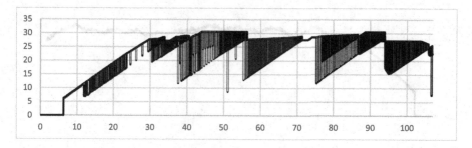

Fig. 4. Travel time of cars in point E during the whole experiment: steady flow, non predictive routing, flow value 50.

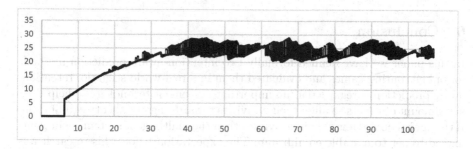

Fig. 5. Travel time of cars in point E during the whole experiment: steady flow, detailed prediction routing, flow value 50.

travel time in this detailed prediction experiment is about 23% higher than the equilibrium value.

The above diagrams show that the intention-aware prediction methods somewhat limit the fluctuation of the congestions in the multi-agent system and the simple prediction method performs better than the detailed prediction method. So **hypothesis H3 was confirmed** in the experiment.

The convergence to the equilibrium is not fully confirmed, because the average travel times are higher than the equilibrium. However we cannot expect that the equilibrium can be achieved exactly, because the formal proof in [15] says that the travel times can come near to the equilibrium only within a threshold. This threshold is due to the fact that the cars enter the road (C, E) from two different roads, and if two cars arrive there close in time, then one of them has to wait a little. This waiting time is not taken into account in the equilibrium model, and this waiting time seems to accumulate considerably in this realistic experiment. So **hypothesis H4 needs further investigations** to define the threshold to the equilibrium.

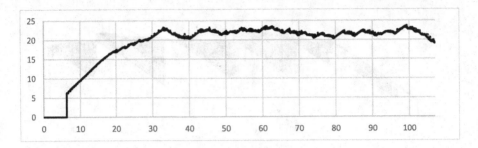

Fig. 6. Travel time of cars in point E during the whole experiment: steady flow, simple prediction routing, flow value 50.

6   Conclusion

In this paper we have defined formally two intention-aware prediction methods for online routing games and evaluated them in a real-world scenario. Intention-aware prediction is regarded as an important agreement technology to help massive amount of agents to align their activities towards a game theory equilibrium. If the agents do not align their activities, then the multi-agent system is not guaranteed to get to a stable equilibrium. The expectation before this research was to confirm in the real world scenario, that the routing strategies using intention-aware prediction methods limit the fluctuation of congestions in online routing games, and they make the system converge to the equilibrium. The experiments more or less confirmed the expectations, because the fluctuation of congestions is reduced by the intention-aware prediction methods. The convergence to the equilibrium needs further investigations, because it seems that the equilibrium cannot be achieved exactly, and the threshold heavily depends on the road network properties.

An unexpected result of this research is that the simple prediction method performs better at higher traffic flow values than the detailed prediction method. The current conjecture is that the intention-aware prediction methods cannot give perfect predictions in online routing games, because they do not take into account the intentions of the agents that arrive afterwards, therefore the detailed method may sometimes give misleading prediction. This needs further research.

This work was supported by the European Union, co-financed by the European Social Fund (EFOP-3.6.3-VEKOP-16-2017-00002).

References

1. Beckmann, M.J., McGuire, C.B., Winsten, C.B.: Studies in the Economics of Transportation. Yale University Press, New Haven (1956)
2. Blum, A., Even-Dar, E., Ligett, K.: Routing without regret: on convergence to nash equilibria of regret-minimizing algorithms in routing games. In: Proceedings of the Twenty-fifth Annual ACM Symposium on Principles of Distributed Computing, pp. 45–52, PODC 2006. ACM, New York (2006)

3. Claes, R., Holvoet, T.: Traffic coordination using aggregation-based traffic predictions. IEEE Intell. Syst. **29**(4), 96–100 (2014)
4. Claes, R., Holvoet, T., Weyns, D.: A decentralized approach for anticipatory vehicle routing using delegate multi-agent systems. IEEE Trans. Intell. Transp. Syst. **12**(2), 364–373 (2011)
5. Fischer, S., Vöcking, B.: On the evolution of selfish routing. In: Albers, S., Radzik, T. (eds.) ESA 2004. LNCS, vol. 3221, pp. 323–334. Springer, Heidelberg (2004). https://doi.org/10.1007/978-3-540-30140-0_30
6. Nisan, N., Roughgarden, T., Tardos, E., Vazirani, V.V.: Algorithmic Game Theory. Cambridge University Press, New York (2007)
7. Rosenschein, J.S.: Multiagent systems, and the search for appropriate foundations. In: Proceedings of the 12th International Conference on Autonomous Agents and Multiagent Systems, AAMAS 2013, pp. 5–6 (2013). www.ifaamas.org/
8. Roughgarden, T.: Routing games. In: Algorithmic Game Theory, pp. 461–486. Cambridge University Press, New York (2007)
9. Sandholm, W.H.: Potential games with continuous player sets. J. Econ. Theor. **97**(1), 81–108 (2001)
10. Varga, L.: On intention-propagation-based prediction in autonomously self-adapting navigation. Scalable Comput. Pract. Exp. **16**(3), 221–232 (2015)
11. Varga, L.Z.: Online routing games and the benefit of online data. In: Klügl, F., Vizzari, G., Vokřínek, J. (eds.) ATT 2014 8th International Workshop on Agents in Traffic and Transportation, Held at the 13th International Conference on Autonomous Agents and Multiagent Systems, 5–6 May 2014, Paris, France, pp. 88–95 (2014)
12. Varga, L.Z.: Paradox phenomena in autonomously self-adapting navigation. Cybern. Inf. Technol. **15**(5), 78–87 (2015)
13. Varga, L.Z.: Benefit of online real-time data in the braess paradox with anticipatory routing. In: Kounev, S., Giese, H., Liu, J. (eds.) 2016 IEEE International Conference on Autonomic Computing, ICAC 2016, 17–22 July 2016, Würzburg, Germany, pp. 245–250. IEEE Computer Society (2016)
14. Varga, L.Z.: How good is predictive routing in the online version of the braess paradox? In: Kaminka, G.A., Fox, M., Bouquet, P., Hüllermeier, E., Dignum, V., Dignum, F., van Harmelen, F. (eds.) ECAI 2016, Frontiers in Artificial Intelligence and Applications, vol. 285, pp. 1696–1697. IOS Press (2016)
15. Varga, L.Z.: Equilibrium with predictive routeing in the online version of the braess paradox. IET Softw. **11**(4), 165–170 (2017)
16. Varga, L.Z.: Game theory models for the verification of the collective behaviour of autonomous cars. In: Bulwahn, L., Kamali, M., Linker, S. (eds.) Proceedings First Workshop on Formal Verification of Autonomous Vehicles. Electronic Proceedings in Theoretical Computer Science, 19 September 2017, Turin, Italy, vol. 257, pp. 27–34. Open Publishing Association (2017)
17. Wardrop, J.G.: Some theoretical aspects of road traffic research. Proc. Inst. Civ. Eng. Part II **1**(36), 352–378 (1952)
18. de Weerdt, M.M., Stein, S., Gerding, E.H., Robu, V., Jennings, N.R.: Intention-aware routing of electric vehicles. IEEE Trans. Intell. Transp. Syst. **17**(5), 1472–1482 (2016)
19. Wooldridge, M.: An Introduction to MultiAgent Systems, 2nd edn. Wiley, Hoboken (2009)

The Multi-agent Layer
of CALMeD SURF

M. Rebollo⑩, A. Giret⑩, C. Carrascosa⑩, and V. Julian⁽⊠⁾⑩

Dpto. Sistemas Informáticos y Computación,
Universitat Politècnica de València, València, Spain
{mrebollo,agiret,carrasco,vinglada}@dsic.upv.es
http://www.gti-ia.upv.es

Abstract. This paper proposes a crowdsourcing approach that deals with the problem of Last Mile Delivery (LMD). The proposed approach is supported by Multi Agent System (MAS) techniques and makes use of a crowd of citizens that are moving in an urban area for their own needs. The idea is to employ those citizens to deliver parcels on their way to their destinations. The complexity of the approach lies in integrating the public infrastructure network of the city for the delivery route planning, and the citizens that are deliverers in the system with their own routes to their destinations. The proposed approach is supported by a MAS framework for open fleets management. Moreover, the executed tests suggest that the LMD by citizens can drastically reduce the emissions of carbon dioxide and other airborne pollutants that are caused by delivery trucks. Moreover it can reduce the traffic congestion and noise in urban areas.

Keywords: Multi Agent Systems · Logistics · Parcel delivery
Complex network analysis

1 Introduction

Over the last few years, urban goods distribution has become a key element of the current economy. Nevertheless, urban transport causes critical problems such as traffic, noise and pollution. Goods transport is required for the people to live but it can be also considered a disturbing activity due to congestion and environmental nuisances, which negatively affects the quality of life. As cities continue to grow at unprecedented rates, providing efficient, safe, and affordable goods distribution is becoming increasingly difficult. Moreover, the increase of parcels delivery in cities is becoming more and more higher adding to the already complex urban mobility.

The problem of urban goods distribution is known as the Last Mile Delivery (LMD), which can be defined as the problem of transport planning for deliver-

F. Belardinelli and E. Argente (Eds.): EUMAS 2017/AT 2017, LNAI 10767, pp. 446–460, 2018.
https://doi.org/10.1007/978-3-030-01713-2_31

ing parcels from urban distribution centers (UDC[1]) hubs to the final destination in the area (for example the end consumers' homes). Current research in this area aims at increasing efficiency in urban distribution by proposing new logistics models as new solutions in the context of parcel delivery and the use of Intelligent Transport Systems (ITS). The current advances in developing and utilizing information and communication technologies in goods distribution offer opportunities to integrate these systems to improve the LMD. In that respect, information and communication technologies would enable and improve practical implementation of the last mile distribution model proposed in this paper.

Specifically, this work is motivated and inspired by the need of ITS software tools/services for sustainable transportation. Currently, the urban delivery scheme consists of a number of vehicles that leave the hub and drive towards the city. Our proposal starts from the opposite side, trying to drastically reduce (in an ideal scenario, eliminate) the use of dedicated vehicles for parcels delivery. To do this, our sustainable LMD is implemented by the idea of crowdsourcing. In our approach the crowd is the set of citizens that already move in the urban area for their own needs and are willing to deliver parcels on their way to their destinations. In this way, the LMD by citizens can drastically reduce the traffic congestion, noise and, of course, emissions of carbon dioxide and other airborne pollutants that are caused by delivery trucks in urban areas. The drastic reduction of conventional delivery vehicles means less number of vehicles, which can be argued to be an approach capable of improving energy and cost efficiency.

The proposed approach follows an open transportation fleet paradigm[2] in which the citizens can become deliverers of the system in a dynamic way (entering and leaving the system when required). Moreover, a parcel delivery is executed in a cooperative way, that is the delivery route can be executed by a chain of different users that engage in an delivery agreement. The deliverers may use their own transportation and/or the public transportation system for delivering the parcel, and there is a continuous tracking of the parcel being delivery in order to offer real-time information on the status of the parcel to the customer.

This paper proposes a framework that seeks to use collaborative strategies in last mile delivery of goods in cities. The main contribution of this work lies in delegating the parcels delivery to the citizens that are going to their own destinations in the urban area. The complexity of the approach lies in integrating the public infrastructure network of the city for the delivery route planning, and the citizens that are deliverers in the system with their own routes to their destinations. To do this, a Multi-agent System Approach based on the SURF framework [2] is proposed in this paper. The approach provides a set of services/facilities for

---

[1] UDC is a concept, where the loads of delivery trucks from different carriers are consolidated at a single facility and transferred to new trucks/vehicles to increase the load factor and to allow for easier time-windowed operations in order to avoid traffic congestion.

[2] Open fleets extend the traditional fleet concept towards a new dimension of openness: vehicles may interact with their environment in a Smart city [9], or join and leave the fleet at any time.

citizens who wish to participate in the delivery of parcels in a collaborative way. The main service of the approach is the intelligent distribution of delivery tasks among registered citizens. This intelligent distribution makes use of a complex network based algorithm which considers the city as a complex network where nodes represent the current location of the system deliverers, and edges connect consecutive system deliverers along a route.

The rest of the paper is structured as follows: Sect. 2 analyses previous works; Sect. 3 presents the proposed approach for the last mile delivery of goods in cities; and, finally, some conclusions are exposed in Sect. 4.

2   Related Work

Current cities can be seen as complex systems formed by different intercon- nected nodes such as citizens, different modes of transport, and communication networks. As commented in [8], the rapid growth faced by several cities has gen- erated traffic congestion, pollution and increasing social inequality. According to this, it is necessary to improve logistics flows in cities by effectively integrating business needs with traffic conditions, geographical, and environmental issues.

Although, passenger travel received the bulk of the attention [1,6], similar contributions to new research and technology are found in modeling the move- ment of parcels (see [9] for a state of the art review on requirements and features of transport, mobility, and logistics in Smart Cities).

The work proposed in [11] is a MAS simulation model capable of optimizing the distribution phase of small and medium packaged parcels in supply chains management. The author also investigates if improvements in efficiency of time, cost and energy can be achieved. To do this, the proposal employs a combina- tion of public transport and e-cargo bikes by the Courier Service for delivery of the parcels. Another interesting work is presented in [3]. The work discuses the different benefits of using an alternative delivery option compared to conven- tional delivery modes such as cars and vans. Specifically, the proposal describes the success of Micro-Carrier Urban Vehicle (MCUV) in pilot tests compared to conventional delivery.

A commercial application that follows the previously commented approach is the solution from DPD parcel delivery brand (https://www.dpd.com/). This application provides a set of services and options for smart urban delivery: an app that accurately informs the users about their shipments delivery times and allows changing or redirecting them if necessary; an alternative zero emission drive system with electric or hybrid vehicles in Stuttgart, and transport bikes in Hamburg. Another example is Green Link (http://green-link.co.uk), in which an emission-free delivery solution that uses electric vehicles, load-carrying tricycles, bicycles and load-carrying trailers for last mile delivery of parcels from their centres to the final destination is provided. The courier companies deliver the parcels to Green Link centers (similar to UDC) and from this point Green Link completes the distribution with their own deliverers and emission-free vehicles to the final customer. Green Link operates in York, Luton and Darlington. Other examples of self-service parcel station are DHL PackStation, LaPoste Pickup Station etc.

Analyzing other related approaches, we can highlight the work proposed in [12] where the authors define a MAS model for evaluating city logistics measures like joint delivery systems (introducing UDCs) and car parking management for logistics efficiency in a city faced with congested urban traffic conditions. On the other hand, [5] proposes a methodological approach in order to apply crowdsourcing solution for LMD. Specifically, the crowd studied is taxi fleet in city, supported by a transport network composed by road network and customer self-pickup facilities such as 24 h shops in city. The system relies on a two-phase decision model, first offline taxi trajectory mining and second online package routing-taxi scheduling. In this work the taxi drivers that are willing to deliver parcels are registered first in the system. Finally, [10] presents a case study in which a crowdsourcing approach is used for library deliveries. In this work the citizens deliver parcels to each other along their way. Despite prevailing regulative challenges, the study found that existing library deliveries can be successfully crowdsourced. Each crowdsourced delivery reduced an average of 1.6 Km driven by car, despite 80% of the deliveries being made within less than a 5 km distance.

As can be seen, different approaches have been developed in order to improve the movement of parcels in today's cities. Nevertheless, few works have addressed that problem using collaborative strategies. Next section will introduce a framework which try to deal with the problem of last mile delivery of goods in cities from a collaborative perspective.

3   SURF City Logistics Approach

This section introduces, in a nutshell, a collaborative crowdsourcing approach for parcels' LMD with the particular aim of reducing the harm to the environment. The complete detail of the approach is described in next sections.

One of the issues to be addressed in Smart Cities concerns the smart transport of parcels inside a city [9]. City logistics refers to the process of optimization of the logistics and transport activities in a urban area considering economic, environmental, social and safety aspects. In our approach the collaborative distribution of parcels is tackle using an open fleet approach [2] where a varying number of vehicles (from different transportation modes: bus, metro, tram, train, taxis, private cars, bicycle, etc.) may be used by different users/deliverers for their individual transportation needs. Moreover, private users or organizations may offer a partial use of their vehicles to others, or may participate with their own vehicles in the transportation of parcels.

This kind of collaborative distribution of parcels is characterized by the following aspects:

- Dynamic service demand: the distribution of parcels should be dynamic in the sense that new tasks may appear dynamically at any time and at any location in the city.

- Dynamic number of vehicles and deliverers: the number of available vehicles that might participate in the distribution of parcels is dynamic. New deliverers with or without their own vehicles may join or leave the fleet at any time and this should not affect normal fleet operation.
- Autonomy control: the usage of private vehicles reduces the control of the fleets operators. Individual goals or needs of vehicles owners, deliverers and parcel customers have to be balanced with the global objectives and goals of the system.
- Size: a crowdsourcing approach for parcels' LMD is conceived to work on large, maybe unlimited, fleet sizes, which can greatly complicate the design.

Our crowdsourcing approach for parcels' LMD is based on and supported by Multi-agent System (MAS) techniques [4] and is implemented by four main components (see Fig. 1). (i) A MAS framework (SURF Framework) that supports the crowdsourcing LMD execution. (ii) A transportation analysis and optimizing module (Transport Network Analysis Module - TNAM) that proposes parcels delivery paths to the crowd. (iii) A transportation ontology that specifies the different concepts that appear in a transportation model. It also facilitates the information sharing among the MAS framework components and the TNAM in order to link the dynamic crowd to a particular city (defined by the city transportation network, the city public transportation system, and the city UDCs locations). (iv) A MAS application that provides running support to the different agent roles in the LMD. The first three components were described in [7], whereas the last component constitutes the main contribution of the current paper.

All these parts will be accessed through a new application that is called *CALMeD SURF* (Crowdsourcing Approach for Last Mille Delivery). This application is mainly supported by the approach described above, and it is addressed as a mobile phone app for: customers that wants to deliver a parcel, and users that want to serve as occasional deliverers in an urban area. The main idea is that the users register in the application (as customer or deliverer), and *CALMeD SURF* will locate them in the city on real-time, sharing their position with the SURF Framework. In this way, when there is a parcel delivery request (step 1 in Fig. 1), the TNAM [7] uses a graph (dynamically generated by the SURF Framework and the instantiated transportation ontology, step 2 in Fig. 1) where each node is either a user (a potential deliverer, and/or customer) or an UDC. As the TNAM calculates how to get the parcel from an origin point of delivery to an end point, it proposes to the crowd of potential deliverers (those who are closest to the calculated delivery path) to participate. If some of the potential deliverers rejects the proposal, it calculates an alternative path (i.e. a new path and a new set of potential deliverers) in order to achieve the parcel delivery goal (step 3 in Fig. 1). The calculated path may include several deliverers that may pass the parcel from one to another (connecting sub-paths). One of the optimization criteria used by TNAM, closely related with the goal of minimizing the harm to the environment, is to minimize the deviation of the deliverers from the path to their own destinations. Trying in this way to minimize new emissions originated

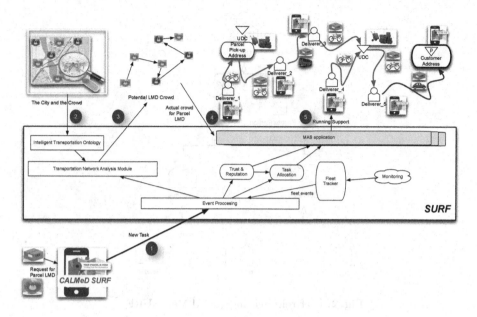

Fig. 1. CALMeD SURF a Crowdsourcing Approach for Last Mille Delivery

by movements that are solely used for parcel deliveries. The MAS layer starts
the running support from step 4 in Fig. 1. The proposed approach is defined as
a set of interaction sequences among the agent roles that built up the system.
The details are described in the following section.

3.1   The MAS Layer of CALMeD SURF

This section focuses in the MAS layer of the CALMeD SURF framework, which
is the focus of the paper.

There is one agent for each user along with a *CALMeD Manager agent*. Users
may play different roles in the system (as can be seen in Fig. 2), either being a
private person or a company. A user can play the role of a customer as the one
that asks for the transport service (being the sender) or the one who will be the
addressee of the transport service (playing the receiver rol). On the other hand,
a user may register in the system as an occasional deliverer, playing that rol
in the system whenever he wants to be an intermediate person in the delivery
process.

User agents are the interface to the system for registered users. These agents
know the different preferences or their users, as if they want to be occasional
deliverers or not, or the maximum distance they consider to turn off their path
to deliver something. They also communicate the current user position to the
frame.

The Manager Agent is in charge of serving the services offered by
the CALMeD SURF application, interacting with the user agents and the

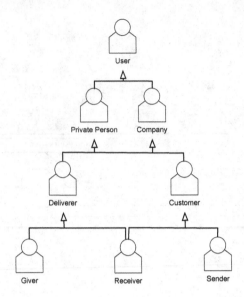

Fig. 2. User roles scheme in CALMeD SURF

different modules of the SURF framework. In this way, when a user wants to send something, it asks to the Manager Agent for it, and the Manager will establish, using the TNAM, not only the path from source position to objective, but also the user agents to ask for being occasional deliverers. If some of such users doesn't agree to play the occasional deliverer role in this situation, then the Manager Agent will ask for another path (and set of agents) to the TNAM.

The rest of the section presents some of the interaction diagrams detailing the coordination of such agents and the CALMeD SURF.

Main Interactions in the MAS Layer. In this section the key cooperation domains are described in order to get a correct understanding of the MAS approach for CALMeD SURF. A total of 28 interaction sequences among the agent roles of CALMeD SURF support the distributed and optimized delivery of parcels. The set of interactions includes: a number of managerial ones devoted to assure the correct management of users (customers and deliverers) of the system; a number of parcel tracking interactions that assures registration of the parcel, query of its status, and its real time GPS location; a number of parcel delivery interactions that are the key for supporting the coordination among the chain of deliverers, the distributed coordination and planning of the parcel delivery route, the movement of the parcel from its origin to its delivery point, and the associated re-planning due to events during the parcel delivery (i.e. a deliverer not available any more, a change in the delivery point, obsolete time frames, etc.).

Figure 3 shows the interaction that constitutes the first step for planning a parcel LMD. The Manager requests to TNAM, from SURF, a list of possible

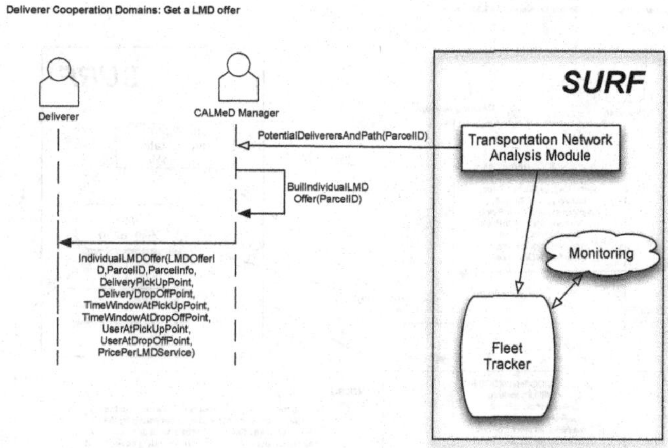

Fig. 3. Interaction sequence for Getting a LMD Offer from TNAM

deliverers (with the delivery path) that will optimize the parcel LMD. From this list of possible deliverers the Manager proposes and sends an offer to every individual deliverer in the list (in general the offer is a sub-path of the complete path for the parcel LMD built by TNAM). The deliverer may opt for accepting the offer at it is (a new interaction is started to fulfill it), reject it (using another interaction sequence) or negotiate it in order to redefine some features of the parcel LMD.

Figure 4 shows the interaction initiated by the Deliverer in order to Negotiate a LMD Offer. The first step is a request from the Deliverer to the Manager with the new parameters for the LMD offer that better suits him/her. The Manager reacts to this message checking with the modules of SURF (Intelligent Transportation Ontology and Task Allocation) to determine the feasibility of the Deliverer proposal. If the LMD offer from the Deliverer is valid, the Manager sends an information message that confirms all the parameters for the LMD offer initially proposed by the Deliverer. On the other hand, if the LMD offer from the Deliverer is not valid, there could be two possibilities. A new counter offer from the Manager which is sent to the Deliverer including the new parameters for the LMD offer calculated by the Manager from the information provided by Task Allocation module. Or a rejection from the Manager sent back to the Deliverer that marks the end of the negotiation. In the counter offer case the message from the Manager is followed by one of the following three possible interactions initiated by the Delivery: accept the counter offer at it is (ending the negotiation), reject it (the negotiation ends) or negotiate it (in this case this same negotiation interaction, Fig. 4, is repeated).

Figure 5 shows the interaction sequence between two Users in order to execute the parcel LMD. The Receiver (the User that might be the Customer of the parcel that receives his/her parcel, or the User that is the next Deliverer in the parcel LDM chain) must move to the pick up point of the given parcel LMD.

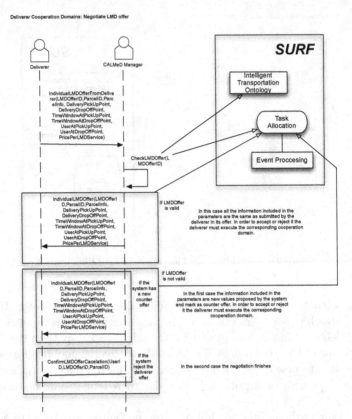

Fig. 4. Interaction sequence for Negotiate a LMD Offer between the Deliverer and Manager

On the other hand, the Giver (a Deliverer who is delivering the parcel or a Sender of the parcel) also moves to the delivery point of his/her current parcel LMD. These actions are recorded by the different modules of SURF in order to track the parcel GPS location and to foresee what will be the sequel of the interchange between the two users involved in the interaction. When any of the two Users is at the pick up point he/she informs it to the other User in order to become acquaintance of each others. When the two Users are in the pick up point, the next step is issued by the Giver by passing the parcel to the Receiver marking the action with Current Time Stamp and GPS location. Whereas the Receiver scans the parcel (a QR code printed in the parcel is read by the mobile phone app) and marks the action with Current Time Stamp and GPS location as well. These two messages are tracked by the Event Processing module of SURF and the last message marks the end of the interaction. On the other hand, if any of the two Users can not make it to the pick up point on time, the Manager informs the two Users of a parcel LMD re-planning and a new interaction of LMD offer (see Fig. 3) is initiated in order to react to this situation.

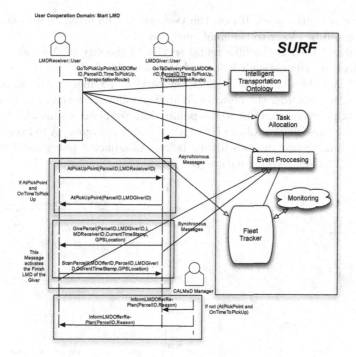

Fig. 5. Interaction sequence for Start a LMD between two Users, one is the Giver, that is the User that has the parcel (a Deliverer who is delivering the parcel or a Sender of the parcel), and the other is the Receiver, that is the User that might be the Customer of the parcel that receives his/her parcel, or the User that is the next Deliverer in the parcel LDM chain.

The interaction depicted in Fig. 5 is repeated until the whole delivery route is executed by the pairs of Users involved in the parcel LMD chain. The successful fulfillment of any sub-route of the parcel LMD by the given Deliverer is rewarded by the monetary compensation in his/her account defined by the PricePerLMD-Service stated in the committed parcel LMD offer. In the same way a failure to accomplish the agreed delivery task by any of the Deliverer, as well as a parcel lost or damage due to the Deliverer fault, is debited from his/her account by the price stipulated in the service contract.

3.2 Case Study. Package Delivery Using Valencia's Bike Sharing Service

To check the validity of the proposal, we have apply it to a delivery scenario in which a bike sharing service is used. The service will use the trips that users make habitually during the day: to study, to work or to do the shopping. These trips are used to deliver a package to the final addressee if they share the same

location (or a nearby one). If not, the package can be given to a intermediate
user that could be closer to the final customer.

The dataset used is the bike rental service of the city on Valencia (Spain),
called Valenbisi. The network is formed by a set of 275 stations in which bikes
are parked and the registered users os the service. To analyze the structure of
the service, let's consider the network created as follows. The city can be divided
into as et of polygons that define the points that are closer to each bike station.
The result is a tessellation of the city with Voronoy polygons. A network can be
created by linking two stations if they belong to adjacent polygons. The result
is known as Delaunay triangulation (see Fig. 6).

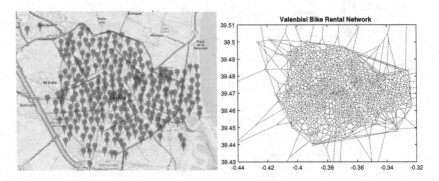

Fig. 6. (Left) distribution of the Valenbisi stations on the city. (Right) Network formed
by the stations with Delaunay triangulation

The network is an undirected graph with 275 nodes and 810 edges. The average degree is 5.9, which means that each station has 5.9 other adjacent stations
in average. The diameter of the network (the maximum path length in the graph)
is 13 links and the average shortest path length is 6.5. The clustering coefficient
is 0.18 (significative, but not very high) and the cumulative degree distribution follows a Poisson distribution. Therefore, the network has some small-world
properties, but because of its construction, there is no hub that concentrates
most of the connections. This can be easily confirmed when the efficiency of
the network is measured and compared with the efficiency of the network when
some nodes are removed. The efficiency indicates how well the exchange if information is performed (or in this case the movement along the city). If a node
fails, it is removed from the network and the new efficiency is compared. This
is done until all nodes are removed. Figure 7 shows the network efficiency under
different strategies. The random one chooses one station at random. The rest,
use different centrality measures to order the stations by importance and try to
force failures beginning with the most relevant ones. It can be seen that there
is no clear difference in the efficiency degradation. We can conclude that the
structure is quite robust under failures, random or deliberate.

To model the trips in the city, information about 3 weeks in three different
years has been considered. Using this information, it has been calculated the

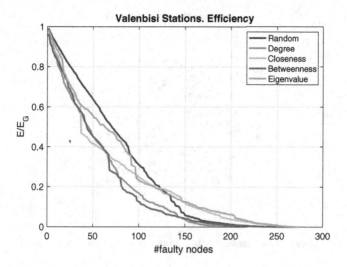

Fig. 7. Efficiency of the network under station failure with different strategies. There is no clear difference, so there is no hubs.

probability of a trip to finish in each station given the starting stations. This model is used to simulate a set of typical trips in the city and they are used to deliver the packages. In this situation, we can confirm the hypothesis that users can be used in a last-mile delivery service with no other movements different from the natural ones they follow in daily basis. Figure 8 shows a sample trip in the city. The user begins in one of the stations. A set of stops are defined (four in this case) according with the most probables destinations from each station. To calculate the path between start and bike return point, the shortest path in the network is considered. Doing that, we consider that a user is under the 'influence' of the nearest station in each point of the trip. Therefore, as the distance between stations typically is under 500 m, we can assume that the package can be delivered at any point in the surrounding area of the station. Or an exchange can be done between two users.

The final experiments show the performance of the proposed method for the last-mile delivering. Four sizes for the deliverer's team have been chosen: 25, 50, 75 or 100 deliverers for the complete network[3]. For each case, 5 different origin and addressee have been chosen for the delivery, and for each one of them, 5 different executions have been made. Figure 9 shows the average path length obtained for each one of them. Results show that a small number of users is better, obtaining shortest paths for the delivery. For 25 or 50 deliverers, the paths are in the order of the diameter of the network (13 steps), whereas for bigger teams the randomness introduced in the movements seems to reduce the performance. Furthermore, the scenario of a dynamic addressee which position changes with time does not affect to the performance.

---

[3] Take into account that the Valenbisi service has nowadays 45,000 registered users.

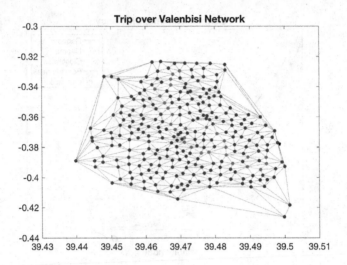

Fig. 8. Individual trip of an user through four stations {215, 19, 221, 203}

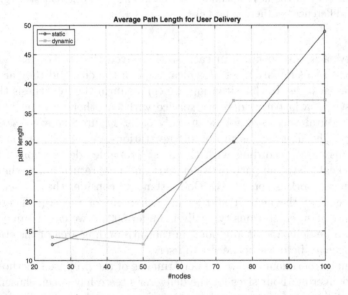

Fig. 9. Delivery by users of Valenbisi bike service. Two cases are considered: static and dynamic final customers.

4   Conclusions

A crowdsourcing approach for parcels' LMD has been presented in this paper. The approach proposes that citizens can become the deliverers of the parcels in a dynamic and collaborative way. To do this, a Multi-agent System has been designed based on the SURF framework. The systems offers an intelligent distribution of goods considering the city as a complex network where registered citizens act as a part of the whole delivery process.

A validation example has been proposed in order to test the utility of the proposal. The example has been implemented over a bike sharing service using the trips that users make habitually during the day in order to deliver packages. Results have shown that users of the service can be used as intermediaries in the LMD service without different displacements than the natural ones they follow in daily basis.

The experiments show that the network of the Valencia bike sharing service is a robust one and it has some properties that eases its usage as a transportation system for a last-mile delivery scenario. Some test have been made using the route patterns of the users of the service.

As ongoing work, we are introducing delivery deadlines in the network analysis. The delivery deadlines can be guaranteed taking into account sub-deadlines between the different sub-deliveries of the participants in the whole delivery route. Moreover, in order to ensure deliveries, we are studying the use of trust and reputation models that can be used to estimate the behavior of the participants in the delivery process.

References

1. Alonso-Mora, J., Samaranayake, S., Wallar, A., Frazzoli, E., Rus, D.: On-demand high-capacity ride-sharing via dynamic trip-vehicle assignment. Proc. Nat. Acad. Sci. **114**(3), 462–467 (2017)
2. Billhardt, H., Fernández, A., Lujak, M., Ossowski, S., Julián, V., De Paz, J.F., Hernández, J.Z.: Towards smart open dynamic fleets. In: Rovatsos, M., Vouros, G., Julian, V. (eds.) EUMAS/AT -2015. LNCS (LNAI), vol. 9571, pp. 410–424. Springer, Cham (2016). https://doi.org/10.1007/978-3-319-33509-4_32
3. Brning, M., Schnewolf, W.: Freight transport system for urban shipment and delivery. In: 2011 IEEE Forum on Integrated and Sustainable Transportation Systems, FISTS 2011, pp. 136–140 (2011)
4. Castelfranchi, C., Lespérance, Y. (eds.): ATAL 2000. LNCS (LNAI), vol. 1986. Springer, Heidelberg (2001). https://doi.org/10.1007/3-540-44631-1
5. Chen, C., Pan, S.: Using the crowd of taxis to last mile delivery in e-commerce: a methodological research. In: Service Orientation in Holonic and Multi-agent Manufacturing, vol. 640, pp. 61–70 (2016)
6. Gentile, G., Noekel, K. (eds.): Modelling Public Transport Passenger Flows in the Era of Intelligent Transport Systems. STTT, vol. 10. Springer, Cham (2016). https://doi.org/10.1007/978-3-319-25082-3
7. Giret, A., Carrascosa, C., Julian, V., Rebollo, M.: A crowdsourcing approach for last mile delivery. Emerging Technologies, Submitted to Transportation Research Part C (2017)
8. Kim, H.M., Han, S.S.: Seoul. Cities **29**(2), 142–154 (2012)
9. Neirotti, P., De Marco, A., Cagliano, A.C., Mangano, G., Scorrano, F.: Current trends in smart city initiatives: some stylised facts. Cities **38**, 25–36 (2014)
10. Paloheimo, H., Lettenmeier, M., Waris, H.: Transport reduction by crowdsourced deliveries - a library case in finland. Journal of Cleaner Production **132**, 240–251 (2016). Absolute Reductions in Material Throughput, Energy Use and Emissions

11. Rajeshwari, C.: Optimizing last mile delivery using public transport with multiagent based control. Master thesis, pp. 1–59 (2016)
12. Wangapisit, O., Taniguchi, E., Teo, J.S.E., Qureshi, A.G.: Multi-agent systems modelling for evaluating joint delivery systems. Procedia Social Behav. Sci. **125**, 472–483 (2014)

AT 2017: Applications

Event-Driven Agents: Enhanced Perception for Multi-Agent Systems Using Complex Event Processing

Jeremias Dötterl[1]([⊠]), Ralf Bruns[1], Jürgen Dunkel[1], and Sascha Ossowski[2]

[1] Department of Computer Science,
Hannover University of Applied Sciences and Arts, Hannover, Germany
{jeremias.doetterl,ralf.bruns,juergen.dunkel}@hs-hannover.de
[2] CETINIA, University Rey Juan Carlos, Madrid, Spain
sascha.ossowski@urjc.es

Abstract. With the increase of existing sensor devices grows the data volume that is available to software systems to understand the physical world. The use of this sensor data in Multi-Agent Systems (MAS) could allow agents to improve their comprehension of the environment and provide additional information for their decision making. Unfortunately, conventional BDI agents cannot make sense of low-level sensor data directly due to their limited event comprehension capabilities: The agents react to single, isolated events rather than to multiple, related events and therefore are not able to efficiently detect complex higher-level situations from low-level sensor data. In this paper, we present Event-Driven Agents as a novel concept to enhance the perception of conventional BDI agents with Complex Event Processing. Their intended use is in environments in which percepts arrive with high speed and are too low-level to be efficiently interpreted by conventional agents directly. In a case study, we show how Event-Driven Agents can be used to address the bicycle rebalancing problem, which bike sharing systems face in their daily operations. Without an intelligent and timely intervention, bike stations of bike sharing systems tend to become empty or full quickly, which prevents the rental or return at these stations. We demonstrate how Event-Driven Agents, based on live data, can detect situations occurring in the bike sharing system in order to initiate appropriate rebalancing efforts.

Keywords: Multi-Agent Systems · Agent perception
Complex event processing · Situation detection

1 Introduction

Nowadays, due to the increased number of mobile phones, tablets, and other sensor devices, there is more data available than ever that can be utilized by software systems to understand the world. If processed appropriately, this *data*

© Springer Nature Switzerland AG 2018
F. Belardinelli and E. Argente (Eds.): EUMAS 2017/AT 2017, LNAI 10767, pp. 463–475, 2018.
https://doi.org/10.1007/978-3-030-01713-2_32

awareness allows systems to comprehend the situations that are taking place in the environment they are operating in and enables them to adapt their behavior accordingly. The immediate understanding of the temporary circumstances is a fundamental prerequisite for a system to be able to act intelligently.

For many years now, Multi-Agent Systems (MAS) [15] are recognized as a useful paradigm for the design and development of distributed intelligent systems. In MAS, autonomous computing entities called *agents* acquire data from the environment in form of percepts. Based on the sensed percepts, the agents perform actions, which result in changes in the environment.

MAS can potentially achieve intelligent behavior if information about the environment is provided on a level that it is understood by the agents. This typically happens in form of high-level percepts that correspond to concepts of the system's application domain. On the other hand, exposing agents to an infinite, high-velocity stream of low-level sensor events as input source makes the agents face a challenge they are not inherently equipped for. The processing and understanding of events generated by sensors are challenging for multiple reasons: Firstly, the events tend to arrive in large volumes, which requires appropriate handling to prevent a collapse of the system. Secondly, the events have to be analyzed in (near) real-time to be of value for the system. Often, a rapid reaction is critical to the system's success. Actions based on delayed and out-dated information might even be counterproductive to the system's goals. Finally, sensor events are typically very technical and lack necessary context. Thus, a single event exhibits little meaning. To achieve a deep understanding of the observed events, they have to be enriched with background knowledge about the domain and the relations between *multiple event occurrences* have to be analyzed.

Conventional MAS are not optimized for operating in sensor data environments. Agent-oriented programming languages and frameworks like Agent-Speak [10], Jason [2] and SARL [11] have their strengths in the expressive and convenient description of agent behavior but struggle with the problems outlined above. Their biggest restriction is their limited event analysis capability: While conventional agents are already event-based in the sense that they react to *single, isolated event occurrences*, they lack the inherent ability to efficiently analyze *multiple, related event occurrences* and their temporal relations in an event stream.

Complex Event Processing (CEP) [8] is an established method for the (near) real-time analysis of massive event streams, which allows inferring complex, high-level situations from a sequence of fast, low-level sensor data. A designated Event Processing Language allows expressing event pattern rules that match when a certain pattern is found in the event stream. The language supports the description of temporal relationships between *multiple events*.

In this paper, we present a novel architectural approach for enhancing the perception of software agents. While the agent's behavior keeps being realized with established MAS technology, we use CEP to make agents perceive complex patterns in event streams that they are typically prone to overlook. This new type of agents, which we denote as *event-driven agents*, because of their improved event comprehension, is compatible with the existing MAS concept. They are intended to be used in environments in which percepts arrive with high speed and are too low-level to be understood by the conventional agents directly.

The remainder of the paper is structured as follows. In Sect. 2 we discuss some related work. In Sect. 3 we present the event-driven agent concept. Based on a case study, we show in Sect. 4 how event-driven agents can be used to balance public bike sharing systems through user cooperation. Finally, in Sect. 5 we draw some conclusions and propose possible future work.

2   Related Work

There exist several prior works that concern themselves with the adaption and advancement of agent perception in order to achieve different improvements. In [14], the authors equip agents in situated MAS with active perception, which lets the agent focus on those environmental aspects that are relevant to its current task. To achieve this goal, the perception process is decomposed into three steps, namely sensing, interpreting, and filtering. The authors introduce *perceptual laws* and *foci filters* as two extension points of their framework that allow system designers to define domain-specific perception-behavior. In [7], the authors introduce the concept *perception management* as a mechanism to enhance available percepts. Perception management is not (only) responsible for acquiring data from sensor devices, but is foremost concerned with the acquisition and fusion of information. The goal is to obtain information that is more valuable compared to the raw, unprocessed data in order to enable situation-dependent decisions. In this paper, we adopt this goal and attempt to shift raw sensor data to the information level with an event-driven approach.

We are not the first who have recognized the potential of adding a stronger event notion to the MAS paradigm. In [9], Omicini proposes first steps towards the integration of event-based systems and MAS. The paper focuses in particular on the idea of a coherent conceptual framework. As one issue, it mentions the need for an interpretation mechanism that finds meaning that might not be inherent in individual events. It names CEP as one possible solution approach to detect complex relationships between multiple events.

When agents act in complex and dynamically changing environments, an appropriate handling of the observed environment state is required. In [1], agents are extended by a *capability* component dedicated to the efficient processing of large event volumes. A *capability* is an event-oriented module that listens to incoming events in order to decide whether to launch a certain task. The paper discusses different capability variants and their effects on the agent's event processing abilities.

We argue that BDI agents can benefit from situational knowledge about their environment to make better decisions. Our view is supported by [3], where the authors identify the existence of a single triggering event as a weakness of the conventional event-plan paradigm used in BDI agents. The use of BDI agents in highly dynamic domains demands a richer event-handling mechanism that is able to detect relationships between multiple events. The proposed Situation-Based BDI Agent performs event correlation and situation recognition in order to select appropriate plans.

3   Enhancing Agent Perception with Complex Event Processing

In this section, we present our approach for the enhancement of agent perception. Figure 1 shows the proposed architecture of the *event-driven agent* (EA), which consists of two major parts:

1. A Complex Event Processing Engine is used to realize the intelligent and effective processing of low-level percepts. Percepts are the input data that the EA acquires by sensing the environment. They are processed in a three-step process (Filtering, Context Enrichment, Situation Detection) to obtain high-level situations. Situations are occurrences in the environment that correspond to domain-level concepts and form the basis of the agent's decision making.
2. A Belief-Desire-Intention (BDI) agent, embedded in the EA, is used to achieve intelligent behavior. The detected situations are provided to the BDI agent in form of high-level percepts. The BDI agent is able to understand these percepts directly as they are given in the expected data format and on the appropriate abstraction level. This enables the BDI agent to make informed decisions and to act intelligently.

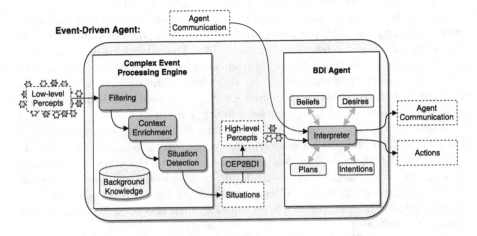

Fig. 1. Event-Driven Agent

The EA is situated in an environment, which provides the EA with percepts. We denote as E the set of low-level percepts available to the EA. Each event

$e_i \in E$ is a tuple consisting of a unique identifier, the timestamp of its occurrence, an event type, and a set of attributes: $e_i = (id, ts, type, attr)$. The possible values for the event type and the event attributes are given by an event model. The measurement of a temperature of $23°$ C at time $t = 300$ could be represented as follows:

$$e_0 = (1, 300, temperature, \{(degrees, 23), (unit, celsius)\})$$

The events of set E enter the CEP engine in form of a stream.

3.1   Complex Event Processing Engine

Complex Event Processing is a paradigm for the near real-time processing of massive event streams. CEP comes with a declarative event processing language, which allows expressing event processing rules consisting of a condition and an action: The condition describes an event pattern, which is a particular sequence of events with a special meaning for the application domain. When the CEP engine detects the pattern in the stream, the rule fires and the corresponding action is executed. Possible actions include in particular the creation of new events, which then can be processed by subsequent rules.

The CEP engine implements the following three-stage percept analysis process to bridge the gap between low-level sensor events and high-level situations:

1. Filtering
2. Context Enrichment
3. Situation Detection

Each of these stages is realized by a dedicated component. To fulfill its task, each component is equipped with its individual rule base.

Filtering: The filtering stage reduces the (potentially) high data volumes and ensures high data quality.

If many sensors are used as data sources, they can produce a large amount of data. If the data was forwarded to the BDI agent directly, it might place a high load on the reasoning mechanism and stall the agent's deliberation. Therefore, the incoming event stream has to be filtered to reduce the number of events that have to be processed by subsequent components. For instance, a sensor might emit its unchanged state repeatedly in a fixed interval, which is unnecessarily redundant; typically, a system only wants to be notified when the state changes. Redundant events that do not provide additional value might be removed from the event stream in order to reduce the load.

Moreover, sensors may report erroneous data. To prevent illegal data values from entering the system, events should be checked against a set of constraints, which describe the acceptable values for each data attribute. Thereby, the EA can avoid decisions based on low-quality data.

Conceptually, the filter stage applies a filter function fil to reduce a stream of incoming events $e \in E$:

$$fil \colon E^k \to E^l$$

Function fil reduces the size of the stream from k to l (with $l \leq k$)[1]. The filter does not only analyze a single isolated event to decide whether to let it pass but can base its decision also on previously seen events.

Context Enrichment: This stage adds context information to the raw sensor events to increase the events' informative value.

Sensor events typically are not self-contained pieces of information that can be understood without consulting other knowledge sources as they often lack necessary context. An event might carry a certain identifier referring to an object or concept that itself is not contained in the event. For example, an event might contain the number of items some machine has produced. Information about the machine, such as its location or last maintenance check, might be stored in a static knowledge base rather than sent within the event itself.

Conceptually, a context enrichment function ctx translates the low-level sensor events of set E into instances of the event set C.

$$ctx \colon E \to C$$

Set C contains contextually enriched events, which are passed to the situation detection stage.

Situation Detection: This stage uses the enriched events to infer complex situations. This component is the most sophisticated part of the architecture and benefits most from the usage of CEP, as CEP allows the near real-time detection of complex situations in event streams [5, 12, 13].

To detect meaningful patterns, the event stream is monitored by the situation function sit.

$$sit \colon C^m \to S$$

Function sit analyzes m events and their relations to detect meaningful situations. Expressed with the event processing language, m events and their relations form the event pattern in the condition part of CEP rule, and the resulting situation is modeled in the action part by creating a new complex event. The resulting set S contains situations,

- which represent occurrences related to the agent's application domain and therefore can serve directly as the basis for the BDI agent's decision making.
- which would not have been detected without the intelligent analysis of a *multitude of events* and their relationships. (The case study in Sect. 4 demonstrates this in more detail.)

Also, the size of set S is expected to be significantly smaller than the size of the original event set E.

---

[1] How this can be achieved with CEP rules is demonstrated in the case study in Sect. 4.

3.2   CEP-to-BDI Mapping

The CEP engine emits situations in form of events. As the BDI agent expects its input in form of percepts, a mapping from events to percepts is required. Therefore, the EA architecture contains a CEP2BDI component that serves as an adapter between the CEP engine and the BDI agent.

A single situation is represented by a single CEP event. However, depending on the concrete language used in the BDI agent, it might be useful to create several percepts. This means, there is not necessarily a 1-to-1 relationship between situations and percepts.

3.3   BDI Agent

The BDI agent, which is embedded into the EA, receives the high-level percepts. To the BDI agent, it appears as if the percepts were directly sensed from the environment. The CEP engine protects the BDI agent from data overload and provides it with percepts it can act upon directly.

The BDI agent listens to the percepts, which might cause it to modify its beliefs and intentions and which might trigger the execution of plans. The plan execution, in turn, can trigger actions, which modify the agent's environment or let the agent enter into communication with other (event-driven) agents.

The BDI agent can be implemented with established agent platforms and agent-based programming languages. In particular, the implementation of the BDI agent does *not* require the development of a situation detection mechanism. Advanced pattern detection in event streams is complicated and should be left to dedicated event processing engines.

4   Case Study: Rebalancing Bike Sharing Systems with Event-Driven Agents

To demonstrate the feasibility of our approach, we show how the EA concept of Sect. 3 can be used to coordinate the use of public bike sharing systems.

Bike Sharing Systems (BSS) allow users to rent and return bikes to undertake short trips. The users rent and return the bikes at dedicated bicycle stations, which are typically placed at a distance of several hundred meters to each other. Each of these stations has a fixed capacity, which determines the number of bikes that can be stored at this station.

While BSS recently have gained popularity as an eco-friendly transportation alternative in big cities, they suffer from the *Bike Sharing Rebalancing Problem* [4]. Operating a BSS without purposeful intervention results in imbalances between the station occupancies: While some stations suffer from a lack of bicycles, which prevents the rental at these stations, others suffer from congestion, which prevents the return of bikes. To assure high user satisfaction and revenues for the operator, an effective rebalancing approach is required to maintain a balanced system state.

4.1   Event-Driven Rebalancing Approach

In [6], we presented a dynamic, agent-based rebalancing approach that tries to reduce imbalances in BSS. The approach offers incentives to users to convince them to modify their cycling routes and return bikes at selected stations in a way that is beneficial for the overall system balance. The user receives the incentive on his smartphone and can then decide if he wants to accept it. If enough users can be convinced to choose beneficial cycling routes, imbalances can be reduced.

The incentives are determined by the rebalancing system based on live data about the environment, which is dynamically changing. The environment is monitored to acquire atomic events. Through monitoring, the system knows the users' positions (GPS) and when rentals and returns take place at the stations. To enable the system to make intelligent decisions about which incentives should be offered to which user, it performs event stream analysis with CEP to obtain higher-level situations, such as movement behavior (*User A is cycling with a speed of 18 km/h*) or proximity information (*User B is cycling near station S*).

To specify the nearness of users to a station more concretely, we introduced the concept of a station's *proximity area*. A user is a member of a particular station's proximity area if he holds a bike and can potentially reach the station within a given time limit. This concept is illustrated in Fig. 2, where the users Alice, Bob, and Carol are expected to be able to reach station s_1 within the given time, whereas Dave is not. The proximity area is useful, as its members are those users who can in the near future increase the station's occupancy, an information that can be used for demand prediction. Furthermore, the members of a station's proximity area are the potential recipients of incentives to return their bikes at this station.

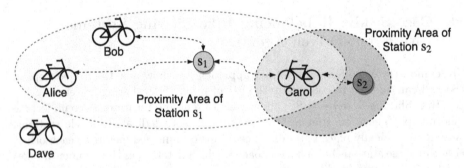

Fig. 2. Proximity areas of two stations s_1 and s_2 [6]

The rebalancing approach consists of two agent types, which exhibit the following behavior (see Fig. 3):

- *User Agent* (UA): UAs represent the users and run on the users' personal smartphones. UAs use CEP to monitor the GPS data provided by the smartphone's GPS sensor in order to infer the user's movement behavior. Based on the user's position and movement behavior, the agent determines the user's temporal distance to the stations of the BSS. When the temporal distance sinks below a specified time threshold, the user is considered near the station and enters the station's proximity area. The UA notifies the station's agent accordingly with an *EnteredAreaEvent*.

– *Station Agent* (SA): SAs represent the stations of the BSS and listen to messages from the UAs. Whenever a user enters or leaves the station's proximity area (as indicated by the UA with an event message), the SA updates its belief about the proximity area accordingly. The SA also monitors the rentals and returns that take place at the station that is under its control. Based on this data, the SA determines its state, which characterizes the station's (predicted) fill level: low, medium, or high. Based on this state information, the agent infers whether it wants to attract bikes from nearby users and whether to offer an incentive.

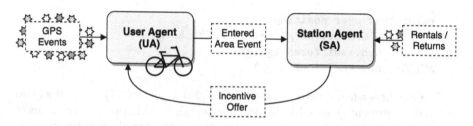

Fig. 3. Interaction between User Agent and Station Agent

Below, we demonstrate how the UA can be realized with the EA approach of Sect. 3. We only show the enhanced perception with CEP. Further information about the rebalancing mechanism can be found in [6].

4.2 Enhanced Perception for the Event-Driven User Agent

The enhanced perception is driven by event processing rules written in a dedicated event processing language (EPL). We introduce a simplified pseudo language, which is easier to understand than the EPL of a productive CEP system. This pseudo EPL supports the following operators:

AND, OR	Boolean operator for events or constraints.
->	Sequence of events.
.within	defines a time interval in which the event has to occur.

For example, the pattern (A -> (B OR C)).within(30 s) matches when the CEP engine detects an event of type A that within 30 s is followed by an event of either type B or C.

The UA uses enhanced perception to detect nearby stations based on a temporal distance measure. Therefore, the user agent accesses the GPS sensor of the smartphone to continuously monitor its current location. The location of the smartphone is assumed to reflect the user's location. Furthermore, the UA has to analyze the user's movement to detect whenever the user enters or leaves the proximity area of some station. In particular, it has to be determined whether the user is moving forward or resting. The goal is to create and send a *EnteredAreaEvent* to the station, as soon as the user enters a station's proximity area.

Filtering: The UA monitors the smartphone's position, which is provided in form of an event stream of *GPS events*. As the UA is only interested in location changes, it uses the following CEP rule to filter out GPS events that are redundant. The GPS events form set E (introduced in Sect. 3), which is reduced according to the following CEP rule.

```
rule: "new user position"
CONDITION GPS-Evt AS g1  ->  GPS-Evt AS g2
    AND Geo.isDifferent(g1,g2)
ACTION  new PositionEvt(g2)
```

The rule fires when it detects a GPS event g2 that follows a GPS event g1 and the events represent geographically different locations. Whether the locations of g1 and g2 are equal, is determined by a function of the Geo class. When the rule matches, a new *position event* is created that contains the user's new location and is forwarded to the next stage. The GPS events are dropped and do not reach the second stage.

Context Enrichment: Context enrichment is used to add context data that is stored in (semi-)static knowledge bases. In this exemplary bicycle sharing scenario, the rebalancing process does not depend on extensive background knowledge. This step can be skipped for simple application domains, where no contextual data from external sources is required.

Situation Detection: Based on the position events, the user's movement can be characterized. The position events of set E are used to construct situation set S.

In a first step, the user's speed is measured with the following CEP rule.

```
rule: "speed of movement"
CONDITION PositionEvt AS p1 -> PositionEvt AS p2
    AND p2.timestamp - p1.timestamp AS timeDiff
    AND Geo.distance(p1, p2) AS distance
    AND distance/timeDiff AS speed
ACTION  new SpeedEvt(p2.userID, p2.pos, speed)
```

For each pair of position events $p1$ and $p2$, it is computed how much time passed between the two events, which can easily be calculated as all events carry a timestamp indicating their time of occurrence. The speed is then calculated dividing the geographical distance of position events $p1$ and $p2$ through the elapsed time. The calculated speed is passed on in form of a newly constructed *speed event*.

Based on the speed measurements of the last 5 min, the user's average speed is inferred. If the average speed is greater than 0, the user has been moving.

```
rule: "user movement"
CONDITION SpeedEvt AS s
    AND avg(s.speed).within(5 min) AS avgSpeed
    AND avgSpeed > 0
ACTION  new MovingEvt(s.userID, s.pos, avgSpeed)
```

The avg-Operator calculates the average value of the given speed measurements. In the action part of the rule, a new moving event is created that contains the user's ID, position, and the calculated average speed.

Finally, on arrival of a *moving event*, the following rule calculates the user's geographical distance to each station and translates it (by division through avgSpeed) into the corresponding temporal distance. If the temporal distance d lies below a certain threshold value, the user and the station are considered near to each other, which is indicated by a respective proximity event.

```
rule: "proximity detection"
CONDITION MovingEvt AS m
    AND Geo.distance(m.pos, station.pos)/m.avgSpeed AS d
    AND d < TIME_THRESHOLD
ACTION  new ProximityEvt(m.userID, station.ID)
```

If the user has not been near to the station before, the UA informs the station's SA about the user's proximity with an *EnteredAreaEvent*. Then, the SA makes an autonomous decision whether to offer an incentive to the user in an attempt to modify his cycling route. If a sufficiently high number of users can be convinced to return their bikes at appropriate stations, an increased service level is expected.

4.3   Prototypical Implementation

To try out the approach, we built a simulation of the BSS of New York City, based on data that is openly available online[2]. Figure 4 shows the graphical user interface of the simulation, which displays the stations of the BSS, which serve as starting and end points for bike trips. The station coordinates and capacities, as well as the users' trips, are directly extracted from the dataset. The simulation generates position events for the simulated users of the system, as well as events for rentals and returns.

---

[2] www.citibikenyc.com/system-data (Accessed: 2017-09-20).

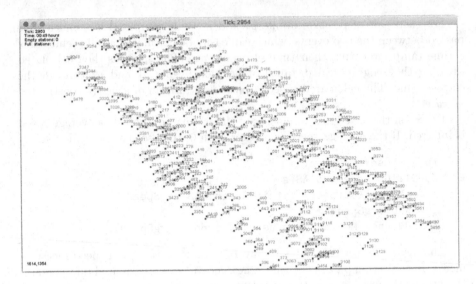

Fig. 4. Simulation of the bike sharing system of New York City

With this simulation, we tested a basic prototype of the rebalancing system. We implemented a simplified version of the UA and SA using the Jason agent framework [2]. In our test setup, the agents run centralized on the same computer and operate on the data that is provided by the simulator. The agent's behavior is programmed with Jason's variant of the AgentSpeak language.

5   Conclusion

In this paper, we have introduced EAs as a novel concept that allows BDI agents to operate in environments with high volumes of fast and low-level sensor data. The three-step percept analysis process consisting of the steps filtering, context enrichment, and situation detection allows the EA to reduce event streams to a manageable size, increase its informative value, and to extract high-level situations. Situations are domain-relevant concepts that are translated to a set of percepts that the BDI agent can sense. The BDI agent is responsible for acting in the environment. Due to the enhanced perception, the BDI agent can base its decisions on situational knowledge rather than raw sensor events. In particular is the action based on knowledge detected in event patterns consisting of multiple events, which would have been lost without the use of an advanced event processing paradigm like CEP.

In a case study, we have shown how EA can be used to realize a dynamic rebalancing of bike sharing systems based on user and station agents. The event-driven approach allows for a decentralized solution based on autonomous agents that can react rapidly to situations occurring in the bike sharing system.

In this paper, we applied CEP to detect patterns in the event stream of environment percepts. In the current EA architecture, messages from other agents are directly exchanged between the embedded BDI agents. Future work could model agent communication as an event stream to process agent messages with CEP. Furthermore, in the current architecture, the integration of BDI and CEP takes place in the CEP-to-BDI component. A stronger and more powerful interplay of the BDI model and CEP could potentially be achieved by constructing a new language that integrates the known BDI concepts and the advanced event processing capabilities of CEP.

References

1. Agüero, J., Rebollo, M., Carrascosa, C., Julián, V.: Agent reactive capabilities in dynamic environments. Neurocomputing **163**, 69–75 (2015)
2. Bordini, R.H., Hübner, J.F., Wooldridge, M.: Programming multi-agent systems in AgentSpeak using Jason, vol. 8. Wiley (2007)
3. Buford, J., Jakobson, G., Lewis, L.: Extending BDI multi-agent systems with situation management. In: 2006 9th International Conference on Information Fusion, pp. 1–7, July 2006
4. Contardo, C., Morency, C., Rousseau, L.-M.: Balancing a dynamic public bike-sharing system. Technical report, CIRRELT, March 2012
5. Cugola, G., Margara, A.: Processing flows of information: from data stream to complex event processing. ACM Comput. Surv. **44**(3), 15:1–15:62 (2012)
6. Dötterl, J., Bruns, R., Dunkel, J., Ossowski, S.: Towards dynamic rebalancing of bike sharing systems: an event-driven agents approach. In: Oliveira, E., Gama, J., Vale, Z., Lopes Cardoso, H. (eds.) EPIA 2017. LNCS (LNAI), vol. 10423, pp. 309–320. Springer, Cham (2017). https://doi.org/10.1007/978-3-319-65340-2_26
7. Ronnie, L., Johansson, M., Xiong, N.: Perception management: an emerging concept for information fusion. Inf. Fusion **4**(3), 231–234 (2003)
8. Luckham, D.: The Power of Events: An Introduction to Complex Event Processing in Distributed Enterprise Systems. Addison-Wesley, Boston (2002)
9. Omicini, A.: Event-based vs. multi-agent systems: Towards a unified conceptual framework. In: 2015 IEEE 19th International Conference on Computer Supported Cooperative Work in Design (CSCWD), pp. 1–6, May 2015
10. Rao, A.S.: AgentSpeak(L): BDI agents speak out in a logical computable language. In: Van de Velde, W., Perram, J.W. (eds.) MAAMAW 1996. LNCS, vol. 1038, pp. 42–55. Springer, Heidelberg (1996). https://doi.org/10.1007/BFb0031845
11. Rodriguez, S., Gaud, N., Galland, S.: SARL: a general-purpose agent-oriented programming language. In: The 2014 IEEE/WIC/ACM International Conference on Intelligent Agent Technology. IEEE Computer Society Press, Warsaw (2014)
12. Stojanovic, N., Artikis, A.: On complex event processing for real-time situational awareness. In: Bassiliades, N., Governatori, G., Paschke, A. (eds.) RuleML 2011. LNCS, vol. 6826, pp. 114–121. Springer, Heidelberg (2011). https://doi.org/10.1007/978-3-642-22546-8_10
13. Teymourian, K., Rohde, M., Paschke, A.: Fusion of background knowledge and streams of events. In: Proceedings of the 6th ACM International Conference on Distributed Event-Based Systems, DEBS 2012, pp. 302–313. ACM, New York (2012)
14. Weyns, D., Steegmans, E., Holvoet, T.: A model for active perception in situated multi-agent systems. In: Proceedings of the First European Workshop on Multiagent Systems (EUMAS 2003) (2003)
15. Wooldridge, M.: An Introduction to MultiAgent Systems. Wiley (2002)

Station Status Forecasting Module for a Multi-agent Proposal to Improve Efficiency on Bike-Sharing Usage

C. Diez[1]([✉]) [iD], V. Sanchez-Anguix[2,3,4] [iD], J. Palanca[1] [iD], V. Julian[1] [iD], and A. Giret[1] [iD]

[1] Dpto. Sistemas Informáticos y Computación, Universitat Politècnica de València, València, Spain
{cardieal,jpalanca,vinglada,agiret}@dsic.upv.es
[2] School of Computing, Electronics, and Maths, Coventry University, Coventry, UK
ac0872@coventry.ac.uk
[3] Florida Universitaria, Catarroja, Spain
[4] Universidad Isabel I, Burgos, Spain
victor.sanchez.anguix@ui1.es
http://www.gti-ia.upv.es

Abstract. Urban transportation involves a number of common problems: air and acoustic pollution, traffic jams, and so forth. This has become an important topic of study due to the interest in solving these issues in different areas (economical, social, ecological, etc.). Nowadays, one of the most popular urban transport systems are the shared vehicles systems. Among these systems there are the shared bicycle systems which have an special interest due to its characteristics. While solving some of the problems mentioned above, these systems also arise new problems such as the distribution of bicycles over time and space. Traditional approaches rely on the service provider to balancing the system, thus generating extra costs. Our proposal consists on an multi-agent system that includes user actions as a balancing mechanism, taking advantage of their trips to optimize the overall balance of the system. With this goal in mind the user is persuaded to deviate slightly from its origin/destination by providing appropriate arguments and incentives. This article presents the prediction module that will enable us to create such persuasive system. This module allow us to predict the demand for bicycles in the stations, forecasting the number of available parking spots (or available bikes). With this information the multi-agent system is capable of scoring alternative stations and routes and making offers to balance bikes across the stations. In order to achieve this, the most proper offers for the user will be predicted and used to persuade her.

Keywords: Multi-agent systems · Vehicle sharing systems

F. Belardinelli and E. Argente (Eds.): EUMAS 2017/AT 2017, LNAI 10767, pp. 476–489, 2018.
https://doi.org/10.1007/978-3-030-01713-2_33

1   Introduction

The Artificial Intelligence community has focused an important part of its efforts in the transportation domain. The interest in this domain is explainable due to the characteristics and complexity of the challenges provided, which are difficult to solve by making use of more traditional techniques. The application of Artificial Intelligence paradigms allows to deal with these problems [2,3,14,16].

As population in cities tends to grow, the need for an urban transport that is able to cope with the demand of inhabitants is an important need to cover [7]. However, the growth of urban transport generates a series of well known problems: large expenditure on creating new infrastructure or adapting and maintaining existent ones, air pollution, acoustic contamination, increase in the number of vehicles, etc. [7]. Because of this, optimizing transportation resources has become an area of great interest for the sectors involved in urban planning. One of the most interesting solutions proposed for urban transportation is the idea of shared vehicles systems. This kind of systems, such as bicycle or car sharing systems, reduces or helps to control intrinsically some of the mentioned problems. Nevertheless, shared vehicles schemes generate new problems. For instance, in the case of bike-sharing vehicles, one of the most important problems is the vehicle distribution along time and space across the different areas. Being used by multiple users, bikes locations depends on their behaviour. User behaviour creates some areas, at specific points in time, that hoard the majority of the bikes. Thus, generating also other areas with a lack of bikes. In the first case, users have difficulties parking to end their trips, while in the second case users have problems borrowing a bike to start their trips. These situations oblige users to wait or find another station, leading to potential dissatisfaction which can also result in a loss of service subscribers and, therefore, an increase in the use of non-shared vehicles. From the point of view of the service providers, bike imbalance across the stations incurs in additional expenses since they have to balance bikes using motorized transport, which means additional costs on vehicles, fuel, and extra staff. Furthermore, if the balance is done improperly this expenses can grow and may generate more traffic in the system.

The problem of optimizing bike sharing systems' resources (i.e., bikes, stations, transportation trucks) has caught the attention of researchers [10,13, 18,20], who have proposed many architectures and algorithms that allow service providers to both predict the incoming/outgoing demand from bike sharing stations, as well as educated balancing strategies that optimize the service provider's resources. All of these proposals are pieces of a global strategy that aims to smartly balance bikes according to future demand. All of the actions and strategies are applied from a service provider perspective, while taking the user behaviour as granted. This means that resources are optimized by modelling the user behaviour, and accepting that behaviour as an external effect that will change the system. As a result, actions aiming at balancing the state of the system are solely carried out by the service provider. This paper takes a slightly different point of view to this problem. What if, instead of taking the

user behaviour for granted, we attempt to slightly modify the user's planned trip
for optimizing the overall bike sharing system?

The paper defines the design of the *bikes and parking availability prediction module* which is an essential component for the proper functioning of a
multi-agent system architecture described on [6]. This multi-agent system aims
to improve the efficiency of bike sharing systems by predicting the future demand
and smartly balancing bikes across stations. In order to achieve this goal, it
introduces user-driven balancing in the loop by means of negotiation and argumentation processes [5,15] that slightly modify the behaviour of users.

2   A General MAS Proposal for Bike Sharing

Our aim is providing a module capable of forecasting the future status of the
stations in the bike-sharing system: predicting the number of free parking slots
that stations will have in the future. This prediction is necessary to efficiently
manage resources (i.e, bikes, stations, transportation trucks, etc.) and it will be
used in a multi-agent system proposed and described in [6]. Due to the nature
of cities and their lifestyle, bikes and parking slots become unequally distributed
across the bike-sharing system stations. This unbalance creates situations where
users do not find available bikes when they decide to start their trips, and there
are no available parking slots when users reach their destinations. Avoiding these
situations is an essential part of optimizing the bike-sharing systems. For dealing
with this problem, service providers redistribute the amount of bikes in the
stations using transportation trucks. However, this redistribution takes some
time, and if its not done when appropriate, it may end up in user dissatisfaction.
Therefore, the real challenge for service providers is predicting future demand
and redistribute bikes accordingly.

Balancing operations carried out by the service provider will always be an
integral part of a bike sharing system, specially for preparing for rush hour.
However, in some scenarios we may be able to employ users as balancing agents,
if individuals are persuaded to slightly deviate[1] from their planned destina-
tion/origin. The reasons, by which these users may be persuaded, vary and
include arguments such as the fact that their destination station may be full at
arrival, the adoption of healthier habits, or the inclusion of small rewards (e.g.,
extra rental minutes, badges, lotteries, etc.). Small deviations can act in benefit
of the system by carrying out pre/after rush hour balancing, and acting as real
time balance for unplanned demands.

In order to tackle this scenario, we propose a multi-agent based architecture.
The proposed system will run on top of *SURF* [4], an agent support framework
for open fleet management. The work we are presenting in this paper is part of
a broader research project, in which the main goal is to provide a set of tools
and applications that foster the efficient and sustainable management of urban
fleets. One of such applications is the one presented in [8] for last mile delivery
in urban areas.

---

[1] We would never expect drastic deviations.

$SURF$ was designed to support general urban transportation fleets, and it provides modules for most general and shared functionalities. As a result, part of the proposed architecture is supported by these general modules such as the fleet tracker module, the event processing module, the trust and reputation module, the transportation network analysis module, and the intelligent transportation ontology [6]. However, we need to include some extra modules to support part of the functionalities of this bike sharing system. The two main components that distinguish our approach to bike sharing are: **The Efficient Bike Trip Module** and the **Bikes and Parking Availability Prediction Module** whose design is the main contribution of this article.

Both the **Bikes and Parking Availability Prediction Module** and the **Efficient Bike Trip Module** will support how users' trips are managed. In order to understand the logic behind the module, let us focus on an example:

1. $User_1$ agent wants to ride from $PreferredBikeStation_x$ to $Preferred$ $BikeStation_y$. The user employs a mobile app to query the availability of bikes at the origin station, and the availability of slots in the destination station.
2. The request is received by the System Manager agent, and then it is analyzed to find out the availability by the time $User_1$ agent may arrive to both preferred origin and destination stations. The expected times are calculated taking into consideration the current GPS location of $User_1$ agent, the possible route that leads to the origin station, the possible route that leads to the destination station, and all the information from the Intelligent Transportation Ontology from SURF concerning traffic, traffic lights, weather, and so forth.
3. With this time frame the System Manager agent requests to the **Bikes and Parking Availability Prediction Module** an estimation for the number of free bikes at $PreferredBikeStation_x$ by the expected departure time. At the same time, the System Manager agent also requests an estimation for the number of free parking slots at $PreferredBikeStation_y$ by the expected arrival time.
4. The
prediction module also computes whether or not $PreferredBikeStation_x$ or $PreferredBikeStation_y$ are likely to suffer from bikes/slots shortage in the short/medium term. In that case, the prediction module retrieves a set of available nearby stations to $PreferredBikeStation_x$ and a set of available nearby stations to $PreferredBikeStation_y$. If they are not likely to suffer from bikes/slots shortage in the short term, then they are also suggested to the System Manager agent.
5. The System Manager agent collects the suggestions from the **Bikes and Parking Availability Prediction Module** and sends those suggestions to the **Efficient Bike Trip Module**. Within this module, the alternatives for both origin and destination are analyzed. The module will select pairs of origin and destination stations, along with arguments or incentives in favor of the slight trip change.

6. The System Manager agent receives the offers from the **Efficient Bike Trip Module** and presents them to the user, who finally selects the one that he/she considers more appealing.

In this paper we introduce the **Bikes and Parking Availability Prediction Module**. The module will predict the occupation of the stations using a machine learning model. The design of this module, and the features that will be used to train the model are described on Sect. 3. The predictions provided by the prediction module for the user's preferred and alternative stations will be passed to the **Efficient Bike Trip Module**. This module, using the bike/slot availability predictions will score the stations taking into account both balancing objectives and potential user preferences. These scores, and the user's behavior model provided by the trust and reputation module, will be used to generate the arguments or incentives for the user.

More specifically, we focus on developing and finding prediction models for bike availability at different stations in Valencia's bike sharing system, our test scenario. This module is the cornerstone to the application of Bike Sharing in Urban Areas, as its outputs are needed to compute the availability of preferred and nearby stations. These stations are later used as building blocks for building arguments in the **Efficient Bike Trip Module**.

3   Prediction Module Design

In order to achieve an appropriate overall performance, we need to obtain an accurate model that estimates the number of empty parking slots[2] for a station in a future time. Since we can use historical data to model users behavior, we are facing a regression problem. Machine learning algorithms have consistently proven to provide accurate regressions for a wide variety of domains [9,12,19]. Hence, we decided to approach this problem by considering two of the most successful machine learning regression algorithms: support vector regression (SVR) [1], and artificial neural networks (ANN) [17]. Given the restriction of 30 min per trip that is established by the service provider, we decided to formulate a regression problem where, given the current state of a station and associated weather variables at that instant, we attempt to predict the number of bikes in the station in the next 30 min.

3.1   Case Study and Data

To design the prediction module, and prove its viability, we employed a real dataset containing bike usage in a large city. We decided to use Valencia's bike sharing system as a case study due to the data access availability, the scale of the system, the interconnection of the bicycle sharing systems with other transport systems, and access to domain expertise.

---

[2] Equivalent to predicting the number of available bikes, as it can be obtained by subtracting the empty parking slots from the total number of slots.

Valencia's bike sharing system is composed of 276 bike stations distributed throughout the city, whose aggregated capacity is 5000 parking slots. There is a total of 2750 bikes available to borrow for the 45.000 users. The data used to test our proposal was collected mainly from two sources: the city's open data repository[3] and a weather information service provider[4]. The first dataset contains the number of available parking slots at the different stations at approximate intervals of approximately one minute. The second dataset contains a variety of weather variables taken approximately every 30 min. After thoroughly studying the characteristics of the city and the system in [6], we concluded that the more suitable characteristics for the prediction module are the following:

- **Date:** Date is an essential feature, since it determines the moment in which the measurement was taken. It also provides other intrinsic information such as season or time of the year. It also helps to determine events that are fixed in the calendar and can influence in the use of the system like holidays.
- **Weekday:** The day of the week is one of the most influential features when modeling user's behavior. For instance, there is a clear difference between working days and weekend days. In addition, there is also a slight difference between working days themselves, being the users a little more active in middle days of the week.
- **Temperature:** Temperature usually affects human behavior. Therefore we made the hypothesis that in this scenario it would be a relevant feature when modeling the problem. When temperature is too low or too high for human comfort, the system usage decreases.
- **Rain & wind speed:** Similarly to the case of temperature, other weather conditions can affect the amount of users using bikes, being rain and wind speed two of the most influential characteristics. This is the case because the rain and the wind speed are two of the most influential weather related characteristics since both directly affect in the ease and comfort when driving a bicycle.
- **Number of available parking slots in the station:** In order to make a future prediction on the availability of the station, one needs to have an accurate measurement of the current status of the station.

3.2 Experiment Design

At first we ran an experiment in order to determine if the chosen variables were actually influential for the prediction model. We observed the model behavior and MSE while adding the features one at time. As seen in Fig. 1 all the characteristics improve the model's performance. Weekday and the current status of the stations are the variables that reduces the MSE in a more noticeable way since they are common to all the cases. Weather related characteristics are essential to forecast the station status when the conditions are not the usual. In our

---

[3] http://gobiernoabierto.valencia.es/en/.
[4] http://www.weatherunderground.com.

case study weather characteristics offer a lower improvement compared to week-day or current station status because the number of days with precipitations or uncomfortable temperatures is low in comparison.

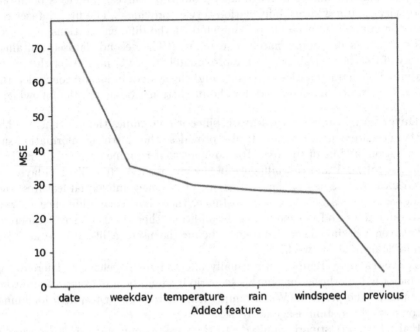

Fig. 1. Feature influence on MSE

Once we had determined what variables may be useful for our prediction module, we prepared an experimental setup to test the accuracy of different machine learning models. First, we describe the general settings for the experiments. Then we describe and analyze how hyper-parameters were optimized for machine learning algorithms. Finally, we analyze the performance of the best models on the test data.

The dataset was divided in two parts: the training and the test dataset. The training dataset was exclusively used as a testbed for hyper-parameter tuning. Then, the performance of the best hyper-parameters was tested against the test set to assess the performance of the models in a realistic setting. Since the quality of the resulting model depends on the quantity and quality of the training dataset, 80% of the total data was employed as training, while the remaining 20% was left for testing purposes. This means that the final performance of the models was tested with approximately three months of data, amount that should be sufficient enough to ensure meaningful results. The test set consisted of the last three months of available data. As for measuring the performance of the model, we employed the average mean squared error (MSE).

3.3 Hyper-parameter Optimization

Due to computational limitations, the fine tuning process was exclusively carried out in a single bike station: *UPV Informática*. The methodology employed for finding the best model hyper-parameters was a grid search over the space of possible values. Following, we describe the hyper-parameter space for each of the selected machine learning algorithms.

- **Support Vector Regression:** We decided to employ a radial basis function kernel in order to model non-linear relationships between the input variables. For the penalty error parameter (C), we tested values in the range of 10^{-5} and 10^4 with increases in powers of base 10. γ was set between the range of 10^{-5} and 10^4, again increasing exponentially with base 10.
- **Artificial Neural Networks:** A 3 hidden-layer topology with ReLU activation functions was chosen for study, the last layer being the only one with a linear activation function. The neurons in each hidden layer varied exponentially from 8 to 2048 with a base of 2. On the other hand, the learning rate of the network also exponentially varied between 10^{-7} and 0.1, but this time the base being 10. Either stochastic gradient descent or RMSProp were employed to optimize the weights of the network.

The best artificial neural network was found to be a 3 hidden layers network with 64 nodes per hidden layer. The best learning rate was found to be 0.01, with smaller learning rates providing almost constant predictions for any input (i.e., a sign that the network does not learn any pattern due to a slow convergence) and larger learning rates providing totally inaccurate predictions. The best network optimizer was found to be RMSProp. With respect to the support vector regression, we found that the optimal value for the penalty error was 10^4, while the best value for γ was found to be 10^{-5}. In general, we found that artificial neural networks tended to produce more accurate predictions than support vector regressions. Detailed results for the grid search can be found in Tables 1 and 2.

3.4 Test Results

Once we had two candidate models, we employed the test set to realistically assess the performance of the models in a deployed application. This time, instead of focusing on a sole station, we trained several stations coming from different city districts. This way, we can better study the accuracy of the models in a realistic setting. In addition to these models, we also introduced two benchmarks for comparability purposes. One of the benchmarks outputs the average number of bikes available in that station throughout history, whereas the other benchmark always outputs the current state of the station as a prediction. If trained correctly, both our models should outperform the benchmarks.

Table 3 shows the results obtained by the four prediction models using the test set. Those results that are statistically better according to a Mann-Whitney test with $\alpha = 0.05$ are highlighted with bold font. As it can be observed, the

Table 1. Results for the grid search carried out for RMSProp optimized neural networks. The best result is highlighted in bold font

Neurons/lr	1.0E−01	1.0E−02	1.0E−03	1.0E−04	1.0E−05	1.0E−06	1.0E−07
8	79.26	11.97	5.15	5.25	5.45	74.21	705.14
16	74.99	9.52	5.01	5.01	5.42	72.13	675.10
32	76.71	8.70	4.20	5.70	4.96	42.26	499.00
64	78.26	14.05	**3.54**	3.81	4.99	6.01	75.64
128	76.43	76.13	5.69	4.69	4.95	5.38	74.18
256	79.36	13.63	5.28	3.71	4.80	5.04	72.64
512	77.31	11.54	5.17	4.33	5.29	5.04	28.38
1024	77.29	11.57	4.40	5.86	4.55	5.28	6.86
2048	75.74	11.54	4.32	4.23	3.99	6.55	5.31

Table 2. Results for the grid search carried out for support vector regression. The best result is highlighted in bold font

C/γ	1.00E−05	1.00E−04	1.00E−03	1.00E−02	1.00E−01	1.00E+00	1.00E+01	1.00E+02	1.00E+03	1.00E+04
1.00E−05	148.40	148.40	148.39	148.34	148.40	148.40	148.40	115.47	115.47	115.47
1.00E−04	148.40	148.40	148.32	147.73	147.12	122.89	115.47	115.47	115.47	115.47
1.00E−03	148.40	148.33	147.55	140.80	135.27	122.29	115.47	115.47	115.47	115.47
1.00E−02	148.30	147.44	140.12	148.34	73.27	116.42	115.46	115.47	115.47	115.47
1.00E−01	147.35	139.15	77.87	27.75	20.45	84.46	115.42	115.47	115.47	115.47
1.00E+00	139.10	148.39	38.03	144.32	14.77	24.05	104.86	115.47	115.47	115.47
1.00E+01	86.27	22.52	279.17	79.11	14.38	18.58	75.89	102.00	115.47	115.47
1.00E+02	22.67	26.16	812.06	35.38	24.93	25.80	89.11	123.14	136.49	136.63
1.00E+03	32.55	21.27	77.22	87.01	42.44	31.40	89.11	123.14	136.49	136.63
1.00E+04	**5.10**	18.66	154.04	301.69	138.33	31.20	89.11	123.14	84.23	84.21

artificial neural network tends to outperform the rest of the models in almost every station tested. More specifically, the artificial neural network was the best choice for 16 out of the 19 stations (approx. 84% of the stations). The support vector regression was one of the best choices for only 8 of the stations, accounting for 42% of the scenarios. In none of the scenarios the benchmarks produced better predictions than the two machine learning models. This information is also represented in Table 4, where the relative improvement of the machine learning models versus the benchmarks are compared. As it is observed, the ANN model improves the predictions of the benchmark that predicts the current status by 16.51%, the benchmark that predicts the average bike availability by 63%, and the SVR model by 10.05%. Overall, it is the best performing model in these scenarios.

However, it should be noted that in some cases the prediction of the machine learning models and the benchmark that outputs the current state of the station are close. This suggests that some stations may require different hyperparameters to distance their outputs from benchmarks. As another sidenote, we observed that, in some stations, there is very little activity throughout the day.

Table 3. Mean squared error for the four prediction models across different stations in the city

Station	ANN	SVR	Current	Average
City hall - Cotanda	**6.01**	8.07	7.80	19.22
Colon station	**5.50**	**5.49**	6.60	13.86
Porta de la Mar	**5.80**	6.75	6.79	17.39
Plaza de los Fueros	8.08	**7.15**	8.50	18.54
Peris y Valero - Luis Santangel	**4.05**	5.01	4.67	9.33
Av. Puerto - Dr. Manuel Candela	**4.83**	**4.81**	5.44	7.35
Av. Puerto - Jose Aguilar	**2.89**	2.96	3.16	5.28
Molinell - Calderon de la Barca	**2.34**	3.16	2.59	10.63
Blasco Ibañez - Poeta Duran Tortajada	6.05	**5.72**	9.11	10.67
Blasco Ibañez, 121	**4.39**	**4.34**	5.42	8.29
UPV Caminos	**11.59**	15.03	13.74	31.46
UPV Informãtica	**3.82**	5.10	5.52	25.46
Benimaclet station	**5.49**	6.73	6.82	7.31
Turia station	**1.34**	1.43	1.41	21.76
Manuel Candela - Rodriguez de Cepeda	**4.53**	**4.60**	5.45	10.82
Reig Genovés - Ramón Contreras Mongrell	**1.70**	2.11	1.96	11.76
Hospital Nueva Fe	**3.16**	4.70	5.94	32.63
Giorgeta, 64	**1.29**	**1.28**	1.39	6.92
Veles e Vents	3.57	**3.53**	3.73	8.76

This means that a benchmark that outputs the current state of the stations, is also likely to produce accurate results many times. It will only produce inaccurate predictions in the few instants when a bike arrives or leaves the station.

Table 4. Relative improvement of model (rows) versus benchmark (columns)

VS.	Current	Average	SVR
ANN	16.51%	63.05%	10.05
SVR	6.09%	59.47%	N/A

Table 3 shows the MSE for different stations distributed across the city. Despite the fact that lower MSEs indicate more accurate predictions, they are not very informative of the practical quality of the best predictive model per se. Therefore, we decided to plot the prediction of our ANN model against the target value for a given day. Figure 2 shows this comparison.

The figure suggests that, in both cases, the ANN model is capable of closely matching the real bike demand. This happens for most of the day, even matching some of the peaks in the bike demand. However, there are some sudden peaks that are not as closely matched as the rest. This suggests that some of the peaks may be accounted by other variables not necessarily included in our dataset.

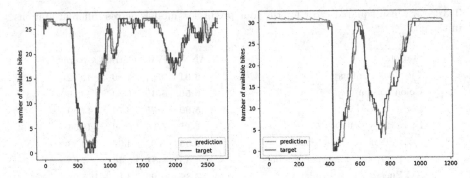

Fig. 2. Prediction of the ANN model versus the target value for the City hall - Cotanda station (left) and UPV Informática (right).

For instance, transportation trucks balance bikes across stations, information that is not included in open access datasets. This problem is also documented in other similar works [10,20]. We are currently working on including more data sources to attempt to better predict some of these sudden outbursts of activity. For instance, we are including data about sport and music events, national, regional, and local holidays, and nearby transportation methods.

Overall, the experiments suggest that ANN is the best current candidate for predicting the bike demand in Valencia, Spain. The predictions also closely match the real demand. This is of crucial importance for our multi-agent system, since, as we described in Sect. 2, the prediction module is the base for the argumentation & negotiation module. We expect that this module will allow us to incentivize users and make them balancing agents that optimize the overall performance of the system.

4   Related Work

Intelligent transportation systems have captured the attention of the AI research community in the last few years. The scale and complexity of the problems faced by the transportation system preclude simple and classic solutions from achieving the desired outcomes, hence the necessity to adopt AI approaches. As a consequence, multiple areas in AI have proposed solutions to different transportation problems. In the specific field of multi-agent systems, the number of papers devoted to applications in traffic and transportation engineering has grown enormously. Bazzan and Klügl [3] present a literature review related to the areas of agent-based traffic modelling and simulation, and agent-based traffic control and management applied to different problems.

Focusing on the domain of bike-sharing systems, we find two main problems that have been tackled by the AI research community: (i) predicting the bike/parking availability, and (ii) optimizing the transportation routing used to balance the bikes/parking positions across stations.

The first problem consists of predicting the number of available bikes and parking positions in the future. The rationale behind this is that, in order to improve the service given by bike sharing systems, users should be able to borrow and leave a bike when needed. Otherwise, users may become dissatisfied with the service and decide to use other transportation methods. The data mining community has made several efforts in this regard. Yoon et al. [20] propose prediction algorithms to predict the number of available bikes at origin and destination stations in Dublin's bike sharing system. The authors propose a modification of the ARIMA model to include information from neighboring stations along with the classic temporal information. The authors trained and tested their approach using approximately 1 month of data per process. While the authors employ important variables such as the available data in neighbor stations, they do not include other well-known factors that impact the usage of bikes such as weather data, nor they account for longer term seasonality such as seasons (e.g., summer, winter, etc.). Li et al. [11] proposed a multilayer data mining approach to predict bike traffic (i.e., bikes in transit) in New York City and Washington D.C.. In their approach, bike sharing stations are clustered together according to both geo-location and transit matrices. The advantage of employing clustering techniques to group stations is that predicting the traffic demand on the overall system and clusters is more robust and accurate than on individual stations. The multilayer approach first predicts overall traffic by using gradient boosted regression trees, and then distributes the overall traffic across cluster according to similarity between past and current data. Finally, the traffic between clusters is also predicted according to historic data. Differently to us, they possess bike trips information (i.e, bike id, origin, destination) whereas our dataset is solely composed by the current state of stations. That preclude us from employing the same approach. In [10], present bike/parking availability data combined with weather data for 27 cities across the globe (including Valencia, Spain). The authors analyze the correlation between weather data and bike demand, and find correlations between temperature, wind velocity, and precipitation with the demand of bikes in different cities. The paper does not propose any prediction mechanism per se, but it finds interesting effects on the bike demand, such as the effect of weather conditions, that are present in Valencia and other cities of the world.

The other main strand in research revolves around the idea of optimizing the routes and trips of the vehicles that balance bikes across the different stations. Given the nature of the problem, many researches have proposed the used of search & optimization techniques for this purpose. For instance, O'Mahony and Shmoys employ integer programming to balance bikes overnight, preparing them for rush time, and mid-rush balancing in New York City. As another example, Schuijbroek et al. [18] present a system that both predicts station demand and balances bikes attending to expected demand and desirable service levels. For prediction, authors rely on queues models and Markov chains using arrival and departure data from Boston and Washington. Due to the intractable nature of the routing problem when the number of stations is large, the authors cluster stations together so that service levels are guaranteed using only within-cluster routing. Then, mixed integer programming is used over the clustered problem.

All of these system rely on prediction and optimization from the system designer perspective. The main difference between these approaches and our proposed architecture is that we rely on both a combination of optimization from the system designer, but also from the user perspective. In order to incorporate the users' actions into the optimization loop, we plan to use technologies such as incentives, persuasion [5], and negotiation [15].

5   Conclusions

This paper has presented the design of the *bikes and parking availability prediction module*, which is key for the multi agent system architecture described in [6]. The prediction module uses a machine learning approach to forecast bike station status based on real historic data. The information generated by this module is crucial for the system, and it is used in other modules to score the user's preferred and alternative stations attending to availability. Using this data we will introduce user-driven balancing in the loop: attempting to persuade users to slightly deviate from their origin/destination stations, and balancing the system in the process. The aim is that of improving the efficiency of bike-sharing systems and helping to provide a better service, increase user satisfaction, and optimize the management of the bike network.

Results have shown that a ANN obtained the best results for this prediction module, as it was showcased in the experimental section of this work. Moreover the experiments have shown that this approach is feasible and accurate.

As ongoing work, the *efficient bike trip module* is being built to be included in the bike sharing system of the city of Valencia (Spain). This module function inside the proposed architecture is to score stations using the *bikes and parking availability prediction module* output. Using this scores the module persuades the user to use the most appropriate stations according to the user preferences and the system balancing. Moreover, the proposed approach will be integrated with other applications running on top of the *SURF* framework, such as [8].

References

1. Basak, D., Pal, S., Patranabis, D.C.: Support vector regression. Neural Inf. Proc. Lett. Rev. **11**(10), 203–224 (2007)
2. Bast, H., et al.: Route planning in transportation networks. In: Kliemann, L., Sanders, P. (eds.) Algorithm Engineering. LNCS, vol. 9220, pp. 19–80. Springer, Cham (2016). https://doi.org/10.1007/978-3-319-49487-6_2
3. Bazzan, A.L., Klügl, F.: A review on agent-based technology for traffic and transportation. Knowl. Eng. Rev. **29**(03), 375–403 (2014)
4. Billhardt, H., et al.: Towards smart open dynamic fleets. In: Rovatsos, M., Vouros, G., Julian, V. (eds.) EUMAS/AT -2015. LNCS (LNAI), vol. 9571, pp. 410–424. Springer, Cham (2016). https://doi.org/10.1007/978-3-319-33509-4_32

5. Costa, A., Heras, S., Palanca, J., Jordán, J., Novais, P., Julián, V.: Argumentation schemes for events suggestion in an e-Health platform. In: de Vries, P.W., Oinas-Kukkonen, H., Siemons, L., Beerlage-de Jong, N., van Gemert-Pijnen, L. (eds.) PERSUASIVE 2017. LNCS, vol. 10171, pp. 17–30. Springer, Cham (2017). https://doi.org/10.1007/978-3-319-55134-0_2
6. Diez, C., Sanchez-Anguix, V., Palanca, J., Julian, V., Giret, A.: A multi-agent proposal for efficient bike-sharing usage. In: An, B., Bazzan, A., Leite, J., Villata, S., van der Torre, L. (eds.) PRIMA 2017. LNCS (LNAI), vol. 10621, pp. 468–476. Springer, Cham (2017). https://doi.org/10.1007/978-3-319-69131-2_29
7. Farahani, R.Z., Miandoabchi, E., Szeto, W., Rashidi, H.: A review of urban transportation network design problems. Eur. J. Oper. Res. **229**(2), 281–302 (2013). http://www.sciencedirect.com/science/article/pii/S0377221713000106
8. Giret, A., Carrascosa, C., Julian, V., Rebollo, M.: A crowdsourcing approach for last mile delivery. Emerging Technologies, Submitted to Transportation Research Part C (2017)
9. Hernández, E., Sanchez-Anguix, V., Julian, V., Palanca, J., Duque, N.: Rainfall prediction: a deep learning approach. In: Martínez-Álvarez, F., Troncoso, A., Quintián, H., Corchado, E. (eds.) HAIS 2016. LNCS (LNAI), vol. 9648, pp. 151–162. Springer, Cham (2016). https://doi.org/10.1007/978-3-319-32034-2_13
10. Kull, M., Ferri, C., Martínez-Usó, A.: Bike rental and weather data across dozens of cities. In: ICML 2015 Workshop on Demand Forecasting (2015)
11. Li, Y., Zheng, Y., Zhang, H., Chen, L.: Traffic prediction in a bike-sharing system. In: Proceedings of the 23rd SIGSPATIAL International Conference on Advances in Geographic Information Systems, p. 33. ACM (2015)
12. Ochando, L.C., Julián, C.I., Ochando, F.C., Ferri, C.: Airvlc: an application for real-time forecasting urban air pollution. In: Proceedings of the 2nd International Conference on Mining Urban Data, vol. 1392, pp. 72–79. CEUR-WS.org (2015)
13. O'Mahony, E., Shmoys, D.B.: Data analysis and optimization for (citi)bike sharing. In: Proceedings of the Twenty-Ninth AAAI Conference on Artificial Intelligence, AAAI 2015, pp. 687–694. AAAI Press (2015). http://dl.acm.org/citation.cfm?id=2887007.2887103
14. Rigas, E.S., Ramchurn, S.D., Bassiliades, N.: Managing electric vehicles in the smart grid using artificial intelligence: a survey. IEEE Trans. Intell. Transp. Syst. **16**(4), 1619–1635 (2015)
15. Sanchez-Anguix, V., Aydogan, R., Julian, V., Jonker, C.: Unanimously acceptable agreements for negotiation teams in unpredictable domains. Electron. Commer. Res. Appl. **13**(4), 243–265 (2014). http://www.sciencedirect.com/science/article/pii/S1567422314000283
16. Satunin, S., Babkin, E.: A multi-agent approach to intelligent transportation systems modeling with combinatorial auctions. Expert Syst. Appl. **41**(15), 6622–6633 (2014)
17. Schmidhuber, J.: Deep learning in neural networks: an overview. Neural Netw. **61**, 85–117 (2015)
18. Schuijbroek, J., Hampshire, R., van Hoeve, W.J.: Inventory rebalancing and vehicle routing in bike sharing systems. Eur. J. Oper. Res. **257**(3), 992–1004 (2017)
19. Ticknor, J.L.: A bayesian regularized artificial neural network for stock market forecasting. Expert Syst. Appl. **40**(14), 5501–5506 (2013)
20. Yoon, J.W., Pinelli, F., Calabrese, F.: Cityride: a predictive bike sharing journey advisor. In: IEEE 13th International Conference on Mobile Data Management (MDM), pp. 306–311. IEEE (2012)

Towards Robots-Assisted Ambient Intelligence

Marin Lujak[1]([✉])(iD), Noury Bouraqadi[1], Arnaud Doniec[1], Luc Fabresse[1],
Anthony Fleury[1](iD), Abir Karami[2], and Guillaume Lozenguez[1]

[1] IMT Lille Douai, Douai, France
{marin.lujak,noury.bouraqadi,arnaud.doniec,luc.fabresse,anthony.fleury,
guillaume.lozenguez}@imt-lille-douai.fr
[2] University of Lyon 2, LIRIS, Lyon, France

Abstract. An integrated network of mobile robots, personal smart
devices, and smart spaces called "Robots-Assisted Ambient Intelligence"
(RAmI) can provide for a more effective user assistance than if the former resources are used individually. Additionally, with the application of
distributed network optimization, not only can we improve the assistance
of an individual user, but we can also minimize conflict or congestion created when multiple users in large installations use the limited resources
of RAmI that are spatially and temporally constrained. The emphasis of
RAmI is on the efficiency and effectiveness of multiple and simultaneous
user assistance and on the influence of an individual's actions on the
desired system's performance. In this paper, we model RAmI as a multi-
agent system with AmI, user, and robot agents. Moreover, we propose
a modular three-layer architecture for each robot agent and discuss its
application and communication requirements to facilitate efficient usage
of limited RAmI resources. Our approach is showcased by means of a
case study where we focus on meal and medicine delivery to patients in
large hospitals.

Keywords: Service robotics · Ambient intelligence ·
Multi-robot team · Patient care

1 Introduction

Ambient Intelligence (AmI) uses multiple sensors fixed in a smart space to assist
user's activities through recommendation, guidance, and appliance control. However, the capabilities of physical interaction in AmI are limited to a tactile
interface, and many applications need physical interaction that is only possible through mobile robots. The service quality provided by mobile robot teams
(MRT) to simultaneous multiple users depends on the efficiency of the robots'
coordination with each other and with humans.

To keep a good MRT performance in simultaneous multiple tasks, an updated
task information is required. Even though the MRT quality of service depends on

© Springer Nature Switzerland AG 2018
F. Belardinelli and E. Argente (Eds.): EUMAS 2017/AT 2017, LNAI 10767, pp. 490–497, 2018.
https://doi.org/10.1007/978-3-030-01713-2_34

the quality of the available information that can be facilitated by maintaining the MRT connectivity [18], MRT task assignment can be performed both in perfect (e.g., [1,3]) and imperfect robot networks, e.g., [11]. Due to the loss in the information quality, the efficiency of a MRT in the task execution can fall rapidly, e.g., [11,12]. The strategy to employ to mitigate this problem depends also on the environment that can be collaborative, neutral, or adversarial [11,12]. Providing redundant robots to keep the network's connectivity is a possible approach to this problem. However, it is costly and can create congestion in narrow spaces. This is why, in this paper, we propose to network mobile robots, users' smart devices, and AmI networks, such that we can use more accurate data for decision-making than when the former are used individually. We call this network of AmI, personal devices, and robots "Robots-Assisted Ambient Intelligence (RAmI)". The emphasis of RAmI is on the quality of service in simultaneous multiple users' assistance and the influence of individual actions on the desired system's performance.

A good use-case example of RAmI is meal and medicine delivery to multiple patients in hospitals. The delivery should be done at given times for each patient while minimizing the crowdedness of the common spaces. By distributed network optimization in RAmI, not only can we improve the assistance of an individual patient, but we can also ensure that actions of multiple robots that are spatially and temporally constrained are coordinated in real-time and do not result in crowding of narrow corridors. To lower the computation time, we should balance between each robot's communication and computation load, but foremost, we should provide for a self-reconfigurable robot architecture that assures fast and efficient decision making at the MRT's level.

The recognition and analysis of the user's activities facilitates better user assistance in the performance of some daily activities like, e.g., vacuum cleaning [7]. For this aim, usually, smart homes are equipped with sensors, actuators and alarms while users dispose of smart devices for the interaction with the smart home. However, service robotics is still limited to a set of predefined activities and is, as such, still far away from the realization of robots that can substitute human care givers.

A step towards RAmI is the concept of ubiquitous robotics that is created by integrating stand-alone robots with web services and ambient intelligence technologies [6]. The main challenge of ubiquitous robotics is how to enhance the quality of living and working of an individual human user. The objective is the creation of a physical and virtual companion that can assist a user in his/her daily activities, and the creation of an autonomic guard capable to protect and rescue people. A distributed ROS-based AmI architecture DAmIA integrating robotic and AmI sensors for human tracking has been proposed in [15]. A survey of cloud robotics that leverages an ad-hoc cloud formed by communicating robots, and an infrastructure cloud was presented in [6]. Moreover, in [10], we proposed ORCAS architecture for manufacturing MRTs that configures and schedules robots based on robots' and tasks' semantic descriptions.

In ORCAS [10], we consider a heterogeneous multi-robot system on a shop-floor requiring the assembly of multiple products. Here, every robot is considered a collaborative agent whose architecture is made of three layers: semantic, scheduling and the execution layer. The objective is to seamlessly optimize robots' performance by dynamic reconfiguration and rescheduling in case of contingencies thus minimizing overall assembly costs and off-line times. Semantic layer finds feasible robots' configurations that can satisfy customer demand given the resource and infrastructure semantic descriptions. The scheduling layer determines robot-task assignments and sequencing of tasks assigned to each robot configuration considering task interrelations and the robot assembly capacities. The solution is found through distributed minimization of total production time and cost considering resource combinations obtained from the semantic layer. We apply a modification of dynamic combinatorial auction-based approach in [11]. The execution layer monitors the correct execution of the schedule in real-time by local actions to minimize the effects of contingencies. The schedule's quality and stability are controlled in real-time, e.g. [5].

The paper is organized as follows. Section 2 describes a modified three-layer robot architecture of RAmI for the case of a team of heterogeneous mobile service robots for assistance of multiple human users when the robot configuration cannot be rearranged during the operation times. The principles of the proposed architecture are demonstrated by means of a case study in Sect. 3. We draw conclusions in Sect. 4.

2   RAmI Robot Architecture

We design RAmI as a multi-agent system made of mobile robot, user, and AmI agents. User agents are installed on an app of a smart device of each user, while AmI agents are distributed throughout the infrastructure where each one monitors certain area in the range of its sensors. The sensors can be cameras and iBeacons. The signals emitted by iBeacon sensors are read by user agents and serve to locate the users and recognize their activities (aided by accelerometers of their smart devices).

The architecture used for the distributed coordination of robots in task assignment and routing is implemented in each one of the robots and is presented in Fig. 1. It contains semantic, scheduling and the execution layer. Contrary to ORCAS, in RAmI, we assume that robot configuration is fixed and that each robot's delivery capacity is limited by maximum item's weight and dimensions. Moreover, all resources and each item delivery are semantically described by a human operator: e.g., meal/medicine, time of delivery, weight, dimensions, and type of a meal/medicine. The semantic storage description contains the information of available items and their hospital locations.

In the semantic layer, a set of compatible robots for each patient demand is found by using a DL inference engine and SPARQL query language. Scheduling layer contains the task assignment and route planning module. Based on the semantically described delivery demand, each robot agent coordinates with

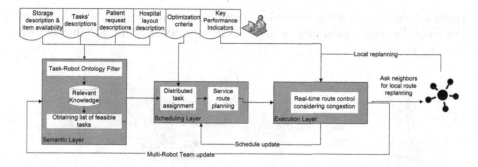

Fig. 1. Proposed RAmI architecture implemented in each robot

other robot agents for the task assignment through the bi-level task assignment algorithm in [9]. While MRT is responsible of the MRT task assignment, the AmI network is responsible of updating the travel times under congestion in the network and distributively optimizing robots' routes by using the route finding algorithm in [13]. Robots receive updated routes and travel times info from the closest AmI agent. In the execution layer, the individual performance is monitored in real time and in case of unpredicted events, a robot tries to coordinate locally with its neighbors to lower their impact. If the local coordination is inefficient, the scheduling layer recomputes the robots' routes. In the case of larger contingencies or the addition of robots that can improve the MRT's performance, RAmI architecture recomputes the routes starting from the semantic layer.

Except of route guidance, RAmI user assistance tasks may include, among others: encouraging physical activity, medical supervision, offering entertainment, maintaining social ties, item delivery (e.g., meal or a medicine) and assisting a user in the case of urgency. These activities should be coordinated based on priorities in the semantic layer of RAmI. We take different user and task requirements into account to find the best possible sequence of tasks. In the patient assistance context, the best sequence is the one that brings the best well-being of the patient. To achieve this goal, we propose a coordination approach involving two steps, Fig. 2. The first step consists in finding all the suitable and consistent sequences of tasks. However, some tasks are not compatible and cannot be performed at the same time. For example, simultaneous eating and medical assistance. Similarly, some sequences of activities are not desirable, as, e.g., two consecutive heavy physical activities. These requirements can be easily integrated by semantic matching and then a classical constraint programming approach to generate all the possible sequences.

In the second step, designing a mathematical program related with the well-being of a patient is a challenging task since it is related to a patient's physical condition, mental state, habits, and the context: time of day, location, etc. This is why the patient should be included in the decision-making preferably by learning his/her preferences according to rewards. These rewards could be awarded directly by the patient depending on the sequence of offered activities or by physiological measures. For example, an evening activity sequence that improves the patient's sleep would have a high reward and we may use a reinforcement learning approach.

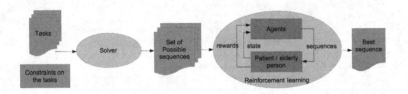

Fig. 2. Overview of the two-step coordination mechanism

Users can be considered as sources of relevant knowledge (Fig. 1). Such knowledge is needed in making adaptive and coherent decisions in the RAmI performance. To better assist patients and caregivers, robots should reply to requests that are declared explicitly or implicitly. In fact, users through their reactions and feedback are an important source of information on how to achieve tasks in an adaptive and personalized way (time to give medicine, route recommendation, etc.). Relatedly, in [4,16], implicit and explicit feedback are used to learn users' preferences in smart homes and for companion robots. Also, analyzing contradictions may help in detecting the need of a more representative model of the current environment. Furthermore, in the RAmI architecture, both AmI agents and robots can help in handling conflicts in gathered data.

To achieve any task (e.g. medicine or food delivery or transporting blood samples), each robot needs to navigate inside a building. MRT performance depends on the navigational maps (i.e. areas where the robots can safely go) by tracking human trajectories and integrating them within the probabilistic map which is built directly through the conventional sensory readings (see, e.g., [14]). Map updating is a background task during other mission execution by merging maps produced by various robots.

Robot's decisions and actions can be improved by using non-local information coming from AmI sensors [17] and AmI actuators, e.g., automatic doors [19]. We are specifically interested in the *dynamic update* of the control software of a robot to deal with it. Previously, we worked on an architectural solution for robotics applications and proposed the MaDcAr model [2]. More recently, we have been working on a general-purpose for dynamic software update (DSU) [20] in the context of dynamic object-oriented languages.

In our use-case scenario, the use of such a DSU mechanism eliminates the stop, install and restart cycle. Updating a running application should preserve its running state and the service provided to the users. Our solution provides guarantee for correct continuation of the application's threads and validation of the application constraints after each update.

The assumption in *RAmI* architecture (Fig. 1, module *service route planning*) is to take advantage of distributed planning (each robot is responsible for its own movements). [8] considers distributed planning in an MRT without human presence.

3   Case Study Setting

We demonstrate the functionality of the Scheduling and Execution Layer of the RAmI robot architecture by means of a simple case study related with item delivery in Fig. 3. Given is a simple scenario of a building network with 5 nodes and 6 arcs. There are two mobile robots positioned at o_1 and o_2, two patients (at d_1 and d_2), and inventory node i. Moreover, given are arcs' travel times t_{ij} in minutes for each arc (i, j). Patients' delivery items are ontologically described through RDF. The objective is to find routes from the robots' positions o_1 and o_2 through inventory i to patients d_1 and d_2 that minimize the overall patient delivery time.

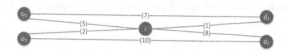

Fig. 3. A simple 5 node AmI network. Arcs' travel times in parentheses

Let us assume that both robots can deliver the demands of both patients d_1 and d_2. Then, in the scheduling layer, the robots get assigned to patients' demands (tasks) following steps in the MRTA algorithm [1] based on the updated paths with shortest travel times given by SAs. The travel time computation is done by the AmI network where SA nodes compute distributively the routes through [13].

Let us analyze this simple example. Robots start the task assignment through [9]. From o_1 to d_1 and from o_2 to d_2, there is only one simple path available passing through i. The overall cost of this assignment is 16. From o_1 to d_2 and from o_2 to d_1, there are four simple paths available for each one of the patient nodes d_1 and d_2. The overall cost of optimal paths $(o_1, i), (i, d_2)$ and $(o_2, i), (i, d_1)$ is also 16. Since both assignments have the same cost, the solution is found lexicographically. In the case of contingencies during the moving from one node to another, the robots try to coordinate among themselves by locally recomputing their routes by following the algorithm in [9]. If the solution is unsatisfactory, they recompute routes in the scheduling layer. If one of them breaks, then the other recomputes its route starting from the semantic layer.

In case of high travel time variations, robots should reroute. This is where AmI agents play a crucial role in observing congestion and updating travel times. The AmI agents compute the routes and inform the robots of the available routes' arrival times.

4   Conclusions

In this work, we proposed "Robots-Assisted Ambient Intelligence (RAmI)" architecture for robots that should work in multi-robot teams integrated with the networks of smart spaces (Ambient Intelligence networks) and users' personal smart devices. We discussed some open challenges to reach fully intelligent multi-robot teams that can assist people in various daily activities. Moreover, we showcased the functioning of the RAmI architecture on a meal or medicine delivery to simultaneous multiple patients needing assistance. The focus of RAmI is on the coordination of robot teams and multiple humans that share the same space resources in their daily activities, related congestion control and the influence of an individual (robot or human) action on the system's performance in such complex systems.

In future work, we intend to analyze the efficiency of our RAmI approach related with unpredictable scenarios through simulations on building networks of varying complexity with varying number of users.

Acknowledgements. This work has been partially supported by the COMRADES project within the framework "Fonds d'amorçage Santé" by Institut Mines Telecom in France.

References

1. Giordani, S., Lujak, M., Martinelli, F.: A distributed algorithm for the multi-robot task allocation problem. In: García-Pedrajas, N., Herrera, F., Fyfe, C., Benítez, J.M., Ali, M. (eds.) IEA/AIE 2010. LNCS (LNAI), vol. 6096, pp. 721–730. Springer, Heidelberg (2010). https://doi.org/10.1007/978-3-642-13022-9_72
2. Grondin, G., Bouraqadi, N., Vercouter, L.: MADCAR: an abstract model for dynamic and automatic (re-)assembling of component-based applications. In: Gorton, I., Heineman, G.T., Crnković, I., Schmidt, H.W., Stafford, J.A., Szyperski, C., Wallnau, K. (eds.) CBSE 2006. LNCS, vol. 4063, pp. 360–367. Springer, Heidelberg (2006). https://doi.org/10.1007/11783565_28
3. Kantaros, Y., Zavlanos, M.M.: Global planning for multi-robot communication networks in complex environments. IEEE Trans. Robot. **32**(5), 1045–1061 (2016)
4. Karami, A.B., Fleury, A., Boonaert, J., Lecoeuche, S.: User in the loop: adaptive smart homes exploiting user feedback–state of art and future directions. Information **7**(2), 35 (2016). https://doi.org/10.3390/info7020035
5. Katragjini, K., Vallada, E., Ruiz, R.: Flow shop rescheduling under different types of disruption. Int. J. Prod. Res. **51**(3), 780–797 (2013)
6. Kehoe, B., Patil, S., Abbeel, P., Goldberg, K.: A survey of research on cloud robotics and automation. IEEE Trans. Autom. Sci. Eng. **12**(2), 398–409 (2015)
7. Kon, B., Lam, A., Chan, J.: Evolution of smart homes for the elderly. In: Proceedings of the 26th International Conference on World Wide Web Companion. WWW 2017 Companion, International World Wide Web Conferences Steering Committee, Republic and Canton of Geneva, Switzerland, pp. 1095–1101 (2017). https://doi.org/10.1145/3041021.3054928

8. Lozenguez, G., Adouane, L., Beynier, A., Mouaddib, A.I., Martinet, P.: Punctual versus continuous auction coordination for multi-robot and multi-task topological navigation. Auton. Robot. **40**(4), 599–613 (2016). https://doi.org/10.1007/s10514-015-9483-7

9. Lujak, M., Billhardt, H., Ossowski, S.: Distributed coordination of emergency medical service for angioplasty patients. Ann. Math. Artif. Intell. **78**(1), 73–100 (2016). https://doi.org/10.1007/s10472-016-9507-9

10. Lujak, M., Fernandez, A.: ORCAS: optimized robots configuration and scheduling system. In: Proceedings of the 30th ACM Symposium on Applied Computing, vol. 1, pp. 327–330 (2015). https://doi.org/10.1145/2695664.2696024

11. Lujak, M., Giordani, S.: On the communication range in auction-based multi-agent target assignment. In: Bettstetter, C., Gershenson, C. (eds.) IWSOS 2011. LNCS, vol. 6557, pp. 32–43. Springer, Heidelberg (2011). https://doi.org/10.1007/978-3-642-19167-1_4

12. Lujak, M., Giordani, S., Ossowski, S.: Value of incomplete information in mobile target allocation. In: Klügl, F., Ossowski, S. (eds.) MATES 2011. LNCS (LNAI), vol. 6973, pp. 89–100. Springer, Heidelberg (2011). https://doi.org/10.1007/978-3-642-24603-6_10

13. Lujak, M., Giordani, S., Ossowski, S.: Route guidance: bridging system and user optimization in traffic assignment. Neurocomputing **151**(1), 449–460 (2015). https://doi.org/10.1016/j.neucom.2014.08.071

14. Papadakis, P., Rives, P.: Binding human spatial interactions with mapping for enhanced mobility in dynamic environments. Auton. Robot. **41**(5), 1047–1059 (2017). https://doi.org/10.1007/s10514-016-9581-1

15. Petitti, A., et al.: A network of stationary sensors and mobile robots for distributed ambient intelligence. IEEE Intell. Syst. **31**(6), 28–34 (2016)

16. Rashidi, P., Cook, D.J.: Keeping the resident in the loop: adapting the smart home to the user. IEEE Trans. Syst. Man Cybern. Part A Syst. Hum. **39**(5), 949–959 (2009)

17. Rodic, A., Katie, D., Mester, G.: Ambient intelligent robot-sensor networks for environmental surveillance and remote sensing. In: 2009 7th International Symposium on Intelligent Systems and Informatics, pp. 39–44, September 2009

18. Sabattini, L., Chopra, N., Secchi, C.: Decentralized connectivity maintenance for cooperative control of mobile robotic systems. Int. J. of Robot. Res. **32**(12), 1411–1423 (2013)

19. Sakaguchi, T., Ujiie, T., Tsunoo, S., Yokoi, K., Wada, K.: Intelligent ambience-robot cooperation - door-closing tasks with various robots. In: 2009 IEEE Workshop on Robotic Intelligence in Informationally Structured Space, pp. 60–65, March 2009

20. Tesone, P., Polito, G., Fabresse, L., Bouraqadi, N., Ducasse, S.: Instance migration in dynamic software update. In: Proceedings of International Workshop on Meta-Programming Techniques and Reflection (META 2016) (2016). http://car.mines-douai.fr/luc/files/pdfs/2016-Tesone-META.pdf

AT 2017: Philosophical and Theoretical Studies

Approximating Agreements in Argumentation Dialogues

Juan Carlos Nieves[✉]

Department of Computing Science, Umeå University, 901 87 Umeå, Sweden
jcnieves@cs.umu.se

Abstract. In many real applications, to reach an agreement between the participants of a dialogue, which can be for instance a negotiation, is not easy. Indeed, there are application domains such as the medical domain where to have a consensus among medical professionals is not feasible and might even be regarded as counterproductive. In this paper, we introduce an approach for expressing goals of a dialogue considering ordered disjunction rules. By applying argumentation semantics and degrees of satisfaction of goals, we introduce the so-called *dialogue agreement degree*. Moreover, by considering sets of dialogue agreement degrees, we define a *lattice of agreement degrees*. We argue that a lattice of agreement degrees suggests different approximations between the current state of a dialogue and its aimed goals. Indeed, a lattice of agreement degrees can show evidence about whether or not it is acceptable to dismiss goals in order to maximize agreements regarding other goals.

1 Introduction

Formal argumentation has been revealed as a powerful conceptual tool for exploring the theoretical foundations of reasoning and interaction in autonomous systems and multiagent systems [1,27]. Different dialogue frameworks have been proposed by considering formal argumentation. Indeed, by considering formal argumentation, the so-called *Agreement Technologies* have been introduced in order to deal with the new requirement of interaction between autonomous systems and multiagent systems [22].

Formal argumentation dialogues have been intensively explored in the last years [5,10,17,23,25] by the community of formal argumentation theory. Most current approaches have been suggested as general frameworks for setting up different kinds of dialogues. Roughly speaking, we can understand a dialogue as a finite sequence of utterances: $[u_1, \ldots, u_n]$. Depending on the followed dialogue approach [5,10,17,23,25], the sequence of utterances follows a protocol of valid moves performed by the participants of a dialogue. Moreover, these approaches are mainly oriented to a particular topic/goal that is usually denoted by a logical formula. Hence, these dialogue approaches are only concerned about validating a particular goal, *i.e.* a given logical formula. Therefore, we can say that these approaches were defined for validating only static goals. This means that there

© Springer Nature Switzerland AG 2018
F. Belardinelli and E. Argente (Eds.): EUMAS 2017/AT 2017, LNAI 10767, pp. 501–515, 2018.
https://doi.org/10.1007/978-3-030-01713-2_35

is an agreement at the end of a dialogue upon whether the given goal holds true in the outcomes of the dialogue; otherwise, there is no agreement at the end of the dialogue.

In many real applications, to reach an agreement between the participants of a dialogue is not easy [28,29]. Indeed, there are application domains such as the medical domain where to have a consensus among medical professionals is not feasible and might even be regarded as counterproductive [16]. In order to illustrate this situation, let us consider a hypothetical scenario from the medical domain in the field of human organ transplanting (the scenario is reported from [21,29]):

Scenario 1 *Let us assume that we have two transplant coordinators, one which is against the viability of the organ (TCA_D) and one which is in favour of the viability of the organ (TCA_R). TCA_D argues that the organ is not viable since the donor had endocarditis due to Streptococcus viridans, then the recipient could be infected by the same microorganism. In contrast, TCA_R argues that the organ is viable because the organ presents correct function and correct structure and the infection could be prevented with post-treatment with penicillin, even if the recipient is allergic to penicillin, there is the option of post-treatment with teicoplanin.*

In the settings of the aforementioned scenario, one can argue that the main goal is to keep alive the recipient; however, finding safe-organs is an issue for a discussion since there are not unique criteria for selecting safe-organs [29].

We argue that managing *dynamic degrees of agreement* during a dialogue can help with the management of disagreements during a dialogue. These dynamic degrees of agreement can be defined by considering preferences between the goals of a dialogue. Currently, dialogue systems manage mainly static goals that usually are introduced as the topic of a dialogue [5,10,17,23,25]. Hence, these approaches do not allow the specification of preferences between goals of a given dialogue.

Depending on the application domain, we can argue that there are *static* and *dynamic goals* during a dialogue. A static goal is a goal that cannot be skipped during a dialogue and a dynamic goal is a goal that can change during a dialogue, *e.g.*, a goal that can be skipped during a dialogue. These assumptions suggest a need for defining methods that can manage *degrees of agreement* on an ongoing dialogue *w.r.t.* each intended goal of a dialogue. In these settings, some research questions arise:

Q1: Given a dialogue, is there *a partial degree of agreement* between the participants of a dialogue?

Q2: Given a dialogue, can we *dismiss goals* in order to maximize agreements *w.r.t.* other goals?

In this paper, we address the aforementioned questions. To this end, we follow Dung style [8] for selecting arguments from a set of arguments with disagreements. We consider structured arguments, which are constructed from extended logic programs. Moreover, logic programs with ordered disjunctions [7] are considered for expressing preferences between the goals of a dialogue. For instance, a possible representation of the dialogue of Scenario 1 is:

$$D = \langle Participants, Goals, Utterances \rangle$$

in which $Participants = \{TCA_D, TCA_R\}$, $Goals = \{keep\_alive\_recipient \leftarrow \top; healthy\_donor \leftarrow \top; safe\_organs \times managed\_disease \leftarrow \top\}$. Let us observe that the rule $safe\_organs \times managed\_disease \leftarrow \top$ suggests that the dialogue looks for safe organs for being transplanted; however, if not possible, the doctors will argue for organs that can be treated post-transplanting. $Utterances = [u_1, \ldots, u_n]$ in which each $u_i (1 \leq i \leq n)$ is an utterance from either TCA_D, TCA_R.

By considering dialogues, argumentation semantics and subsets of goals, we introduce the so-called *dialogue agreement degree*. This dialogue agreement degree considers different sets of goals such that each goal has a satisfaction agreement degree in terms of satisfaction degrees of ordered-disjunction rules. Considering sets of dialogue agreement degrees, we define a *lattice of agreement degrees*. We consider that both dialogue agreement degrees and lattices of agreement degrees are novel ideas that have not been explored in the settings of formal argumentation dialogue before. Indeed, to the best of our knowledge, we are introducing the first argumentation dialogue system that considers degrees of agreements based on preferences among the goals of a dialogue. We argue that a lattice of agreement degrees suggests different approximations between the current state of a dialogue and its aimed goals. Indeed, a lattice of agreement degrees can show evidence about whether or not it is acceptable to dismiss goals in order to maximize agreements regarding other goals.

The rest of the paper is split as follows: In Sect. 2, basic concepts of logic programming are introduced. Moreover, an approach for building arguments from logic programs is presented. In Sect. 3, we introduce our approach for defining dialogues considering preferences between the goals of a dialogue. In Sect. 4, the concepts of dialogue agreement degree and lattice of agreement degrees are introduced. In the last section, our conclusions and future work are outlined.

2   Background

In this section, a basic background in logic programming is presented. Mainly, extended logic programs and logic programs with ordered disjunctions are presented. We are assuming that the reader is familiar with basic concepts of Answer Set Programming (ASP). A good introduction to ASP is presented in [2]. In terms of argumentation, we present an approach for building arguments from an extended logic program.

2.1   Extended Logic Programs

Let us introduce the languace of a propositional logic, which consists of propositional symbols: $p_0, p_1, \ldots$; connectives: $\leftarrow, \neg, not, \top$; and auxiliary symbols:

$(\,,\,)$, in which $\wedge, \leftarrow$ are 2-place connectives, $\neg$, not are 1-place connectives and $\top$ is a 0-place connective. The propositional symbols, the 0-place connective $\top$ and the propositional symbols of the form $\neg p_i$ $(i \geq 0)$ stand for the indecomposable propositions, which we call *atoms*, or *atomic propositions*. The atoms of the form $\neg a$ are also called *extended atoms* in the literature. In order to simplify the presentation, we call them atoms as well. The negation symbol $\neg$ is regarded as the so-called *strong negation* in the Answer Set Programming literature [2], and the negation symbol not as *negation as failure*. A literal is an atom, a (called a positive literal), or the negation of an atom $not\ a$ (called a negative literal). A (propositional) extended normal clause, C, is denoted:

$$a \leftarrow b_1, \ldots, b_j, not\ \ b_{j+1}, \ldots, not\ \ b_{j+n} \tag{1}$$

in which $j + n \geq 0$, a is an atom, and each b_i $(1 \leq i \leq j + n)$ is an atom. We use the term *rule* as a synonym of *clause* indistinctly. When $j + n = 0$, the clause is an abbreviation of $a \leftarrow \top$ (a *fact*), such that $\top$ is the propositional atom that always evaluates to true. In a slight abuse of notation, we sometimes write a clause $C = a \leftarrow \mathcal{B}^+ \wedge not\ \mathcal{B}^-$, in which $\mathcal{B}^+ := \{b_1, \ldots, b_j\}$ and $\mathcal{B}^- := \{b_{j+1}, \ldots, b_{j+n}\}$. We denote by $head(C)$ the head atom a of clause C.

An extended logic program P is a finite set of extended normal clauses. When $n = 0$, the clause is called an *extended definite clause*. By $\mathcal{L}_P$, we denote the set of atoms that appear in P.

Let A be a set of atoms and P be an extended (definite or normal) logic program. $r = a_0 \leftarrow \mathcal{B}^+, not\ \mathcal{B}^- \in P$ is applicable in A if $\mathcal{B}^+ \subseteq A$. $App(A, P)$ denotes the subset of rules of P which are applicable in A. $C = a_0 \leftarrow \mathcal{B}^+, not\ \mathcal{B}^- \in P$ is closed in A if C is applicable in A and $head(C) \in A$.

Since we are using a comma for denoting the $\wedge$ binary connective in the body of the rules, we will use semicolon for separating elements in sets of rules.

2.2   Logic Programs with Ordered Disjunction

The formalism of *Logic Programs with Ordered Disjunction* (LPODs) was created with the idea of expressing explicit context-dependent preference rules, which select the most plausible atoms to be used in a reasoning process and to order answer sets [7].

Technically speaking, LPODs are based on extended logic programs augmented by an ordered disjunction connector $\times$ which allows for the expression of qualitative preferences in the head of rules [7]. An LPOD is a finite collection of rules of the form:

$$r = c_1 \times \ldots \times c_k \leftarrow b_1, \ldots, b_m, not\ b_{m+1}, \ldots, not\ b_{m+n} \tag{2}$$

where c_i's $(1 \leq i \leq k)$ and b_j's $(1 \leq j \leq m + n)$ are atoms. The intuitive reading behind a rule like (2) is that if the body of r is satisfied, then some c_i must be true in an answer set, if possible c_1, if c_1 is not possible then c_2, and so on. As previously stated, from a nonmonotonic reasoning point, each of the c_i's can represent alternative ranked options for selecting the most plausible (default) rules of an LPOD.

The LPODs semantics was defined in terms of split programs. Split programs are a way to represent every option of ordered disjunction rules with the property that the set of all answer sets of an LPOD corresponds exactly to the answer sets of the split programs. An alternative and more straightforward characterization of the LPODs semantics was also given in terms of a program reduction defined as follows:

Definition 1 (×-reduction) [7]. *Let* $r = c_1 \times \ldots \times c_k \leftarrow b_1, \ldots, b_m, \text{ not } b_{m+1}$, ..., *not* b_{m+n} *be an ordered disjunction rule and* M *be a set of atoms. The* ×*-reduction of a rule* r *is defined as:*

$$r_\times^M = \{c_i \leftarrow b_1, \ldots, b_m | c_i \in M \wedge M \cap (\{c_1, \ldots, c_{i-1}\} \cup \{b_{m+1}, \ldots, b_{m+n}\}) = \emptyset\}$$

The ×*-reduction is generalized to an LPOD* P *in the following way:*

$$P_\times^M = \bigcup_{r \in P} r_\times^M$$

Based on the ×-reduction, the LPODs semantics is defined by the following definition:

Definition 2 (SEM_{LPOD}) [7]. *Let* P *be an LPOD and* M *be a set of atoms. Then,* M *is an answer set of* P *if and only if* M *is closed under all the rules in* P *and* M *is the minimal model of* $P_\times^M$. *We denote by* $SEM_{LPOD}(P)$ *the set of answer sets of* P.

One interesting characteristic of LPODs is that they provide a means to represent preferences among answer sets by considering the satisfaction degree of an answer set *w.r.t.* a rule [7].

Definition 3 (Rule Satisfaction Degree) [7]. *Let* M *be an answer set of an LPOD* P. *The satisfaction degree* M *w.r.t. a rule* $r = c_1 \times \ldots \times c_k \leftarrow b_1, \ldots, b_m$, *not* $b_{m+1} \ldots$, *not* b_{m+n}, *denoted by* $deg_M(r)$, *is*

- 1 *if* $b_j \notin M$ *for some* j $(1 \leq j \leq m)$, *or* $b_i \in M$ *for some* i $(m+1 \leq i \leq m+n)$,
- j $(1 \leq j \leq k)$ *if all* $b_l \in M$ $(1 \leq l \leq m)$, $b_i \notin M$ $(m+1 \leq i \leq m+n)$, *and* $j = min\{r \mid c_r \in M, 1 \leq r \leq k\}$.

The degrees can be viewed as penalties, as a higher degree expresses a lesser degree of satisfaction. Therefore, if the body of a rule is not satisfied, then there is no reason to be dissatisfied and the best possible degree 1 is obtained [7]. A preference order on the answer sets of an LPOD can be obtained by means of the following preference relation.

Definition 4 [7]. *Let* P *be an LPOD, and* M_1 *and* M_2 *be two answers of* P. M_1 *is preferred to* M_2 *(denoted by* $M_1 >_p M_2$*) if and only if* $\exists\, r \in P$ *such that* $deg_{M_1}(r) < deg_{M_2}(r)$ *and* $\nexists r' \in P$ *such that* $deg_{M_2}(r') < deg_{M_1}(r')$.

2.3   Constructing Arguments from Extended Logic Programs

In this section, an approach for building arguments from a logic program is presented [14]. In the construction of these arguments, the well-founded semantics (WFS) is used [12]. By lack of space, the definition of WFS is not presented, see [12] for the formal definition of WFS. We just mention that WFS is a three-valued semantics that infers a unique partial interpretation of a given logic program. Hence, given a logic program P, $WFS(P) = \langle T, F \rangle$ such that the atoms that appear in T are considered true, the atoms that appear in F are considered false, and the atoms that are neither in T nor in F are considered undefined.

The following definition introduces an approach for constructing arguments from an extended normal logic program.

Definition 5 [14]. *Given an extended logic program P and $S \subseteq P$, $Arg_P = \langle S, g \rangle$ is an **argument** under WFS, if the following conditions hold:*

1. *$WFS(S) = \langle T, F \rangle$ such that $g \in T$.*
2. *S is minimal w.r.t. the set inclusion satisfying 1.*
3. *$\nexists g \in \mathcal{L}_P$ such that $\{g, \neg g\} \subseteq T$ and $WFS(S) = \langle T, F \rangle$.*

By $Arg(P)$ we denote the set of all of the arguments built from P.

Given an argument $A = \langle S, g \rangle$, S is usually called the *support* of A, g the *conclusion* of A, $Cl(A) = g$ and $Sp(A) = S$. Given a set of arguments Ag, Δ_{Ag} denotes $\{Cl(A) | A \in Ag\}$.

Let us mention that there are other approaches for constructing arguments from a logic program [6,8,11,26]. We are considering an approach that has shown to be a conservative approach since it does not allow problematic arguments such as the self-attacked arguments. For instance, the construction of arguments suggested by Definition 5 will not construct arguments such as the argument $arg_1 = \langle \{a \leftarrow \ not\ a\}, a \rangle$; nevertheless, arg_1 can be constructed by other approaches for constructing arguments [26]. arg_1 can be understood as a self-attacked argument.

Formally attacks between arguments are binary relations between arguments; moreover, these binary relations express disagreements between arguments. Intuitively, an attack between two arguments emerges whenever there is a *disagreement* between these arguments. Attacks between arguments can be identified by the following definition:

Definition 6 (Attack relationship between arguments) [14]. *Let $A = \langle S_A, g_A \rangle$, $B = \langle S_B, g_B \rangle$ be two arguments such that $WFS(S_A) = \langle T_A, F_A \rangle$ and $WFS(S_B) = \langle T_B, F_B \rangle$. We say that A attacks B, denoted by (A, B), if one of the following conditions holds:*

1. *$a \in T_A$ and $\neg a \in T_B$.*
2. *$a \in T_A$ and $a \in F_B$.*

$At(\mathcal{A}rg)$ denotes the set of attack relationships between the arguments belonging to the set of arguments $\mathcal{A}rg$.

It has been shown that this definition of attack between arguments generalizes other definitions of attacks between arguments based on logic programs [19]. Like Dung's style, we define the resulting argumentation framework from a logic program as follows:

Definition 7. *Let P be an extended logic program. The resulting argumentation framework w.r.t. P is the tuple: $AF_P = \langle Arg_P, At(Arg_P) \rangle$.*

Following Dung's style [8], argumentation semantics are used for selecting arguments from the resulting argumentation frameworks from logic programs. An argumentation semantics σ is a function that assigns to an argumentation framework AF_P w.r.t. P a set of sets of arguments denoted by $\mathcal{E}_\sigma(AF_P)$. Each set of $\mathcal{E}_\sigma(AF)$ is called σ-extension. Let us observe that σ can be instantiated with any of the argumentation semantics that has been defined in terms of abstract arguments [3].

3   Dialogues and Relations Between Them

In this section, we introduce an approach for defining dialogues between agents. These dialogues will have the property of expressing preferences between their goals by using ordered disjunction programs. As was argued in Sect. 1, the main aim of this paper is to study the outcomes (*i.e. agreements*) of an ongoing dialogue by considering the current *active knowledge* of a dialogue and the set of goals of this dialogue. Hence, we put less attention to the protocols that lead the moves of the participants of a dialogue. The protocols that lead the moves of the participants of a dialogue mainly depend on the kind of dialogue that a dialogue-based system aims to implement [23, 24].

Let us start by introducing the basic piece of a dialogue that is called *utterance*.

Definition 8. *An utterance of a given agent a is a tuple of the form $\langle a, A \rangle$ in which A is an argument according to Definition 5.*

For the sake of simplicity of presentation, the following notation is introduced. Given an utterance $u = \langle a, A \rangle$, $u^* = A$. Given a set of utterances $\mathcal{U}$, $\mathcal{U}^* = \{u^* \mid u \in \mathcal{U}\}$.

An utterance is a suggested argument by an agent a in an ongoing dialogue. Considering utterances, dialogues between a set of agents are defined as follows:

Definition 9. *A dialogue is a tuple of the form $\langle \mathcal{I}, G, D_r^t \rangle$ in which G is a logic program with ordered disjunction and D_r^t is a finite sequence of utterances $[u_r, \ldots, u_t]$ involving a set of participating agents $\mathcal{I}$, where $r, t \in \mathbb{N}$ and $r \leq t$, such that:*

1. $Sender(u_s) \in \mathcal{I}$ $(r \leq s \leq t)$,

in which Sender $: \mathcal{U} \longmapsto \mathcal{I}$ *is a function such that Sender*$(\langle Agent, Argument \rangle) = Agent$ *and* $\mathcal{U}$ *denotes the set of all the possible utterances of the participating agents* $\mathcal{I}$.

Given a dialogue, $D = \langle \mathcal{I}, G, [u_r, \ldots, u_t] \rangle$, $\mathcal{U}_D = \{u_i | r \leq i \leq t, [u_r, \ldots, u_t]\}$.

Let us illustrate Definition 9 considering the following simple abstract example.

Example 1. Let $D_1 = \langle \mathcal{I}, G, D_1^2 \rangle$ such that $\mathcal{I} = \{1, 2\}$, $G = \{a \times c \leftarrow \top; b \leftarrow \top\}$, $D_1^2 = [u_1, u_2]$, $u_1 = \langle 1, \langle \{a \leftarrow not\ b\}, a \rangle \rangle$ and $u_2 = \langle 2, \langle \{c \leftarrow \top; b \leftarrow c\}, b \rangle \rangle$. Hence, D_1 is a dialogue between two agents. D_1 has as goals the topics expressed in terms of two ordered disjunction rules: $a \times c \leftarrow \top$ and $b \leftarrow \top$. D_1 has two utterances: u_1, u_2. We can see that $\mathcal{U}_{D_1} = \{u_1, u_2\}$.

Let us observe that given a dialogue D, we can get an *active knowledge base*, *i.e.* an extended logic program, *w.r.t.* D. Moreover, we can get the set of conclusions of the utterances *w.r.t.* D.

Definition 10. *Let* $D = \langle \mathcal{I}, G, \mathcal{U}_r^t \rangle$ *be a dialogue.*

- *The active knowledge base w.r.t.* D, *denoted by* $\mathcal{A}_D$, *is* $\mathcal{A}_D = \bigcup_{u \in \mathcal{U}_D} Sp(u^*)$.
- *The argument-conclusions of the utterances w.r.t.* D, *denoted by* $\mathcal{C}_D$, *is:* $\mathcal{C}_D = \bigcup_{u \in \mathcal{U}_D} Cl(u^*)$.

The active knowledge of a dialogue is the information that the participating agents of a dialogue have shared by means of arguments.

Example 2. Considering the dialogue D_1 introduced by Example 1, we can see that:

$$\mathcal{A}_{D_1} = \{a \leftarrow not\ b; c \leftarrow \top; b \leftarrow c\}$$
$$\mathcal{C}_{D_1} = \{a, b\}$$

Considering the information of a dialogue in terms of utterances, active knowledge and arguments, we define four kinds of sub-dialogues.

Definition 11. *Let* $D = \langle \mathcal{I}, G, \mathcal{U}_r^t \rangle$, $D' = \langle \mathcal{I}', G', \mathcal{U}_i^j \rangle$ *be two dialogues.*

- D' *is a sub-dialogue w.r.t. utterances of* D $(D' \sqsubseteq_u D)$ *iff* $\mathcal{U}_{D'}^* \subseteq \mathcal{U}_D^*$.
- D' *is a sub-dialogue w.r.t. active-knowledge of* D $(D' \sqsubseteq_{ak} D)$ *iff* $\mathcal{A}_{D'} \subseteq \mathcal{A}_D$.
- D' *is a sub-dialogue w.r.t. argument-conclusions of* D $(D' \sqsubseteq_{ac} D)$ *iff* $\mathcal{C}_{D'} \subseteq \mathcal{C}_D$.
- D' *is a sub-dialogue w.r.t. goals of* D $(D' \sqsubseteq_g D)$ *iff* $G' \subseteq G$.

We illustrate Definition 11 in the following example.

Example 3. Let D_1 be the dialogue introduced by Example 1 and $D_2 = \langle \mathcal{I}_2, G_2, D_1^1 \rangle$ such that $\mathcal{I}_2 = \{1, 2\}$, $G_2 = \{a \times c \leftarrow \top; b \leftarrow \top\}$, $D_1^1 = [u_1]$ and $u_1 = \langle 1, \langle \{a \leftarrow not\ b\}, a \rangle \rangle$.

We are assuming that D_1 and D_2 have the same participating agents. Following Definition 11, the following sub-dialogue relations hold: $D_2 \sqsubseteq_u D_1$, $D_2 \sqsubseteq_{ak} D_1$, $D_2 \sqsubseteq_{ac} D_1$, $D_2 \sqsubseteq_g D_1$ and $D_1 \sqsubseteq_g D_2$.

Given that the definitions of sub-dialogues, introduced by Definition 11, are basically defined in terms of subsets, the equality between dialogues is defined by the classical definition of set-equality.

Definition 12. *Let $D = \langle \mathcal{I}, G, U_r^t \rangle$, $D' = \langle \mathcal{I}', G', U_i^j \rangle$ be two dialogues and $\epsilon \in \{u, ak, ac, g\}$. D and D' are ϵ-equal ($D' =_\epsilon D$) iff $D' \sqsubseteq_\epsilon D$ and $D \sqsubseteq_\epsilon D'$ holds.*

It is easy to see that if two dialogues are utterances-equal, then they are active-knowledge and argument-conclusions equal. However, if two dialogues are active-knowledge equal, it does not imply that they are utterances-equal and argument-conclusions-equal. The main reason for this is because one can construct two arguments with same conclusions but with different supports. This property is quite common in different approaches for constructing arguments from a knowledge base [6,18,26].

Considering a dialogue, two argumentation frameworks can be derived from it.

Definition 13. *Let $D = \langle \mathcal{I}, G, U_r^t \rangle$ be a dialogue.*

- *The resulting argumentation framework AF_D^u w.r.t. D and its utterances is $\langle \mathcal{U}_D^*, At(\mathcal{U}_D^*) \rangle$.*
- *The resulting argumentation framework AF_D^{ak} w.r.t. D and its active-knowledge is $\langle Arg(\mathcal{A}_D), At(Arg(\mathcal{A}_D)) \rangle$.*

AF_D refers to either AF_D^u or AF_D^{ak}.

We can illustrate Definition 13 with the following simple example:

Example 4. Let D_1 be the dialogue introduced by Example 1.

$$AF_{D_1}^u \text{ w.r.t. } D_1 \text{ is } \langle \{arg_1, arg_2\}, \{(arg_2, arg_1)\} \rangle$$

$$AF_{D_1}^{ak} \text{ w.r.t. } D_1 \text{ is } \langle \{arg_1, arg_2, arg_3\}, \{(arg_2, arg_1)\} \rangle$$

in which $arg_1 = \langle \{a \leftarrow not\ b\}, a \rangle$, $arg_2 = \langle \{c \leftarrow \top; b \leftarrow c\}, b \rangle$ and $arg_3 = \langle \{c \leftarrow \top\}, c \rangle$.

Let us observe that the arguments of AF_D^u are the arguments that the participating agents of D have explicitly shared by means of utterances in the dialogue. However, considering the active-knowledge of a dialogue new both arguments and attacks can emerge; hence, AF_D^{ak} suggests a different view of the shared information in a dialogue. Nevertheless, we can identify a relationship between AF_D^u and AF_D^{ak}.

Proposition 1. *Let $D = \langle \mathcal{I}, G, U_r^t \rangle$ be a dialogue, $AF_D^u = \langle A^u, At^u \rangle$ and $AF_D^{ak} = \langle A^{ak}, At^{ak} \rangle$. It holds the following subset relations: $A^u \subseteq A^{ak}$ and $At^u \subseteq At^{ak}$.*

We consider that AF_D^u and AF_D^{ak} show different perspectives of an ongoing dialogue. Hence, these two views of an ongoing dialogue can be taken in consideration for defining strategic plans of dialogue-moves by the participating agents in a dialogue, *e.g.*, in a negotiation dialogue.

4   Agreement Degrees of Dialogues

Up to now, we have seen how to deal with the information that has been shared by the participating agents of a dialogue in terms of argumentation frameworks; however, we have not seen how this information can be understood regarding the goals of the dialogue. As was mentioned in the previous section, the shared information in a dialogue can define different argumentation frameworks regarding the active knowledge of a given dialogue. Now in this section, we will use these argumentation frameworks for exploring the satisfiability of the goals of a given dialogue.

The inference from argumentation frameworks is usually led by considering argumentation semantics. Hence, we will use σ-extensions of a σ argumentation semantics for defining answer sets of ordered disjunction rules as follows:

Definition 14. *Let $D = \langle \mathcal{I}, G, U_r^t \rangle$ be a dialogue, $G' \subseteq G$ and σ be an argumentation semantics. A σ-extension $E_\sigma \in \mathcal{E}_\sigma(AF_D)$ is a σ-model of G' iff $M = \mathcal{L}_{G'} \cap \Delta_{E_\sigma}$ is an answer set of G'. $\mathcal{M}_\sigma(AF_D, G')$ denotes the set of all σ-models inferred by the argumentation semantics σ w.r.t. AF_D and G'.*

Let us observe, in Definition 14, that the σ argumentation semantics is suggesting sets of atoms that can be considered for satisfying the goals of a dialogue. As was mentioned in Sect. 2.2, an answer set infers a satisfaction degree of an ordered disjunction rule. Hence, considering this satisfaction degree of each goal (an ordered disjunction) we define a satisfaction degree of a set of goals as follows:

Definition 15. *Let $D = \langle \mathcal{I}, G, U_r^t \rangle$ be a dialogue, $G' \subseteq G$, σ be an argumentation semantics. The satisfaction degree of $M \in \mathcal{M}_\sigma(AF_D, G')$ w.r.t. AF_D and G' is:*

$$deg_M(AF_D, G') = max\{deg_M(r)|r \in G'\}$$

Let us observe that $deg_M(AF_D, G')$ is capturing the satisfaction degree of the ordered disjunction rule that was worst satisfied. It is worth mentioning that according to Definition 4, an ordered disjunction rule with higher degree expresses a lesser degree of satisfaction. Hence if a dialogue and an argumentation semantics suggest that the $deg_M(AF_D, G') = 1$ means that all the goals of G' were satisfied in its best case. However, if $deg_M(AF_D, G') = 2$ means that at least one of the decisions (*i.e.* an ordered disjunction rule) of G' took the second option.

We can define preferences between σ models considering the satisfaction degree defined by Definition 15.

Definition 16. *Let $D = \langle \mathcal{I}, G, U_r^t \rangle$ be a dialogue, $G' \subseteq G$ and σ be an argumentation semantics. If $M_1, M_2 \in \mathcal{M}_\sigma(AF_D, G')$, M_1 is preferred to M_2 (denoted by $M_1 >_p M_2$) if and only if $deg_{M_1}(AF_D, G') < deg_{M_2}(AF_D, G')$.*

It easy to see that $>_p$ defines a partial ordered set considering all the σ models suggested by an argumentation semantics σ. Let us denote by $Upp(D, G', \sigma)$ the satisfaction degree of the members of the upper bound of $(\mathcal{M}_\sigma(AF_D, G'), >_p)$.

Now we are ready for defining the dialogue agreement degree suggested by an argumentation semantics σ regarding a given dialogue.

Definition 17 (Dialogue agreement degree). *Let $D = \langle \mathcal{I}, G, U_r^t \rangle$ be a dialogue, $G' \subseteq G$ and σ be an argumentation semantics. The dialogue agreement degree of D w.r.t. AF_D and σ (denoted by $D\text{-}Deg(D, AF_D, G', \sigma)$) is a tuple of the form $\langle i/n, Upp(D, G', \sigma) \rangle$ such that $i = |G'|$ and $n = |G|$.*

According to Definition 17, a dialogue D reaches *a total agreement* whenever $D\text{-}Deg(D, AF_D, \sigma) = \langle 1, 1 \rangle$, which means that all the goals were satisfied and all of them took the best option.

Example 5. Once again, let us consider the dialogue D_1 introduced by Example 1. Hence, $D_1 = \langle \mathcal{I}, G, D_1^2 \rangle$ such that $\mathcal{I} = \{1, 2\}$, $G = \{a \times c \leftarrow \top; b \leftarrow \top\}$, $D_1^2 = [u_1, u_2]$, $u_1 = \langle 1, \langle \{a \leftarrow not\ b\}, a \rangle \rangle$ and $u_2 = \langle 2, \langle \{c \leftarrow \top; b \leftarrow c\}, b \rangle \rangle$.

As we saw in Example 4, $AF_{D_1}^{ak}$ w.r.t. D_1 is $\langle \{arg_1, arg_2, arg_3\}, \{(arg_2, arg_1)\} \rangle$ in which $arg_1 = \langle \{a \leftarrow not\ b\}, a \rangle$, $arg_2 = \langle \{c \leftarrow \top; b \leftarrow c\}, b \rangle$ and $arg_3 = \langle \{c \leftarrow \top\}, c \rangle$.

If we consider the grounded semantics [8], denoted by gs, $\mathcal{E}_{gs}(AF_{D_1}^{ak}) = \{\{arg_2, arg_3\}\}$. We can see that $\Delta_{\{arg_2, arg_3\}} = \{b, c\}$. Moreover, one can see that $M_{gs} = \mathcal{L}_G \cap \Delta_{\{arg_2, arg_3\}}$ is a gs-model of G.

Let us denote by $r_1 = a \times c \leftarrow \top$ and $r_2 = b \leftarrow \top$. We can see that $deg_{M_{gs}}(r_1) = 2$ and $deg_{M_{gs}}(r_2) = 1$. Therefore, $deg_{M_{gs}}(AF_{D_1}^{ak}, G) = 2$.

Since the grounded semantics only infers a unique gs-model, we get a unique element in $\mathcal{M}_{gm}(AF_{D_1}, G)$. One can see that $D\text{-}Deg(D_1, AF_{D_1}^{ak}, G, gs) = \langle 1, 2 \rangle$. By removing goals from G, one can get different agreement degrees w.r.t. AF_D^{ak} and gs. For instance, by considering the sets $\{a \times c \leftarrow \top\}$ and $\{b \leftarrow \top\}$, we get:

$D\text{-}Deg(D_1, AF_{D_1}^{ak}, \{a \times c \leftarrow \top\}, gs) = \langle 0.5, 2 \rangle$.
$D\text{-}Deg(D_1, AF_{D_1}^{ak}, \{b \leftarrow \top\}, gs) = \langle 0.5, 1 \rangle$.

In Fig. 1, it is depicted the different agreement degrees that can be committed considering the current sequence of utterances of D_1. Let us point out that Fig. 1 suggests different readings regarding dismissing some of the goals of the D_1. For instance, $D\text{-}Deg(D_1, AF_{D_1}^{ak}, \{b \leftarrow \top\}, gs) = \langle 0.5, 1 \rangle$ suggests that one of the goals is satisfied in its optimal value; however, it is skipping other goals of the dialogue.

One can observe that agreement degree values are monotonic regarding the size of the set of goals.

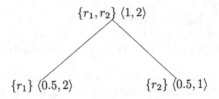

Fig. 1. A lattice of agreement degrees of Example 5.

Proposition 2. *Let $D = \langle \mathcal{I}, G, U_r^t \rangle$, $D' = \langle \mathcal{I}', G', U_i^j \rangle$ be two dialogues and σ be an argumentation semantics.*

- *If $D =_u D'$ and $D' \sqsubseteq_g D$, then $j' \le j$ such that $D\text{-}Deg(D, AF_D, G, \sigma) = \langle i, j \rangle$ and $D\text{-}Deg(D', AF_{D'}, G', \sigma) = \langle i', j' \rangle$.*

As we can see in Fig. 1, if we consider all the possible subsets of the set of goals of a dialogue, we can identify different understanding of an ongoing dialogue in terms of agreement degrees. Therefore, by having a list of utterances U_r^t, we can identify the best possible agreements that are possible to reach by considering different subsets of goals. Hence, a lattice of agreement degrees is defined as follows:

Definition 18 (Lattice of agreement degrees). *Let $D = \langle \mathcal{I}, G, U_r^t \rangle$ be a dialogue, σ be an argumentation semantics. The lattice of agreement degrees w.r.t. D and σ is $\Omega_D^\sigma = (L, \le_\Omega)$ in which:*

- *$L = \{ \langle G', Upp(D', G', \sigma) \rangle | G' \in 2^G \setminus \emptyset, D' = \langle \mathcal{I}, G', U_r^t \rangle \}$*
- *$\le_\Omega$ is a lexicographical order considering the $\subseteq$ relation for the first element of the tuple and the numerical relation $\le$ for the last element of the tuple.*

Let us observe that one can also define a lattice of agreements considering all the possible tuples suggested by Definition 17. The unique difference will be the first element of the tuples.

Let us point out that Ω_D^σ is defined in terms of a particular argumentation semantics σ. Nevertheless, by considering different argumentation semantics, one can identify different evaluations of the elements of Ω_D^σ.

Before ending this section, let us mention that the big issue regarding the construction of Ω_D^σ is the computational complexity of the argumentation semantics σ. An important concern in argumentation semantics is the *computational complexity* of the decision problems that has been shown to range from NP-complete to $\Pi_2^{(p)}$-complete [9].

5   Conclusions and Future Work

Currently, formal argumentation dialogue systems see the disagreements of a dialogue from the perspective of a unique argumentation framework [5,20]. However, in open environments of agents, the participating agents of a dialogue can join a dialogue and have different interpretations of the shared knowledge by the participating agents. From this perspective, we consider that a given share knowledge base can give place to different argumentation frameworks. In this paper, we show that the active knowledge of a dialogue at least can give place to two different argumentation frameworks AF_D^{ak}, AF_D^u (see Definition 13). Considering Proposition 1, it is easy to see that AF_D^{ak} is an expansion [4] of AF_D^u. We have considered an approach, for constructing arguments, that does not allow us to construct self-attacked arguments. However, considering other constructions of arguments (*e.g.*, [26]), one can identify different argumentation frameworks from the same active knowledge base of a dialogue. From this perspective, the use of self-attacked arguments can be an interesting topic for defining strategies in order to decide the next moves of an ongoing dialogue.

We show that by considering an argumentation semantics approach we can manage ordered disjunctions rules such that these ordered disjunctions rules capture preferences between goals of a dialogue. We show that argumentation semantics can define different satisfaction degrees of the goals of a dialogue, which are captured by ordered disjunctions rules. Hence, considering the active knowledge of a dialogue and an argumentation semantics, we introduce an approach for measuring an agreement degree of a dialogue. Considering this agreement degree of a dialogue, we introduce an approach for answering the research question **Q1**. It is clear that if we change the argumentation semantics, the dialogue agreement degree can change. Hence, a new research question arises:

Q3: Which argumentation semantics infers the maximum (or minimum) agreement degrees of a dialogue and its goals?

Answering **Q3** will be part of our future work. Let us point out that by considering different argumentation semantics one can define different lattices of agreement degrees. It is known that there are different sub-contention relations between different well-acceptable argumentation semantics [3]. Hence, to see the effect of these sub-contention relations in agreement degrees of dialogues will be also part of our future work.

Considering the lattice of agreement degrees, we introduce an approach for answering **Q2**. Let us observe that $\Omega_D^\sigma = (L, \leq_\Omega)$ shows a picture of the pros and the cons of eliminating goals of a dialogue since L is defining different agreement degrees by considering different subset of goals of the initial set of goals of a dialogue.

Let us point out that in this paper we are introducing a novel approach for modeling dialogues with preferences in their goals. Moreover, the satisfaction degree of a dialogue is a novel approach for defining heuristics to decide the next move in an ongoing dialogue. In this regard, let us highlight that the process of deciding which set of rules to disclosure from a private knowledge has been shown to be NP-complete even when the problem of deciding whether a given theory entails a literal can be computed in polynomial time [13]. Hence, the suggested lattice of agreement degrees can define heuristics in the settings of strategic argumentation [13].

From our applied research, we have observed that considering only static goals in a dialogue do not work in real applications. For instance, let us consider the case of persuasive software agents. If a given persuasive software agent has as a goal to persuade a given human agent, the persuasive software agent will need take into consideration different possible scenarios of agreement where different user preferences can be partially satisfied during a dialogue. Hence, we consider that by modeling preferences between the goals of a dialogue, one can incorporate user preferences into dialogues between software agents and human agents [15].

Acknowledgements. The author is very grateful to the anonymous referees for their useful comments.

References

1. Atkinson, K., et al.: Towards artificial argumentation. AI Mag. **38**(3), 25–36 (2017)
2. Baral, C.: Knowledge Representation. Reasoning and Declarative Problem Solving. Cambridge University Press, Cambridge (2003)
3. Baroni, P., Caminada, M., Giacomin, M.: An introduction to argumentation semantics. Knowl. Eng. Rev. **26**(4), 365–410 (2011)
4. Baumann, R., Woltran, S.: The role of self-attacking arguments in characterizations of equivalence notions. J. Logic Comput. **24**(14), 1293–1313 (2014)
5. Black, E., Hunter, A.: An inquiry dialogue system. Auton. Agents. Multi-Agent Syst. **19**(2), 173–209 (2009)
6. Bondarenko, A., Dung, P.M., Kowalski, R.A., Toni, F.: An abstract, argumentation-theoretic approach to default reasoning. Artif. Intell. **93**, 63–101 (1997)
7. Brewka, G., Niemelä, I., Syrjänen, T.: Logic programs with ordered disjunction. Comput. Intell. **20**(2), 335–357 (2004)
8. Dung, P.M.: On the acceptability of arguments and its fundamental role in non-monotonic reasoning, logic programming and n-person games. Artif. Intell. **77**(2), 321–358 (1995)
9. Dunne, P.E.: Computational properties of argument systems satisfying graph-theoretic constraints. Artif. Intell. **171**(10–15), 701–729 (2007)
10. Fan, X., Toni, F.: A general framework for sound assumption-based argumentation dialogues. Artif. Intell. **216**, 20–54 (2014)
11. García, A.J., Simari, G.R.: Defeasible logic programming: an argumentative approach. Theory Pract. Logic Program. **4**(1–2), 95–138 (2004)
12. Gelder, A.V., Ross, K.A., Schlipf, J.S.: The well-founded semantics for general logic programs. J. ACM **38**(3), 620–650 (1991)
13. Governatori, G., Olivieri, F., Scannapieco, S., Rotolo, A., Cristani, M.: Strategic argumentation is NP-complete. In: ECAI 2014–21st European Conference on Artificial Intelligence, vol. 263 of Frontiers in Artificial Intelligence and Applications, pp. 399–404. IOS Press (2014)
14. Guerrero, E., Nieves, J.C., Lindgren, H.: Semantic-based construction of arguments: an answer set programming approach. Int. J. Approximate Reasoning **64**, 54–74 (2015)
15. Guerrero, E., Nieves, J.C., Lindgren, H.: An activity-centric argumentation framework for assistive technology aimed at improving health. Argument Comput. **7**(1), 5–33 (2016)

16. Kljakovic, M.: Clinical disagreement: a silent topic in general practice. NZ. Fam. Physician **30**(5), 358–360 (2003)
17. Kraus, S., Sycara, K.P., Evenchik, A.: Reaching agreements through argumentation: a logical model and implementation. Artif. Intell. **104**(1–2), 1–69 (1998)
18. Modgil, S., Prakken, H.: The ASPIC$^+$ framework for structured argumentation: a tutorial. Argument Comput. **5**(1), 31–62 (2014)
19. Nieves, J.C.: Expansion and equivalence relations on argumentation frameworks based on logic programs. In: Criado Pacheco, N., Carrascosa, C., Osman, N., Julián Inglada, V. (eds.) EUMAS/AT-2016. LNCS (LNAI), vol. 10207, pp. 375–389. Springer, Cham (2017). https://doi.org/10.1007/978-3-319-59294-7_32
20. Nieves, J.C., Lindgren, H.: Deliberative argumentation for service provision in smart environments. In: Bulling, N. (ed.) EUMAS 2014. LNCS (LNAI), vol. 8953, pp. 388–397. Springer, Cham (2015). https://doi.org/10.1007/978-3-319-17130-2_27
21. Nieves, J.C., Osorio, M., Cortés, U.: Supporting decision making in organ transplating using argumentation theory. In: LANMR 2006: 2nd Latin American Non-Monotonic Reasoning Workshop, pp. 9–14 (2006)
22. Ossowski, S.: Agreement Technologies. Springer, Dordrecht (2013). https://doi.org/10.1007/978-94-007-5583-3
23. Parsons, S., Wooldridge, M., Amgoud, L.: Properties and complexity of some formal inter-agent dialogues. J. Logic Comput. **13**(3), 347–376 (2003)
24. Prakken, H.: Coherence and flexibility in dialogue games for argumentation. J. Logic Comput. **15**(6), 1009–1040 (2005)
25. Prakken, H.: Formal systems for persuasion dialogue. Knowl. Eng. Rev. **21**(2), 163–188 (2006)
26. Prakken, H., Sartor, G.: Argument-based extended logic programming with defeasible priorities. J. Appl. Non-Classical Logics **7**(1), 25–75 (1997)
27. Rahwan, I., Simari, G.R. (eds.): Argumentation in Artificial Intelligence. Springer, Boston (2009). https://doi.org/10.1007/978-0-387-98197-0
28. Sierra, C., de Mantaras, R.L., Simoff, S.: The argumentative mediator. In: Criado Pacheco, N., Carrascosa, C., Osman, N., Julián Inglada, V. (eds.) EUMAS/AT - 2016. LNCS (LNAI), vol. 10207, pp. 439–454. Springer, Cham (2017). https://doi.org/10.1007/978-3-319-59294-7_36
29. Tolchinsky, P., Cortés, U., Nieves, J.C., López-Navidad, A., Caballero, F.: Using arguing agents to increase the human organ pool for transplantation. In: Proceedings of the Third Workshop on Agents Applied in Health Care (IJCAI 2005) (2005)

An Ontology for Sharing Touristic Information

Carmen Fernández ⓘ, Alberto Fernández⁽⊠⁾ ⓘ, and Holger Billhardt ⓘ

CETINIA, University Rey Juan Carlos, Madrid, Spain
carmen.urjc@gmail.com, {alberto.fernandez,holger.billhardt}@urjc.es

Abstract. E-Tourism applications require reliable means for sharing and reusing information and the possibility to add intelligence and inferred knowledge. In this paper, we focus on developing an ontology or common vocabulary for the tourism domain and, in particular, to represent resources from Croatia. We evaluate some of the most popular ontology development methodologies for this case. As a result of this assessment we present a proposal for a methodology that combines activities from both traditional and simplified methods.

Keywords: Ontologies · Knowledge sharing
Semantic search engines · Semantic technologies
Touristic information · E-Tourism

1 Introduction

As the amount of touristic information and services available online increases, the challenge is how to coordinate the activities that all involved agents, both humans and machines, need to carry out, including searching for information, planning transportation, accommodation, etc. In order to facilitate agent interaction, it is necessary to represent and share common representations of a given domain. Ontologies are useful for common knowledge sharing. For heterogeneous agents to interact, they need to share the terminology they use in their models. Otherwise, ontology alignment [2] is necessary, which is a more difficult task. Ontologies not only provide the basics for representing knowledge but also provide the means for reasoning possibilities, which are important for automatically inferring knowledge. Therefore the tourism industry can benefit of these technologies by improving the search and browsing for tourists and enterprises.

The work presented in this paper contributes to the interoperability in the tourism domain by proposing a new general ontology for representing touristic information. In our case, we were inspired and created a specific ontology for the case of Croatia. Most common ontology development methodologies are difficult for not experienced users. For this reason we also propose a new methodology which follows a simple and common software engineering lifecycle with not so many activities and phases.

© Springer Nature Switzerland AG 2018
F. Belardinelli and E. Argente (Eds.): EUMAS 2017/AT 2017, LNAI 10767, pp. 516–522, 2018.
https://doi.org/10.1007/978-3-030-01713-2_36

The paper is organised as follows. In Sect. 2 we present some related works. Section 3 describes the proposed ontology. A new methodology for developing ontologies is described in Sect. 4. We conclude the paper with Sect. 5.

2   Related Works

Several ontologies and vocabularies have been proposed for tourism applications. The *Harmonise*[1] *Ontology* was developed as a mediating ontology to map different tourism ontologies. The core ontology contains concepts and properties mainly related to accommodation and events. The *OnTour* [9] is an OWL ontology focused on accommodation and activities. *Hi-Touch* [5] created an ontology that contains over 1000 concepts focusing on tourism and cultural products offered, packages and consumer needs for travel agency assistants The project *Satine* [4] developed an ontology to annotate tourism Web Services. The *IMA@GINE IT* [1] project developed ontologies for transport and tourism recommendation systems depending on user location.

With the goal of structuring the tourism ontology development process we used four well-known methodologies. For each of them we tested the general utility, the number of activities of stages, the duration of the "design" activity, at what stage of lifecycle is considered the reusing of other ontologies - which could unnecessarily lengthen the development process-, and if the name of the activities and phases is confusing and differs excessively from a traditional software engineering lifecycle. In the following we briefly describe each of those ontologies.

- *Ontology Development 101.* This is a simplified methodology [8] recommended for beginners in ontology design. After practical experience in the development of tools such as Protégé2000, Ontolingua and Chimaera they came up with a set of heuristics as a conclusion. The methodology includes seven activities: (1) *Determine scope,* (2) *Consider reuse of ontologies,* (3) *Enumerate important terms,* (4) *Define classes and class hierarchy,* (5) *Define properties,* (6) *Define constraints,* and (7) *Create instances.*
- *Horrocks method.* The simplified method proposed by Horrocks [6] focuses on simple ontology development. The methodology has two phases: (1) *Set how the domain works* and (2) *Build the OWL ontology.*
- *METHONTOLOGY.* This methodology [3], inspired by the IEEE software development process and previous knowledge engineering methodologies, contains seven phases: (1) *Specification,* (2) *Knowledge Acquisition,* (3) *Conceptualization,* (4) *Integration,* (5) *Implementation,* (6) *Evaluation* and (7) *Documentation.*
- *ON-TO-KNOWLEDGE.* This methodology [10] is process-oriented with an evolutionary approach and contains five mains phases: (1) *Feasibility study,* (2) *Kickoff,* (3) *Refining,* (4) *Evaluation* and (5) *Application and Evolution.*

Table 1 summarises several characteristics that we consider important.

---

[1] http://www.harmo-ten.org/.

Table 1. Comparative methodology analysis

Methodology	Type	Software engineering life cycle coverage	When reusing of ontologies in life cycle	Descriptive level
Ontology development 101	Simplified	Incomplete-Lacks evaluation	Early (Consider reuse of ontologies)	Intuitive
Horrocks	Simplified	Not following lifecycle pattern	Not reusing	Not very detailed-intuitive
Methontology	Prototype improvement	Yes	Late (Integration)	Quite detailed
On-To-Knowledge	Process-oriented	Emphasis on early stages, not design	Early (kick-off)	Detailed-lacks design

3   Proposed Tourism Ontology

We created a generic ontology as well as instances for the specific case of Croatia. As domain information sources, we mainly used the Croatian official tourism website. We navigated the whole site and looked for every name or substantive that would give back terms with meaning. Touristic and geographic information was gathered. We also relied on the knowledge of domain experts to complete some categories. Special emphasis was made in describing natural resources such as mountain, river, lake, island, islet, which could be of interest in the future for other neighboring countries with similar resources. Figure 1 shows a partial radial view of the first two levels of the class hierarchy. The ontology is organised in eight main parts corresponding to the first level of classes, which we describe in the following paragraphs.

- *Document*: is intended to control the type of access to driving, international routes, etc.
- *Touristic resources*: allow describing types of accommodation, cultural historic attractions, events, points of interest, routes, social attractions and transportation infrastructures.
- *Place*: includes classes and properties for describing uninhabited and natural spaces, such as archipelagos, beaches, islands, forests, etc.
- *Person*: it represents different types of users: tourists and owners of touristic resources. We distinguish between EU and non-EU people, which may be useful for mobility reasons and visa applications, among others.
- *TouristRegion*: describes the regions or places most visited and that could be linked to a particular geographic area, coastal or administrative region.
- *Activity*: is intended to represent activities available for tourists, such as sports (fishing, football, hiking, scuba diving, surfing?), sightseeing and nightlife.

- *TransportationMeans*: different possible means of transportation are represented (aircraft, airplane, helicopter, boat, ship, train, tram?).
- *Geographic Area*: entities that describe natural and geographic areas, such as coastal settlements, countries, counties, cities, squares, streets, ways.

The generic tourism ontology[2] contains 183 classes and 92 properties, while 537 individuals[3] were created representing Croatia resources.

The proposed tourism ontology was implemented from scratch following first an intuitive approach and then improved with a structured methodology. Later, we checked for logic consistence and domain coherence and query capabilities.

We carried out three different activities to evaluate the proposed ontology. First, we used Ontology Pitfall Scanner![4], a tool for analysing good practices. Then, we executed several SPARQL queries[5]. Finally, we created a prototype of app for searching information about ferries in Croatia.

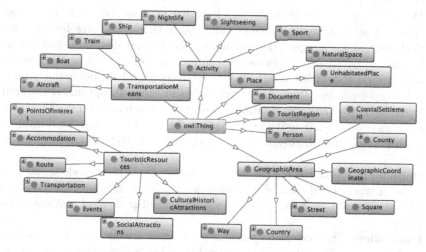

Fig. 1. Partial view of the first two levels of the ontology. All arcs represent subClassOf relations. The top concept (owl:Thing) of the hierarchy is in the center of the picture.

4 Proposed Methodology

Most common ontology development methodologies are difficult for not experienced users. We propose a methodology that follows a simple and common software engineering lifecycle with not so many activities and phases, so the learning curve for non-experts in ontologies is reduced. After a careful analysis of the strengths of the four well-known methodologies described in Sect. 2, we propose a new methodology that combines some of the activities and suggests optional activities.

---

[2] http://www.ia.urjc.es/ontologies/tourism.ttl.

[3] http://www.ia.urjc.es/ontologies/croatia_tourism.ttl.

[4] http://oops.linkeddata.es/.

[5] SPARQL is a language for querying RDF data.

1. **Requirement specification/scope.** As suggested in [8], it is recommendable to start the development of an ontology defining its domain and scope. The first activities from *Ontology Development 101 and Methontology* would be wholly contained in this stage. In addition, we should identify information in use cases of ontology, text analysis, and questions to domain experts or local citizens. This phase includes a subactivity *Reusing existing ontologies*, which is convenient to be carried out in an early phase of development.

2. **Analysis.** For the analysis phase, we again focus on the information available (e.g. on a website) to get a comprehensive list of relevant terms. We brainstorm possible hierarchies and without worrying about overlapping entities. It is better to avoid flooding with terms. Restructuring a hierarchy afterwards or eliminating redundancies could affect efficiency. At the same time, competence questions are evaluated looking for further substantives resulting in more concepts.

3. **Design.** Design is a difficult and iterative process. We take into consideration the recommendations of different authors. Looking for efficiency, Uschold and Grüninger [11] recommend be precise designing but not too specific or detailed. Otherwise, this approach could overflow the ontology with several redundant terms. The so-far-recommended middle-out strategy is far more efficient than other approaches to build an optimised hierarchy. It means applying generalization just for the crucial concepts. This phase includes two optional activities: (i) *Design Refinement* (assimilated from *On-To-Knowledge* and highly recommended) and (ii) *Atypical entities elimination* [7].

4. **Implementation.** During the implementation phase the knowledge acquired so far is represented explicitly using a description language (e.g. OWL) and an edition tool (e.g. Protégé). The ontology itself is the end product of this phase.

5. **Evaluation.** The evaluation phase is not always present in other traditional methodologies. The ontology is assessed technically according to the requirements document. The evaluation checks throughout the whole lifecycle to guarantee that the ontology is correct and in sync with the original idea. Every error found could be compiled in an evaluation document.

6. **Maintenance.** Even though in some analysed methodologies, evaluation and maintenance are combined in only one activity, we recommend a separate activity to test any requisite changes along the lifecycle. Some guidelines could be produced as a result of this phase that could serve as additional documentation of the ontology.

5   Conclusions

In this paper, we have presented a vocabulary for representing touristic information using ontologies, and a specific ontology populated with instances of Croatia resources. Furthermore, we have proposed a methodology for ontology development by non-expert users that takes into account existing methodologies and software engineering lifecycle. Thus, we provided with a reduced and clear set of activities, which we expect contribute to easy the ontology development process for non-expert users.

The resulting ontology was tested, firstly through SPARQL queries to prove the possibilities of querying the vocabulary and secondly with an Android prototype. We tried to lie our focus just in a subset of the ontology - Islands of Croatia and natural resources. In fact, it was not an arbitrary decision; there was real need of a search application or search engine applied to Croatia islands, due to the complexity of transport for tourists among islands.

In the future, we plan to extend our ontology to add more geographical and geological features, which could be of interest for bordering countries with common natural resources such as Slovenia. In addition, we plan to extend the set of instances of Croatia touristic information, and working on automating the extraction of instances from texts. We also intend to continue assessing the correctness and possibilities of the new methodology and understanding what explicitly requires a methodology for a proper development.

Acknowledgments. Work partially supported by the Autonomous Region of Madrid (grant "MOSI-AGIL-CM" (S2013/ICE-3019) co-funded by EU Structural Funds FSE and FEDER), project "SURF" (TIN2015-65515-C4-4-R (MINECO/FEDER)) funded by the Spanish Ministry of Economy and Competitiveness, and through the Excellence Research Group GES2ME (Ref. 30VCPIGI05) co-funded by URJC and Santander Bank.

References

1. Bekiaris, E.: Factsheet ICT for transport and the environment center for research and technology Hellas/Hellenic institute of transport. Technical report, Certh/HIT (2004)
2. Ehrig, M.: Ontology Alignment: Bridging the Semantic Gap (Semantic Web and Beyond). Springer, Secaucus (2006). https://doi.org/10.1007/978-0-387-36501-5
3. Fernandez-Lopez, M., Gomez-Perez, A., Juristo, N.: Methontology: from ontological art towards ontological engineering. In: Proceedings of the AAAI 1997 Spring Symposium, pp. 33–40, March 1997
4. Flgge, M.: Satine: semantic-based interoperability infrastructure for the tourism industry. Technical report (2006)
5. HTW Group: Semantic web methodologies and tools for intra-European sustainable tourism. Technical report (2003)
6. Horrocks, I.: An example owl ontology. Technical report (2003)
7. Jouis, C., Bourdaillet, J.: Representation of atypical entities in ontologies. In: Proceedings of the International Conference on Language Resources and Evaluation, LREC 2008, 26 May–1 June 2008, Marrakech, Morocco (2008)

8. Noy, N.F., Mcguinness, D.L.: Ontology development 101: a guide to creating your first ontology. Technical report (2001)
9. Prantner, K.: Ontour: the ontology. Technical report (2004)
10. Sure, Y., Staab, S., Studer, R., Gmbh, O.: On-to-knowledge methodology (OTKM). In: Staab, S., Studer, R. (eds.) Handbook on Ontologies. International Handbooks on Information Systems, pp. 117–132. Springer (2003). https://doi.org/10.1007/978-3-540-24750-0_6
11. Uschold, M., Gruninger, M.: Ontologies: principles, methods and applications. Knowl. Eng. Rev. **11**, 93–136 (1996)

Analyzing the Repercussions of the Actions Based on the Emotional State in Social Networks

Guillem Aguado$^{(\boxtimes)}$, Vicente Julian(iD), and Ana Garcia-Fornes(iD)

Departamento de Sistemas Informáticos y Computación (DSIC),
Universitat Politècnica de València,
Camino de Vera s/n, Valencia, Spain
{guiagsar,vinglada,agarcia}@dsic.upv.es

Abstract. The present work is a study of the detection of negative affective or emotional states that people have using social network sites (SNSs), and the effect that this negative state has on the repercussions of posted messages. We aim to discover in which grade an user having an affective state considered negative by an analyzer (Sentiment Analyzer and Stress Analyzer), can affect other users and generate bad repercussions, and to know whether its more suitable to predict a bad future situation using the different analyzers. We propose a method for creating a combined model of sentiment and stress and use it in our experimentation in order to discern if it is more suitable to predict future bad situations, and in what context. Additionally, we created a Multi-Agent System (MAS) that integrate the analyzers to protect or advice users, which uses the trained and tested system to predict and avoid future bad situations in social media, that could be triggered by the actions of an user that has an emotional state considered negative. We conduct this study as a way to help building future systems that prevent bad situations where an user that has a negative state creates a repercussion in the system. This can help avoid users to achieve a bad mood, or help avoid privacy issues, in the way that an user that has a negative state post information that he don't really want to post.

Keywords: Agents · Multi-Agent System · Social Networks
Sentiment Analysis · Stress · Stress Analysis · Advice · Privacy · Users

1 Introduction

In the actual society, we are immersed on a constant stream of on-line applications. One of the most important of them are Social Networks or Social Network Sites (SNSs). There are plenty of situations when we can be at risk or suffer negative consequences of being in a SNS [1]. Teenagers face several risks at SNSs and have some characteristics that make them more vulnerable to those risks [2]. Publishing a post can have negative consequences and lead to regret [3].

© Springer Nature Switzerland AG 2018
F. Belardinelli and E. Argente (Eds.): EUMAS 2017/AT 2017, LNAI 10767, pp. 523–537, 2018.
https://doi.org/10.1007/978-3-030-01713-2_37

Moreover, it has been proved that a negative emotional state can lead to a poor decision making, In [4], a study demonstrates the role of cognitive bias, emotional distress and poor decision making in the gambling disorder. More specifically, and related to the emotional state, [4] demonstrates that pathological gambling correlated with negative emotional states. The more individuals have a problematic gambling involvement, the more they experience anxiety and depression.

In [5], the effects that incidental moods, discrete emotions, integral affect and regret can have in the decision making process are reviewed. By incidental moods and discrete emotions we mean affective states that are not linked directly with the task at hand (e.g., moods and emotions at the time of making a decision); Integral affect is affect that arises from the task that is being performed [5]. They show that incidental moods proved to affect decision making by altering people's perception. Discrete emotions, integral affect and regret also shown to affect it and regret can do it in the form of anticipated regret (thinking of the bad outcome before it happens).

Since the stress has been observed to be associated with a concrete emotional state [6], it is suitable for building a system that analyzes the emotional state of the users. Our aim is to build a system capable of recognizing the potential bad outcomes when an user in a SNS is interacting with the network, and more concretely we focus on the case of the publication of messages on it. Being able to predict a bad consequence we would advice users to protect them and to make their experience in SNSs more satisfactory and safe. For this purpose we designed a MAS that has multiple agents, that perform different kinds of analysis (sentiment, stress, combined), and interacts with the users advising them at the moment of publishing a message. This system has been integrated in a SNS to perform advices to the users according to their emotional states, in order to help them with the decision making process, and for avoiding bad future situations that could be triggered by, for example, publishing something that you don't really want to post (due to the emotional state causing cognitive distortions). In this paper we focus on the agents Sentiment Analyzer, Stress Analyzer and combined version. A design of the whole system is detailed in Sect. 3.

For that intention, we present the current work as an study for determining how the emotional state or stress level when writing a message can determine the repercussion of publishing a message, as the emotional state or stress of the messages that come as a result of it. Concretely we will analyze the sentiment polarity and stress levels of the replies of a message to determine if it caused a bad repercussion or not. We analyze the state with our set of analyzers (Sentiment, Stress and combined model), of both the messages and the replies of them, for the purpose of determining whether being in a concrete emotional state or having a level of stress (or a combination of both), can cause a future situation of bad consequences (other people with a similar state). Also, we want to study what kind of analysis can predict better a potential bad outcome (sentiment, stress or combined), and in which cases.

2   Related Work

In this section we are going to discuss the previous works related to the topic of study, which are the Sentiment Analysis and Stress Analysis work, the work on risk prevention on SNSs, and on modeling user state.

Sentiment Analysis, is a field of research that intends to study the phenomena of opinions, sentiments, evaluations, appraisal, attitude and emotion through different kinds of media (e.g. written messages, images, etc.) [7]. When we look into the literature searching for previous works in Sentiment Analysis in texts (which is the most common), we will find that there are four well differentiated techniques: document-level Sentiment Analysis, sentence-level Sentiment Analysis, aspect-based Sentiment Analysis and comparative Sentiment Analysis [8]. The kind of analysis depends on the level of fine grained Sentiment Analysis that we choose to perform, starting out from the document level Sentiment Analysis (sentiment from the entire document), to sentence level (sentiment in a sentence), and finally to the aspect based Sentiment Analysis (sentiment in concrete aspects, as sequences of words that can be one word, found in the text). Finally comparative Sentiment Analysis is an exception, where comparative sentences are used to learn which are the preferred entities, associated to comparative words appearing in the sentences (the sentiment words for the model) [8]. For the present study we choose to use aspect based Sentiment Analysis on texts, so we can perform a fine grained analysis, focusing on terms that may contain sentiment and not entire sentences or documents, which may contain more than one.

There are two main issues that appear recurrently in the literature when working with Sentiment Analysis, that are aspect extraction and sentiment classification. We can also find works that use hybrid approaches, and there are several techniques that intend to solve those topics [9].

1. Aspect detection: For aspect detection we can find frequency based methods, which use the frequency of the terms in the training corpus to put them as aspects or not in the aspect set (the most frequent terms are added) [10]; Detection through generative models (e.g. Conditional Random Fields or CRF), that use a variated set of features [11]; Non supervised machine learning techniques (e.g. Linear Discriminant Analysis or LDA) [12]. We will use a frequency based method because it helps to know what aspects are the most frequently mentioned in a SNS.
2. Sentiment classification: We have a variety of methods for sentiment classification, such as dictionary based methods and machine learning methods (supervised and not supervised). Dictionary based methods use a dictionary of aspects with a polarity assigned to them, and a method for extracting polarities later from texts using the dictionary, they also use a method for training the aspect set for assigning the polarities [9]. Machine learning methods use Support Vector Regression and various other techniques to obtain the features for training the model, and non supervised methods use other techniques like relaxation labeling [9]. We choose a dictionary based method because that

way we will be able to have a set of sentiment and stress aspects (sequences of words) with associated sentiment polarities or stress levels.

3. Hybrid works: Hybrid approaches try to detect aspects and assign polarities at the same time [9], but those are not worked in this paper.

TensiStrength is an algorithm derived from the SentiStrength algorithm for sentiment strength detection, that uses a set of terms associated with stress and another set of terms associated with relaxation, previously trained like the dictionary based methods of Sentiment Analysis, and uses them to detect stress and relaxation levels in sentences of written texts, with some improvements implemented in the algorithm such as detecting exclamation marks and boosting the strength of stress or relaxation within a sentence. It assigns levels of stress and relaxation to its aspect sets first with an unsupervised method that use annotated tweets with strengths, and then refining the values with a hill-climbing method [6].

There are works trying to model the information of the user on a system that can be found on the literature. A nearest-neighbor collaborative approach, used to train user-specific classifiers, which were combined with user similarity measurement in a Sentiment Analysis task [13]; Gao et al. [14] used a model for a task of sentiment classification that computes user and product specific sentiment inclinations; Rincon et al. [15] created a social emotional model that detects the social emotion of a group of entities. They used the PAD three-dimensional emotional space for representing the emotions of the entities and a neural network to learn the emotion of the group in the context of some event that has just happened.

Privacy aiding in SNSs has been worked on in [16], where privacy improving in SNSs has been addressed designing the user interface of the system for that purpose (e.g. having the core features of privacy visible and privacy reminders, also having customized privacy settings), and to the best of our knowledge, there is not an approximation that use the combined analysis of sentiment and stress levels of the users to advice them in SNSs, so we will try to address this case with the present study.

3   System Proposed

Our system has been designed as a MAS to be able to analyze data from written short messages, so it can give recommendations to the user in order to help him or her in the social experience. We designed the system as agents, that are components of the MAS. These agents perform different tasks on the system and communicate with other agents in order to accomplish their tasks. They use the SPADE multi-agent platform for the implementation of their behaviors.

The MAS proposed has three layers, which follow the classic presentation, logic and persistence layer architecture. The system is structured into diverse agent types that operate in the different layers and each one has a different task to perform. The presentation layer has an agent to show information to the user and to get the information of the user and send it to the logic layer. The logic layer has agents that perform all the analysis and calculations of the system and generate recommendations, it gets input from the presentation layer and retains the information via the persistence layer. Finally, the persistence layer has the agent that stores the data into the database and provides it to the logic layer when it is needed. The architecture of the MAS can be seen at Fig. 1. As it can be seen on the image, the advisor agent can get the information about the sentiment polarities and stress levels from the agents at the moment when an user is about to make a post or from the database (for if we need to implement an advice based on old data).

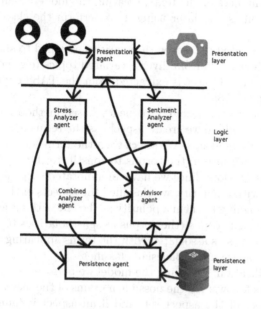

Fig. 1. Architecture of the MAS

The agents that are the focus of the current work are used at the logic layer of the MAS, and correspond to the agents that will perform the analysis on the text data. As we can see in Fig. 1, there are three different analyzer agents, that correspond to the Sentiment Analyzer agent, the Stress Analyzer agent and the Combined Analyzer agent. Each of those agents will be performing the different kinds of analysis on the system. The combination agent will be interacting with the other two agents to perform a combined analysis. Other auxiliary artifacts have been built, to pre process and translate tweets and to extract data from twitter, but those aren't agents in the MAS, just auxiliary code for the MAS agents and for launching experiments.

3.1 Sentiment Analyzer Agent

The Sentiment Analyzer agent can be viewed as a black box that takes as input the content of a short text message (e.g., from a social network), and analyzes it using a previously trained model, for giving as a result its sentimental polarity (positive, negative or neutral). For designing it, various decisions have been made:

1. Aspect based Sentiment Analysis: The kind of Sentiment Analysis chosen for the system was aspect-based. This type of Sentiment Analysis, as explained in the previous works section, performs an analysis based on concrete aspects found in the sentences of the texts, creating the model as an aspect set with associated polarities and later using it to perform the classification on text messages.

   We used an annotated dataset with polarities assigned to short written messages (tweets), extracted from diverse variated topics (e.g. politics) for training the model. This dataset is extracted from the TASS experimental evaluation workshop [17, 18].

2. Aspect extraction: We selected a frequency-based method for performing the aspect extraction, where we create aspects as the terms found in the training corpus, which are unigrams. We select then the terms or aspects with higher frequency of appearance in the corpus to constitute the aspect set.

3. Sentiment classification: Since we have an annotated corpus of data with sentences labeled with a polarity, we classified the aspects of the aspect set using those labels, assigning to them a polarity as the one with major appearance on the training labeled corpus (the corpus assigns polarities to sentences, so we took those polarities as associated with the terms appearing in the sentence), which means that we use a Bayesian classifier.

4. Sentence classification: For using the model we perform classification of short written texts as follows: All the possible n grams of the message are compared with each aspect of the aspect set, and if an aspect is found we store that information. Finally, when all the aspects of the aspect set are compared, we determine the sentiment of the message as the most predominant polarity found from the previous exploration. Either positive, negative or neutral.

3.2 Stress Analyzer Agent

The Stress Analyzer agent is similar to the Sentiment Analyzer agent, but it assigns levels of stress to the aspects in the aspect set instead of sentiment polarities. In that manner we can find low stress level, normal stress level and high stress level associated to an aspect. The dataset used to train the model is also a dataset of messages written in a context in which stress is normally present.

We used an annotated corpus of stress-related tweets with stress strengths coming from the work on TensiStrength [6], extracted from twitter monitoring a set of stress and relaxation keywords.

3.3   Combination Analyzer Agent

We use the combined values of sentiment and stress from the text messages. We determined that when stress is in low or normal levels, we assign the polarity of the message as the polarity of the Sentiment Analysis, but when the stress levels are high we directly assign the polarity of the message being analyzed with this combined model as negative. This is done in this way to determine the effect of high levels of stress in the repercussion of a message in a SNS, we don't experiment with normal levels of stress because those are present in a multitude of situations for different reasons and we choose not to consider a medium level of stress as a negative state. Instead we study the negative bad repercussions and user negative states as high levels of stress or negative sentiment polarity.

4   Experimentation

4.1   Design of the Experiment

We have taken corpus of data extracted from the popular social network site Twitter.com, composed of real text messages of real people from all around the world and characterized for having a thematic on each corpus (e.g. political, cultural, etc.). The corpus has been created using the twitter API for streaming tweets, and it has been processed using a function to clean them up for the Sentiment, Stress, or Combined Analyzer, which searches possible sources of error for the future analysis and corrects them. We have two corpus for the main experimentation:

1. Champions League (A leisure dataset about the famous football championship The 'Champions League'). This is a small corpus (less than a million of tweets).
2. Podemos (A political corpus made of messages related to the politic party 'Podemos'). This is a very large corpus (millions of tweets).

We used also the annotated corpus Stompol for the calculation of the recall of the analyzers.

In this work, we will try to determine the effect that the messages detected as negative or dangerous by the hand of the Sentiment and Stress Analyzers have in the messages that are a repercussion (we used the replies of the messages in this case) of them.

We want to determine the effect that tweets analyzed by our combined model (which uses different analyzers), have on the replies as well, and compare this effect to the effect that we observed in the previous stage (using only one analyzer at a time). With this information we aim to determine whether it is more useful or informative to use only one analyzer or both combined, and in what situations.

We coded a function that read and load a tweet in JSON format and then analyzes it for knowing if it is a Spanish tweet (since our aspect sets for Sentiment Analysis and Stress Analysis are in Spanish), and if is a reply of another tweet.

If it passes the two filters, then we proceed to look at a dictionary where we store the analyzed replies, and if the original tweet that generated a reply is not present, then we search that tweet using the twitter API. We calculate the sentiment and stress of both messages and store it at the dictionary (if the original message was already present we only calculate the ones of the reply).

When we have all the corpus analyzed, for all the tweets that generated replies we do:

1. Calculate its combined value using both the sentiment and stress value in the way we explained in the Subsect. 3.3.
2. Calculate the predominant sentiment in the replies of that tweet, by predominant we understand the most present.
3. Calculate the predominant stress level in the replies of the tweet.
4. Calculate the combined value of the replies using both predominant sentiment and stress from them.

With this done, we finally proceed to calculate which tweets correspond to its replies in terms of comparing their calculated values (using sentiment, stress and combined values), with the calculated final values in the replies (using predominant sentiment, predominant stress and combined values on the replies). If it is the same value (positive, negative or neutral for sentiment, stress levels or combined value), we conclude that this tweet has generated a repercussion, according to what the model predicted.

Finally we just accumulate the percentage of generated replies that are in line (have the same emotional polarity associated, stress level or combined value), with the prediction of the model for the original tweet (the calculation of the value for the original tweet that generated them), and store it as the result of the experiment.

Metrics of the Experimentation. We performed an experiment with an annotated corpus with tweets associated to a sentiment polarity, in order to discover the recall of the analyzers. For calculating the recall we took the tweets that were classified as negative by the classifier and the total amount of tweets annotated as negative (or annotated as having a stress level associated as negative by the classifier). We used the following metrics for calculating the result of the experiments:

1. For Sentiment Analysis, percentage of concordance sentiment (PCsen):
   tweetsConc = Amount of tweets with the same emotional polarity than the predominant in its replies.
   tweetsTotal = Amount of total tweets with replies analyzed.

$$PCsen = \frac{tweetsConc}{tweetsTotal}$$

2. For Stress Analysis, percentage of concordance stress (PCstr):
   tweetsConc = Amount of tweets with the same stress levels than the predominant in its replies.
   tweetsTotal = Amount of total tweets with replies analyzed.

$$PCstr = \frac{tweetsConc}{tweetsTotal}$$

3. For the combined analysis, percentage of concordance combined (PCcomb):
   tweetsConc = Amount of tweets with the same value, combining emotional polarity and stress levels than the predominant in its replies.
   tweetsTotal = Amount of total tweets with replies analyzed.

$$PCcomb = \frac{tweetsConc}{tweetsTotal}$$

4. Recall for the Sentiment Analyzer (RecallSA):
   NegativeTweetsDetected = amount of tweets considered negative that the analyzer detected.
   NegativeTweets = Amount of tweets considered negative in the corpus.

$$RecallSA = \frac{NegativeTweetsDetected}{NegativeTweets}$$

5. Recall for the Stress Analyzer (RecallStr):
   NegativeTweetsDetected = amount of tweets considered negative that the analyzer detected (which in this case is associated to the stress level considered negative).
   NegativeTweets = Amount of tweets considered negative in the corpus (again it is associated to the stress level considered negative).

$$RecallStr = \frac{NegativeTweetsDetected}{NegativeTweets}$$

6. Recall for the Combined Analyzer (RecallCombined):
   NegativeTweetsDetected = amount of tweets considered negative that the analyzer detected.
   NegativeTweets = Amount of tweets considered negative in the corpus.

$$RecallCombined = \frac{NegativeTweetsDetected}{NegativeTweets}$$

Plan of the Experiments. We will explain in this subsection how many experiments we launched, of what kind and with what corpus of data. As stated above, we launched an experiment with a corpus of annotated tweets called Stompol for calculating the recall of the analyzers. We used the amount of tweets classified as negative and that actually had a negative polarity label coded by an human, and the total amount of tweets coded as negative. The fraction of negative tweets detected by the analyzer (NegativeTweetsDetected), and negative tweets in the corpus (NegativeTweets), are shown following for the three analyzers:

$RecallSA = 79.12\%$; $RecallStr = 0.012\%$; $RecallCombined = 79.12\%$

The Stress Analyzer agent has a very low recall, this may be caused because we only use the high levels of stress to determine whether an user has a dangerous stress level or not. Nevertheless, it has proved to make a difference in the tests over large amount of data (which will be shown following).

The recall for the Sentiment Analyzer resulted the same as the Recall Combined, this is because it is a small corpus, and the small amount of detections from the Stress Analyzer part were also detected (mostly or completely) be the Sentiment Analyzer.

1. Experimentation with the corpus Champions League: We prepared an experimentation with the corpus related to the Champions League as follows:
   We partitioned the corpus in parts of different sizes, and for each size we launched 3 different experiments with the three cases (Sentiment Analysis only, Stress Analysis only and the combined analysis). For partitioning the corpus, we understand that we will analyze a percentage of the total tweets that are replies in the corpus. Since this was a small corpus (around 3000 replies), we could only perform two partitions. The first partition was to divide the corpus in parts of 1/3 of the total replies, so we had three different experiments with around 1000 replies each, and those were made with the three analyzers. The second partition was made in parts of 1/2 of the total replies of the corpus, this was done in three experiments, using one of three partitions at a time and with the three analyzers again. We used the first half of the corpus in the first partition, the central part of the corpus for the second, and the second half for the third. This was done because the information that an experiment will give is different even if we use part of the tweets used in another, because when the total set of tweets analyzed is different from any other experiment the replies associated to each tweet may change, and so the result. We did it in this case because there was not another way to get enough partitions to make an experiment that was comparable to the previous. We show in Table 1 the results for all the experiments with the corpus Champions League.

2. Experimentation with the corpus Podemos: We prepared an experimentation with the corpus Podemos in the following way: We partitioned this corpus, but this time, since it is a very large corpus, we decided to make six different partition sizes, doing four different experiments for each partition size. This was done in this way because the largest partition size was 1/4 of the corpus replies, and the maximum amount of parts that we could perform without using a tweet more than one time was four. Again, we performed each experiment using the three different analyzers.
   The first partition is 1/128 of the total replies of the corpus for each experiment (around 1700 replies); The second partition is 1/64 of the replies; In this same way, the following four partitions are of 1/32, 1/16, 1/8 and 1/4 of the total replies, and the final results of the experimentation can be seen at Table 2.

We show in Fig. 2 the results of all the experiments launched for the corpus Champions League, the values of the three experiments for each corpus size have been represented as one single point as the average of the three experiments.

Table 1. Experimentation with the corpus Champions League

Partition size	Experiment	PCsen	PCstr	PCcomb
1/3 of replies	1	0.6435	0.9196	0.6167
	2	0.736	0.912	0.688
	3	1.0	1.0	1.0
1/2 of replies	1	0.6453	0.9359	0.6239
	2	0.6667	0.9815	0.6481
	3	0.6365	0.9668	0.6276

We also show the results of the experiments in the same way for the corpus Podemos in Figs. 3 and 4, but this time we separated the information about the Stress Analyzer experiments from the others, because the high percentage of concordance of this analyzer (PCstr) is very high and it made difficult to appreciate well the results of the others when they were shown in the same figure. In the following three figures, the legend stands for:

1. SA and Stress A: Sentiment Analysis combined with Stress Analysis.
2. SA: Only Sentiment Analysis.
3. Stress A: Only Stress Analysis.

4.2   Results of the Experimentation

We discovered that both analyzers separately (Sentiment and Stress) are success-fully able to predict a bad outcome through bad emotional states in the replies. This can be seen for the experiments at both corpus. Regarding the Stress Ana-lyzer, despite of having a general tendency of high concordance with the replies, we have to remember that it has a very small recall (RecallStr), so it may be less suitable than the other analyzers in a variety of cases.

In the case of the Champions League corpus, we can see that it is shown to be unstable results because they switch from 65% to 100% concordance in the case of only around 1000 replies analyzed. This is caused by the small amount of replies analyzed, that make the experiment little representative in the case of this corpus. That is not the case with the Podemos corpus, since we perform experiments with up to around 55000 replies (1/4 of the total for each experi-ment). The Sentiment Analyzer agent shows to be better at first in the 1/3 sized experiments (PCsen), but it gets closer to the Combined Analyzer (PCcomb) in the 1/2 sized experiments. The Stress Analyzer by its own is in the 90%–100% range of concordance (PCstr). We can see some variation in that case as well, that may be caused by the small size of the corpus.

In the case of the Podemos corpus, we can see that there is a big varia-tion at the smallest sized experiments (1/128), but the results are considerably more stable at the big partition size experiments, starting to get more variation again when it comes to the biggest size experiment. This could be caused by

Table 2. Experimentation with the corpus Podemos

Partition size	Experiment	PCsen	PCstr	PCcomb
1/128 of replies	1	0.5975	0.9752	0.5944
	2	0.5594	0.9752	0.5644
	3	0.5881	0.9611	0.5943
	4	1.0	1.0	1.0
1/64 of replies	1	0.5789	1.0	0.5789
	2	0.4583	1.0	0.4583
	3	0.5680	0.9813	0.5697
	4	0.4706	1.0	0.4706
1/32 of replies	1	0.5	0.9833	0.5
	2	0.5682	1.0	0.5682
	3	0.5261	0.9799	0.5281
	4	0.5824	0.9780	0.5824
1/16 of replies	1	0.5132	0.9737	0.5
	2	0.5156	0.9778	0.52
	3	0.5616	0.9726	0.5616
	4	0.5375	0.95	0.525
1/8 of replies	1	0.5508	0.9786	0.5508
	2	0.5546	0.9738	0.5611
	3	0.5493	0.983	0.5511
	4	0.5864	0.978	0.5864
1/4 of replies	1	0.5591	0.9694	0.5577
	2	0.5948	0.9752	0.6020
	3	0.5638	0.9741	0.5618
	4	0.5674	0.9787	0.5686

the excessive amount of information when more and more replies are added to the analysis. As a general tendency (except for one case, which are the 1/16 partition size experiments), we see that the Combined Analyzer performs better than the Sentiment Analyzer alone, from what we can conclude that at least at the domains where there is stress involved (such as politics in this case), the Combined Analyzer performs better than just the Sentiment Analyzer. Again we can see a tendency of the Stress Analyzer agent to fluctuate in the 90%–100% range.

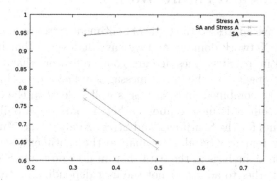

Fig. 2. Results of the experiments with the corpus Champions League

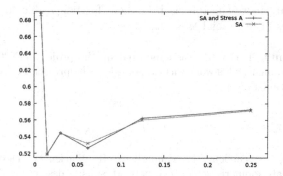

Fig. 3. Results of the experiments with the corpus Podemos for the Sentiment Analyzer and the Combined Analyzer

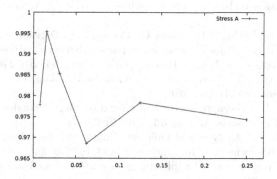

Fig. 4. Results of the experiments with the corpus Podemos for the Stress Analyzer

5   Conclusions and Future Work

In this work we have addressed the topic of Sentiment, Stress and combined analysis in the Social Network domain, and we have discovered that both sentiment and stress found in a written message are good indicators that this polarity or stress level will propagate to the future messages influenced by this message. We discovered that the combined analysis works well at least in the domains where stress is present, but it is unsure about other domains. We built a MAS that incorporates agents for the Sentiment and Stress Analysis and a novel combined analysis. This system will be able to analyze the sentiment, stress levels and perform a combined analysis in the data that an user post in a SNS, and will be able to decide whether to advice or not the user depending on those values and the concrete case.

For future lines of work we will be performing a deeper analysis with more data, and we will aim to create new agents capable of performing new types of analysis (e.g. with other media like images), and discovering in what domains and situations are more suitable each of them for being able to help the user ever better in his or her social experience.

Acknowledgments. This work was supported by the project TIN2014-55206-R of the Spanish government. This work was supported by the project TIN2017-89156-R of the Spanish government.

References

1. Vanderhoven, E., Schellens, T., Vanderlinde, R., Valcke, M.: Developing educational materials about risks on social network sites: a design based research approach. Educ. Tech. Res. Dev. **64**, 459–480 (2016)
2. Vanderhoven, E., Schellens, T., Valcke, M.: Educating teens about the risks on social network sites. An intervention study in secondary education. Comunicar **22**(43), 123–132 (2014)
3. Christofides, E., Muise, A., Desmarais, S.: Risky disclosures on facebook: the effect of having a bad experience on online behavior. J. Adolesc. Res. **27**, 714–731 (2012)
4. Ciccarelli, M., Griffiths, M.D., Nigro, G., Cosenza, M.: Decision making, cognitive distortions and emotional distress: a comparison between pathological gamblers and healthy controls. J. Behav. Ther. Exp. Psychiatry **54**, 204–210 (2017)
5. George, J.M., Dane, E.: Affect, emotion, and decision making. Organ. Behav. Hum. Decis. Processes **136**, 47–55 (2016)
6. Thelwall, M.: TensiStrength: stress and relaxation magnitude detection for social media texts. Inf. Process. Manag. **53**, 106–121 (2017)
7. Liu, B.: Sentiment Analysis and Opinion Mining. Synthesis Lectures on Human Language Technologies, vol. 16. Morgan, San Mateo (2012)
8. Feldman, R.: Techniques and applications for sentiment analysis. Commun. ACM **56**(4), 82–89 (2013)
9. Schouten, K., Frasincar, F.: Survey on aspect-level sentiment analysis. IEEE Trans. Knowl. Data Eng. **28**(3), 813–830 (2016)

10. Hu, M., Liu, B.: Mining opinion features in customer reviews. In Proceedings of the 19th National Conference on Artificial Intelligence, pp. 755–760 (2004)
11. Jakob, N., Gurevych, I.: Extracting opinion targets in a single-and cross-domain setting with conditional random fields. In: Proceedings of the 2010 Conference on Empirical Methods in Natural Language Processing, pp. 1035–1045 (2010)
12. Blei, D.M., Ng, A.Y., Jordan, M.I.: Latent dirichlet allocation. J. Mach. Learn. Res. **3**, 993–1022 (2003)
13. Seroussi, Y., Zukerman, I., Bohnert, F.: Collaborative inference of sentiments from texts. In: De Bra, P., Kobsa, A., Chin, D. (eds.) UMAP 2010. LNCS, vol. 6075, pp. 195–206. Springer, Heidelberg (2010). https://doi.org/10.1007/978-3-642-13470-8_19
14. Gao, W., Yoshinaga, N., Kaji, N., Kitsuregawa, M.: Modeling user leniency and product popularity for sentiment classification. In: Proceedings of IJCNLP, Nagoya, Japan (2013)
15. Rincon, J.A., de la Prieta, F., Zanardini, D., Julian, V., Carrascosa, C.: Influencing over people with a social emotional model. In: International Conference on Practical Applications of Agents and Multiagent Systems (2016)
16. Xie, W., Kang, C.: See you, see me: teenagers self-disclosure and regret of posting on social network site. Comput. Hum. Behav. **52**, 398–407 (2015)
17. Villena-Roman, J., Lana-Serrano, S., Martinez-Camara, E., Gonzalez-Cristobal, J.C.: TASS - workshop on sentiment analysis at SEPLN. Procesam. Leng. Nat. **50** (2013)
18. Villena-Roman, J., Garcia-Morera, J., Lana-Serrano, S., Gonzalez-Cristobal, J.C.: TASS 2013 - a second step in reputation analysis in Spanish. Proces. Leng. Nat. **52**, 37–44 (2014)

Challenges on Normative Emotional Agents

Karen Y. Lliguin, Vicente Botti🆔, and Estefania Argente[(✉)]🆔

Dpto. Sistemas Informáticos y Computación, Universitat Politècnica de València,
Camino de Vera s/n, 46022 Valencia, Spain
`kallileo@inf.upv.es`, {`vbotti,eargente`}`@dsic.upv.es`

Abstract. Most people's choices, including economic ones, are largely based on normative-affective considerations, not only with regard to the selection of goals but also of means. However, although emotions are inherent in human behaviour, and they are also relevant when dealing with the decision making processes, the relationship between norms and emotions has hardly been considered in the agent field, and most normative multi-agent systems do not take emotions into account, as a variable for their computation. In this paper, we analyse the advantages of including emotions in a normative system, how emotions and norms affect to each other and the work done in this field so far. To do this, we (1) identify and describe the relationships between emotions and norms; (2) review the state of art of normative emotional agents; and (3) discuss future directions for research in this field.

Keywords: Normative MAS · Emotion · Multi-agent system
Affective agent · Norm

1 Introduction

The majority of choices people make, including economic ones, are completely or largely based on normative-affective considerations not merely with regard to selection of goals but also of means, and that the areas in which other logical-empirical considerations are paramount, they are also defined by normative/affective factors that legitimate and otherwise motivate such decision-making [1]. Emotions are, therefore, inherent in humans. They play a crucial role in social relationships, they motivate actions and influence our perception. Moreover, as we are social beings, norms have been used to regulate human interaction. Thus, our behaviour towards norms is also influence by emotions, as any other action.

Nowadays with the increase of multi-agent systems where cooperation and coordination mechanism are needed, normative systems are used to regulate the interaction among the agents. The combination of emotional models and normative models in *Normative Emotional Agents* (NEA) seems interesting for

© Springer Nature Switzerland AG 2018
F. Belardinelli and E. Argente (Eds.): EUMAS 2017/AT 2017, LNAI 10767, pp. 538–551, 2018.
https://doi.org/10.1007/978-3-030-01713-2_38

modelling agents capable of dealing with the norms of the group and also dealing with the emotions related to the regulations and consequences of these norms.

There are two very straight forward links between norms and emotions. The first one is how both norms and emotions interfere in the decision making processes of agents. Bagozzi and Pieters [2] studied this relation and proposed a model of goal-directed emotions that takes into account the *anticipated emotions*, which refer to the emotions that will be triggered if the related goal is achieved or not. In this way, the influence of emotions in the decision making process can be considered as a parameter of the utility function of the agents. In a normative system, emotions will intervene in the decision of whether to follow the norm or not. Not only because of the punishment or reward associated with the norm, but also, even if there is not such consequences, the positive or negative emotions (shame, embarrassing, guilt, pride, disappointment, admiration, respect, comfort, etc.) that will be triggered will affect the agent itself and its relationship with the rest of agents. For example, the consequences of a negative emotion can be considered as harmful to the agent, and this consideration will prevent the agent from violating the norm again.

The second link between norms and emotions is regarding on how social norms influence emotions. Emotional theories allow establishing a link between specific actions (of oneself or others) and the emotions that these actions arise in the individual. Thus, since there are some set of emotions that can be expected given an event, an appropriate response to the social norm can also be determined.

Another interesting thing to point out is that when taking into account emotions, the personality of the agent is directly involved too. Therefore emotions allow flexibility in the event interpretation and response depending on the personality given to the agent. This aspect can be related with the role that emotions play in the society.

Next, in Sect. 2 we will briefly explain the concepts of norms, emotions and their relationships, and we will also provide a description of what a Normative Emotional Agent (NEA) should offer. In Sect. 3, a revision of the state of art on NEAs is given. In Sect. 4 we propose several challenges to be addressed when dealing with Normative Emotional Agents. Finally, our conclusions are given in Sect. 5.

2   Norms and Emotions

In this section, a brief revision of the concepts of norms and emotions is given, as well as how these terms have been related in the literature of multi-agent systems.

2.1   Norms in Multi-Agent Systems

Norms have been defined as a mechanism for organising and controlling a society [3]. In the Artificial Intelligence field, norms have been proposed to deal with coordination and security issues in multi-agent systems (MAS) [4]. Normative multi-agent systems (NMAS) have been defined as MAS that use norms as a mechanism for persuading autonomous and heterogeneous agents to behave according to the stated social order [5]. Therefore, NMAS define norms, which are immaterial entities that exist thanks to their acceptance by the society members, so as to avoid conflicts and ensure social order [6]. Therefore, a NMAS combines models for normative systems with models for multi-agent systems.

As described in [4], the role of norms in human societies has been analysed from different disciplines such as philosophy, sociology, or law. From the philosophical point of view, deontic logics [7] are mainly used to formalise norms in terms of permissions, prohibitions and obligations. Norms have been proposed in MAS research as formal specifications of deontic statements aimed at regulating the life of software agents and the interactions among them [8].

From the sociological point of view, Elster characterises social norms as [9]: "norms that must be shared by other people and partly sustained by their approval and disapproval. They are also sustained by the feelings of embarrassment, anxiety, guilt and shame that a person suffers at the prospect of violating them. A person obeying a norm may also be propelled by positive emotions, like anger and indignation". According to this, the emotional and social dimensions of norms are the key factors that allow the distinction among social norms and other kinds of norms such as private ones.

Several authors have proposed different classifications of norms, such as those of Tuomela [10], Dignum [11], Boella [12], Savarimuthu [13] or Peng [14]. From all these proposals, we can differentiate four main types of norms (see Table 1): institutional norms, conventions (or social norms), interaction norms and private norms.

Table 1. Norm classification.

Norm type	Promulgated by	Target	Enforcement	Description
Institutional	Institutional authority	Society	Sanctions/Rewards	YES (Deontic)
Convention	Emerge from social relationships	Society	Social mechanisms (emotions)	NO
Interaction	Participants of the interaction	Participants of the interaction	Sanctions/Rewards	YES (Deontic)
Private	Individual agent	Individual	Moral, emotions	NO

Institutional norms [10,11,14] are promulgated by an organisation authority or the institution itself and their violation is considered to be an illicit act that entails sanctions or punishments, for [13] modelled as laws. They generally describe the ideal behaviour by means of obligations, prohibitions and permissions [12].

Conventions or *social norms* [10,13] indicate the established and approved ways of doing things, and their violation does not imply an institutional sanction or punishment but there can be social consequences, such as being unpopular or even an outcast from a group. Both institutional and social norms govern the coordination of individuals in a society or group of agents. However, social norms are not enforced by any entity representing the institution, but they represent behaviours that emerge from repeated interactions between individuals, such as a convention within a society that has not been imposed by a central authority. Being emergent norms, they are generally not explicitly described in the society, nor define sanctions or rewards for persuading agents to respect them. But they are enforced by social mechanisms such as ostracism, recrimination, etc., being emotions an interesting mechanism for this enforcement [4].

Interaction norms [11,14] are formed by legal contracts and informal agreements between entities, which are created explicitly for a limited period of time as a consequence of an interaction among individuals, and they are also based on the notion of obligation, prohibition and permission and normally include sanctions and rewards.

Finally, *private norms* [11,14] are formed by norms internal to the agent that are self-imposed and ensure the agent autonomy. These private norms are created inside agents' minds, normally as a result of the internalization of an interaction or social norm, and they are accepted as principles.

2.2 Emotions in Multi-Agent Systems

An emotion is an affective state of consciousness in which joy, sorrow, fear, hate, or the like, is experienced, as distinguished from cognitive and willing states of consciousness[1]. The *computational models of emotions* (CMEs) [15] are software systems designed to provide autonomous agents with proper mechanisms for the processing of emotional information, elicitation of synthetic emotions and generation of emotional behaviour, in order to endow agents with abilities for the recognition of emotions from human users and artificial agents, the simulation and expression of emotional feelings, and the execution of emotional responses. The most notable theoretical approaches that have influenced the development of CMES are: appraisal theories of emotion, dimensional theories of emotion and hierarchical theories of emotion.

The *appraisal theories* of emotion differentiates emotions on the basis of the relationship between individuals and their environment [16–18], so emotions arise from the evaluation of situations, objects, and agents existing in the environment that directly or indirectly impact the individual's goals, plans, and beliefs [15]. Several instances of this theory have been proposed, being the OCC appraisal model [16] by Ortony et al. one of the most implemented in CMEs [19–21]. This model considers 22 different emotions as positive or negative reactions elicited by the aspects of *objects* (likes, dislikes, love, hate), the actions of *agents* (pride, admiration, shame, reproach), and the consequences of *events* (happy-for, hope, satisfaction, fear, joy, distress). Another notable appraisal theory is Frijda's model [17], which focuses on the emotion process, defining three steps:

---

[1] WordReference Rando House Unabridge Dictionary of American English, 2017.

appraisal (from the environment), impulse (instigation of an action tendency), and generation of cognitive actions, possibly in the form of mostly expressive behaviour such as facial expressions. A considerable number of CMEs have been developed on the basis of the appraisal theory, such as EMotion and Adaptation (EMA) [22] (see [15] for a deeper review).

The *dimensional theories* of emotion represent emotions from a structural perspective, establishing what can be differentiated on the basis of dimensional parameters, such as arousal and valence [15]. Relevant examples of this theory are the Russell's two-dimensional framework proposal [23], which characterises with pleasantness (pleasure/displeasure) and activation (arousal/non-arousal) a variety of affective phenomena such as emotions, mood and feelings; and the Russell and Mehrabian' three-dimensional framework proposal [24], also known as PAD model, which describes emotions based on their level of pleasantness, arousal and dominance. This PAD model has also been used to represent temperament scales and describe personality types [25]. Examples of CMEs based on dimensional theories are WASABI (Affect Simulation for Agents with Believable Interactivity) [26], Alma (A Layered Model of Affect) [27] and GENIA3 (a General Purpose Intelligent Affective Architecture) [28]. This last proposal also provides an extension to Jason [29], the language of reference for BDI agents. This extension allows defining personality traits for agents, rationality, coping strategies and different affective categories, based on the PAD model.

Finally, in the *hierarchical theories* of emotions, there is a small set of basic, primary or fundamental emotions, which have an evolutionary basis and are innate and instinctive, and they have been extensively investigated and identified. These basic emotions are considered as building blocks that enable the construction of more complex emotions. The most accepted group of basic emotions was established by Ekman [30]. Examples of CMEs based on hierarchical theories are Cathexis [31] and WASABI (which combines dimensional theories with hierarchical theories).

2.3   Emotions and Norms Relationship

Different relationships between norms and emotions can be determined. For example, the violation of a social norm can trigger negative emotions such as shame or guilt in the norm violator, even if nobody can observe that the norm has been violated [32]. So emotions can arise as negative internal consequences of a norm violation and thus they can serve as mechanisms for enforcing or sustaining social norms, in addition to external sanctions. Moreover, these resulting emotions can also differ depending on who is violating the social norm. For example, shame and guilt are contingent upon a norm violation by oneself, while contempt and anger are contingent upon a norm violation by another [32]. Staller and Petta claim that people will feel embarrassed if they get isolated when not following the social norms (for example, wearing jeans in formal dinner). Therefore, emotions are used as a way of sanctioning social norms [32].

Virtual environments are another example in which it is crucial that the virtual agents show emotional reactions related to the importance of the norms which are fulfilled or violated [33], in order to increase the believability (or realism) of these agents. For intelligent agents to be believable they must respect and follow the social rules (institutional norms and/or conventions) established within the social virtual environment. Emotional reactions of agents not only result from the fact that their goals are satisfied, but also from the actions performed in the social environment such as the violation of an important social norm, even if that action contributed to the success of a personal goal [33].

Moreover, emotions can also be considered during the normative decision processes of the agent, known as *norm compliance dilemma* [4]. Thus, making a decision about violating (or complying with) a norm must consider the expected utility of this decision in terms of the effect on agent's goals, the coherence of this decision with respect to the agent's cognitions, and the emotional consequences of these decisions. As Criado et al. [4] argue, decisions about whether or not comply with a norm do not only have to be based on rational decisions (which is normally the case) but also emotions should be taken into account so as to provide a more realistic and complex solution to the decision-making problem.

Joffily et al. [34] analyse the relation among emotions, sanctions and cooperation. For us, cooperation can be seen as the decision of following the rules. Their work shows that the emotions triggered (in other agents and itself) as a consequence of the decision made by the agent will affect its behaviour so that the agent will be more willing to follow the norm. So emotions influence in the enforcement of the norm, in the behaviour of the agent and ultimately in its social relationships.

Regarding social norms, the role of emotions in the enforcement of social norms is particularly interesting [4]. There are works in social science that argue that the anticipation of emotions promotes the internalization and the enforcement of norms [35]. For example, the work described in [36] models the emotion-based enforcement of social norms in agent societies. In this approach, the society monitors norm compliance and generates social emotions such as contempt, or disgust in the case of norm violation, and admiration or gratefulness in the case of norm fulfilment. Similarly, agents observe the expression of these emotions and are able to generate emotions such as shame or satisfaction in response.

As a result, we propose that a *Normative Emotional Agent* (NEA) is an agent that integrates an emotional model and a normative model, following at least one these relationships:

- *Norm Enforcement*: emotions are used as mechanisms for enforcing norms, so emotions arise as positive (negative) internal consequences of a social norm fulfilment (violation), being emotions the main result of the application of the norm. Therefore, positive emotions are related with rewards whereas negative emotions are related with sanctions.
- *Norm Compliance dilemma*: emotions are considered in the normative decision process as an additional parameter, apart from rational decisions.
- *Private Norm inference*: emotions can be used as a mechanism for promoting or inferring private norms. From emotions appraised from certain actions and

behaviours within the society, agents can construct private norms that help them to improve their relationship within the group.

3   Normative Emotional Agents: State of Art

Tables 2 and 3 shows a comparison of the works that have considered the relationship between emotions and norms. All of them have used the appraisal theory as the basis for their emotional model. As agent architectures, they are based on BDI approaches in which they incorporate norms, mainly as *if-then-else* rules (hard-wired in the deliberative process); or explicitly represented and managed by normative components. Only in this last case, these agent architectures can also be considered as Normative Multi-agent Systems (NMAS). Next, a brief description of the analysed proposals is given.

Table 2. Normative emotional agents state of art. (I)

Proposals	Staller [32]	Bazzan [39]	von Scheve [40]
Year	2001	2003	2006
Appraisal Theory	Frijda's	OCC	OCC
Emotional Archit.	TABASCO	OCC translation in Rule-Based system	MULAN
Agent Architecture	JAM (BDI)	Not specified	SONAR
Is it a NMAS?	NO	NO	NO
Norm Represent.	If-then-else rules	If-then-else rules	Petri Nets
Norm/Emotion Rel.	Norm compliance	Norm compliance	Norm compliance
Scenario	Aggression control	Aggression control	
Final Architecture	TABASCO$_{JAM}$		

Staller and Petta [32] proposed TABASCO$_{JAM}$, which is an agent-based architecture that combines the emotional-agent TABASCO architecture [37] and a BDI architecture, named JAM [38]. The TABASCO$_{JAM}$ architecture captures the main components of the emotion process (appraisal, impulse and cognitive actions), detailed by Fridja appraisal theory [17]. Its main steps are: (i) the Observer component senses the world and updates the World Model (a database representing the beliefs of the agent); (ii) the Appraisal component maps beliefs of the World Model to the appraisal outcome and computes an intensity value, which (iii) the Impulse component uses for posting a goal to the Intention Structure; (iv) the plans in the Plan Library applicable to the goals posted by the Impulse component contain the actions to be executed; and (v) a regulatory process at the Appraisal component determines whether the execution of a plan instance results in a norm violation, and the meta-level plan uses the appraisal outcome and the intensity value for determining whether to obey or violate the norm. Therefore, social norms are implemented here as a general behaviour regulation, by means of *If-then-else* rules hard-wired in the agents. At the JAM

Table 3. Normative emotional agents state of art. (II)

Proposals	Ahmad [41]	Ferreira [33]
Year	2012	2014
Appraisal Theory	OCC	OCC
Emotional Archit.	OCC translation in Rule-Based system	FAtiMA
Agent Architecture	OP-RND	FAtiMA (BDI)
Is it a NMAS?	NO	YES
Norm Represent.	Normative Goals	Normative Envir.
Norm/Emotion Rel.	Plan Generation	Emotion generation
Scenario	EPMP	Smoking
Final Architecture	OP-NRD-E	

architecture, norm deliberation or norm reasoning have not been taken into account, so it cannot be considered as a normative architecture.

Bazzan et al. [39] define a framework that allows users to define the characteristics of a given interaction, the emotions agents can display, and how these emotions affect their actions and interactions. Norms are related here with the interactions that agents follow when they meet. For the emotional part of their framework, they translate the OCC model into a rule-based system that generates cognitive-related emotions in an agent. These *If-then-else* rules test either the desirability (of a consequence of an event), the praiseworthiness (of an action of an agent) or the appealingness (of an object). The rule determines the potential for generating an emotional state accordingly. Moreover, similarly to Staller and Petta's work, social norms are here directly implemented in the agents as part of these *If-then-else* rules.

Von Scheve et al. [40] mainly outline the social functions of emotions, so that emotions can be used to acknowledge and maintain social norms. Therefore, authors establish the relation between norms and emotions according to the violation of the norm and the emotions that will arouse. They use SONAR (a socionic multi-agent architecture) and MULAN (a multi-agent architecture) to model social entities formed by different layers; they use MULAN for implementing key concepts like autonomy, mobility, cooperation and adaptation; and the SONAR architecture to model the internal representations of an entity (acknowledgement, observation and actions). For them the interaction of norms is seen as explicitly represented mental objects and emotions as processes with non-propositional output. Moreover, the activities of an agent are modelled as protocol Petri nets. This proposal lacks of a explicitly representation of norms; and their Petri Net modelling implies reference nets (with recursive nets that are tokens of nets again) that might make the modelling of emotions and norms very complex.

Ahmad et al. [41] propose the OP-RND-E framework, based on the OP-RND normative framework [42], in which norms are modelled as obligations to the authority to do a specific action in a time-constrained situation. Their emotional model is based on the OCC theory, from which they only consider "joy", "pride", "distress" and "shame" emotions for representing the positive and negative categories of emotions, respectively. Events are represented by the occurrence of goals, which can be normative goals, mandatory personal goals and discretionary personal goals. Therefore, norms are modelled here as normative goals, which represent the actions that should be done within a stipulated time. Emotions are triggered when unexpected events occur, and the agent needs to use its resources and efforts to complete the tasks to achieve the normative goal. For example, a positive emotion (joy) is triggered for getting extra time to achieve the normative goal and "pride" for the ability to do the action within time; whereas a negative emotion (distress) is triggered for losing time to achieve the normative goal and "shame" for the inability to do the action within time. Thus, changes of events determine the positive or negative elicited emotions, which influence the agent's desirability. If the elicited emotion is negative, the agent needs to re-evaluate its plans. Therefore, emotions motivate an agent to plan for better actions in achieving the normative goal.

Finally, Ferreira et al. [33] focused on how to increase the believability of agents with virtual character representation by generating emotions not only from the events that affect a character's goals, but also from other sources of emotions, such as norms and standards. Therefore, they proposed a model for the generation of emotions based on the appraisal of actions associated with norm-related events, such as the fulfilment or violation of a norm. They make use of the agent architecture FAtiMA [43], a BDI architecture that endows agents with the ability to generate emotional reactions to events, based on the OCC model but in which there was no explicit notion of norms. Thus, they complemented this architecture with a normative model, in which norms include: activation conditions, expiration conditions, normative conditions (prescriptions for behaviour of agents), targets (agents expected to fulfil the norm) and salience (importance of the norm). Moreover, their emotional model triggers Attribution Emotions, i.e. "pride" and "shame" occur when the agent is appraising its own actions as praiseworthy (when fulfilling a norm) or blameworthy (when violating a norm), respectively, while "admiration" and "reproach" arises from appraising the actions of others as praiseworthy or blameworthy. In their proposal, agents constantly check if any norm becomes active or expires. Every time that an agent perceives a new event, it will check if it is an action of an agent that causes the fulfilment or violation of a norm. When a norm fulfilment is detected, the agent appraises that event and computes its praiseworthiness and expectation-deviation to determine the intensity of the resulting emotion.

Regarding case studies, some works have based their experiments on the Conte and Castelfranchy [44] control of aggression case study. In their example, agents perform some elementary routines for surviving in a situation of food scarcity (e.g., moving, eating, attacking an eating agent). Each agent has a strength, which is increased by eating and decreased by moving and attacking. In one condition, each agent owns a number of food items and all agents follow a normative strategy for aggression control: they do not attack agents eating their own food (this is the institutional norm, named "finder-keeper" norm). In another condition, all agents follow a utilitarian strategy for aggression control: they do not attack eating agents whose strength is higher than their own. The normative strategy has been found to reduce aggression (i.e., the number of attacks) to a much greater extent than the utilitarian strategy [44]. In [32], the appraisal of concern relevance is also considered, i.e. the optimal state of feeding is a basic concern for agents, so as long as this concern is not satisfied, food is considered as relevant. Therefore, their "normative emotional agents" were capable of deciding whether to obey or violate the institutional norm (i.e. the finder-keeper norm), based on the strengths of their concerns for the optimal state of feeding and for norm compliance. In [39] they conducted a similar experiment, but they used emotions also to represent different types of agents: joyful, resentment, pitiful or angry agents. All these experiments showed that normative emotional agents in a social normative system are more efficient than just a social normative agent because the first ones ended up with higher strength and the lowest rate of being attacked, thus having better performance than just "normative agents".

In [41], their OP-RND-E framework was validated using the "Examination paper preparation and moderation process" (EPMP) case study, where they compared rational normative agents vs. emotional normative agents. This case study attempts to determine the actions and emotions of a Lecturer in executing the process of preparing and submitting the examination paper to the Examination Committee.

Finally, in [33] their proposal was tested in a scenario inspired by the existing no-smoking law in bars and restaurants in many European countries. In this scenario, the user's avatar is seated with other characters inside a bar where the norm "Do not smoke inside bars" is active. After an initial conversation, which states which agents are friends and which are complete strangers, one of the agents begins to smoke (because it considers its goal of smoking more important than the norm), and the remaining agents react emotionally to that norm violation. They experimented different versions of this scenario, varying the salience of the norm and the group of the smoker (i.e. friends or strangers). Their model was able to generate emotions in synthetic characters similar to those felt by humans in analogous situations.

4   Challenges on Normative Emotional Agents

As we have seen, the study and implementation of NEAs is rather a recent field. Here we present some open branches to explore in future works:

- **Norm Compliance Dilemma.** Normative agents should be endowed with capabilities for recognising, representing, and accepting norms, and for solving possible conflicts among them. As Criado et al. argue [4], decisions about whether or not comply with a norm do not only have to be based on rational decisions but also emotions should be taken into account so as to provide a more realistic and complex solution to the decision-making problem. Currently, the works that have focused on this issue have mainly implemented norms using *if-then-else* rules hard-wired in the agents. However, there is still a need for mechanisms that make use of an explicit representation of emotions as well as an explicit representation of norms, so as to consider phenomena such as shame, honour, gratitude, etc. in the decision-making processes of any type of norms (institutional norms, conventions, interaction norms and private norms). Emotions to be taken into account should be not only current emotions appraised from previous events of the environment, but also the *anticipated-emotions* [2] that are assumed to be triggered when individuals fulfil or violate the norm. Moreover, since emotions are related with the personality of the agent, they should also be considered when calculating the salience of the norm. Thus, agents showing different emotions to events will also be able to give different saliences to the same norm.

– **Emergence and Detection of Social Norms.** Norm detection responds to the ability of an agent to infer the correct rules of an unknown context in which he is not aware of the current norms. For institutional norms, there can be institutional authorities capable of communicating the norms to the agents of the system. However, for social norms that emerge from agent interactions, we need mechanisms that enable agents to infer these social norms through the observation of the rest of agents, their responses and their interactions. Although there is quite a huge work on social norms and norm emergence, there is still a need for inferring social norms from the emotional reactions of agents to social interactions. This also might imply a need for inferring the emotions of other agents given a specific event, for instance by paying attention to the response given by the other agents that are familiar with the social context and determine the emotions that are appraised.

– **Creation of Private Norms (Morality).** As explained before, private norms are those that are self-imposed by the agent. It would be interesting that an agent could be able not only to decide whether it follows or not the norms of the system but also to be proactive and by analysing the environment it could infer its own private norms, using its own experience on what works better. This experience also includes emotions. When combining private norms with emotions, then they can be considered as morality rules. Pankov and Dastani proposed a semi-formal specification of three moral emotions (anger, contempt and disgust) [45]. These moral emotions should be mainly considered by the agent when inferring its private norms.

– **Self-enforcement.** Norm enforcement has been mainly implemented by [4]: second-party entities, where agents directly involved in an interaction are in charge of monitoring and taking coercive measures accordingly; or third-party entities in charge of applying sanctions in case of norm violation. However, self-enforcement has been hardly considered. As explained before, emotions could be used as a suitable mechanism for enforcing norms without needing second or third parties, but only the own personal judgment of the agent, modelled by means of its own emotions. This self-enforcement can be applied to institutional, conventions and private norms.

- **Usage of Emotion Theories.** All current approaches of NEAs only focus on the appraisal theory, mainly on the OCC model. However, dimensional theories and hierarchical theories propose interesting features that could also be integrated in a normative emotional agent in order to better model the emotional issues. For example, in GENIA3 the dimensional theory is used [28], by means of the PAD model.
- **Description of Case Studies.** There is a need of more case studies in which the relationships between norms and emotions can clearly be represented. These case studies should be able to represent different types or norms (institutional, conventions, interactions, and private norms), different types of agents (with different emotional appraisals, different personalities), and the representation of norms should be done in an explicit way, by means of normative models. These case studies should also offer a visual representation of their scenario, with virtual characters that allow an interpretation of the agent emotions by human users.

5   Conclusions

This paper has revised the relationship between norms and emotions and how normative multi-agent systems can profit by including emotional models into their decision processes. From the analysis of the state of the art, we have proposed a Normative Emotional Agent (NEA) which is the one that coalesce norms and emotions so that it is able not to only represent, recognize and solve possible conflicts among norms but also to represent, recognize and include emotions as a part of its reasoning process of goal selection. Moreover we present open challenges for the design and implementation of NEA multi-agent systems. As future works, we intend to present a case study for NEAs that clearly allows describing norms and emotions and tests the capabilities of NEAs compared to normative agents.

Acknowledgments. This work was supported by the Spanish Government projects TIN2014-55206-R and TIN2017-89156-R.

References

1. Etzioni, A.: Normative-affective factors toward a new decision-making model. J. Econ. Psychol. **9**, 125–150 (1988)
2. Bagozzi, R.P., Pieters, R.: Goal-directed emotions. Cogn. Emot. **12**(1), 1–26 (1998)
3. Posner, E.: The regulation of solidary groups: the influence of legal and nonlegal sanctions on collective action. Univ. Chicago Law Rev. **63**, 99–133 (1996)
4. Criado, N., Argente, E., Botti, V.: Open issues for normative multi-agent systems. AI Commun. **24**(3), 233–264 (2011)
5. Boella, G., van der Torre, L., Verhagen, H.: Introduction to the special issue on normative multiagent systems. J. Auton. Agents Multi Agent Syst. **17**, 1–10 (2008)
6. Boella, G., van der Torre, L., Verhagen, H.: Introduction to normative multiagent systems. In: Normative Multi-agent Systems. Dagstuhl Seminar Proceedings, vol. 07122 (2007)

7. von Wright, G.H.: Deontic logic. In: Logical Studies, pp. 58–74 (1957)
8. Rubino, R., Sartor, G.: Preface. J. Artif. Intell. Law **16**(1), 1–5 (2008)
9. Elster, J.: Social norms and economic theory. J. Econ. Perspect. **3**(4), 99–117 (1989)
10. Tuomela, R.: The Importance of Us. Stanford University Press, Stanford (1995)
11. Dignum, F.: Autonomous agents with norms. J. Artif. Intell. Law **7**(1), 69–79 (1999)
12. Boella, G., van der Torre, L.: Substantive and procedural norms in normative multiagent systems. J. Appl. Logic **6**(2), 152–171 (2008)
13. Savarimuthu, B.T.R., Cranefield, S.: Norm creation, spreading and emergence: a survey of simulation models of norms in multi-agent systems (2011)
14. Peng, Y.B., Gao, J., Ai, J.Q., Wang, C.H., Guo, H.: An extended agent BDI model with norms, policies and contracts. In: 2008 International Conference on Wireless Communications, Networking and Mobile Computing, WiCOM 2008 (2008)
15. Rodriguez, L.F., Ramos, F.: Development of computational models of emotions for autonomous agents: a review. Cogn. Comput. **6**(3), 351–375 (2014)
16. Ortony, A., Clore, G.L., Collins, A.: The Cognitive Structure of Emotions. Cambridge University Press, Cambridge (1990)
17. Frijda, N.H., Kuipers, P., Ter Schure, E.: Relations among emotion, appraisal, and emotional action readiness. J. Pers. Soc. Psychol. **57**(2), 212–228 (1989)
18. Roseman, I.J., Spindel, M.S., Jose, P.E.: Appraisals of emotion-eliciting events. J. Pers. Soc. Psychol. **59**(5), 899–915 (1990)
19. Hudlicka, E.: Guidelines for designing computational models of emotions. Int. J. Synth. Emot. **2**(1), 26–79 (2011)
20. Marsella, S., Gratch, J., Petta, P.: Computational models of emotion. In: Blueprint for Affective Computing: A Source Book. Oxford University Press, Oxford (2010)
21. Lin, J., Spraragen, M., Zyda, M.: Computational models of emotion and cognition. Adv. Cogn. Syst. **2**, 59–76 (2012)
22. Marsella, S.C., Gratch, J.: EMA: a process model of appraisal dynamics. Cogn. Syst. Res. **10**(1), 70–90 (2009)
23. Russell, J.A.: Core affect and the psychological construction of emotion. Psychol. Rev. **110**(1), 145–172 (2003)
24. Russell, J.A., Mehrabian, A.: Evidence for a three-factor theory of emotions. J. Res. Pers. **11**(3), 273–294 (1977)
25. Mehrabian, A.: Pleasure-arousal-dominance: a general framework for describing and measuring individual differences in temperament. Curr. Psychol. **14**(4), 261–292 (1996)
26. Becker-Asano, C., Wachsmuth, I.: Affective computing with primary and secondary emotions in a virtual human. Auton. Agents Multi Agent Syst. **20**(1), 32–49 (2010)
27. Gebhard, P.: ALMA: a layered model of affect. In: 4th International Joint Conference on Autonomous Agents and Multiagent Systems, pp. 29–36 (2005)
28. Alfonso, B.: Agents with affective traits for decision-making in complex environments. Ph.D. thesis, Universitat Politecnica de Valencia, Spain (2017)
29. Bordini, R.H., Hbner, J.F.: Jason, manual, release 0.7 edition, August 2005. http://jason.sf.net/
30. Ekman, P.: Basic emotions. In: Handbook of Cognition and Emotion, pp. 45–60. Wiley, New Jersey (1999)
31. Velasquez, J.D.: Modeling emotions and other motivations in synthetic agents. In: 14th National Conference on Artificial Intelligence and 9th Conference on Innovative Applications of Artificial Intelligence, pp. 10–15. AAAI Press (1997)
32. Staller, A., Petta, P.: Introducing emotions into the computational study of social norms: a first evaluation. J. Artif. Soc. Soc. Simul. **4**(1), U27–U60 (2001)

33. Ferreira, N., et al.: Generating norm-related emotions in virtual agents. In: Nakano, Y., Neff, M., Paiva, A., Walker, M. (eds.) IVA 2012. LNCS (LNAI), vol. 7502, pp. 97–104. Springer, Heidelberg (2012). https://doi.org/10.1007/978-3-642-33197-8_10

34. Joffily, M., Masclet, D., Noussair, C.N., Villeval, M.C.: Emotions, sanctions and cooperation. South. Econ. J. **80**(4), 1002–1027 (2014)

35. Elster, J.: Rationality and the emotions. Econ. J. **106**(438), 1386–1397 (1996)

36. Fix, J., von Scheve, C., Moldt, D.: Emotion-based norm enforcement and maintenance in multi-agent systems: foundations and petri net modeling. In: Proceedings of the Fifth International Joint Conference on Autonomous Agents and Multiagent Systems, pp. 105–107 (2006)

37. Staller, A., Petta, P.: Towards a tractable appraisal-based architecture for situated cognizers. In: Grounding Emotions in Adaptive Systems, Workshop Notes of 5th International Conference of the Society for Adaptive Behaviour (SAB 1998), pp. 56–61 (1998)

38. Huber, M.J.: JAM: a BDI-theoretic mobile agent architecture. In: Proceedings of the Third International Conference on Autonomous Agents, Seattle, pp. 236–243 (1999)

39. Bazzan, A.L.C., Adamatti, D.F., Bordini, R.H.: Extending the computational study of social norms with a systematic model of emotions. In: Bittencourt, G., Ramalho, G.L. (eds.) SBIA 2002. LNCS (LNAI), vol. 2507, pp. 108–117. Springer, Heidelberg (2002). https://doi.org/10.1007/3-540-36127-8_11

40. Von Scheve, C., Moldt, D., Fix, J., von Luede, R.: My agents love to conform: norms and emotion in the micro-macro link. Comput. Math. Organ. Theory **12**(2–3), 81–100 (2006)

41. Ahmad, A., Ahmad, M.S., Mohd Yusoff, M.Z., Ahmed, M.: Formulating agent's emotions in a normative environment. In: Lukose, D., Ahmad, A.R., Suliman, A. (eds.) KTW 2011. CCIS, vol. 295, pp. 82–92. Springer, Heidelberg (2012). https://doi.org/10.1007/978-3-642-32826-8_9

42. Ahmad, A., Ahmad, M.S., Mohd Yusoff, M.Z., Mustapha, A.: A novel framework for normative agent-based systems. In: MJCAI (2009)

43. Dias, J., Paiva, A.: Feeling and reasoning: a computational model for emotional characters. In: Bento, C., Cardoso, A., Dias, G. (eds.) EPIA 2005. LNCS (LNAI), vol. 3808, pp. 127–140. Springer, Heidelberg (2005). https://doi.org/10.1007/11595014_13

44. Conte, R., Castelfranchi, C.: Understanding the functions of norms in social groups through simulation. In: Artificial Societies: The Computer Simulation of Social Life, pp. 252–267. UCL Press (1995)

45. Pankov, A., Dastani, M.: Towards a formal specification of moral emotions. In: 2nd International Workshop on Emotion and Sentiment in Social and Expressive Media: Opportunities and Challenges for Emotion-Aware Multiagent Systems, vol. 1351, pp. 3–18, May 2015

Author Index

Printed in the United States
By Bookmasters